The Making of Urban America

THE MAKING
OF URBAN AMERICA

A HISTORY OF CITY PLANNING

IN THE UNITED STATES

BY JOHN W. REPS

PRINCETON UNIVERSITY PRESS · PRINCETON · NEW JERSEY

Published by Princeton University Press, 41 William Street,
Princeton, New Jersey 08540
in the United Kingdom, Princeton University Press, Oxford

Library of Congress Card No. 64-23414
ISBN 0-691-04525-9 (hardback)
ISBN 0-691-00618-0 (paperback)
Third printing and first Princeton Paperback printing, 1992

Princeton University Press books are printed on acid-free paper, and meet
the guidelines for permanence and durability of the Committee on Production Guidelines
for Book Longevity of the Council on Library Resources

10 9 8 7 6 5 4 3

Printed in the United States of America

To my wife Constance Peck Reps

Table of Contents

List of Illustrations

Preface

THE year 1965 marks the end of four centuries of continuous urban development in the United States of America. This book is an attempt to describe and assess the planning of those towns and cities founded from the time of colonial settlement to the beginning of the present era. My purpose is to provide a general survey and basic history of this neglected aspect of the nation's growth.

Although several excellent articles and a few fine books have been written about the planning of individual cities or those of a state or region, no comprehensive and documentary treatment of American city planning exists. Urban historians have dealt mainly with social, political, and institutional affairs, while the physical aspects of city growth have been described chiefly by architectural historians. The present work is intended to supplement the valuable studies of such scholars.

The emphasis throughout this book is on town and city plans and the planning process, not on the architecture of individual buildings or even on civic design. While such a distinction would be highly artificial in a history of European city planning, in this country urban architecture and urban planning can be readily distinguished if not completely separated. Unfortunately, with but rare exceptions, American city planning has been essentially a two-dimensional pursuit.

I had several objectives in undertaking this study and during the course of the research others began to take shape. While these are implied in the pages to follow, a brief, explicit statement of them seems appropriate at the outset.

My chief interests lay in discovering to what extent city planning was rooted in the nation's tradition and in tracing the main influences that have governed the form of America's cities for some four hundred years. I also hoped to document what I had long suspected—that, contrary to general opinion, the United States was not a country where all cities had been designed on an undeviating gridiron pattern.

Another objective was to investigate the fate of the original plans for the cities—the extent to which predetermined patterns had been followed in later years. I was concerned as well with the quality of the plans in the light of conditions and technical knowledge prevailing at the time of first settlement. I also found myself becoming interested in the persons responsible for the layout of our cities and in their backgrounds. Finally, I hoped to relate city planning activities to other events in American history.

The organization of the book is relatively simple. Aside from the first chapter, which deals with the European background of American city planning, and the two which follow on French and Spanish colonial towns, its scope is generally limited to cities and towns of the continental United States. The period covered is from the beginning of European settlement to the first World War. The first half is devoted to the planning of colonial cities and to the design and early development of the national capital. Because of the manner in which the country was settled it was possible to arrange this material not only in rough chronological order but also by region and by the European country responsible for colonization.

The next three chapters take up the three major design forms used in American city layout. The five chapters that follow discuss the planning of cities under a variety of special influences, while the concluding chapter reviews the events leading up to the beginning of modern urban planning in the America of our own period.

Maps, plans, and views are vital to an understanding of city planning. More than three hundred reproductions have thus been included to illustrate the topics discussed in the text. Notes on these plates and a summary of the research methods employed in obtaining them will be found at the end of the book.

The scope and objectives of this work are ambitious. I am under no illusion that I have succeeded in all that I set out to do or that I have done justice to the rich material at hand. Errors of fact, interpretation, judgment, and omission are certain to be found. I ask the reader's charity as he discovers such shortcomings. I can only hope that the merits of this pioneering work exceed its flaws and that its appearance will stimulate other scholars to undertake similar studies.

CHAPTER 1

European City Planning on the Eve of American Colonization

THE first settlers of the New World were Spanish, French, English, Dutch, and Swedish. They were not yet Americans. Their language, their dress, their political, social, and religious beliefs, and their architecture were those of their homelands. Gradually in some instances, more rapidly in others, these cultural and physical characteristics changed to meet the opportunities and requirements of the American environment. Although European influences continued, with the passing of time their power waned, and new modes of life more appropriate to the changed circumstances of the settlers emerged.

No crude environmental determinism is implied by the foregoing statement. Complex and subtle forces caused these changes, and cultural factors seem to have exerted as much influence as the more obvious physical elements. The fact remains that, from the beginning of settlement, the European way of life, as represented by the various colonizing groups, began its metamorphosis to a new and different pattern.

During the early period of colonization innovations in community layout rarely appeared. The plans of villages and towns, and their surrounding agricultural lands, closely resembled, if they did not actually duplicate, traditional patterns of land division and allotment already familiar to those coming to America from the colonizing countries of Europe. But new or modified community plans emerged in response to novel requirements or changed circumstances.

In this book we shall be examining the adaptation of those community planning forms to the evolving American scene. This introductory and preliminary chapter will survey the status of European city planning on the eve of colonization in an attempt to summarize the body of knowledge dealing with urban layout available to the founders of America's first cities. Those readers already familiar with the rich history of late medieval and renaissance European planning will find this at best a mere outline of an incredibly interesting and complicated period of urban growth. Others less aware of these events may at least gain some understanding of the extent to which European town planning had developed by the time the first settlers left for the New World and during the formative period of colonial life.[1]

What were these elements of the European planning tradition? Aside from the legacy of ancient Greece and Rome, half a dozen fairly distinct aspects of European town planning stand out. There were, first of all, a whole series of architectural treatises dealing at least in part with the principles of planning, urban reconstruction, town extensions, and the layout of new cities. Of these the works of Alberti and Palladio exerted greatest influence on their contemporaries and remain the best known. Similar in some respects but forming a group somewhat apart were the various ideal city proposals put forward by utopian philosophers, economic reformers, and military engineers.

The European tradition could also boast of scores of "new" towns, completely preplanned and built largely as designed. While most of these date from the late middle ages, many were creations of the Renaissance and Baroque periods and came into being shortly before and during the early periods of American colonization. Ur-

[1] In this background essay on the European roots of American city planning I have not attempted the same kind of documentary treatment that will be found in subsequent chapters. In such a compressed summary the number of references would be excessively burdensome to the reader. Moreover, there are a number of excellent books that deal with the history of European planning comprehensively or with city planning in particular countries. Those secondary sources listed in the bibliography should be consulted by the reader who may wish to verify the statements or judgments appearing herein. Most of these works contain bibliographies of primary and other source materials. There is in addition the annotated bibliography compiled by Thomas W. Mackesey, *History of City Planning*, Council of Planning Librarians, Exchange Bibliography 19, Oakland, 1961.

ban extension projects also provided examples of large-scale planning and construction.

An important aspect of European planning influential in many New World towns was the development of residential squares and public piazzas or *places*. Not so extensive in scale as new towns or new suburban quarters, the squares nevertheless provided a sense of order otherwise often lacking.

Finally, the European tradition included a history of evolution in garden and park design, which in turn strongly influenced the layout of cities and especially the alignment of major streets and boulevards. The similarity in scale and design between the gardens of Versailles and the plan of Washington, D.C. was no mere coincidence, as we shall see in a later chapter. Still later the sinuous lines of the English garden appeared in the winding roads of the romantic suburban developments of America's *nouveau riche*.

We now turn to an examination of each of these elements of European planning. While they are discussed separately, this is more a matter of convenience than an accurate representation of their true positions. In fact, many of these elements are closely connected with one another.

Bastide Towns of Medieval Europe

As Europe began to emerge from the Dark Ages and as a limited revival of commerce and trade developed, a new period of town founding began. These new towns were primarily military in character and were designed to protect a frontier or to consolidate military and political domination of a region. Their founders were usually locally powerful lords who claimed or aspired to the rule of a domain larger than the traditional feudal estate and who were in positions to make that claim effective. In the countries with which we are concerned these fortress or *bastide* towns are to be found chiefly in southwestern France, in the northern portions of Spain, and on the Welsh and Scottish borders of England.

The history of the *bastide* towns can be found in the works of several authorities. There is no need to repeat this material here, but some brief description of these communities is warranted. The extent to which these *bastide* communities served as models for American colonial town planning remains undetermined, but, as will be seen, many of the early American towns bore close resemblance to them. In at least one case—French Detroit—there appears to be some direct connection between a *bastide* plan and that of an American town. Certain similarities in form suggest that these medieval towns may have been influential in other European colonial communities. Yet we cannot be certain that these points of resemblance resulted from direct or even unconscious copying of the features of the *bastides*.

The plan of Monpazier in France is fairly typical of these cities, although such complete regularity is not often encountered in the scores of other such towns in southern France, the few in northern Spain, or the half-dozen or so in the British Isles, of which Flint, Winchelsea, and Hull are perhaps the best known. The gridiron plan, market square, walled perimeter, and restricted size characterize them all with but few exceptions. The plan of the town as it was established near the end of the thirteenth century is reproduced in Figure 1. The walls of the town enclose a rectangle about 1,300 feet long and 600 feet wide, divided into blocks approximately 125 feet wide and 150, 250, and 300 feet long. Near the center, surrounded by arcaded streets—a feature of many of the French *bastides*—is the market square. The church and its adjacent open space are located nearby off one corner of the market square. The main streets were only 24 feet wide, the minor ways 16 feet, and the alleys but 6 feet in width.

In most instances the *bastides* were established as frontier outposts or to dominate actual or potentially hostile territory. Towns on the American frontier came into being for similar reasons. The *bastide* type plan met the requirements of these stern conditions, and it is little wonder that it was used by some of the earliest town planners in the New World. The relative unimportance of most of the European *bastides* and the remoteness in time of their founding suggests that functional requirements rather than historical imitation was largely responsible for the use of this plan in America. If the *bastides* did not directly provide models for our colonial towns, they at least furnished a background of examples of planned towns for subsequent European planning activities. These in turn supplied many of the concepts and design details later to be incorporated in American colonial towns.

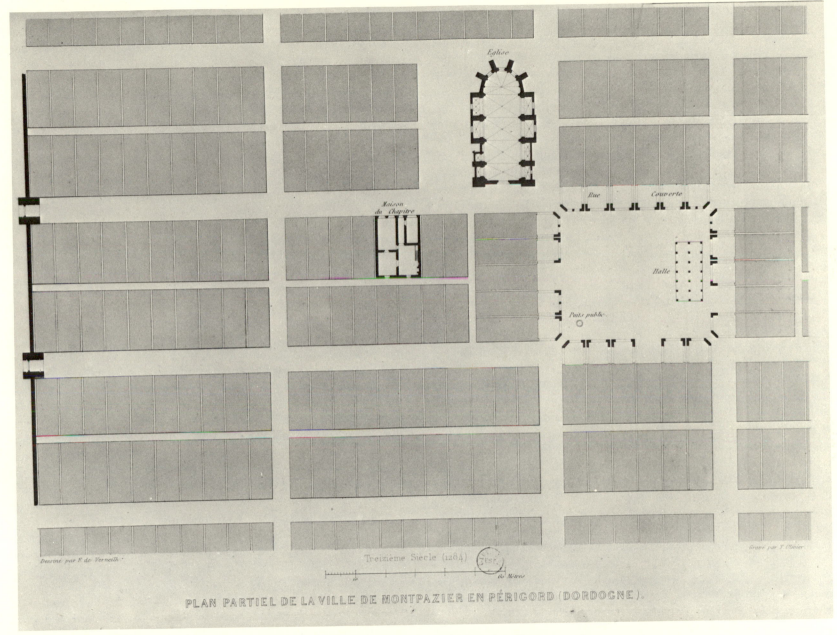

Églilse

Maison
du Chapitre

Rue   Couverte

Halle

Puits public

Dessiné par F. de Verneilh.

Treizième Siècle (1284)

Gravé par F. Olivier.

60 Mètres

PLAN PARTIEL DE LA VILLE DE MONTPAZIER EN PÉRIGORD (DORDOGNE).

Figure 1. Plan of a Portion of Monpazier, France: 1284

Europe's New Vitruvians

The *bastides* mark a transitional stage between the feudal castle with its confined community huddled at its base and the bustling, expanding cities of the Renaissance and Baroque eras. Renaissance city planning did not lack for theoreticians. Books expounding architectural principles appeared almost as soon as the new printing press came into widespread use. Most of these works contained at least some reference to the ideal layout of cities, and many of them emphasized this aspect of architecture as of importance equal to that of the design of individual buildings. In this the Renaissance writers followed the model of Vitruvius, who wrote in the first century B.C. and whose rediscovery in the fifteenth century stimulated a long series of similar theoretical works.

The earliest important treatise of this kind in the Renaissance was Leon Battista Alberti's *De Re Aedificatoria*, published posthumously in 1485. Alberti was one of the acknowledged masters of the early Renaissance and the architect for important buildings in Mantua, Rimini, Florence, and elsewhere in Italy. His manual of architecture drew on this experience, on the principles laid down by Vitruvius, and on the practice of his less illustrious contemporaries in the design of dwellings, civic and palatial buildings, and urban open spaces.

Alberti, like Vitruvius, began with a consideration of desirable site conditions for cities. The shape of towns, their walls and fortifications, and such matters as water supply and sewerage all received his attention. The design of the street system also was considered. For large and important towns Alberti felt the streets should be straight and broad. Smaller and less heavily fortified towns should be planned with winding streets to increase their beauty and to give the impression of greater size. Alberti singled out other streets leading to public places as deserving of special architectural treatment for the buildings along their path. He advocated the development of piazzas and recreational areas for each district of the city. Finally, he suggested that certain industrial activities, offensive because of odor or noise be prohibited from towns altogether and that the various crafts and industries be grouped together in districts set aside for that purpose.

A century later, in 1570, Andrea Palladio published a similar work. Palladio's *I Quattro Libre dell' Architettura* bulged with sumptuous views and plans of magnificent palaces and public buildings. The relative simplicity and restraint of Alberti's day had given way to the elaborate devices of the Baroque. Palladio's chief concern lay in the city as a visual experience. Mundane problems of water supply and sewage disposal he dismissed in a few short lines. Broad streets lined with imposing buildings leading to great squares embellished with fountains and statues are admiringly described. The image of the Baroque city of pomp and pageant appears in these pages—and it soon began to take shape as powerful princes, both secular and spiritual, began to remake European cities into these new patterns.

Every European country produced architectural theoreticians of the Vitruvian mold, although the Italians remained best known. The works of both Alberti and Palladio were translated into other languages and were widely read throughout Europe. These books, and the many others of similar character, exerted a powerful influence on the design of Renaissance and Baroque towns, urban extension projects, the layout of squares and plazas, and the character of new streets and boulevards.

Along with the theoretical works of Alberti, Palladio, and their followers appeared other books by engineers dealing with the city primarily as a military stronghold and fortress. With the introduction of gunpowder into Europe in the fourteenth century, the traditional types of fortification became obsolete. The castle walls which had served so well as a defense against more primitive weapons now stood open to breaching fire from cannon. Clearly some way was needed to keep artillery at bay. The method finally devised involved the construction of various types of outworks, either as separate strongpoints or as projections from the main wall. These outworks or bastions were usually flat, thus presenting a small target area, and so laid out that the flanks of salients received protection from adjoining points.

Such new methods of fortifying cities gave rise to a host of theories and proposals. Francesco Martini was one of the earliest and most prolific theoreticians, the designer of several ideal military city plans dating from the late fifteenth century. Cattaneo, nearly a century later, refined and elaborated these studies of Martini. Palma Nova, designed by Vincenzo Scamozzi and built in 1593 north of Venice, was one of the earliest examples of a city whose entire plan stemmed from these theories of military engineering. At the beginning of the seventeenth century, Scamozzi described a similar ideal fortress town with twelve sides, a bastion at each angle, and the whole town surrounded by a moat. At least a dozen other architects and engineers, chiefly Italian, advanced like proposals.

In all these schemes two general types of street patterns stand out: the rectangular and the radial. Most designers employed squares and open spaces—the architects for their visual appeal and as sites for major buildings, the engineers for their utility as mustering places for troops. The perimeters of these plans were normally circular. The architects evidently found this more satisfying aesthetically, and the engineers wanted to minimize the length of the required fortifications. Both advocated straight, wide streets—the architects because of the monumental character it would give to the city and the engineers because of the facility such streets would provide for troop movements and the use of artillery. To a remarkable degree, then, the desires of architects and military engineers coincided and blended. While actual city building in the Renaissance rarely approached the symmetrical perfection shown in these theoretical plans, the many executed projects for enlarged fortifications or for civic embellishment followed ideal proposals in general outline.

Another group of treatises influenced the layout of cities. These were works dealing with the art of castrametation, that is, the layout of military camps. These castrametation books were based largely on Roman writings. Niccolo Machiavelli's *Arte della Guerra*, which appeared in 1521, was but the first of a long list of such works. Most of them contained illustrations and diagrams of camp layout, and there are many similarities between these illustrations and the plans used in certain American colonial settlements.

Renaissance Utopians

Other theoretical sources inspired Renaissance town planning. These were the writings of the utopian philosophers, chiefly Thomas More, Tomasso Campanella, Eximenic, Johann Valentin Andreae, and Francis Bacon. The utopian tradition, as well as the word itself, begins with More. His *Utopia* appeared in 1516 and describes an imaginary island containing 54 cities, each the center of a little city-state. Amaurot, the capital city, like the others was limited in size to six thousand families. More's cities had three-story row houses "so uniform, that a whole side of a street looks like one house." Each city contained four neighborhoods grouped around market squares. Like Alberti, More suggested that offensive uses be banned from the city proper and located nearby in the countryside.

Campanella's *City of the Sun*, published in 1623, in many ways resembled More's work. His city, however, consisted of seven rings, the outermost being two miles in diameter. Four streets and four gates facing the cardinal points of the compass provided access and the main lines of transportation to the center. The concentric rings were to be formed by fortified walls, and the buildings of the city would be connected directly to them on the inside of the circumference.

In all the literature on utopias appearing in the sixteenth and seventeenth centuries the most complete and painstaking description of an ideal city appears in Andreae's *Reipublicae Christianopolitanae Descriptio*, published in 1619. Andreae furnished both ground plan and perspective of his proposed city. It was to be square, 700 feet on each side, and strongly fortified. Four great squares of buildings were to form the town, beginning with an outer square just inside the walls. Successively smaller squares were to fit inside this frame. In the middle was a quadrangle, 190 feet square, containing in its center a great temple. Each side of the squares of buildings was to be devoted to a separate use or function, with the inner building square used for a college, laboratories, galleries, and archives. Four streets leading from as many gates set in the middle of the sides of the enclosing walls led through arched tunnels to the central square and temple.

The other utopian writers of the period were concerned less with the details of city design than with the social or political systems advocated for ideal commonwealths. Bacon's fragment, *The New Atlantis* (1622), mentions only a walled seaport community. Gaspar Stiblinus, in his *Commentariolus de Eudaemonensium Republica* (1555), tells of a circular city with three concentric walls and a large open space for military maneuvers. And Harrington's *Oceana* (1656) contains the details of a complete constitution for a model society with scarcely a word on its physical organization. The Catalan, Eximenic, writing in the fifteenth century, described a square, fortified city with a large central open space and four smaller plazas in the four quarters of the town.

The contribution to European town planning by these utopian writers can not be precisely measured. Their direct effects were negligible. Indeed the authors themselves scarcely hoped for practical results; the descriptions of communities in their writings were intended primarily to lend an air of realism to programs for social and political reform. Indirectly, these writers may well have stimulated further thinking about the function of cities and how they could be planned by holding out the possibility of new ways of ordering society.

New Cities for a New Era

In the foregoing we have explored some aspects of the theoretical base for Renaissance town planning. Now we come to an examination of town building itself. Completely new towns were rare in Renaissance Europe despite the frequency with which they were created on paper by architects, military engineers, and utopians. Their creation is significant, however, since they represent the practical application of the art and science of town planning of the time. As symbols of the status of planning on the eve of American colonization, they deserve attention.

France provides the best and most numerous examples both of the use of all the devices of the Renaissance architects and planners and of the reversion to simpler forms reminiscent of the *bastides*. These begin about half a century before the establishment of the first French colonies in the New World. Thus, by the time Champlain and his successors began to found French colonial towns, a body of knowledge concerning the new techniques of town planning was at hand. In a later chapter the extent to which French colonial planners employed these doctrines will be reviewed.

In this period the first important city planning project was the new town of Vitry-le-François, laid out in 1545 by order of Francis I. An Italian engineer, Hieronimo Marino, prepared the plan which is reproduced in Figure 2. Doubtless he drew heavily on the already rich literature dealing with the planning of fortified towns and strongpoints. The plan of Vitry shows a symmetrical

system of fortifications enclosing a grid street pattern. The main entrance stood at the west, across the Marne bridge. From here a main street led to a central square, as did three other principal streets running north, east, and west. A smaller open area set aside as a market place opened off the north-west corner of the main square.

The design of the main square is worth noting. The four main streets entered at the mid-points of the enclosing sides. This differed from almost all of the earlier *bastides*, whose market places were simply unbuilt-on blocks of the regular grid and whose access streets ran along the sides of the squares. The Vitry plan certainly afforded maximum accessibility to the fortifications from the central square, one function of which was to serve as a mustering place for troops. But Marino must also have considered the advantages of this form as an element in civic design. As used by later Renaissance planners with persistent consistency, the center of the square served as the site of a fountain, statue, or column. On axis of the four approach streets this monumental architectural feature provided a terminal point and an easily understood symbol marking a spot of importance. When combined with uniform façades and cornice lines along the approach streets and used as the site for civic or royal buildings the Renaissance square took on added significance.

Vitry still resembled the *bastide* towns more than the vision of civic grandeur that had been described by Alberti. Navarrins, built in the south of France only three years later, also followed the *bastide* form. It was at Charleville, founded in 1608 on the Meuse River by Charles of Gonzaga, Duke of Nevers and Mantua, that the principles of Alberti and particularly those of Palladio found expression in new town planning. The plan of Charleville undoubtedly drew also on the new town of Nancy, planned in 1588 by an Italian, Jerome Citoni, under the direction of Duke Charles III and built adjacent to the much older settlement of the same name. Here Citoni traced a system of straight streets intersecting at right angles, with several of the regular blocks left open as sites for major buildings.

The Charleville plan shown in Figure 3 carried these and other precedents to a climax of Baroque design. Generally rectangular, the plan was interrupted by the introduction of several squares and *places* where minor streets terminated. The noble ducal palace

VITRY·LE·FRANÇOIS

Figure 2. View of Vitry-le-François, France: 1634

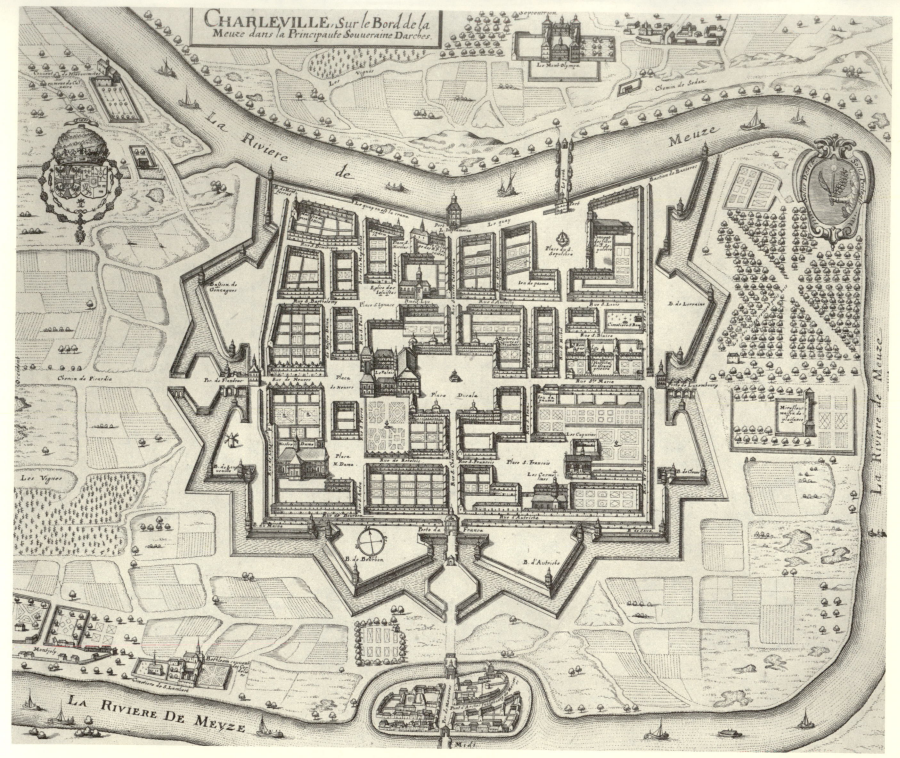

Figure 3. Plan of Charleville, France: 1656

fronted the central square that was developed with uniform façades on the remaining three sides. Three major streets, one from the riverfront and two from land gates standing behind the moat and surrounding fortifications, led directly to this central place. A fourth street from the western gate ended at the rear of the palace. No more consistent expression of Palladian principles can be found. The clear differentiation of major and minor streets, the subsidiary squares, the *Place Ducale*, the careful attention to street façades, and the skillful placement of important buildings on axis with approaching streets, all demonstrate an understanding of the chief devices of Baroque town planning.

Other new French towns of the period lack the impact of Charleville but are nonetheless interesting and not without importance. Henrichemont, also planned in 1608, owed its existence to the Duke de Sully. Sully's downfall in 1610 prevented the completion of the town entirely as planned, but significant parts remain. The plan resembled one of the ideal city proposals of Perret, on which it may well have been modeled. A grid four blocks square was overlain by four diagonal streets running to the corners from a central square. Four smaller squares appeared where the diagonal streets intersected the basic grid pattern.

Quite different in form and function, Richelieu, planned in 1638 by Lemercier under the direction of the cardinal, was created to house the servants and workmen of the chateau belonging to the famous French churchman and politician. The design was rectangular with two squares, one at each end of the village. One of the squares opened off the entrance gate; on the other, nearest the chateau, fronted the village church. Five streets running lengthwise and three crossing at right angles provided access to neat rows of cottages each with gardens at the rear. Even at this domestic scale, many of the Baroque devices of axial relationships, uniform façade treatment, and reciprocal vistas were employed.

France was not the only country in which new towns developed. In the Low Countries much the same evolution occurred, although *bastide* communities were rare, and fully developed Renaissance new towns were less important and smaller in scale. Of the *bastides*, Elburg and Naarden, among others, show similarities to those of southern France. The need for additional urban development, how-

ever, normally was met through the careful expansion of existing towns.

A few examples of the application of Renaissance planning theories do exist. One of the earliest is Philippeville, planned in 1555 by Sebastian van Noyen and named in honor of Philip II of Spain. The plan appears in Figure 4. This border fortress town guarding the approaches from France closely followed the theories of the Italian military engineers. The five walled sides and the bastions at the points of intersections formed a star-shaped city, slightly irregular because of the site. In the center stood the square from which radiated eleven streets leading to the bastions, walls, and gates. Between the square and the perimeter and roughly equidistant from both ran a secondary street nearly circular in outline although broken at two points. Even more clearly deriving its inspiration from the Italian fortress town models was Coeworden in Holland, planned in 1597. Coeworden, like Palma Nova, was completely symmetrical, with a spider web plan of radial and concentric streets between the open square at the center and the elaborate fortifications and moat around the exterior.

Two other Dutch towns deserve mention—Klundert and Willemstad, laid out in the mid 1560's on almost identical plans. The earliest drawings show rather elaborate fortifications, but these apparently were later additions by William the Silent. Both towns evidently were intended originally as market towns for areas recently reclaimed from the sea and converted to agricultural land. Willemstad, the plan of which is reproduced in Figure 5, is a tidy example of Renaissance town planning, not unlike the later Richelieu in scale and general form. The town hall square near the harbor connects with a rather larger rectangular space at the other end of the town by way of a broad and rather short avenue. The church in this second square stands on axis with the avenue and faces toward the watergate and harbor. Two secondary streets in each direction complete the little composition, as simple as it is effective and well ordered.

Although Spain controlled the Low Countries during the period we have been reviewing, and Spanish architects certainly knew the doctrines of Vitruvius, Alberti, Palladio, and the military engineers, the impact of Renaissance planning in the home country was not as great as might be expected. Wholly new towns of the

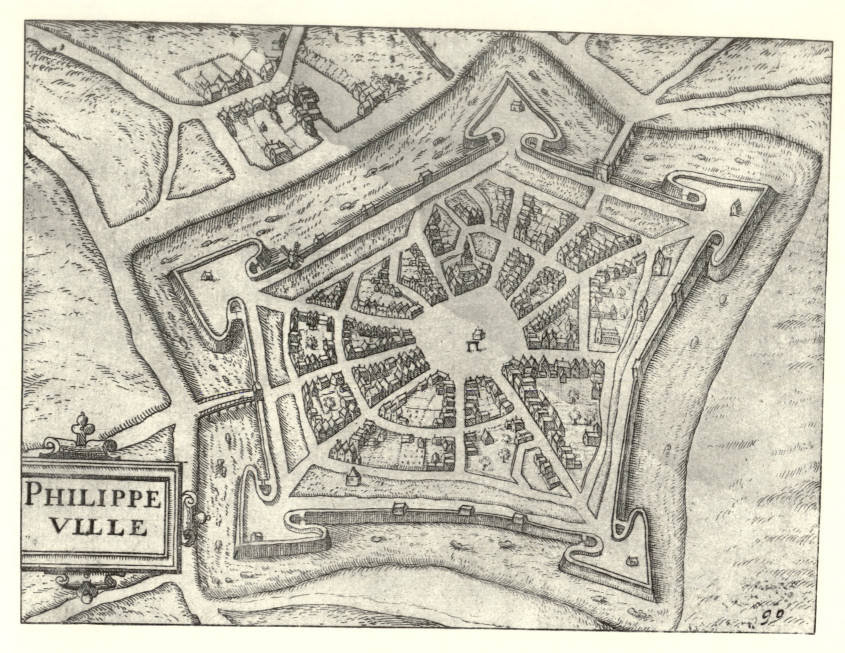

Figure 4. Plan of Philippeville, Belgium: date unknown

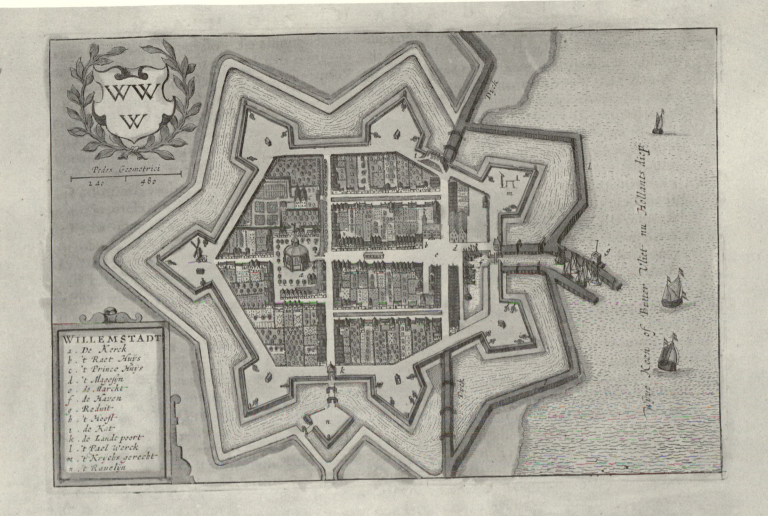

WILHELMOSTADVM.

ILHELMOSTADUM in Ruy-genhillensi tractu, qui anno mil-lesimo quingentesimo sexagesi-mo quarto exaggeratus dicitur à Wilhelmo Auriaco, ad inhibendos hostium è Brabantia insultus, exstrui cœptum est. Do-minium ejus Wilhelmo, Principi de publici egregii bono optime merito, tradiderunt. Aër hic gravissimus est; quod ante aliquot annos cives Leydenses experti; quorum plerique morbo gravissimo contacti vitam cum morte commutarunt.

Figure 5. Plan of Willemstad, Holland: 1647

period seem to be lacking, and Renaissance planning techniques found expression mainly in the creation of new plazas in older towns.

Spanish colonization of the New World began more than a century before successful attempts by France, England, and Holland, and possible models for Spanish colonial town planning must be sought in an earlier era. As we shall see in the next chapter, the form of Spanish-American towns established itself at an early date and in its essentials scarcely changed during two and a half centuries.

The one new town in Spain that may have been influential in subsequent colonization efforts is almost medieval in origin. It dates from 1492, the very year that Spanish exploration led her to a new and unsuspected continent. Ferdinand and Isabella, by their marriage in 1469, had brought together the separate kingdoms of Aragon, Castile, and Leon. When Columbus departed on his first voyage of discovery the new Spanish nation was engaged in the last efforts to drive the Moors from the Iberian peninsula. Near Granada, the remaining Moorish stronghold, the Spanish rulers established the siege town of Santa Fé, a modern air photo of which is shown in Figure 6. More than a temporary camp, Santa Fé even then had the appearance of a permanent community, and its plan remains little changed in the almost five hundred years that have intervened.

Santa Fé, in its small scale and regular street plan, follows the familiar *bastide* pattern. The central square differs, however, from those with which we are familiar. On one side it is bordered by the main street of the town running lengthwise from gate to gate. A short cross street enters the sides of the square near their midpoints, thus conforming in part to the canons of Renaissance planning. Here at Santa Fé may be the genesis of the remarkable Laws of the Indies that were to guide the planning of hundreds of Spanish colonial towns during the coming centuries. The close royal connection with Santa Fé and the planning of a number of colonial towns during the remaining years of the king and queen suggests that the Spanish-American towns owe their form in part to this specialized military community.

In turning to England we are struck by the almost complete absence of new town planning at the time such activities were at their height on the continent. The Renaissance came to insular

England later than to other European countries, and its effect on town planning was not in the direction of the creation of wholly new communities. Yet in the seventeenth century two examples, widely separated in space, scale, and design, must be mentioned. The first occurred early and resulted in the creation of several small new towns in northern Ireland. The second resulted from the famous London fire of 1666 and consisted of no less than eight separate plans for rebuilding the city. These were essentially new town schemes and properly belong in the present group of plans we have been describing.

The Irish venture has at last been properly treated in a recent study.[2] Its significance for an understanding of English colonization is considerable. Many of the English participants were also active in the settlement of Virginia and New England, and it is only logical to assume that some of the experience gained in town building in northern Ireland under English direction found application in the American colonies.

The province of Ulster in Ireland came under the jurisdiction of the English crown at the beginning of the seventeenth century following the flight of the Irish earls. Their feudal holdings were declared forfeit and became the property of the crown. In effect a regional development plan was then prepared, which included proposals for land disposal and the development of a series of towns. By 1609 the plan for the six counties of the area had been completed, and twenty-three new town sites were designated. The crown enlisted the financial support of the wealthy city companies of London, and in the following year all or part of five counties came under the direction of the Irish Society, a colonizing company created by the Common Council of the City of London. Finally, the society reached agreements with certain of the London companies for the settlement and development of designated portions of the area, retaining as its own responsibility the building of the two towns of Derry and Coleraine.

Both plans date from about 1611 and are similar in that each had a gridiron layout with straight streets crossing at right angles. Each had a central square, but of different design. That of Coleraine resembles the *bastide* type, although it is about twice as long as it is broad and streets entering on the narrow sides intersect the square at the midpoints of the sides. Londonderry, the

[2] Gilbert Camblin, *The Town in Ulster*, Belfast, 1951.

Figure 6. Vertical Aerial View of Santa Fé, Spain: 1958

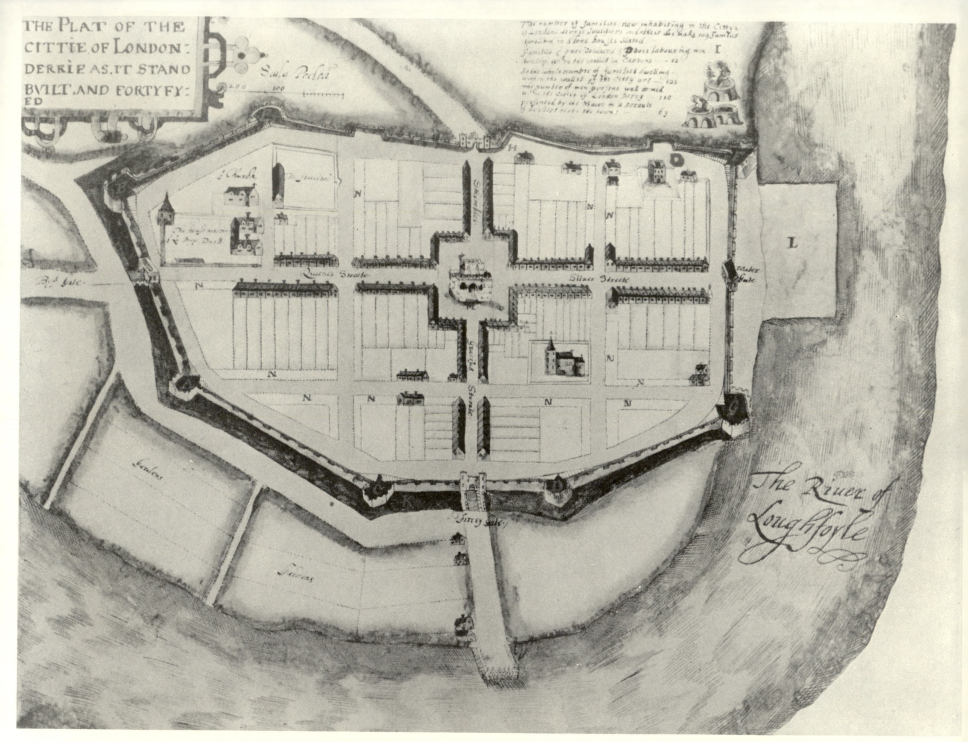

Figure 7. Plan of Londonderry, Northern Ireland: 1622

plan of which is reproduced in Figure 7, had a more regular and interesting layout. Its central square had sides of equal dimensions and all four streets providing access to the square enter at the midpoints of its sides. An early plan shows in perspective uniform rows of attached houses lining the four approach streets and the sides of the square. In the center of the square stood the most imposing building of the town, housing a market, prison, and town hall. One cannot escape the feeling that Coleraine was essentially medieval in concept while Londonderry drew its inspiration from the Renaissance towns of the continent.

Other early town plans of the period, including those of Bangor, Holywood, Comber, Killyleagh, and Bellaghy, were less sophisticated. Some were simple grids lacking any central open space; others were merely linear settlements along a single street. These same forms were to appear within a few years in New England, at Jamestown in the expansion of the original stockaded settlement, and in other towns in tidewater Virginia. At Ulster, the frontier of English seventeenth century colonization, these simple village and town patterns had their first trial.

Too late to influence the design of the earliest English colonial towns but of considerable importance to later communities, the eight plans for rebuilding London after the fire of 1666 reveal the diversity of English planning toward the end of the seventeenth century. The widely known three plans by John Evelyn and the even more famous plan of Christopher Wren illustrate the attractions of continental Baroque urban patterns to the more sophisticated and artistic of Englishmen. Wren's plan and one of Evelyn's appear in Figures 8 and 9. Great diagonal avenues, rond-points, ovals, and squares appear in these schemes as though sketched by Palladio himself. Both Wren and Evelyn employed the spider web pattern in portions of their plans. From great plazas radiated eight streets, connected by octagonal circumferentials. At other points radial streets converged on sites for major buildings, in Wren's plan St. Paul's cathedral and the Royal Exchange. This was a new vocabulary, translated from continental expression and reproduced with only the slightest English accent.

While Wren and Evelyn did employ the grid system in portions of their schemes, this remained subordinate to the diagonal boulevards and monumental plazas to which they ran. The other four recorded plans demonstrated the force which

simpler and more orthodox grid systems still exerted on more traditional minds.

The plan of Captain Valentine Knight was the simplest. No less than twenty-four east-west streets were proposed, two of them sixty feet in width, the rest thirty. Twelve cross streets thirty and fifty feet wide ran north and south. Knight also suggested that all streets should have arcaded sidewalks. Knight's plan received little general consideration, but we do know it came to the attention of the king. Knight ended up in prison for proposing the construction of a great canal and for daring to suggest that the crown could profit from fines and tolls levied for its use. Charles evidently reacted strongly to this idea that he might profit from the city's misfortune.

The plan shown in Figure 10 and attributed to Robert Hooke, a physicist, mathematician, and astronomer at Gresham College, was rather more elaborate. Hooke, too, proposed an almost undeviating grid, but with square blocks rather than the long and narrow ones appearing in Knight's plan. Hooke also proposed four great plazas 375 by 460 feet and, like Evelyn and Wren, advocated an open embankment along the Thames.

The two other grid schemes came from Richard Newcourt, whose map of London published in 1658 was the most detailed and accurate of any yet produced. Newcourt's two plans, one of which is described in Chapter 6 and reproduced in Figure 98, differed only in the number and size of blocks, the first having a greater number. Five open squares appear on the plan. The great one in the center occupied an area equal to four of the standard blocks. Four others, each one block in extent, were symmetrically located in the four quadrants of the replanned city. The most unusual feature was the treatment of the block interiors. Each block formed a separate parish. The parish church was to be located in a churchyard 260 by 140 feet at the center of each block, surrounded by a street with four points of egress to the main streets of the city along the frontage of the block. Newcourt thus provided a unique combination of splendid civic open spaces and the more intimate, domestic neighborhood or parish squares.

As it turned out, London adopted none of the various plans submitted for its rebuilding. But from the discussion of these proposals surely came a wider understanding of the problems involved in laying out cities. The effects on colonial town planning were

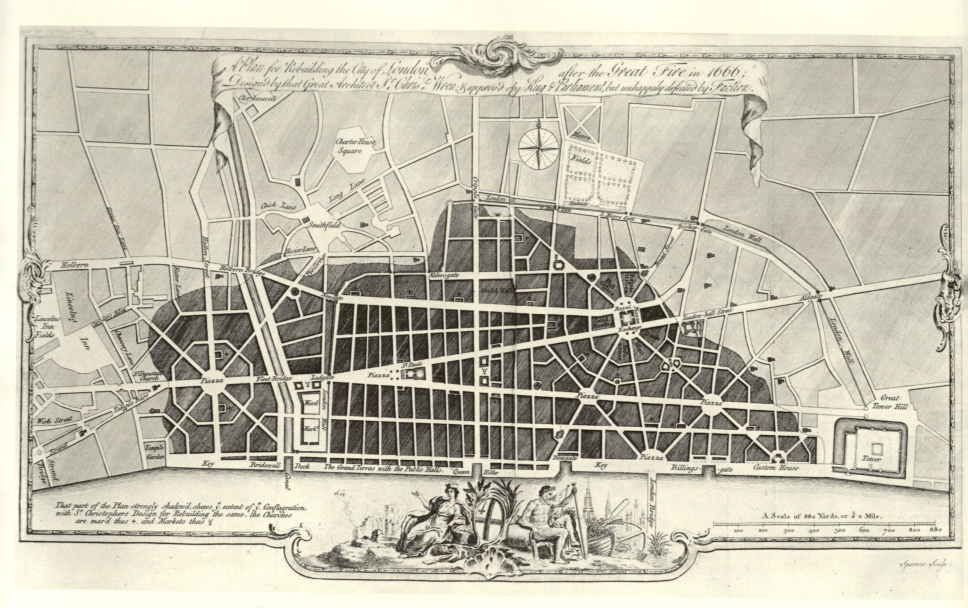

Within the map illustration:

A Plan for Rebuilding the City of London after the Great Fire in 1666; Designed by that Great Architect S.r Chris.r Wren, & approv'd of by King & Parliament, but unhappily defeated by Faction.

Clerkenwell

Charter House Square

Moore Fields

Bedlam

Chick Lane

Long Lane

London Wall

Cripple Gate

Moore Gate

Bishop Gate

London Wall

Smithfield

Hosier Lane

Holborn

Holborn Bridge

Newgate

Aldersgate

Guild Hall

South Sea Ho.

Royal

Excise Office

Aldgate

Lincolns Inn Fields

Lincolns Inn

Chancery Lane

St Dunstans Church

Piazza

Fleet Bridge

Ludgate

Piazza

St Pauls

Gold Smiths

Royal Exchange Bank

Leaden-hall Street

London Wall

Temple Barr

Wick Street

London Wall

Wood

Mark.t

Piazza

Piazza

Piazza

Great Tower Hill

Strand

Temple Garden

Key

Bridewell

Dock

The Grand Terras with the Public Halls.

Queen Hithe

Dowgate

Key

Billings-gate

Custom House

Tower

Canal

London Bridge

That part of the Plan strongly shadow'd, shews ÿ extent of ÿ Conflagration, with S.r Christophers Design for Rebuilding the same, the Churches are mar'd thus + and Markets thus ※

A Scale of 880 Yards, or ½ a Mile.

100   200   300   400   500   600   700   800   880

Sparrow Sculp:

Figure 8. Christopher Wren's Plan for Rebuilding London after the Fire of 1666

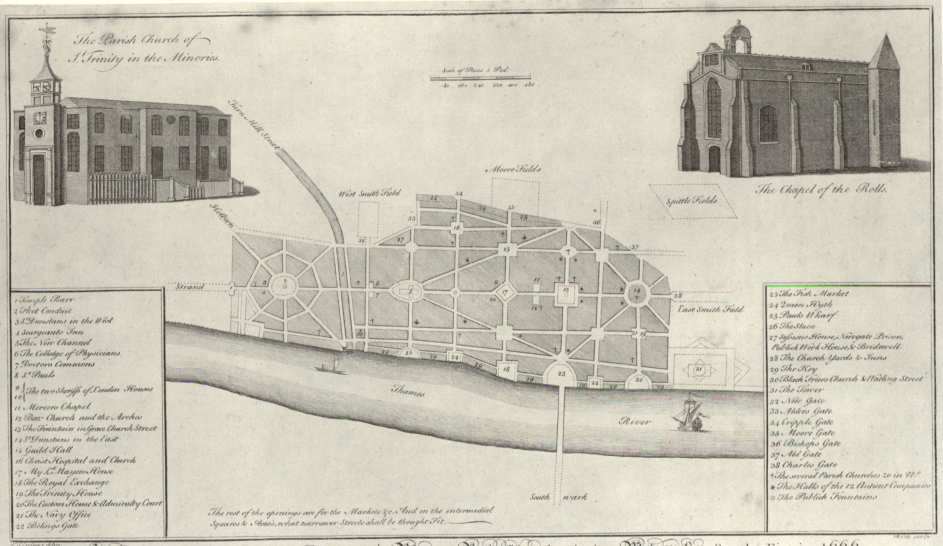

The Parish Church of S.t Trinity in the Minories.

The Chapel of the Rolls.

Scale of Paces 5 Ped.
80 160 240 320 400 480

Moore Fields

Spittle Fields

West Smith Field

Turn Mill Street

Holborn

Strand

Thames

River

South wark

East Smith Field

1 Temple Barr
2 Fleet Conduit
3 S.t Dunstans in the West
4 Seargeants Inn
5 The New Channel
6 The Colledge of Physicians
7 Doctors Commons
8 S.t Pauls
9 The two Sheriffs of London Houses
10
11 Mercers Chapel
12 Bow Church and the Arches
13 The Fountain in Grace Church Street
14 S.t Dunstans in the East
15 Guild Hall
16 Christ Hospital and Church
17 My L.d Mayors House
18 The Royal Exchange
19 The Trinity House
20 The Custom House & Admiralty Court
21 The Navy Office
22 Billings Gate

23 The Fish Market
24 Queen Hyth
25 Pauls Wharf
26 The Sluce
27 Sessions House, Newgate Prison, Publick Work House & Bridewell
28 The Church Yards & Inns
29 The Key
30 Black Friers Church & Watling Street
31 The Tower
32 New Gate
33 Alders Gate
34 Cripple Gate
35 Moore Gate
36 Bishops Gate
37 Ald Gate
38 Charles Gate
+ The several Parish Churches 20 in N.o
* The Halls of the 12 Antient Companies
o The Publick Fountains

The rest of the openings are for the Markets &c. And in the intermedial Squares & Areas, what narrower Streets shall be thought Fit.

J. Evelyn delin.

B. Cole sculp.

London Restored Or SIR IOHN EVELYN'S Plan for Rebuilding that Antient Metropolis after the Fire in 1666.

Figure 9. John Evelyn's Plan for Rebuilding London in 1666

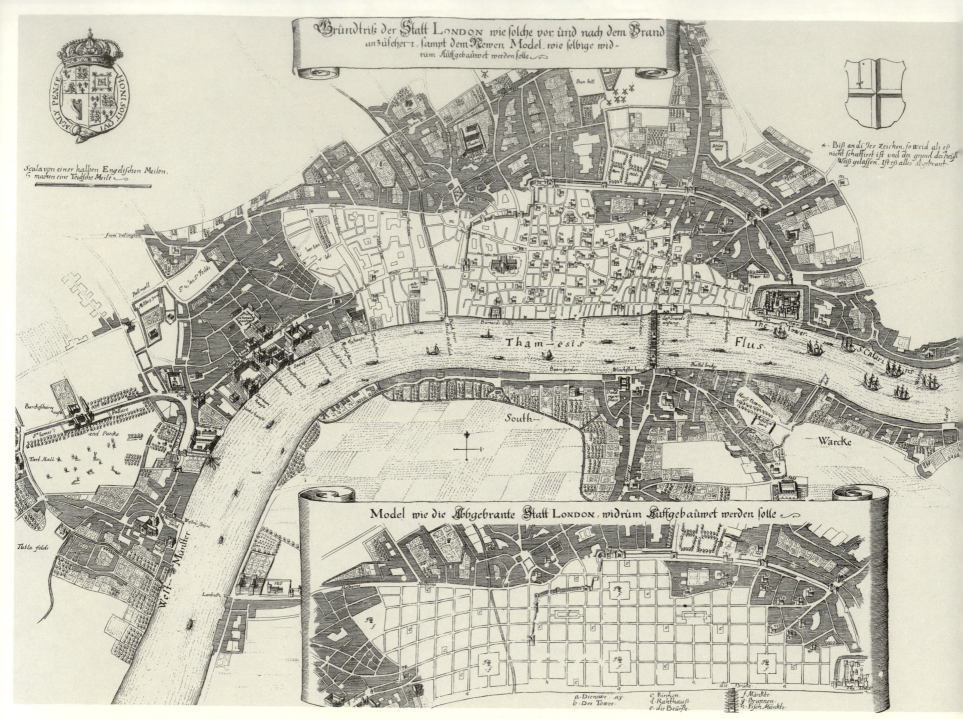

Figure 10. Plan of the Great Fire of London in 1666 and Robert Hooke's Proposal for Rebuilding the City

indirect and, as is often the case with elements of European planning, cannot be measured with precision. The new style of Baroque layout put forward by Wren and Evelyn for the capital of the Empire may well have had its first tentative application in the tiny capital city of Maryland some thirty years later. In 1681, William Penn or his surveyor Thomas Holme may have recalled Newcourt's plan when they came to lay out the streets and squares in Philadelphia. But the London plans of 1666 probably had an impact first on the design of individual urban improvement and extension projects in England and, through them, on the form of similar elements in the American colonial towns.

Piazza, Place, and Urban Square

In no other aspect of city planning did the Renaissance produce such numerous and magnificent results as in the development of great civic open spaces. As a practical matter, such projects were obviously less difficult to bring into reality than whole towns. First in Italy and then later throughout Europe, kings and popes, cardinals and princes sponsored the creation of planned urban spaces as settings for palaces, churches, and monumental groups of buildings. Many of Europe's greatest architectural glories date from this era.

Two general types of squares can be distinguished. The first to appear were the public squares—those conceived as settings for major buildings or as gathering places for religious, royal, or civic pageants and festivals. In some cases these planned squares were not entirely new. The great Piazza di San Marco in Venice, for example, functioned as a market and approach to St. Mark's as early as 1000. But a series of enlargement and building projects extending over several hundred years transformed this medieval open space into perhaps the grandest of all Renaissance urban compositions. Florence's Piazza della Signoria and Michelangelo's Piazza di Campidoglio in Rome shared similar origins. Other great open spaces, such as the Piazza di San Pietro, Bernini's masterpiece in the Vatican, were wholly or largely new creations.

In France the great civic squares developed at a later date, and in England later yet. Such Parisian landmarks as the Place de la Concorde and the Place de l'Opera were creations of the eighteenth and nineteenth centuries. And, in London, planned civic open spaces of the type developed on the continent scarcely existed before John Nash's bold scheme for Regent Street and the construction of Piccadilly Circus.

But, if France and England lagged behind Italy in such Renaissance and Baroque compositions, they led in the creation of the second major type of enclosed urban space, the residential square. The earliest complete example of any consequence of the residential square appeared in France. This was the Place Royale (now the Place des Vosges), begun in 1605 by Henry IV as one of the many improvements to Paris carried out by this energetic monarch. As early as 1563 Catherine de' Medici had conceived of a square here bordered by identical houses, and perhaps Henry recalled this earlier scheme when he issued orders for his own project.

The Place Royale, as shown in Figure 11, was square. Houses were built by individuals to designs established at the outset. Henry himself constructed the two larger buildings on the north and south sides somewhat taller than the others. Entrances opened off an arcaded sidewalk on the four sides. The center of the square was at first left in sand and for several years was used for tournaments. Then it was covered with turf; only in relatively recent times has it been planted with trees and decorative flower gardens.

Henry's square quickly became a fashionable place of residence for the minor aristocracy and wealthy commoners. During the eighteenth century it became less desirable as other quarters of the city assumed new importance. But for well over a century the Place Royale was properly regarded as a place of residence of quiet elegance. It remains virtually unchanged today, a monument to the aristocratic good taste and uncommonly sound judgment of its founder.

Henry also created another residential precinct of similar scale and character. The Place Dauphine, enclosing a triangular space at the point of the Ile de la Cité, was started in 1607. The base of the triangle has since been removed and only one of the original houses remains but much of the early atmosphere of this private residential close can still be appreciated. Both the Place Royale and the Place Dauphine represent significant departures from previous square planning. The domesticity, the quiet, the privacy all contrast with the imposing monumentality and bustle of the civic squares previously described. This urban innovation of the early seventeenth century soon found its way into town planning

Liure de diuerſes Veuës, Perſpectiues, et Payſages faicts ſur le naturel.
DEDIEZ AV ROY, par Iſrael auec Priuilege de **SA MAIESTE**.
A Paris Chez Iſrael Henriet. rue de larbre ſec au logis de Monſieur le Mercier Orſeure de la Reyne proche la croix du Tiroir. 1651.

Figure II. View of the Place Royale in Paris, France: 1652

practice, either as isolated elements in older towns or as part of the original plan of completely new communities.

But it was in Britain, first in London, then in such provincial cities as Bath, that the residential square achieved the highest order of development. The first London square was a frank imitation of continental models. Inigo Jones, retained by the Earl of Bedford in 1630 to design a residential development on the Bedford estate at the then outskirts of London, produced a neat arcaded rectangle of houses with the Tuscan church of St. Paul's at the south end. Although Covent Garden was never quite complete and soon became a market square, the concept of the residential square which it introduced into London quickly seized the public fancy.

This handy device for organizing urban residential space came at a time when the great estates at London's fringe offered financially attractive opportunities for land development. Fortunately the visual results were equally attractive—an almost unique example of land speculation producing urban design of a high order. In rapid sequence new squares appeared. They differed from models such as the Place Royale in their more restrained architecture and in the grassed or tree-shaded circles, ovals, or rectangles at their centers. Often the building façades were not exactly uniform, but they were almost always harmonious in scale, materials, colors, and general proportions.

The several hundred residential squares in London today testify to the popularity of this element of urban form in large-scale estate development. And it was not only in London but in towns throughout the British Isles that this pattern came to be employed. It is little wonder, therefore, that in the English colonial cities we shall see evidences of the influence of this popular plan.

Planned Extensions of European Cities

In addition to the planning of completely new towns and to the development of civic and residential squares, the European tradition included experience with guided and directed urban growth. In Rome, for example, several of the fifteenth- and sixteenth-century popes changed the face of classical and medieval Rome, cutting new streets, building bridges, and constructing new piazzas. Under Sixtus V (1585-1590), and with the advice of

Domenico Fontana, these improvements were consolidated and extended. Such new town extensions conformed to the doctrines of Alberti and Palladio in their formal layout and attention to the details of impressive street vistas and harmonious façade treatment.

Early in the seventeenth century Paris began to experience a period of growth aided by the vigorous policies of Henry IV. His Place Royale served as a node around which many new houses were constructed. New streets in this quarter generally followed rectangular alignments, although they deviated somewhat from a completely regular grid. Similar growth occurred in the Faubourg St. Germain across the Seine from the Tuileries Gardens. Here, too, the street pattern took rectangular form.

The most regular of these early seventeenth-century town addition projects was for the development of the Ile St. Louis. In 1608 Christophe Marie, a contractor, and his two financial partners, Poulletier and Le Regrattier, acquired the rights to develop the island and receive ground rents for sixty years. In return they agreed to construct embankments, two bridges, and to fill in the canal which divided the island. They adopted a simple grid plan that remains essentially unchanged today. One street bisected the island running down its center in the longest direction. Two others paralleled this along the two new quais. Three shorter streets crossed at right angles connecting one side of the island with the other. Important town extension schemes elsewhere in France generally followed similar patterns of regular layout. Not until the eighteenth century did the more elaborate diagonal boulevards of the Baroque planners begin to appear in these plans.

The form of town extension in England has already been mentioned in the previous section dealing with the London squares. Examination of seventeenth-century maps reveals the typical contrast of new rectilinear urban expansion surrounding a core of irregular narrow streets and lanes dating from medieval times. There were exceptions. Towns of Roman origin, such as Chester, or the rarer medieval planned towns, such as Salisbury, began with grid layouts in the center. And, beginning in the eighteenth century, notably at Bath, town extensions included crescents, circles, and ovals along with the more regular grid.

In Holland the art of planned town expansion reached a level of skill and perfection that has seldom been equaled. By the middle of the sixteenth century the basic patterns of such typical *grach-*

tensteden ("water towns") as Amsterdam, Leiden, and Delft had already taken shape. The late sixteenth-century plan of Delft appears in Figure 12. From the middle ages modest extensions had been made, each apparently carefully considered and the alternatives weighed before development was allowed. Extensive public works improvements were necessary in each case because of the engineering difficulties presented by the high water table and poor bearing qualities of the soil. Virtually every town extension involved the reclamation of land, extensive canal construction, and the sinking of piles on building sites. Speculative development by even the wealthiest of builders seemed unattractive under these circumstances. It was perhaps inevitable that urban extension projects thus depended on advance planning by municipal authorities. The cost of site engineering also made virtually impossible the development of piecemeal, scattered suburbs. The Dutch towns typically grew in an annular pattern through the addition of contiguous rings or limited off-shoots. The result was a compact town, yet one in which open space was not lacking because of the numerous drainage and navigation canals.

These town extensions, like those of the French and English, were generally rectangular in form, with small blocks facing on canals having streets on both sides. Behind the houses with their party walls stretched narrow gardens. Domestic in scale, yet urbane and dignified, these Dutch town planning projects attained such marked urban character that they still may serve as models from which modern planners can learn much.

The pilgrims who fled from England at the beginning of the seventeenth century first settled in Amsterdam at about the same time that one of these town additions took form. When they moved to Leiden they found a similar extension under way. Its effect on their own later planning appears to have been slight, but the same careful ordering of a town pattern can be seen in the somewhat later Dutch settlements at New Amsterdam and along the Hudson River.

Gardens, Parks, and the Design of Towns

We come now to the final element of the European planning tradition that influenced the design of American towns, both in colonial times and in the years following independence. For our exploration of this subject we must go back to the earliest years of the Renaissance in Italy and the development of ducal palaces, villas, and estates. Following perhaps medieval monastic herbal garden design and the descriptions of Roman gardens in such works as Pliny's, designers of early Renaissance villas included garden design as an integral part of the whole composition. These gardens commonly were divided into many groups of plant materials separated by paths. Geometric arrangements prevailed. Major paths normally divided the entire garden into some kind of grid pattern, although the resulting beds or *parterres* were not all the same dimensions. Minor paths further subdivided the *parterres* into smaller planning groups. At the beginning of the Renaissance these too were rectilinear in pattern.

These gardens were designed to be seen from above, from the terraces, the porches, and balconies of the villa or palace. To dazzle the eye of the beholder, more intricate and elaborate patterns were sought. Within individual *parterres* the paths and planted beds were now laid out with diagonal and circular lines. Within the basic grid pattern of the major garden paths an almost bewildering variety of *parterre* design could be seen. These principles of landscape architecture became widely accepted throughout Europe.

In the layout of these gardens we can find the same techniques that Renaissance architects advocated for the design of new towns and the reconstruction of old ones. The use of major and minor axes, the introduction of buildings, fountains, or statues as terminal points of major circulation routes, the planning of open spaces at intervals to add interest and variety—these features were shared by town and garden design. Even the use of uniform façade and cornice lines along major city streets had its counterpart in the dense clipped hedges and trees lining the edges of garden *parterres*. One can find, also, in *parterre* design almost exact duplicates of the dozens of ideal city layouts that have previously been mentioned. This does not imply that one was copied from the other; it indicates only that the same philosophy of design and the same techniques of layout were generally accepted as being equally appropriate to town and garden.

Garden design reached its height in France during the last half of the seventeenth century under André Le Nôtre. First at Vaux-le-Vicomte for Fouquet and then at Versailles for Louis XIV, Le Nôtre elaborated and vastly extended the Italian garden concept.

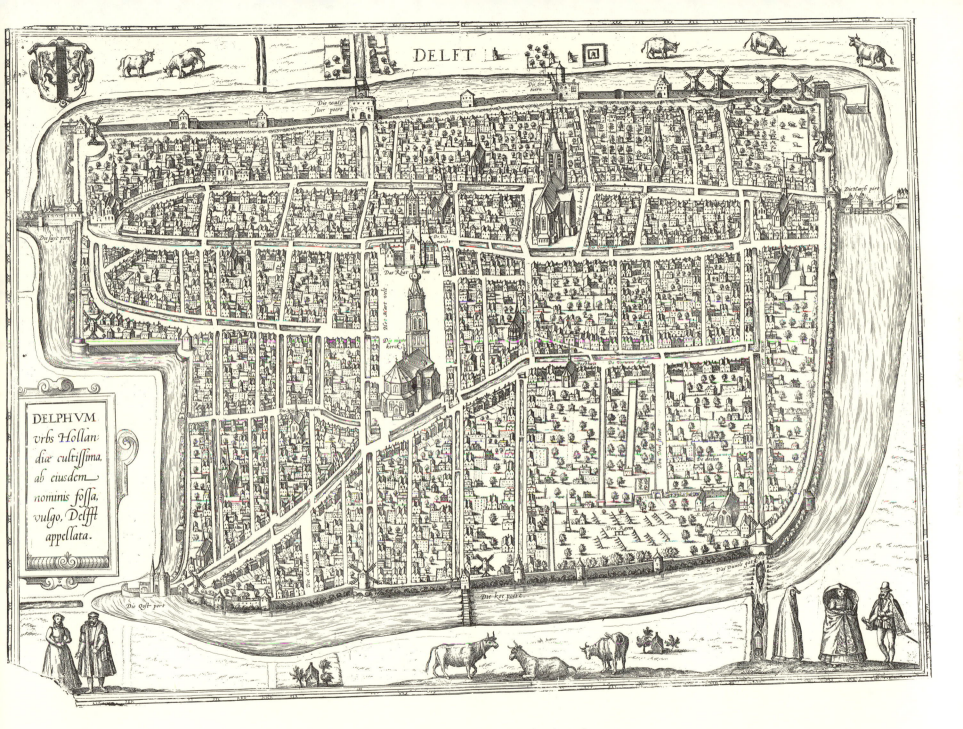

DELFT

Die water
sloer poert

Die Stel
toern

Die Tacch port

Die syck port

Die oude Gasthus   Ceren maer

Het oude Galhuis

Die Voer kraet

Die oude kercke

Das Raet hus

De Vis
marckt

Aglen kelter

Die nicuer
kerck

Die nieu
volck

Die Coer

De Verwens dyck

Peft hus

Den Duel Trast

De doelen

Die Corr welt

Die Hol wer brueder

S. Clare

Den Raem

DELPHVM
*vrbs Hollan-
diæ cultissima,
ab eiusdem
nominis fossa,
vulgo, Delfft
appellata.*

Die Cokelarn

Das Dunels gate

Die Qost port

Die koe poert

Figure 12. Plan of Delft, Holland: 1582

For our purposes it is sufficient to note at Versailles the introduction of an additional element, as the plan in Figure 13 clearly shows. Beyond the garden proper, with its intricate *parterres*, each vying with the other, stretched the great royal park. Here Le Nôtre ran tree-lined *allées* radiating outward from *rond-points* in bold diagonal lines. These were echoed on the opposite side of the chateau by two diagonal streets running through the town of Versailles and meeting the main approach road in a great forecourt stretching out from the chateau.

This new scale of design was soon to be employed in Paris itself. The Avenue des Champs-Elysées and the streets radiating from the Place de l'Etoile repeat Versailles in an urban setting. Much later, in the last half of the nineteenth century, Haussmann continued the same style of planning in his gigantic undertaking to remake Paris. These planning projects in Paris occurred after the pattern of French colonial towns had already been established, but they affected strongly the course of American city planning. We will indicate later the extent to which L'Enfant, the planner of Washington, drew on his familiarity with Versailles and Paris in his design for the new capital city of an infant nation. And at the beginning of the present century the fathers of modern American city planning turned once again to French and particularly Parisian models to guide their own efforts in beautifying American cities.

Later developments in European garden design were important as sources of inspiration first for American cemetery layout, then for public park design, and finally for the romantic patterns of new suburban developments. These will be discussed in a later chapter; they are mentioned here to emphasize the impact on city planning that garden and landscape design has had from medieval times to the present.

Enough has now been said to provide the reader with some understanding of the state of European town planning just prior to American colonization. We are now ready to examine the planning of towns in the New World and to analyze the ways in which these European devices for bringing order to urban settlements were applied in a new environment and under new economic, social, and political institutions.

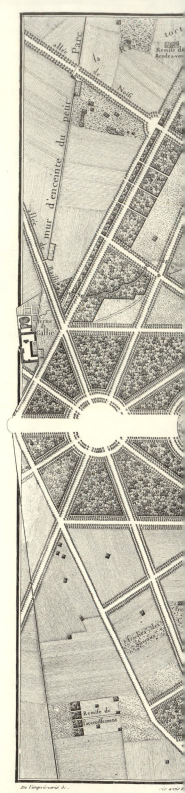

Figure 13. Plan of the Town, Chateau, and Gardens of Versailles, France: 1746

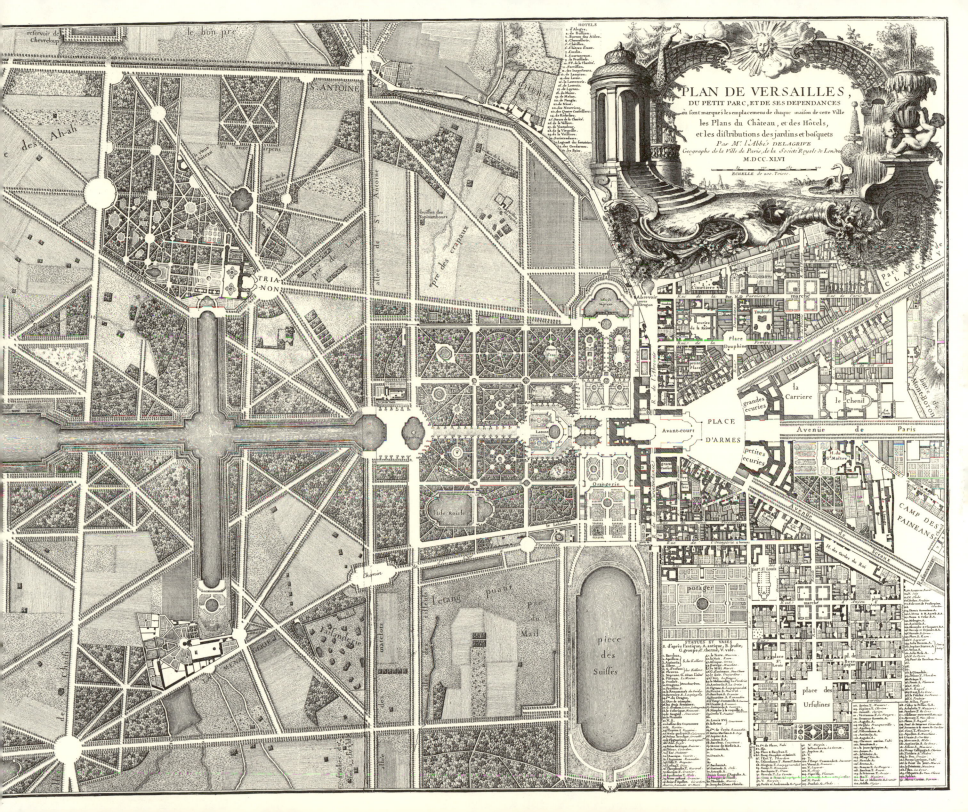

CHAPTER 2

The Spanish Towns of Colonial America

THE Spanish empire in North America was nearing its end. Within the cool walls of Mission San Gabriel, shielded from the hot August sun in the year 1781, sat Philipe de Neve, Governor of the province of Upper California. Finally he put down his pen and reread the document on which he had been working so carefully:

"For the establishment of the Pueblo of Los Angeles . . . there shall be included all the lands that may be benefited by irrigation. . . .

"The site where the pueblo is to be established shall be marked out, on land slightly elevated, exposed to the north and south winds. Measures shall be taken to avoid the dangers of floods; the most immediate vicinity to the river . . . shall be preferred, taking care that from the pueblo the whole or greatest portion of the planting lands be seen.

"The plaza ought to be 200 feet wide by 300 long, from said plaza four main streets shall extend, two on each side, and besides these two other streets shall run by each corner. . . . For the purpose of building there shall be marked out as many building lots as there may be agricultural plots susceptible of irrigation. Also, a tract of land 600 feet wide between the planting lands and the pueblo shall be left vacant.

"Every building lot shall measure 60 feet wide by 120 feet long. . . .

"The front of the plaza looking towards the east shall be reserved to erect at the proper time the church and government buildings and other public offices, and the adjoining lots shall be allotted to settlers."[1]

---

[1] *Instruccion para la fundacion de Los Angeles*, from a translation of the document in the Archives of California, State Papers, Missions and Colonization, I, used in evidence in the case of *Annis Merril v. J. S. Joerenhout, et al.*, filed in California Superior Court, Los Angeles County, May 10, 1869. Slightly edited for form by the author.

With these instructions de Neve began the settlement of one of America's great cities and, although he could not know it, the last civil settlement by the Spanish to survive within the limits of the United States. Los Angeles was the last of these Spanish towns, but the first, St. Augustine, had been founded more than two hundred years earlier. During that interval dozens of military, ecclesiastical, and civil settlements arose under Spanish rule.

To a far greater degree than any other colonizing power in the New World Spain followed a system of land settlement and town planning formalized in written rules and regulations. Although time and man have succeeded in obliterating many of the results of this period of American city building, much still remains. In a great arc from the Gulf States to New Mexico and up through California to the Golden Gate curves the land once subject to Spanish rule. Here and there, now almost hidden by later urban accretions, may still be seen the precious heritage of this era in our urban history.

For an understanding of the urban pattern established by the Spanish we must go back to the very discovery of the land itself —to the end of the fifteenth century, when the voyages of Columbus revealed a new continent and the way was opened for white settlement in America.

Española and its Colonial Towns

When, in December 1492, Christopher Columbus built a crude fortress from the timbers of the wrecked *Santa Maria* on the northern coast of the island of Española, he began an era of city planning in the Americas. La Navidad, that first primitive military outpost of Europeans in the New World, did not survive, nor did the thirty-nine men Columbus left behind as its first settlers when he sailed back to Spain to report his discoveries. The first true city was laid out the following year when Columbus returned with

URBS DOMINGO IN HISPANIOLA

Figure 14. Plan of Santo Domingo, Dominican Republic: 1671

twelve hundred colonists and founded the town of Isabella some miles to the east of the abandoned La Navidad. But Isabella, too, failed to survive, and it was not until 1496 that a permanent settlement was finally established. This was Santo Domingo, on the southern side of the island, the oldest existing city founded by Europeans in America.

We do not know what the original plan of that city was like, for in 1501 the city was moved across the river to the west and re-established on its present site. A few early views of Santo Domingo exist, but their sketchy details or stylized representation furnish little information about the original form of the city. Accurate and detailed plans or views, such as the one reproduced in Figure 14, date from a much later period and cannot be relied on as depicting the original layout. This view shows the city in 1671. By that time Santo Domingo served as one of the most important Spanish administrative centers and the regular plan, central plaza, and imposing buildings quite likely represent later additions not foreseen in the original plan.

Columbus and other early voyagers were dispatched from Spain to open up trade routes to China and Japan. For the first decade or so they were under the impression that the land they had reached was part of fabulous Cathay. The Spanish crown was totally unprepared for the task of exploring an unknown continent, selecting sites for cities, bringing in colonists, distributing land, and administering the affairs of an enterprise based on farming and mining rather than trade and plunder. Only gradually did it become apparent that a new empire lay before them, one which must be settled and subjugated before it could yield the riches that were so confidently expected.

Further exploration soon revealed the vast dimensions of the new discovery. Port towns were needed first to serve as outfitting points for expeditions and as bases for supplies and anticipated trade. Leaders of expeditions setting out from Spain were evidently given great latitude in deciding on the location and layout of these early colonial towns. For example, Ferdinand in 1501 instructed Orviedo only in these general terms:

"As it is necessary in the island of Espanola to make settlements and from here it is not possible to give precise instructions, investigate the possible sites, and in conformity with the quality of the land and sites as well as with the present population outside present settlements establish settlements in the numbers and in the places that seem proper to you."[2]

Within a few years, however, much more precise instructions were being issued. The following directive to Pedrarias Davila indicates that as early as 1513 a body of town planning experience and principles had developed and that closer central control over colonial planning was being asserted:

"One of the most important things to observe is that . . . the places chosen for settlement . . . be healthy and not swampy, good for unloading goods; if inland to be on a river if possible . . . good water and air, close to arable land. . . .

"In view of these things necessary for settlements, and seeking the best site in these terms for the town, then divide the plots for houses, these to be according to the status of the persons, and from the beginning it should be according to a definite arrangement; for the manner of setting up the *solares* will determine the pattern of the town, both in the position of the plaza and the church and in the pattern of streets, for towns newly founded may be established according to plan without difficulty. If not started with form, they will never attain it."[3]

As settlements extended into the Caribbean islands, Mexico, and Central and South America, and as the pace of colonization accelerated, the issuance of individual orders and directives for each expedition was found to be inefficient and unnecessary. In 1573 the Laws of the Indies established uniform standards and procedures for planning of towns and their surrounding lands as well as for all the other details of colonial settlement. The Laws of the Indies, at least as they affected town planning, represented a codification of practices that had become fairly standardized some years earlier. A study of the plans of cities founded before 1573 indicates that the

[2] Colección de documentos inéditos relativos al descubrimiento, conquista y colonización de las posesiones españolas en América y Oceanía, sacodos, en su mayor parte, del Real Archivo de Indias, XXXI, 1879, 17-18, as quoted by Dan Stanislawski, "Early Spanish Town Planning in the New World," *The Geographical Review*, XXXVII, January 1947, 95.
[3] *ibid.*, XXXIX, 284-85, as quoted by Stanislawski, 96.

· 28 ·

town planning regulations of the Laws of the Indies must have been generally followed at least as early as 1561.[4]

Because of the relative inflexibility of Spanish colonial policy the regulations of 1573 remained virtually unchanged throughout the entire period of Spanish rule in the Western Hemisphere. Even beyond that time they influenced the plans of towns laid out in North America by the Mexican government after its separation from Spain. Literally hundreds of communities in the Western Hemisphere were planned in conformity to these laws—a phenomenon unique in modern history. Because of their influence and because the urban forms prescribed by these regulations are of such interest, the Laws of the Indies deserve more than casual examination.

The Laws of the Indies: America's First Planning Legislation

Philip II proclaimed the royal ordinances governing the planning of new cities on July 3, 1573, but the real author of these regulations is not known. Whoever he may have been we know one thing about him: he was thorough and conscientious, for there are more than three dozen specifications or admonitions set forth as guiding principles. They begin, as might be expected, with the selection of a suitable site. One on an elevation surrounded by good farming land and with a good water supply and available fuel and timber was favored. The plan was to be decided upon before any construction, and it was to be ample in scope. As the regulations stated:

"The plan of the place, with its squares, streets and building lots is to be outlined by means of measuring by cord and ruler, beginning with the main square from which streets are to run to the gates and principal roads and leaving sufficient open space so that even if the town grows it can always spread in a symmetrical manner."[5]

Several paragraphs of the regulations dealt with the plaza, that distinctive element in all Spanish-American towns. For coastal cities the regulations prescribed a location for the plaza near the shore; for inland cities, in the center of the town. As to shape, the regulations specified that the length should be at least one and a half times the width since "this proportion is the best for festivals in which horses are used. . . ." Planners were instructed to consider the eventual size of the town in deciding on the dimensions of the main plaza. Here the regulations were quite specific:

"It shall not be smaller than two hundred feet wide and three hundred feet long nor larger than eight hundred feet long and three hundred feet wide. A well proportioned medium size plaza is one six hundred feet long and four hundred feet wide."[6]

The main plaza was to be oriented so that its four corners pointed to the four cardinal points of the compass. This feature was designed to prevent exposure "to the four principal winds," which would otherwise result in "much inconvenience." In other parts of the towns smaller, "well proportioned" open spaces were to be provided as sites for churches and other religious buildings.

From the main plaza principal streets were to lead from the middle of each side, with two minor streets also diverging from each corner. The regulations called for another distinctive aspect of Spanish colonial towns:

"The whole plaza and the four main streets diverging from it shall have arcades, for these are a great convenience for those who resort thither for trade. The eight streets which run into the plaza at its four corners are to do so freely without being obstructed by the arcades of the plaza. These arcades are to end at the corners in such a way that the sidewalks of the streets can evenly join those of the plaza."[7]

Other streets were to be located "consecutively around the plaza," and, although nowhere do the regulations so state, it is obvious that the laws envisaged a gridiron or checkerboard pattern of straight streets with intersections at right angles.

[4] The plans of two settlements in Argentina, Mendoza in 1561 and San Juan de la Frontera in 1562, are virtually identical to later towns planned under the Laws of the Indies. These plans and more than three hundred others can be found in *Planos de Ciudades Iberoamericanas y Filipinas Existentes en el Archivo de Indias*, Madrid, 1951, I.

[5] The translation used throughout is from Zelia Nuttall, "Royal Ordinances Concerning the Laying Out of New Towns," *The Hispanic American His-* *torical Review*, v, 1922, 249-54. The original document is Archivo Nacional Ms. 3017, "Bulas y Cedulas para el Gobierno de las Indias."

[6] *ibid.*

[7] *ibid.*

The regulations provided precise guides for the location of the important buildings of the town. The main church of a coastal city was to face on the plaza and set near the harbor, so constructed that it might be used as a defensive fortification in the event of attack. In inland towns, however, the church was to be at a distance from the plaza, separate from other buildings and if possible on an elevated site. Other sites around the plaza were to be assigned for the town hall, the customs house, arsenal, a hospital, and other public buildings. Remaining sites on the plaza were to be allotted for shops and dwellings for merchants.

As for the location of ordinary dwelling sites and for future expansion, the regulations stated:

"The remaining building lots shall be distributed by lottery to those of the settlers who are entitled to build around the main plaza. Those left over are to be held for us to grant settlers who may come later or to dispose of at our pleasure."[8]

After the drawing for lots the regulations provided that a settler should erect a tent or temporary hut on his site and then join in the construction of a palisade around the plaza for immediate safety against Indian attack.

The town itself was to be but one element in the settlement unit. Surrounding the central or urban core,

"A common shall be assigned to each town, of adequate size so that even though it should grow greatly there would always be sufficient space for its inhabitants to find recreation and for cattle to pasture without encroaching upon private property."[9]

Beyond the common were to be located the agricultural lands. There were to be as many parcels as there were town lots, and these were also to be distributed by drawing lots. If within the community territory there were lands capable of being irrigated these were also to be subdivided into farming tracts and similarly distributed. Remaining farm land was reserved to the crown for distribution to settlers who might come at a later time.

There were many additional regulations governing such matters as construction of houses, planting, cattle breeding, and other de-

tails important in establishing a self-sufficient colony with efficiency and dispatch. One brief regulation covered the appearance of the community: "Settlers are to endeavor, as far as possible, to make all structures uniform, for the sake of the beauty of the town."

And, finally, the town founders were admonished not to permit any Indians to enter the community during its construction until the fortifications and the houses were complete,

". . . so that when the Indians see them they will be filled with wonder and will realize that the Spaniards are settling there permanently and not temporarily. They will consequently fear the Spaniards so much that they will not dare to offend them and will respect them and desire their friendship."[10]

These regulations stand out as one of the most important documents in the history of urban development. The fact that almost without exception they were followed in the construction of so many towns throughout the Spanish possessions in the Americas makes them doubly significant. Because this study is concerned with tracing the sources of ideas that contributed to city form, the background of the town planning sections of the Laws of the Indies must be examined.

Many of the regulations doubtless grew out of the experience gained in the first city planning efforts by the Spanish. The results of these colonization activities received the attention of the Council of the Indies in Spain, and by the first quarter of the sixteenth century a substantial number of reports would have been available. Royal instructions for each successive colonization expedition probably incorporated the lessons learned from the previous settlement.

This explanation fails to account for the detailed and highly sophisticated doctrines of planning embodied so early in the Laws of the Indies. If the regulations of 1573 are regarded as largely a codification of rules that had been established perhaps fifty years earlier, the hypothesis that the laws emerged entirely from a trial and error process seems even more remote. There were other sources from which the Spanish could draw.

As the previous chapter has indicated, two comprehensive treatises on town planning and civil architecture existed before the beginning of Spanish colonization. The earliest and probably best

[8] *ibid.*
[9] *ibid.*

[10] *ibid.*

known was the *Ten Books on Architecture* of Vitruvius, written about 30 B.C. and rediscovered early in the fifteenth century. On many points the regulations in the Laws of the Indies closely resemble the principles of city planning established by Vitruvius. To select but a few examples, Vitruvius suggested that the forum should be rectangular, that its dimensions should be in the ratio of three to two; the forum should be located near the harbor if in a coastal city or in the center of the town if inland; public buildings should be given sites around the forum; and religious buildings should be located on an elevation. The similarity is unmistakable, and we have every reason to believe from internal evidence that the Spanish planners and colonial administrators drew heavily on Vitruvius in formulating their own regulations for town development.[11]

Another possible source, and one closer in time to the period of Spanish colonization, was the great work on architecture by Alberti. In addition to his own recommendations for the planning of towns and the siting and design of buildings, Alberti's work contained a summary of the suggestions of Vitruvius and other Roman and Greek authorities on the main elements of civic design. Alberti also advocated a gridiron plan with straight streets and right-angle intersections and that certain noxious uses, like tanneries, be located apart and downwind from the city. Both points find their counterparts in the Spanish regulations.

There were in addition actual examples of city planning on which the Spanish might have based some of their regulations. In Spain itself were many Roman colonial cities planted on the Iberian Peninsula centuries before. Santa Fé, the siege town laid out near Granada, and the *bastide* type communities in northern Spain may also have been partial models. North of the Pyrenees in south-

ern France lay dozens of planned communities. Most of them were planned on a gridiron pattern with central colonnaded squares on which the church and other principal buildings fronted. These *bastide* communities were so numerous and so located on strategic land routes that it is difficult to believe they were unknown to the Spanish, isolated as they were at the end of the great peninsula of Europe.

Then, too, almost on the scale of complete towns were the great monastic complexes throughout Europe. Many of them were planned on roughly rectangular lines and usually included a colonnaded cloister surrounding some open court or green. Philip II was himself responsible for one of the greatest and most regular of these—San Lorenze el Real del Escorial, begun in 1563, a decade before the Laws of the Indies were proclaimed. It is at least possible that the architectural and planning experience gained in the layout of these ecclesiastical building complexes may have influenced the pattern of the towns in New Spain, where the power and authority of religious orders seemed at times to rival that of the king.

The Spanish also were aware of the results of the Renaissance in Italy. In Rome under Pope Sixtus IV (1471-1484), in Florence, and in other Italian cities, great urban extension and reconstruction projects had been completed or planned by the beginning of the sixteenth century. Cultural and economic ties to Italy were closer than with any other European country, and the election of the Spanish pope, Alexander VI (1492-1503), undoubtedly gave rise to more frequent contacts with Italian culture. The new, formal principles of architecture symbolized by Alberti and his fellows must have been thoroughly familiar to Spanish architects.

Finally, in view of the strong military character of most of the early Spanish settlements, the influence of writers on castrametation should not be underestimated. The previous chapter mentioned and briefly described some of the theories of military encampment that had begun to appear early in the sixteenth century. The Spanish obviously were acquainted with these treatises and, through their involvement in the Italian wars as allies of the Kingdom of Naples, they had every opportunity to observe theories of encampment in action. Machiavelli's *Arte della Guerra* first appeared in 1521 and included an encampment plan with a central

---

[11] Stanislawski has made a detailed comparison of Vitruvian principles and the regulations of the Laws of the Indies. See pp. 102-104 of his "Early Spanish Town Planning." Stanislawski, however, is under the impression that Vitruvius advocated a gridiron plan, and his claim for Vitruvius as virtually the only source of inspiration for the Laws can thus hardly be sustained. In fact, Vitruvius clearly indicates his belief that there were eight principal winds and that streets and alleys should "be laid down on the lines of division between the quarters of two winds." Vitruvius, *The Ten Books on Architecture*, translated and edited by Morris Hicky Morgan, Cambridge, 1926, p. 27. The Vitruvian city thus had a radial street system and was either octagonal or circular in outline.

square, rectangular perimeter, and gridiron streets essentially similar to the Santa Fé of Ferdinand and Isabella. The works of Polybius describing Roman castrametation practices were published in 1530, and another treatise on Roman encampment appeared in 1555 by Guillaume du Choul. This latter was translated into Spanish in 1579, an indication that the subject had already stimulated interest in Spain. These and later writers all advocated the grid system of planning within a square or rectangular enclosure and called for some kind of open area or square near the center for command headquarters.

The Roman *castra* often developed into towns and cities with building blocks replacing the camp squares marked out for the cohorts of legions and auxiliaries. For communities planned in the beginning as civil settlements the Romans merely adapted the *castrum* plan for permanent use. The Spanish were familiar with this aspect of the history of Roman colonial towns. It seems likely that the advisers to the Spanish crown on colonial settlement policy would lean heavily on castrametation theory and practice in drafting the town planning sections of the Laws of the Indies.[12]

What has been said about the possible origins of the city planning principles given legal form in the Laws of the Indies indicates that many diverse sources were available during the development of Spanish colonial policy. The history of ideas is never a simple matter, particularly when dealing with a series of events so distant in time and so meagerly documented. One fact is clear: the Laws of the Indies represented a unique combination of town planning doctrines and prescribed practices. They stemmed from a number of diverse European sources, modified by experience in the islands and on the mainland of Hispanic-America, and represent the best efforts by Spanish authorities to provide detailed guides for the founders of future colonial towns.

Now we turn to the practical results of the Laws of the Indies as they governed the towns established within what is now the United States. The approach will be from east to west, coinciding roughly with the chronological development of Spanish cities in our country. Examples of these towns in the Gulf States and in the Southwest will be discussed, with a more detailed treatment of

land division in and around these towns being reserved for the concluding sections dealing with California.

St. Augustine

By the middle of the sixteenth century New Spain had become a rich source of treasure for the mother country. Twice each summer convoys of merchant ships, guarded by Spanish men-of-war, sailed northward from Havana between the Florida coast and the Bahamas. In the vicinity of Bermuda they set an eastward course for the Azores and then to Seville. Their cargoes had been loaded at a dozen or more important and thriving port cities in the Caribbean islands, the northern coast of South America, and along Central America and Mexico. In half a century a European urban culture had been established in these tropical lands.

The Florida Straits were perilous waters for the clumsy, heavily laden treasure ships, and many of them failed to survive the tropical storms that drove them ashore and left them wrecked on the Florida beaches. Pirate ships and raiders from countries unfriendly to Spain constituted another and different kind of menace. It soon became apparent to Spanish colonial authorities that a strong base on the eastern coast of Florida was needed. From here counterattacks against the pirates and privateers could be launched, and a port could also shelter rescue ships needed to render aid to merchant vessels that might founder along that uninhibited coast.

Earlier efforts to establish mission settlements in Florida, Georgia, and the Carolinas had been only partially successful. A few had survived for a time, but ultimately they had all been abandoned. Spain was soon spurred to action by the unwelcome news that a French expedition under one Jean Ribaut had sailed in 1561 to establish a fortress colony somewhere along the southeast coast of the American continent. Although this colony did not succeed, a second party set out in 1564 commanded by René de Laudonnière. Not only did this group represent a rival European power but the French expedition consisted of Huguenots, thus posing a double threat to Catholic Spain.

Laudonnière's party landed near the mouth of the St. John's River, built a fortification named Fort Caroline, the plan of which appears in Chapter 16 as Figure 260, and laid out a little village on an adjoining meadow. Here a hundred and fifty soldiers, four

[12] Turpin C. Bannister was the first, so far as I am aware, to point out the importance of the castrametation literature as a possible influence on the early plans of American cities.

women, and perhaps fifty artisans and servants began a perilous existence. Discipline was weak, and at least two groups abandoned the colony to begin a series of attacks on Spanish shipping in the vicinity. In 1565 a third group of French arrived, led again by Ribaut, and the reinforced colony began to spread along the coast.

Philip II began a series of negotiations with the French in an effort to bring about the withdrawal of the colony from territory claimed by the Spanish; when these broke down he ordered Don Pedro Menéndez de Avilés, an experienced soldier and skilled mariner to remove the French and establish a Spanish base on the Florida coast. In return for military and trading privileges in Florida, Menéndez was to transport five hundred colonists, including a hundred soldiers and an equal number of sailors; three hundred artisans, craftsmen, and laborers, two hundred of which were to be married; four Jesuits and ten or twelve monks of some other order; and five hundred slaves for the purpose of establishing at least two towns and appropriate fortifications. In July 1565 the fleet sailed from Cadiz, and after calling in Caribbean ports for supplies arrived at what is now the site of our earliest city on St. Augustine's day, August 28. Sailing up the coast, Menéndez had a preliminary skirmish with the little French fleet off Fort Caroline, and then returned to his original landfall on September 6 to disembark his troops and erect a temporary fortification. During the following two days the other colonists came ashore, and Menéndez formally took possession of the territory in the name of the Spanish king. Although the next year the settlement was moved some distance away to a more advantageous location, the year 1565 properly dates the founding of the city. It was a community established in blood, since Menéndez within a short time overwhelmed Fort Caroline and mercilessly cut down one hundred and thirty-two of the captured garrison.[13]

Plans of St. Augustine showing the city soon after its founding provide only limited details of its plan. The map reproduced in Figure 15 shows the harbor, fort, and town at the time of Francis Drake's attack in 1586. The fort was located to command the nar-row entrance to the harbor from the sea. The town itself may be seen in the upper left corner as a little gridiron settlement of eleven blocks of various sizes. The open space where the twelfth block might be expected may indicate the plaza, which, according to the Laws of the Indies specifications for seaport towns, would have opened to the water.

A more detailed plan of the town nearly two centuries later appears in Figure 16. The generally rectangular street system is readily apparent, and, in the size and location of the plaza, the city generally conforms to the regulations established by the Laws of the Indies. But many irregularities in the street alignment and size of blocks appear, indicating either a more casual plan or laxity in guiding development not exhibited in later colonial settlements. Menéndez, in 1565, was of course not guided by the Laws of the Indies, and he had evidently been given almost complete freedom in deciding on the plan of his settlement.

One feature that can be noticed on the plan is the open character of the community. Houses fronted directly on the streets, leaving generous areas to the rear for lawns and gardens. As in most of the Spanish colonial towns, houses usually rose two stories high. The roofs were generally flat. Balconies at the upper levels over porticoed entrances added interest to the street façades.

Town life focused on the plaza. At its upper end stood the governor's house with a balcony on the front and galleries along its sides. The main church and guardhouse were on the plaza itself, while other churches were located along the principal streets. At the northern edge of the city stood the fortress surrounded by a ditch and earth bastions. The entire community was enclosed by a palisade, strengthened at intervals by watchtowers and minor fortifications.

St. Augustine combined three distinct functions in one community. The city was, first of all, a military post with its fort and military garrison. Secondly, it was designed as a civil settlement for trade, farming, and handicraft industry. And, finally, it was intended as a center from which religious orders would begin the work of converting the Indians to Christianity. Toward the end of the sixteenth century it became the policy of Spain to establish separate settlements for these three types of activity: missions for religious orders and the Indians who were being converted; *presidios* for military establishments with their ancillary activities;

---

[13] In this summary account of the beginnings of French and Spanish colonization in Florida I have relied chiefly on Woodbury Lowery, *The Spanish Settlements Within the Present Limits of the United States: Florida, 1562-1574*, New York, 1911.

Saint Augustine.

A The place where the whole Fleete came to ancker.
B The place where the Pinnaces and Shipboats did set vs on shore.
C A Beacon or high scaffolde standing on the sand hils, wherein the Spaniards did vse to discouer ships at sea.
D The way which our army marched along the sand by the sea side towardes their fort.
E The place where our Pinnaces put our ordinaunce on land.
F A lowe plaine or meadow ground through the which our troupes passed to go towards the woods right ouer against the Spaniards forte.

G A wood growing hard by the riuer side, hauing betweene it and the riuer side a high bancke of sande, in which wood our men encamped themselues, and in the said great bancke of sand, being fitted for the purpose was placed also two peeces of ordinaunce to beate the Spanish forte, which was done with such expedition as they were planted and discharged twise or thrise the same day we landed, meaning the next day to haue had more ordinaunce brought, and to haue it planted on the same side of the riuer wherein the fort is, whither Master Carleill our Lieutenant generall was minded the same night to transport him-
self & some part of the army, to lodge himself in some trenches close by the fort, but the Spaniards perceiuing the approch abandoned the place before the day.
H A Pinnace which the Spaniards had lying hard by their forte in the little riuer.
I The fort which the Spaniardes had made of the bodies of Cedar trees, they placed therein some fourteene great and long peeces of artillery, which at our arriuall there to the sand bancke played vpon vs, the forte was called Saint John de Pinos which afterward we burned.

K Our Pinnaces as they rowed vp the riuer being all full of men, who because the way was not passable were faine to embarke them selues to take the towne of Saint Augustine, which being wonne was at our departure burned to the ground.
L The towne of Saint Augustine where dwelled a hundred and fifty Spanish souldiers.
M The towne house.
N A high scaffold for a watchman.
O The Church.

P The liuely purtraicture of a fish called the Dolphin, which is of three seuerall coullours: the top of his backe and all his fins be blue, all his sides are of light greene, the belly white, his head almost all blue, the taile one parte blue, and the lower parte greene, he is very pleasant to beholde in the sea by day light, and in the night he seemeth to be of the coullour of gold, he taketh pleasure as other fishes do by swimming by the ship, he is excellent sweete to be eaten, this fish liueth most by chasing of the flying fish and other small fishes, they are caught most commonly by our mariners with harping irons or fisgigs.

Figure 15. View of the Harbor, Fort and Town of St. Augustine, Florida: 1586

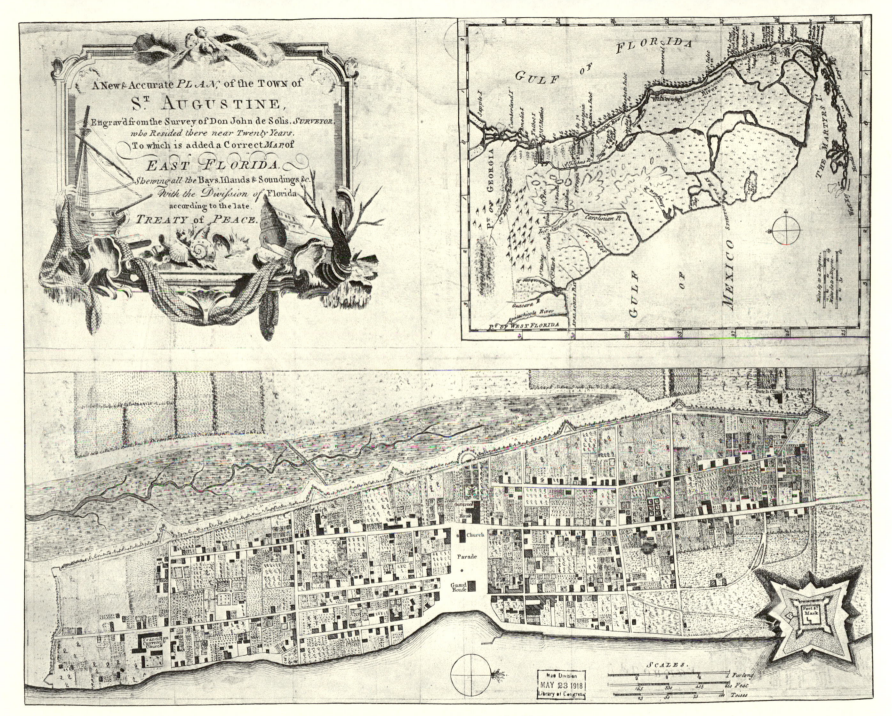

Figure 16. Plan of St. Augustine, Florida: ca. 1770

and *pueblos* or *villas* as civil settlements for farming, trade, and town life.

Two matters should be made clear at this point. First, the Laws of the Indies applied to the *pueblo* type of settlement—that is, to civil communities. Second, the distinction between the three types of communities, clear enough in theory, often disappeared in practice. The mission communities, for example, were intended to be temporary arrangements for the "reduction" of the Indians to Christianity at the same time they were being instructed in self-government. At the end of the period of tutelage, the mission community was to become a civil *pueblo*. The Indians would then assume all the rights and duties of Spanish citizens, the mission church would be converted to a parish church, and the missionaries themselves would be relieved of all powers of direction over the Indians. This, at least, was the stated intention of secular authorities in Spain; clerical powers, however, continually resisted efforts to secularize the missions.

Nor did the *presidios* remain exclusively military in character. Married soldiers and other settlers not under military direction gave these fortress outposts something of the air of a civil settlement. In many cases, too, *pueblos* were founded by groups of settlers that included soldiers who remained under military discipline. Finally we find several instances where one or more missions, *presidios*, and *pueblos* were established in such close proximity to one another that the distinction became further blurred.

Towns of the Gulf and Southwest

Just such a mixture of civil, military, and religious settlements by the Spanish is part of the history of San Antonio, Texas. The *presidio* of San Antonio de Béjar had been founded by Martin de Alarcon, Governor of Coahuila, in 1718. Near it was the mission later to become famous as the Alamo, the Mission of San Antonio de Valero. Four other missions existed along a twelve-mile stretch of the San Antonio River. Yet this section of Texas remained far from secure, and Spanish authorities determined that a *pueblo* should also be established in the area.

Families from the Canary Islands were recruited as the first settlers, and late in the fall of 1730 the group set out for their new home. At that time the viceroy issued a series of orders to various provincial officials directing them to provide proper transportation, military protection, and other assistance for the expedition. The governor received orders to select a suitable site and to lay out the town, which was named San Fernando. According to this order, common pasture lands were to surround the town, and beyond this land farm tracts were to be located. One-fifth of the commons and farm lands was to be reserved for later settlers and as *pueblo* land.[14]

Figure 17 shows the original plan of the *pueblo* of San Fernando. The rectangular blocks are neatly arranged around the plaza, on which fronted the church and the royal house. This plan is an excellent example of a Laws of the Indies town, following, as it does, virtually all the principles laid down by those regulations.

Modifications were made in this plan, as Figure 18 indicates. This is a drawing made about 1777 by Father Juan Agustín Morfi, who also recorded this unflattering description of the community following his tour of inspection of the region:

"On the west bank of the San Antonio river . . . is situated the villa of San Fernando and the presidio of San Antonio de Bexar, with no other division between them than the parochial church. To the west of the presidio is San Pedro creek, in such a manner that the villa and the presidio are both situated within the angle formed by the juncture of the two streams. The church building is spacious and has a vaulted roof, but the whole is so poorly constructed that it promises but a short life. The town consists of fifty-nine houses of stone and mud and seventy-nine of wood, but all poorly built, without any preconceived plan, so that the whole resembles more a poor village than a villa, capital of so pleasing a province."[15]

Father Morfi's comment about the lack of any "preconceived plan" apparently refers to the houses of the town rather than to the layout of the *pueblo* itself. The changes in the original plan merely reduced the plaza in size and resulted in the church being placed at one end instead of facing it on its own block. Around

[14] A full account of the founding of the *pueblo* of San Fernando and a summary of the various orders from the viceroy is I. J. Cox, "The Founding of the First Texas Municipality," *Texas Historical Association Quarterly*, II, 1899.

[15] Fray Juan Agustín Morfi, *History of Texas, 1673-1779*, translated by Carlos Eduardo Castañeda, Albuquerque, 1935, I, 92.

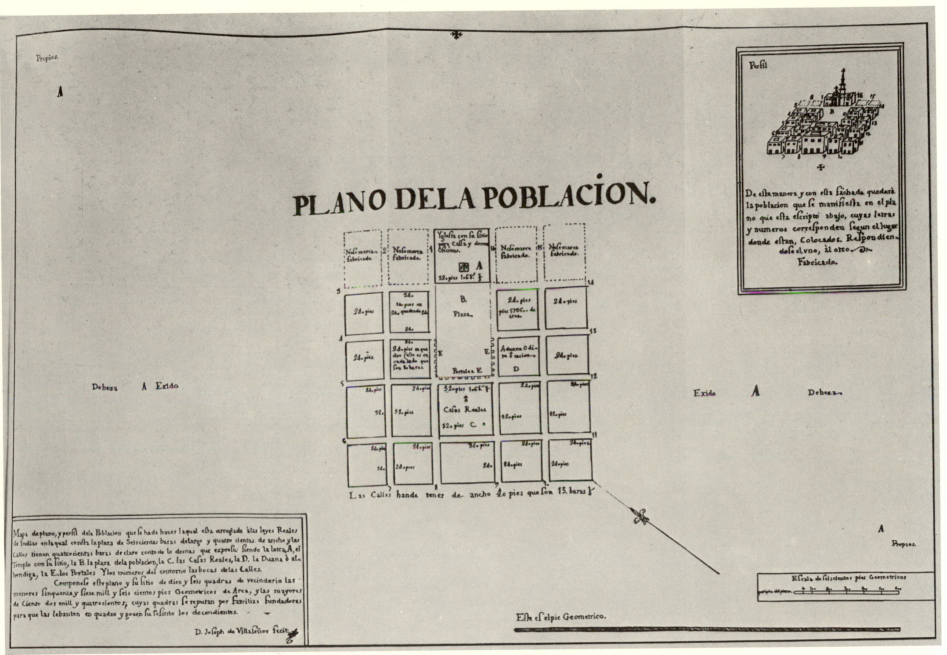

Figure 17. Plan of the Pueblo of San Fernando de Béxar (San Antonio), Texas: ca. 1730

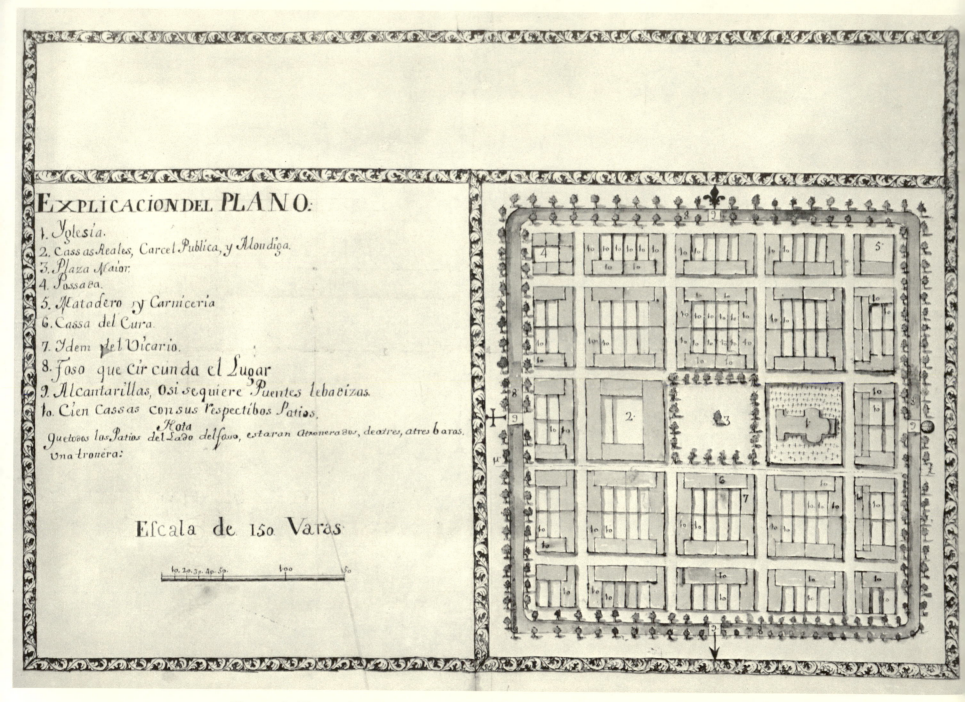

EXPLICACION DEL PLANO:

1. Yglesia.
2. Cassas Reales, Carcel Publica, y Mondiga.
3. Plaza Maior.
4. Possaca.
5. Matadero y Carniceria
6. Cassa del Cura.
7. Idem del Vicario.
8. Foso que circunda el Lugar
9. Alcantarillas, Osi sequiere Puentes lebacizas.
10. Cien Cassas con sus respectibos Patios.

Nota
que todos los Patios del Lado del fosso, estaran Atronerados, de a tres, a tres baras,
una tronera:

Escala de 150 Varas

Figure 18. Plan of the Pueblo of San Fernando de Béxar (San Antonio), Texas: ca. 1777

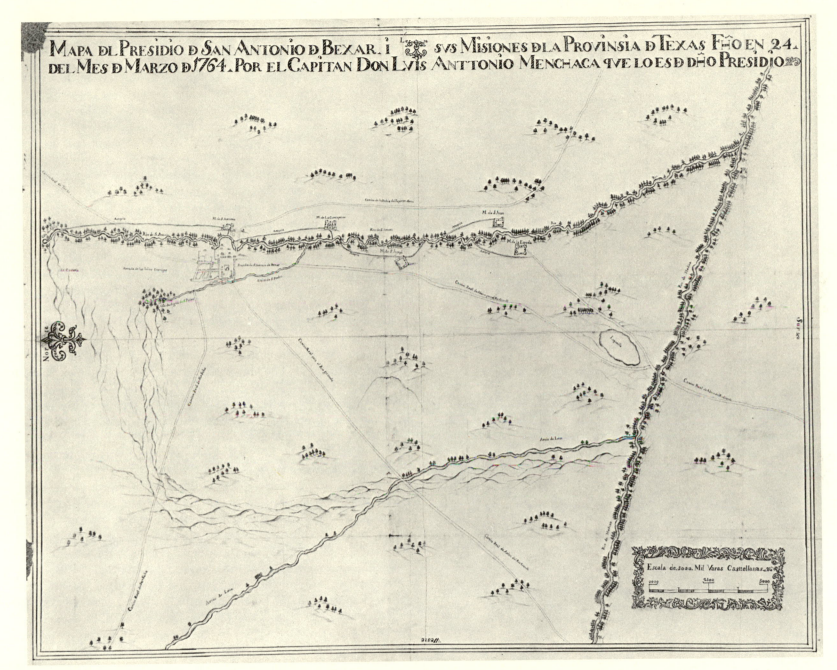

Figure 19. Map of San Antonio, Texas and Vicinity: 1764

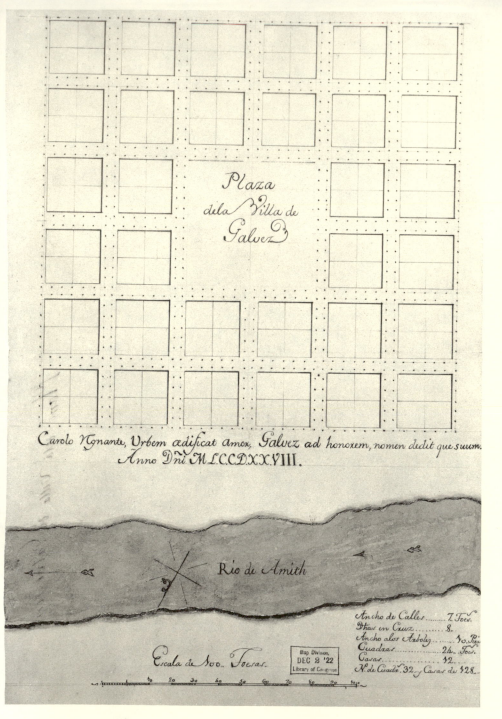

Plaza
dela Villa de
Galvez

Carolo Ygnante, Urbem ædificat amox, Galvez ad honorem, nomen dedit que suum.
Anno Dñi M.LCCDXXVIII.

Rio de Amith

Ancho de Calles.........7. Toes.°
Dhas en Cruz.............8.
Ancho alos Arbolg.......4o. Pies
Cuadras................24. Toes.
Casas..................52.
N. de Cuadr. 32 y Casas de 528.

Escala de 800. Toesas.

Map Division
DEC 2 '22
Library of Congress

Figure 20. Plan of Galvez, Louisiana: 1778

the perimeter only half blocks were laid out, but otherwise the original design was followed.

The complex mission, *presidio*, and *pueblo* settlements in the area referred to by Father Morfi are shown in Figure 19. The *presidio* and *pueblo*, side by side, appear faintly in the upper left. Across the river lies the mission of San Antonio. Stretching along the river to the right are no less than four additional mission communities.

The quality of building construction that so distressed Father Morfi typified at least the early years of Spanish colonization north of Mexico. This part of New Spain was full of such settlements, boldly conceived on an elaborate plan but carried out with little attention to details.

Galvez, Louisiana, serves as another example. The plan of this town, reproduced in Figure 20, dates from 1778. Here the unknown planner modified somewhat the regulations of the Laws of the Indies by making the plaza a perfect square and indicating arcades along all of the streets instead of only on those entering the plaza.

Galvez, like San Fernando, sheltered a group of settlers from the Canary Islands. The site was located on the border of Spanish Louisiana and English West Florida. The town enjoyed a brief period of prosperity when, in 1779, Spanish troops reinforced the garrison and prepared to attack the British. At that time the population reached its peak of four hundred persons. With the fall of Florida to the Spanish, Galvez had no further reason for existence, and within a few years the site lay deserted.

Farther to the east along the Gulf of Mexico stands an earlier Spanish settlement, one that passed rapidly from Spanish to French to English hands with such bewildering frequency that its real character is difficult to classify. Yet the original plan of this town, Pensacola, was Spanish, and its later occupants merely modified its original design. Pensacola Bay was first settled in 1698, when three hundred settlers began a town on Santa Rosa Island at its entrance to the Gulf. Captured by the French in 1719 and restored to Spain in 1723, the town was finally destroyed in 1754 by a hurricane. The residents then reestablished the town on its present site, coming under British rule from 1763 to 1781.

The view in Figure 21 shows the first settlement on Santa Rosa Island, but it reveals more about the primitive nature of the build-

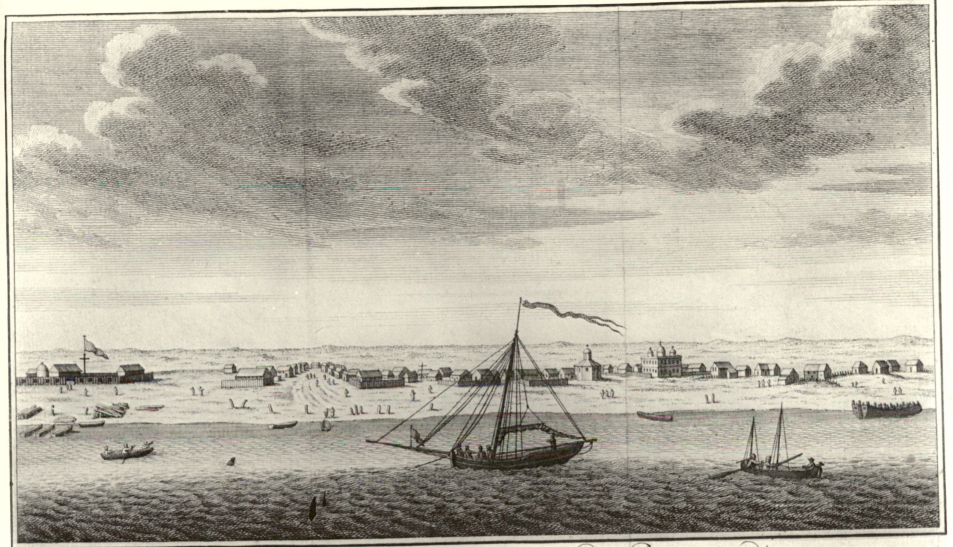

Gezigt van 't Spaansche Vlek PENSACOLA, aan de Baay van dien naam, in de Golf van Mexiko, bevosten den uitloop van de Rivier Misfisippi.

Naar een Tekening, die op de Plaats zelve, in 't jaar 1743. is gemaakt.

Figure 21. View of Pensacola, Florida: 1743

Figure 22. Plan of Pensacola, Florida: 1778

ings than of its plan. Figure 22 shows the plan of the town on its new site toward the end of British occupation and about twenty-five years after its construction. The fort in the center represents British reconstruction and enlargement of the Spanish fortress that had previously existed. Yet the great rectangle left uncrossed by streets was apparently provided in the original Spanish plan. From this fact and the strategic location of the town one can conclude that its purpose was primarily military. This would explain the obvious departures from the regulations of the Laws of the Indies. Philip Pittman's account of Pensacola in 1763, when the British took possession, would seem to support this conclusion:

"[Pensacola] . . . consisted of a fort and a few straggling houses; the fort was constructed of high stockades, enclosing in a very small space a house for the governor, and several miserable huts, built with pieces of bark, covered with the same materials, and most of them without floors; so that in the summer they were as hot as stoves, and the land engendered all sorts of vermin: in these wretched habitations the officers and soldiers dwelt."[16]

Older than all of the Spanish towns in the United States except St. Augustine was Santa Fé, New Mexico. Originally La Villa Real de la Santa Fé de San Francisco (The Royal City of the Holy Faith of Saint Francis), the city was founded in 1609 by Don Pedro de Peralta. The capital of the province was established here, having been moved from San Juan de los Caballeros, also known as San Juan Bautista and San Gabriel del Yunque, which had been settled in 1598. Except for a period of Indian occupation from 1680 to 1698, Santa Fé has served continuously as capital, first of the Spanish and then Mexican province, then the territory, and now the state of New Mexico.

The old Governor's Palace, which now stands much altered but restored on the north side of the plaza, was one of the first buildings erected. Today's plaza is only a portion of the more generous area set aside in Peralta's original plan. Unfortunately, the design of early Santa Fé has not survived in graphic form. Virtually the only map showing the details of the city in the Spanish era is reproduced in Figure 23. This probably dates from between 1766 and 1768. During that period Father Francisco Atanasio Domin-

guez visited the town and recorded his impression in 1776. Like Morfi a year later in San Antonio, Dominguez found Santa Fé scarcely to his liking:

"Surely when one hears or reads 'Villa of Santa Fé,' along with the particulars that it is the capital of the kingdom . . . such a vivid and forceful notion or idea must be suggested . . . that it must at least be fairly presentable, if not very good. . . . The location or site, of this villa is as good as I pictured it . . . but its appearance, design, arrangement, and plan do not correspond to its status as a villa nor to the very beautiful plain on which it lies, for it is like rough stone set in fine metal. . . .

"The Villa of Santa Fé (for the most part) consists of many small ranchos at various distances from one another, with no plan as to their location, for each owner built as he was able, wished to, or found convenient."[17]

Passing from these generally unfavorable comments, Dominguez continues with a more detailed description of the center of the city:

"In spite of what has been said, there is a semblance of a street in this villa. It begins on the left facing north shortly after one leaves the . . . parish church and extends down about 400 or 500 varas. Indeed, I point out that this quasi-street not only lacks orderly rows, or blocks, of houses, but at its very beginning, which faces north, it forms one side of a little plaza in front of our church. The other three sides are three houses of settlers with alleys between them. The entrance to the main plaza is down through these. The sides or borders, of the latter consist of the chapel of Our Lady of Light, which is to the left of the quasi-street mentioned. . . . The other side is the government palace. . . . The remaining two sides are houses of settlers, and since there is nothing worth noting about them, one can guess what they are like from what has been said. The government palace is like everything else there, and enough said."[18]

[16] Philip Pittman, *The Present State of the European Settlements on the Mississippi* (London, 1770), Frank H. Hodder, ed., Cleveland, 1906, p. 25.

[17] Fray Francisco Atanasio Dominguez, *The Missions of New Mexico, 1776*, translated by Eleanor B. Adams and Fray Angelico Chavez, Albuquerque, 1956, pp. 39-40.
[18] *ibid*.

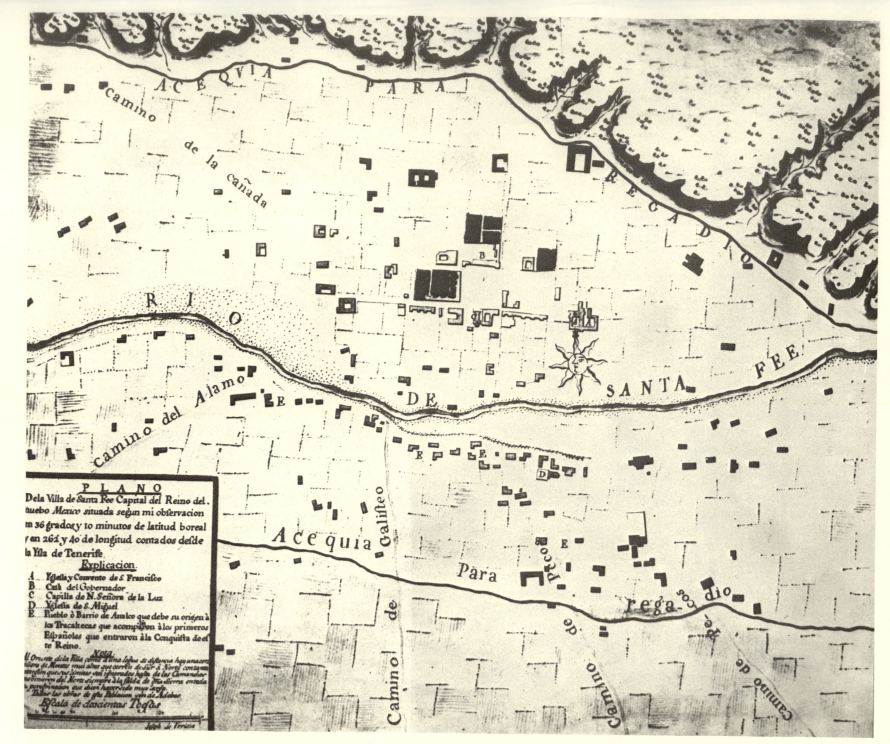

Figure 23. Plan of Santa Fé, New Mexico: ca. 1766

Figure 24. *View of Santa Fé, New Mexico: 1848*

Certainly the view of Santa Fé in 1848 shown in Figure 24, at the beginning of American influence, would seem to confirm Dominguez's much earlier impression of haphazard growth and development. Only with difficulty can anything resembling streets be discerned, and the outskirts of the town appear particularly disorganized.

There is no reason to believe that the city appeared any more attractive at the time Dominguez commented so scathingly. Even after allowances are made for the differences that often arose between civil and religious authorities and which commonly colored their descriptions of the other's activities, we can only conclude that Morfi's and Dominguez's opinions were not unjustified. The North American settlements of the Spanish colonial empire were always frontier outposts far removed from the prosperity that characterized the cities at the heart of Spain's colonial enterprise in the Western Hemisphere. Like frontier outposts at any period, conditions were primitive and unsophisticated. For all that the Laws of the Indies might say about the details of land settlement, their administration, at least along the Gulf and in the southwest, appeared to be tempered with a measure of freedom that has been characteristic of all frontiers at the edge of permanent settlement. Nor were these conditions to be different in the last efforts by the Spanish to settle previously unoccupied portions of the continent.

Mission, Presidio, and Pueblo in California

Although Spanish explorers from Mexico had ventured north along the California coast as early as 1542, when Cabrillo entered San Diego Bay, attempts at settlement were not made until more than two hundred years later. In 1769 two expeditions, one by land and the other by sea, set out to establish three missions and two *presidios*. Thus began the final chapter of Spanish community planning within the area of the United States.

The first mission was founded at San Diego in July, the beginning of a chain of religious settlements that eventually stretched northward beyond San Francisco Bay as far as Sonoma. The mission communities followed the well-known pattern established over the years in New Spain. They are described by Eugène Duflot de Mofras, sent in 1840 by the French to report on con-

ditions in California, then under Mexican rule. De Mofras pointed out that all of the missions resembled one another closely. He chose to describe one of the last to be founded and perhaps the most impressive—San Luis Rey, established about fifty miles north of San Diego and a few miles inland in 1798. The illustration from de Mofras' own work, published in 1844, appears in Figure 25 accompanied by this description:

"Mission San Luis Rey de Francia is built in the form of a quadrangle, 150 meters in width, with a chapel occupying one of the wings. Along the façade extends an ornamental cloister. The building, which is one story high, is raised a few feet above the ground. The interior, in the form of a court, is adorned with fountains and planted with trees. Off the surrounding cloister open doors lead into rooms occupied by priests, majordomos, and travelers, as well as the main rooms, schools, and shops. Infirmaries for men and women are placed in a secluded corner of the mission. Nearby the school is situated.

"Surrounding the mission are the workshops, the huts of the neophytes, and the houses of a few white settlers. In addition to the main buildings, 15 or 20 subsidiary farms and some auxiliary chapels lie within a radius of 30 or 40 square leagues. Across from the mission are the quarters of the priests' bodyguard, an escort consisting of four cavalrymen and a sergeant."[19]

The Spanish government expected these Indian mission communities to become self-governing within a few years. This hope was ill-founded. The Indians failed to adjust to this changed mode of life, often they rebelled against what in reality was a system of conscript labor, and there is substantial evidence that the religious authorities resisted strongly the attempts by civil officials to secularize the missions. Not until 1833, by which time California had passed to Mexico, was a general decree passed for the secularization of the missions. Actual accomplishment of this order took several years. The results were quite different from what had been hoped. In most cases the Indians were quickly dis-

[19] Eugène Duflot de Mofras, *Exploration du Territoire de L'Oregon, des Californies et de la mer Vermeille* (Paris, 1844), translated and edited by Marguerite Eyer Wilbur, *Duflot de Mofras' Travels on the Pacific Coast*, Santa Ana, 1937, I, 134-35.

Figure 25. View of the Mission of San Luis Rey, California: 1840

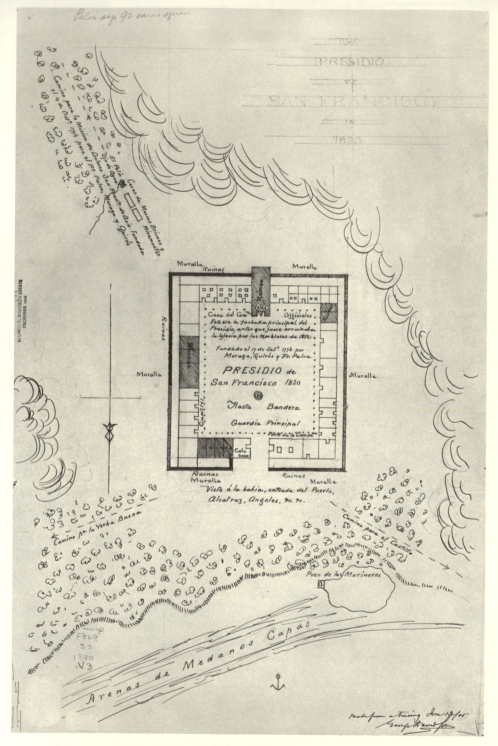

Figure 26. *Plan of the Presidio of San Francisco, California: 1820*

possessed of both lands and political power by white settlers from both Mexico and the United States.

Four California *presidios* or military communities were also founded: San Diego in 1769, Monterey in 1770, San Francisco in 1776, and Santa Barbara in 1782. These, too, were essentially similar in design, and de Mofras again furnishes the details:

"Presidios were invariably built in the following uniform manner: After a suitable place had been chosen, a trench about 4 meters broad and 2 deep was then excavated. What earth was removed was used for an outer embankment. The presidio was then enclosed by a quadrangle that measured approximately 200 meters on each side. The rampart, or wall, constructed of adobes, was 4 or 5 meters high and a meter thick, with small bastions at each corner. The presidio had only two gates. These fortifications were never protected by more than eight bronze cannon, usually of 8, 12, or 16 pounds. Although incapable of resisting a serious attack by warships, these fortifications were adequate to repulse Indian raids. Not far from the presidios, at a point selected to conform with the local topography, stood the outpost batteries, inappropriately designated as the *castillo*, or fort. Within the presidio, the church, barracks for officers and soldiers, the houses of a few settlers, and the stores, shops, stables, wells, and cisterns were provided. Outside stood more groups of houses."[20]

Figure 26 shows the *presidio* of San Francisco as it existed in 1820. The features described by de Mofras can be seen in this plan, and, happily, many of the old *presidio* buildings stand today on the original site surrounded by the modern military reservation of the Presidio of San Francisco. The plan in Figure 26 is misleading in one respect. It does not show the houses and farm structures that sprang up beyond the walls of the *presidio* proper. These features of civil life, as has already been mentioned, tended to give these military communities a closer resemblance to the purely civil towns than the laws and regulations governing their founding indicated. A view of Monterey in 1842 is reproduced in Figure 27. This shows the development that had taken place around the military post founded seventy years earlier. As in the case of the *presidio* at San Francisco the settlement at Monterey soon attracted many of the farming and trading activities that changed the purely

[20] *ibid.*, 142-43.

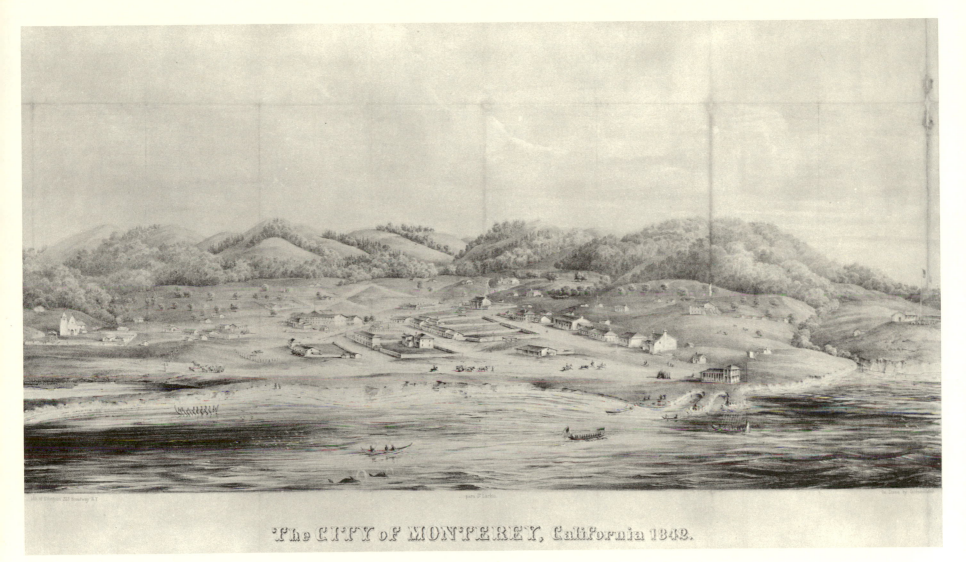

The CITY of MONTEREY, California 1842.

Figure 27. View of Monterey, California: 1842

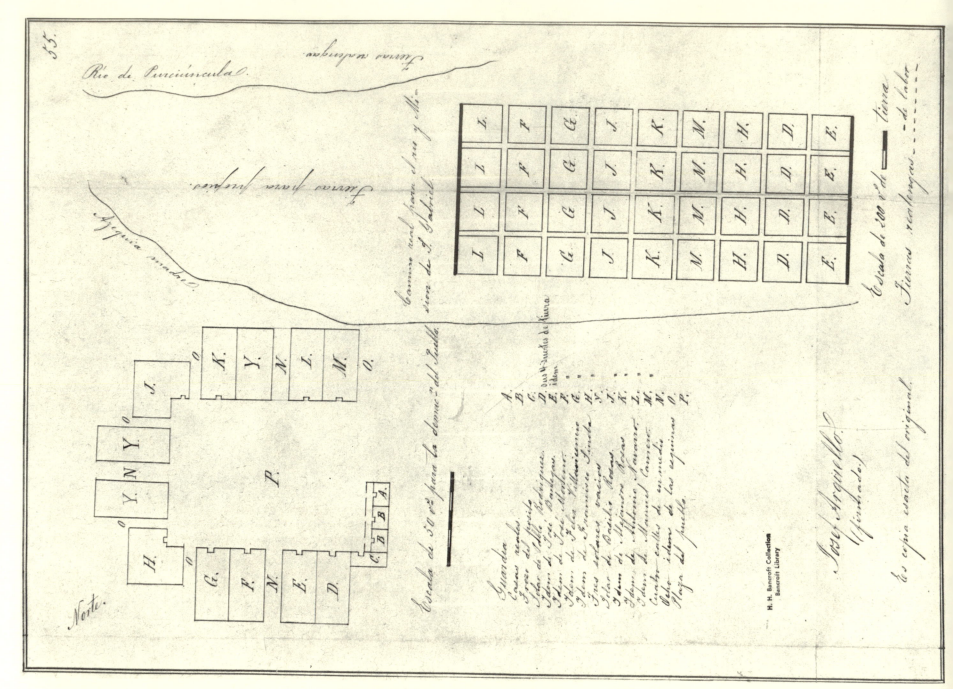

Figure 28. Plan of Los Angeles, California: 1781

garrison community into a diversified frontier town with important civil functions.[21]

The missions and *presidios* were numerically more important in California, but the *pueblo* towns and their land system are of greater interest. The California *pueblos* owe their founding to Philip de Neve, governor of the province. In 1775 the Spanish king ordered him to take up residence in Monterey. De Neve faced two problems: securing the province against encroachments by other powers and increasing the supply of farm produce for the military garrisons then supplied with wheat and other foodstuffs from Lower California and Mexico. He reasoned that further colonization of the province by Spaniards in civil communities would assist in solving both problems. After a tour of the province he selected two sites for the proposed settlements. Without waiting for approval from the viceroy or the king he chose nine soldiers from the Monterey *presidio* who had some farming experience and five other settlers and set out for one of the sites he had picked on the Guadalupe River. There, in 1777, he laid out the *pueblo* of San José and made preliminary allotments of land subject to later confirmation of his action by his superiors.

Four years later he began plans for the second *pueblo* at Los Angeles. The order by Neve establishing that settlement has already been quoted at the beginning of this chapter. It was preceded, however, by the drafting of a general regulation governing the future planting of settlements in the province. Evidently Neve hoped to found a number of such communities as part of his general policy of stimulating colonization. In these regulations Neve provided for increased assistance to prospective settlers in the form of agricultural equipment, an annual payment for five years, and sufficient livestock to begin farming operations. In return the settlers were to repay the government for the tools and livestock in horses and mules, and the surplus food produced by the *pueblo* was to be sold to the *presidios*.[22]

Figure 28 shows the *pueblo* of Los Angeles as planned by Neve in 1781. The town proper appears in the upper left-hand corner and the location of the principal buildings around the rectangular plaza is indicated. The regular gridiron in the lower right-hand corner represents the farm lots allocated to the settlers. The drawing uses two different scales, with the town exaggerated in size to five times that of the farming area.

Under Spanish, and, later, Mexican rule, the *pueblos* remained small and relatively unimportant settlements. A view of Los Angeles in 1853 is reproduced in Figure 29 and shows the condition of the town as it must have looked within a few years of its founding. Even in 1857 following a period of substantial growth, Los Angeles retained the character of a sleepy Mexican or Spanish provincial village, as the view in Figure 30 makes clear. It was from this unpromising nucleus that the present sprawling metropolis has grown. The plaza has survived, but only nearby Olvera Street, with its synthetic Mexican bazaar, suggests the humble but carefully planned origins of America's most disorderly metropolis.

Both San José and Los Angeles in the arrangement of central plaza and building lots followed closely the forms prescribed in the Laws of the Indies. Undoubtedly this was true also in the case of the third and last Spanish *pueblo* in California. This was Branciforte, established in 1797 but never fully completed because of lack of funds. There was yet another town planned in America partially following the regulations laid down by the Laws of the Indies, although by Mexican, not Spanish authorities. In many ways it is the most interesting of all and one which, because of its relatively isolated location, has retained much of its original character.

Sonoma was founded in 1835 as a check by the Mexican government against possible Russian expansion from that country's settlement north of San Francisco at Fort Ross. Governor José Figueroa instructed General Alferez Mariano Vallejo to establish a town in the Sonoma Valley near the mission of San Francisco Solano which had been built in 1823. Vallejo's orders seemed to allow him considerable discretion in determining the form of the town:

"In conformity with orders and instructions issued by the Supreme Confederation respecting the location of a village in the

[21] A reproduction of the original plan of the Monterey *presidio* may be found in Irving B. Richman, *California Under Spain and Mexico, 1535-1847,* Boston, 1911, following p. 338. Sketches of the Monterey *presidio* and the nearby mission of San Carlos Borromeo (Carmel) made in 1791 appear in Donald C. Cutter, *Malaspina in California,* San Francisco, 1960.

[22] The text of the regulations may be found in *Regulations for Governing the Province of the Californias,* translated by John Everett Johnson (San Francisco, 1929). Further discussion of the background of the San José

and Los Angeles *pueblos,* as well as much useful material on the system of land division and tenure, appears in Frank W. Blackmar, *Spanish Institutions of the Southwest,* Baltimore, 1891, and in Hubert Howe Bancroft, *History of California,* San Francisco, 1884, I.

Figure 29. View of Los Angeles, California: 1853

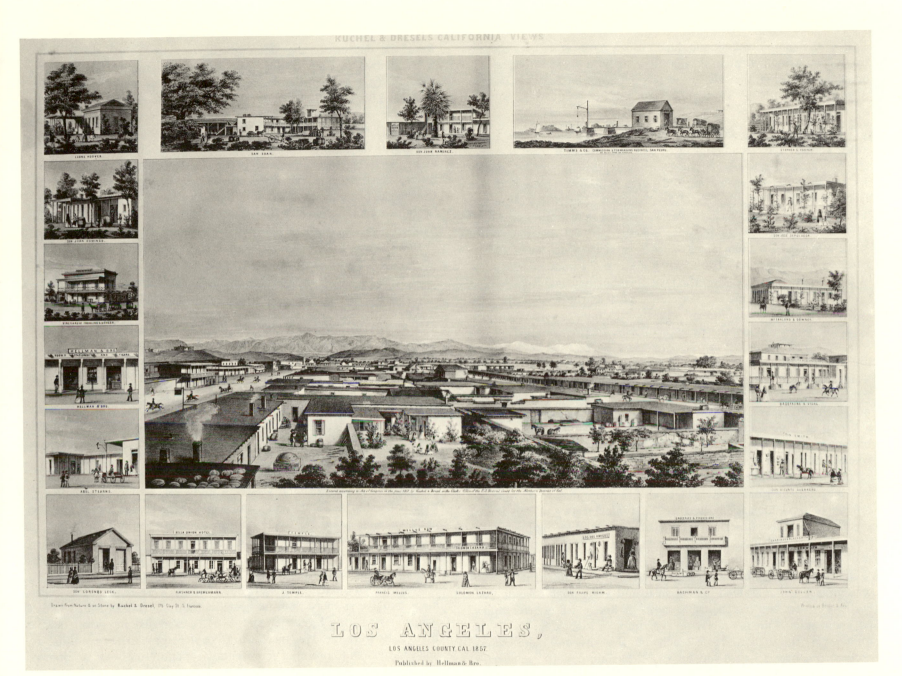

Figure 30. View of Los Angeles, California: 1857

Valley of Sonoma, this comandance urges upon you that, according to topographical plan of this place, it be divided into quarters or squares, seeing that the streets and plazas be regulated so as to make a beginning. The inhabitants are to be governed entirely by said plan."[23]

Vallejo's charming little city obviously owes much to the Laws of the Indies, but elements of originality can be seen from the plan reproduced in Figure 31. The enormous plaza is square, nearly six hundred feet on each side, a departure both in shape and size from most of the other cities of Spanish origin in North America. The most obvious novelty, however, is the great avenue one hundred and eleven feet wide, entering the plaza from the south. Vallejo located his own home and a four-story watchtower on the north side of the plaza from which he could command the view of that great open space and the broad avenue beyond.

The plaza unfortunately was later used as the site of the city hall and courthouse buildings, but its generous expanse can still be appreciated. Facing the plaza or nearby can be found the carefully restored mission, the Mexican army barracks, two hotels of the period, Vallejo's house, and other residences. The modern visitor needs little imagination to picture Sonoma as it must have appeared when Vallejo ruled the town. Mexican jurisdiction did not last many years, however, for it was in the Sonoma plaza that a group of Yankee settlers in 1846 ran up the star and grizzly bear flag of the "Republic of California," not replaced until three weeks later when American occupation began.

The plan of Sonoma shows also the farm or "outlot" division of land beyond the town itself. Here, also, Vallejo departed from the system of land allocation used in the typical Laws of the Indies towns. A detailed description of that pattern may help in comparing the Spanish settlement system with those of the French and English which are discussed in the following two chapters.

The Spanish colonial *pueblo* was more than a town; it was intended as a self-contained urban-rural unit. The *pueblo* lands generally were square, ten thousand *varas* or five and a quarter miles, on each side. The town proper occupied a site in or near the middle of this tract. Here each of the original settlers, or *pobladores*, had a house lot, or *solar*. Farming plots, or *suertes*,

were laid out in rectangular fields beyond the town proper and were allotted to each settler. Apparently settlers did not receive absolute title to their lands, holding them instead in perpetuity subject to prescribed duties of cultivation. Nor could lands be sold. In this respect the *suertes* closely resembled the common fields of the New England communities.

Certain farm tracts were reserved to the king, the *realengas*, and were to be used in making grants to later settlers. Other farm tracts, called *propios*, remained *pueblo* property to be rented, with the income being devoted to community purposes. Common pasture lands and common woodlands were also set aside for general community purposes and not allotted to individuals. Finally, on one or more sides of the town, or completely surrounding it, were the *ejidos*. These also were common lands not under individual jurisdiction and apparently were for the purpose of permitting the enlargement of the town should additional streets and *solares* be needed.

The Spanish *pueblo* pattern of land division closely resembles that of the early New England towns. In the case of the English colonies this system of land distribution clearly stemmed from the conditions of land tenure in rural England at the time of American colonization. This in turn had slowly evolved from feudal land law. It seems a justifiable hypothesis that the Spanish *pueblo* land system similarly owed its origins to the pattern of feudal land holding in Spain. Indeed, throughout most of Western Europe these feudal patterns were common. In America the municipality, Spanish *pueblo* or New England town, replaced the feudal lord. It was, in fact, a fairly sophisticated concept of collective ownership and communal land management that guided the early years of these relatively simple communities.

Despite the more than two and a half centuries of Spanish town planning in North America, the influences and tangible remains of the Laws of the Indies are slight. Within the area of the present United States, Spanish colonial efforts rarely were regarded in the home country as more than marginal activities. Undermanned and underfinanced, the Spanish reach always exceeded its grasp, and the results were meagre. In efforts to explore past urban traditions and in attempts to preserve representative examples of our architectural and planning heritage, an awareness of this dearth of the Spanish legacy should warn us against squandering what little is left of this irreplaceable treasure.

[23] Orders from Figueroa to Vallejo, Monterey, June 24, 1835, as quoted in Tom Gregory, *History of Sonoma County California*, Los Angeles, 1911, p. 36.

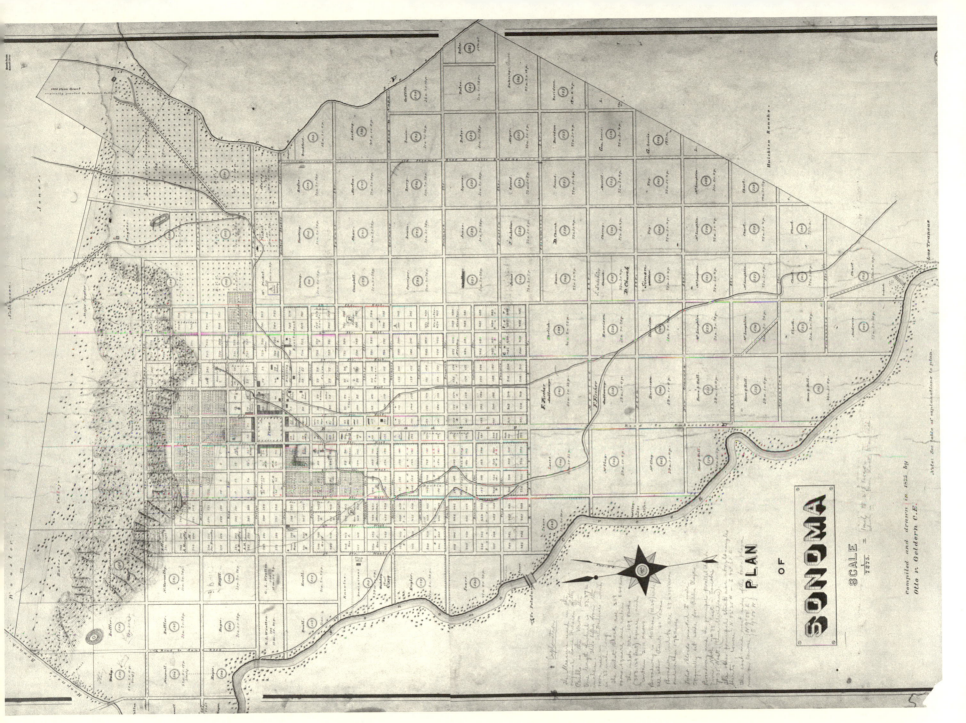

Figure 31. Plan of Sonoma, California: 1875

CHAPTER 3

The Towns of New France

IN the great valleys of the St. Lawrence and the Mississippi the French developed a line of trading posts, missions, and civil settlements along the northern and western boundaries of colonial America. Unlike the Spanish communities far to the south, these French settlements were not laid out on a common pattern established under a Gallic equivalent of the Laws of the Indies. French colonial policy was less vigorous than in Spain, and exploration and settlement in the early years of French colonization were carried out by individuals who were granted trading rights and whose motives were primarily personal gain. Thus, French communities came into being as adjuncts to a commercial enterprise—not, as in the case of the Spanish colonial towns, under the careful supervision of the monarch.

Each settlement was planned according to the circumstances prevailing at the time and the skill and knowledge of its founder. It is not surprising that, under these conditions, variety in the urban pattern was the rule. Yet certain common elements existed in most of the important French towns and identify them as springing from the same culture and in response to similar conditions. Because of their variety, the main elements of the French colonial towns have somewhat more charm and interest than can be found in the Spanish settlements. Indeed, in such cities as Quebec or New Orleans, where the original French character has not been entirely obliterated, the quality of the urban scene or townscape surpasses virtually anything else of its kind in North America.

From their beginnings along the Canadian coast, French settlements spread to the St. Lawrence Valley. Later communities were planted along the Great Lakes, in the Mississippi Valley, and on the coast of the Gulf of Mexico. Even after the French were eliminated as a colonizing power in America small groups of Frenchmen came to found small cities not unlike those developed under the colonial empire. Gallipolis, on the Ohio River, for example, has a plan virtually identical with the elongated layouts of Montreal, St. Louis, New Orleans, or Mobile. And in the person

of Pierre Charles L'Enfant, France was to furnish the new nation with the planner of its national capital and, through him, with a typical French baroque street pattern. Still later Haussmann's bold reconstruction of Paris in the last century provided an example for Daniel Burnham as he set about the remaking of such cities as Chicago, San Francisco, and Manila. In a variety of ways, therefore, French planning has exercised a considerable influence on the layout of American cities.

Champlain and the Beginnings of Settlement in New France

French colonization of North America lagged more than a century behind that of Spain. The exploration of Jacques Cartier during the period 1534-1542 did not result in any permanent settlements, although Cartier penetrated the St. Lawrence Valley as far as the Indian village of Hochelga on the site of the present Montreal. In South Carolina and Florida the tiny fortress colonies of French Huguenots soon succumbed to Spanish attack. Not until the last years of the sixteenth century did a few scattered French fur traders manage to establish themselves along the St. Lawrence. They survived only by marrying into the Indian tribes, and no attempts were made to construct towns. Serious colonization efforts awaited more favorable circumstances.

In 1604 Pierre du Guast, Sieur de Monts, received from the French king the exclusive fur trading rights for Canada. De Monts was a wealthy Huguenot and a favorite of Henry IV, whose cause he naturally had championed. He fitted out an expedition to explore the area covered in his patent and to establish one or more settlements to serve as trading centers. De Monts was fortunate in securing as official geographer for the expedition Samuel de Champlain who, in the previous year, had made a voyage of exploration to Canada. Champlain was a superb cartographer, and most of his maps, including several showing the details of the

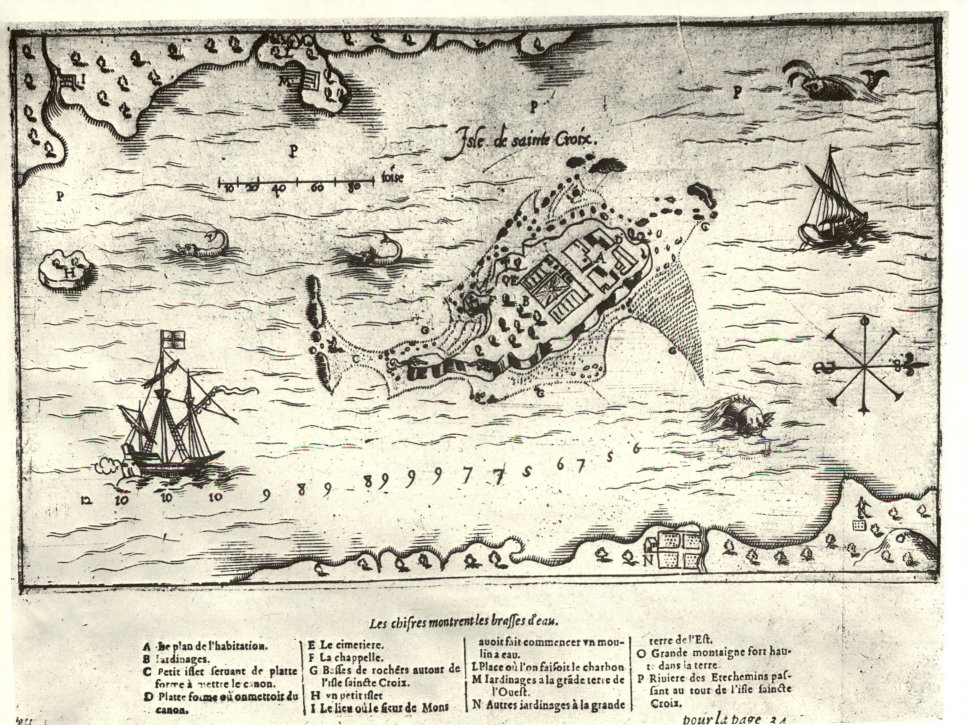

Les chifres montrent les brasses d'eau.

A   Le plan de l'habitation.
B   Iardinages.
C   Petit iſlet ſeruant de platte forme à mettre le canon.
D   Platte forme où onmettoit du canon.
E   Le cimetiere.
F   La chappelle.
G   Baſſes de rochers autour de l'iſle ſaincte Croix.
H   vn petit iſlet
I   Le lieu où le ſieur de Mons auoit fait commencer vn moulin a eau.
L   Place où l'on faiſoit le charbon
M   Iardinages a la gráde terre de l'Oueſt.
N   Autres iardinages à la grande terre de l'Eſt.
O   Grande montaigne fort haute dans la terre.
P   Riuiere des Etechemins paſſant au tour de l'iſle ſaincte Croix.

pour la page 21

Figure 32. Map of Sainte Croix (Douchet) Island, Maine: 1604

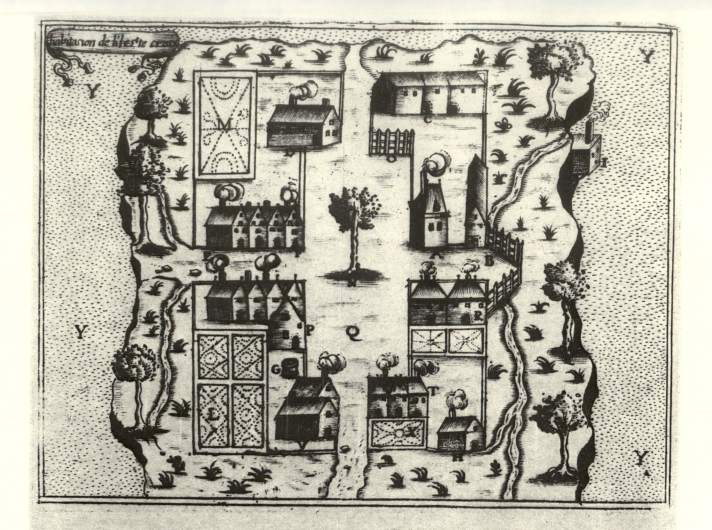

Habitation de lisle ste croix

A Logis du sieur de Mons.
B Maison publique ou l'on passoit le temps durant la pluie.
C Le magasin.
D Logement des suisses.
E La forge.
F Logement des charpentiers
G Le puis.
H Le four ou l'on faisoit le pain.

I La cuisine.
L Iardinages.
M Autres Iardins.
N La place où au milieu y a vn arbre.
O Pallissade.
P Logis des sieurs d'Oruille, Champlain & Chandore.
Q Logis du sieur Boulay, & autres artisans. ∫

R Logis ou logeoiét les sieurs de Genestou, Sourin & autres artisans.
T Logis des sieurs de Beaumont, la Motte Bourioli & Fougeray.
V Logement de nostre curé.
X Autres iardinages.
Y La riuiere qui entoure l'isle.

Figure 33. View of Champlain's Settlement on Sainte Croix (Douchet) Island, Maine: 1604

settlements he helped to found, have survived. Moreover, in his written works dealing with his voyages to Canada we have available an authoritative account of the country and unusually detailed descriptions of the towns laid out by the expeditions.

Champlain was uniquely qualified to act as town planner. From 1599 to 1601 he had commanded a Spanish merchant ship on a voyage to the Americas. During this time he visited virtually all the important seaports as well as major inland towns, including Mexico City, San Juan, Vera Cruz, Porto Bello, Santo Domingo, Panama, and Havana. They are all mentioned and described in his *Brief Narrative of the Most Remarkable Things that Samuel Champlain of Brouage Observed in the West Indies, 1599-1601.* He must have become thoroughly familiar with the town planning provisions of the Laws of the Indies, and perhaps already had begun to formulate his own ideas.

The expedition's first settlement was established in 1604 on the island of Douchet, now part of the State of Maine, which de Monts named Isle de Sainte Croix. Champlain's map of the island showing the general plan of settlement appears in Figure 32. On it can be seen the little town with its central square and outlying gardens. We also have Champlain's detailed perspective of the town itself, reproduced in Figure 33. Identified in this drawing are the houses of the settlers, a storehouse, blacksmith shop, carpenter's dwelling, a cook-house, and other structures, as well as the central square, palisade, and garden plots. Champlain tells of the building of this little community, revealing himself as its planner:

"Without loss of time, the Sieur de Monts proceeded to set the workmen to build houses for our residence, and allowed me to draw up the plan of our settlement. After the Sieur de Monts had chosen the site for the Storehouse, which was fifty-four feet long, eighteen broad, and twelve feet high, he settled the plan for his own house, which he had built quickly by good workmen. Then he assigned a place to each one, and immediately they began to collect in fives and sixes, according to their preferences. After that all set to work to clear the island, to fetch wood, to cut timber, to carry earth, and other things necessary for the construction of the buildings."[1]

[1] Samuel de Champlain, *The Voyages of the Sieur de Champlain* (Paris, 1613), in H. P. Biggar, ed., *The Works of Samuel de Champlain*, Toronto, 1922, I, 275-76.

Champlain also mentions the building of an oven and a hand-powered mill for grinding wheat, and the creation of the gardens on the island and the nearby mainland. It is extremely doubtful, however, that the little settlement at Sainte Croix ever bore much resemblance to Champlain's neat perspective drawing. The location proved so inhospitable, because of the exposed site and the severe winter, that the following year de Monts decided to abandon it and establish another settlement. The site of this second colony was on the western coast of Nova Scotia at a sheltered harbor off the Bay of Fundy. The site for this new settlement, named Port Royal, was selected by Champlain, who again furnished a description:

"The plan of the settlement was ten fathoms in length and eight in breadth, which makes thirty-six in circumference. On the eastern side is a storehouse of the full width, with a very fine cellar some five to six feet high. On the north side is the Sieur de Monts' dwelling, constructed of fairly good woodwork. Around the courtyard are the quarters of the workmen. At one corner on the western side is a platform whereon were placed four pieces of cannon; and at the other corner, towards the east, is a palisade fashioned like a platform, as can be seen from the following picture."[2]

The "picture" is reproduced in Figure 34. As with Champlain's drawing of Sainte Croix, the actual buildings could hardly have presented as finished an appearance as the drawing indicates. In plan this second settlement is much less elaborate than the first. The compact, enclosed quadrangle form was undoubtedly selected as a more practical plan for a site without natural defenses and as one better adapted to the severe winter climate. This type of fortified village was used in other frontier locations in North America: in certain New England settlements, at the frontier stations in Kentucky, at Marietta, Ohio, and in many parts of the west. As at these later communities, Champlain's village was intended mainly as a place of residence, with the garden and farm tract being located beyond the enclosure.

Champlain relates how the forty-five persons making up the tiny colony soon began to plant gardens on allotted plots and to make other preparations for a permanent settlement. Champlain

[2] *ibid.*, 373.

abitasion du port royal

A Logemens des artisans.
B Plate forme où estoit le canon.
C Le magasin.
D Logemét du sieur de Pont-graué & Champlain.
E La forge.

F Palissade de pieux.
G Le four.
H La cuisine.
O Petite maisonnette où l'on retiroit les vtansiles de nos barques; que de puis le sieur de Poitrincourt fit

rebastir, & y logea le sieur Boulay quand le sieur du Pont s'en reuint en France.
P La porte de l'abitation.
Q Le cemetiere.
R La riuiere.

Figure 34. View of Champlain's Settlement at Port Royal, Nova Scotia: 1605

himself continued to explore much of the coast of northeastern America and then returned to France to report to de Monts, who had left the expedition after the founding of Port Royal.

In 1608 a new expedition set out from France to establish a post well inland on the St. Lawrence River. Only July 3 Champlain reached the site of Quebec, which he had noted on his earlier travels. Here, he relates:

"I looked for a place suitable for our settlement, but I could not find any more suitable or better situated than the point of Quebec. . . . I at once employed a part of our workmen . . . to make a site for our settlement, another part in sawing planks, another in digging the cellar and making ditches. . . . The first thing we made was the storehouse, to put our supplies under cover, and it was promptly finished by the diligence of everyone and the care I took in the matter."[3]

Champlain's attention was then diverted by a plot against his life by four members of the party, but when this was overcome he once again resumed supervision of the Quebec colony. Figure 35 is his drawing of the fortified settlement, which he described as follows:

"I continued the construction of our quarters, which contained three main buildings of two stories. Each one was three fathoms long and two and a half wide. The storehouse was six long and three wide, with a fine cellar six feet high. All the way round our buildings I had a gallery made, outside the second story, which was a very convenient thing. There were also ditches fifteen feet wide and six deep, and outside these I made several salients which enclosed a part of the buildings, and there we put our cannon. In front of the building there is an open space four fathoms wide and six or seven long, which abuts upon the river's bank. Round about the buildings are very good gardens, and an open place on the north side of a hundred, or a hundred and twenty, yards long and fifty or sixty wide."[4]

From this fortified *habitation* by the bank of the river, Quebec began its slow growth. The arrival of Recollect missionaries in 1615 helped to establish the basis for true colonization. Their little chapel and living quarters were built near Champlain's first structures, and around these buildings the first houses were constructed. But France's policy of granting trading concessions in Canada proved a poor device to bring about colonization, even though trade privileges frequently were conditioned by obligations to settle Frenchmen in the new country. In practice these conditions were often ignored or followed only with great reluctance. English occupation of Quebec from 1629 to 1632 still further slowed the pace of French colonization.

Champlain at last persuaded Richelieu to modify French colonial practices. Under the cardinal's leadership the company of the One Hundred Associates was formed to take over the activities of the old trading companies. This association was to settle four thousand persons in New France within the following fifteen years, a modest enough program, but far more vigorous than any previously attempted. Although many of the plans of the Associates went unrealized, the groundwork for additional colonization had been established. When, in the 1660's, rule by the Associates ended and Canada became a royal province, renewed and more effective colonization measures were possible.

One important feature of Canadian settlement came into being under the Associates. Under the terms of its grant the company was authorized to establish a system of feudal land holding—seignorial tenure—which in effect recreated in the New World conditions that were dying in the Old. The priest and the *seigneur* became the dominant forces in French Canada, and in the towns the spires of the churches and the towers of the fortress symbolized these twin powers. The view of Quebec in 1759, reproduced in Figure 36, shows the series of striking architectural features that by the latter part of the seventeenth century had given Quebec much of the character of some medieval city in Western Europe.[5]

A century older than the view just mentioned is the plan of Quebec in 1660 shown in Figure 37. Here is the city as it existed just prior to the establishment of Canada as a royal province. Both the view of Quebec in 1759 and this plan show clearly the division of the city into upper and lower towns. At the time the map was prepared, the company of the One Hundred Associates was still in control of settlement and had been active in planning the portion

[3] *ibid.*, II, 24.
[4] *ibid.*, 35-36.

[5] An earlier view of Quebec in 1691 can be found in *Nouveaux Voyages de Monsieur le Baron de Lahontan*, The Hague, 1707, I.

Figure 35. Champlain's View of the First Buildings at Quebec: 1608

QUEBEC, *The Capital of* NEW-FRANCE, *a Bishoprick, and*
Seat of the Soverain COURT.

1. *The* Citadel. 2. *the* Castle.
3. Magazine. 4. *ye* Recolets.
5. Ursulines. 6. Jesuits. 7.

7. Cathedral of Our Lady.
8. *The* Palace 9. *ye* Seminary.
10. *The* Hôtel Dieu.

11. *St* Charles River.
12. *The* Common Hospital.
13. *The* Hermitage of the Recolets.

14. *The* Bishop's House. 15. *The*
Parish Church of the Lower Town.
16. *The* Upper Town 17. *ye* Lower Town.
18. *The* Platform & Battery of Cannon
19. *The* Isle of Orleans. 20. Point Lievi.

Engrav'd & Printed By Thos. Johnston for Step. Whiting.

Figure 36. View of Quebec, Canada: 1759

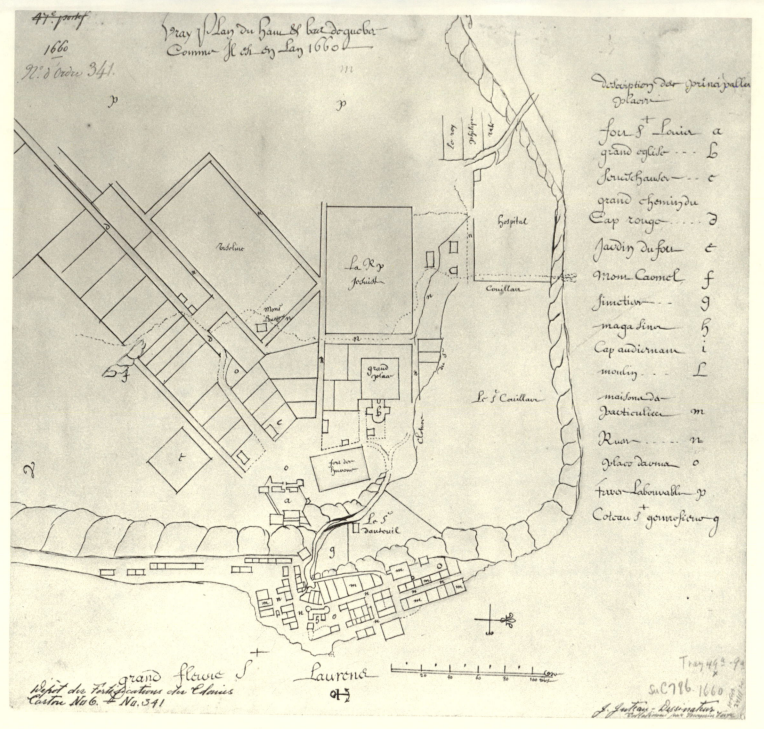

Figure 37. Plan of Quebec, Canada: 1660

of the city on the heights above the river. The eventual result of this work can be seen most clearly in Figure 38, a detailed plan of Quebec in 1759 at the end of French domination.

There are many excellent descriptions of Quebec during the years between 1660 and 1759, but none is better than the one furnished by that perceptive Jesuit priest, Father Pierre Charlevoix, who arrived in Canada in 1719 and spent the next three years observing French settlements along the St. Lawrence, the Great Lakes, and the Mississippi. Like all visitors to Quebec, Charlevoix began his tour of the city at the lower town near the site of Champlain's *Habitation*:

"The first thing you meet with on landing is a pretty large square, and of an irregular form, having in front a row of well built houses, the back part of which leans against the rock, so that they have no great depth. These form a street of a considerable length, occupying the whole breadth of the square, and extending on the right and left as far as the two ways which lead to the upper town. The square is bounded towards the left by a small church, and towards the right by two rows of houses placed in a parallel direction."[6]

The plan of the lower town, then, was quite regular, and, as can be seen on the map, most of the streets, while narrow, are straight and intersect one another at right angles. The regular plan and the single open square before the church, which served as a market place, are reminiscent of Champlain's first venture in town planning at Sainte Croix. Whether he consciously directed the planning of the lower town into this pattern is not known. To a considerable extent the plan was dictated by topography, and the town was forced to grow in this linear pattern in front of the steep cliff and along the narrow shelf of rocky bank at the edge of the river. The lower town remains today much as it existed at the time of Charlevoix's visit, although many of the buildings he observed have been replaced.

The upper town on the heights overlooking the river was much less restricted by topography; moreover, its growth, while slow by contemporary standards, was relatively more rapid than the settlement by the river. It seems evident that no over-all plan for the

[6] Pierre François Xavier de Charlevoix, *Journal of a Voyage to North America* (London, 1761), Chicago, 1923, I, p. 104.

development of this part of Quebec was ever established. That is not to say that no planning was carried out. A study of the map reveals many sections in which regularity of streets and orientation of buildings indicate attempts at directing the growth of individual quarters of this part of the city. Charlevoix describes this newer portion of the city reached by a steep lane from the lower town:

"The first building worthy of notice you meet with . . . is the bishop's palace. . . . When you are got about twenty paces farther, you find yourself between two tolerably large squares; that towards the left is the place of arms, fronting which is the fort or citadel, where the governor-general resides; on the opposite side stands the convent of the Recollects, the other sides of the square being lined with handsome houses.

"In the square towards your right you come first of all to the cathedral, which serves also for a parish church to the whole city. Near this, and on the angle formed by the river St. Lawrence and that of St. Charles, stands the seminary. Opposite to the cathedral is the college of the Jesuits, and on the sides between them are some very handsome houses."[7]

Also to be seen on the map and described by Charlevoix are the hospital and the convent of the Ursuline nuns. A substantial group of buildings stood on the lower elevation along the St. Charles River. Here were the principal docks, the residence of the intendant, who was the commercial representative of the king, miscellaneous manufacturing plants, and a number of residences backed against the steep escarpment.

The plan of the upper town of Quebec represents one type of urban form established by the French in North America. Here the general configuration of the community is non-linear, thus resembling most European cities of the time. Another, and much more regular, example of this urban type is Louisburg on Cape Breton Island, the site for which was selected in 1712. Louisburg was intended as the main French fortress town in Canada, and the plan of the town in 1764, reproduced in Figure 39, shows the extent of the French commitment to this concept. In all, thirty million francs were poured into the construction of this mighty fort, and its building took twenty years. The main ramparts ex-

[7] *ibid.*, 105.

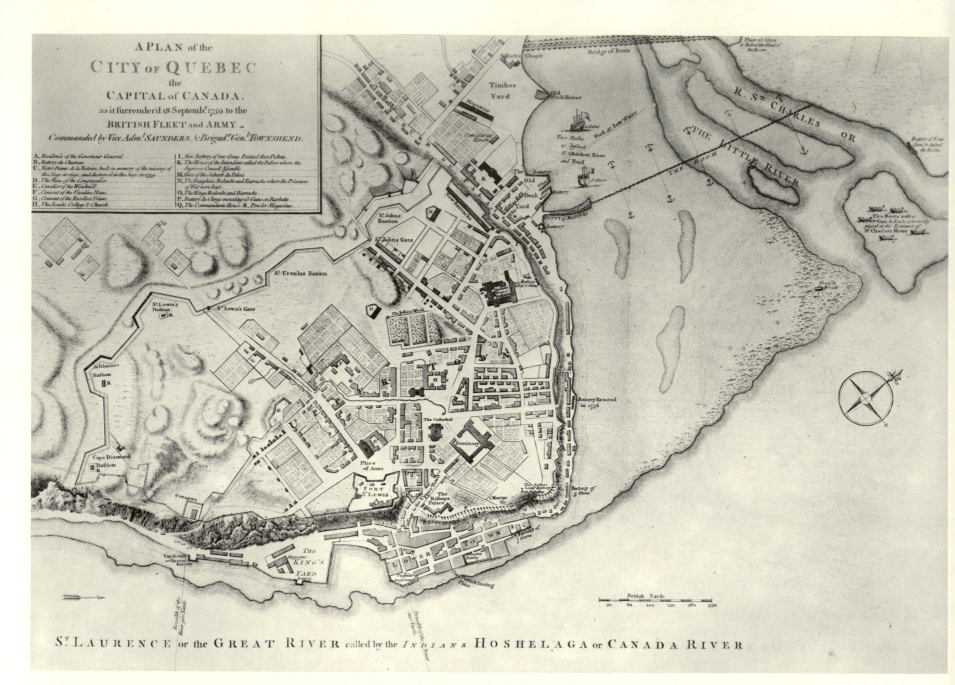

Figure 38. Plan of Quebec, Canada: 1759

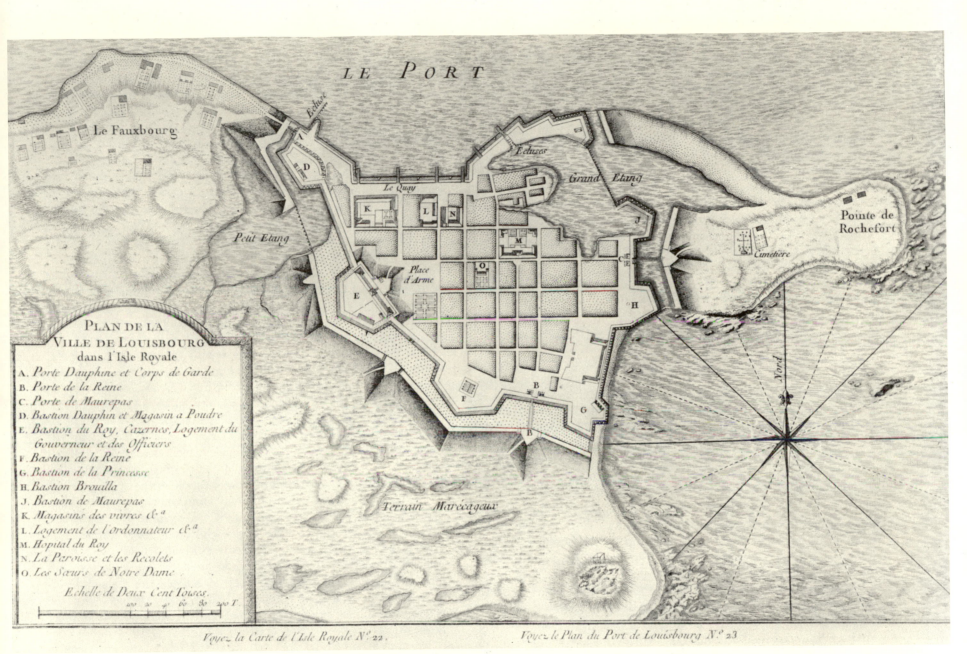

LE PORT

Le Fauxbourg

Petit Etang

Voyez la Carte de l'Isle Royale N.º 22.

Ecluse

Le Quay

Ecluses

Grand Etang

Pointe de Rochefort

Cimetière

Place d'Arme

Nord

Terrain Marécageux

PLAN DE LA
VILLE DE LOUISBOURG
dans l'Isle Royale

A. Porte Dauphine et Corps de Garde
B. Porte de la Reine
C. Porte de Maurepas
D. Bastion Dauphin et Magasin a Poudre
E. Bastion du Roy, Cazernes, Logement du
   Gouverneur et des Officiers
F. Bastion de la Reine
G. Bastion de la Princesse
H. Bastion Brouilla
J. Bastion de Maurepas
K. Magasins des vivres &.ª
L. Logement de l'Ordonnateur &.ª
M. Hopital du Roy
N. La Paroisse et les Recolets
O. Les Sœurs de Notre Dame

Echelle de Deux Cent Toises.

Voyez le Plan du Port de Louisbourg N.º 23

Figure 39. Plan of Louisbourg, Canada: 1764

tended for two miles, and, in addition, there were extensive outworks beyond the principal walls.

The plan of Louisburg followed the town and garrison layout theories and principles of the great French military engineer, Sebastian Vauban. With its *place d'armes*, elaborate fortifications, protected harbor, and gridiron street system, Louisburg could have been one of the several hundred cities planned or remodeled by Vauban in Europe. Although Louisburg served primarily as a garrison town, it was planned for a population of four thousand persons and was developed as an important commercial port as well. Yet for all its seemingly impregnable fortifications, Louisburg fell to the English twice, once in 1745 and again in 1758. Some years after its final capture the English demolished the fortifications, and the town virtually ceased to exist. A national park of some three hundred acres now contains the site of the old town and fort.

Montreal and the Linear Plan

Quebec and Louisburg must have seemed familiar to new colonists or travelers from Europe, the first growing like a replica of some medieval city, the second springing into existence as a Renaissance community. Quebec's great rival, Montreal, developed in quite a different pattern. The plan of Montreal in 1758, reproduced in Figure 40, can be compared with the previous map of Quebec just one year later. It is obvious that the general form of this city—a narrow, linear pattern—was strongly influenced by topography. As at the lower town of Quebec, the narrow level area along the St. Lawrence River restricted the community's growth in depth. But it is equally obvious that the plan reflects some over-all direction of town development. Topographic restrictions were also present in the case of Mobile, New Orleans, and St. Louis, whose plans closely resemble that of Montreal. It is likely that the planners of those later cities consciously imitated the Montreal plan.

Montreal's original plan, however, may have been derived from Champlain's first venture in town planning at Isle Sainte Croix. That plan, recently discovered in manuscript, is reproduced in Figure 41.[8] The plan apparently dates from the first year of set-

[8] The Montreal plan is one of a group of drawings of Canadian forts by Jehan Bourdon. Facsimile copies of these manuscripts were published in a limited edition by the McGill University Library in a portfolio entitled

tlement in 1642, when a group of missionaries, soldiers, nuns, and settlers arrived at Montreal Island. The site and its advantages were already well known. Cartier had visited here, and Champlain had constructed a rude trading post which he named Place Royale. Yet during the early years of Quebec's building the Montreal site remained unoccupied except for a few traders and trappers who camped there during the summer months.

The group that took up residence in 1642 had ventured to Canada as the pioneers of a movement supported from France by money and prayers designed to bring the Indians into the fold of Christianity. On the narrow point of land formed by the St. Lawrence River and the stream called the St. Pierre the first buildings were erected around a little square. The hospital, a small fort, and a number of residences made up the settlement during the bitter early years when Indians raids, the severe winters, and spring floods made life hazardous for these first settlers. By 1665 the population had reached 500, and within a few years expansion of the town became necessary.

The growth of Montreal coincided with changes in the colonial status of New France. The Sulpician order received the seigneurial rights for the Island of Montreal, and in 1672 Dollier de Casson, the Superior of the Sulpicians, supervised surveys for new streets and building sites. St. Paul Street, which on the map in Figure 40 can be seen connecting the Market Place and the Parade along the river, already existed as a curving lane serving the few houses that had been built beyond the confines of the original settlement. This was now surveyed and building lines established.

Parallel to St. Paul Street and away from the river, Notre Dame Street was laid out 30 feet broad and in a straight line above and below the site set aside for the parish church of Notre Dame. The right-of-way for this street lay across cultivated fields, and for a year or so some of the proprietors ignored the surveyor's monuments. In 1673 these settlers received notices that the right-of-way must be observed and, further, that in accordance with the terms of the land grants they must enclose their lots and erect houses on them to prevent forfeiture of their lands.[9]

Plans of the First French Settlements on the Saint Lawrence, 1635-1642, Montreal, 1958.

[9] For a more complete account of these and other events in the early planning of Montreal see William H. Atherton, *Montreal*, Montreal, 1914, I, 241-46.

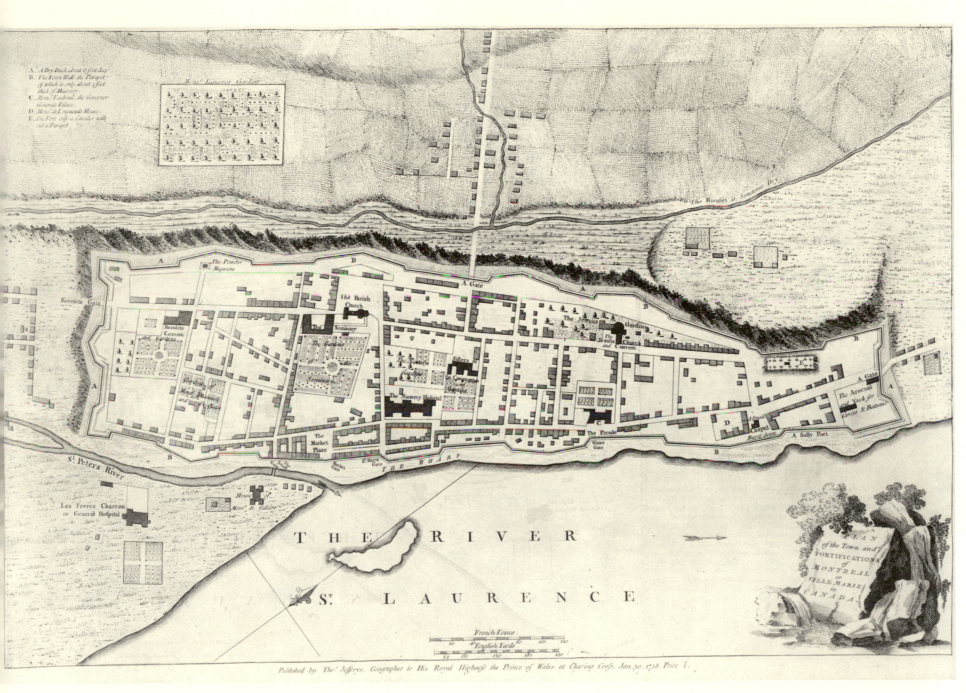

Figure 40. Plan of Montreal, Canada: 1758

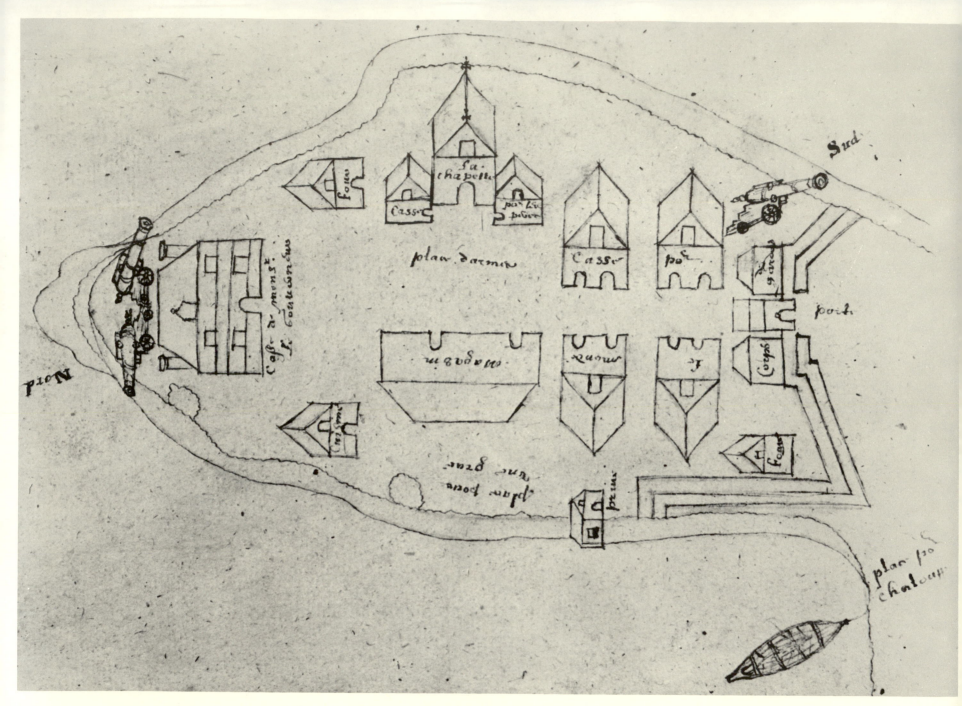

Figure 41. Plan of Montreal, Canada: ca. 1644

Other streets were laid out at right angles to St. Paul and Notre Dame. Some of these were completely new, although most of them followed generally the location of lanes and trails affording access to scattered dwellings that were in existence at the time. These cross streets were quite narrow, 18 or 24 feet being the dimensions of most of them. In 1678, the same year that marked the completion of the church of Notre Dame, a third street parallel to the river, St. James, was surveyed. Within the framework of the newly established linear grid pattern the town began to grow. By 1680 the population was about 1,400, and in 1750, toward the end of the French regime, more than 8,000 persons lived in Montreal.

Charlevoix's description of the city in the spring of 1721 indicates the development that had taken place in the first eighty years of the town:

"The city of Montreal has a very pleasing aspect, and is besides conveniently situated, the streets well laid out, and the houses well built. . . .

"Montreal is of a quadrangular form, situated on the bank of the river, which rising gently, divides the city lengthwise into the upper and lower towns, though you can scarcely perceive the ascent from the one to the other; the hospital, royal-magazines, and place of arms, are in the lower-town, which is also the quarter in which the merchants for the most part have their houses. The seminary and parish-church, the convent of the Recollects, the Jesuits, the daughters of the congregation, the governor, and most of the officers dwell in the high-town. Beyond a small stream coming from the north-west, and which terminates the city on this side, you come to a few houses and the hospital general; and turning towards the right beyond the Recollects, whose convent is at the extremity of the city, on the same side, there is a kind of suburb beginning to be built, which will in time be a very fine quarter."[10]

Scarcely a month after Charlevoix's departure a disastrous fire swept the town, destroying many of the frame buildings. This led to a series of regulations encouraging the use of stone in rebuilding and providing for new street lines, since, in the words of the regulations,

"... they are not large enough nor straight enough; that while this cannot be done without individuals suffering, yet at the present moment, seeing that there are only ruins in the streets, it would be easy for individuals, before rebuilding, to conform with the alignment which shall be drawn up by the Engineer. . . ."[11]

And so the first replanning of the city began, a process that continues to the present day as old plans and buildings are modified to meet the changing conditions of a new era. The modern metropolis of Montreal sprawls for miles beyond the boundaries of the old town, yet much of the seventeenth-century character remains. As in the lower town of Quebec, this older section of Montreal preserves the results of an earlier age of town planning, a precious heritage almost unique on a continent where all too frequently the residue of the past has been destroyed.

French Towns in the American Interior

With Quebec and Montreal established along the St. Lawrence, French traders, explorers, and missionaries pushed on into the great central lake and river valleys of America. Champlain, Nicolet, Jolliet, Marquette, La Salle—these were but a few of the hardy Frenchmen who established a great empire in North America. It was a different kind of domain than the English were carving from the forests along the Atlantic coast. Based on a string of frontier forts and missions, with here and there a settlement large enough to be called a town, New France depended heavily on water transportation as the only reasonably speedy and effective means of communication and trade. The waterfront, or a military installation controlling water transportation, was the important feature of most of these French colonial settlements.

The plan of Detroit, which was founded in 1701 by Antoine de la Mothe Cadillac, expressed its function as a fortress town dominating the Detroit River connection between Lakes Erie and St. Clair. The drawing reproduced in Figure 42 strongly suggests one of the *bastide* towns of southern France in Cadillac's native Gascony. The fortifications enclosed a space about 600 by 400 feet. Streets were extremely narrow. The widest, Rue Sainte Anne,

[10] Charlevoix, *Journal*, I, 198-200.

[11] As quoted by Atherton, *Montreal*, I, 347.

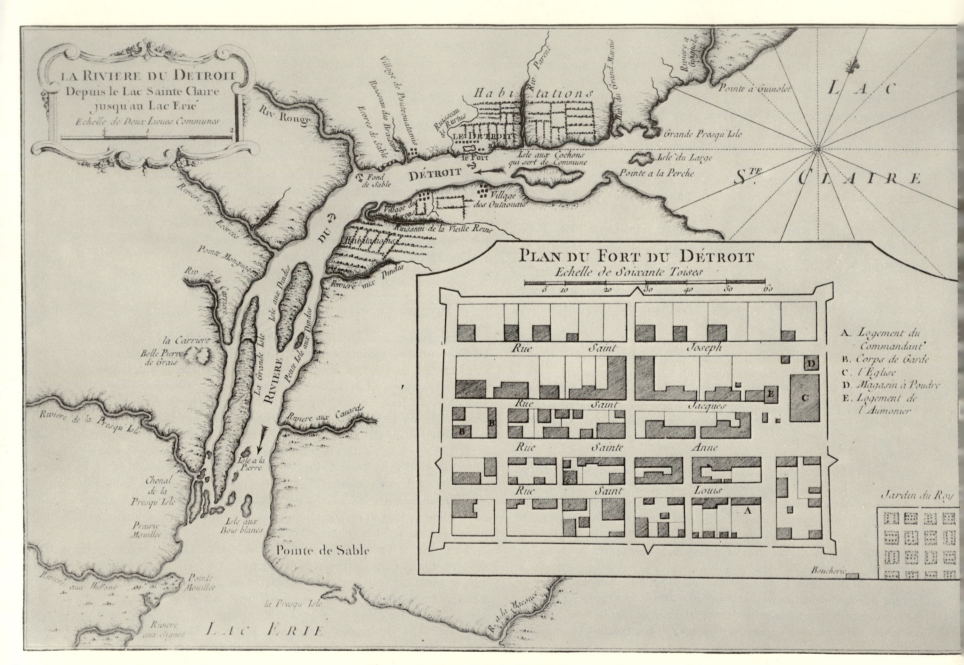

La Rivière du Détroit
Depuis le Lac Sainte Claire
jusqu'au Lac Erié

Echelle de Deux Lieues Communes

Riv. Rouge

Village de Poutcouatamis
Ruisseau des Brasans
Ecorce de Sable

Habitations

Riv. Parent

Riv. du Grand Marais

Riviere a Quiquelet

Pointe a Guinolet

LAC

Ruisseau de Rubis

LE DÉTROIT

le Fort

Fond de Sable

DÉTROIT

Isle aux Cochons
qui sert de Commune

Grande Presqu'Isle

Isle du Large

Pointe a la Perche

STE CLAIRE

Village des Hurons

Village des Outaouais

Ruisseau de la Vieille Reine

Habitations

Riviere aux Ecorces

Pointe Monguagon

Riv. de la Carriere

Riviere aux Dindes

la Carriere
Belle Pierre
de Grais

La Grande Isle

Isle aux Dindes

Petite Isle aux Dindes

RIVIERE DU D

Riviere aux Canards

Riviere de la Presqu Isle

Isle a la Pierre

Chenal
de la
Presqu Isle

Prairie
Mouillée

Isle aux
Bois blancs

Pointe de Sable

Riviere aux Hufons

Pointe
Mouillée

la Presqu Isle

Riviere aux Cignes

R. à la Maconce

LAC ERIE

PLAN DU FORT DU DÉTROIT
Echelle de Soixante Toises

5   10   20   30   40   50   60

Rue   Saint   Joseph

Rue   Saint   Jacques

Rue   Sainte   Anne

Rue   Saint   Louis

A. Logement du
     Commandant
B. Corps de Garde
C. l'Eglise
D. Magasin à Poudre
E. Logement de
     l'Aumonier

Jardin du Roy

Boucherie

Figure 42. Plan of Detroit, Michigan: 1764

measured less than 30 feet, and the others were between 10 and 20 feet wide.[12]

Outside the little town lay the farm plots of the settlers. The map shows the major field lines in the vicinity of Detroit, with the typical French pattern of long, narrow farms running back from the water's edge. This pattern was even more pronounced in the Canadian settlements along the St. Lawrence and, later, on the lower Mississippi in the neighborhood of New Orleans. In the case of New Orleans the pattern of rural land holdings helped to shape the expansion of the city. At Detroit, however, the French system of field division had little influence. After the town passed to the British and still later into American hands, a fire completely destroyed the settlement. Congress authorized its replanning and gave jurisdiction over 10,000 acres of land in the vicinity to the governor and judges of Michigan Territory. Their plan, as is described in a later chapter, completely wiped out the last traces of the French town and its surrounding farm lands.

There were many other fortress communities erected by the French. Some, like Fort Duquesne, at the present Pittsburgh, were intended to stop the westward march of the English colonies. Others were established in an effort to consolidate French control over the vast interior valleys of the Great Lakes and the Mississippi River. While most of these settlements began as military garrison communities, they often included groups of missionaries and usually attracted traders and farmers.

By the end of the seventeenth century, French settlements began to appear along the Mississippi and tributary rivers. Cahokia, near the mouth of the Illinois River, was established as a mission in 1699 and developed into a small village.[13] Around Fort Pimitoui

[12] In M. M. Quaife, *This is Detroit: 250 Years in Pictures*, Detroit, 1951, there is a reproduction of what may be Cadillac's original plan for Fort Detroit. This shows a square fortification with a pointed bastion at each corner and with an elongated, rather narrow parade ground extending from the river gate almost to the other site of the fort. Another interesting plan of Detroit is a manuscript plan of 1803 by Georges de Bois St. Lys in the collections of the Chicago Historical Society. This shows in greater detail many of the features indicated in Figure 42. Of special importance is the small but elaborately planned "King's Garden" laid out in intricate *parterres* with what appears to be a series of pavilions at one side.

[13] For a reproduction of a manuscript plan showing the French settlement pattern in the Cahokia area see John Francis McDermott, *Old Cahokia*, St. Louis, 1949, following p. 16. A mid-nineteenth-century view of Cahokia by J. C. Wild also appears as the frontispiece.

or Fort St. Louis, built at Peoria in the winter of 1691-1692, another group of Frenchmen settled. At Kaskaskia, a mission originally founded by Marquette and moved once to Peoria was established on its third site at the southern end of the long, fertile, alluvial plain called the American Bottom, on the east side of the Mississippi southward from St. Louis. Here, as Pittman tells us, developed

". . . by far the most considerable settlement in the country of the Illinois, as well from its number of inhabitants, as from its advantageous situation. . . . The principal buildings are, the church and Jesuits house, which has a small chapel adjoining to it; these, as well as some other houses in the village, are built of stone, and, considering this part of the world, make a very good appearance. . . . Sixty-five families reside in this village, besides merchants, other casual people, and slaves."[14]

The plan of the village at the time of Pittman's visit is reproduced in Figure 43. Although some semblance of an over-all plan is apparent, Kaskaskia grew up without much thought or control from the original Jesuit establishment. One feature appearing on the map is the designation of common lands surrounding the village. Alvord, in his splendid history of early Illinois, describes how individual farmers received allotments in the common fields, separated by two furrows, and stretching backward from the river in strips from 100 to 500 feet in width and occasionally as long as one mile. A common fence separated the village from the fields, and each farmer was made responsible for maintaining his strip of fence. In addition to these cultivated fields, there were open common lands for cattle grazing.[15] This system of common lands was similar to that of the Spanish communities and was also a feature of the New England communities as described in a later chapter.

Between Cahokia and Kaskaskia, along the 70-mile extent of the American Bottom, there were a number of smaller settlements. Opposite Kaskaskia on the Missouri side of the river was Ste.

[14] Philip Pittman, *The Present State of the European Settlements on the Mississippi* (London, 1770), Frank H. Hodder, ed., Cleveland, 1906, pp. 84-85.

[15] Clarence Walworth Alvord, *The Illinois Country: 1673-1818*, Springfield, 1920, p. 207. Maps of the common fields may be found in *American State Papers*, Public Lands Series, II.

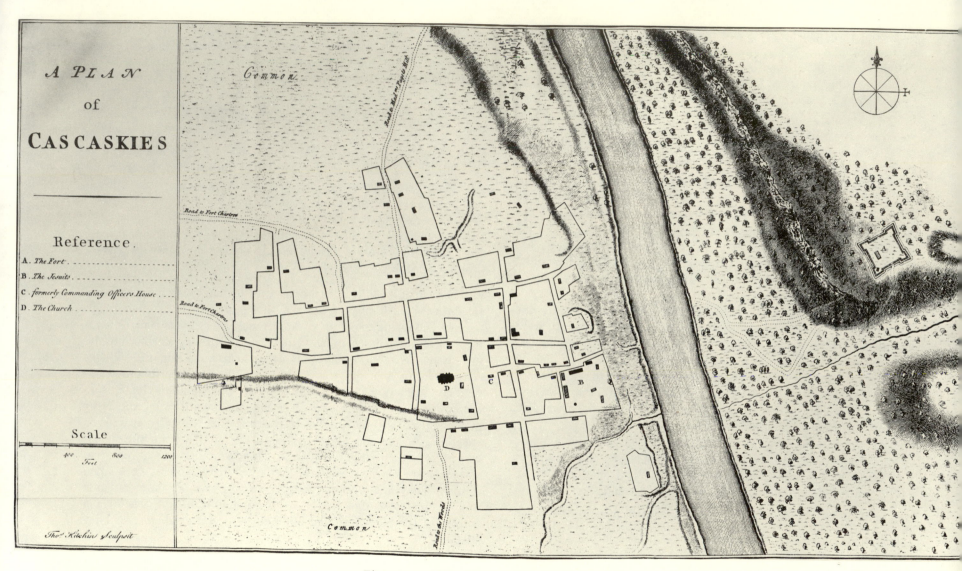

A PLAN
of
CASCASKIES

Reference.

A. *The Fort* . . . .
B. *The Jesuits* . . . .
C. *formerly Commanding Officers House* . . . .
D. *The Church* . . . .

Scale

400   800   1200
Feet

Common

Common

Road to Fort Chartres

Road to Fort Chartres

Thos. Kitchin Sculpsit

Figure 43. Plan of Kaskaskia, Illinois: 1770

Genevieve, founded in 1732. Far to the east on the banks of the Wabash lay Vincennes, where a fort had been built in 1731. During the first half of the century, aside from scattered trading posts, these villages and forts constituted the extent of French settlement in the middle Mississippi Valley.

The largest and most important of the mid-Mississippi French towns was, of course, St. Louis. Here the French reverted to their former practice of granting trading privileges to a private company, in this case one headed by Pierre Laclede. Laclede in 1762 secured exclusive trade rights west of the Mississippi for an eight-year period. He explored the area below the mouth of the Missouri and finally fixed on the site of St. Louis for his trading post and settlement. Auguste Chouteau, one of Laclede's associates, tells us of the establishment of the town:

"Navigation being open in the early part of February, he fitted out a boat . . . and he gave the charge of it to Chouteau, and said to him: 'You will proceed and land at the place where we marked the trees; you will commence to have the place cleared, and build a large shed to contain the provisions and the tools, and some small cabins to lodge the men. . . .' In the early part of April, Laclede arrived among us. He occupied himself with his settlement, fixed the place where he wished to build his house, laid a plan of the village which he wished to found, (and he named it St. Louis, in honor of Louis XV, whose subject he expected to remain, for a long time;—he never imagined he was a subject of the King of Spain;) and ordered me to follow the plan exactly, because he could not remain there any longer with us."[16]

Such was the beginning of St. Louis. The modern visitor to the city seeking the majestic river on which St. Louis has turned its back will find a vast stretch of the sloping bank stripped of buildings, a curious gap in the otherwise solidly built downtown district. This is the future site of the Jefferson Memorial and a complex of civic and cultural buildings. It was on this site that Laclede laid out the last city under French jurisdiction planned in America.

An early plan as drawn by Chouteau in 1764 appears in Figure 44. This copy of Chouteau's map shows some additional blocks added to the north and south that were not part of the original plan. The resemblance to Montreal is obvious; Laclede's Louisiana background may also have been influential, for the linear plan first used at Montreal also was followed at Mobile and New Orleans.

The Chouteau plan shows a square opening to the river and two other unsubdivided blocks on the other side to the west. One or more of these may have been intended as the *place d'armes*, that central feature of most of the French colonial towns. At least one later map shows a similar location but a quite different treatment of this square. Figure 45 reproduces a manuscript plan prepared in 1796, during the last years of Spanish rule. Chouteau's account mentions that, unknown to Laclede, Spain had acquired by treaty the territory in which St. Louis stood. The square shown on the 1796 map could well be a Spanish modification, according to the prescriptions of the Laws of the Indies, of Laclede's *Place d'Armes*. The streets bordering it on the north and south evidently were cut through following the lot lines in the middle of the boundary blocks.

Under Spanish rule St. Louis enjoyed no particular prosperity, but with the Louisiana Purchase and the opening of the west the city rapidly assumed a commanding position. Henry Brackenridge, who viewed it in 1811, felt sure St. Louis was destined to become a great mercantile city. But he was unimpressed by its plan and appearance.

"It is to be lamented that no space has been left between the town and the river; for the sake of the pleasure of the promenade, as well as for business and health, there should have been no encroachment on the margin of the noble stream. The principal place of business ought to have been on the bank. From the opposite side, nothing is visible of the busy bustle of a populous town; it appears closed up. The site of St. Louis is not unlike that of Cincinnati. How different would have been its appearance, if built in the same elegant manner! its bosom opened to the breezes of the river, the stream gladdened by the enlivening scene of business and pleasure, compact rows of elegant and tasteful dwellings, looking with pride on the broad wave that passes!"[17]

[16] Fragment of Col. Auguste Chouteau's Narrative of the Settlement of St. Louis as quoted in Ina Faye Woestemeyer, *The Westward Movement*, New York, 1939, pp. 201-202.

[17] Henry M. Brackenridge, *Views of Louisiana Together with a Journal of a Voyage up the Missouri River, in 1811*, Pittsburgh, 1814, pp. 120-21.

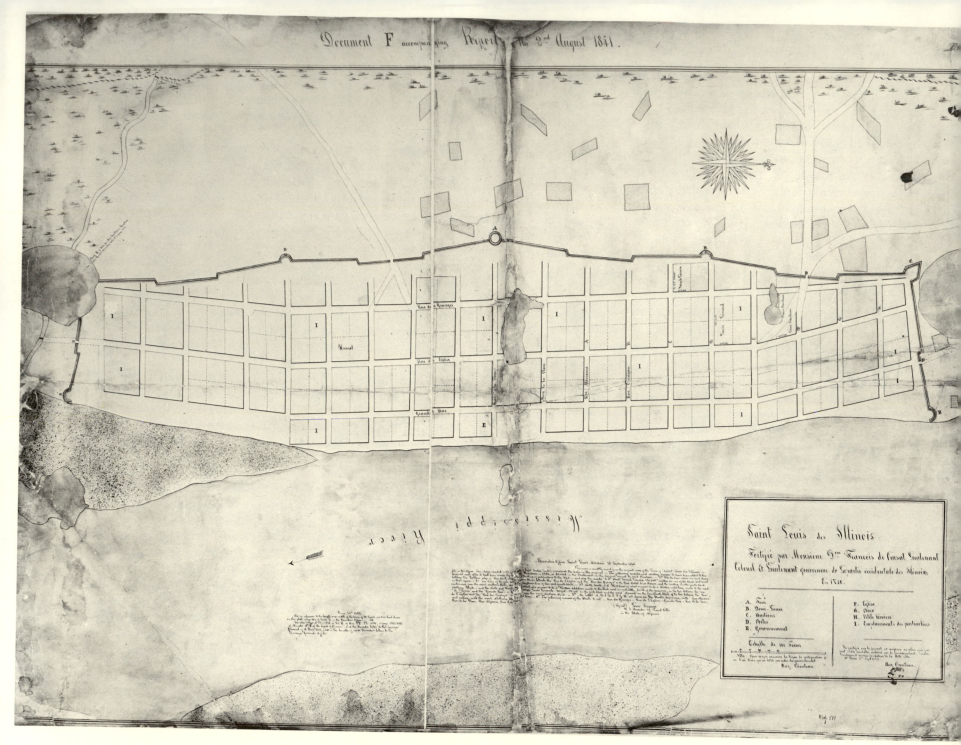

Figure 44. Plan of St. Louis, Missouri: 1780

Figure 45. Plan of St. Louis, Missouri: 1796

Brackenridge might have added that so insensitive were the early builders of St. Louis to the most elementary principles of planning that the cathedral itself was assigned a miserable location on a site totally inadequate in size. Only with the recent demolition for the Jefferson Memorial has it emerged from the surrounding rubble to achieve at last some kind of architectural prominence.

Bienville and the Planning of Mobile and New Orleans

One of the most prominent of the early settlers of Montreal was Charles le Moyne, whose seigneury of Longueuil across the river from the city was once almost as important and influential as that of Montreal itself. Eleven of his sons brilliantly served the cause of New France. Two of them were responsible for important cities: Pierre, Sieur d'Iberville; and Jean Baptisti, Sieur de Bienville. It was Iberville who, in 1698, sailed from Brest in command of an expedition under orders to discover the mouth of the Mississippi and to secure the lower end of the great valley for France.

Early the following year Iberville and his brother reached the mouth of the Mississippi and explored its lower reaches. Then, sailing eastward to Biloxi Bay, Iberville constructed a fort near its entrance as a temporary post. After further explorations, he sailed for France, but in 1701 he returned with a new party, this time to establish a settlement on Mobile Bay. Early in 1702 Fort Louis was located on the Mobile River, and a rectangular gridiron village plan was marked out.[18] Bienville, who had assisted his brother throughout these years, was installed as governor of the French settlement, and on the death of Iberville in 1706 became the leading figure in the Gulf possessions of France.

The original settlement survived only eight years. After a flood in 1710 had covered the site, Bienville determined to reestablish the town on a more favorable site, this time at the mouth of the

Mobile River. The plan for this second Mobile was similar to the first, although more elaborate and more carefully laid out. A reproduction is shown in Figure 46, on which appears a detailed description of the city. In reading this, one should know that the French *toise* measured approximately 6 feet. After a description of the fort and its method of construction, the explanation continues.

"There is in the fort only the governor's house, the *magasin* where are the king's effects, and a guardhouse. The officers, soldiers, and residents have their abode outside the fort, as is indicated, being placed in such manner that the streets are six toises wide and all parallel. The blocks are fifty toises square except those opposite the fort, which are sixty toises wide and fifty deep, and those nearest the river, which are fifty wide and sixty deep.

"The houses are constructed of cedar and pine upon a foundation of wooden stakes. . . .

"They give to all who wish to settle in this place land 12 1/2 toises wide, facing a street, by 25 deep."[19]

The letters on the map and the accompanying key show the allotments of land made at that time. The most prominent settlers were given sites nearest the fort and bordering the tree-lined parade. One feature is of interest: the streets and blocks shown by dotted lines projected inland from those first laid out for the settlers moved from the old site. Evidently Bienville was confident that his new city would grow and that additional land would be needed. Note, too, the proportions of the city, ten blocks long by five blocks deep, and the parade ground or *place d'armes* opening to the river bank and centrally located.

Under the Treaty of Paris in 1763 Mobile passed to the English. Pittman's map accompanying his account of the Mississippi country shows Mobile shortly after French occupation ended. Shown in Figure 47, the map indicates that with the passage of time some of the regularity of Bienville's plan had been lost. When the capital of the French territory was shifted from Mobile many years earlier the city lost some of its initial importance, and encroachments were made on the original straight streets and carefully surveyed city blocks. Yet the original plan can still be seen clearly on Pittman's map and may yet be traced in the streets of the modern city.

[18] A reproduction of this first plan for Mobile may be found in Peter J. Hamilton, *Colonial Mobile*, Boston, rev. ed., 1910. I have relied on Hamilton's excellent history for my treatment of the planning of Mobile. There is also a brief but detailed contemporary account of the first plan for Mobile in André Pénicaut, *Fleur de Lys and Calumet: Being the Pénicaut Narrative of French Adventure in Louisiana*, translated and edited by Richebourg Gaillard McWilliams, Baton Rouge, 1953, pp. 58-59. The Pénicaut narrative is a fascinating chronicle of the early years of French colonization of the Gulf Coast and lower Mississippi Valley.

[19] Hamilton, *Colonial Mobile*, p. 87.

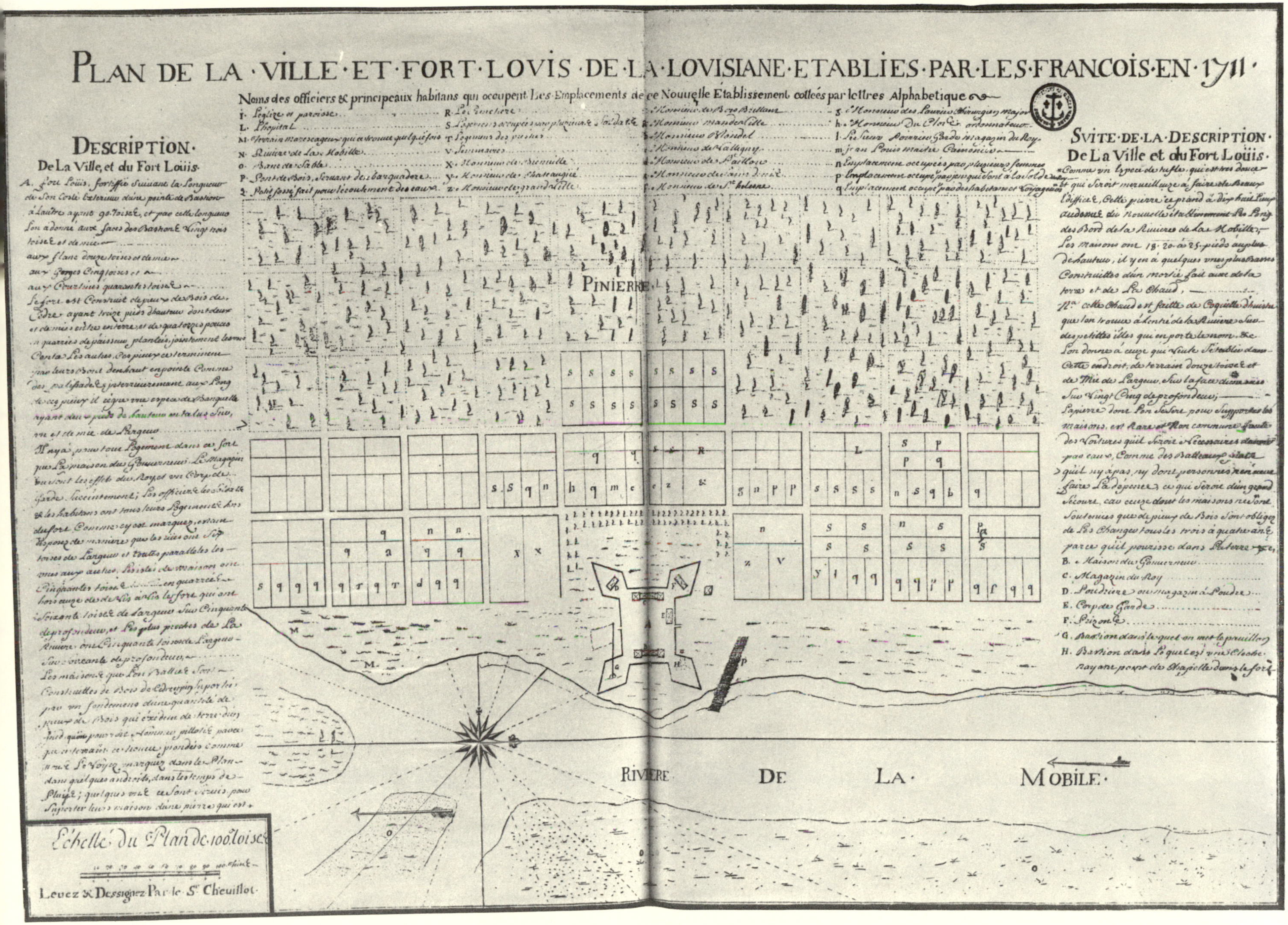

Figure 46. Plan of Mobile, Alabama: 1711

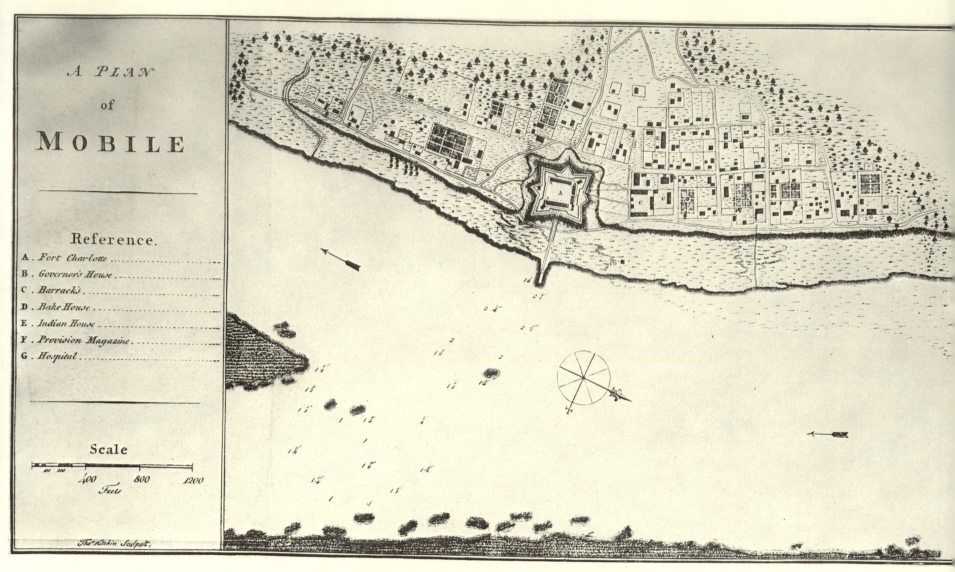

A *PLAN*
of
MOBILE

Reference.

A . *Fort Charlotte* ....
B . *Governor's House* ....
C . *Barrack's* ....
D . *Bake House* ....
E . *Indian House* ....
F . *Provision Magazine* ....
G . *Hospital* ....

Scale

80 200   400   800   1200
Feet

Tho.ʳ Kitchin Sculpsit.

Figure 47. Plan of Mobile, Alabama: 1770

Of all the French settlements in the United States, however, it is mainly in New Orleans that substantial portions of the French legacy remain today. New Orleans, too, was a product of the energy of Bienville, who applied there what he had learned in laying out the two Mobiles. Bienville had always favored a city on the Mississippi. His interest was renewed by the promotional activities of one John Law, who had received a charter from the French government for his Western Company, one of the early examples in America of a speculative real estate promotion. Law's enterprise received wide publicity in France as he advanced extravagant claims for Louisiana's fertility, ease of settlement, and potential wealth.

As early as 1718 Bienville sent a few emigrants from Canada to clear the site and to erect temporary buildings, but not until 1722 did the actual planning and town building begin. In this year Charlevoix visited the site accompanied by Adrien de Pauger, the engineer who Bienville put in charge of running the surveys and laying out the city. Charlevoix mentions that Pauger

". . . has just shown me a plan of his own invention; but it will not be so easy to put it into execution, as it has been to draw it out upon paper."[20]

Charlevoix no doubt had expected to find the city already in existence, since before he left France for Canada he had read in *Le Mercure de France* and other newspapers the exaggerations by Law, who described the great city on the banks of the Mississippi as something only slightly less imposing than Paris itself. Charlevoix refers to these false impressions in his descriptions of the actual conditions at New Orleans as he saw them:

"If the eight hundred fine houses and the five parishes, which our Mercury bestowed upon it two years ago, are at present reduced to a hundred barracks, placed in no very good order; to a large ware-house built of timber; to two or three houses which would be no ornament to a village in France; to one half of a sorry ware-house, formerly set apart for divine service, and was scarce appropriated for that purpose, when it was removed to a tent: what pleasure, on the other hand, must it give to see this . . . become the capital of a large and rich colony."[21]

[20] Charlevoix, *Journal*, II, 274.
[21] *ibid.*, 257-58.

An early drawing of the Bienville-Pauger plan and the surrounding area appears in Figure 48. Although in its details of the city the drawing is inaccurate in some particulars and in its depiction of the countryside it is highly stylized rather than precise, it gives a good general picture of the new settlement. Charlevoix's comment about its difficulty of execution may well have been directed to the problems of construction in the low-lying, marshy terrain. The swamps and ponds that show on the map long caused severe health hazards, and the high water table still creates problems for building construction.

An accurate plan of the town forty years after its founding is shown in Figure 49. The focal point of the city is the *place d'armes*, the modern Jackson Square. As at Mobile, this appears at the water's edge. But this open square was plainly intended as more than a parade ground. On the inland side, facing the square and the river beyond, stood the principal church. To give this building further architectural prominence the planners introduced an extra street dividing the central range of blocks terminating at the square. This strong axial treatment doubtless reflected the intentions of Bienville to create a capital city of beauty as well as utility. Stretching each way from the central square along the river ran the quay, broadening at either end where the river curved away from the town site.

As the capital city, New Orleans became the favored spot for French settlers, and it enjoyed a mild prosperity. Above and below the city on both sides of the Mississippi plantations were developed, laid out on the typical French pattern with relatively narrow river frontages and stretching back from the river for great distances. Yet even by 1797 we are told that not all of the land within the original city boundaries enclosed by its fortifications had been built on. Francis Baily's account of the city at that time is of considerable interest for his description of the *place d'armes*, the buildings around it, and the appearance of the city from the river bank:

"The church is a plain brick building of the Ionic order. . . . Not far from the square in which this church stands is the government-house, a plain edifice, in which the governor of the province resides: it stands facing the water at the corner of a street; it is built (as many houses in this place are) with open galleries fac-

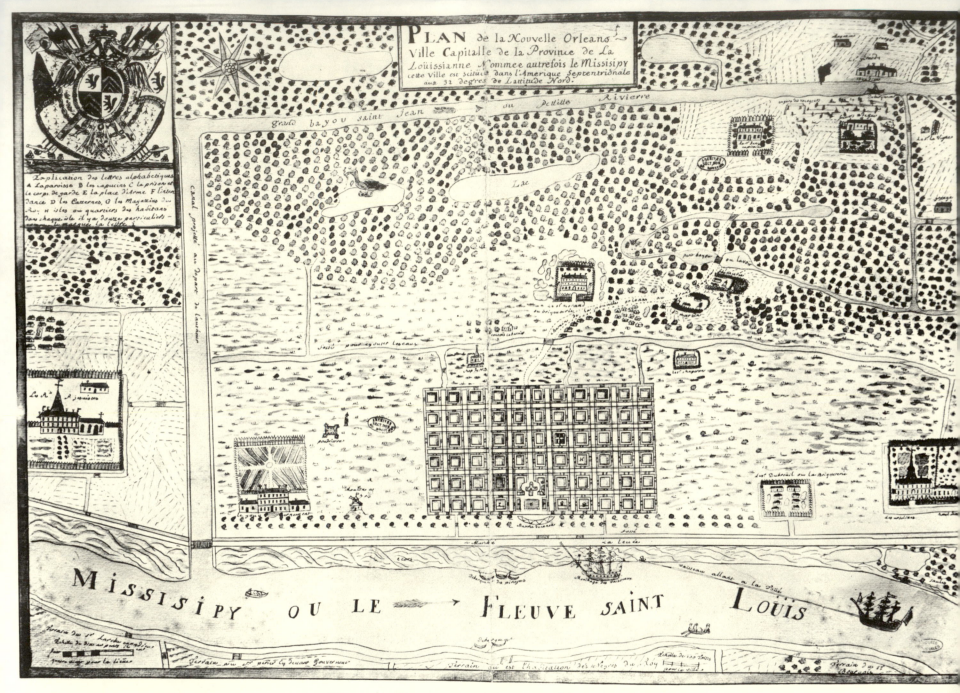

Figure 48. Plan of New Orleans, Louisiana: ca. 1720

Figure 49. Plan of New Orleans, Louisiana: 1764

ing the street, and is surrounded at the back by a garden. At an equal distance from the church, on the opposite side, and immediately facing the water, is a magazine of stores. . . . At the eastern corner of the city are the barracks. . . . Immediately adjoining the barracks is the convent, which is another very plain edifice, and holds about thirty or forty nuns. . . . The levee . . . here was a handsome raised gravel walk, planted with orangetrees; and in the summer-time served for a mall, and in an evening was always a fashionable resort for the beaux and belles of the place."[22]

Baily's impressions were thus not entirely favorable. The "plain edifices" he encountered doubtless seemed to him unimpressive, and it is true that they would have been unfashionable in Georgian London. New Orleans at this time was under Spanish rule, a period lasting from 1763 to 1801, and little was done to further the development of the city. France regained possession for a brief period, and then, with the Louisiana Purchase in 1803, American control began. It is from this time that the city began its steady expansion beyond the original boundaries, expansion that in its initial years at least was orderly and controlled.

Figure 50 shows the enlarged city in 1817. As in many European walled cities, when the old fortifications of New Orleans were pulled down broad boulevards replaced them: the Canal Street, North Rampart Street, and Esplanade Avenue of the present day. This ring established a pattern followed in other sections of the city. Above and below the old city new suburbs or "faubourgs" were laid out. The curving river bank suggested a new orientation for the grid plan of these city extensions, a change in street directions that could have been disastrous except for the skill with which these were connected to the streets of the old city. This was done with particular effectiveness downriver, where the Faubourg Marigny was joined to the city with great care so that only three streets rather than four come together at the angled intersections.

Good planning and the influence of topography combined in another way to fashion a street pattern of beauty and interest as well as one that functions well even with modern traffic loads. As the long, narrow plantations adjoining the expanding community were

subdivided, each was laid out in a little gridiron strip. But, because the land back from the river was the least desirable owing to its location and its swampy character, the first subdivision of land occurred along the river. Each grid developed independently and rather slowly. Developers recognized the importance of short cross streets and arranged for connections across property lines.

New Orleans adopted one feature of its original plan, which was repeated at intervals as its boundaries expanded. This was the open square, often combined as a space opening off or terminating one of the numerous boulevards. Many of these, with their variety of forms, are shown in Figure 51, a view of the city in 1883 which shows the pattern of growth along the Mississippi and to the northwest in the direction of Lake Pontchartrain. In this respect, although the city was under American rule, it remained European in its use of the urban square as a major element of planning and growth.

Timothy Flint, whose eye for the details of townscape makes him a valuable source of information about early cities along the Mississippi, was charmed by New Orleans. Here is how he found the city in 1823:

"The ancient part of the city, as you pass down Levee street towards the Cathedral, has in one of the clear, bright January mornings . . . an imposing and brilliant appearance, I am told, far more resembling European cities, than any other in the United States. The houses are stuccoed externally, and this stucco is white or yellow, and strikes the eye more pleasantly than the dull and sombre red of brick. . . . There are in the limits of the city three malls, or parade grounds, of no great extent, and not yet sufficiently shaded, though young trees are growing in them. They serve as parade grounds, and in the winter have a beautiful carpet of clover, of a most brilliant green."[23]

In New Orleans, as in Quebec and Montreal, the French colonial plan survives, a precious remnant that should be guarded and preserved. Fortunately, relics of the past are not without value as tourist attractions, aside from their historic worth. The modern city has

[22] Francis Baily, *Journal of a Tour in Unsettled Parts of North America in 1796 and 1797*, London, 1856, pp. 300-302.

[23] Timothy Flint, *Recollections of the Last Ten Years*, Boston, 1826, pp. 302-303.

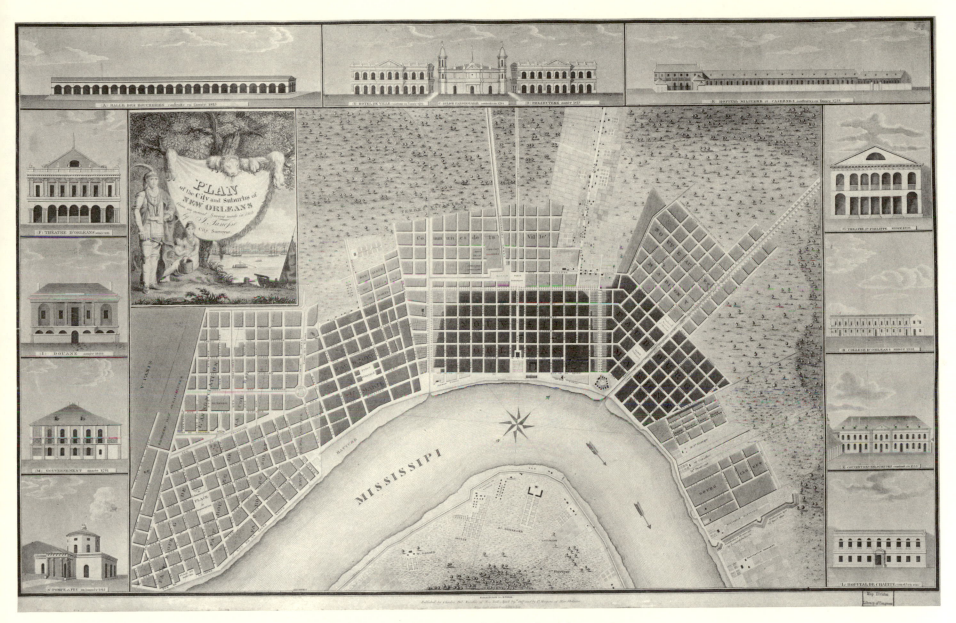

Figure 50. Plan of New Orleans, Louisiana: 1815

Published by GUSTAVE KOECKERT. 1 ANNUNCIATION SQUARE. 5 MARGARETS PLACE. 7. SHOT TOWER.   9. COURT BUILDING. 11. CITY HALL.   13 CANAL ST FERRY.   15. U. S. CUSTOM HOUSE   16 LA. SUGAR REFINERY. 17 SUGAR EX.   BIRDS EYE VIEW OF THE   21. CHRIST CHURCH.   22. 2ND DISTRICT FERRY.   23 JACKSON SQUARE   25 CONGO SQUARE   27 ESPLANADE FERRY.   29. U S MINT   31 LAKE PONTCHARTRAIN.   Copyright. GRAUWEDELS Thos PUBLISHING Co.

1. JACKSON ST FERRY.   2 EXPOSITION PARK.   4 COLISEUM SQUARE.   6 LEE CIRCLE.   8. ST PATRICK'S CHURCH.   10 LAFAYETTE SQUARE 12 PRODUCE EX. 14. CUSTOM EX.   24 ST LOUIS CATHEDRAL.   26 FRENCH MARKET.   28 LOWER CITY PARK.   30 WEST END.

18 PICKWICK CLUB.   19 CLAY STATUE.   20 SUGAR SHEDS.   AND SUBURBS.

CITY OF NEW ORLEANS.

Figure 51. View of New Orleans, Louisiana: 1883

already taken some steps to preserve the unique flavor of the *vieux carré* by regulations governing architectural changes and through the encouragement of restoration projects. Much has already been lost through neglect and barbaric commercialization of some of the finest parts of old New Orleans. Today's visitor must restrict his vision to escape the visual intrusions of neon signs, the ubiquitous automobile, and the dominating billboard. Yet, in the little oasis of Jackson Square and in some of the surrounding streets, one may recapture the atmosphere of French New Orleans and imagine himself in Bienville's little capital of the great province of Louisiana.

What were the lasting contributions of French colonial town planning? One is forced to conclude that few elements of French planning were retained when France ceased to be a colonizing power in the New World. Except in the Province of Quebec and in small, isolated, and unimportant pockets elsewhere, French culture has ceased to exist in America. Those aspects of town planning we think of as distinctly French—the grand plan with diagonal boulevards, *rond points*, and strong axial treatment of principal buildings —came to us indirectly from other sources. Within the limits of the United States the French were always too few, too lacking in resources, and too often forgotten by a mother country busy with what appeared to be more pressing affairs in Europe to make a significant lasting impact in the face of the advancing English. What remains in Quebec, Mobile, New Orleans, Montreal, and a few other spots thus deserves all the more our most sensitive treatment and careful efforts at preservation lest these precious remnants of a vanished past disappear forever.

CHAPTER 4

Town Planning in the Tidewater Colonies

NOT until the sixteenth century was drawing to a close did English interest in North America extend beyond occasional voyages of exploration, periodic raids on Spanish ports, and the use of the fishing banks off the mouth of the St. Lawrence. The first organized attempt at permanent settlement took place in 1585. It was then that Sir Walter Raleigh dispatched seven ships carrying 108 persons in the ill-fated effort to establish a colony on Roanoke Island off the Carolina coast. Raleigh's step-brother, Sir Humphrey Gilbert, had previously received a patent from Elizabeth in 1578 to explore and settle "remote heathen and barbarous lands," but he had died in an unsuccessful voyage to Newfoundland. Raleigh succeeded Gilbert, by charter from the Queen, and financed an expedition to the coast of Carolina in 1584. It was the favorable report on Roanoke brought back by this expedition that led to the establishment of the first, short-lived English colony in the New World.

This first settlement was laid out by Ralph Lane, the governor appointed by Raleigh. It consisted of a small fort and an unknown number of small houses nearby. No contemporary drawings survive, but recent archaeological work indicates the fort was square, with pointed bastions along its sides and an octagonal tower at one corner.

Temporarily abandoned within a year, Roanoke was reoccupied in July 1587 by a new colonizing group sent over by Raleigh, including a number of women. The fort had been largely destroyed, but some of the houses remained and others were soon built. Governor John White returned to England in August for additional provisions, and the enterprise seemed well established.

Here, however, the story ends. The open conflict between Spain and England prevented relief voyages to Roanoke, and not until the summer of 1590 was White able to return. He found Roanoke abandoned. Inside the palisade the settlers had constructed, the dwellings had been destroyed and the place was overgrown with weeds. Only the word "CROATOAN" carved on one of the logs of the enclosure gave a clue to the fate of the inhabitants. This was a sign, as had previously been agreed on with White, that the settlers had moved to Croatoan Island, where lived a friendly tribe of Indians.

But unfavorable weather prevented White from reaching Croatoan, and Raleigh's interest had momentarily been directed to his estates in Ireland. Although in 1602 Raleigh did send another expedition to try to determine the fate of his lost colony, the matter remains an unsolved mystery. The first English colonial effort in the New World ended in total failure.[1]

Jamestown, St. Mary's and the First Tidewater Towns

Some twenty years after Raleigh's first attempt at colonization, the settlement that was to open a new era in North America was finally established. At Jamestown the English succeeded in gaining a toehold on the new continent and thus began one hundred and seventy years of colonization and town building.

The Virginia Colony came into being through the formation of a joint-stock enterprise with a royal charter. The two divisions of the company—almost separate enterprises—were granted settlement rights along the American coastline. Curiously enough, the designated jurisdictions overlapped, although the charter specified that neither group should establish a settlement within one hundred miles of one already made by the other. The Plymouth Company, whose activities will be examined in the next chapter, could colonize between the 38th and 45th parallels of north latitude. The London Company received settlement rights between the 34th and 41st parallels.

[1] Contemporary accounts by Lane, White, and Sir Richard Grenville are given in full in Stefan Lorant, ed., *The New World*, New York, 1946, pp. 135-79.

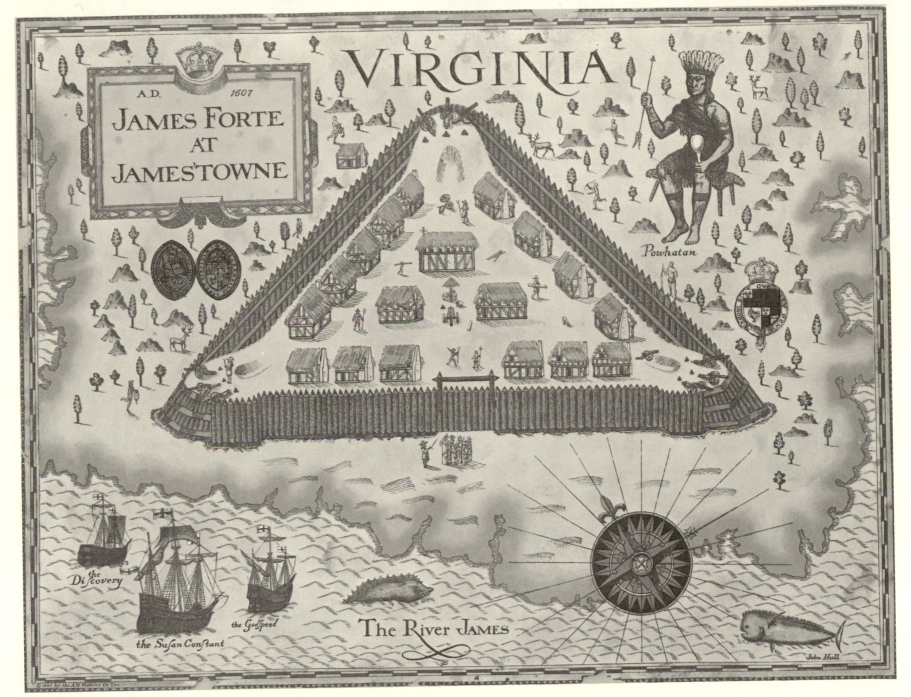

Figure 52. *View of Jamestown, Virginia: 1607*

In December 1606, the London Company dispatched three ships carrying some one hundred settlers on the long voyage to Virginia. The expedition arrived off the Virginia coast late in April and made their first landing at Cape Henry, near present-day Norfolk. Then began a two-week search for a suitable site for the first town. A thorough exploration of the lower course of the James River was carried out. Finally, the site named Jamestown was selected some thirty miles from the coast where a narrow isthmus connected the mainland to a near-island in the James River.

The selection of this location followed closely the instructions given to the first group of colonists on their departure from England. This directive pointed out that a site well inland on a navigable river would be far easier to protect against attack. However, in one important respect the instructions were ignored. They warned against "a low or moist place because it will prove unhealthful," and unfortunately Jamestown, with its nearby swamps and brackish water, proved to be exactly this type of site.

The instructions also included these general directions on the order of construction of the buildings:

"It were necessary that all your carpenters and other such like workmen about building do first build your storehouse and those other rooms of publick and necessary use before any house be set up for any private persons, yet let them all work together first for the company and then for private men."[2]

As to the layout of the town itself, the instructions were brief but admirably clear:

"And seeing order is at the same price with confusion it shall be adviseably done to set your houses even and by a line, that your streets may have a good breadth, and be carried square about your market place, and every street's end opening into it, that from thence with a few field pieces you may command every street throughout, which market place you may also fortify if you think it need full."[3]

On May 14th work on the fort began. Within a month the little fortified settlement had begun to take shape. A palisade, triangular in plan extending 400 feet along the river and with the other two sides 300 feet long, enclosed the one-acre site. At the corners "bulwarkes," each shaped "like a halfe moone and foure or five pieces of artillerie mounted in them," were erected. Inside were the church, storehouses, and the first houses, probably in a double row flanking a single street.

No plan of this first settlement is known to exist, and the original location of the settlement disappeared long ago when the river bank gave way before flood waters of the James. From contemporary descriptions, however, modern scholars have constructed a full-size reproduction of James Fort not far from its actual site. The plan of this reconstruction, shown in Figure 52, is a modern map in ancient style and corresponds in all essentials with what we know of the community's pattern.[4]

Certainly little appears here reflecting the status of civic design in the Europe of that era. Not even the *bastide* towns of the late Middle Ages in France, Spain, and England were so modest in scale and primitive in character. The triangular form, of course, represents the least effort required to enclose a protected space; the limited resources and skills of the colonists, the threatening environment, and the urgency of time permitted little else. If the first settlers had ever believed that they could at once create an English country village in the New World, those misconceptions were quickly dispelled.

The history of Jamestown and the other early settlements in Virginia is one of famine, disease, misfortune, and disappointments. By fall, half of the original settlers were dead. Although reinforcements and new supplies reached the town the following January, that same month saw a fire destroy most of the buildings, many of the supplies, and even a portion of the palisades protecting the town from the increasingly hostile Indians. In October 1608, the first women arrived, along with a number of skilled artisans and

---

[2] "Instructions given by way of Advice by us whom it hath pleased the King's Majesty to appoint of the Counsel for the intended voyage to Virginia . . . ," September 10, 1606; quoted from the complete text in Alexander Brown, *The Genesis of the United States*, Boston, 1890, I, 84.

[3] *ibid.*, 84-85.

[4] For descriptions of early Jamestown and archaeological investigations of the site see the following: Samuel H. Yonge, *The Site of Old "James Towne" 1607-1698*, Richmond, 1926; Henry Chandlee Forman, *Jamestown and St. Mary's, Buried Cities of Romance*, Baltimore, 1938; and Charles E. Hatch, Jr., *Jamestown, Virginia, The Townsite and its Story*, National Park Service Historical Handbook Series No. 2, Washington, rev. ed., 1957.

the second shipment of supplies. During that winter and spring additional farming land was cleared, and new buildings were built under the direction of Captain John Smith, recently designated president of the colony. But in the winter of 1609-1610 the population that had increased to 500 dwindled to 60 as a result of disease, Indian attacks, and starvation.

When, in May 1610, Sir Thomas Gates arrived to assume the governorship he found the settlement more a ruin than a town. A month later Gates decided that conditions were hopeless and resolved to abandon the town and, indeed, the entire colony. Packing the surviving settlers aboard his ships he began the short passage down the James to the open sea. But while still making his way downstream he learned that Lord Delaware had just arrived at the coast with 150 new colonists and ample supplies. At the eleventh hour the colony had been saved by Delaware's timely arrival.

A new period began. The hardships were by no means past, but after the first three years the survival of Jamestown no longer seemed in doubt. But from this time also Jamestown ceased to be the only town of the colony. While only small military outposts had previously existed, now new settlements began to appear. Hampton was established in 1610, and the following year Thomas Dale, deputy governor under the ailing Delaware, set out to settle a new site farther up the James River. Captain John Smith has left an account of this venture and the following description of the new settlement:

"In the beginning of September, 1611 he [Dale] set saile, and arrived where he intended to build his new town: within ten or twelve daies he had environed it with a pale, and in honor of our noble Prince Henry, called it Henrico. The next worke he did, was building at each corner of the Towne a high commanding Watch-house, a Church, and Storehouses: which finished, he began to thinke upon convenient houses for himselfe and men, which with all possible speed he could, he effected, to the great content of his companie, and all the Colonie.

"This towne is situated upon a necke of a plaine rising land, three parts invironed with the maine River, the necke of land well impaled, makes it like an Ile; it hath three streets of well framed houses, a handsome Church, and the foundation of a better laid (to bee built of Bricke), besides Storehouses, Watch-houses, and such like. Upon the verge of the River there are five houses, wherein live the honester sort of people, as Farmers in England."[5]

Captain John Smith was not above exaggeration, and his description of Henrico may not be accurate. What is apparently the only graphic record of Henrico, shown in Figure 53, is of little help in reconstructing the original plan. In its general representation of the coast and the James River, this map is highly inaccurate. Henrico (here called Henryville) appears as a small, regularly concentric town similar to the symmetrically planned fortified towns of the late Renaissance in Europe. Probably Henrico bore little resemblance to the town plan shown on the map, and it is doubtful that the cartographer ever set eyes on the place. The map is also of interest, although for our purposes no more helpful, in that it shows Jamestown, indicated by the name "Jacqueville."

Bermuda City, fourteen miles above Henrico, was also laid out about this time, and there were other settlements. In all of these towns, continued difficulties were encountered in preventing the buildings and fortifications from falling into ruins. The early records of the colony contain repeated accounts of new governors arriving to find Jamestown in a state of decay and their efforts to promote rebuilding. Henrico itself was abandoned within a few years, and constant attention had to be given to the buildings in the other towns to prevent their complete disintegration. Flimsy construction with unseasoned timber, excessive moisture in the low-lying townsites, inattention to regular maintenance, and destruction by frequent fires contributed to the difficulties of sustaining the physical basis for town life.

[5] Captain John Smith, *Generall Historie of Virginia, New England and the Summer Isles* (London, 1624), in Lyon Gardiner Tyler, ed., *Narratives of Early Virginia, 1606-1625,* New York, 1907, pp. 304-05. An almost identical description appears in Ralph Hamor, *A True Discourse of the Present Estate of Virginia . . . ,* London, 1615, pp. 31-32. Hamor's account of Jamestown in 1614 is of interest: "The Towne . . . is reduced into a handsome forme, and hath in it two fair rowes of howses, all of framed Timber, two stories, and an upper Garret, or Corne loft high, besides three large, and substantiall Storehowses joyned togeather in length some hundred and twenty foot, and in breadth forty, and this town hath been lately newly, and strongly impaled, and a faire platforme for Ornance in the west Bulworke raised . . . ," p. 33.

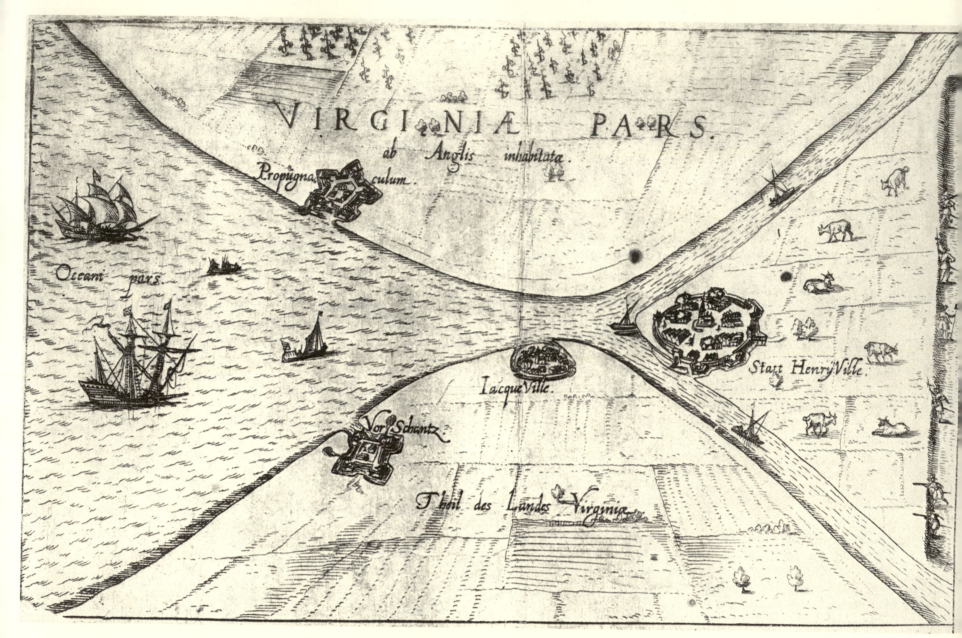

VIRGINIÆ PARS.

ab Anglis inhabitata.

Propugnaculum.

Oceani pars.

Iacque Ville.

Vor Schantz.

Statt Henry Ville.

Theil des Landes Virginia.

Figure 53. Map of the Coast of Virginia and the James River: 1611

The problem of establishing towns as focal points in the new colony was aggravated by two related factors. One was topography. The Virginia coast was penetrated at frequent intervals by wide, slow-flowing, deep rivers that were navigable for many miles inland by the largest ships then used in commerce. With so many excellent and protected anchorages, no single site had any particular advantage over the others.

The second factor causing a dispersed pattern of settlement which made town development difficult was the early adoption of tobacco as the dominant product of the colony. With the growing demand for tobacco in England, the crop itself began to serve as a medium of currency. The most economical and efficient method of tobacco production lay in large plantations. As plantations developed and cheap labor was introduced with the beginning of slavery, individual plantations became small communities with warehouses, shops, slave quarters, and the plantation residence. And because of the proximity to tidewater channels, docks and other port facilities were soon built on each of the great tobacco plantations. While this pattern developed most noticeably in Virginia, the same forces operated in neighboring Maryland, and the same difficulties in town development were encountered in that colony.

While such a pattern of plantation communities might have been satisfactory to the great landowners, it had its drawbacks when viewed by the government in Westminster. Under the mercantile theory that prevailed, the chief concerns there were the proper collection of customs duties and the control of trade. There must have been some feeling, too, that the affairs of the colony would be furthered if one town in each district clearly became the center of trade, administration, and cultural activities. As early as 1623 rules were established requiring all cargoes to be shipped through Jamestown. These rules were naturally resisted by the planters, as were later directives authorizing the use of a limited number of other ports. The first century of the colony saw a continued struggle between the planters, who favored shipment directly to and from individual plantations, and the crown, which desired town and port development through which all commerce would be channeled.

By 1623 the original bounds of Jamestown became inadequate. West of the old town the surveyor general, William Claiborne, laid out "the New Towne," and several additional houses were erected. In 1636 an act of the General Assembly granted house lots at nominal rentals to anyone who would build in Jamestown, and this provision resulted in some further enlargement of the settlement. Five years later, with the arrival of Governor Berkeley, a new attempt was made to enlarge and improve the town. All persons to whom lots were granted were then required to build brick structures at least 16 by 24 feet with cellars. The royal instructions to the governor also authorized him to remove the capital to a new town if he found the site of Jamestown was unhealthful or the buildings too dilapidated. Berkeley chose not to exercise this authority, but it foretold the eventual abandonment of Jamestown as the center of the colony.

The most ambitious attempt to rehabilitate Jamestown came in 1662. Instructions from England directed the governor to build towns on each of the major rivers in Virginia and to begin these new efforts at Jamestown. It is a striking commentary on the conditions in that town that, after more than half a century, it should be necessary to establish it virtually from the beginning.

The "Act for building a towne" became the model for subsequent legislation, both in Virginia and Maryland. The law specified

"That the towne to be built shall consist of thirty two houses, each house to be built with brick, forty foot long, twenty foot wide, within the walls, to be eighteen foote high above the ground, the walls to be two brick thick to the water table, and a brick and a halfe thick above the water table to the roofe, the roofe to be fifteen foote pitch and to be covered with slate or tile.

"That the houses shall be all regularly placed one by another in a square or such other forme as the honorable Sir William Berkeley shall appoint most convenient."[6]

Each of the 17 counties was directed to build one house. A tax of 30 pounds of tobacco a head was levied, and from these proceeds 10,000 pounds of tobacco were to be granted each county or person erecting a dwelling of the prescribed size within two years. The act further required that all tobacco from the counties of James City, Charles City, and Surry should be stored in the town.

[6] William Hening, *The Statutes at Large . . . of Virginia*, New York, 1823, II, 172.

The tobacco tax would apply during the first year to stimulate the development of Jamestown and then in successive years to sites on the York, Rappahannock, and Potomac Rivers and in Accomac. In order that the necessary craftsmen could be obtained, counties were authorized to impress building workmen at wages established in the act.

This elaborate legislation failed to accomplish its goals. One account indicates that only four or five houses were completed. By 1675 the population probably did not exceed one hundred freemen, and, while buildings for the government remained, Jamestown was hardly more than a village. The final blow, from which the town never fully recovered, was the burning of Jamestown by discontented small farmers and traders during Bacon's Rebellion in 1676.

Meanwhile, across Chesapeake Bay in the Maryland colony, new attempts at town founding were being made. In many respects the development of towns in Virginia and Maryland followed parallel courses. In both colonies the first settlers brought with them instructions for choosing a site and laying out the first town. Legislation aimed at promoting town development followed within a few years after initial colonization. In both colonies topography, tobacco economy, and the resistance of planters largely nullified these urbanizing efforts. And in both colonies the original capitals were finally moved to new, planned towns of considerable interest and character.

The Jamestown of Maryland was St. Mary's, located near the point of land between the mouth of the Potomac and Chesapeake Bay. Cecilius Calvert, the second Lord Baltimore, had been granted a patent from Charles I for this colonizing venture on terms quite different from the London Company's grant in Virginia. Maryland, so named in honor of the Queen, was to be a kind of feudal domain where the lord proprietor would be not only the owner of land to be disposed of as he pleased but the ruler as well, subject only to general restrictions of English law.

Baltimore's father had made an unsuccessful attempt to plant a colony in Newfoundland in 1627. Now in a friendlier climate and in close proximity to the established colony in Virginia, the Calverts were finally to succeed. Landing in March 1633, the settlers established themselves in a town they called St. Mary's. The instructions from Baltimore to the leaders of the expedition

were detailed and explicit, and there can be little doubt that they were based on the previous experience in Newfoundland and in Virginia. The high bank overlooking the river which emptied into the bay a short distance away met the requirements of a healthful site; certainly in almost every respect it was a location superior to that of Jamestown. The instructions further directed

". . . all the Planters to build their houses in as decent and uniforme a manner as their abilities and the place will afford, and neere adjoyning one to an other, and for that purpose to cause streetes to be marked out where they intend to place the towne and to oblige every man to buyld one by an other according to that rule and that they cause divisions of Land to be made adjoyning on the back sides of their houses and to be assigned unto them for gardens and such uses. . . ."[7]

The instructions also specified that a plat of the town should be sent to Baltimore at the earliest opportunity. Unfortunately this has apparently not survived, and the exact layout of St. Mary's remains unknown. Although St. Mary's never encountered the difficulties that Jamestown endured, neither did it become a community of great importance. Charles Calvert, in 1678, described the town in a letter to the Lords of the Committee for Trade and Plantations in these words:

". . . the principal place or town is called St. Mary's where the General Assembly and provincial court are kept, and whither all ships trading there do in the first place resort; but it can hardly be called a town, it being in length by the water about five miles, and in breadth upwards towards the land not above one mile,—in all which space, excepting only my own house and buildings wherein the said courts and offices are kept, there are not above thirty houses, and those at considerable distance from each other, and the buildings (as in all other parts of the Province), very mean and little, and generally after the manner of the meanest farm-houses in England."[8]

[7] "Instructions . . . directed by the Right Honorable Cecilius Lord Baltimore and Lord of the Provinces of Mary Land and Avalon . . ." (November 13, 1633), in Clayton Colman Hall, *Narratives of Early Maryland, 1633-1684*, New York, 1910, pp. 20-22.
[8] As quoted by Justin Winsor, *Narrative and Critical History of America*, Boston, 1884, III, 558.

In the same document Calvert refers to the absence of towns and the preference of the planters "to have their houses near the water for convenience of trade, and their lands on each side of and behind their houses. . . ." In this, as in other characteristics, Maryland was one with Virginia.

The New Town Acts of Virginia and Maryland

The Virginia Act of 1662 for the rebuilding of Jamestown also specified four other sites where towns were to be built in subsequent years. Through its tobacco tax provisions it further provided a means of financing town building and established a procedure for town development. The act became the precedent for a whole series of legislative enactments in Virginia and Maryland. Passed at the request of the crown, these laws designated sites for towns, established the method of land acquisition and land valuation, provided for their layout, and made provision for disposition of town lots. The motives for these legislative programs stemmed from the desire to promote town life generally as the best means of stimulating the development in the two colonies and the wish to control trade and customs collections for the benefit of the mother country.[9]

A feature of the laws was the requirement that all or specified types of imports and exports were to pass through these towns and that agricultural products were to be warehoused there pending the departure of merchant ships bound for England. Although some of the acts established maximum charges for these mandatory warehouse services and for transporting products from plantations to ports, these laws were unpopular with the planters and with the English merchants who bought their products. In Virginia the three main acts and in Maryland the governor's proclamation and the subsequent two acts were each in turn repealed by the legislatures or voided by the crown under pressure exerted by the planters and traders. Despite this erratic record of legislative vacillation, many towns were laid out. Although most of the

[9] A discussion of these town acts can be found in Edward M. Riley, "The Town Acts of Colonial Virginia," *The Journal of Southern History,* xvi, August 1950, pp. 306-323, and Philip Alexander Bruce, *Economic History of Virginia in the Seventeenth Century,* New York, 1896, ii, Chapter 20.

original plats are no longer extant, the few that have survived provide interesting evidence of the state of colonial town planning.

The first effort appears in Maryland when, in 1668, the governor, by proclamation, designated thirteen locations for port towns. Apparently this failed to produce the desired results; the proclamation was repeated in 1669 and again in 1671. Doubtless these later attempts met with the same fate. In Virginia the history of the new town legislation begins in 1679. In that year the Virginia governor received instructions from the crown directing him to

". . . endeavor all you can to dispose the planters to build towns upon every river, and especially one at least on every great river. . . . And in order thereunto, you are to take care that after sufficient notice to provide warehouses and conveniences, no ships whatsoever be permitted to load or unload but at the said places where the towns are settled."[10]

In the meeting of the General Assembly of that same year an act was passed granting land to Captain William Bird and to a Major Smith for two settlements on the Rappahannock and the James Rivers. The law concluded with a general enabling clause extending the same privileges to any proprietor who would similarly settle 250 persons on the initiative of private individuals.[11]

In the following year, however, direct public action for town development was provided. In an Act for Cohabitation and Encouragement of Trade and Manufacture, the General Assembly directed each county to acquire 50 acres of land for a town on 20 sites specified in the act. A flat sum of 10,000 pounds of tobacco was established as the acquisition price for each site. Each person agreeing to build a house and warehouse in the new town could acquire a half-acre plot on payment of 100 pounds of tobacco.[12]

While this enactment was nullified by the king in December 1681, evidence exists indicating that about half of the 20 town

[10] Royal Instructions to the Governor of Virginia, 1679, Leonard W. Labaree, ed., *Royal Instructions to British Colonial Governors 1670-1776,* New York, 1935, ii, 545.
[11] Act xi of the laws enacted at a General Assembly in James City, April 25, 1679. Hening, *Statutes,* ii, 448-454. The William Bird referred to was probably William Byrd (1652-1704), the first of an illustrious Virginia family.
[12] Act v of the laws enacted at a General Assembly in James City, June 8, 1680, Hening, *Statutes,* ii, 471-75.

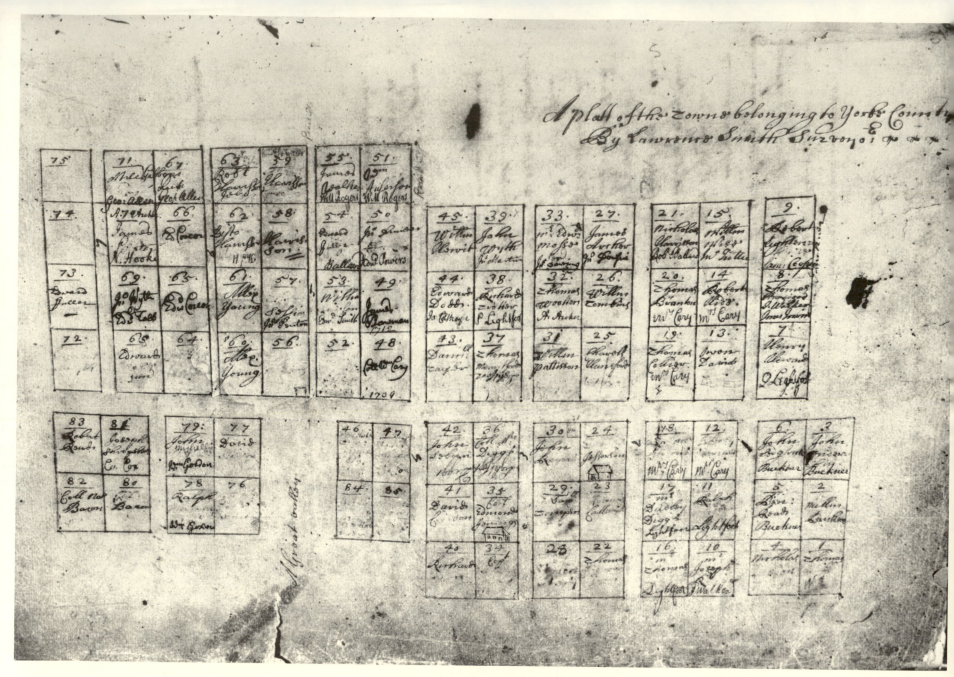

Figure 54. Plan of Yorktown, Virginia: 1691

sites had been acquired, surveyed into streets and lots, and plots conveyed for buildings. A few of these town plats still exist, although since the towns designated in 1680 were renamed in the two subsequent acts of 1691 and 1706, their plans as shown here may be of slightly later date.

A simple grid system was evidently regarded as the logical plan for these new towns. Figure 54 shows the layout adopted for Yorktown, where a main street runs parallel to the shore of the York River and is crossed by eight shorter streets leading back from the river. Tappahannock, which became the county seat of Rappahannock County and later of Essex County, had a more regular plan, reproduced in Figure 55. One entire block of four lots was set aside for public use. Three different street widths were used, with the widest streets, which flanked the public square and divided the town in half, being 82½ feet wide. Three other streets were 66 feet wide, with the two narrower "lanes" being 49½ feet in width. All lots were platted with the same dimensions, 165 by 132 feet, to equal exactly half an acre as prescribed by the statute.

Marlborough on the Potomac in Stafford County no longer exists, although it once enjoyed a brief period of prosperity. Its plan, shown in Figure 56, is curious. Perhaps the surveyor could not decide which shore line to follow as the main axis for the town. Evidently he decided to use both, with the result that the blocks and lots are parallelograms without a right angle to be seen.

Ten years after the Act of 1680 had been suspended, the General Assembly passed a new and somewhat revised law. The Act for Ports differed from its predecessor chiefly in its provisions for land acquisition. Instead of establishing a fixed price for all town sites, the law authorized the justices of each county to purchase the required land at a reasonable price. If the owner was unwilling to sell, the justices could then empanel twelve freeholders to fix a fair price for the land. Half-acre lots could then be granted outright to persons agreeing to build a house 20 feet square within four months.[13]

Further building was carried out under this second new town law, but again the act was repealed—this time by the Assembly

itself on the grounds that the crown had not specifically signified its approval of the measure. Subsequently, in 1699 the Assembly approved an enactment confirming land titles in these towns, indicating that construction had taken place on the sites despite the action to rescind the original legislation.[14]

Finally, and again following royal instructions to the new governor, a third general town act was passed by the Assembly in 1706. Like the previous legislation, this law specified a number of sites, in this case 15. It also contained detailed and liberal provisions for town government, including freedom from certain taxes for the residents.[15] This law met a fate similar to the earlier ones and was suspended by the crown in 1709. This marked an end to the general town acts of Virginia; from that time individual towns were created by special acts as the need arose with the westward progression of settlement.

Fredericksburg, Virginia, the plan of which is reproduced in Figure 57, is one example of a town created by a specific act, dating from 1727. With its simple grid plan and sites for church and market place, Fredericksburg is typical of many such towns laid out in the eighteenth century. Alexandria, whose plan appears in Figure 58, is another, and similar, example. This plan was prepared after the General Assembly, in 1748, authorized a town for the new county of Fairfax. The following year the county surveyor, John West, Jr., and his assistant, a young man named George Washington, laid out the usual grid system of streets and 84 half-acre lots. Both Fredericksburg and Alexandria indicate that the rather elementary but serviceable plan forms first used to carry out the provisions of the town acts of the seventeenth century persisted for many years after those general acts were repealed.

A more interesting plan was that proposed by William Byrd

[13] Act VIII of the laws enacted at a General Assembly in James City, April 1691, Hening, *Statutes*, III, 56-60.

[14] A modern plan reconstructed from old records and surveys of Delaware Town, one of the port towns designated in the legislation of 1691, appears in Malcolm H. Harris, " 'Delaware Town' and 'West Point' in King William County, Va.," *William and Mary College Quarterly*, 2nd Ser., XIV, No. 4 (October 1934), 342-351. This town had two parallel streets 660 feet apart leading to the water. Between the streets were the house lots. A third street crossed at right angles and terminated at the public wharf located at a bend in the river.

[15] An Act for Establishing Ports and Towns, Chapter XLII of the laws enacted at a General Assembly in Williamsburg, October-June, 1705-1706, Hening, *Statutes*, III, 404-419.

Figure 55. Plan of Tappahannock, Virginia: 1706

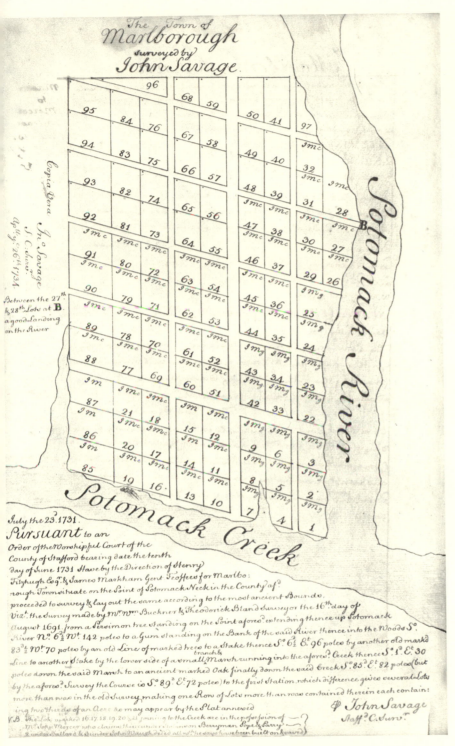

Figure 56. Plan of Marlborough, Virginia: 1691

in the 1730's for a group of Swiss settlers. The layout of his model community appears in the upper left-hand corner of the drawing reproduced in Figure 59. With its nine squares, the central one being left open as a green, the plan of the Eden settlements closely resembles that of New Haven of a century earlier. Byrd planned a series of these settlements to be developed along the Roanoke River, as can be seen in the drawing. However, despite the publication of the proposal in Switzerland the colony apparently never developed.

Also dating from the early years of the eighteenth century are the remarkable, isolated court house square compounds of Virginia. These may be regarded as an expression of and a concession to the essentially rural character of the early commonwealth. Seats of local government, the basic unit of which was the county, were clearly needed. If towns stubbornly refused to spring up as county seats, then the only solution was to provide county buildings in a rural setting as centrally located within the county as possible. Some of these eventually became the centers of towns, as in the case of Gloucester. Others, such as King William Court House, stand as solitary symbols of government.

Typically the compounds are surrounded by a brick wall. Inside can be found the courthouse, a jail, a caretaker's residence, and a row of lawyers' offices. Nearby usually stood a tavern and inn. These little administrative and legal communities came to life only when the court was in session or other sporadic governmental activities occurred. Architecturally they are like fine gems with no elaborate setting to distract from their beauty. A carefully prepared documentary history of these unusual settlements remains to be written.[16]

The new town legislative record in Maryland was almost identical to that of Virginia, and the results were similar. Following the governor's ineffective proclamations, a town development law was passed in 1683, supplemented by acts in 1684 and 1686. More ambitious than the Virginia legislature, the Maryland Assembly designated no less than 57 sites for new communities. Maryland was also more generous in the amount of land to be set aside for these towns, specifying 100 acres, or twice that of the Virginia towns.

[16] A useful beginning is Gerda Mayer-Rotermund, *Alte Gerichtsbegäude in Virginia*, Dr.-Ing. dissertation, Technischen Hochschule Braunschweig, 1958.

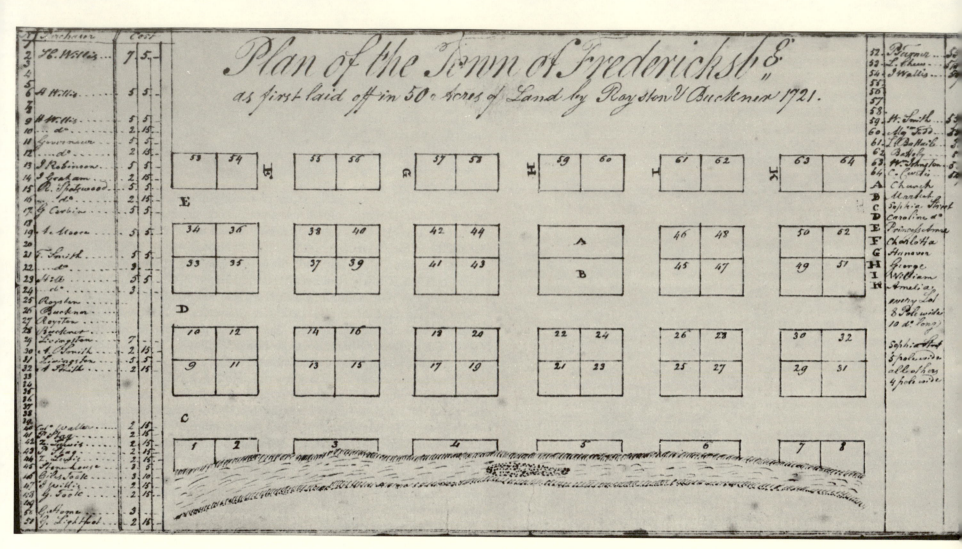

Figure 57. Plan of Fredericksburg, Virginia: 1721

Figure 58. George Washington's Plan of Alexandria, Virginia: ca. 1749

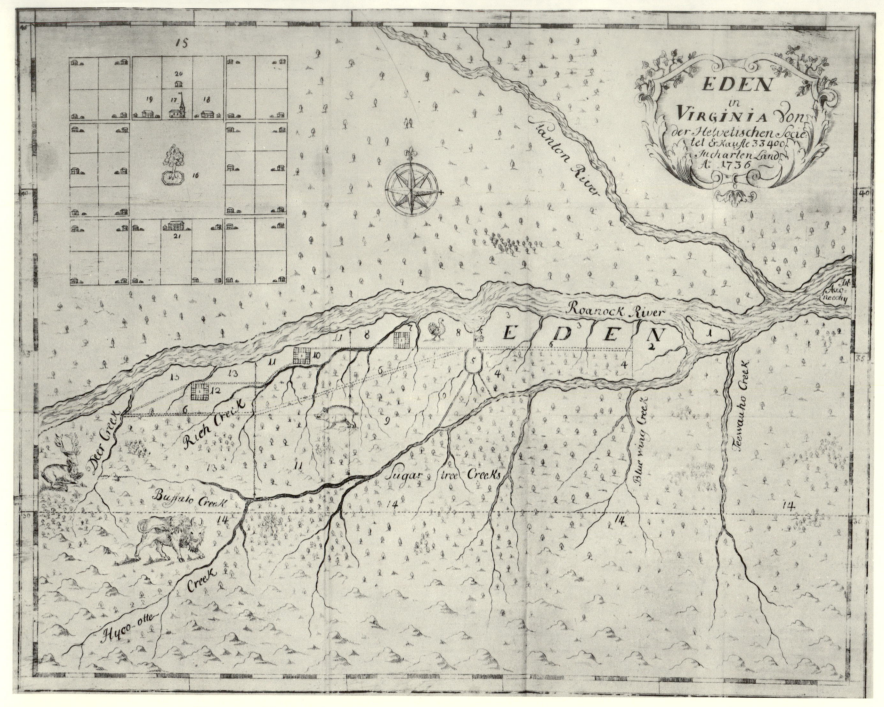

Figure 59. Map of Eden in Virginia with a Plan of one of the Proposed Towns: 1736

Maryland legislation was more specific in describing the land to be set aside for public use. The commissioners appointed to oversee the establishment of the towns in each county were directed to have the site

". . . marcked staked out and devided into Convenient streets, Laines & allies, with Open Space places to be left on which may be Erected Church or Chappell, & Marckett house, or other publick buildings, & the remaining part of the said One hundred acres of Land as neare as may be into One hundred equall Lotts. . . ."[17]

The same pressures exerted in Virginia were directed against the Maryland town development program, and in 1692 the acts were repealed. In 1706 the last general town act became law, but it too disappeared from the statute books when the crown failed to approve it because of its ambiguity with respect to the ports through which trade was directed.

The cartographic record of the Maryland experiment with wholesale town building is apparently as fragmentary as Virginia's. At least one legible contemporary plat survives, that of Vienna Town, illustrated in Figure 60. Three streets run parallel to the Nanticoke River, providing access to the long, narrow lots, two tiers of which have double frontage. At right angles to these are three narrower streets leading to the river. In one corner, occupying one large block and another smaller one, appears the legend, "Publick Lands of Vienna Towne." Evidently the surveyor took the easiest course in deciding on the location of the various public sites specified in the law and simply left a large, unplatted section for this purpose. The only other interesting feature of the plan is that "The Strand called Thames-Street" along the river insured that the waterfront would not be obstructed by private buildings.[18]

[17] An Act for Advancement of Trade 1683, William H. Browne, ed., *Archives of Maryland*, Proceedings and Acts of the General Assembly of Maryland (October, 1678-November, 1683), Baltimore, 1889, p. 612.

[18] A reproduction of the 1707 plan of Oxford, Maryland, referred to as Williamstadt in the Act of 1694 can be found in M. V. Brewington, *Chesapeake Bay: A Pictorial Maritime History*, Cambridge, Md., 1953. A redrawing of one of the towns established under the legislation of 1683, Wye in Talbot County, appears in Henry Chandlee Forman, *Tidewater Maryland Architecture and Gardens*, New York, 1956.

In Maryland, as in Virginia, towns of the eighteenth century came into being through special, rather than general, legislation. Beginning in 1728 a series of acts provided for the creation of single towns using much the same procedure as in the earlier laws. At least 23 such laws were passed between 1728 and 1751. Figure 61 is the plan of one of these later communities, Charlestown, in Cecil County at the head of Chesapeake Bay. The plan shows a common of 300 acres surrounding the town proper. In the center, marked "M," is the market place and the two lots for the lord proprietors, designated "A" and "B." The two other large squares were set aside for "meeting houses or other public occasions," while the site marked "L" was reserved for a courthouse or other public building.[19]

However interesting these ventures in town development might be, one can scarcely contend that the surviving plats indicate any great skill in or attention to the planning of towns. Furthermore, all evidence points to the conclusion that their planners scarcely considered the third dimension of architecture at the time of their layout. Certainly in this respect, whether due to conscious intent or simply the happy result of individual taste furthering the design of the whole, the New England communities of the same period emerge as clearly superior.

It is just this lack of noteworthy features in the early tidewater towns that makes so remarkable the achievements in planning the capital cities of the two colonies at the turn of the seventeenth century. It is to these related projects that we now turn.

The Annapolis of Francis Nicholson

Many of the cities important in the history of American planning have been the inspirations of single men who were, as often as not, administrators rather than technicians. The Philadelphia of William Penn, the Savannah of James Oglethorpe, the Detroit of Augustus Woodward are among the more famous. Less well known but equally important is the contribution to the tradition of American city planning by Francis Nicholson.

[19] The planning of three other towns in Cecil County, Ceciltown, Fredericktown, and Georgetown, is described in George Johnston, *History of Cecil County, Maryland*, Elkton, Md., 1881.

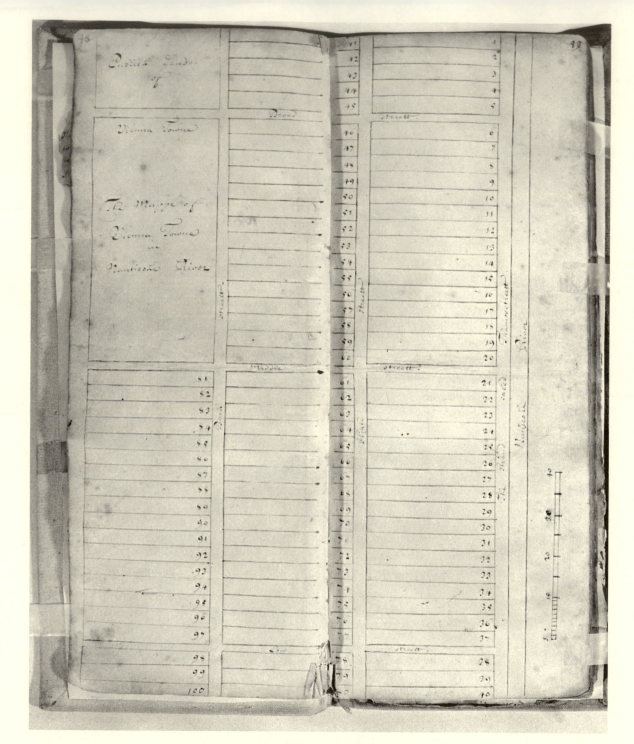

Figure 60. Plan of Vienna Town, Maryland: 1706

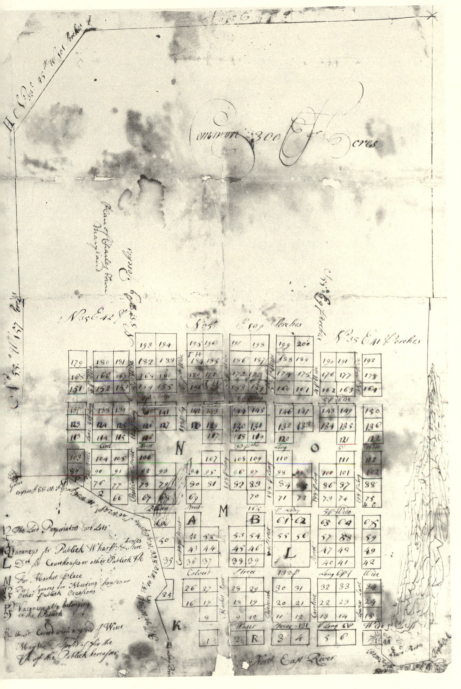

Figure 61. Plan of Charlestown, Maryland: 1742

Nicholson was a remarkable person. He might be regarded as one of the fathers of American public administration, since he served as lieutenant governor or governor of no less than six colonies. He helped to found America's second oldest institution of higher learning, and he was directly responsible for the establishment and design of two of the country's most interesting cities. He was also short of temper, often overbearing, and inclined to be self-righteous. That no even partially satisfactory study of Nicholson exists is surely an indictment of English and American biography.[20]

He was born in 1655, probably the natural son of Lord St. John, later the Duke of Bolton. A Francis Nicholson graduated from Magdalene College, Cambridge, in 1677, presumably the same Nicholson who received an Ensign's commission the following year. After military duty in Tangier, Nicholson served as a courier of important dispatches to the British ambassador in Paris in 1682 and 1683. Three years later he was appointed lieutenant governor of New York, returning to England in 1689 and taking up an appointment as lieutenant governor of Virginia in 1690. While in that post he helped to secure the passage of the town planning act of 1690 and also assisted Commissary James Blair to establish the College of William and Mary. For that project he made a personal contribution of £300 and was named by the charter to its first Board of Visitors.

In 1693 Nicholson was again in England. It is mere speculation but by no means inconceivable that on this visit he may have consulted with Christopher Wren about the design of the so-called "Wren" building at William and Mary. It is also possible that Nicholson might have discussed town planning theory and practice with the designer of the great baroque scheme for rebuilding London after the fire in 1666.

By the time that Nicholson was appointed governor of Maryland in 1694 he thus had already acquired some familiarity with the problems of town planning in a plantation economy. He had also seen something of urban life in Paris and doubtless other places on the continent, including Versailles; and, through his frequent visits to London, he would have witnessed the typical pat-

[20] Aside from the usual biographical dictionaries, the chief source of information about Nicholson comes from Charles Dalton, *George the First's Army 1714-1727*, London, 1912, II, 54-62.

tern of residential expansion as exemplified by such projects as Bloomsbury Square, Red Lion Square, and St. James's Square. Further, his education as an English gentleman and his position in the leisured class would have exposed him, if only superficially, to something of the history and accepted practices of architecture, garden and landscape design, and civic embellishment. From his military training he presumably would have learned the elements of fortification, garrison town layout, and castrametation. It is not unlikely that he encountered in his reading some of the Renaissance theorists of military and civil architecture and town design. Perhaps also when he assumed the Maryland governorship he had come to the conclusion that town development efforts were more likely to be successful if concentrated on one or two towns rather than on a great many.

Nicholson's impressive background was not to be wasted. In his first year in office he was instrumental in obtaining legislation to found two communities. One was Oxford, originally called Williamstadt. The other was named Anne Arundel, strategically located at the mouth of the Severn River on Chesapeake Bay and virtually in the center of the colony. From the early days of Maryland this site had been occupied by a settlement of sorts originally called Providence, later referred to as "The Town at Proctor's." In the supplemental town act of 1684 it was made a port of entry, one of the 57 towns named in the legislative program, but it is doubtful if its original condition was much affected.

When Nicholson took office he no doubt learned of the repeated attempts of the past half-century to move the capital from St. Mary's to some more central and convenient location. When the act was passed designating Oxford and Anne Arundel as towns, the town fathers of St. Mary's may have realized that a new effort of this sort loomed ahead. For the provisions of the law specifying how town lots were to be granted provided that

". . . his Excellency Francis Nicholson Esquire Governor of this Province . . . shall have the next Immediate Choice of one, two, or three Lotts in each or either of the said Towns if his Excellency so pleases. . . ."[21]

Their fears were soon realized, since a second act in the same session officially designated Anne Arundel town as the capital of the colony. In 1695 the name of the town was changed to Annapolis, honoring Princess Anne, soon to become Queen.

Direct evidence is lacking, but there is every reason to believe that Governor Nicholson himself assumed responsibility for the design of the town. We do know that Richard Beard acted as surveyor and that he carried out his duties under difficulties not usually encountered in city planning. When the officials called on Beard for his finished plat of the town, he reported ". . . that for want of some Large Paper to draw the same on, it is not yet done. . . ." It seems unlikely that Beard had the imagination to produce the plan which was finally adopted. Nicholson, in his first position as full colonial governor, with his European, New York, and Virginia background, and with apparent ambitions to make his mark in Maryland, doubtless furnished the inspiration.

The Annapolis plan, shown in Figure 62, was a novelty for North America. With its two great circles, the imposing "Bloomsbury Square," and the several radiating diagonal streets, the layout introduced a new concept of civic design to colonial America. All the original drawings perished in the statehouse fire of 1704, but the Stoddert plat of 1718 faithfully reproduces the first layout, adding only the 20 lettered lots to the east of the town, which were provided in 1718 as accommodations for tradesmen. This addition followed a law of 1695 which provided

". . . that when any baker, brewer, tailor, dyer, or any such tradesmen, that, by their practice of their trade, may any ways annoy, or disquiet the neighbors or inhabitants of the town, it shall and may be lawful for the commissioners and trustees . . . to allot and appoint such tradesmen such part or parcel of land, out of the present town pasture, as . . . shall seem meet and convenient for the exercise of such trade, a sufficient distance from the said town as may not be annoyance thereto. . . ."[22]

The immediate sources on which Nicholson drew are unknown. The general inspiration must have been the achievements of French baroque designers, first applied in garden layout, as at Versailles,

[21] Browne, *Archives*, Proceedings and Acts . . . September, 1693-June, 1697, p. 111.

[22] An Act for Keeping Good Rules and Orders in the Port of Annapolis, as quoted in Elihu S. Riley, *"The Ancient City: A History of Annapolis*, Annapolis, 1887, pp. 63-64.

Figure 62. Plan of Annapolis, Maryland: 1718

then to town extension and remodeling schemes on the continent, and later adapted by Christopher Wren and John Evelyn for the rebuilding of London after the great fire.

Following accepted planning practice of this style, Nicholson set aside the highest and most commanding sites for the statehouse and church. The "Public Circle" within which the statehouse now stands measured slightly over 500 feet in diameter, while the "Church Circle" was approximately 300 feet across. The other great open space, "Bloomsbury Square" is some 350 feet on each side. It may be sheer coincidence, but the proportions of these three open spaces are such that the square just fits neatly inside the larger circle, while the smaller circle can be contained in the square, although with some room to spare. The other open area shown is the market square, 100 feet on each side. There were other public reservations as well: a school site, public landings, and common lands beyond the town proper.

The derivation of Bloomsbury Square is suggested by its name; Nicholson would have known the elegant square of the same name in London, which gave its name to an entire district of that city. Unfortunately, this portion of the Annapolis plan was not developed, and the interesting combination of the English residential square and the French *rond-point* was never achieved.

One curious detail is in the diagonal streets. Those leading into the statehouse circle have a pinwheel alignment, with not one directly on axis with the center of the circle. It is hard to believe that this was anything but deliberate, if we except the possibility of a surveying error, but the motives are unclear. It may well have been that Nicholson did not fully comprehend one of the aims of baroque design—that is, to create as many terminal vistas as possible by ending diagonal streets at some great public building or monument and with the center line of the street precisely on axis with the center of the structure.

The many lots bisected by the diagonal streets and the resulting awkward shapes of building sites also testify to the planner's unfamiliarity with some of the problems inherent in this type of layout. Indeed, the plan of Annapolis is almost a caricature of baroque design.

Something of the character of Annapolis as it slowly developed during the century following its planning may still be captured by today's visitor, although modern development has relentlessly intruded. It is fortunate that the center of commerce did not develop in the political capital of Maryland, for many of the older buildings of Annapolis no doubt thus escaped the destruction that would have accompanied an era of mercantile expansion. The growth of nearby Baltimore as the commercial and industrial center for the state happily spared Annapolis. The view of the city in 1864, reproduced in Figure 63 reveals the pleasantly irregular character of the site and the charm of its architecture.

The Annapolis of this view, however, was not Nicholson's. His attempts to promote swift development of the town encountered difficulties, and even a dozen years after its planning it remained little more than a village. One contemporary account describes the governor's efforts and the condition of the community in 1708:

"Gov. *Nicholson* has done his Endeavor to make a town of that Place. There are about 40 Dwelling Houses in it, 7 or 8 of which can afford a good Lodging and Accommodations for Strangers. There are also a State-House, and a free School, built with Brick, which make a great Show among a Parcel of Wooden Houses; and the Foundation of a Church is laid, the only Brick Church in *Maryland*. They have two Market Days in a Week; and had Gov. *Nicholson* continu'd there a few years longer, he had brought it to Perfection."[23]

Williamsburg: Nicholson's Second Capital

Nicholson's plan for Annapolis was not completely successful, but he was soon to have a second opportunity to create a capital city. In 1698 he found himself again in Virginia, this time with the full authority of the governor's office. He cared for Jamestown as little as he had for St. Mary's, and the burning of the Virginia statehouse earlier in the year he took office furnished the excuse he needed to shift the capital site to a new location and away from the scene of so much discomfort and so many disasters.

Late in April of 1699 the General Assembly met at Middle Plantation to select a new capital site. At that time Middle Plantation, located on ground midway between the James and York Rivers, was second in population only to Jamestown. Certainly

[23] From an account sent to the Royal Society of London as quoted in John Oldmixon, *The British Empire in America*, London, 1708, i, 195.

Figure 63. View of Annapolis, Maryland: 1864

the location was more healthful than that of Jamestown—almost any site would have been. Here for a brief period following Bacon's Rebellion and his destruction of Jamestown the General Assembly had met some years before. Most persuasive, the infant College of William and Mary had been established here, the buildings of which might be used as temporary quarters for the legislature.

At the College May Day celebration attended by the governor, members of the General Assembly and the trustees, five student speakers skillfully pleaded the cause of Middle Plantation as the site for the capital. Nicholson exerted all his influence to bring about the move, and within the month the General Assembly agreed. On May 27, 1699, Theodoric Bland and Edwin Thatcher were appointed to survey the site for the new town. The protests of the people of Jamestown were to no more avail than had been those of St. Mary's in neighboring Maryland.[24]

Nicholson soon became deeply involved in the planning of the town, the name of which was changed from Middle Plantation to the more dignified Williamsburg. The legislation of 1699 which established the new town, and which doubtless Nicholson helped to draft, was beyond a doubt the most detailed piece of town planning law yet adopted in the English colonies. It specified the exact amount of land to be set aside for the town proper, the capitol building site, the public landing areas on the two rivers, and the roads leading from the town proper to these outlying river port areas. In great detail the law also defined the form and principal dimensions of the capitol building, including the pitch of the roof, the size of windows, and many elevational specifications.

The principal street, the Duke of Gloucester Street, was named in the act. All houses built on this street were to be set back six feet and to "front alike." For other streets the directors of the town, Nicholson among them, were authorized to adopt rules and orders governing dwelling size and setbacks. The town was to be divided into half-acre lots to be sold after public notice. Each purchaser was required to construct a dwelling within two years. Minimum house sizes were specified, with the larger houses required along the Duke of Gloucester Street. All lots on the main

street had to be enclosed with "a wall, pails, or post and rails" within six months after the dwelling was completed.

Indeed little was omitted from this unique statute that the General Assembly could provide to guarantee a capitol building and a town which would, in the words of the act, result in a

". . . convenient sitting . . . at a healthy, proper and commodious place, suitable for the reception of a considerable number and concourse of people, that of necessity must resort to the place where the general assemblies will be convened, and where the council and supreme court of justice for his majesty's colony and dominion will be held and kept."[25]

The evidence is fragmentary but strongly suggests that two plans for Williamsburg were prepared and that for reasons unknown the first was abandoned or rejected. Robert Beverly, a Jamestown landowner and foe of Nicholson, alluded to this first plan in his history of the colony written in 1707. Nicholson, he said,

". . . flatter'd himself with the fond Imagination, of being the Founder of a new City. He mark'd out the Streets in many Places, so as that they might represent the Figure of a W, in Memory of his late Majesty King William. . . ."[26]

Hugh Jones, writing a few years later, mentions that Nicholson planned the city "in the Form of a Cypher, made of W. and M." for William and Mary. Then, in his description of Williamsburg as actually built, Jones refers to the Duke of Gloucester Street as "a noble Street mathematically straight (for the first Design of the Town's Form is changed to a much better)."[27]

Do these suggest that Nicholson drew on his experience at Annapolis and first proposed a town plan incorporating a number of diagonal streets? No copies of this first plan are known to exist, and the exact manner in which Nicholson planned to incorporate

[24] Richard L. Morton describes the May Day events in his *Colonial Virginia*, Chapel Hill, 1960, I, 357-59. The texts of the student speeches are in the William and Mary College *Quarterly Historical Magazine*, 2nd Ser., X, 323-37.

[25] For the text of the law of 1705 which confirmed the act of 1699 see Hening, *Statutes*, III, 419-32, Chapter XLIII of the Laws of 1705, An Act Continuing the Act directing the building the Capitol and the City of Williamsburg.

[26] Robert Beverly, *The History and Present State of Virginia* (London, 1705), Louis B. Wright, ed., Chapel Hill, 1947, p. 105.

[27] Hugh Jones, *The Present State of Virginia*, London, 1724, reprinted for Joseph Sabin, New York, 1865, pp. 25, 28.

the initials of the sovereigns in his city can only be conjectured. One possibility is that the two diagonal streets diverging from the end of the Duke of Gloucester Street and bordering the college grounds are the remnants of one of the letters. It is just possible that Nicholson's original scheme for Williamsburg was quite different from its eventual plan and was based firmly on his recent town planning experience in Maryland. We do know that Nicholson retained a fondness for Annapolis, or at least the name. In 1710, when he led the force that captured the French stronghold of Port Royal, he renamed the town Annapolis.

Whatever may have been the merits of Nicholson's first plan, it is just as well that he abandoned it. The revised layout of Williamsburg was, along with the plan of Savannah and perhaps one or two others, the most successful essay in community planning of colonial America. Unfortunately, contemporary drawings no longer exist; the earliest is the so-called Frenchman's Map of 1782. This plan, reproduced in Figure 64, shows the main features of the town as conceived by Nicholson.

The principal axis of the composition is the Duke of Gloucester Street, 99 feet wide and three-quarters of a mile long, laid out to run along the divide between the two rivers. This followed generally the lane that once led from the college buildings past Bruton Parish Church and along the ridge. Several houses were moved to accommodate this broad, straight street.

The College of William and Mary stands at the western end of the street, where two roads diverge at equal angles. The Capitol terminates this axis at its other end, rising from the center of a square 475 feet on each side set aside by the legislature for this purpose. Midway along the Duke of Gloucester Street appears the Market Square, on or near which are sites for the court house, magazine, and the church.

Close to this point a secondary axis opens at right angles to the north. This is the palace green, somewhat over 200 feet wide and approximately 1,000 feet long. Furnishing the terminal vista for this tree-lined expanse, the governor's palace rises impressively. Beyond the palace, although concealed from the eyes of the ordinary viewer, the secondary axis continues for some distance as the formal gardens to the rear of the mansion.

The view to the south down the palace green is unchecked, since the site on the Duke of Gloucester Street facing the governor's palace remains open. Whether this feature was intentional or not is open to some doubt, since baroque planning principles usually dictated the closing of all internal town vistas and the stopping of axes by architectural devices.

Nicholson provided additional building sites of special prominence by changing the spacing of the streets paralleling the Duke of Gloucester Street east and west of palace green. Opposite the termination points of these streets houses were erected from which long views could be enjoyed and which in turn closed the views from the other ends of these minor axes.[28]

Many of these features show more clearly on the recently discovered nineteenth-century plan of Williamsburg reproduced in Figure 65. Although this plan is inaccurate in many details, notably the location of the governor's palace off the axis of the palace green, it contains some additional points of interest. One of these is the street leading at right angles from the Duke of Gloucester Street as a continuation of the axis of the palace green.

More intriguing is the pattern of streets near the Capitol. Two short diagonals diverge from the Duke of Gloucester Street near its end and connect with the parallel streets on each side. The ends of these diagonals bend sharply so that their outer intersections are at right angles. Here, perhaps, is the evidence that Nicholson did indeed succeed in incorporating the initials of England's rulers as part of the street pattern of his little city, for the peculiar arrangement of these streets plainly traces a "W" or an "M."

Both of these features may represent later additions made to the original plan; this would explain why they do not appear on the much earlier version shown in Figure 64. That map, however, was prepared during the Revolutionary War, probably by a French officer who was not entirely familiar with the city. Moreover, it is vague in some of its details, which may indicate that it shows only conditions as they then existed rather than street and property lines as they may have been laid out.

[28] A helpful analysis of the elements of the Williamsburg plan is Arthur A. Shurcliff, "The Ancient Plan of Williamsburg," *Landscape Architecture*, XXVIII, 1938, 87-101. Marcus Whiffen, *The Public Buildings of Williamsburg*, Williamsburg, 1958, should also be consulted. Whiffen reproduces a manuscript plan of Williamsburg and vicinity from the Rochambeau Collection in the Library of Congress that provides helpful topographic information about the site.

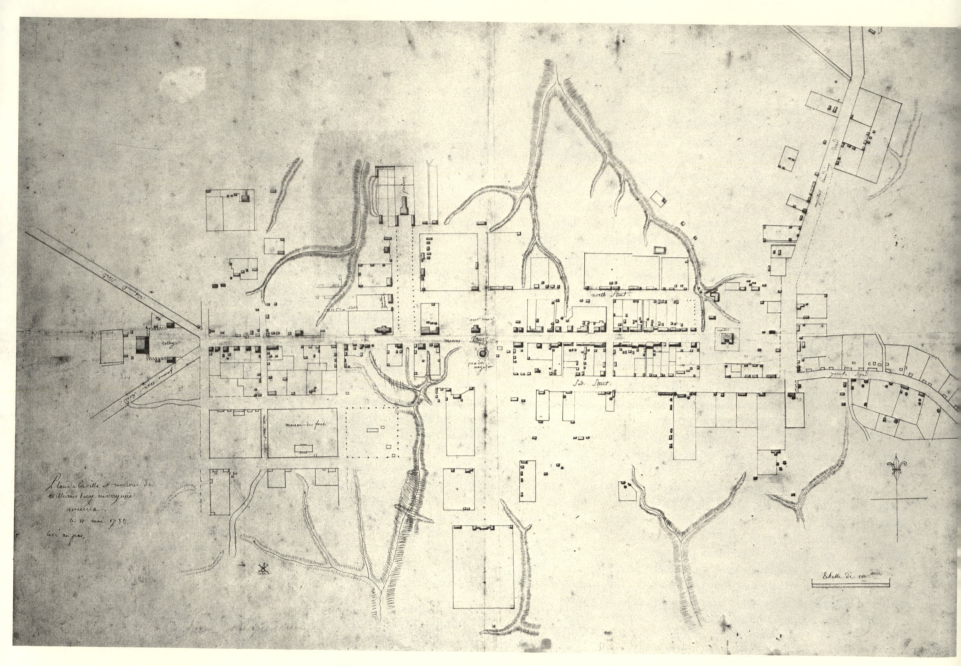

Figure 64. Plan of Williamsburg, Virginia: 1782

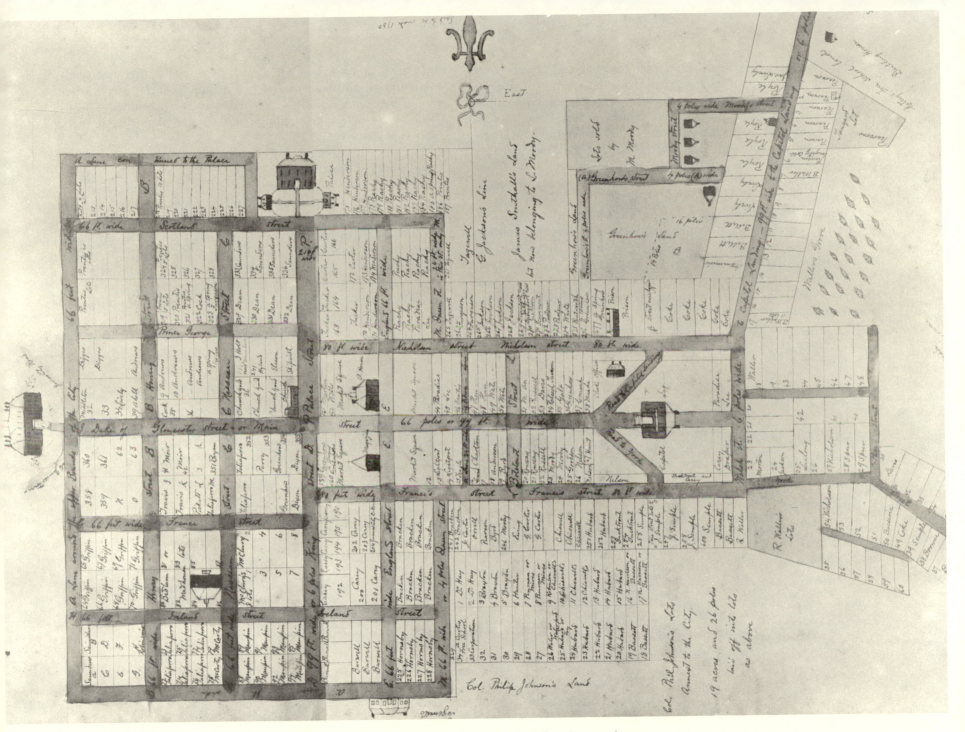

Figure 65. Plan of Williamsburg, Virginia: date unknown

The case for believing that at least the diagonal streets were part of Nicholson's plan is strengthened by their apparent uselessness as routes of transportation and their ineffectiveness as aesthetic devices. For the latter purpose one would expect them to lead inward toward the Capitol from the parallel streets and thus provide multiple vistas to and from that important building. Baroque planners employed this motif widely in Europe, and it was just such an effect that Nicholson himself had attempted at Annapolis.

Whether or not Nicholson was responsible for this feature of the Williamsburg plan may never be known. He did achieve in his neatly conceived plan an urban design of a very high order, a vast improvement over his earlier effort at Annapolis. At Williamsburg the mere eccentricities that mar the plan of Maryland's capital city disappear; nearly every feature is deftly placed. Here is a disciplined exercise in axial planning—formal, yet never pompous.

Part of the success of the Williamsburg plan is surely due to its scale. Designed for a population of about 2,000, the little city must always have had an air of domesticity that balanced its miniature grand plan. And part of its appeal surely stems from its three-dimensional quality—the architectural planning of at least some of the principal buildings at the same time that its ground plan was conceived.

For slightly more than three-quarters of a century Williamsburg served as the capital of Virginia. Then, in 1779, the recently constituted independent Commonwealth of Virginia resolved to move the seat of government to Richmond. From that time Williamsburg began to decline, its plan and buildings finally being rescued from further encroachments and destruction through the generosity of John D. Rockefeller, Jr., in 1927. The elaborate and painstaking restoration of the old colonial capital provides us today with an unusual opportunity to observe one of the noteworthy accomplishments of our town planning tradition. Even in an age where mechanization has taken command, the merit of this plan for a town in a simpler era can still be appreciated and is not without lessons for modern planners.

CHAPTER 5

New Towns in a New England

DURING the first two decades of the seventeenth century virtually all of the European powers that were to contend for supremacy in North America were active in colonization and the planning of towns. The French at Isle Sainte Croix, Port Royal, and Quebec began to stake out an empire that would ultimately include Canada and the Mississippi Valley. In the southwest the Spanish, thrusting northwards from secure bases in Mexico, established a new outpost at Santa Fé in 1609. Along the majestic Hudson the Dutch founded their short-lived colony with forts at Albany in 1614 and Kingston in 1615, preceding the settlement on Manhattan Island by ten years. The English finally gained a precarious grasp on the New World, after a number of failures, with the founding of Jamestown in 1607.

New England was not neglected. The Plymouth Company, the group of merchants granted settlement rights in northern "Virginia," was initially as active as the London Company, which settled at Jamestown. The leaders of this northern group, Sir John Popham and Sir Ferdinando Gorges, organized an expedition that set out from Plymouth in May 1607. Two months later the two ships carrying 100 would-be colonists arrived off the coast of Maine. At the mouth of the Kennebeck River, according to a contemporary account,

"They all went ashore, and there made choise of a place for their plantation, at the mouth or entry of the river on the west side (For the river bendeth itself towards the nor-east, and by east), being almost an island, of a good bigness. . . ."[1]

The work of fortifying the point and building dwellings for the winter began immediately. Within a few weeks, if our informant can be believed, they had "full finished the fort, trencht and fortefied yt with twelve pieces of ordinaunce, and built fifty howses therein, besides a church and a storehowse. . . ."

[1] William Strachey, *The Historie of Travaile into Virginia Britannia*, R. H. Major, ed., London, 1849, p. 172.

The plan of the settlement, called St. George, was sent back to England in October. This drawing is reproduced in Figure 66, but it seems extremely unlikely that it is an accurate representation of what the colonists had managed to accomplish by that time. Rather, it must be regarded as a plan for eventual construction. The elaborate fortifications were almost certainly never built; much more likely was a stockade of tree trunks set vertically around the perimeter of the fort, possibly with a ditch beyond. Whatever was constructed was soon abandoned, for the next year the entire colony withdrew after a severe winter and the death of several of the leaders. Like Roanoke, Fort St. George was soon covered with underbrush and in time all but forgotten.

"Two Rows of Houses and a Fair Street"

The first permanent English settlement in New England was, of course, at Plymouth. Here a tiny group of Separatists who had broken with the established church in England and who had endured exile in Holland in exchange for religious freedom erected their crude dwellings to begin the urbanization of New England. The Pilgrims planned to settle in Virginia and had obtained a grant for that purpose from the authorities. When they tried to proceed southward from their first landfall on Cape Cod, unfavorable seas forced them to reconsider; finally, although they lacked authority to do so, they decided to plant their colony on the bleak shore of Plymouth Bay.

The spot selected was one of the Indian "oldfields," partially cleared and formerly used by one of the tribes for growing corn. The land sloped up from the sea to a hill, and along one side of the site ran a "very sweet brook" which supplied water and the mouth of which formed a little harbor for the smaller boats.

Winter was already upon the land, and, as the following contemporary account implies, the colonists already felt the effects of the unfriendly climate:

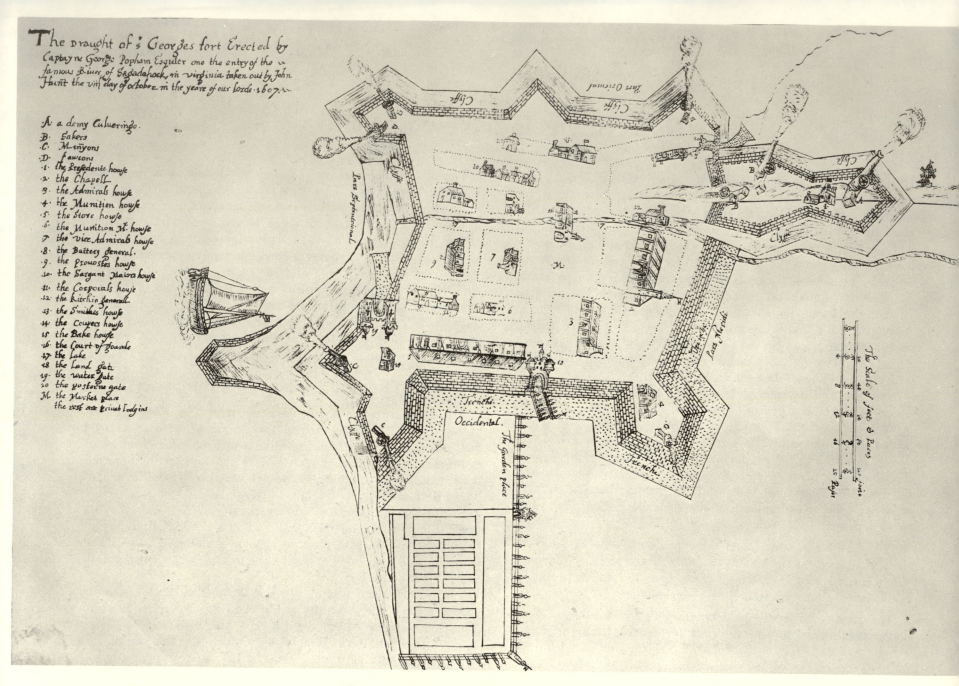

The draught of S. Georges fort Erected by
Captayne George Popham Esquier one the entry of the
famous River of Sagadahock, in virginia taken out by John
Hunt the viii day of october in the yeare of our lorde 1607

A. a demy Culueringo.
B. Bakers
C. Minyons
D. fawcons
1. the Presedent house
2. the Chapell
3. the Admirals house
4. the Munition house
5. the Store house
6. the Munition Nt house
7. the Vice Admirals house
8. the Buttery Generall
9. the Prowostes house
10. the Sargant Maiors house
11. the Corporals house
12. the Kitchin Generall
13. the Smithes house
14. the Coupers house
15. the Bake house
16. the Court of goarde
17. the Jake
18. the Land gate
19. the water gate
20. the postorne gate
M. the Market place
the rest are priuat lodgins

Figure 66. Plan of St. George's Fort, Maine: 1607

"Thursday, the 28th of December, so many as could went to work on the hill, where we proposed to build our platform for our ordinance, and which doth command all the plain and the bay, and from whence we may see far into the sea, and might be easier impaled, having two rows of houses and a fair street."[2]

In order to reduce the amount of work necessary and to hasten the construction of the town the Pilgrims agreed that all single men should be assigned to live with one of the families. This reduced the number to nineteen groups. Then the account continues:

"To greater families we allotted larger plots; to every person half a pole in breadth and three in length; and so lots were cast where every man should lie, which was done, and staked out. We thought this proportions was large enough at the first, for houses and gardens to impale them round, considering the weakness of our people, many of them growing ill with colds. . . ."[3]

No plan of this simple settlement has survived, although a crude diagram of the order of the house lots appears in one of Governor Bradford's journals. There is, however, an excellent description of the town at the end of its first decade. The observer was one Isaack de Rasieres, the chief commercial agent of the Dutch colony of New Netherland, who visited Plymouth briefly sometime between 1628 and 1630. His observations are both interesting and detailed:

"New Plymouth lies on the slope of a hill stretching east towards the sea-coast, with a broad street about a cannon shot of 800 feet long, leading down the hill; with a . . . [street] . . . crossing in the middle. . . . The houses are constructed of hewn planks, with gardens also enclosed behind and at the sides with hewn planks, so that their houses and court-yards are arranged in very good order, with a stockade against a sudden attack; and at the ends of the streets there are three wooden gates. In the centre, on the cross street, stands the governor's house, before which is a square stockade upon which four patereros are mounted, so as to enfilade the streets. Upon the hill they have a large square house, with a flat roof, made of thick sawn plank, stayed with oak beams, upon the top of which they have six cannon, which shoot iron balls of four and five pounds, and command the surrounding country. The lower part they use for their church. . . ."[4]

The view in Figure 67 is a modern conjectural sketch of how Plymouth must have looked toward the end of its first decade of existence. It shows a portion of the village from a point above Fort Hill with the town creek and Plymouth Bay in the background.

The neat regularity of this little village plan reflected the tight social and economic organization of the Pilgrim group. Under the terms of their grant the Pilgrims had bound themselves for seven years to pool any profits from their trade, fishing, and farming enterprises. At the end of that period, land, capital, and profits were to be divided between the Pilgrims and the joint-stock company in England that had underwritten the costs of the venture. Socially, the Pilgrims were united as an oppressed minority religious sect, who had suffered common hardships and privations. Physically, as the only white settlers in a strange land, they naturally drew closely together and relied on one another.

The early years at Plymouth resembled those at Jamestown, with the added suffering brought by the cruel Massachusetts winters. Somehow the colony managed to survive and even to increase in numbers as new recruits arrived from time to time. Plymouth, however, despite its early establishment soon found itself outstripped by the Massachusetts Bay settlements to the north. In 1691 it was absorbed by this later colony.

As for the village of Plymouth, its character evidently changed with the gradual pacification of the Indians and the growing demand for larger farms and gardens. In the early years, all the settlers lived in the little village and tilled the fields just beyond the stockade and the gardens within. At first all labor was performed in common, but general dissatisfaction with this arrangement led to its abandonment as early as 1623. Then fields were allotted temporarily to individuals and families, with each entitled to their own

[2] *Relation or Journall of the Beginning and Proceedings of the English Plantation Settled at Plimoth. . . .* London, 1622. Commonly called *Mourt's Relation*, this was probably written by Edward Winslow and William Bradford. This interesting account is reprinted in full in Alexander Young, *Chronicles of the Pilgrim Fathers of the Colony of Plymouth, From 1602 to 1625*, Boston, 1841. The portion quoted appears on pp. 169-70.

[3] *ibid*. The personal allotment was thus 8¼ by 49½ feet, a pole being equal to the 16½-foot rod.

[4] De Rasieres' letter appears in J. Franklin Jameson, ed., *Narratives of New Netherland 1609-1664*, New York, 1909, pp. 111-12.

Figure 67. View of Plymouth, Massachusetts: 1630

products. Later this temporary allotment became permanent, and the settlers acquired full title to their land. Further allocation of lands became necessary to accommodate new settlers and in response to the demand for larger holdings. By 1623 the effects of these changes in the original system of organization became so marked that Governor Bradford expressed fear for the future of the town:

"For now as their stocks increased . . . there was no longer any holding them together, but now they must of necessitie goe to their great lots; they could not other wise keep their katle; and having oxen growne, they must have land for plowing and tillage. And no man now thought he could live, except he had catle and a great deale of ground to keep them; all striving to increase their stocks. By which means they were scatered all over the bay, quickly, and the town, in which they lived compactly till now, was left very thine, and in a short time allmost desolate. . . . And this, I fear, will be the ruine of New-England, at least of the Churches of God ther."[5]

Bradford's lament over the partial abandonment of the compact agricultural village pattern was not the last to be heard. The frontiersman in his ceaseless quest for more and better land, which was to have so profound an effect on America in the nineteenth century, had already taken his first stride from the earliest colonial footholds on the new continent. Bradford was witnessing only the first stage in the breakdown of the nucleated farming community, a European institution that failed to survive in the American environment of boundless land peopled by resourceful and rootless colonists.

Village and Town: The New England Land Pattern

Within three years after Plymouth was settled, a small fishing colony was established to the north on Cape Ann in what is now Gloucester. The leaders of this little outpost succeeded in obtaining a patent for settlement of a much larger area in 1628. The territory included the land from three miles north of the Merrimac River to three miles south of the Charles and extending westward

[5] William Bradford, *History of Plymouth Plantation*, W. T. David, ed., New York, 1908, pp. 293-94.

to the Pacific Ocean. Sixty colonists were soon on their way to Naumkeag, the present Salem, to which the Cape Ann settlers had moved. In 1629 a new charter was obtained directly from the crown, and by it the Massachusetts Bay Company was created with both territorial and governmental powers. The General Court, which within a few years evolved into a bicameral body, became the legislative body, and the charter also provided for a governor as chief executive officer.

Like the Plymouth Colony, that of Massachusetts Bay involved religious motives. Many of its stockholders were Puritans who were dissatisfied with the established church, although they were not willing to make a complete break as the Pilgrim Separatists had done. Under Charles I the lot of these Nonconformists grew more uncomfortable, and, when the king dissolved Parliament in 1629 to begin a ten-year dictatorial rule, matters became worse. The drastic step of emigration seemed to many the only safe course.

Coinciding with this religious unrest were serious economic difficulties in the textile crafts of the southeastern counties in England. This area was the stronghold of Puritanism; thus economic motives reinforced those of a religious nature stimulating removal from the Old World to the New. In 1630 the exodus referred to as the Great Migration got under way. Eleven ships left for Massachusetts in the spring of that year, and more than a thousand settlers arrived in the colony by the end of the summer. Additional immigrants arrived later in the year.

Settlement of so many numbers and different groups in a single place being out of the question, several favorable locations were selected for towns and surrounding farm fields. William Wood, in his account, *New Englands Prospect*, published in London in 1634, mentions settlements at Weymouth, Dorchester, Roxbury, Charlestown, Newtown (Cambridge), Watertown, Medford, Chelsea, Saugus, Salem, and Boston. Other towns prior to 1635 included Newbury, Ipswich, Beverly, Danvers, Concord, Quincy, Hingham, and Scituate. Thus, in less than a decade the Massachusetts Bay Company was instrumental in the founding of a series of communities along the shores of the great bay and inland on the principal rivers draining into it.

Virtually all of these communities and those that followed as the colony grew were laid out on a common pattern. The details varied from place to place, but the principles remained constant. While in later years the New England land system was modified to meet changing conditions and new requirements, this basic pattern of land development continued to guide the progress of settlement until the Revolution.

Agriculture formed the base for the New England community. Although fishing contributed to the economy, land quickly became and remained for many years the most important economic element. The New England community was thus from the beginning an agricultural community, but it was not entirely rural. Unlike the later settlement pattern in farming areas beyond the Appalachians, the agricultural community in New England centered on the village. Farmers lived in the village in a relatively compact community and daily went to their fields that stretched outward from the cluster of buildings. The complete rural-urban settlement was called a town or township, the term for which survives to the present. So in New England the word "town" did not and does not connote only a nucleated urban-type settlement but instead the entire community of village lots and farm fields.

Most of the older portion of New England was settled by groups of persons bound together by ties of kinship, religion, economic interest, or other reasons, who received by gift or purchase a grant of land with defined boundaries and who proceeded to occupy, settle, and cultivate it. These original purchasers or grantees were known as the proprietors, who allotted land among themselves and their families following some agreed-on formula. Allotments were usually based on the financial share in the enterprise, the total "estate" or wealth of the person, the size of the family, profession or occupation, or some combination of these factors. Early records reveal little dissatisfaction with the methods adopted; this can be understood if we remember that the groups normally were small in size, often related, and that the system used was the result of mutual agreement.

Near the center of the township a site for home lots was selected. Usually these were grouped around an open space on or fronting which the meetinghouse was erected. The planning of these villages will be described in detail in a later section. All that need be said here is that, as at Plymouth, all or nearly all the members of the community resided in the village. Not until later years did the isolated farmstead, so familiar in the midwest, become common.

Large fields suitable for cultivation were then roughly surveyed. These were divided into many strips, usually rather long and narrow. The strips were then numbered, and the settlers drew lots to determine their strips. Each settler ordinarily had more than one strip, the number depending on his share in the allotment. The purpose of this system was to assure each person land that was no better and no worse than his neighbors. While the strips themselves were not fenced, it was the usual practice to enclose the entire field by a wooden paling. Each farmer then became responsible for the maintenance of his proportionate share of fencing. These great fields were referred to as the common fields, but, except in the earliest years of some of the townships, common ownership was not the usual rule. On the other hand, in a number of the settlements the proprietors as a group determined what crops would be grown, when they would be harvested, and what land should be left fallow. Common cultivation was thus carried out, although apparently crops harvested from each strip belonged to the person to whom the strip had been allotted. After the harvest and before the spring sowing the fields were also used in common, with cattle turned loose to graze on the stubble.

These "common fields" or "proprietor's commons" were thus not open to subsequent settlers unless these newcomers were formally granted commoners' rights. The remaining lands, however, were open to all inhabitants of the town. These were the common pasture lands and common woodlands. Cattle and sheep were entrusted to cowherds and shepherds. These herdsmen were paid a salary by the owners of the animals under their care. Like the pasture lands, the wooded areas of the town were also held in common ownership. Subject to town regulations, residents could fell timber and quarry stone for individual use, but the title to the land itself remained with the community.

Thus the land system of the typical early New England town combined ownership in severalty and ownership in common. Even where home lots and strips in the common fields were in individual ownership, by custom and by town regulations the welfare of the community as a whole predominated over individual desires or advantage. For communities who were only one crop removed from starvation and engaged in subduing a harsh wilderness, no other system would have met their requirements so well.

This pattern of land distribution, however, arose only in part because of the special environment of the frontier. In fact, a pattern essentially similar, although not so regular in its boundaries, prevailed in England at that time. The narrow strip cultivation practices grew out of feudal systems of land tenure. Common pasture and woodland, too, marked many areas in England. Indeed, throughout most of Europe, the land was occupied by tightly grouped agricultural villages surrounded by strip fields interspersed with irregular pasture and forest plots.

The close similarity between the New England town and the Spanish colonial *pueblo* is obvious. This suggests that the village-farm unit used in both English and Spanish settlements had its origin in European land tenure systems as they had evolved from feudalism. There were, of course, differences between older European systems and that used throughout New England. Generally the holdings of land were larger in New England. Field lines were also more regular, a feature to be expected where land was being divided at one time rather than gradually over the centuries. Yet there can be little doubt that the New England towns were based on existing practices in England, modified and regularized to meet economic and environmental requirements, and reproduced on the New England landscape.

The graphic evidence of these early land allotments is fragmentary. In some towns apparently no general town plat was prepared. Individual fields were surveyed, but their boundaries and the individual farming plots were often described by metes and bounds. Moreover, the mortality rate for such plats as may have been drawn was high. Fortunately modern scholars have painstakingly reconstructed early property lines from town records, and the general pattern of land division can now be understood.

Figure 68 shows the field lines and roads of Wethersfield, Connecticut, in 1640. The home lots appear on streets leading to the central green. Strip fields surround the town. Those to the east of the Connecticut River are approximately three miles long, but such extreme length was not typical of most of the early New England communities. Beyond this subdivided area lay the common pasture and woodlands. At Springfield, Massachusetts, settled in the mid 1630's, a much simpler pattern of layout and less variation in the size of fields is evident. Here, as Figure 69 indicates, the home lots ranged backwards on either side of a road parallel to the Connecticut River. Adjacent to these lots and on the other side of the river were the fields, pastures, and woodlands. The plan of Little Compton, Rhode Island, in 1681, reproduced in

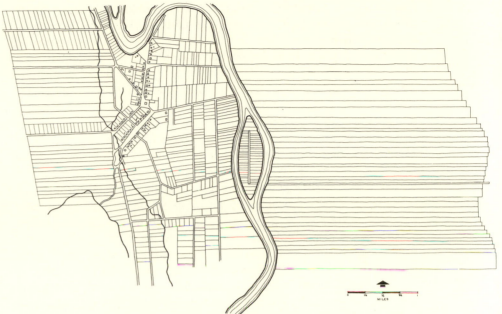

Figure 68. Map of Wethersfield, Connecticut: 1640

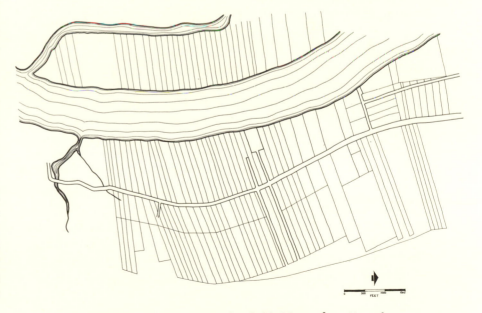

Figure 69. Plan of Springfield, Massachusetts: 1640

Figure 70, shows several different sizes of fields. These represent allotments made at different times as additional land became available for cultivation.

Increased population forced adjustments in the settlement system. One solution seemed obvious: to parcel out the hitherto undivided common lands to the newcomers. All of the towns used this method to accommodate new residents, although by no means all of these later settlers acquired the rights of commoners. The practical result of this gradual process of subdivision was that after some years, the time depending on the rate of immigration and the policies of the proprietors, all or most of the common lands in the earlier towns became divided. Original proprietors benefitted from this process, since in subsequent divisions of land they were frequently given additional allotments. In a number of towns, as the supply of common land became scarce, a final division was made at which time all the proprietors or their heirs received proportionate shares of the remaining undivided land.

The second method of providing for an increased population was the "hiving off" of groups of settlers from the old town and the establishment of a new town on newly granted land nearer the frontier. An early example is the founding of Sudbury through a grant made in 1637 by the Massachusetts General Court, a portion of which read as follows:

"Whereas a great part of the chief inhabitants of Watertown have petitioned this court, that in regard to their straightness of accommodation, and want of meadow, they might have leave to remove and settle a plantation upon a river which runs to Concord . . . it is hereby ordered that they . . . shall take view of the places upon said river and shall set out a place for them by marks and bounds sufficient for 50 to 60 families. . . . And it is ordered further, that if the said inhabitants . . . shall not have removed their dwelling to their said new plantation, before one year after the plantation be set out that then the interest of all such persons, not so removed . . . shall be void and cease."[6]

In the same manner the three early Connecticut River towns of Wethersfield, Hartford, and Windsor were established by groups moving from the Massachusetts Bay settlements. In turn, these three river towns subsequently sent out new groups in the

[6] D. H. Hurd, *History of Middlesex County, Massachusetts*, Philadelphia, 1890, ii, 377.

vicinity which led to the founding of ten additional towns. Until 1675, when King Phillip's War marked the beginning of a period of organized Indian resistance to further expansion, group settlement of new plantations and towns continued steadily.

The pattern of settlement changed in the eighteenth century. Where previously grants were made mainly to organized groups desiring land for their own use, now an element of land speculation appeared. Large tracts of land, sizeable enough for several of the standard six-mile square townships of previous years, were granted to a group of proprietors. These persons as often as not had no intention of settling the land but, in turn, laid out one or two townships, offered lots free to those who would settle, and then made their profit from the sale of farms in the remaining townships. The plat of Meredith, New Hampshire, in 1770, shown in Figure 71, reveals the tendency during this period to use a modified gridiron system in the arrangement of farm lots. A typical farm in Meredith measured approximately one-quarter of a mile in width and one-half mile in depth.

Coincident with this development and to some extent because of it, there developed a trend toward larger home lots and away from the compact village design of the earlier years. In part this was simply a reflection of the deficiencies of the multi-field strip system of agricultural land allotment. As individuals began to consolidate their land holdings into contiguous and larger parcels, maintaining their residence in the village became a hardship. Then, too, the decreased danger of Indian attacks made the compact settlement pattern less necessary as a defense measure. Home lots of 10 and 20 acres and even larger became common, where earlier custom had dictated lots of 1, 2 or perhaps 6 acres.

In summarizing this brief discussion of the New England system of land distribution, the importance of the group or community basis of settlement should be re-emphasized. The public welfare was paramount, and public control over land distribution and land use was regarded as essential. In these small communities a rough but workable democracy prevailed. Whatever changes were made were subject to group discussion and approval. Dissension there must have been, but one has the impression that rarely since that time have important decisions been made about community planning in America with such harmony. The other feature to note is that the settlement of New England was an experiment

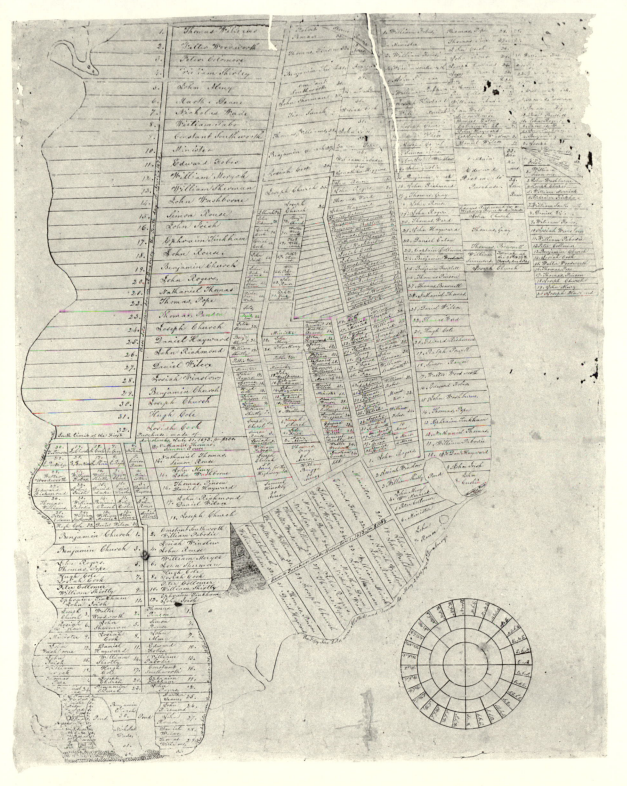

Figure 70. Map of Land Division in Little Compton, Rhode Island: 1681

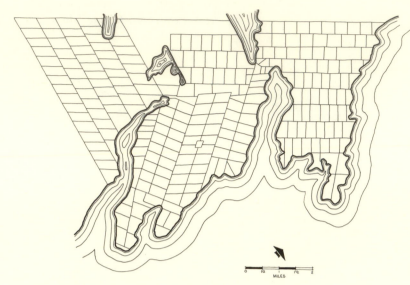

Figure 71. Map of Meredith, New Hampshire: 1770

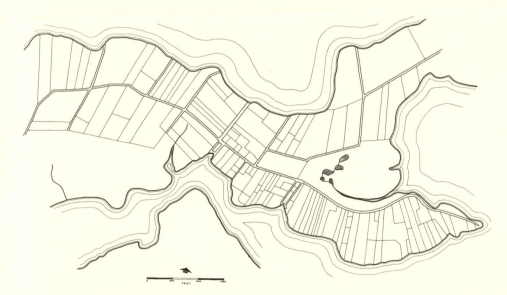

Figure 72. Plan of Salem, Massachusetts: 1670

in genuine regional planning. Both urban and rural development were subject to conscious forethought and community controls. Only the Spanish *pueblo* rivaled the New England town in this respect.

New England Village Planning

The other element in the New England land planning system was the village. The simple plan of New England's first village—Plymouth—has already been discussed. While many of the later village plans were rather more elaborate, it was characteristic of the New England communities that the elements used in their planning were few in number and elementary in nature. New England never possessed counterparts of Annapolis or Williamsburg. Such formal planning in the baroque tradition would not have been in keeping with the spartan, almost stern, philosophy adhered to by the Puritan founders. But if the New England villages lacked the long, axial vistas of a Williamsburg, they achieved an intimate charm of their own which many of them have retained to the present day.

What were the distinguishing features of the New England villages? First of all, the villages were planned to accommodate a limited population. Once the home lots were taken up, with perhaps some modest expansion possible through platting undivided land, the expectation was that a new settlement would be formed elsewhere to accommodate newcomers. In actual practice, many of the villages did continue to increase in size as farm lots became divided into home lots, but in the early years at least community size remained within bounds.

Many, though not all, New England villages centered on some form of central open space—the village green or common. The motives behind this element of the plan appear mixed. The green often served as a site for the meetinghouse and later for other public buildings as well. It was also used as a mustering place and training ground for adult males who served as the local militia or village guard. While apparently some of the larger greens provided space for cattle grazing, this was not often a normal function. The green did, however, offer itself as a space into which cattle from the common pastures could be herded in case of a threatened Indian attack. Doubtless also the early village planners must have consciously attempted to create open spaces for purposes of community amenity and as an advantageous setting for dwellings.

Care was used in the siting of buildings. In some cases dwellings were required to sit back from the street line some prescribed distance. Even where such requirements were lacking, builders seemed to observe good taste in locating buildings with respect to the street line and adjacent structures. The church or meeting-house in this theocratic society naturally assumed great importance. A location on the green itself or facing it was favored.

Another feature of the New England village community was the sharp break between village and countryside. Although the eighteenth-century villages, with their much larger home lots blurred this distinction between town and country, the earlier villages exhibited a compact group of houses and home lots quite apart from the surrounding farm lands. Modern suburban growth has obliterated this crisp distinction in the larger New England communities, but it can still be observed in the hill villages of New Hampshire and Vermont.

The oldest of the Massachusetts Bay villages was Salem. One of its early residents has left us this account of its condition in 1629 and the hopes its settlers had for the future:

"When we first came to Nehum-kek, we found about half a score houses, and a fair house newly built for the Governor. . . .

"There are in all of us, both old and new planters, about three hundred, whereof two hundred of them are settled at Nehum-kek, now called Salem, and the rest have planted themselves at Masa-thulets Bay, beginning to build a town there, which we do call Cherton or Charles town.

"We that are settled at Salem make what haste we can to build houses, so that within a short time we shall have a fair town.

"We have great ordnance, wherewith we doubt not but we shall fortify ourselves, in a short time to keep out a potent adversary."[7]

A reconstruction of the original home lots plat appears in Figure 72. Here the informality that characterized many of the village

plans is evident. The main street, now the present Essex Street, ran along the high ground forming the drainage divide between North and South Rivers. From this street at irregular intervals short streets led to the water's edge. A large plot near the center was retained as town property. Its western half now forms the large Salem Common on which front elegant three-storied brick houses built at the height of Salem's commercial prosperity in the late eighteenth and early nineteenth centuries.

Charlestown, located on a peninsula formed by the estuaries of the Charles and Mystic Rivers, was the second oldest town among the Massachusetts Bay Company settlements. It was intended as the capital of the colony, but although the first meetings of the Court of Assistants took place there the shortage of water and an outbreak of fever caused Governor Winthrop to transfer the seat of government.

The intended importance of Charlestown is indicated by the assignment of Thomas Graves, an engineer, to accompany the settlers and to assist them in laying out the town and its fortifications. The fragmentary records of the period indicate that the first inhabitants,

". . . jointly agreed and concluded . . . that Mr. Graves do model and lay out the form of the town, with streets about the Hill; which was accordingly done, and approved of by the Governor."[8]

It is not known if Graves was responsible for the plans of any of the other Massachusetts Bay villages. The company records show some concern over his salary, and one letter from England to officials in the colony requested a statement as to how long his services might be required. It would seem likely, therefore, that his talents would have been put to use in other town planning ventures. This, however, is mere speculation; all that is known is that Graves is the first town planner in the English colonies whose name has been recorded.

Among the earliest towns of the period, along with Salem, Charlestown, and Boston, were Watertown and Medford on the Charles and Mystic Rivers, and Newtown, later named Cambridge on the tidal estuary of the Charles. It was here in December 1630 that the Court of Assistants resolved to:

[7] *New-England Plantation* (London, 1630), in Alexander Young, *Chronicles of the First Planters of the Colony of Massachusetts Bay*, Boston, 1846, pp. 258-59.

[8] *Charlestown Town Records* in Young, *ibid.*, 376. According to Young the original records no longer exist. They were copied in 1664 from the originals written by Increase Nowell in 1636 or 1637.

". . . build houses at a place a mile east from Watertown, near Charles River, the next spring, and to winter there the next year; that so by our examples, and by removing the ordnance and munition thither, all who were able might be drawn thither and such as shall come to us hereafter, to their advantage be compelled so to do; and so, if God would, a fortified town might grow up there. . . ."[9]

While only a few of the assistants built their houses in Newtown under this agreement, development began in the new community in the spring of 1631. Apparently it was not until the following year that any formal village plan was adopted, but with the arrival of a new group of colonists from Essex, streets were laid out and house lots chosen. Perhaps the earliest record of a front yard regulation in the English colonies dates from this period when the newly formed town government decreed that "houses shall range even and stand just six feet in their own ground from the street." By 1634 William Wood, in his survey of all the bay settlements, could write of the new town:

"This is one of the neatest and best compacted towns in New-England, having many fair structures, with many handsome contrived streets. The inhabitants, most of them, are very rich, and well stored with cattle of all sorts, having many hundred acres of ground paled in with one general fence, which is about a mile and a half long, which secures all their weaker cattle from the wild beasts. On the other side of the river lieth all their meadow and marsh ground for hay."[10]

Cambridge, like Charlestown, served for a time as the seat of government, but the central and strategic location of Boston was finally selected for this purpose in 1636. If Cambridge lost the government, however, it soon gained the first institution of higher learning in the colonies. Harvard College, the first building of which was completed in 1637, began its existence at a time when the first settlements were barely secure against the Indians or the threat of famine, and its creation bears testimony to the thirst for knowledge and the respect for learning of the New England colonists.

[9] Letter from Thomas Dudley, Deputy Governor, to the Countess of Lincoln, Boston, March 12, 1631, in Young, *ibid.*, 320.
[10] William Wood, *New-Englands Prospect* (London, 1634), in Young, *ibid.*, 402.

· 126 ·

The first building of Harvard appears as the northernmost structure in the village on the map reproduced in Figure 73. The Cambridge plan, which may have been prepared by Graves, is quite different from that of Salem. As Wood pointed out, possibly to distinguish its character from other contemporary settlements, the plan is compact in contrast to the elongated, rambling layout of Salem. The average home lot measured about 100 by 80 feet. Most of the streets were 30 feet wide. The market square in the northwestern part of the village was approximately 150 feet by 200. Midway along the principal northwest-southeast street stood the meetinghouse on a plot only slightly larger than those allotted for houses. Virtually the entire village with its little gridiron of streets occupied a site hardly more than 1,000 feet square. In its scale and the clear definition between village and countryside the Cambridge plan resembles the tiny *bastide* towns of southern France or the similar settlements in Britain like Winchelsea, Flint, Salisbury, or Hull.

Cambridge was the prototype for one kind of New England village pattern—the compact, "squared" community in which gridiron streets were normally employed, where the home lots were usually small in comparison with the farm fields, and where some kind of central open space or market formed a distinct center for the settlement. This is not to say that the plan of Cambridge was consciously imitated; the general pattern of such a community form owes its origins to Old-World practice and to man's almost instinctive use of geometry in laying out new towns when speed and simplicity are dominant requirements.

Salem represents another community form, probably at least as old. This is the linear pattern, where a single street forms the spine of the settlement. In New England, as in Europe, linear villages were normally less regular in their design although not necessarily less pleasing in their appearance. Relatively few settlements of this type can be observed in their original form in New England today, since the single streets of these early villages now are but a part of the larger community. In the process of growth the essential linear form has become obscured as new development has taken place in depth at right angles to the original axis.

Although most of the New England villages fall into one of these two general plan forms, the variations within each category are almost endless. We can also distinguish within each type two subgroups: those where the layout is more or less regular or geometric and those where the plan is informal, irregular, or "organic." The problem of classification is made more difficult by the fact that some villages combine the geometric layout in some parts with the informal plan in others. Because most of the cartographic evidence is not contemporary with the original settlement but is either from much later periods or in the form of modern conjectural plans based on old land records, generalizations about early New England village planning are at best tentative and hypothetical.

One fact remains clear: the stereotype image of the New England village with its lofty meetinghouse spire rising from a crisply painted, green-shuttered building fronting a central green and dominating a cluster of large, comfortable "colonial" houses does not fairly represent conditions during the early years of settlement. The grace and charm of the New England was long in the making. These were pioneer communities. Some, like Windsor, Connecticut, in 1637 began as small fortress stockades enclosing a square of dwellings that were little more than huts. In others, such as Salem, the first places of residence were tiny dugouts scooped out of a bank or were bark-covered sapling-framed shelters built in imitation of Indian dwellings. Even the surviving larger houses from the middle and late seventeenth century, with their unpainted plank or clapboard siding and their small windows, bear witness to the stern requirements of a frontier existence. In many of the early settlements it was not until nearly half a century or so after original settlement that the architectural qualities we associate with the New England community began to take form.

During this period of development in building types and design, the village plans themselves doubtless underwent many changes. Agricultural lanes became residential streets as population increased, and planting fields became village house lots. Streets that may have been surveyed as straight lines developed irregularities as travelers took the easiest path around rock outcrops or low-lying wet spots in the right-of-way. Portions of the central green, where one existed, were occasionally sold for building lots or allocated for public uses. Building encroachments on street lines apparently were fairly frequent and, when tolerated, resulted in minor shifts in street direction or width. Then, too, the sites of important buildings were sometimes changed; in Hartford, for example, the first meetinghouse site evidently was in

Figure 73. Plan of Cambridge, Massachusetts: 1637

one corner of the meetinghouse square some distance from the site used for its replacement a few years later.

There can be little doubt, however, that in addition to the irregularities that occurred, almost imperceptibly, in the original plans there were many "planned" irregularities from the beginning. Some of these seem deliberate—the sudden widening of a main street to form a narrow green or market space, as in Waterbury, Connecticut, or Greenfield, Massachusetts, are cases in point. Others may have been "planned" only in the sense that existing topographic features too strong to ignore were recognized and the otherwise regular pattern adjusted accordingly. The neat precision of a New Haven with its nine equal, straight-sided blocks is something of a rarity among these early settlements.

It is just these frequent departures from regular geometry that give the charm of the unexpected and the variety in building siting to the New England village today. That this resulted from deliberate attempts on the part of the early planners to create a community-wide aesthetic experience seems highly unlikely. This is not to deny that good taste and foresight in the advantageous siting of individual buildings was practiced. The location of the meetinghouse at Ipswich, Massachusetts, atop a lofty and rocky acropolis-like site or the site chosen at Topsfield, Massachusetts, fronting a spacious common are but two examples of such micro-planning.

Close study of these town plans leads inescapably to the conclusion that the very real visual distinction of the New England village stems less from the merits of their two-dimensional plans than from the combination of buildings and plant materials that developed by semi-accident many years after their layout. Perhaps this merely proves that simple plans often adapt best to changing circumstance. So while the plans were simple but varied, it is the third dimension of the villages that is cherished. The scale, the materials, the architectural designs inherited from abroad but modified to meet the new environment—all combined with the village layout to produce a total quality of community that has yet to be equalled in America except in isolated towns of outstanding character.

A more detailed examination of representative examples of both the compact and linear village forms is of value in gaining an understanding of the town planning in this period. The compact or "square" villages, including the regular and irregular variations, will be examined first, followed by a discussion of those whose pattern was essentially linear.

The most regular of these compact settlements has already been mentioned. The colony of New Haven was settled in 1638 by a group of settlers recently arrived in Massachusetts from England. Previous explorations had indicated that the northern shore of Long Island Sound seemed favorable for settlement, and two or three years earlier three new towns had been established to the north and east along the Connecticut River. At the mouth of that river, 30 miles or so east of New Haven, the fort and town of Saybrook had also been erected.

The plan of New Haven in 1748 as redrawn in 1806 appears in Figure 74. It faithfully follows the original layout. According to tradition, John Brockett was the surveyor of the party and in charge of the town's layout. The two streams entering the harbor were doubtless responsible in part for the form and dimensions of the settlement. Probably a square layout had already been decided on if the site would permit. By tilting the square so that the streets ran generally northwest-southeast and southwest-northeast, the town plot fitted neatly between two streams with its southern corner nearest the harbor. George and State Streets, two of the boundary streets, thus ran roughly parallel with the streams.[11]

Each of the nine great blocks measured 16 rods, or 825 feet, square. The central square was set aside as a market place. In addition to that function, by the time the map was prepared, New Haven green had become the site of the meetinghouse, jail, grammar school, and county court house. When the infant Yale College was moved to New Haven from Saybrook in 1717 it was only natural that the first building should be located on a site facing the green.

As in the other New England communities the village formed

[11] Anthony N. B. Garvan in his *Architecture and Town Planning in Colonial Connecticut*, New Haven, 1951, advances the argument that the orientation of New Haven resulted from the application of the town planning principles of Vitruvius. The argument is at best tortured, and demonstrates more ingenuity than sound historical judgment. The reader is, however, urged to weigh the evidence and judge for himself. Garvan's work is otherwise informative, well-written, and thoroughly documented and stands as a model for other needed regional studies of its type.

one part of a rural-urban community unit. Farm fields stretched out beyond the boundary streets and were supplemented by the common pasture and woodlands of the town. Perhaps it was done in other towns as well, but the New Haven records are the earliest to describe allotments of farm lands so arranged that those owning home lots in each sector of the village could reach their fields with a minimum of time and distance. For a distance of one mile from the village bounds the land was divided into "quarters." The fields or out-lots granted in each quarter were assigned to those living in the village block contiguous to the inner line of these great farm divisions. The map of 1748 shows several of the streets leading outward from the village in radial fashion. Possibly these streets were planned at the time the fields were allotted, although they may simply have developed from paths and lanes used by the colonists. As will be noted elsewhere, this pattern of square village surrounded by a radial field system was later used in Gravesend, Long Island, in 1646 and by William Penn in a somewhat modified version in 1683. Although direct evidence is lacking, a tenable hypothesis is that both of these agricultural village plans were based on the system first devised at New Haven.

The precise regularity of the plan and the manner in which it was oriented so as to fit the site suggest strongly that the form and dimensions of New Haven had been determined well in advance, probably before the group departed from Massachusetts. Theophilus Eaton, one of the leaders of the new colony, had visited the site several months before the founding of the town, reported its desirability, and, in company with others, may at that time have drafted a plan. This conjecture is supported by two facts. One is that the original company numbered about 250 persons; this number was increased considerably by residents of Massachusetts who decided to accompany the group from Boston to the chosen town site in the Spring of 1638. Thus at the last moment the new colony suddenly acquired unexpected reinforcements.

The plan itself furnishes additional evidence. Between the two creeks and adjoining the southwestern part of the grid, the location of many additional homes can be seen. These were not, as might be thought, more recent additions in the first century of the village's existence. Instead, these lots formed part of the original design— a kind of suburb added to the town proper almost as an after-

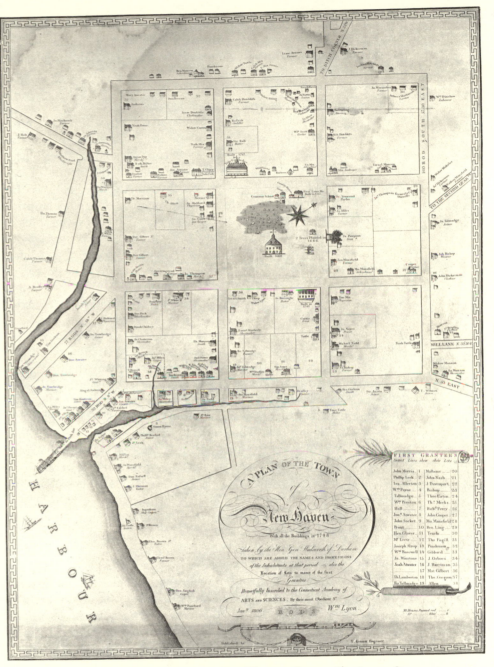

Figure 74. Plan of New Haven, Connecticut: 1748

thought. The only reasonable explanation is that this addition was made to an already conceived town plan in order to accommodate the increased number of colonists who had elected to join the enterprise at almost the last minute.

If it can be tentatively concluded that the New Haven plan, with its generous provision for open space, was no sudden inspiration of the moment, there is no ready explanation for the source of its form or dimensions. That one-ninth of the village, exclusive of the land in streets, should be forever dedicated to open space and sites for public buildings is truly remarkable. None of the earlier New England villages approached this figure. Nor, so far as can be determined, did any village layout in England afford a model. Of the open spaces in London only Lincoln's Inn Fields, some 600 by 800 feet, approximated the scale of New Haven's green. Geometric plans were, of course, not unknown in England, although limited to the relatively few deliberately founded towns of Edward I and a handful of later planned communities. The new towns of the Ulster Plantation in Ireland also employed the gridiron system. But, in its combination of a very large central open space and the regular checkerboard street system, the plan of New Haven was something of an innovation.

The large residential blocks did not long retain their original form. Intended to provide generous garden plots adjacent to residences, these deep squares were eventually divided into four smaller blocks by new streets running at right angles from the midpoints of their sides. The central green itself was divided into two parts, one of which contained the churches and public buildings with the remaining section left in open park. The modern visitor to New Haven can still grasp the generous scale of the central green, but the character of the eight other original blocks has been lost with the development of the business district on one side and Yale University on the other.

Although the plan of New Haven was perhaps the most striking of the early New England geometric compact villages, there were others that deserve mention. Quite different in scale was the fortress settlement of Windsor, Connecticut. Windsor, like Wethersfield and Hartford, was settled in the mid 1630's after a group of colonists successfully petitioned the Massachusetts General Court for a grant of land. It was a Dorchester congregation that established Windsor, just as groups from Watertown and Cambridge settled at Wethersfield and Hartford.

· 130 ·

The earliest pattern of home lots is not known, but in 1637 with the outbreak of the Pequot War, a new although perhaps temporary arrangement became necessary. On the north bank of the Farmington River just above its mouth at the Connecticut the settlers hastily constructed a rectangular stockade and moved their possessions to new dwellings built within the enclosure. A contemporary account describes the details of its layout:

"About 1637, when the English had war with the Pequot Indians, our inhabitants . . . gathered themselves nearer together from their remote dwellings, to provide for their safety, set upon fortifying and with palizado, which some particular men resigned up out of their properties for that end; and was laid out into small parcels, to build upon; some four rods in breadth, some five, six, seven, some eight. . . .

"These building places were at first laid out of one length, that was sixteen rods. . . . Also on all sides within the outmost fence, there was left two rods in breadth for a common way, to go round within the side of the Palizado."[12]

The outer limits of the stockade formed an enclosure with four unequal sides, the shortest being somewhat over 800 feet and the longest about 1,300 feet. Inside, the central open space measured roughly about 300 by 500 feet. At the northeast corner was the town house; diagonally opposite was the burying ground. Grouped around the central square were the houses occupied during the Indian uprising. This was, however, but a temporary arrangement. Although a few persons remained on the new location and, with town consent, enlarged their lots by adding adjacent land, most of the residents moved back to their former places of residence.

The early settlers of Hartford also erected a stockade fortress, but there is no record that it was anything more than a military strongpoint. The village plot at Hartford does, however, belong to the group of rectangular, compact settlements, as can be seen from the layout as it appeared in 1640 reproduced in Figure 75. When first settled the plan consisted only of the long block in which the meetinghouse square is located, but within five years

[12] From an account by Matthew Grant in 1654 as quoted in H. R. Stiles, *The History of Ancient Windsor*, New York, 1859, pp. 121-22. Stiles reproduces a rough drawing showing the division of land within the stockade.

new settlers required additional home lots. These additions were rather less regular than the original layout, but on the whole the initial plan was merely extended as the need arose. Not quite so large as in New Haven, the central square measures a generous 500 by 650 feet. The splayed lines of the square and of the short street entering it from the river side could have been mere accidents; one is tempted, however, to believe that the planner adopted this device to emphasize the importance of the central open space and to enhance the vista into it from without. The location of the meetinghouse is conjectural, since early accounts are unclear; but if located as shown on the drawing the purpose and shape of the short street seems clear enough.

Following the Pequot War in 1639, Roger Ludlow established the new settlement of Fairfield on Long Island Sound east of the New Haven colony. The first lots were laid out by Ludlow in that year, and in 1640 he completed the remainder of the village plan. The layout appears in Figure 76 and shows the simple pattern of four square blocks with the village green and meetinghouse and school sites cut from the central corners of two of the blocks. While some of the village lots were as large as 8 acres, most of them were about 3½ acres in size. The central green contained approximately 10 acres, measuring roughly 850 by 500 feet. Its placement in the village plan appears less skillfully done than at New Haven or Hartford from the standpoint of providing a focus on the meetinghouse or other public buildings. One might also question the desirability of splitting the central open space into two equal portions. Yet the plan is not without merit in its simplicity and compact grouping.

Many other regular, compact villages were created throughout the colonial period of New England. Stratford and Litchfield, Connecticut; Pittsfield, Massachusetts; Hanover, New Hampshire; and Newport, Rhode Island, are among the better documented. In one sense these village plans present no special problem in analysis: all of these regular layouts obviously resulted from advance planning and some degree of continued control, at least over the lines of streets and dedicated open spaces. Much more difficult to determine is the extent to which a preconceived plan or plans governed the development of those villages where the pattern is irregular or non-geometric.

Exeter, New Hampshire, is one example. It was founded in 1638 by John Wheelwright at the fall line of the Exeter River.

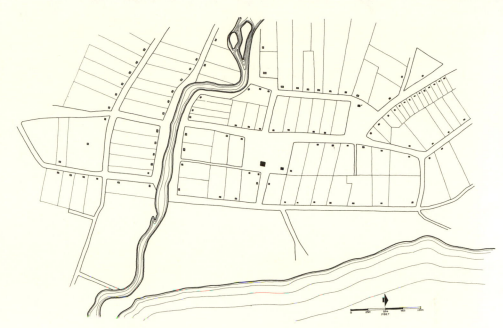

Figure 75. Plan of Hartford, Connecticut: 1640

Figure 76. Plan of Fairfield, Connecticut: 1640

Figure 77 shows the street pattern, the houses, and other buildings as they existed in 1802, probably little changed in most essentials from how the town must have looked a century before. The town was and is a fascinating place, with one main street winding along the riverfront and the other leading inland to what is now the Phillips Exeter Academy. The widened space at the intersection of these two streets, where the map shows the court house, appears to be intentional, perhaps laid out as a market place near the wharves. Spring Street and Cross Street, two of the few straight streets that can be found on the map, appear to have been laid out with at least routine care. But these may well have been later additions; the New England town records are full of documents of such street changes and openings.

The plan of one of New England's most delightful villages—Woodstock, Vermont—differs in form but raises the same questions. Figure 78 shows a nineteenth-century map of Woodstock, which was first settled in 1768. The layout reveals one of the elements which often occurred in these villages of irregular plan. Streets converging at acute angles at both ends of the town's center merge to form an irregular elongated space. In Woodstock the center of this space was developed as a sharp-pointed oval green on which houses and public buildings fronted, shaded in summer by lofty trees planted in the green along the streets. A local tradition has it that the shape and dimensions of the green duplicate the plan of the main deck of a ship once commanded by one of the town fathers.

Did this irregular pattern of the Woodstocks and the Exeters of New England come about through over-all village planning? The answer must be tentatively and cautiously in the negative. But if there was no comprehensive plan at Woodstock, for example, the visual satisfaction one discovers there is no mere accident. The plan shows the product of a century of fitting dozens of individual building projects into a harmonious pattern that makes less sense in two dimensions than it does in three. True, we can see in the plan something of the dignity of the central green, the commanding position of the church sites at the intersection of Prospect and Church Streets, and the quite different but equally effective treatment of the church placement at the terminus of Pleasant Street. But the plan alone cannot convey the pervading qualities of fitness, serenity, and congruity one encounters on the

spot. This, too, is surely no mere accident; but such an architectural atmosphere was not necessarily the result of plans, regulations, and administrative controls. It came about because of a limited architectural vocabulary, limitations of major building materials to timber, brick, and stone, and a feeling of responsibility both to immediate neighbors and the greater community to build wisely and well. Our own era contrasts sharply in outlook and output. It would not be unfair to suggest that if Woodstock were to be planned today the two church sites mentioned would be occupied by gasoline stations, and the central green would no doubt be set aside as a metered parking lot.

Two examples of still another type of irregular compact village are shown in Figure 79, a view of Lebanon, New Hampshire, and Figure 80, the plan of Fair Haven, Vermont. Both of these eighteenth-century villages lack geometric street patterns, but both center on large rectangular greens of near-perfect regularity. In both cases, too, the green sits on the first level of land encountered above the nearby river. Lebanon now has become a small city, and the buildings surrounding the green have an urban quality that contrasts pleasantly with the broad stretch of tree-studded lawn on which they front.

Fair Haven has remained a village, and the character of all but the southeastern corner of the town center is domestic and quiet. Whether by accident or design the green is not quite symmetrical; a small rectangular addition extends eastward at the southern boundary. For the visitor entering from the south this arrangement acts much like a reception chamber, stopping the views ahead momentarily, directing attention to the left, and providing a neat transition from the narrow roadway to the spacious open area ahead. This sequence of spatial experiences occurs only because this has become the business section of the village and the buildings are built to the street line; thus space and those who occupy it become confined and directed by the plan forms. Because the road from the south climbs steeply from the river below, the experience of moving through this series of changing spaces gains added excitement.

Another plan combining the formal and the informal is that of Ipswich, settled in 1634, whose nineteenth-century development is illustrated in Figure 81. Here two greens or commons exist in almost total contrast with one another. The original north

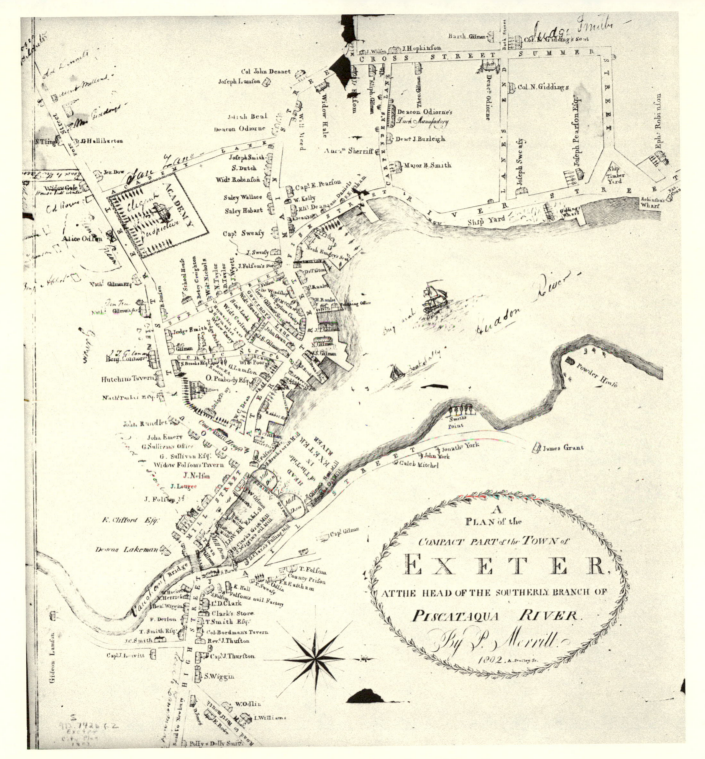

Figure 77. Plan of Exeter, New Hampshire: 1802

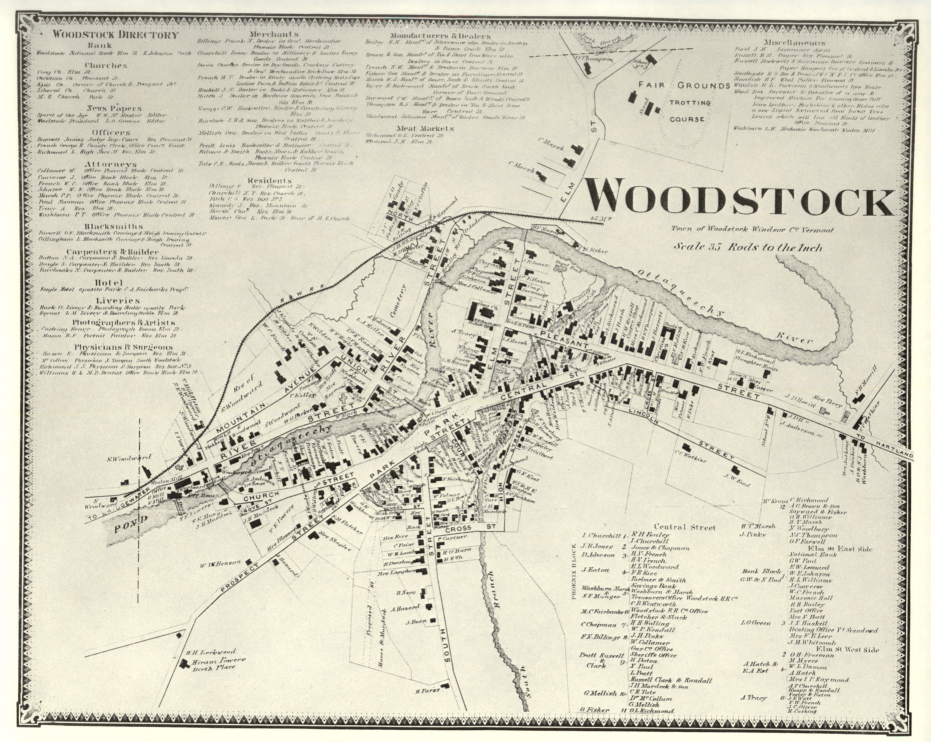

Figure 78. Plan of Woodstock, Vermont: 1869

Figure 79. View of Lebanon, New Hampshire: 1884

Figure 80. Plan of Fair Haven, Vermont: 1869

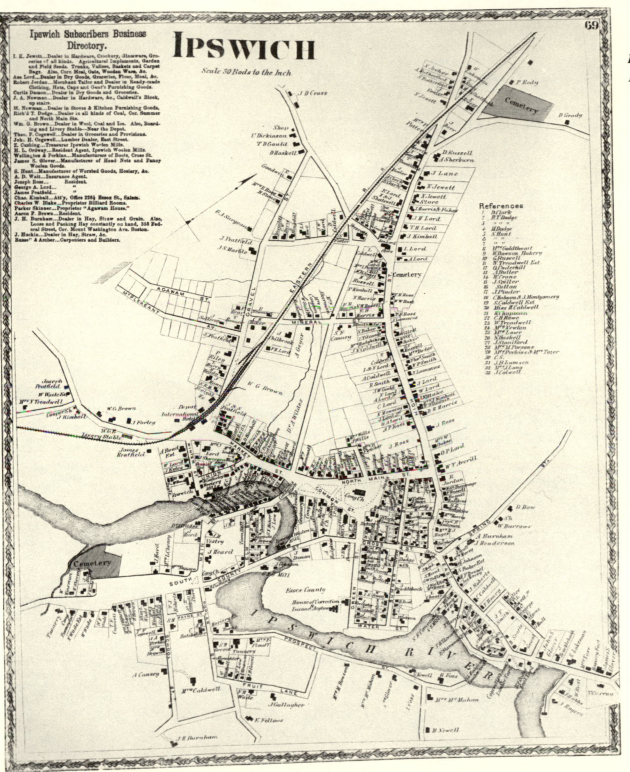

Figure 81. Plan of Ipswich, Massachusetts: 1872

common shows on the plan as the irregular open space with the church in the center. The church site may well have been located first on this highest point where it would be visible from the surrounding countryside and even from the sea two miles east through the marshland. The irregularity of the common reflects the broken topography; rock outcrops and steep slopes dictated the alignment of the streets leading from the river and forming the boundaries of the common. At the foot of the common lay the market, and Market Street leading westward was extended on axis with the church. Whether or not this was fortuitous, influenced by the bend of the river and the slope of land, or deliberately designed to provide a focus on the church will never be known. The view provided, marred considerably in modern times by telephone and power lines, testifies to the good luck or good sense of the New England villagers.

In contrast to the bustle of the market place, now turned business district, and the tumbled rock masses of the main common, the south common of Ipswich is flat, reposed, and rather formal. This area was a later addition to the original village, but since at least one of the houses fronting the common dates from the seventeenth century the south common too is of fairly ancient origin. As can be seen from the map, one side opens to the river through a cemetery; the other is lined with houses. At the western end the common narrows, partially closing the view in that direction. At the eastern end, square on axis, is the imposing Congregational Church. Either one of these open spaces might be envied by any community; the two combined give Ipswich a rare treasure architecturally and a capsule history of New England town planning.

Of the linear villages, the plan of Springfield, Massachusetts, has already been described. Generally these plans are of less interest, and they certainly lack the variety of the compact villages. Providence, Rhode Island, laid out in 1638 on a site selected by Roger Williams, was one of the earliest of the linear communities. The plan, reproduced in Figure 82, shows one unusual and perhaps unique feature: home lots appear only on one side of "Towne Street," the north-south road that formed the spine of the village. Topography determined this peculiar plan and influenced the shape of the long, narrow home lots which ranged from 100 to 135 feet wide, 1,600 to 3,000 feet long, and 4½ to 8½ acres in area.

· 138 ·

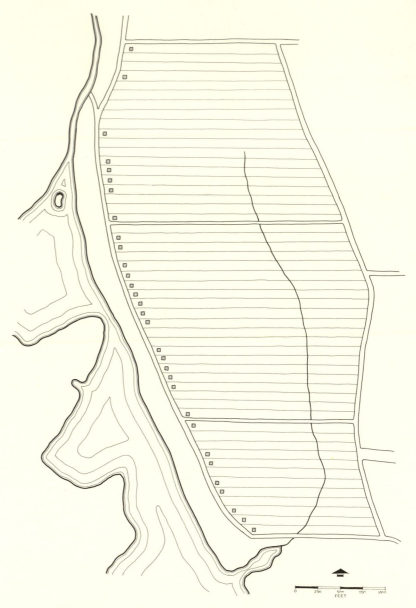

Figure 82. Plan of Providence, Rhode Island: 1638

Towne Street was, of course, laid out to follow the shore line. To the west of the street enough level land extended for houses and out-buildings. Then the land sloped steeply upward to the crest of the ridge midway between Towne Street (now South Main) and Hope Street, the eastern boundary. The plan resembles those of the French colonial settlements of the St. Lawrence and Mississippi Valleys. Here, as there, settlers desired water frontage. To make that possible and still maintain a relatively close grouping of dwellings, very long, narrow house and garden lots were used. Farm fields in the customary New England pattern were allotted beyond the village home lot boundaries.

In Providence a good deal of this original plan survives today, although in quite different form. The two north-south streets remain on their original alignment. The two southernmost east-west streets shown on the plan also exist as Power Street and Meeting Street. Many additional streets have been added with the east-west streets following or paralleling the old field lines. This gridiron pattern which began to develop in the eighteenth century was ill-suited to the steep slopes. It is of interest to note that this College Hill section of Providence, three and a half centuries after its original design, is once again the scene of a major planning program attempting to conserve the many fine houses erected here in the heyday of the city's commercial prosperity and to rebuild those areas that have crumbled into decay during years of civic neglect.

A more typical linear village plan appears in Figure 83, which shows the design of Greenfield, Massachusetts, on the eve of the Revolutionary War. Greenfield was incorporated as a separate town in 1753. Formerly it had been a part of Deerfield, one of the early towns formed in Massachusetts along the Connecticut River. Deerfield's plan, dating from 1670, was also a linear pattern; quite possibly the earlier plan of nearby Springfield was an influence. It was thus only natural that the settlers of Greenfield should repeat a method of land development that had already been used at least twice in the immediate vicinity. As at Deerfield, a small green was introduced on one side of the central street to provide a focus of sorts to the elongated community. At Greenfield, as in Springfield, development at right angles to the original axis has obscured the linear character of the original plan. Deerfield, however, preserves its original form almost intact—a miraculous sur-

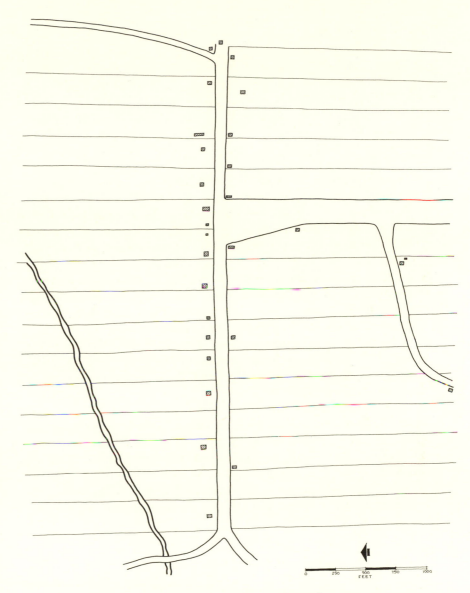

Figure 83. Plan of Greenfield, Massachusetts: 1774

vival in the automotive era of a simple settlement form once widely encountered in New England and now almost vanished. The local museum displays an early manuscript drawing of the village lots and farm fields, most of which can still be seen. The village itself is one of those precious architectural and civic treasures now happily protected from incongruous "improvements" by its residents, who recognize that they hold their property in trust from history.

Boston

In the summer of 1630 Governor John Winthrop decided that because of a lack of good water at Charlestown another site should be found for the principal city of the Massachusetts Bay Colony. Across the Charles River to the south lay a hilly peninsula barely connected to the mainland by a low, marshy, narrow neck of land leading toward Roxbury. The present day Beacon Hill is the much reduced survivor of one of many such elevations that then provided a jagged silhouette against the sky when viewed from the Charlestown shore. Good level farm land was lacking, but the harbor facilities seemed excellent and the narrow neck leading to the mainland could easily be defended. By the fall of that year, Winthrop's group began the task of creating a new town, named Boston for the town of the same name far behind in East Anglia.

The Boston settlers must have been an energetic band, for four years later William Wood could write: "This towne although it is neither the greatest, nore the richest, yet it is the most noted and frequented, being the Center of the Plantations where the monthly Courts are kept."[13]

Two decades later another observer, obviously impressed by what he had seen, described the city in these words:

"The chiefe Edifice of this City-like Towne is crowded on the Seabankes, and wharfed out with great industry and cost, the buildings beautifull and large, some fairly set forth with Brick, Tile, Stone and Slate, and orderly placed with comly streets, whose continuall inlargement presages some sumptuous City. The wonder of this modern Age, [is] that a few yeares should

[13] William Wood, *New-Englands Prospect* (London, 1634), as quoted in Nathaniel B. Shurtleff, *A Topographical and Historical Description of Boston*, Boston, 1871, p. 41.

bring forth such great matters by so meane a handfull, and they so far from being inriched by the spoiles of other Nations. . . ."[14]

The usual lack of contemporary street plans prevents absolute certainty about the disposition of the "beautiful and large" buildings in their "comly streets," but the general arrangement of the land pattern in the 1640's has been reconstructed by a modern scholar and appears in Figure 84. The Boston of three centuries ago and only a decade after its founding already had become a sizeable village and seemed destined indeed to develop into a "sumptuous city."

[14] Edward Johnson, *Wonder Working Providence* (London, 1654), as quoted in Shurtleff, *ibid.*, 44.

Figure 84. Plan of Boston, Massachusetts: 1640

Although Boston's plan could hardly be clasified as regular, it was no more confusing than those of, say, Salem or Ipswich. Men not cows, as legend would have it, created the Boston street system, and by the standards of the seventeenth century it was reasonably well suited to the early community. The exact location of the rocky banks, the marshes, the low and muddy sinks of the virgin site never were recorded. The odds are, however, that these minor topographic variations shaped the early street pattern that has so persistently remained to plague the modern driver.

The longest street ran from the neck of land northeastward to the cove where the town dock was located. Here Dock Square provided space for the handling of merchandise and the loading of cargo. A hundred yards or so south of Dock Square, Great Street (now State Street) led from the harbor to the main highway. This intersection formed the center of the village. Great Street here widened to 113 feet to provide space in its center for an open market. Fronting the market was the meeting house. In 1657 the town house was built on the market square, and the governor's house was located nearby.

Much of this is described by John Josselyn in 1674 after eight years' residence in what had already become a small city.

"The houses are for the most part raised on the sea-banks and wharfed out with great industry and cost, many of them standing upon piles, close together on each side of the streets as in *London* and furnished with many fair shops . . . with three meeting Houses or Churches, and a Town-house built upon pillars where the merchants may confer. . . . Their streets are many and large, paved with pebble stone. . . . On the South there is a small but pleasant common, where the Gallants a little before Sunset walk with their *Marmalet*-Madams, as we do in *Moorfields*. . . ."[15]

Josselyn's account indicates that many of the prominent features appearing on the first published map of Boston in 1722 were well under way fifty years earlier. John Bonner's map, reproduced in Figure 85, provides our first detailed glimpse of the city's progress. No great change in the street system of the 1640's appears. The density of buildings is somewhat greater, although gardens still exist to the rear of the houses. The vaguely defined common men-

tioned by Josselyn shows between the closely built-up section and the western shore. Greater changes have taken place along the harbor. Wharfs now extend into the water, the most notable being the Long Wharf, which was begun in 1710. Bonner's map also shows the "Old Wharfe" connecting the two sides of the harbor. Started in 1673, this was intended to provide harbor defenses. Although completed, it soon fell into disuse, and outbound vessels used the stone from which it was constructed as ballast.

Figure 86 is a closer view of the Long Wharf and the Boston skyline, drawn and engraved by Paul Revere. The wharf simply continued Great Street on a straight line some 1,500 feet into the harbor. Shops and warehouses along one side furnished excellent shipping facilities and incidentally provided a dramatic entrance directly into the center of the city. Other wharfs and docks can be seen in this print and on the Bonner map. These projects marked the beginning of Boston's reclamation of underwater land. During the eighteenth century additional wharfs were projected into the harbor. Often these were joined by cross wharfs, and eventually the spaces between were filled and built on or occupied by buildings constructed on piles. Today every point on the water front extends well beyond the original shoreline. The scramble for urban land that was to mark the last century as an era of speculation was early anticipated in the colonial capital of New England.

At the time Bonner drew his map of the city, Boston's population stood about 12,000, the largest of the English colonial settlements. Some fifty years later, at the time of the Revolution, the city had grown to 16,000, but by then Philadelphia and New York outstripped it. This modest growth made possible the city's expansion on the peninsula and resulted in a compact community of restricted dimensions. The Boston of 1800, as it appears in Figure 87 shows few changes east of the Common. But from the Mill Pond, which had been dammed in the mid sevententh century, to the Common many new streets had been built. Cambridge Street led to the first bridge across the Charles River; this had been completed in 1786 as a private toll bridge and at once stimulated development on both sides of the river in the vicinity of its approaches. The grid pattern adopted here on the northern slope of Beacon Hill shows on a version of the Bonner Map reprinted in 1743 and indicates a fairly early attempt to break away from the rambling alignment of the city's streets elsewhere.

[15] John Josselyn, *An Account of Two Voyages to New-England* (London, 1674), as quoted in Shurtleff, *ibid.*, 45-46.

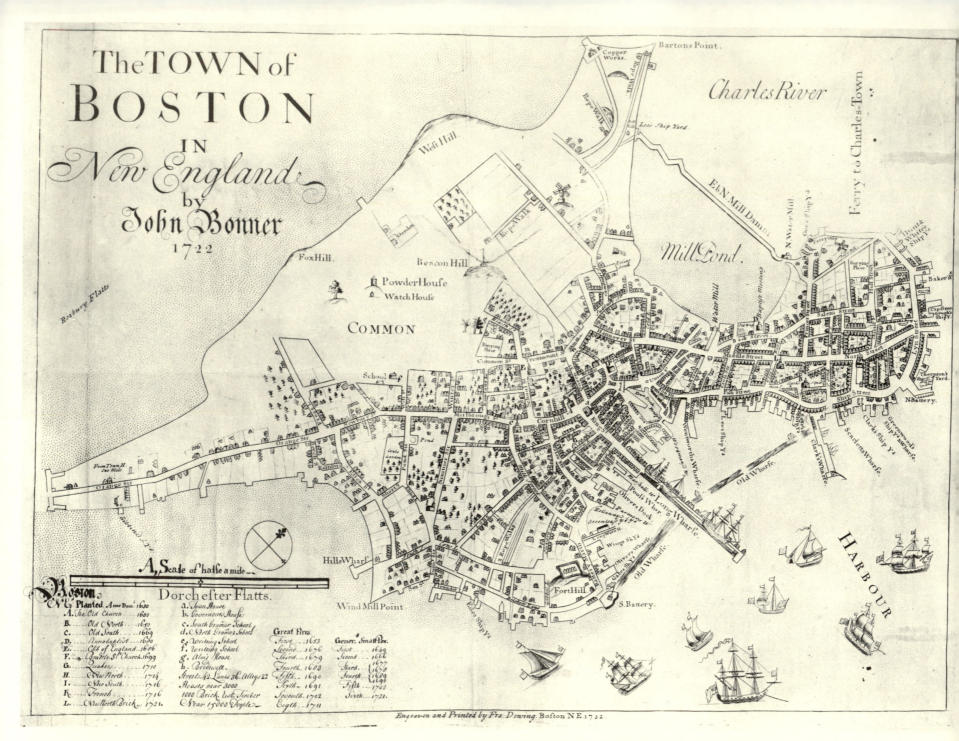

Figure 85. Plan of Boston, Massachusetts: 1722

Figure 86. View of the Harbor at Boston, Massachusetts: 1768

Figure 87. Plan of Boston, Massachusetts: 1800

Figure 88. View of Boston, Massachusetts: 1850

The plan of 1800 shows two of Charles Bulfinch's many contributions to Boston. The State House appears north of the Common on the slope of Beacon Hill. Completed in 1798 this improvement led to the residential development of the Beacon Hill slopes to the west. Here the Mount Vernon Proprietors used a grid pattern to develop the former pasture lands in the vicinity. The early years of the last century witnessed the construction on this site of some of America's most dignified town houses. The development included also some of the unaccountably few American residential squares on the London models. Louisburg Square, built from a plan prepared in 1826 but not substantially completed until about 1840, remains intact as a monument of urbanity and a model of what dignified city dwelling could be.

An earlier Bulfinch residential development also appears on the map. This is Franklin Place, midway between Fort Hill and the Common. Here in 1793 Bulfinch laid out a great crescent of 16 brick row houses facing a straight line of 8 houses in four units. Between lay a half oval, tree-planted green 300 feet long. The resemblance of this project to those of the Adams and the Woods in England is surely no coincidence, for Bulfinch had returned from a grand tour of Europe during which his previous interest in building design grew keen enough to take him from his counting-house job into architecture as a profession. Financially the project proved a failure; if it had been successful Boston might well have become an American Bath, transformed into a city of elegant crescents, squares, and circuses.

The planning of Boston beyond this period cannot be followed in any detail. One look at the mid-nineteenth-century city must suffice. The view of 1850 in Figure 88 is toward the northeast from a point over the then unreclaimed Back Bay. In the center, Boston Common stands out, trim and cropped, in bold contrast to the untended pasture it had once been. To the left of the Common and south of the majestic State House dome lie the handsome town houses fronting Beacon Street and the quieter residential streets to the north. In front appears a newer development. This is the Public Garden, approved by the voters in 1824, as an addition to the Common. Originally its site had been under water; then in 1794 the city permitted reclamation and use of the area for rope manufacturing; now it was added to the great central open space to be enjoyed by all the city's residents—one of the earliest examples in America of public acquisition of land for recreational purposes.

Soon the city would be extended in a great grid pattern southwesterly from the Public Garden as the Back Bay was filled to provide more land for the now rapidly growing city. The beginning of this can be seen at the lower left corner of the view. Western Avenue was built in the 1820's as a continuation of Beacon Street along the mill dam constructed between the old peninsula and Brookline. There were many plans for filling the Back Bay; work began in the 1850's and continued for many years. The present Commonwealth Avenue, terminating at the Public Garden, forms

the spine of this impressive project that still further altered the shoreline of original Boston.[16]

We have come well beyond the era of New England colonial planning in following the growth of Boston. Only for that city have the changing influences and shifting styles of subsequent town layout been mentioned. In other New England cities where substantial growth took place, the same influences were felt. Only the details of development differed. In later chapters these newer trends and fashions of city planning will be examined, and, although more recent communities to the west of New England will be the chief examples, most of the forces of subsequent planning were felt to some degree in the old towns of New England.

The pattern of land utilization that evolved in New England also influenced the layout of towns in other colonial ventures and even beyond. William Penn's agricultural villages may well have been based on the layout of New Haven. The frequently encountered system of in-lots and out-lots in the town plans of the Northwest Territory probably stems from the New England pattern of home lots and farm fields. In northeastern Ohio, in the Western Reserve of Connecticut, dozens of little New England villages were recreated in regularized form by Connecticut settlers following the Revolution. The architectural heritage of New England is well known and is reflected in thousands of well- or ill-designed imitations of Cape Cod cottages, Salem or Boston town houses, or a Deerfield village residence. The planning heritage, buried for the most part under the clutter of the automobile, remains little known but hardly less important. Modern planners concerned with central city renewal and suburban expansion alike could do worse than study the lessons of New England town and village design.

[16] In the section of this chapter dealing with the planning and development of Boston I have drawn heavily on Walter Muir Whitehill's splendid *Boston: A Topographical History*, Cambridge, 1959. This work treats in detail and with ample illustrations the growth of the city from colonial to modern times. It is a superb example of the type of study all of our major cities deserve and most lack.

CHAPTER 6

New Amsterdam, Philadelphia, and Towns of

The Middle Colonies

WITHIN a comparatively short distance of one another two of America's greatest cities were planned in the seventeenth century. Each was located at the mouth of an important river reaching into the interior and on a splendid natural harbor. They quickly became the dominant cities of the Middle Atlantic region, a position they have never relinquished. They differed in one important respect. New York was originally planned as a compact, regular little fortress town, which, however, during its first century of growth developed on an almost medieval pattern with irregular winding streets. Then, during the eighteenth century, extensions of the city began to be made on a more orderly plan, finally culminating in 1811 in the famous gridiron scheme stamped on the entire island of Manhattan. Philadelphia, on the other hand, enjoyed from its beginnings in 1682 a plan with generous scope and public open spaces ample in area for the kind of city envisioned by its founder. The city grew according to this plan for many years, but in later extensions failed to follow the original concept of orderly growth and adequate open space. This chapter describes the planning of these two cities as well as the lesser communities associated with them.

New Amsterdam on the Island of Manhattan

One of the earliest and certainly the best publicized real estate transaction in American history was the purchase of Manhattan Island by Peter Minuit for twenty-four dollars in 1626. While this may have legalized Dutch occupation of the area, Minuit's purchase actually followed the first settlement on Manhattan and the planning of New Amsterdam on its southern tip. After Henry Hudson's explorations of the region almost twenty years earlier, Dutch trading companies began a series of voyages up the Hudson

River and along the coast near its mouth. In 1614 one group of merchants established a small fort and trading post near the present site of Albany, and apparently there were also a few crude buildings erected at the lower end of Manhattan to serve as temporary quarters for trading expeditions.

Plans for permanent settlement began in 1621 when the Dutch West India Company received exclusive trading rights in New Netherland. As in the early French colonies the role of the parent government was relatively unimportant. The commercial trading company not only received a monopoly of commercial activities but was granted governmental powers and the right to dispose of land as it saw fit. In 1623 thirty families were transported to the Albany location, and in the following year preparations were made to bring other colonists.

The first permanent settlement on Manhattan Island was made by a group of Protestant Walloons from Flanders who had accepted the West India Company's terms of settlement and who, with later arrivals from Holland, began the building of New Amsterdam. The orderly Dutch directors of the company sent with these settlers detailed instructions on how the town should be laid out and delegated to company officials accompanying the expedition the power to put these into effect.

These plans came to modern attention only in 1910 when documents in the possession of the van Rappard family were sold at auction. Eventually they were purchased for the Huntington Library and became available in translation in 1924. Document E, "Special Instructions for Cryn Fredericksz Regarding the laying out of the fort" dated April 22, 1625, is of greatest interest. The maps and plans referred to in the instructions have, unfortunately, been lost, but a modern Dutch historian, Frederic C. Weider, has attempted to reconstruct the drawings from the descriptive material and from comparisons with earlier Dutch planned towns, notably Phillipeville, shown in Fig. 4, laid out in 1555 on a symmetrical pattern. Weider's "concepts" of the lost drawings are reproduced in Figure 89 and reveal the details of the first attempt at city planning in New York.[1]

Engineer Fredericksz, who accompanied the settlers, was first of all directed to survey a ditch 24 feet wide and 4 feet deep enclosing a rectangle extending back 1,600 feet from the water and 2,000 feet wide. Then, as shown in Weider's Concept A, the instructions stated:

"The outside of the surrounding ditch having been staked out as above, 200 feet shall be staked off from the inside along all three sides, A, B, C, for the purpose of locating therein the dwellings of the farmers and their gardens, and what is left shall remain vacant for the erection of more houses in the future."[2]

Ten house and garden plots, each being 200 by 200 feet, were to be laid out for the first farmers and were to be assigned by lot.

Concept B shows the plan of the entire community, indicating the location of the farms beyond the enclosing ditch. Farms were to be long and narrow, varying in width from 55 to 80 rods and 450 rods long. A rectangular pattern of roads and ditches, the latter presumably for controlled drainage and irrigation on the Dutch pattern, was specified to serve the farm parcels. The remaining land on either side of the fort was to be used for vineyards.

The town proper was to be located within the five-pointed fortification. The distance from one of the points to the central square was to be about 500 feet so that a fairly generous area for buildings was provided. A street 25 feet wide was to connect the two gates, and along this street 25 house lots, each 25 by 50 feet, were to be laid out. The dimensions of the "market square" in the center were given as 100 by 165 feet, at one end of which were to be located the school, hospital, and church. Other streets, house lots, and sites for storehouses and shops were to be planned as specified in the

instructions and as located on the accompanying map of which Weider's Concept C is a reconstruction.

This neat symmetrical pattern conceived in the security and comfort of the company's offices in Amsterdam never governed the development of the little colony. Construction of a fortress on the scale contemplated obviously exceeded the resources of the settlement, and, if it had been built, it most certainly would have been impossible to man properly. Nor did the first colonists exhibit much enthusiasm for engaging in such building efforts when there were farmlands to plow and crops to sow. While the large fortress may have been started, as Weider contends, the best evidence indicates that the first fortification completed was much smaller than specified in the Fredericksz instructions and it enclosed only the buildings necessary for defense and company trading operations.

The town began to grow with no over-all plan for its development. New streets were laid out from time to time as they were needed, usually following the lanes that had become established naturally as men and animals followed the most convenient paths between houses, farms, and the fort. This method of growth resulted in streets of irregular alignment and width. As the population increased and land near the fort became more valuable, encroachments on the streets added to the lack of order. At the same time persons who had been allotted land and had not yet built on their plots hindered the town's growth. Thus, in 1647, we find the director general and his council taking action to eliminate these twin evils. Their ordinance, one of many aimed at improving municipal affairs and eliminating the hazards of fires, read in part:

"As we have seen and remarked the disorderly manner . . . in building and erecting houses, in extending lots far beyond their boundaries, in placing pig pens and privies on the public roads and streets, in neglecting the cultivation of granted lots, the Director General Petrus Stuyvesant and Council have deemed it advisable to decide upon the appointment of three Surveyors . . . whom we hereby authorize and empower, to condemn all improper and disorderly buildings, fences, palisades, post, rails, etc. . . . Likewise we warn all and everybody, who may heretofore have been granted lots, that they must erect on their lots good and con-

[1] Weider's studies and the van Rappard documents are described and analyzed in Fred Roy Frank, *The Development of New York City: 1600-1900*, unpublished Master's Thesis, Cornell University, Ithaca, 1955. I have drawn heavily on Frank's work for the material in this section as the best treatment of the subject.

[2] *Documents Relating to New Netherland 1624-1626*, translated and edited by A. J. F. van Laer, San Marino, 1924, Document E, 135.

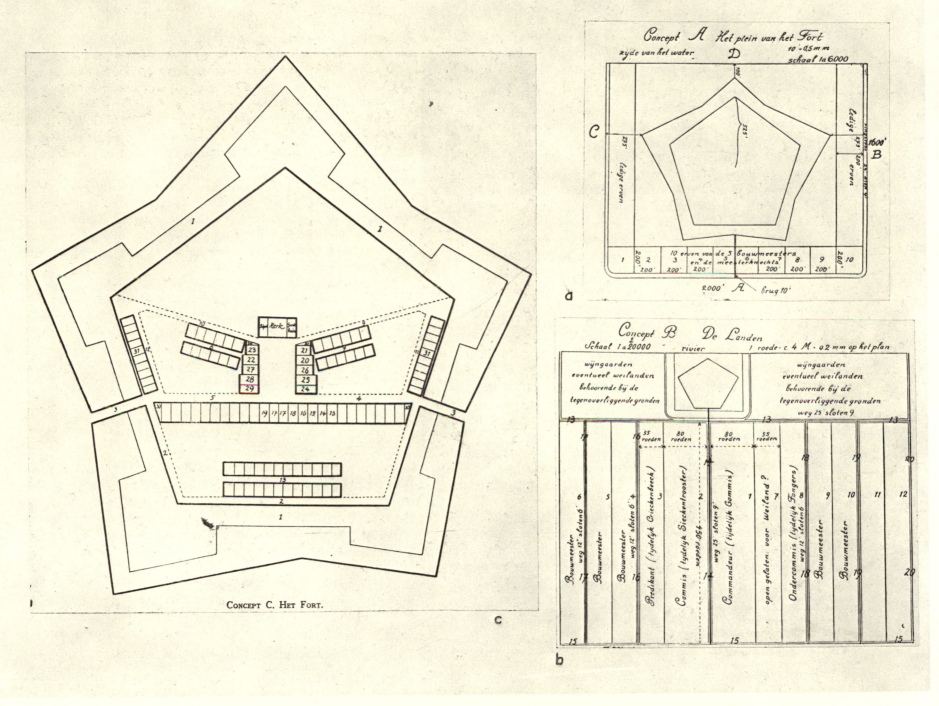

Figure 89. Dutch Plans for the Fort and Town of New Amsterdam (New York City): 1625

venient houses within 9 months . . . or in default thereof such unimproved lots shall fall back to the Patroon or Landlord, to be given by him to such, as he pleases."[3]

Many of the streets surviving today had their origin in the early years of New Amsterdam. Some of these can be seen on the superb map of the city drawn in 1660 reproduced in Figure 90. Leading northward from the fort is the beginning of Broadway. This was the important road connecting the settlement at the tip of the island with the farms and estates beyond. So well established had this highway become that it was virtually the only existing street not fitting the gridiron pattern that survived the Commissioners' Plan of 1811. The map also shows the street running from the East River to Broadway and following the line of fortifications marking the northern limit of the city. This was and is Wall Street, originally built to serve the wall or palisade hurriedly erected in 1633 when an English attack threatened. In the little plot of grass before the fort at the foot of Broadway can be discerned the beginnings of Bowling Green.

A minute description of New Amsterdam just one year later, toward the end of the Dutch period, furnishes us with other details of conditions in the city. We are told of the "gutte" or canal, "whereby at high water boats goe into the towne," and of the town hall on Pearl Street, which followed the bank of the East River. The four-pointed fort contained "the Church, the Governors house, and houses for soldiers, ammunition, etc." The city already had developed as a center of trade, with products from New England and Virginia as well as furs from inland areas being bought, sold and transported by "severall sorts of trades men and marchants and mariners."[4]

New Amsterdam was not the only Dutch settlement on Manhattan. Beyond the city were a number of villages, only the names of which remain. Bowery Village was one of these. Farther to the north along the Harlem River another little settlement developed. At Harlem each settler had a town plot about 90 feet square, a garden lot approximately one-third of an acre, and a 12-acre farm. Harlem was planned with two parallel straight streets leading in-

land from the river, with the town plots located between them, the garden lands beyond the village to the southwest and bordered by the two main streets, and with the farm parcels laid out at right angles to the streets and stretching away to the northwest and southeast across the streets from the houses.

Several other settlements sprang up along the Hudson River. Here were the great estates of the patroons, the feudal lords under the Dutch system of land distribution. At a ferry or perhaps a natural harbor along the river, little villages developed. Wiltwyck, renamed Kingston by the English, was typical of these river communities. The plan of the town as it appeared in 1695 is shown in Figure 91. The stockade and blockhouse were constructed by Stuyvesant in 1658 as added protection for the little gridiron town that had been laid out five years before on the site of a Dutch trading post dating from 1615.

Most important of all was Albany, near the mouth of the Mohawk River and well situated for trade with the Indians in the interior. The plan of the town and fort in 1695, reproduced in Figure 92, shows the street plan established by Stuyvesant in 1652 when he called the town Beverwyck. Settlement at the fort had occurred much earlier, of course, and Stuyvesant's plan merely extended and regularized the street system that had begun to take shape.[5]

English New York

In 1664 Dutch rule came to an end, except for the brief period from 1672 to 1674. Within a year after the English assumed control the corporate existence of the city of New York was established by charter. In 1696 this first charter was supplemented and municipal powers extended by the so-called Dongan Charter. Governor Dongan reaffirmed the corporate existence of the city, and his charter conferred municipal jurisdiction over the entire island of Manhattan. It further granted ownership to the city of all land between high and low water marks, thus fixing the basis for the present system of municipal piers and wharfs. In addition, and more far-reaching in its effects, the Dongan Charter granted to

---

[3] *The Records of New Amsterdam*, I, 4, as quoted in James Ford, *Slums and Housing*, Cambridge, 1936, I, 28.

[4] *Description of the Towne of Mannadens, 1661*, in J. Franklin Jameson, ed., *Narratives of New Netherland, 1609-1664*, New York, 1909, pp. 421-24.

[5] Irving Elting, A. B. Baltimore, and N. Murray, *Dutch Village Communities on the Hudson River*, Johns Hopkins University Studies in Historical and Political Science, 4th series, I, Baltimore, 1886.

Figure 90. Plan of New Amsterdam (New York City): 1660

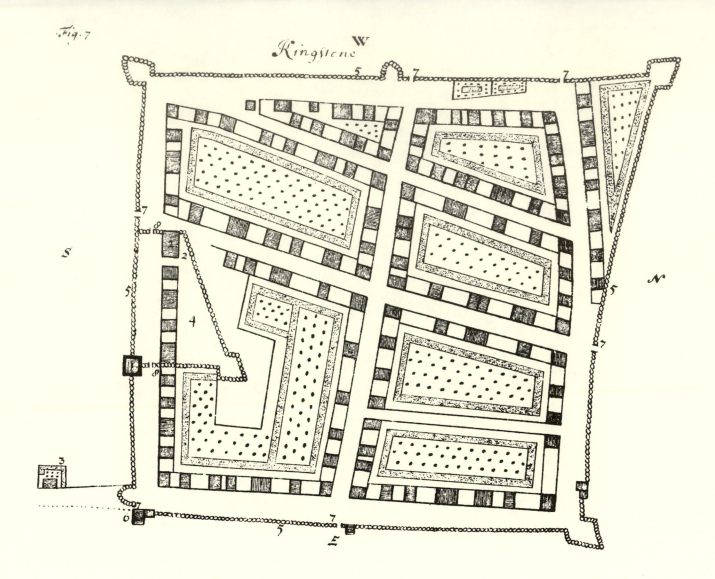

Fig. 7

Kingstone

W

S

N

E

THE EXPLANATION OF FIG. 7.

1. The blockhouse
2, 2. The church and burying place
3. The minister's house
4. The part separated and fortified
5. The stockado
6. The house where the governor is entertained
7, 7. The town gates
8, 8. The gates to the separate fortified part.

Figure 91. Plan of Kingston, New York: 1695

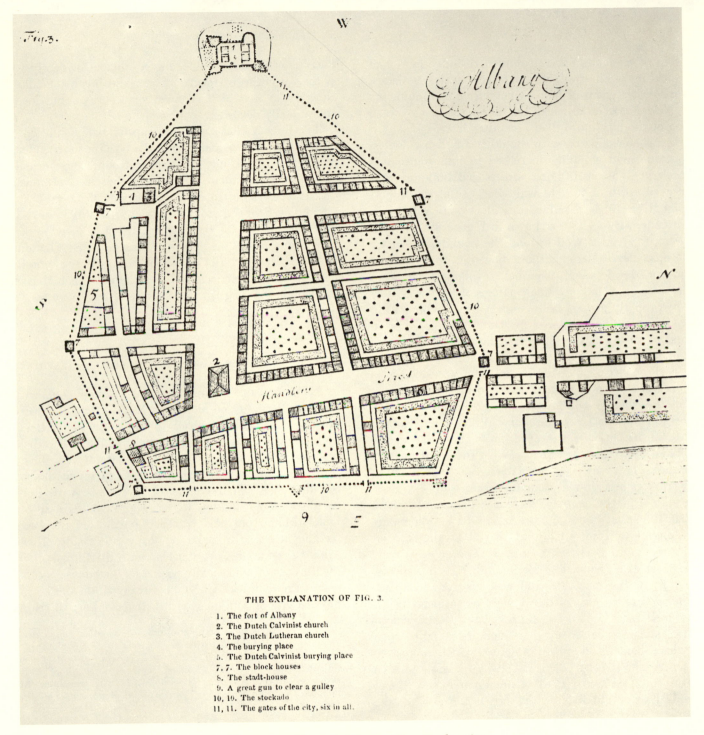

W

Albany

N

THE EXPLANATION OF FIG. 3.

1. The fort of Albany
2. The Dutch Calvinist church
3. The Dutch Lutheran church
4. The burying place
5. The Dutch Calvinist burying place
7, 7. The block houses
8. The stadt-house
9. A great gun to clear a gulley
10, 10. The stockado
11, 11. The gates of the city, six in all.

Figure 92. Plan of Albany, New York: 1695

the city ownership of all lands not yet allotted to individuals and to all land occupied by public buildings or used for streets, lanes, or alleys. This wholesale grant of land ownership to the municipal corporation of New York established the basis for a vast plan for the extension of the city more than a century later.

As New York was consolidated with the other English colonies, manufacturing, trade, and shipping increased in importance and growth was accelerated. By 1700 new streets and building sites were being surveyed north of the old wall. Because of the importance of the East River for harbor facilities, development first extended in this direction. By 1728, as shown in Figure 93, the area occupied by the city extended well beyond the boundaries set by the Dutch. The map clearly demonstrates, however, that no comprehensive plan for development was being followed. Instead, street by street, lot by lot, relatively small parcels of land were surveyed and sold by property owners following their own whims as to design. While the English had replaced the Dutch dictatorial form of municipal control with a more democratic system of local government, the old method of physical growth continued.

Perhaps the earliest large-scale subdividing was carried out as a result of the enforced move of tanners and shoemakers from the older portions of the city. In 1680 a group of them purchased a tract of land north of Maiden Lane and along William and Nassau Streets, and in 1696 the land was surveyed into rectangular streets and lots, and offered at public sale. This was not the usual method of land development, however, and elsewhere sales continued to be made one or two lots at a time as demand arose.

Toward the middle of the century, increased demand for land finally resulted in the subdivision of large tracts for building purposes. Lands belonging to Trinity Church lying along the Hudson were platted in a rectangular pattern by the city surveyor, Francis Maerschalck. He was also responsible for two other such projects. One lay to the west of Bowery Lane and was surveyed in 1763. The other was located to the east of the Bowery on property originally belonging to James DeLancey. Both of these subdivisions were rectangular, and the DeLancey plan included a large open square. These three land development schemes which helped to establish the rectangular street system in New York may be seen on Figure 94, the Ratzen Plan of 1767. Unfortunately the "Great Square" of the DeLancey subdivision did not last, for after the

· 154 ·

Revolution the land came into municipal ownership as the result of the forfeiture of former crown and loyalist lands. The square, New York's first planned open space, was subdivided and sold to obtain badly needed revenues.

The Ratzen Plan shows the approximate condition of New York immediately before and during the war for independence. With the occupation of the city by British troops, the normal commercial and land development activities in the city were suspended. Two disastrous fires destroyed large portions of New York, and the civil population dropped from 20,000 to 10,000 by 1783. It was not until the late 1780's that the expansion of New York regained the momentum of the first years of English rule. Planning of the city following the war will be described in a later chapter, and, as will be seen then, the piecemeal development that characterized both the Dutch and English periods finally gave way to a more orderly pattern of growth.

New Sweden on the Delaware

A few years after the Dutch began their colonization efforts at New Amsterdam and along the Hudson, another European power attempted to establish itself to the south in territory claimed by both the Dutch and the English. In 1638 a Swedish colony was planted on the shores of the Delaware River. The organization of this enterprise was a strange one, involving financing by both Swedish and Dutch commercial interests with backing by the Swedish crown. Oddly, it was the Peter Minuit of the famous Dutch Manhattan land transaction who led the expedition to its landing at Paradise Point on the western side of Delaware Bay. Minuit repeated his negotiations with the Indians, purchased from them a tract of land, neatly posted its boundaries as "New Sweden," and at the mouth of Christina Creek within the boundaries of the modern city of Wilmington constructed Fort Christina.[6]

[6] The best and most complete study of Swedish colonization is Amandus Johnson, *Swedish Settlements on the Delaware*, Philadelphia, 2 vols., 1911. See also Christopher Ward, *Dutch and Swedes on the Delaware, 1609-1664*, Philadelphia, 1930, and Thomas Campanius, *A Short Description of the Province of New Sweden* (Stockholm, 1702), translated by Peter S. Du Ponceau, *Memoirs of the Pennsylvania Historical Society*, Philadelphia, 1834, III.

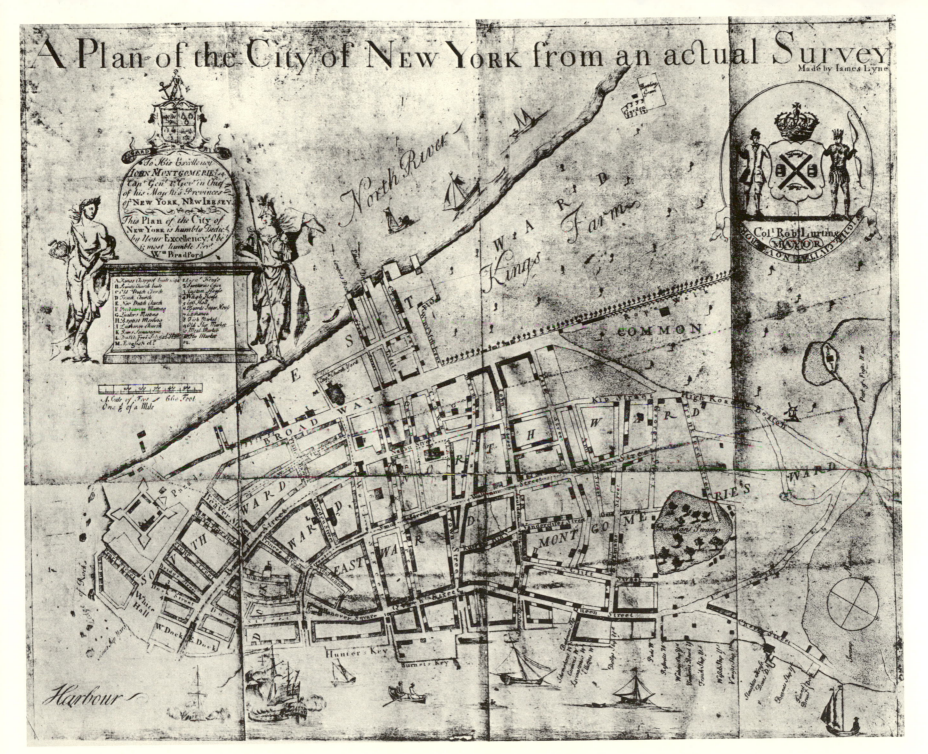

Figure 93. Plan of New York City: 1731

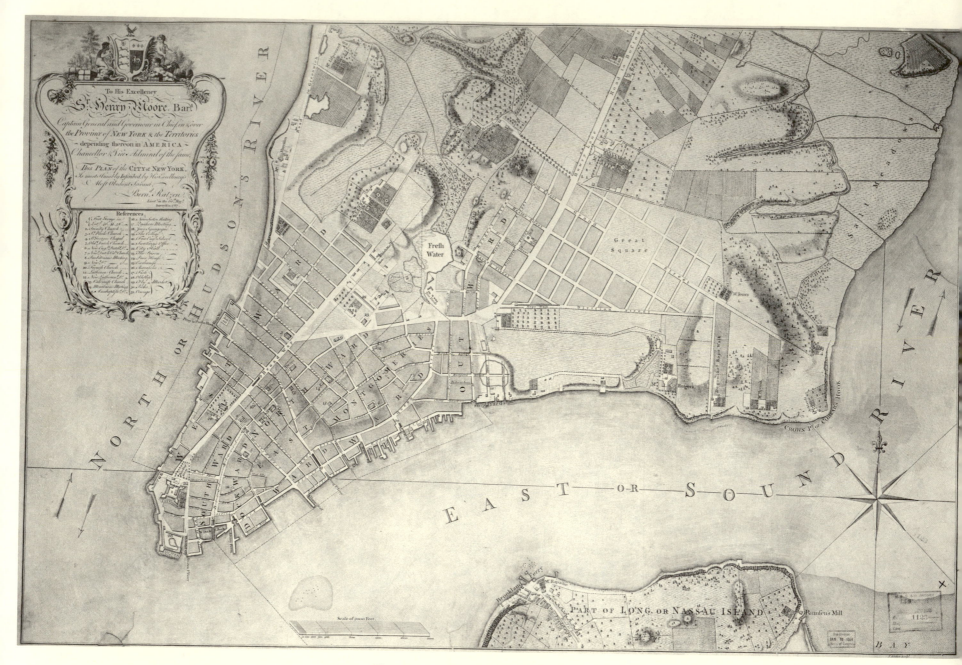

Figure 94. Plan of New York City: 1767

In the spring of 1639 and again in 1641 new arrivals at Fort Christina strengthened the little colony, and in 1642 two additional forts, called New Gothenburg and New Elfsborg, were built. Around these three fortifications little villages developed, but the total population probably did not exceed two hundred. In 1654 Queen Christina determined to expand the colony and to remove the Dutch settlers who had entered the Delaware and built Fort Casimir south of Fort Christina on the site of the present New Castle. This time a major expedition was equipped, and more than 350 colonists left Gothenburg for New Sweden. Fort Casimir was captured, and with the territory apparently secure the first real town was planned. Peter Lindstrom, a military engineer, laid out the little community near Fort Christina. The plan of this town, Christinahamm (Christina Haven), is shown in Figure 95.

Lindstrom's town was a little gridiron with three main streets and one cross street, if the map is an accurate plan of the settlement. It certainly contains nothing remarkable and is of very little interest. The settlement had only a brief existence under the Swedes. The year after its establishment the Dutch appeared with an army of 600 troops under Peter Stuyvesant and soon overwhelmed the colony. Most of the Swedish settlers remained on the Delaware under Dutch and then English rule, but Sweden's experiment in American colonization and town planning had come to an end.

Between the Delaware settlements and New York stretched the flat coastal plains of New Jersey and eastern Pennsylvania. With the removal of the Dutch as a colonial power in North America this territory now lay open to English settlement. Here was to be planned the most important city of colonial America.

William Penn and the Planning of Philadelphia

"That so soon as it pleaseth God . . . a certain quantity of land or ground plat shall be laid out for a large town or city . . . and every purchaser and adventurer shall, by lot, have so much land therein as will answer to the proportion which he hath bought or taken up upon rent."[7]

With these words, published in July 1681, William Penn announced the beginning of English settlement in Pennsylvania, per-

[7] "Certain Conditions and Concessions Agreed upon by William Penn . . . 1681," Samuel Hazard, *Annals of Pennsylvania*, Philadelphia, 1850, p. 516.

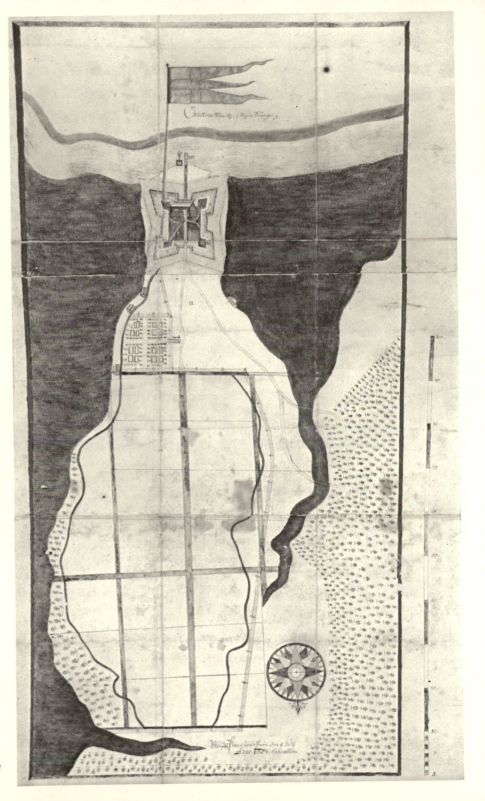

Figure 95. Fort Christina and Christinahamm, Delaware: 1654

haps the most successful English colonization scheme in the New World. Penn's "holy experiment," an achievement in political and religious toleration, also became an experiment in urban planning. In no other colony, with the possible exception of Georgia, did the related problems of city and regional planning receive such attention. Ample evidence exists that Penn—himself London bred and a visitor to the urban centers of Europe—was as fascinated by the prospect of founding a great city as he was concerned with establishing religious freedom for his fellow Quakers.

Philadelphia was Penn's great accomplishment in city building, but his experience in the planning of towns and the development of land not only began with an earlier effort but extended to later attempts to duplicate the success of his capital city. For twenty-five years William Penn exercised his sense of practical idealism in the planning of cities. The full story of these activities is one of the most absorbing episodes in the history of American city planning.

In 1674 Lord John Berkeley sold his interest in the Province of West Jersey to John Fenwick and Edward Byllynge. The new owners disagreed over their land interests, and Penn was asked to arbitrate the difference. He awarded Byllynge nine-tenths of the province, and, when Byllynge was found to be heavily in debt, Penn and two creditors were appointed trustees of his West Jersey estate with full power to manage its affairs for the benefit of the creditors. Virtually all persons concerned were fellow Quakers, and Penn seized on this opportunity to promote the establishment of settlements in West Jersey where they might be free of religious persecution.

Penn drew up a charter of government, and instructions were prepared governing the distribution of land. In 1677 two groups of Quakers, one from London and the other from Yorkshire, arrived in Jersey. Land was purchased from the Indians, and the town of Burlington was laid out by Richard Noble, whose name also appears on some early Philadelphia land surveys. The plan of Burlington was simple, with the High Street dividing the separate holdings of the two groups of settlers. Figure 96 shows the town more than a hundred years after the first settlement, but the original plan had scarcely been modified.[8]

[8] For early descriptions of the development of Burlington see George DeCou, Burlington: *A Provincial Capital*, Philadelphia, 1945; and Samuel

Five years later the adjoining Province of East Jersey was put up for auction. Penn and eleven associates purchased proprietary rights to this land as an additional location for Quaker-sponsored settlements. They lost no time in seeking to attract new settlers. In 1682 the proprietors published "A Brief Account of the Province of East-Jersey . . ." describing the location and condition of the province. This broadside concluded with a statement of their immediate intentions:

"Our purpose is, if the lord permit, with all convenient expedition, to erect and build one principal town; which by reason of situation must in all probability be the most considerable for merchandize, trade and fishery in those parts; it is designed to be placed upon a neck or point of rich land, called Ambo point, lying on Rariton River, and pointing to Sand-Hook bay, and near adjacent to the place where ships in that great harbour commonly ride at anchor; a scheme of which is already drawn. . . .

"And all such persons who desire to be concerned, may repair to Thomas Rudyard or Benjamin Clark, in George-Yard, in Lombard-street; where they may view the constitutions, the scheme of the intended town, the map of the country, and treat on terms of purpose."[9]

The settlement at Ambo point, later given its present name of Perth-Amboy, followed soon after. According to another statement of the proprietors, the town was ". . . set out into streets according to rules of art," and there were reserved ". . . four acres for a market place, town-house, &c. and three acres for publick wharfage."[10] Perth-Amboy, like Burlington, became the provincial capital and steadily increased in population.

This experience in colonization guided Penn when he set about the settlement of his own colony. Although he retained an interest in the Jersey colonies, his new venture in Pennsylvania was soon to require all his energy and attention.

Smith, *The History of the Colony of Nova-Caesaria or New Jersey*, Burlington, 1765, 2nd ed., Trenton, 1877.

[9] Smith, *History*, Appendix III, 542-43.

[10] "Proposals by the Proprietors of East-Jersey . . . for the Building of a Town on Ambo Point . . . ," Smith, *History*, 544. For a description of the planning of Perth Amboy see the Introductory essay by George J. Miller in Board of Proprietors of the Eastern Division of New Jersey, *The Minutes of the Board . . . from 1685 to 1705*, Perth Amboy, 1949, pp. 35-38. The plan itself was unremarkable: a grid of streets, with a single central square.

When Admiral Penn had died in 1670 he had left to his son a substantial estate, including a sizeable but uncertain asset of £16,000 in the form of a debt owed by Charles II. Penn undoubtedly saw in this royal obligation an opportunity to further his colonization schemes. The necessary petitions were filed. Persons influential with the king were approached. The Duke of York, under whom the Admiral had served with distinction in the Dutch wars, was sympathetic. Finally, in March 1681, Charles put his signature to a charter which established Penn as governor and proprietor of Pennsylvania. In return the troublesome debt was canceled.

Within four months Penn produced his general scheme of colonization. In July he published the conditions of settlement, to be binding on him and those who accepted his terms. The first paragraph of that document containing the statement of intention to found a great city has already been quoted. Following this appeared the details of settlement and the method of land distribution. Each purchaser of a tract in the colony was to receive city lots proportionate to the extent of his holdings. As the conditions stated: ". . . the proportion of lands that shall be laid out in the first great town or city, for every purchaser, shall be after the proportion of ten acres for every five hundred acres purchased, if the place will allow it."[11]

Penn then selected three commissioners to accompany the first group of settlers. To them he handed a long and detailed memorandum of instructions dealing with the establishment of his proposed city. These instructions, dated September 30, 1681, are specific, practical and to the point—the work of a man to whom town planning was no longer a novelty.

The instructions first considered the selection of a suitable site and the amount of land which would be required:

". . . let the rivers and creeks be sounded on my side of Delaware River, . . . and be sure to make your choice where it is most navigable, high, dry, and healthy; that is, where most ships may best ride, of deepest draught of water, if possible to load or unload at the bank or key side, without boating or lightening of it. It would do well if the river coming into that creek be navigable, at least for boats, up into the country, and that situation be high,

at least dry and sound, and not swampy, which is best known by digging up two or three earths, and seeing the bottom.

"Such a place being found out, for navigation, healthy situation, and good soil for provision, lay out ten thousand acres contiguous to it in the best manner you can, as the bounds and extent of the liberties of the said town."[12]

Penn, in trying to foresee every contingency, suggested what could be done if the best site for the town was already occupied by earlier settlers:

". . . you must use your utmost skill to persuade them to part with so much as will be necessary, that so necessary and good a design be not spoiled . . . urging my regard to them if they will not break this great and good contrivance, and in my name promise them what gratuity or privilege you think fit, as having a new grant at their old rent; nay, half their quit rent abated, yea, make them as free as purchasers, rather than disappoint my mind in this township. . . ."[13]

Once the site was selected and made available, the commissioners were to proceed with the planning of the city. Penn was quite definite in specifying a regular street pattern and uniform spacing of buildings:

"Be sure to settle the figure of the town so as that the streets hereafter may be uniform down to the water from the country bounds; let the place for the storehouse be on the middle of the key, which will yet serve for market and statehouses too. This may be ordered when I come, only let the houses built be in a line, or upon a line, as much as may be. . . .

"Let every house be placed, if the person pleases, in the middle of its plat, as to the breadth way of it, that so there may be ground on each side for gardens or orchards, or fields, that it may be a green country town, which will never be burnt, and always be wholesome."[14]

Penn had been a resident of London during the outbreak of the plague in 1665, and he had seen the terrible results of the Great

[11] Hazard, *Annals*, p. 517.

[12] "Instructions Given by me, William Penn . . . to . . . my Commissioners for the Settling of the . . . Colony . . . ," Hazard, *Annals*, pp. 527-30.
[13] *ibid.*
[14] *ibid.*

Fire in the following year. He was evidently determined that neither catastrophe would be duplicated in his new city.

The commissioners left for the new colony in the autumn of 1681. It was not until the following year that a surveyor general was selected, when Penn appointed Captain Thomas Holme. Holme's commission is dated April 18, 1682, and he did not arrive in Pennsylvania until June. It seems likely that Holme did not actually participate in selecting the city's site since a letter dated July 24, from one of the prospective Quaker settlers in London mentions, "I have 100 acres where our capital city is to be, upon the river near Schuylkill. . . ."

By the summer of 1682, then, the location of Philadelphia had been determined, Holme had arrived and was preparing to lay out the city, and Penn himself was making ready for his first visit to the colony. The tedious preliminaries were at last complete; the stage was set for the planning of the city.

Between June and September, 1682, Holme and the commissioners were busy planning Philadelphia. The town they laid out encompassed only a part of what is always referred to as the original plan. No plat of their work survives, and we can only infer that it encompassed the area between the Delaware River and a point roughly midway to the Schuylkill. A drawing for lots in this portion of the town was held on September 9, and a list of lot owners was certified by Holme and the commissioners. Whether or not the plan as then established provided for the public squares which appear on the first published map of the city cannot be determined.

Penn arrived in the colony in October of that year. Whatever other changes he may have made in the city's plan, his major contribution was to extend the bounds of the city westward to the Schuylkill River. The evidence of this is fragmentary but conclusive. Penn, in a published report of his activities appearing in 1685, wrote: "Tho this Town seemed at first contrived for the Purchasers of the first hundred shares . . . I added that half of the Town, which lies on the Skulkill, that we might have Room for present and after Commers . . . ,"[15] and Holme, in his description of the city which appeared two years earlier observed: "The City

is so ordered now, by the Governour's Care and Prudence, that it hath a Front to each River, one half at Delaware, the other at Skulkill. . . ."[16]

By the beginning of 1683, then, the basic plan had been prepared, lots surveyed and conveyed to their owners, a whole new portion of the town added, and the first buildings erected. In an effort to attract new settlers, a plan and description of the city was prepared by Holme and published in London later that year. Figure 97, "A Portraiture of the City of Philadelphia," shows the plan of the city, which Holme described in these words:

"The City of Philadelphia, now extends in Length, from River to River, two Miles, and in Breadth near a Mile. . . .

"The Model of the City appears by a small Draught now made, and may hereafter, when time permits, be augmented; and because there is not room to express the Purchasers Names in the Draught, I have therefore drawn Directions of Reference, by way of Numbers, whereby may be known each mans Lot and Place in the City. . . .

"The City, (as the Model shews) consists of a large Front-street to each River, and a High-street (near the middle) from Front (or River) to Front, of one hundred Foot broad, and a Broad-street in the middle of the City, from side to side, of the like breadth. In the Center of the City is a Square of ten Acres; at each Angle are to be Houses for Publick Affairs, as a Meeting-House, Assembly or State-House, Market-House, School-House, and several other Buildings for Publick Concerns. There are also in each Quarter of the City a Square of eight Acres, to be for the like Uses, as the Moore-fields in London; and eight Streets (besides the High-street), that run from Front to Front, and twenty Streets, (besides the Broad-street) that run cross the City, from side to side; all these Streets are of Fifty Foot breadth."[17]

What were the origins of the plan of Philadelphia as laid out by Penn and Holme? What were the models from which its regular streets and neatly balanced open spaces were drawn? No satisfactory answers are possible, but there are remarkable similarities between the Philadelphia pattern and earlier city planning concepts

[15] William Penn, *A Further Account of the Province of Pennsylvania* (London, 1685), in Albert C. Myers, *Narratives of Early Pennsylvania, West New Jersey and Delaware, 1630-1707*, New York, 1912, pp. 261-73.

[16] *A Short Advertisement upon the Situation and Extent of the City of Philadelphia and the Ensuing Plat-form thereof, by the Surveyor General* (London, 1683), in Myers, *Narratives*, pp. 242-44.

[17] *ibid.*

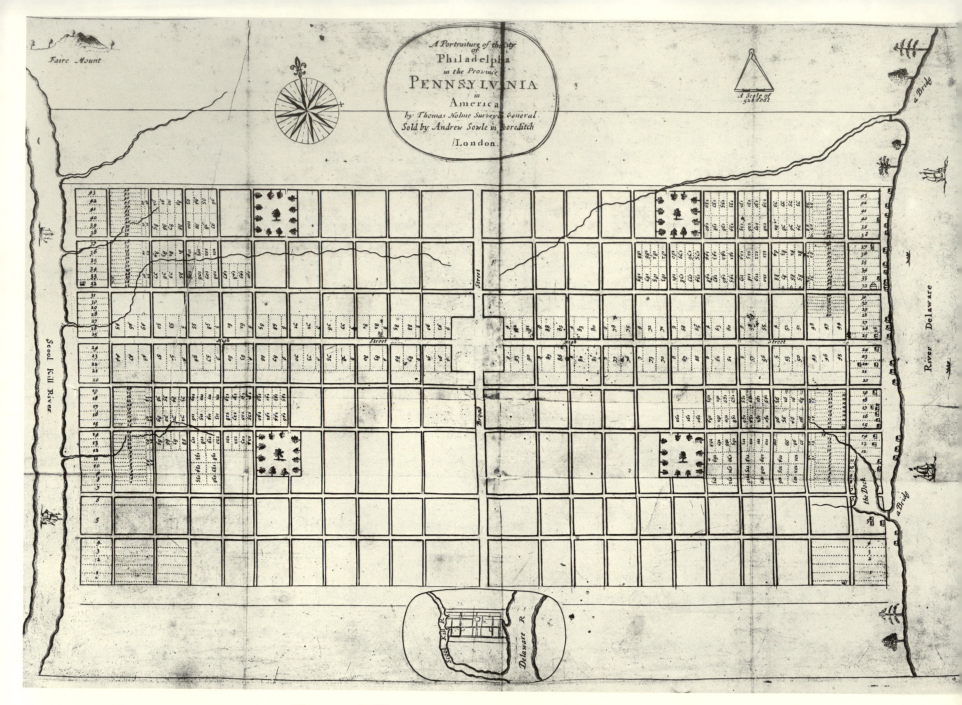

Figure 97. William Penn's Plan for Philadelphia, Pennsylvania: 1682

and achievements. The application of the gridiron pattern for colonial towns was well established. Spanish towns consistently followed this type of plan, and the first plans of Champlain were also little grids. The best known of the English colonial rectangular plans was that of New Haven, and Penn must have drawn also on his earlier associations with the settlements at Burlington and Amboy. In his youth Penn spent some time in Ireland managing his father's estates near Cork, and it is possible he visited the Londonderry plantations of northern Ireland where several gridiron towns had been laid out. More likely, he may have examined in London the plans and records of this colonization program, as Oglethorpe was to do later before beginning his own venture in land development.

Other sources of city planning ideas may have influenced Penn. In 1665 he was at Lincoln's Inn, the result of his father's desire for him to learn a profession. Adjoining were Lincoln's Inn Fields, where extensive building operations had created a regular residential square, flanked by the uniform façades of speculative houses. Here was a daily reminder for young Penn of an emerging element in the design of towns. It may also be significant that Lincoln's Inn Fields, unlike the other new squares of Covent Garden, Leicester Square, and Bloomsbury, was not reserved for the exclusive use of its aristocratic residents. Holme referred to the four smaller squares of Philadelphia by comparing their intended use to that of London's Moorfields, another of that city's few public open spaces. The idea of residential squares was thus accepted, but with the open area to be available for all of the city's residents and not merely those whose property fronted on the square.

But perhaps most influential in furnishing the ideas on which the plan of Philadelphia was based was that greatest of all seventeenth-century city planning events—the reconstruction of London after the Great Fire in 1666. There is no need here to review the history of that catastrophe or the series of plans submitted for the rebuilding of the city. What should be noted is simply this: that the gridiron concept was used in a majority of the known reconstruction plans—those by Hooke, Knight, and Newcourt—and grid planning constituted an important element in the better known schemes of John Evelyn and Christopher Wren. And in all of the plans except Knight's, the symmetrical distribution of open spaces and sites for public buildings was an important element.

The case for the influence of the London plans on the plan of Philadelphia does not rest solely on these general comparisons. The most persuasive evidence is the close parallel in so many details between the city of Penn and Holme and the new London proposed by Richard Newcourt. As shown in Figure 98, Newcourt's plan would have embraced a rectangular area about one by one and a half miles, including a substantial portion of London not damaged by fire. Blocks were uniform in size, 855 by 570 feet—somewhat larger than Philadelphia blocks, most of which were between approximately 425 by 675 feet and 425 by 500 feet. All streets were to be 80 feet wide, compared to Philadelphia's 50 and 100 feet. The most striking similarity is, of course, the pattern and proportions of the five squares, a feature common to both plans. Viewed broadly, the resemblance is unmistakable.[18]

Was Newcourt's plan of London known to Penn or to Holme? We shall probably never be satisfied on this point, but the possibility remains. Newcourt's plan and the accompanying description may have been published, although only the manuscript has survived. In any event, Penn could hardly have escaped seeing or hearing of the various schemes for reconstruction, and Newcourt's may have been among those which came to his attention. It is possible too that Holme, who evidently had experience as a surveyor or military engineer, may have known Newcourt, the surveyor and cartographer of the most accurate map of London prior to the fire.

Although in his published conditions for the settlement of the colony Penn implied that 2 percent of all purchasers' lands would be ". . . laid out in the first great town or city," his instructions to the commissioners were somewhat different. He had directed them to select a town site and then to ". . . lay out ten thousand acres contiguous to it in the best manner you can, as the bounds and extent of the liberties of the said town." Whatever may have been Penn's intention or the understanding of land purchasers, only 1,280 acres were set aside for the city proper. This was insufficient land for the allotment of 2 percent of the area already subscribed

[18] Newcourt's plans for London are reviewed in T. F. Reddaway, "The Rebuilding of London After the Great Fire: A Rediscovered Plan," *The Town Planning Review*, XVIII (1939), 155-61. An alternate plan, similar to the one reproduced here, provided for a reduced number of larger blocks.

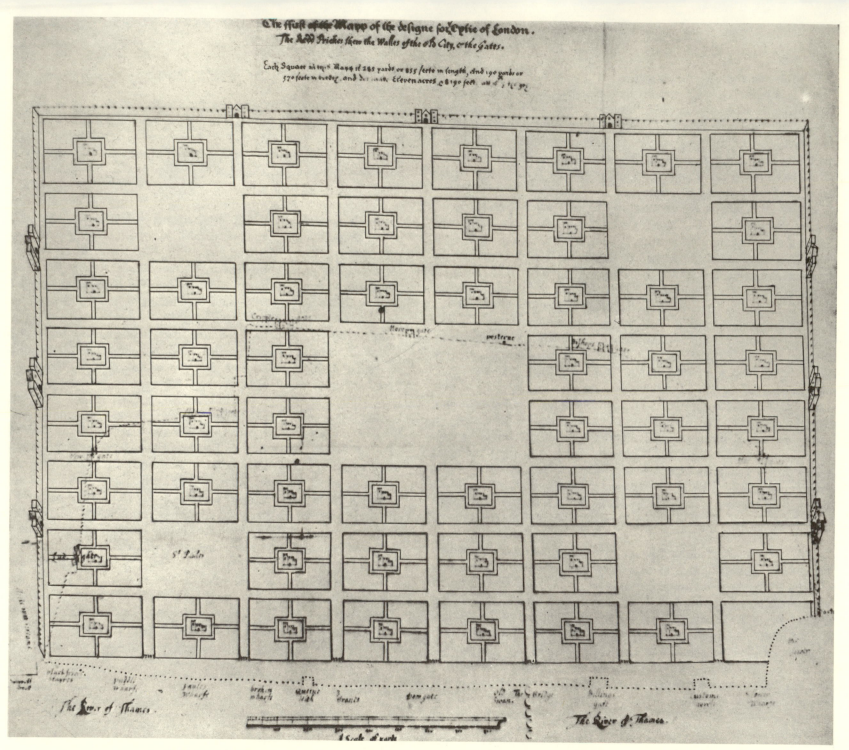

Figure 98. Richard Newcourt's Plan for London: 1666

to by English purchasers. According to one source a tract of six to seven thousand acres would have been needed for this purpose.

Penn's solution was to survey a tract of approximately ten thousand acres immediately adjacent to and north of the city as so-called "liberty lands." The dubious legality of this procedure was noted by an annotator of the laws of Pennsylvania who, in 1810, commented: "Not a single memorial can be found of this plan, nor any record of the alteration, or any written evidence of the consent of the inhabitants to the new arrangement; but a regular series of uniform facts, upon the books of the Land Office establish it beyond a doubt."[19] It might be added that there is no record of any complaints about this questionable breach of faith. Perhaps it was understood that liberty lands were considered part of the city proper. Since apparently the area of the city lots was not counted as part of the 2 percent, purchasers may have felt that they, and not Penn, had benefited.

At least part of the liberty lands were surveyed by August 1683, since Penn, writing then to the Free Society of Traders, a joint stock company established to promote commerce in the colony and one of the largest land purchasers, mentioned the liberty lands of the Society. It was perhaps about this time that city blocks were laid out on the western bank of the Schuylkill. This addition to the city and the location of the liberty lands, appear on Holme's "*A Mapp of ye Improved Part of Pennsilvania*," probably printed about 1687 and reproduced here as Figure 99.

The same map is also a revealing source of information on the planning of rural settlements. Penn's own description of the layout of agricultural villages follows:

"Our Townships lie square; generally the Village in the Center; the Houses either opposit, or else opposit to the middle, betwixt two houses over the way, for near neighborhood. We have another Method, that tho the Village be in the Center, yet after a different manner: Five hundred Acres are allotted for the Village, which, among ten families, comes to fifty Acres each: this lies square, and on the outside of the square stand the Houses, with their fifty Acres running back, where ends meeting make the Center of the 500 Acres as they are to the whole. Before the Doors of the Houses lies the high way, and cross it, every man's 450 Acres of Land

that makes up his Complement of 500, so that the Conveniency of Neighbourhood is made agreeable with that of the land.

"I said nothing in my last of any number of Townships, but there are at least Fifty settled before my leaving those parts, which was in the month called August, 1684."[20]

The map clearly shows two of the second type of townships to the north of the city, near the right-hand edge of the plate. Penn may have known about the similar plan for the little village of Gravesend on Long Island, planned by English settlers from Connecticut on land granted by the Dutch governor of New Netherland in 1645. According to some accounts, later settlers at Gravesend were Quakers, and Penn could well have learned of the unusual plan from them. Talon, the French Intendant at Quebec was also responsible for two or three farm village layouts of almost identical form in the 1670's, but it seems unlikely that Penn would have known of their existence.

Penn was also concerned that his colony should be served by good lines of communication. In the published conditions of settlement he promised that the planning of a road system would receive early attention and that no encroachments on public rights-of-way would be permitted.

". . . the surveyors shall consider what roads or highways will be necessary to the cities, towns, or through the lands. Great roads from city to city not to contain less than forty feet in breadth, shall be first laid out and declared to be for highways, before the dividnt of acres be laid out for the purchaser, and the like observation to be had for the streets in the towns and cities, that there may be convenient roads and streets preserved, not to be encroached upon by any planter or builder, that none may build irregularly, to the damage of another. In this custom governs."[21]

In the breadth of his outlook and his attention to detail Penn was unsurpassed as a colonial regional planner and administrator.

Construction of houses in Philadelphia began immediately after the allocation of city lots. In his letter to the Free Society of Traders in August 1683 Penn mentioned the progress that had been made in the city's development: "It is advanced within less than a Year to about four Score Houses and Cottages, such as they are, where

[19] *Laws of the Commonwealth of Pennsylvania*, printed and published by John Bloren, Philadelphia, 1810, II, 107.

[20] Penn, *A Further Account*.
[21] "Certain Conditions and Concessions," Hazard, *Annals*.

Figure 99. Plan of Philadelphia, Pennsylvania and Vicinity: ca. 1720

Merchants and Handicrafts, are following their Vocations as fast as they can, while the Country-men are close at their Farms. . . .[22] And by the time Penn left to return to England about a year later, he could report:

". . . the Town advanced to Three Hundred and fifty-seven Houses; divers of them large, well built, with good Cellars, three stories, and some with Balconies.

"There is also a fair Key of about three hundred foot square, built by Samual Carpenter, to which a ship of five hundred Tuns may lay here broadside, and others intend to follow his example. . . ."[23]

Penn also commented on the increase in land values, chiding those who were financially interested in the colony but who remained in England as absentee owners:

"The Improvement of the place is best measur'd by the advance of Value upon every man's Lot. I will venture to say that the worst Lot in the Town, without any Improvement upon it, is worth four times more than it was when it was lay'd out, and the best forty. And though it seems unequal that the Absent should be thus benefited by the Improvements of those that are upon the place, especially when they have serv'd no Office, run no hazard, nor as yet defray'd any Publick charge, yet this advantage does certainly redound to them, and whoever they are they are great Debtors to the Country. . . ."[24]

By the end of the summer of 1685 the town was bustling with activity. In a letter to Penn, Robert Turner described the accelerated pace of construction:

"Now as to the Town of Philadelphia it goeth on in Planting and Building to admiration, both in the front and backward, and there are about 600 Houses in 3 years time. . . . Lots are much desir'd in the Town, great buying one of another. We are now laying the foundation of a large plain Brick house, for a Meeting House. . . . A large Meeting House . . . also going up, on the front of the River, for an evening Meeting the work going on apace. . . ."[25]

The growth of Philadelphia continued at the same rapid rate for many years. Gabriel Thomas, a Welsh Quaker who had arrived with the first band of settlers in 1681, wrote an account of the city in 1698:

". . . the Industrious (nay Indefatigable) Inhabitants have built a Noble and Beautiful City, and called it Philadelphia, which contains above two thousand Houses, all Inhabited; and most of them Stately, and of Brick, generally three Stories high, after the Mode in London, and as many as several Families in each. . . .

"Here is lately built a Noble Town-House or Guild-Hall, also a Handsom Market-House, and a convenient Prison. . . ."[26]

But Thomas also records the beginning of a practice that was to create many later problems. He describes the cutting up of Holme's generous city blocks by additional streets, most of which were extremely narrow. Thus began a tradition of overcrowding that was to turn much of Penn's "green country town" into a city of tightly packed row houses and alley dwellings.

These new streets, and others added later, can be seen in Figure 100, a map of the city in 1762 prepared by Nicholas Scull, surveyor general. One major addition, the street paralleling Front Street between it and the Delaware River, is explained in an account of the colony written in 1755 by Thomas Pownall, who had been governor of Massachusetts and lieutenant governor of New Jersey:

"Another idea in the plan of this town was, that Front-street, next the Delaware, should have no houses immediately on the bank, but a parapet: the banks are pretty high, and had a large beach at the foot of them. After the first settlers had bought these lots on Front-street, it was found more convenient for the merchants and traders to build their warehouses, and even dwelling-houses, on the beach below, which they wharfed out. This part of the soil was not sold; several took long leases; and this became

[22] "A Letter from William Penn . . . to the Committee of the Free Society of Traders . . . ," Myers, *Narratives*, pp. 239-42.
[23] Penn, *A Further Account*.
[24] *ibid*.

[25] Turner's letter was printed with Penn's *A Further Account*.
[26] Gabriel Thomas, *An Historical and Geographical Account of Pennsilvania and of West New-Jersey* (1698), in Myers, *Narratives*, pp. 317-31.

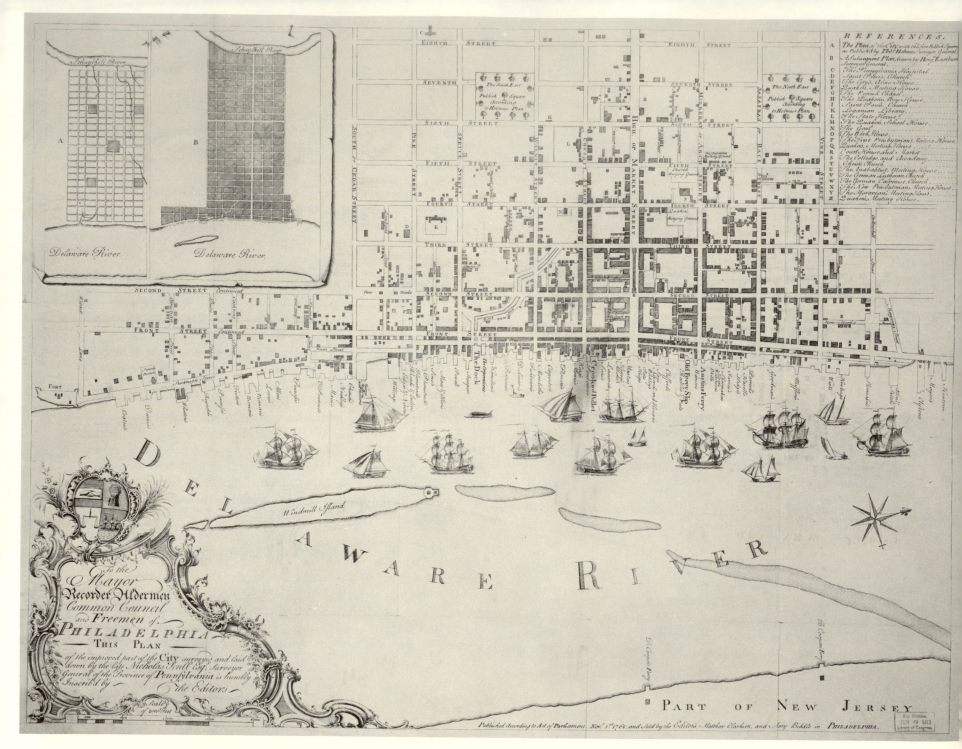

Figure 100. Plan of Philadelphia, Pennsylvania: 1762

a street of the dwelling-houses, &c. of all the principal merchants and rich men of business, and was called Water-street. . . ."[27]

Pownall also stated that the population of the city in 1755 had reached 20,000. As can be seen from the map, the built-up portion of the city was concentrated along the Delaware and had spread north and south along the river bank beyond the original boundaries.

More important alterations were made to the city plan as originally laid out by Holme and Penn. The insert maps of the city in the corner of Scull's map provide the evidence of this. These changes are shown more clearly on Folie's detailed map of the entire city published in 1794, reproduced in Figure 101. Broad Street, the main north-south street, was moved two blocks to the west of the location indicated on Holme's plat; the street pattern along the Schuylkill River was rearranged; and the public squares are nowhere to be seen. What appears to be the south-eastern square on the Folie map is identified as a "Potters field grave yard"! When these changes were made and under whose direction remains a mystery.

Nicholas Scull entertained no doubts at all that his predecessor, Benjamin Eastburn, surveyor general from 1733 to 1741, was the guilty party. Scull identified the insert plans in the corner of his city map as "The Plan of the City with the Five Public Squares as published by Thomas Holmes, Surveyor General" and "A Subsequent Plan, Drawn by Benjamin Eastburn, Surveyor General."

John Reed, who in 1774 published a detailed property map of the Philadelphia area, agreed with Scull and backed up his charges in a long report entitled "An Explanation of the Map of the City and Liberties of Philadelphia." Reed, in his accusation of Eastburn, referred to marked portions of an enlarged plan of the city appearing as an insert on his property map of the liberty lands.

This city map is shown in Figure 102 and is a key document in Reed's indictment of Eastburn, a portion of which follows:

"The streets of the city continued as they were then laid out, until Benjamin Eastburn was appointed surveyor general; when a subsequent plan was made by him, marked A. D. in the map. By what authority that plan was made, I know not; but the design in making of it is easily understood: as it not only takes 132 feet off the square on the west sides of Broad-Street, moving all the streets on Schuylkill front that distance to the eastward; but leaves out one whole square on the front of Schuylkill, from Cedar to Vine-Streets, making Front-Street D parallel with the other streets, at the distance of 528 feet on High-Street; (east of the real Front-Street) as you may see laid down in the plan: whereby the proprietors endeavoring to take back (for their own use) all the land lying between the street D and Schuylkill, then laying out the first purchasers lots on the east side of that street D which they call Front-Street, and observing the numbers regular as they are marked down in Thomas Holme's plan; this, of course, pushes the lots so far to the eastward, that they fall on the publick squares. So that the public is not only deprived of the front on Schuylkill, but likewise those squares. . . ."[28]

But Eastburn is not without defenders. Holme's biographer maintains that the change in the location of the central square and the streets to the west was made as early as 1684. A more recent historian states that it was Penn, in 1683, who ordered the change so that Broad Street would lie along a slight ridge, the highest ground between the two rivers. Neither man mentions the abandonment of the public squares.[29]

The theory that Holme or Penn changed the original plan within a matter of months after its preparation fails to explain a number of conflicting facts. How, for example, could Penn write in the pamphlet accompanying Holme's 1683 plan, "Philadelphia . . . is at last laid out to the great content of those here . . . ." if he

[27] "Governor Thomas Pownall's Journal" appeared in *The Remembrancer, or Impartial Repository of Public Events for the Year 1777*, London, 1778. The portion quoted is from an extract of his description of Pennsylvania in 1754 and 1755 in Historical Society of Pennsylvania, *The Pennsylvania Magazine of History and Biography*, XVIII (1894), 211-12. Regulations governing the building of houses and warehouses on this land were established by Penn's commissioners in 1690. They can be found in *A Digest of the Acts of Assembly Relating to the City of Philadelphia . . . and of the Ordinances of the Said City . . . .* Philadelphia, 1865, pp. 713-14.

[28] Reed's *Explanation* is printed in full in *Pennsylvania Archives*, 3rd ser., III (1894), 295-401.

[29] See Oliver Hough, "Captain Thomas Holme, Surveyor-General of Pennsylvania and Provincial Councillor," *The Pennsylvania Magazine of History and Biography*, XIX (1895), 413-27, and XX (1896), 128-31, 248-56; and William E. Lingelbach, "William Penn and City Planning," *Pennsylvania Magazine*, LXVIII (1944), 398-418.

Figure 101. Plan of Philadelphia, Pennsylvania: 1794

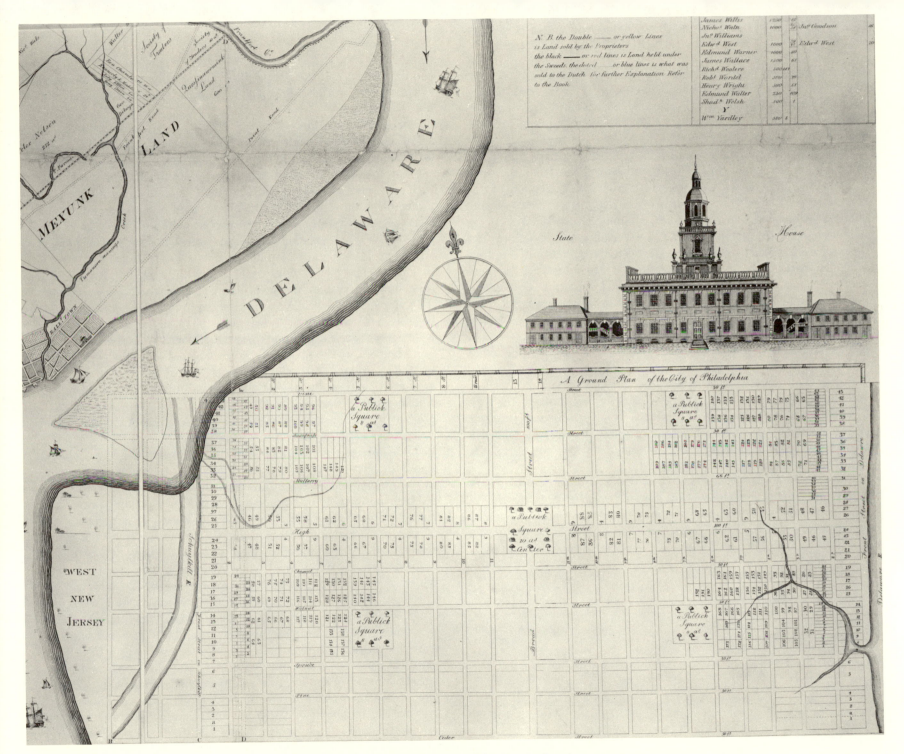

Figure 102. Plan of Philadelphia, Pennsylvania: 1774

were not satisfied with the plan and were not certifying that the engraved plat represented the official plan? Or why, even if the change was made after publication of the Holme drawing, did edition after edition of his map of the province continue to show the city on its original plan?

Whoever ordered the changes, the results were not, after all, of much consequence. The shifting of Broad Street to the west and the modification of the street system in that portion of the city hardly affected the pattern of development. The missing squares reappeared and exist today, although in modified form, as valuable open spaces in an overcrowded city. A series of city ordinances passed in the early part of the nineteenth century officially named the squares, prohibited their use as burying grounds or as dumps, appropriated funds for their improvement, and, as a final reassertion of Quaker respectability, even provided for a fine of two dollars for any person smoking "a segar or segars, pipe or pipes, in any of the public squares. . . ."

The city as it appeared in 1855 is shown in the fine view from the west reproduced in Figure 103. The Fairmount water works and a portion of what was soon to become Fairmount Park show at the lower left. Market Street runs directly east, cutting through the great central square which within a few years became the site of the new city hall. The other four original squares show clearly on either side of Broad Street. Numerous church towers, spires, and domes add interest to the skyline.

Penn in 1690 announced plans to lay out another city somewhere in the vicinity of the present city of Lancaster.[30] Undoubtedly the experience at Philadelphia would have materially influenced the pattern of the proposed new community. However, Penn's attempt to duplicate his earlier achievement failed to attract support,

[30] William Penn, *Some Proposals for a Second Settlement in the Province of Pennsylvania* (London, 1690), in Julius F. Sachse, "Penn's City on the Susquehanna," Lancaster County Historical Society *Papers*, II (1898) 223-37. Penn wrote: "It is now my purpose to make another settlement, upon the river of Susquehannagh. . . . There I design to lay out a plan for the building of another city, in the most convenient place for communication with the former plantation on the East. . . ." In 1701 Penn actually published the conditions of settlement for this area, including the following: "That a Chief Town shall be hereaftre laid out by ye purchassors on any place within the S. Tract in such form and maner as they shall think fitt. . . ." F. R. Diffenderffer, "Early Local History as revealed by an Old Document," Lancaster County Historical Society *Papers*, II (1897), 1-27.

and the influence of the Philadelphia plan on the subsequent course of American town planning was less direct, although of considerable importance.

Philadelphia, as the first large American city to be laid out on a grid pattern, has always been identified, usually unkindly, as the inspiration of the great era of rectangular town planning throughout the last two and a half centuries. The influence of the Holme and Penn plan is undeniable, but it was not always unfortunate. Even where the results were unhappy, part of the blame must be assessed against those who disregarded the good features of the gridiron or who extended an original settlement with mechanical regularity in disregard of topography.

The original city of Philadelphia was built on flat land, and a regular street system was not illogical. Street widths were more than ample for the traffic of the time and were almost extravagant by European standards. Moreover, the plan provided for even wider major streets, a feature often overlooked by subsequent gridiron planners. If the provision of open spaces is judged inadequate by the standards of today, that is simply an indication that standards have changed—not that the original plan was deficient. The location of four squares for "like Uses, as the Moore-fields in London" certainly anticipated modern principles of neighborhood park distribution.

The Philadelphia of Penn and Holme, while large by colonial standards, was a city in which the human figure was never dwarfed by either the plan or the buildings. All parts of the city could be reached comfortably on foot, and even the chief buildings remained almost domestic in size. They clearly intended a compact yet uncrowded settlement with a sharp distinction between the urban core and the surrounding rural region. The liberty lands to the north of the city functioned as a green belt that crisply defined the boundary between town and country.

Penn and Holme, as generous in their vision as they were, did not foresee today's sprawling metropolis that has stretched into the countryside and blurred this distinction between what is urban and what is rural. Nor did they anticipate what might have been more obvious—the early development of the city north and south along the banks of the Delaware, outside the bounds of the original plan, instead of westward toward the Schuylkill. It was unfortunate that these later extensions did not incorporate the same sense of

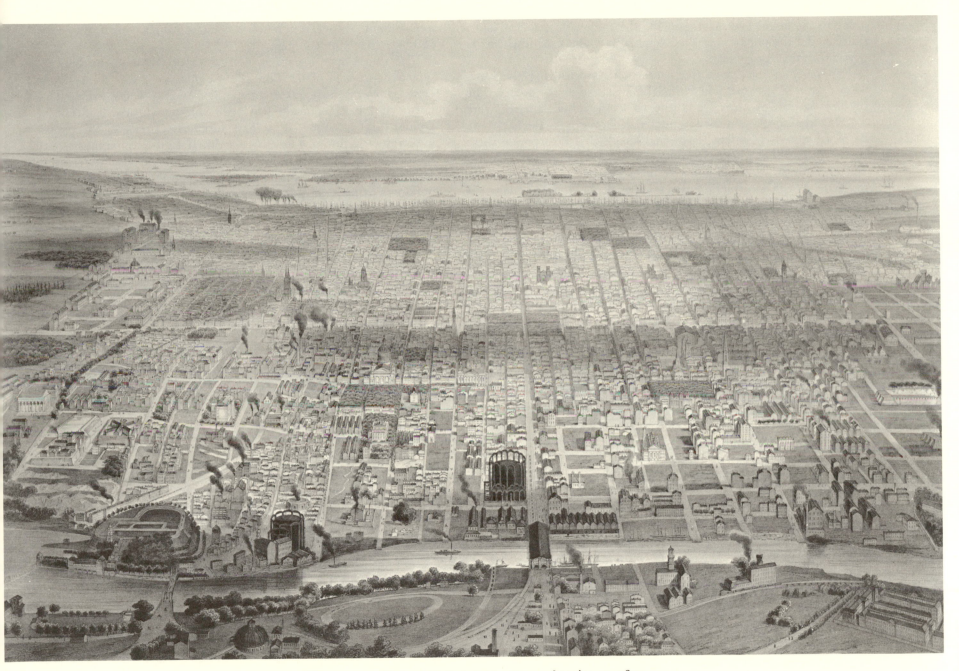

Figure 103. View of Philadelphia, Pennsylvania: ca. 1855

order in the street system or provide the same proportion of open space as did the planners of Philadelphia in what is still the central portion of that great city.

For many of the towns that were built later during the westward march of urbanization Philadelphia served as the model. The regular pattern of streets and one or more public squares were features that became widely imitated. Throughout Pennsylvania there are dozens of towns, large and small, that incorporate these elements in their plans. Reading, Allentown, Lancaster, York, and Pittsburgh were laid out with open squares or rectangles having four streets intersecting the middle of the square's sides. In Lancaster County alone at least six communities use the Philadelphia square as the central motif.

This pattern of grid and public square appears throughout the south and midwest and beyond, copied from Philadelphia or from another imitation. In at least two state capitals, Raleigh and Tallahassee, the identical distribution of five open squares may be found, and a half-dozen or so smaller and less important cities also imitated this plan. As population spread beyond the first colonies westward migrants must have had a strong psychological motivation to duplicate a familiar community element in the midst of unfamiliar surroundings.

The single open square in the center of the town became the typical expression of the Philadelphia plan as it was transplanted west. However inadequate the public square of the midwestern towns may be as a symbol of civic consciousness or a focus of architectural attention, it at least supplies a break in the almost intolerable rhythm of a relentless grid. If Philadelphia must share the blame for the ubiquitous gridiron, it should also be credited as the source of an occasional open square occupied by public buildings or used for park purposes.

Perhaps speculation on the influences of the Philadelphia plan is less important than understanding its place in the American tradition of city planning. Well before the great urban revolution of the nineteenth century there was wealth of experience in the planning of towns and a realization that some degree of municipal control over land development was not incompatible with a democratic society. New Haven, Annapolis, Williamsburg, Charleston, and Savannah are all a part of that tradition. Not the least among them is the Philadelphia of William Penn.

CHAPTER 7

Colonial Towns of Carolina and Georgia

AS the seventeenth century drew to a close, the English had established control of the American eastern seaboard from Maine to Virginia. The Dutch, who earlier had absorbed the Swedish settlements along the Delaware, were themselves removed as a colonizing and town-founding power, and their towns soon became indistinguishable from the other growing settlements originally established under English rule. By the 1660's only Pennsylvania and the southern flank of Anglo-America remained for new colonial expansion.

Both of these areas were to provide interesting and novel examples of city planning. William Penn's great city of Philadelphia has already been described. The Carolina colony, a contemporary of Pennsylvania, and Georgia, the last of the English colonies within the limits of the United States, remain to be examined. Carolina produced Charleston as its chief city—one of the half-dozen largest and most important, both commercially and intellectually, of all American colonial communities. Georgia was the location of Savannah, attractive not only because of the merit of its original plan but because, for more than a century, its growth followed the generous concept of its founder.

Charleston, New Bern, and Edenton

When Charles II was crowned in 1660 the country stretching south from Virginia to Spanish Florida remained virtually unoccupied by white settlement. Along the shores of Albemarle Sound a few hardy families resided, and a group of New England adventurers had established a temporary settlement to the south at Cape Fear. Otherwise the land lay vacant, an invitation to further colonization. As a reward to eight court favorites, Charles in 1663 established the Carolina territory as a proprietary colony and conferred on the Lords Proprietors powers similar to those previously granted Lord Baltimore in Maryland. John Locke drafted a plan of government which turned out to be an extremely cumbersome

as well as reactionary system for administration and land tenure. A hierarchy of nobility was established with such titles as "landgrave" and "cacique." Manorial privileges were specified, and a class of "leet-men" was provided for with roughly the same status as medieval serfs. In practice this governmental framework never fully functioned, and within a few years all but a few of the elaborate provisions were forgotten.

While gradual extensions of the settlements just south of Virginia took place without much guidance or planning from the proprietors, they soon attempted a coordinated settlement in South Carolina. In 1669 they sent an expedition from England with prospective settlers, and a few additional recruits joined the party when the ships put in at Barbados. In April 1670, they entered the harbor at the mouth of the Ashley and Cooper Rivers and laid out a little town on the Ashley a short distance from the coast, which they called Albemarle Point. For a few years this tiny colony managed to survive the miserably unhealthy site, but the leaders soon realized that a location on the peninsula between the two rivers held greater possibilities. About 1672 Lord Anthony Ashley-Cooper instructed Sir John Yeamans, the governor, to lay out a town on this site. An irregular grid of eight blocks surrounded by a line of fortifications was platted fronting on the Cooper River.

Figure 104 shows the plan of Charleston as originally established. Maurice Mathews, writing in 1680, described the site of the new town in these words:

"The cituation of this Town is so convenient for public Commerce that it rather seems to be the design of some skilfull Artist than the accidentall position of nature. For the tide on ebb brings the people to it from all parts branches and Creeks of Cooper and Ashley rivers. . . .

"You see that a fort built upon the point will command both Rivers. There are also convenient places for Fortresses upon the

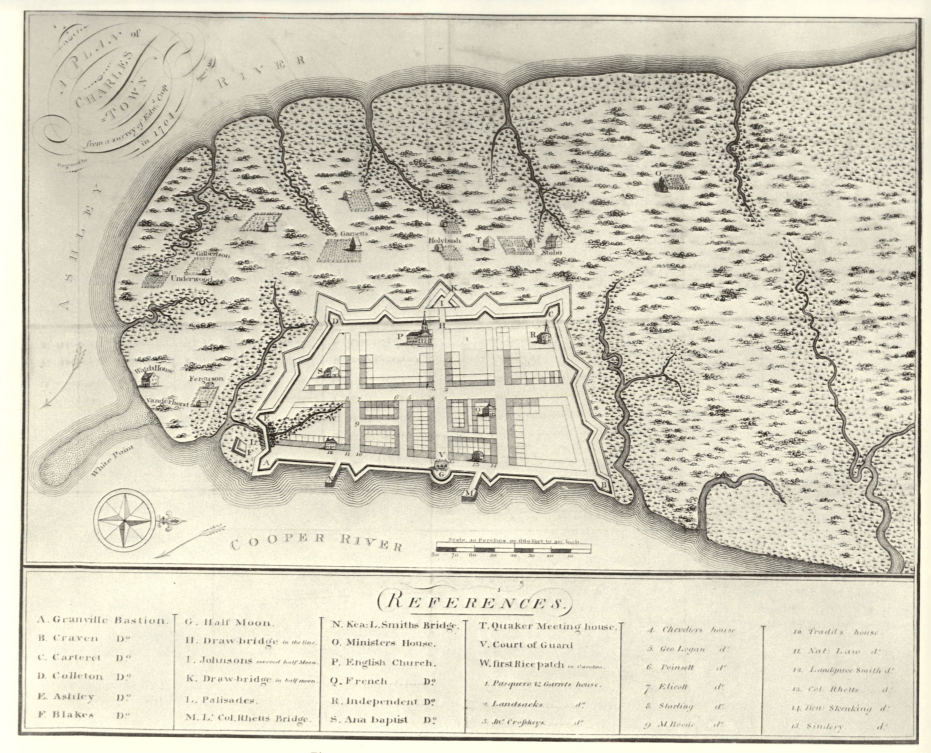

Figure 104. Plan of Charleston, South Carolina: 1704

opposit sides of both Rivers. . . . Upon Cooper Rivers side there is a clean landing the whole length of the Town and also a most plesant prospect out to the Sea. . . ."[1]

Then, turning to the details of the settlement, Mathews continued his account:

"The Town is run out into four large streets. The Court house which we are now building is to be erected in the midle of it, in a Square of two ackers of land upon which the four great streets of 60 foot wide doe center, and to the water side there is laid out 60 foot for a publick wharfe as also for other conveniences as a Church yard, Artillery ground, etc., and without there is care taken that the front lines be preserved whereby wee shall avoid the undecent and incommodious irregularities which other Inglish Collonies are fallen unto for want of ane early care in laying out the Townes."[2]

Mathews' description apparently was of the so-called "Grand Modell" for the city prepared at about the time Locke and the proprietors devised the elaborate scheme of government for the colony. The plan shown in Figure 104, however, represents only a portion of this more generous design, and until 1717 only this part of the town had been completed. By that year Charleston had grown to some 1,500 persons, the hostile Indians had been subdued, and expansion of the little stockaded settlement appeared both necessary and feasible. A new survey was made, the original street pattern was extended following the "Grand Modell," and a new line of fortifications was constructed across the neck of land between the two rivers. Figure 105, published in 1739, shows these and later additions.

The plan is simple enough: a gridiron design with an open square at the center where the two principal streets intersect. There is nothing particularly noteworthy about the scheme; indeed, when compared to New Haven or Philadelphia, the Charleston plan comes off distinctly second best. The Lords Proprietors were never known for particularly lavish expenditures on behalf of the well-being of the colony, and one is forced to conclude that they carried over this niggardly attitude when they decided on the

plan of their capital city. In fact, they might well have copied the plan of Londonderry, doubled the scale, added an extra tier of blocks all around, and laid it off on their delta site in the Carolinas.

The square and the harbor promenades are the city's most interesting features. However, so little attention was given over the years to preserving the square as an open plaza that one corner was occupied by the market as early as 1739, a church was constructed in another corner in 1761, and in 1780 and 1788 the remaining two corners furnished the sites for an arsenal and the courthouse.[3] The park and promenade along the Ashley River belong to a later era and appear in Figure 106, which shows the city from the south looking north on Meeting Street in the middle of the last century. It is this Charleston with its handsome buildings erected after the fire in 1740 that is rightly so highly regarded and widely admired.

While other settlements in the Carolinas never rivaled Charleston's size or prosperity, two North Carolina towns deserve at least passing mention. The first of these was New Bern, after Bath, which was founded in 1705, the second oldest town of the state. A Swiss nobleman, the Baron Christopher von Graffenried, sponsored the first settlement on the site in 1710, aided by a grant from the English crown to assist in the transportation of the Swiss and refugee Palatines who made up the original settling group. In September 1710, Graffenried, with the help of John Lawson platted the town on a site at the juncture of the Trent and Neuse Rivers. The following account of the planning of the town comes from Graffenried's own pen:

"Since in America they do not like to live crowded, in order to enjoy a purer air, I accordingly ordered the streets to be very broad and the houses well separated one from the other. I marked three acres of land for each family, for house, barn, garden, orchard, hemp field, poultry yard and other purposes. I divided the village like a cross and in the middle I intended the church. One of the principle streets extended from the bank of the river Neuse straight on into the forest and the other principle street

[1] "A Contemporary View of Carolina in 1680," *The South Carolina Historical Magazine*, LV (1954), 153-54.
[2] *ibid.*, 154.

[3] Sketches showing the building on the square as well as a critical analysis of Charleston's plan and architecture may be found in Frederick R. Stevenson and Carl Feiss, "Charleston and Savannah," *Journal of the Society of Architectural Historians*, X (December 1951), 3-9.

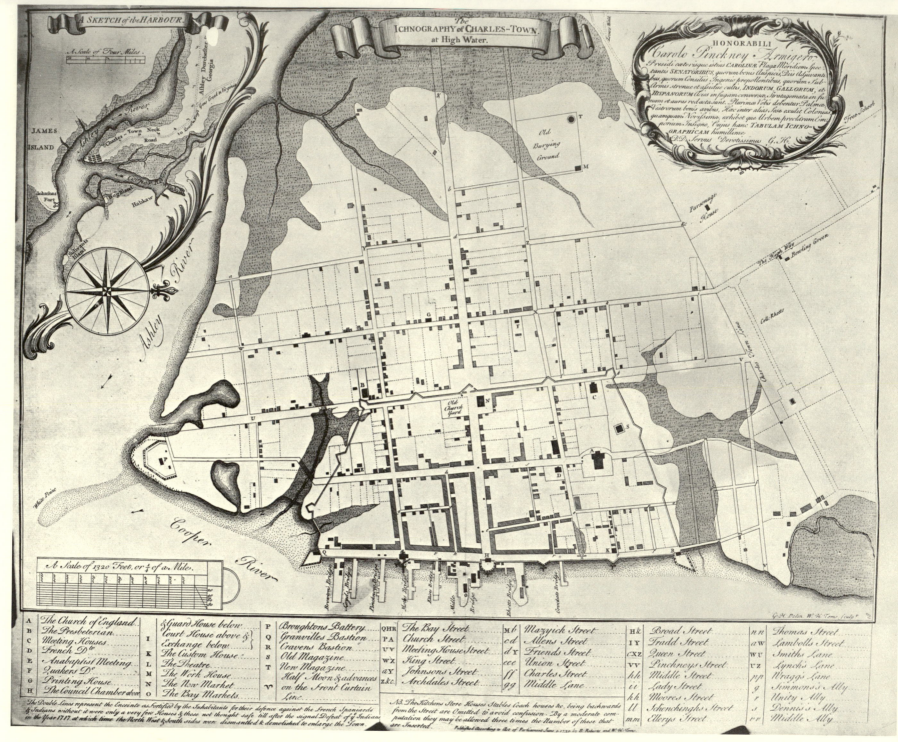

Figure 105. Plan of Charleston, South Carolina: 1739

Figure 106. View of Charleston, South Carolina: 1850

crossed it, running from the Trent River clear to the Neuse River. After that we planted stakes to mark the houses and to make the first two principal streets along and on the banks of the two rivers, mine being situated at the point."[4]

Within a few months the infant settlement was all but obliterated by the Tuscarora Indian uprising in 1711. Many of the settlers, disillusioned by this event and other unexpected hardships of frontier life, left to return to Europe. Graffenried himself, after attempting unsuccessfully to find a site for a second settlement in Virginia, returned to Carolina for a short time and then departed for his native Bern.

Sometime after the destruction of New Bern, possibly as early as 1712 but more probably in 1723, a new plan was apparently established for the town. A plan dating from 1733 shows only 4 streets, and in 1741 a census revealed only 21 families residing in the town. New Bern assumed greater importance when the colonial assembly met there from 1745 to 1761. In 1767 Governor William Tryon began construction of an imposing residence regarded by many as the most beautiful building of colonial America. It was shortly thereafter that the plan of New Bern, reproduced in Figure 107, was drawn by C. J. Sauthier.

This plan bears some resemblance to that of Edenton, shown in Figure 108 as drawn by Sauthier in the same year. Edenton was established in 1712 near the western end of Albemarle Sound at the direction of the General Assembly. Very much as the Virginia and Maryland legislatures had done somewhat earlier, the North Carolina law-makers approved an act ". . . to build a courthouse and House to hold the Assembly in . . ." and appointed commissioners to plan the town where these facilities would be located.

Growth took place at a modest rate. The first lot was not sold until 1714, and in 1730 there were, by one report, only 60 homes. Because the governor's house was nearby and since the assembly

often met in the town during its early years, Edenton assumed a more important role than New Bern during its first three decades. At first known as "ye town on Queen Anne's Creek," in 1722 the more dignified and concise name of Edenton was conferred to honor the memory of the late governor, Charles Eden.

Neither plan shows any great qualities of originality, although both towns were and are pleasant and dignified communities. In New Bern the blocks are square or nearly so, while the street pattern of Edenton provides for somewhat longer and narrower blocks. In Edenton a single strand runs along the bay frontage with no buildings on the water side. The riverfront streets in New Bern offer somewhat greater variation in treatment, and the town faintly resembles Charleston on a similar site.

The siting of public buildings in the two towns also differs. The New Bern courthouse, marked "C" in the Sauthier plan, is skillfully located to provide a vista and to stop the views from two major streets leading inland from both the Trent and the Neuse Rivers. The church, indicated by "A," occupies an important site at the intersection of two streets near the center of the community. The courthouse site must have been at or near the middle of the town as laid out by Graffenried where the street joining the two rivers intersected the highway leading from the point of the peninsula into the interior. It may well be that the lane shown in the northeast corner of Sauthier's map running at a 45 degree angle to the grid street pattern is a surviving remnant of the original street system.

The treatment of the courthouse site in Edenton is quite different. Shown by the letters "B" and "C," the courthouse and jail occupy the center of a wide, grassy mall leading up from the waterfront. The church is located some distance away, fronting on the wide main street that runs roughly north and south and divides the town into two parts. West of this street, along the strand, another mall appears to lead inland almost symmetrically with that of the courthouse mall. Still farther west another stretch of unbuilt land extends inward from the water. The purpose of these latter two plan elements is not clear. Perhaps they were intended to provide views to and from sites for important buildings that would have faced the Sound from the first or second street inland running parallel to the shore.

[4] Christopher von Graffenried, *Account of the Founding of New Bern*, ed. and translated by Vincent H. Todd in *Publications of the North Carolina Historical Commission*, Raleigh, 1920, p. 377. A facsimile of Graffenried's map is reproduced as the frontispiece of this work. The map also appears as redrawn and with the German words translated into English in Alonzo Thomas Dill, *Governor Tryon and His Palace*, Chapel Hill, 1955.

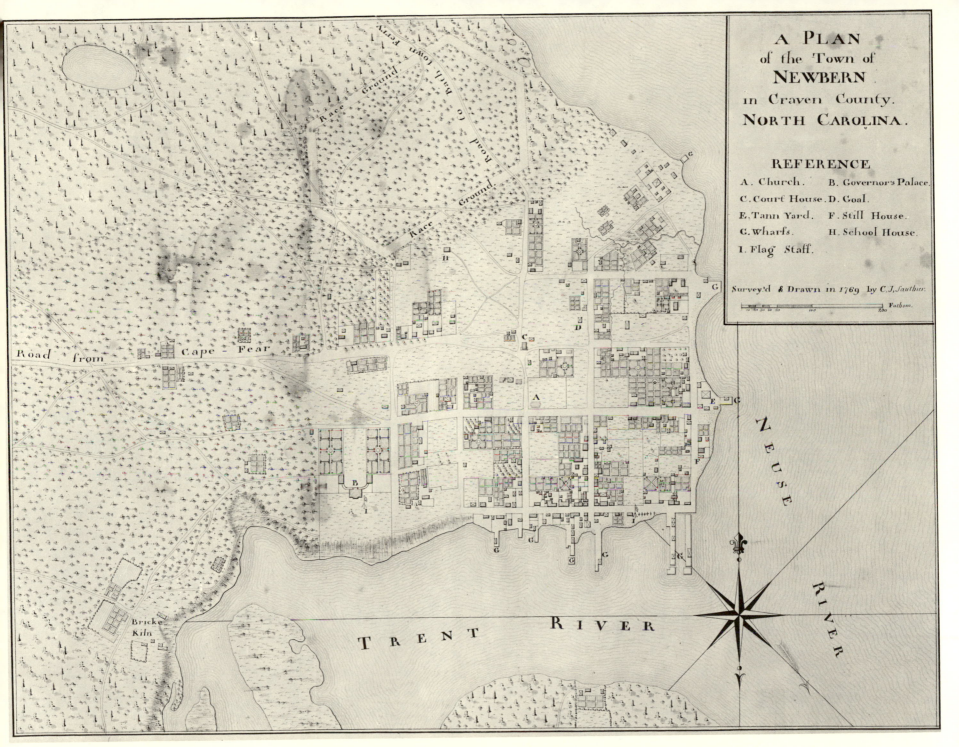

Figure 107. Plan of New Bern, North Carolina: 1769

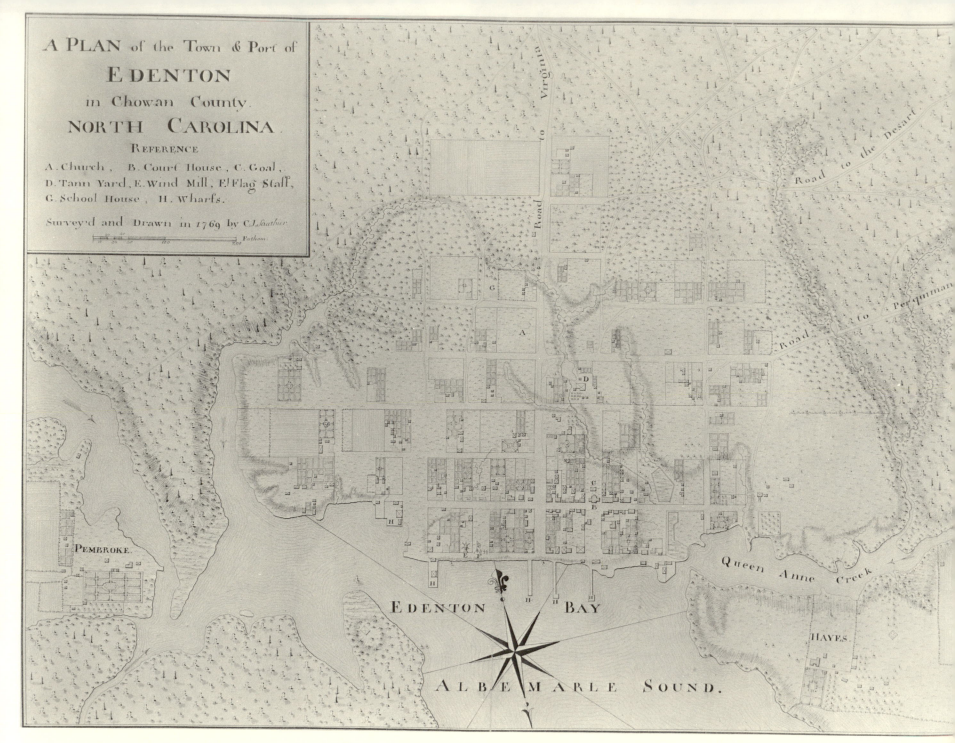

Figure 108. Plan of Edenton, North Carolina: 1769

The plans of these and other Carolina settlements are far from uninteresting.[5] However, the urban designs and land policies employed in the Georgia colony were considerably more novel and arresting. In this last of the colonies founded by England in the New World the best planned community of all was to be established. In the capital city, Savannah, not only did the original plan possess distinctive qualities not found elsewhere but both the form and spirit of its original pattern were followed for more than a century during the city's gradual expansion. The immediate forerunner of this great town planning experiment was itself a unique and interesting venture.

Sir Robert Mountgomery's Margravate of Azilia

Originally the lands of the Georgia colony formed part of the royal grant made to the Lords Proprietors of Carolina. They, however, made little attempt to develop the southern portion of their domain. The king and his military advisors, on the other hand, were anxious to encourage colonization in this area to strengthen the English claim of sovereignty contested by the Spanish. While the treaty of 1670 between England and Spain supposedly composed the differences in conflicting land claims, the exact boundary between Florida and Carolina had not been fixed.

In June 1717, the Carolina proprietors were persuaded to grant to Sir Robert Mountgomery permission to create a separate province between the Savannah and Alatamaha Rivers, to be called the Margravate of Azilia. The proprietors stipulated that unless settlement was undertaken within three years the grant would become void.

Sir Robert lost no time in attempting to promote colonization. Within a few months he published *A Discourse Concerning the Design'd Establishment of a New Colony to the South of Carolina in the Most Delightful Country of the Universe*, in which he set forth his scheme of settlement. Accompanying this tract was a plan of one of the districts or "county divisions" of the Margravate.

This remarkable proposal for an integrated urban-rural unit is reproduced in Figure 109.

Mountgomery's scheme rejected the idea of a series of isolated forts as a means of securing the colony against attack. Instead, he proposed enclosing each county with a continuous line of fortifications, the area to ". . . be in just proportion to the number of men they inclose." The ultimate result would be the neatly developed and highly organized settlement form that he described in considerable detail.

"You must suppose a level, dry, and fruitful tract of land in some fine plain or valley, containing a just square of twenty miles each way, or two hundred and fifty-six thousand acres. . . .

"The district is defended by sufficient numbers of men, who, dwelling in the fortified angles of the line will be employed in cultivating lands which are kept in hand for the particular advantage of the Margrave: these lands surround the district just within the lines, and every where contain in breadth one mile exactly.

"The men thus employed . . . shall have a right of laying claim to a certain fee-farm, or quantity of land ready cleared. . . . The lands set apart for their purpose are two miles in breadth, quite round the district, and lie next within the Margrave's own reserved lands above-mentioned. The 116 squares, each of which has a house in the middle, are every one a mile on each side, or 640 acres in a square, bating only for the highways which divide them. These are the estates belonging to the gentry of the district. . . .

"The four great parks, or rather forests, are each four miles square, that is, 16 miles round each forest, in which are propagated herds of cattle of all sorts by themselves, not alone to serve the uses of the district they belong to, but to store such new ones as may from time to time be measured out on affluence of people."[6]

Then Mountgomery mentioned the urban area to occupy the center of the county district. One interesting point to note is his proposal for a distinct greenbelt separating city from country.

[5] Reproductions of plans of Halifax, Wilmington, Salisbury, and Hillsborough, all drawn by Sauthier, may be found in Francis Benjamin Johnston's valuable work, *The Early Architecture of North Carolina*, Chapel Hill, 1941. See also Lawrence E. Lee, "Old Brunswick, The Story of a Colonial Town," *North Carolina Historical Review*, XXIX (1952), 230-45.

[6] Sir Robert Mountgomery, *A Discourse Concerning the Design'd Establishment of a New Colony to the South of Carolina in the Most Delightful Country of the Universe* (London, 1717), reprinted in George P. Humphrey, *American Colonial Tracts*, No. 1, Rochester, 1897.

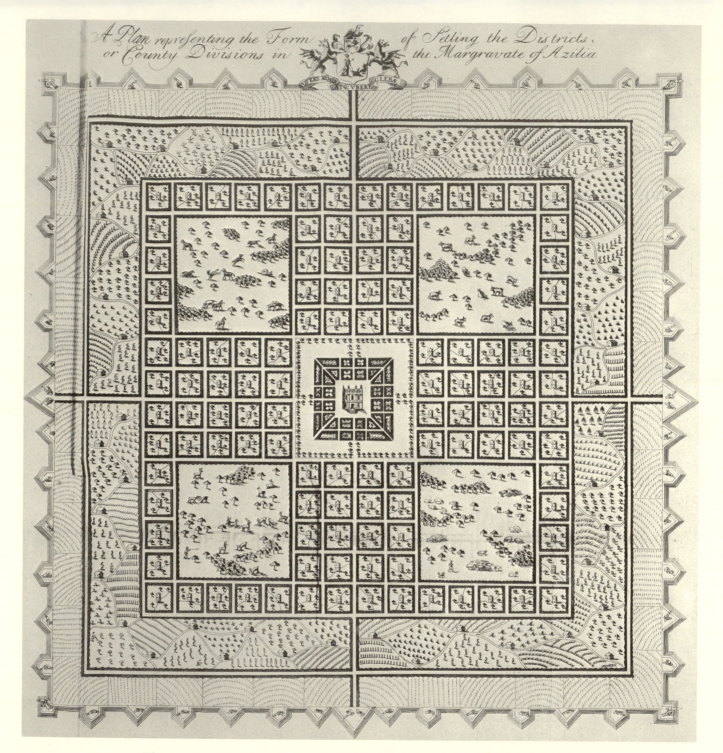

Figure 109. Plan for the Proposed Margravate of Azilia in Georgia: 1717

"The middle hollow square, which is full of streets crossing each other, is the city, and the bank which runs about it on the outside surrounded with trees, is a large void space, which will be useful for a thousand purposes, and among the rest, as being airy and affording a fine prospect of the town in drawing near it.

"In the center of the city stands the Margrave's house, which is to be his constant residence, or the residence of the Governor, and contains all sorts of public edifices for dispatch of business; and this again is separated from the city by a space like that, which as above, divides the town from the country."[7]

Mountgomery's attempts to raise funds for this venture failed, and under the terms of the grant his right to colonize these southern lands lapsed, but if nothing came directly of his visionary scheme, Mountgomery's concept of land division was to influence the pattern of settlement that was adopted a few years later under Oglethorpe. His basic division of country lands into rectangles one mile square was eventually duplicated seventy years later when the Continental Congress established the system of western land surveys.

Oglethorpe and the Establishment of the Georgia Colony

Not only did the Carolina colonists regard the Spanish settlements to the south as a potential threat to their interests but from time to time they were subject to Indian attacks and occasional raids by coastal pirates. The Lords Proprietors of the colony, unable or unwilling to provide sufficient military protection, surrendered their rights to the crown in 1729. In June 1732, George II conveyed the southern territory to The Trustees for Establishing the Colony of Georgia in America.

The leading figure among the trustees was James Oglethorpe, and it was under his immediate supervision that the towns of the new colony were planned and built. Oglethorpe had served in the English army and later under Prince Eugene of Savoy. Returning to England to take over his family estate, he was elected to the House of Commons in 1722. Oglethorpe soon interested himself in prison reform, particularly the treatment of debtors. In 1728 he was chosen chairman of a House of Commons committee formed

[7] ibid.

to investigate the conditions of the London jails. Out of this experience grew his ideas for promoting a colony in the New World where, among others, those confined to English jails by their creditors could find opportunity for a new beginning in life. Not only debtors would be sought for the venture but persons of modest means and little future from England and the continent who, for economic or religious reasons, felt the weight of oppression or discrimination.

Oglethorpe successfully interested persons of wealth and prestige in his cause. It was to this group that King George granted the charter for the Georgia colony. Proprietary colonies had been a source of trouble to the crown, and the Georgia charter contained a number of features designed to provide a more satisfactory form of settlement. The charter, for example, specified that the trustees' jurisdiction would expire at the end of 21 years, at which time the form of government would be reexamined. The trustees were empowered to make grants of land to colonists, but no colonist could obtain more than 500 acres. Moreover, the charter prohibited trustees from owning any land individually while members of the corporation.

The conditions of land tenure established by the trustees reinforced these provisions, designed to eliminate the element of land speculation and profit. Land grants for colonists to be transported and settled at the trustees' expense were set at 50 acres; the right of sale of this land was denied to prevent accumulation of large holdings in one ownership; and succession in title was to be to the male heir only to prevent breaking up of plots into holdings of uneconomic size.

The trustees possessed means and influence and in a short time succeeded in raising sufficient funds for the first settlement. One hundred and fourteen persons signified their willingness to meet the conditions for joining the colony. In November 1732, they sailed from Depford, accompanied by Oglethorpe, who characteristically had volunteered to lead the first group, paying his own expenses and acting as the trustees' representative.

The Founding of Savannah

After two months at sea the colonists arrived at Charleston, where they were welcomed by the governor and his council who assigned Colonial William Bull to accompany Oglethorpe and assist him in locating and laying out a town site. Early in February 1733 Oglethorpe wrote to the trustees describing the beginnings of their colonization venture:

"GENTLEMEN,—I gave you an account in my last, of our arrival at Charlestown, The governor and assembly have given us all possible encouragement. Our people arrived at Beaufort on the 20th of January, where I lodged them in some new barracks built for the soldiers, while I went myself to view the Savannah river. I fixed upon a healthy situation on about ten miles from the sea. The river here forms a half-moon, along the south side of which the banks are about forty foot high, and on the top flat, which they call a bluff. The plain high ground extends into the country five or six miles, and along the river side about a mile. Ships that draw twelve foot water can ride within ten yards of the bank. Upon the river-side in the centre of this plain I have laid out the town. . . . The whole people arrived here on the first of February. At night their tents were got up. Till the seventh we were taken up in unloading, and making a crane, which I then could not get finished, so took off the hands, and set some to the fortification, and began to fell the woods. I marked out the town and common; half of the former is already cleared, and the first house was begun yesterday in the afternoon. . . ."[8]

A few days later Oglethorpe reported further information about the site:

"I chose the situation for the town upon an high ground, forty feet perpendicular above high water mark; the soil dry and sandy, the water of the river fresh, springs coming out from the sides of the hill. I pitched upon this place not only for the pleasantness of the situation, but because from the above mentioned and other signs I thought it healthy; for it is sheltered from the western and southern winds (the worst in this country,) by vast woods of pine trees, many of which are an hundred and few under seventy feet high."[9]

[8] Letter to the trustees, February 10, 1733, in *Reasons for Establishing the Colony of Georgia* (London, 1733), reprinted in Georgia Historical Society, *Collections*, I, Savannah, 1840.
[9] Letter to the trustees, February 20, 1733, in Benjamin Martyn, *An Account, Showing the Progress of the Colony of Georgia* (London, 1741), reprinted in Georgia Historical Society, *Collections*, II, Savannah, 1842.

On March 16 three gentlemen from Charleston arrived in Savannah to observe what was taking place. Their impressions were recorded in the *South-Carolina Gazette* the following week.

"Mr. Oglethorpe is indefatigable, takes a great deal of pains, his fare is but indifferent, having little else at present but salt provisions. . . . There are no idlers there—even the boys and girls do their parts. There are four houses already up but none finished, and he hopes when he has got more sawyers, which I suppose he will have in a short time, to finish two houses a week. . . . He was pallisading the town round, including some part of the common, which I do suppose may be finished in about a fortnight's time. In short, he has done a vast deal of work for the time, and I think his name justly deserves to be immortalized.

"Colonel Bull, who had been sent by Governor Johnson to assist in laying out the town, and to describe to the people the manner of felling the trees, and of clearing, breaking up, and cultivating the ground, was a very efficient helper."[10]

By July substantial progress on the town had been made. Oglethorpe called the colonists together to reveal the plan of the town, the names of streets and wards, and the assignment of town, garden, and farm lots to individual colonists. A contemporary observer told of this event in the *South-Carolina Gazette*:

"On the 7th of July at Day-break, the Inhabitants were assembled, on the Strand Prayers were read, by way of Thanksgiving. The people proceeded to the Square. The Wards and Tythings were named, each Tything consisting of ten Houses, and each Ward of four tythings. An House Lott was given to each Freeholder. All the people had had a very plentiful Dinner, and in the Afternoon, the Grant of a Court of Record was read, and the Officers for that Court were appointed."[11]

But the occasion was not entirely a happy one, since, as the *Gazette* account continues, "Some of the People having privately drank too freely of Rum are dead; and that Liquor which was always discountenanced here, is now absolutely prohibited."[12]

Although the division of land was carried out in July, it was

[10] *South-Carolina Gazette*, No. 62, March 24, 1732 [1733].
[11] *South-Carolina Gazette*, No. 84, August 25, 1733.
[12] *ibid*.

not until December that the first deeds were given to the settlers. A portion of one of them, interesting because of its details of the peculiar method of land grants, reads as follows:

"Whereas . . . James Oglethorpe hath set out and limited . . . a town called Savannah, with Lotts for Houses, and left a Common round the Town for convenience of Air; And, adjoining to the Common, hath set out Garden Lotts of Five Acres each, and beyond such Garden Lotts hath set out Farms of Forty Four Acres and One Hundred and forty and one Pole each, and hath drawn a Plan of the Town, and Plot of the Garden Lots and Farms respectively, with proper Number, references, and Explanations for the more easy understanding thereof. . . .

"Now know Ye, that we . . . do Grant and Enfeoff unto John Goddard one House Lot . . . containing sixty feet in front and Ninety feet in depth, and one Garden Lot containing Five acres . . . and one Farm . . . To have and To Hold the said Fifty Acres of Land."[13]

The deeds further specified that within 18 months the grantees must erect a house on their town lot and within 10 years clear and cultivate at least 10 acres of the land lying outside the town.

The map referred to in the deeds—evidently a detailed plat of all parcels—has unfortunately been lost. Figure 110, however, shows the general pattern as it existed in 1735. The town proper is the tiny rectangle near the river shown divided into six parts. To the north and east are the 5-acre garden lots. The next larger divisions are the farms of 44 acres. Beyond the farms the map shows 39 wooded squares, most of them slightly less than one mile on a side. It seems likely that these tracts were set aside for land grants of 500 acres authorized by the trustees to persons of means who would emigrate to the colony at their own expense and undertake to clear and cultivate a portion of the land.

The common referred to in the deeds does not show on this map, but its boundaries may be seen in Figure 111, a redrawing of the original land divisions. The common evidently was intended to provide additional space for the city as it grew and not as a permanent open belt of land. In this feature, Savannah resembled many of the earlier New England communities. The map shows

[13] As quoted in Charles C. Jones, *The History of Georgia*, Boston, 1883, I, 156-60.

another unusual feature—the triangular shape of the 5-acre garden lots indicated by the dotted lines running diagonally through the squares 10 acres in area. In modern Savannah a few diagonal streets exist which developed from the original lanes or roads leading to the garden plots and following the old boundary lines.

Here certainly is an example of a true regional plan—one as highly organized as Mountgomery's Azilia but without some of the impractical features of that earlier scheme. In many respects the disposition of town and country land grants resembles that put into effect half a century earlier in Philadelphia by William Penn. There the so-called "liberty lands" contained the farm parcels of colonists residing in the city itself. Both Savannah and Philadelphia, of course, owe much to the agricultural village pattern established in New England at the very beginning of English settlement in North America. At Savannah the irregular field divisions of these Pennsylvania and New England communities were brought into geometric order.

Most remarkable, however, was Oglethorpe's plan for the town lots, streets, and open spaces in Savannah itself. As the basic unit he created a number of wards, each consisting of 40 house lots 60 by 90 feet. Fronting the squares on two sides were trustee lots, set aside for churches, stores, places of assembly and other public or semi-public uses. Main streets measured 75 feet in width, with minor streets half that, and lanes 22½ feet wide to the rear of the house lots.

A view of Savannah in 1734, showing the four wards then laid out, is reproduced in Figure 112. The crane at the river bank, the beginning of the palisade around the town, and the dense forest in which the clearing was made may be observed. The plan of the city as extended, possibly as early as 1735, appears in Figure 113. A detailed description of the city as it then appeared is of interest:

"She is laid out 2115 by 1425 ft: square in her Bounds, this again in 24 Tidings, each of them in 10; in all 240; and 48 Trustee Lots, with six Market Places, each 315 by 270 ft. square. Three broad Streets 75 feet wide, running perpendicular from the Bay, and three other 75 feet wide parallel with the Bay, centrically crossing each other, divides the City in six equal Quarters, each Quarter has four Tidings, each Tiding is run through (parallel with the Bay) by a Lane 22½ feet wide, each half Tiding consists

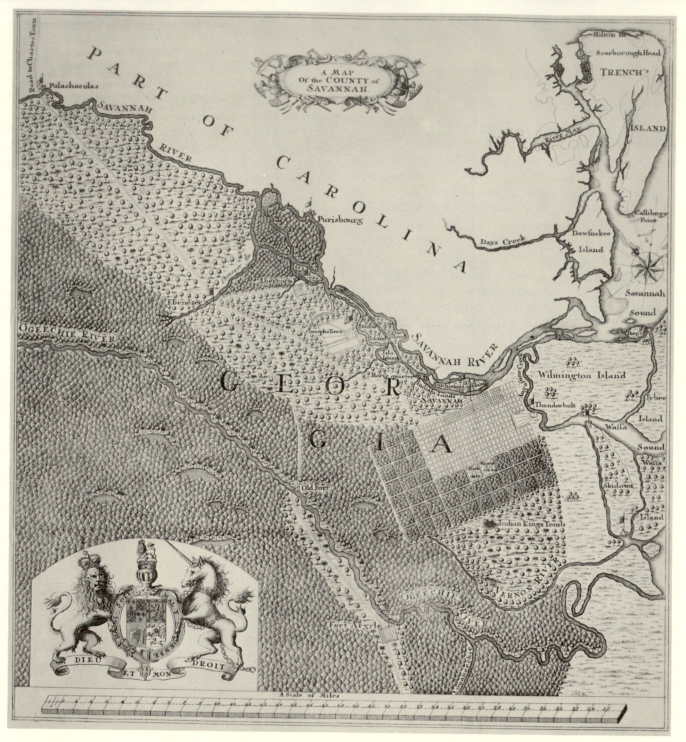

Figure 110. Map of the County of Savannah, Georgia: 1735

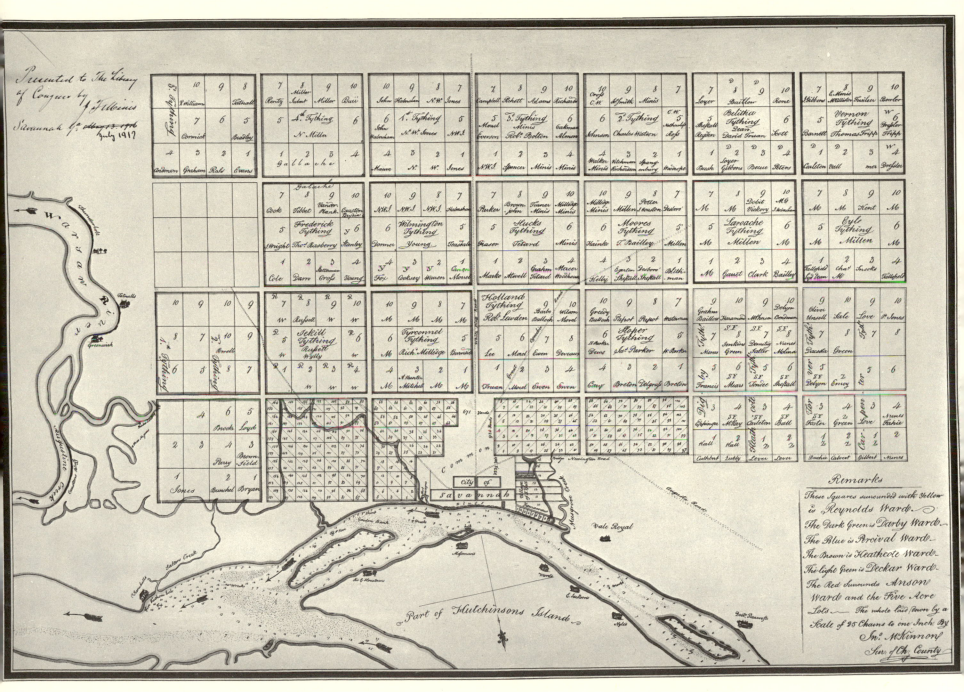

Figure III. Map of the City of Savannah and its Garden and Farm Lots: ca. 1800

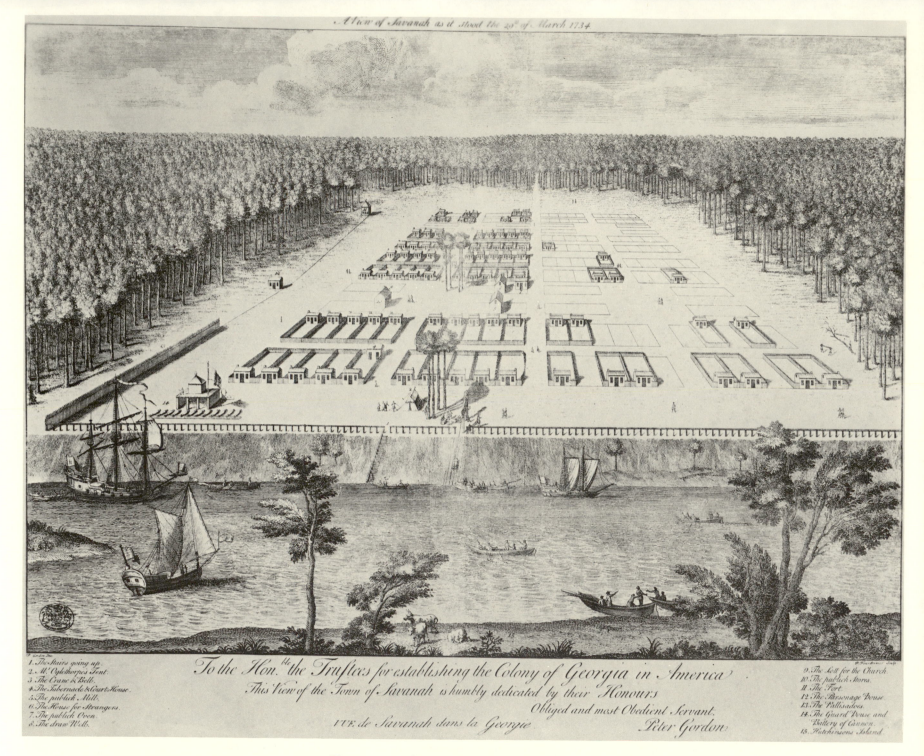

A View of Savanah as it stood the 29th of March 1734

To the Hon.ble the Trustees for establishing the Colony of Georgia in America

This View of the Town of Savanah is humbly dedicated by their Honours

Obliged and most Obedient Servant.

VUE de Savanah dans la Georgie.

Peter Gordon

Figure 112. View of Savannah, Georgia: 1734

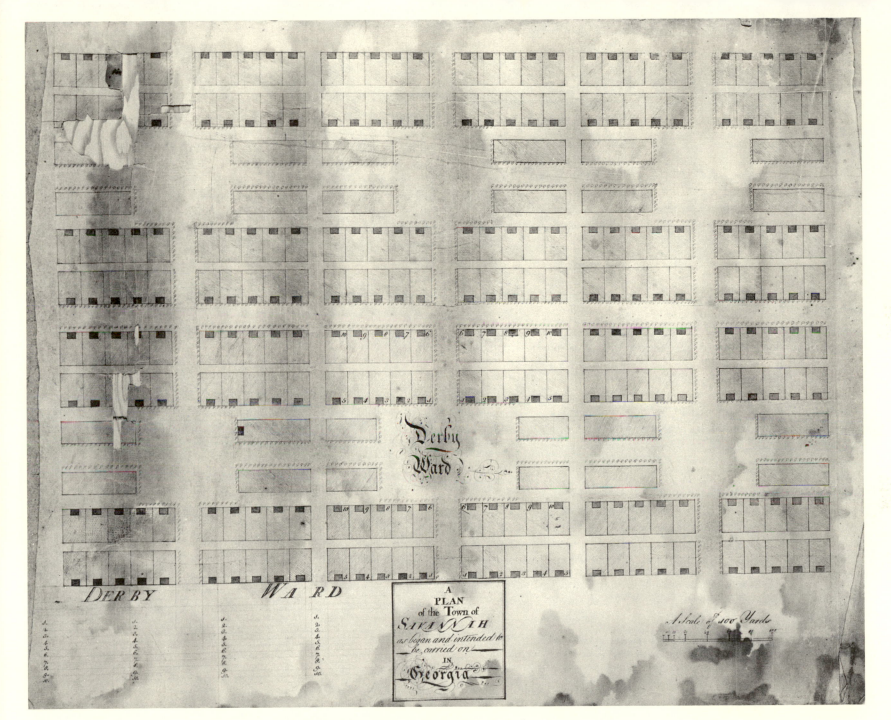

Figure 113. Plan of Savannah, Georgia: ca. 1740

in five contiguous Lots, each Tiding-, as well as Trustee-Lot is 60 feet in front, and 90 feet in depth. Trustee Lots are divided from each other as well as from Tiding Lots by Streets 75 and 37½ ft. wide. The City consists of 400 Houses; a Church, an independent Meeting-House, a Council-House, a Court-House, and a Filatur. . . ."[14]

The possible origins of this novel and effective plan will be discussed later.

The Georgia trustees continued to recruit new colonists. Although population growth was slow, by 1745 the *London Magazine* could report that Savannah:

"has very near 350 Houses, Huts and Warehouses in it, beside the public Buildings, which are, the storehouse of the Trustees, an handsome Court-House, a Gaol, a Guard-House, and a public Wharf, projected out many feet into the River. The Streets are wide and commodious, and intersect each other mostly at Right Angles: The whole Town is laid out very commodiously, and there are several large Squares. Many of the Houses are very large and handsome, built generally of Wood, but some Foundations are brick'd. . . .

"The Houses are built some Distance from each other, to allow more Air and Garden Room, and prevent the Communication, in Case of any Accident by Fire. . . . They have a publick garden, in a very thriving Way, which is a Kind of Nursery for the Use of the Inhabitants. The Town stands about ten Miles from the Sea up the River, (which is navigable some hundred Miles up the Country,) and is, certainly a very good Harbour, and well seated for Trade. The land, a considerable Space round the Town, is well clear'd, and the Passages lie open: a handsome Road-Way running above a Mile from it, and making the Prospect very lightsome."[15]

By the Revolution the population of Savannah exceeded three thousand persons, and the city ranked as the twentieth largest town in the American colonies.

[14] John Gerar William De Brahm, *History of the Province of Georgia,* privately printed by George Wymberley-Jones, Wormsloe, Georgia, 1849, 36. De Brahm served as British surveyor general for the Southern District of North America. In 1757 he directed the construction of fortifications at Savannah. A plan of the town, probably dating from 1757, is included in his *History,* which was submitted in 1798 to the "Consul General of Great Britain for the States of America" in manuscript form.

[15] *London Magazine* (1745), p. 603.

Ebenezer, Darien, and Frederica

The Georgia trustees hastened to develop other settlements throughout the colony. They extended their charitable aid to a group of Protestant Salzburgers who had been driven from their home by religious persecutions. The first group of Salzburgers arrived at Savannah in March 1734 under the leadership of Philip George Frederick Baron Von Reck. Oglethorpe and Von Reck selected a site for the settlement several miles north of Savannah which the Salzburgers named Ebenezer. During the next few months they cleared the land and laid out a town. Presumably the pattern established at Savannah was followed, although apparently no plat of Ebenezer has survived. Other Salzburgers were attracted to the colony, and the little settlement grew. However, the location proved to be a poor choice. It was isolated from Savannah, the soil was not fertile, and the inhabitants were plagued by illness. In 1736 the Salzburgers requested Oglethorpe to permit them to move to a new location on the Savannah River a few miles to the east. The plan of this second settlement, New Ebenezer, is shown in Figure 114. The town common appears to the west of the town lots, the 5-acre garden lots were along the north and south boundaries, with the farm lots ("Plantationes") beyond. In its arrangement of streets and house lots, the Ebenezer plan is virtually identical to that of Savannah. The only difference is that the sites for public uses facing the open squares are not bisected by the short streets appearing in the Savannah plan.[16]

The Georgia trustees also arranged for a settlement of Scots to the south of Savannah near St. Simons Island in 1735. Called New Inverness, or Darien, this tiny community had a single open square surrounded by four ranges of town lots arranged like one of the wards in Savannah or Ebenezer. A portion of Darien appears in the lower left-hand corner of Figure 115, which shows St. Simons Island and vicinity, including the town of Frederica.[17] The latter settlement dates from 1735, when the town and fortifications were

[16] A plan of New Ebenezer also appears in De Brahm, *History.* His version shows only three wards and squares in a line along the river. The De Brahm plan is reproduced in Charles C. Jones, *The Dead Towns of Georgia* in Georgia Historical Society, *Collections,* IV, Savannah, 1878, where there is a full account of Old and New Ebenezer, Frederica, and other early Georgia settlements no longer in existence.

[17] The only plans of Darien known to the author are two re-surveys of the town and commons made in 1767 which are among the records in the Surveyor-General Department of the Georgia Department of State.

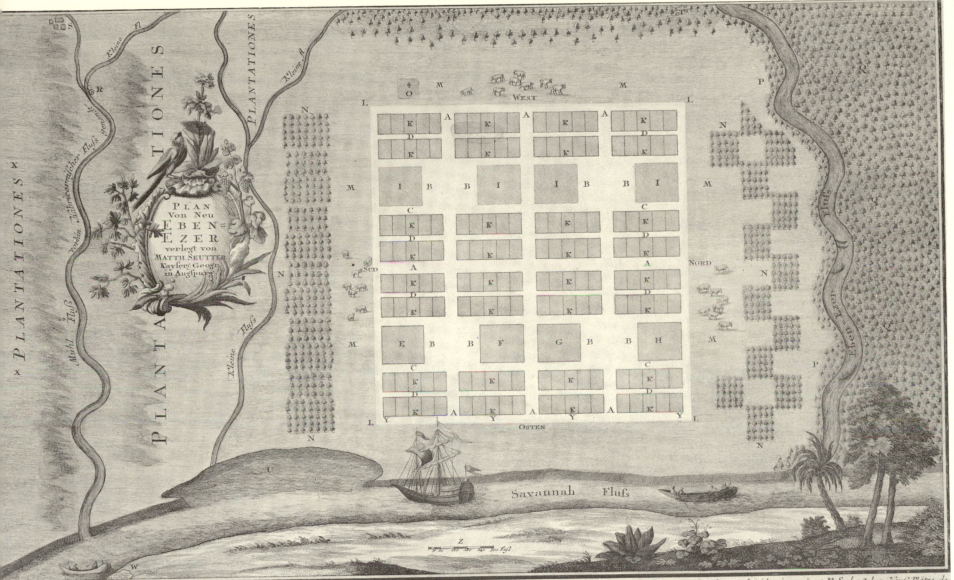

Figure 114. Plan of New Ebenezer, Georgia: 1740

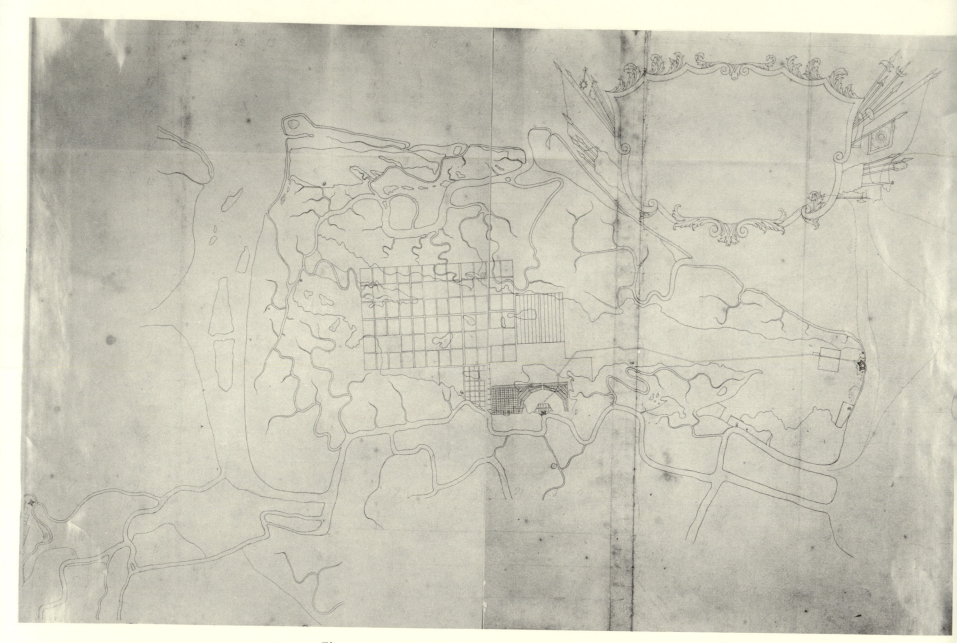

Figure 115. Map of St. Simons Island, Georgia: ca. 1740

laid out under Oglethorpe's direction. Figure 115 shows the division of land into garden and farm lots similar to the Savannah pattern. The inner boundary of the garden lots is a line describing one-half of a dodecagon. Between this line and the town proper appears a semi-circular open space approximately one thousand feet wide, which apparently was the town common.

Frederica itself appears on this map as the small symmetrical trapezoid above the fort at the bend in the river. A larger plan of the town is reproduced in Figure 116.[18] One of the original settlers has left this description of the town at the time of its construction:

"The Main Street that went from the Front into the Country was 25 yards wide. Each Free-holder had 60 Foot in Front by 90 Foot in Depth, upon the high Street, for their House and Garden; but those which fronted the River had but 30 Foot in Front, by 60 Foot in Depth. Each family had a Bower of Palmetto Leaves, finished upon the back Street in their own Lands: The Side towards the front Street was set out for their Houses: These Palmetto Bowers were very convenient Shelters, being tight in the hardest Rains; they were about 20 Foot long and 14 Foot wide, and, in regular Rows, looked very pretty, the Palmetto leaves lying smooth and handsome, and of a good Colour."[19]

Frederica was scarcely completed before it began to decline. After the weakening of the Spanish position in Florida, the town was no longer needed as a border fortress; within a quarter of a century or so the population had dwindled to a few dozen, and by the 1800's only traces of the fortress and some of the foundations of the houses remained.

Other communities were planned during this period. Oglethorpe founded Augusta, named for the mother of George III, in 1735. This town, like Frederica, was an outpost of defense, and the pattern of wards with open squares was not used.[20] In 1737 Ogle-

[18] Another plan of Frederica is in the John Carter Brown Library. This differs only in minor details from the re-survey of 1796 reproduced here.

[19] Francis Moore, *A Voyage to Georgia Begun in the Year 1735* (London, 1744), reprinted in Georgia Historical Society, *Collections*, I, Savannah, 1840.

[20] A plan of Augusta in 1780 appears in Berry Fleming (comp.), *Autobiography of a Colony: The First Half-Century of Augusta, Georgia*, Athens, 1957, p. 134.

thorpe reported that in addition to the settlements already discussed "there were several villages settled by gentlemen at their own expense." The villages referred to probably included such minor settlements appearing in Figure 110 as Josephs Town, Abercorn, Thunderbolt, Highgate, and Hampstead. The latter two were located south of the Savannah farm lots. If the map is an accurate representation of the land division in the villages, it would appear that the plots of land were wedge shaped, radiating outward from a central point where the houses were probably grouped in a small village cluster. This pattern may have been borrowed from the villages laid out by William Penn near Philadelphia half a century previously, or from the earlier town of Gravesend on Long Island, and there also is a resemblance to the similar plan for agricultural villages used in two or three places by the French along the St. Lawrence River near Quebec.

These communities, too, were short lived. Hampstead was soon abandoned, and in 1740 only two families resided at Highgate. Josephs Town, Abercorn, and Thunderbolt also soon disappeared. New Ebenezer maintained its existence until after the Revolution when it also gradually declined and eventually disappeared.

A similar fate awaited a later Georgia town planned in 1754 under the direction of John Reynolds, the first royal governor of the colony. Reynolds intended to move the seat of government from Savannah to a new site on the Ogeechee River. His plan of George Town, later renamed Hardwick, appears in Figure 117. Traces of the Savannah pattern can be seen in the design of the open squares, although they are not so numerous as in Savannah. The common land and the several sites reserved for public use also reflect the influence of Oglethorpian planning. However, plans for moving the capital to George Town were dropped, and within a century this community lay virtually abandoned.

The Urban Pattern in Georgia:
Tradition and Invention

It is highly improbable that the planning of these Georgia towns resulted from some inspiration of the moment. Oglethorpe and his fellow trustees carefully planned all other aspects of their colonization enterprise, as is amply demonstrated by surviving

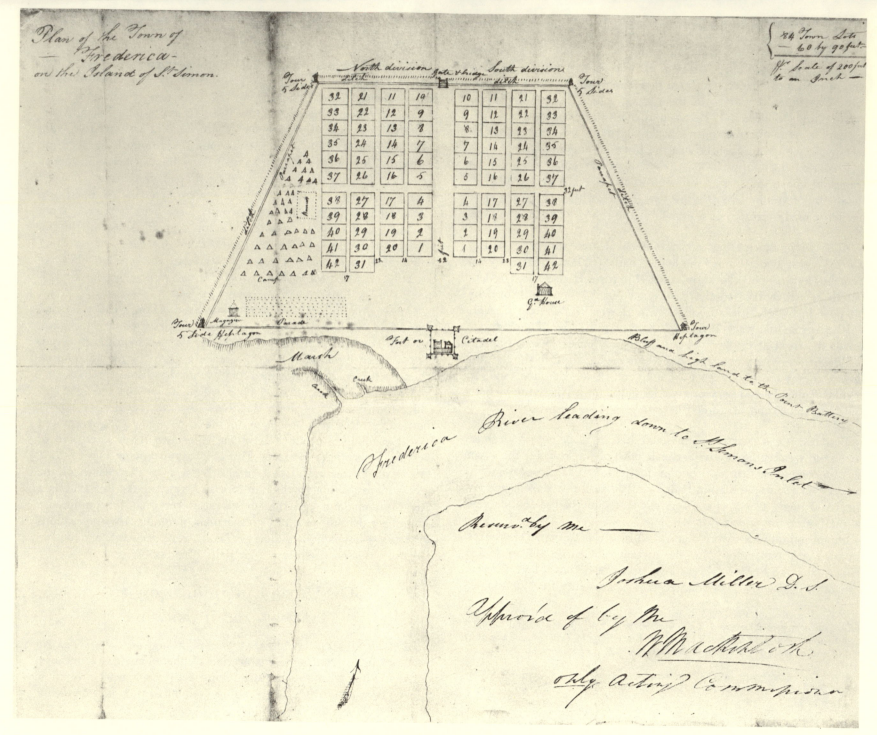

Figure 116. Plan of Frederica, Georgia: ca. 1735

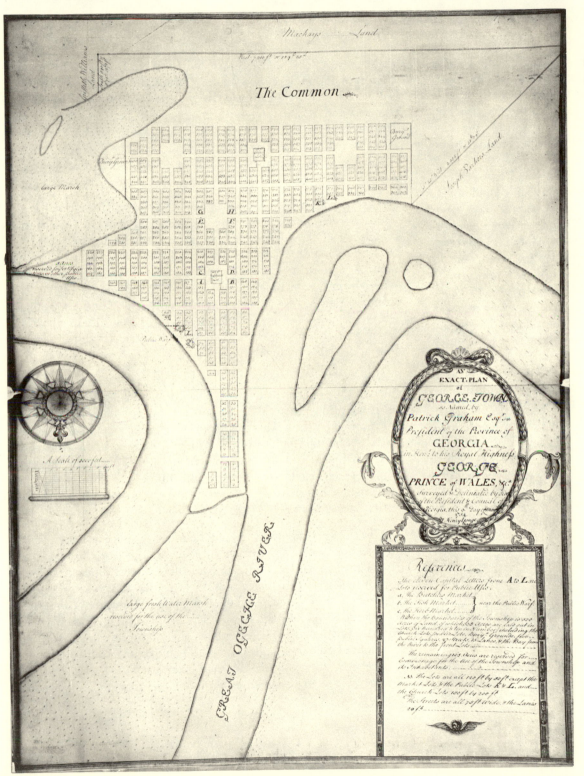

Figure 117. Plan of George Town (Hardwick), Georgia: 1754

records. Perhaps they prepared at least preliminary plans for the towns they hoped to establish before the first boatload of emigrants left England; certainly they had available to them a considerable body of previous town building experience both in the colonies and in England. In addition, Mountgomery's abortive plan for the very area the trustees proposed to settle must have been thoroughly reviewed.

The most obvious parallel in the New World was Pennsylvania, established by William Penn in 1682. The plan of Philadelphia, which had been widely advertised in England, would have been familiar to the Georgia trustees. Indeed, Thomas Penn, then proprietor of the colony, wrote to the trustees in March 1733 commending the establishment of the new colony and contributing £100 to its treasury. The similarity of the small agricultural villages of Hampstead, Highgate, Abercorn, and others to those laid out earlier by Penn has already been noted. The open squares in the Philadelphia plan may also have had some influence on the pattern used at Savannah, Ebenezer and Darien. The liberty lands at Philadelphia, while irregular in their field lines, may have furnished the model for the Savannah garden and farm lots.

One of the presumed influences on the planning of Philadelphia, New Haven, and other early towns had been the even earlier English planning experience in northern Ireland at the beginning of the seventeenth century. In the case of Georgia there is evidence from the highest authority—Oglethorpe himself—that these Ulster Plantation towns inspired the Georgia trustees. In 1732 Oglethorpe published anonymously a tract entitled *A New and Accurate Account of the Provinces of South Carolina.*[21] This was designed to rally support for the initial settlement in Georgia. In the preface to that work Oglethorpe refers to

". . . a Precedent of our own for planting Colonies, which perhaps, in Part, or in the Whole, may be worthy of our Imitation.

"England was more than four Hundred Years in Possession of a great Part of Ireland. . . . In the Days of King James the First, the Londoners were at the Charge of sending into the most dangerous Part of that Kingdom more than four Hundred poor Families.

[21] Printed in London in 1732, this bore the following subtitle: "With many curious and useful Observations on the Trade, Navigation and Plantations of *Great-Britain*, compared with her most powerful maritime Neighbors in ancient and modern Times."

There were a City, and a Town built, as had been agreed on: The City of London-derry contained three Hundred, the Town of Colerain a Hundred Houses; these were fortified with Walls and Ditches, and established with most ample Privileges. . . . The City of London-derry, and its Liberties (which I think are three Miles round it) the Town of Colerain and the Fisheries, belong to the Twelve Companies of London consider'd as one aggregate Body."[22]

The plan of Frederica, with its regular grid, city walls, and central strong point, may owe its origin in part to Oglethorpe's knowledge of the fortified towns in northern Ireland.

Of greater interest is the genesis of the Savannah plan and its minor variations at Ebenezer and Darien. One explanation of the generous provision of open squares has been left us by an early visitor, Francis Moore, who sailed with the band of colonists bound for the new town of Frederica in 1735. Moore described the system of town, garden, and farm lots used at Savannah and then added this statement:

". . . every forty houses in town make a ward, to which four square miles in the country belong; each ward has a constable, and under him four tithing men. Where the town lands end, the villages begin; four villages make a ward without, which depends upon one of the wards within the town. The use of this is, in case a war should happen, the villages without may have places in the town, to bring their cattle and families into for refuge, and to that purpose there is a square left in every ward, big enough for the outwards to encamp in."[23]

This is an ingenious explanation and cannot wholly be disregarded. Moore's account of the Georgia colony, however, was designed in part as a vindication of the trustees' land and governmental policies, then under attack by critics in the colony and in England, and also as a piece of promotional literature. His description of the Savannah squares as a place of refuge for settlers outside the town may well have been an attempt to allay the fears of potential colonists apprehensive about Indian raids.

The plan of Savannah has also been attributed to a design by Robert Castell in his volume *Villas of the Ancients*. Oglethorpe's

[22] *ibid.*, iv-v. [23] Moore, *Voyage*.

name appears among the list of patrons in Castell's book, and, when Castell was confined in debtors' prison, it was his plight among others that awakened Oglethorpe's interest and sympathy in prison reform. This activity, of course, led directly to the establishment of the Georgia colony. But Castell's volume contains no town plan; what does appear are drawings of villas of classical times surrounded by neat rectangular *parterres*. This grid pattern of solids and voids is similar to the Savannah plan, but this scarcely establishes a valid claim for Castell as the source for the Savannah plan.

Mountgomery's design was almost certainly an influence. The scale is different, but the proportions of open space are almost identical if we compare all of Azilia with the much smaller area occupied by the Savannah town lots. It is not inconceivable that the Georgia trustees simply reduced the size of the Azilia plan in keeping with the more modest land grants contemplated for their own colony.

Both Mountgomery and the sponsors of the Georgia colony were well aware of the emerging pattern of land subdivision in London. During the preceding century a series of speculative building developments surrounding existing open spaces or newly created private residential squares had sprung into existence. It is worth recalling that Penn's surveyor described the four neighborhood squares in Philadelphia "to be for the like uses, as the Moorefields in London." At that time Leicester Fields, Covent Garden, Lincoln's Inn Fields, Bloomsbury Square, and Soho Square also had been developed. By the time of the Georgia colony a number of new squares had been created: Red Lion Square (1684), St. James's Square (1684), Grosvenor Square (1695), Hanover Square (1712), and Cavendish Square (1720), among others. John Roque's great map of London, begun in 1737 and published in 1746 is perhaps the best record of this new pattern in Georgian London.

Some of the Georgia trustees were active participants in the development of these squares. Sir William Heathcote built what is now Chatham House in St. James's Square in 1734. General Carpenter and several fellow officers were among the first residents of Hanover Square. No doubt other trustees, generally persons of affluence, had similar first-hand familiarity with the residential square as a unit of urban growth. It is difficult not to conclude that the squares of Georgian London furnished the models after which the plans of Savannah and the other towns of the colony were fashioned.[24]

Yet having duly noted all these possible sources in town planning tradition, one must grant that Oglethorpe, aided perhaps by a person or persons unknown, fashioned a new community pattern out of these older models. The Georgia settlements constituted real innovations in urban design. The basic module—ward, open square, and local streets—provided not only an unusually attractive, convenient, and intimate environment but also served as a practical device for allowing urban expansion without formless sprawl. These little neighborhood units, scaled to human size, must also have established a social pattern desirable for a frontier settlement where cooperation and neighborly assistance was essential for survival.

For many years the six wards of early Savannah provided sufficient space for the nearly stabilized population. Following the Revolution, Savannah began a steady expansion, faithfully retaining the original concept of its founders until the middle of the nineteenth century. Figure 118 is a map of the city in 1856. On it can be noted the wards and squares added over the years. One can also observe at the fringes of the city the first evidences of urban development on the more usual pattern of a gridiron unrelieved by public open space.

[24] In Frederick Doveton Nichols, *The Early Architecture of Georgia*, Chapel Hill, 1958, an otherwise excellent treatment of town planning in Georgia is marred by a conclusion, unsupported by any evidence, that Savannah was laid out by Gabriel Bernard, uncle of Jean Jacques Rousseau, a surveyor and engineer then residing in Charleston. Mr. Nichols underestimates Oglethorpe's versatility, disregards the London square as a likely source of inspiration, and was evidently unaware of Oglethorpe's citation of the Ulster Plantation experience as a partial model for the Georgia colony. The most exhaustive analysis is Turpin C. Bannister's "Oglethorpe's Sources for the Savannah Plan," *Journal of the Society of Architectural Historians*, xx (May 1961), 47-62. This scholarly and interesting study puts greatest weight on the castrametation plans of Renaissance military theorists. Bannister points out that Oglethorpe would have been familiar with these ideas and could have drawn on them in working out the Savannah plan. A military encampment plan by Robert Barret, dating from 1598, which Bannister reproduces, closely resembles the Savannah plan, with open squares at the intersections of the principal streets. Bannister's argument fails to explain why Oglethorpe used a quite different pattern for the very towns where one would expect castrametation theories to be applied—at the fortress communities of Frederica and Augusta.

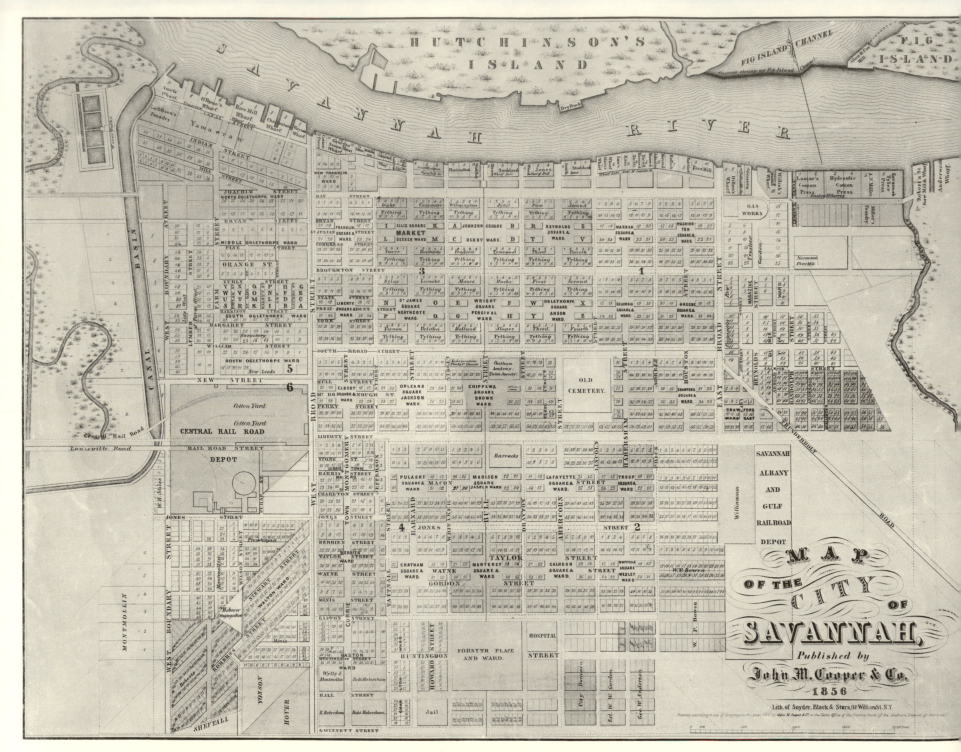

Figure 118. Plan of Savannah, Georgia: 1856

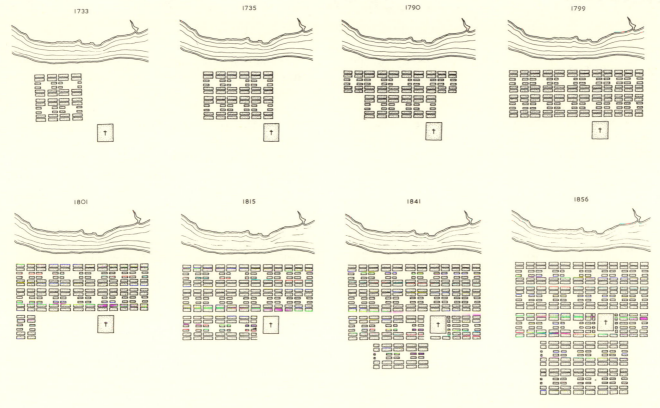

Figure 119. The Growth of Savannah, Georgia: 1733-1856

The gradual but systematic additions to the city are shown in Figure 119, revealing the orderly development of the city from its original boundaries.[25] This history of a century and a quarter of controlled and planned urban growth is all the more remarkable because elsewhere on the continent municipal authorities and land developers alike ignored the spirit of the many fine plans established during the colonial period. New Haven and Philadelphia, for example, originally were laid out with comparatively generous provision for open spaces. As these towns began to grow the in-

[25] Figure 119 is based on a number of sources, the most important of which is Harry A. Chandler, "Map of a Portion of Historical Savannah" appearing in the *Georgia Historical Quarterly*, I, December 1917. While the exact dates of development of some of the wards are uncertain, the general pattern of growth shown in Figure 119 is substantially correct. See Bannister, "Oglethorpe's Sources," for a slightly different graphic depiction of Savannah's expansion.

tentions of the original planners were forgotten. Only Savannah escaped for a time the speculative mania for developing the maximum number of building lots on a given tract that characterized much of nineteenth-century American town development. When Buckingham visited the city in 1840 he was quick to note the unique qualities of the city:

". . . there are no less than eighteen large squares, with grass-plots and trees, in the very heart of the city, disposed at equal distances from each other in the greatest order; while every principal street is lined on each side with rows of trees, and some of the broader streets have also an avenue of trees running down their centre. . . .

"Along the bank of the river, and on the edge of the bluff on which the city stands, is a long and broad street, having its front to the water, and built only on one side. The part nearest the water is planted with rows of trees, having seats placed between; and this street, which is called 'The Bay' is the principal resort for business. The counting-houses, warehouses and best shops, are along this bay; the Exchange and Post Office as well as the city offices, are here; and underneath the bluff, or cliff, are the warehouses and wharfs, alongside which the vessels load with cotton, while the tops of their masts are a little higher only than the level of the street, the height of the cliff from the water varying from forty to seventy feet."[26]

The splendidly urban and urbane community which so charmed Buckingham is shown in the view of Savannah in 1855 reproduced in Figure 120. In the distance, at the end of Bull Street, are the commercial and warehouse buildings along the Savannah River. In the foreground is Monterrey Square, typical in appearance to the two dozen other open spaces of similar character that had resulted from the careful planning and land development control exercised since Oglethorpe's time. These other open spaces can be seen evenly located throughout the town.

One of the great misfortunes of American town planning was that the Savannah plan seemingly exercised no influence on the design of towns outside of Georgia. Even in the later Georgia communities, only Brunswick, planned in 1771, followed the novel and effective neighborhood pattern.[27] The peripheral location of the city in relation to the westward movement of population undoubtedly accounts for this. Had Savannah been located, as were Philadelphia and New York, on the main routes leading to the interior, at least some of our midwestern cities might have achieved part of the charm and urbanity still retained in Oglethorpe's Savannah.

[26] James Silk Buckingham, *The Slave States of America*, London, 1842, I, 118-19.

[27] An early plan of Brunswick is reproduced in Nichols, *Architecture of Georgia*.

Figure 120. View of Savannah, Georgia: 1855

CHAPTER 8

Pioneer Cities of the Ohio Valley

FOR the first century and a half following the English colonization of North America the mountain barrier of the Appalachians and the menace of unfriendly Indians restricted the growth of settlement to the west. As the coastal plain gradually filled with farms and plantations and as the first primitive hamlets slowly grew into respectable towns and small cities, the pressures of an expanding population and the hunger for land caused the colonists to look longingly to the back country. Scotch-Irish immigrants from Ulster and Germans from the Rhineland in the early part of the eighteenth century found little opportunity in the settled portions of the original colonies, and, stimulated by somewhat exaggerated accounts of the piedmont and mountain lands, they too looked to the western country.

Slowly, and with many interruptions because of wars and Indian raids, an irregular penetration of the mountain region began. A few of the hardier adventurers pushed on to the Ohio Valley. Except on the friendlier eastern slopes of the mountains where isolated farmsteads might be maintained with less risk of Indian attack, the first settlements were in tight groups designed for defense. Thus where there were people there were towns. Many of these settlements vanished long ago, and some that remain are small and play an insignificant role in our modern urban civilization. Yet a few rank with the great cities of the country. All, however, are important in understanding how our country developed and how our cities were planned.

The Town at the Forks of the Ohio

The defeat of the French, who controlled the Mississippi and Ohio Valleys, opened the path for settlement in western Pennsylvania. Here, at the strategic point formed by the Monongahela and Allegheny Rivers, the French had built Fort Duquesne. In 1758 this fell to a British force and was renamed Fort Pitt. By 1760, according to an early account, there were 200 houses clustered around the fort, although the civil population numbered only 150, including but 29 women. An early plan, dating from 1764, shows a tiny grid of rectangular blocks along the Monongahela. Aside from the military garrison most of the inhabitants were fur traders. Visiting the community in 1770, George Washington wrote the following comment:

"We lodged in what is called the town, distant about three hundred yards from the fort, at one Semple's who keeps a very good house of public entertainment. The houses which are built of logs, and ranged in streets are on the Monongahela and I suppose may be about twenty in number, and inhabited by Indian traders."[1]

At the historic treaty of Fort Stanwix in 1768 the Indians ceded title to many of their western lands. By this action William Penn's heirs acquired a vast territory in western Pennsylvania, including the site of Pittsburgh. The proprietors, Thomas and Richard Penn, determined to reserve the site from immediate sale and had it surveyed as the Manor of Pittsburgh. Following the Revolution, in 1784, John Penn and his son, who had then become the proprietors, had a plan prepared for the city. Although not the original plat, Figure 121 shows the plan of Pittsburgh as it was then laid out.

The Penns established a new base line parallel with the Allegheny River, running two streets, Penn and Liberty in a roughly east-west direction. The old grid settlement, originally bounded by Ferry, Market, Water, and Second Streets, was extended in both directions so as to fill most of the triangular area between the rivers. A court house square was reserved between Fourth and

[1] Quoted in Neville Craig, *The History of Pittsburg*, Pittsburgh, 1851, p. 95.

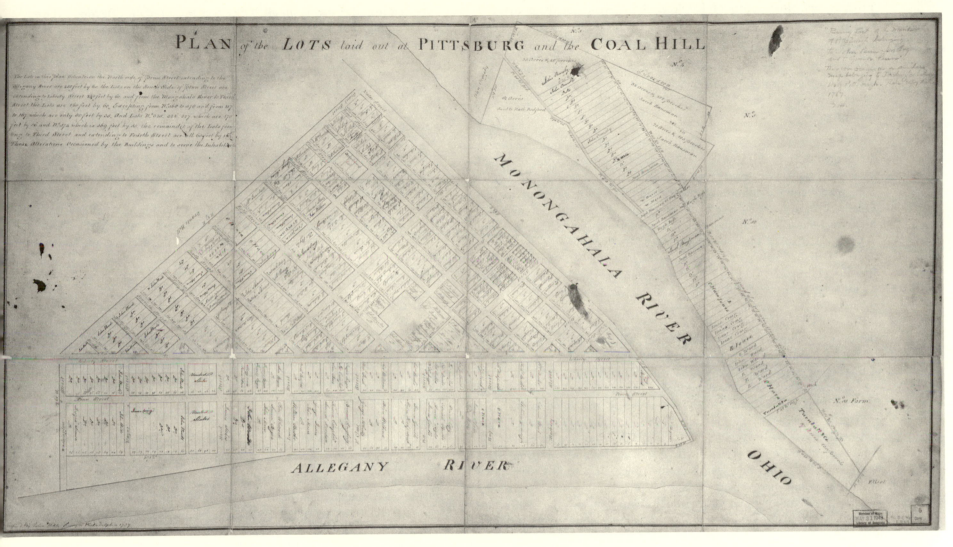

Figure 121. Plan of Pittsburgh, Pennsylvania: 1787

Fifth Streets just south of Liberty. As Melish noted on his visit to the city in 1806:

"The plan was meant to accommodate the town to both rivers, but it is by no means so well designed as it might have been. The streets are generally too narrow, and they cross one another at acute angles, which is both hurtful to the eye and injurious to the buildings."[2]

While Liberty Street was made 80 feet wide, the other principal streets were only 60 and 40 feet, and the alleys, some of which later became business streets were only 10 and 20 feet in width. The plan shows evidence of haste and very little attempt to provide any of the amenities that an earlier Penn did not overlook in laying out Philadelphia. It is no surprise to learn that the surveyors were so careless as to use a chain too long by 1 inch to every 10 feet. Perhaps the Penns were in a hurry to forestall conflicting claims by Virginia to the site. More likely, they desired to take advantage of Pittsburgh's strategic location with respect to westward migration.

The city rapidly developed as the place of departure for settlers bound for points along the Ohio River. By far the easiest method of travel was by water, and dozens of flatboats and rafts started the journey down the river each week from Pittsburgh, which had become the terminus of Braddock's Road from Baltimore and Washington and Forbes' Road, which led from Philadelphia.

While a visitor in 1784 could write that the city was ". . . inhabited almost entirely by Scotts and Irish, who live in paltry log houses, and are as dirty as in the north of Ireland, or even Scotland . . . ,"[3] by the early years of the nineteenth century the town was a busy and prosperous, if not elegant, community. Figure 122 shows the Pittsburgh area in 1815. One can see the additional growth along the rivers beyond the original confines of the Penn plan and the new communities that had been laid out in the vicinity to share the trade and manufacturing wealth of the area. Of particular interest is the town of Allegheny, planned in a neat square of 32 blocks, with an open central green 4 blocks in area.

Surrounding the town on all sides was a common. Beyond, the land was laid out in large garden or farm lots. The origin of this settlement is not known, but the plat of the village is similar to the original plan of New Haven, and the common and farm lot division has a New England touch.[4]

The later development of Pittsburgh is beyond the scope of this work, but its growth was steady and at times rapid. With the development by Congress of the National Road following the War of 1812, Pittsburgh lost some of its importance as a stopover and outfitting station on the way west. But coal and iron, canal and railroad, provided a new basis for prosperity. By the middle of the century Pittsburgh's reputation as a manufacturing city was assured. It also had already acquired a reputation for another feature which despite achievements of our own day it has not lived down. James Silk Buckingham, who spent a few days there in 1840, noted

". . . the unavoidable accumulation of soot and dirt upon everything you see or touch. Sheffield, in England, is sometimes called 'The City of Soot,' but its atmosphere is clear and transparent in comparison with that of Pittsburgh, which is certainly the most smoky and sooty town it has ever been my lot to behold. The houses are blackened with it, the streets are made filthy, and the garments and persons of all whom you meet are soiled and made dingy by its influence."[5]

The Town in the Hills of Kentucky

At the conclusion of the French and Indian War the British government proclaimed the trans-Appalachian region closed to further settlement. While this action helped in establishing friendlier relations with the Indians, who were naturally opposed

[2] John Melish, *Travels Through the United States of America in the Years 1806-07*, Philadelphia, 1812, p. 54.

[3] Arthur Lee, as quoted in Isaac Harris, *Pittsburgh Business Directory for the Year 1837*, Pittsburgh, 1837, p. 6.

[4] Allegheny was located on a tract of land reserved for land grants to soldiers of the Revolutionary War. The Supreme Executive Council of Pennsylvania directed that a town site should be surveyed in 1784. David Redick was the surveyor and planner, and it may have been he who set aside the town commons as common pasture land. The first lots were sold in November 1788, with the purchaser of each town lot receiving an outlot. Pittsburgh Regional Planning Association and Pittsburgh City Planning Commission, *North Side Study*, Pittsburgh, 1954, pp. 2-4.

[5] James Silk Buckingham, *The Eastern and Western States of America*, London, 1842, II, 185.

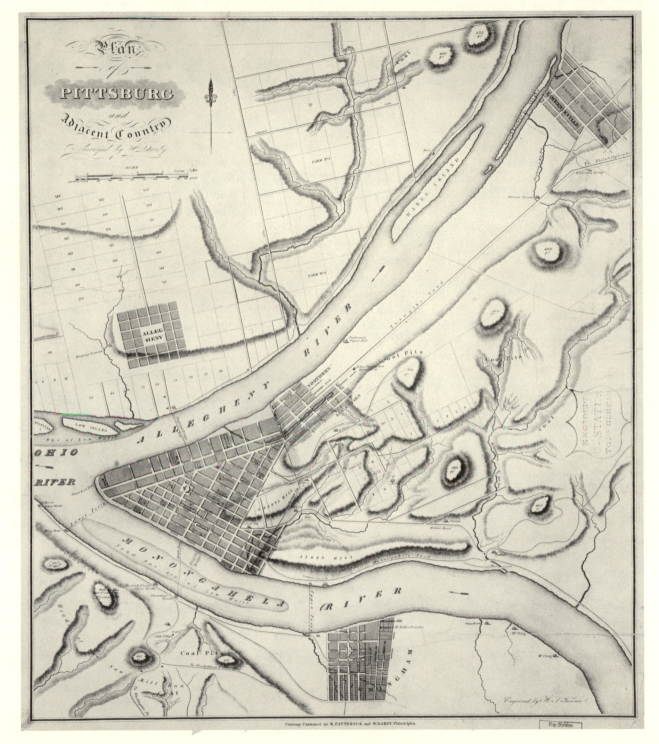

Figure 122. Plan of Pittsburgh, Pennsylvania: ca. 1815

to white encroachment, it aroused immediate resentment among colonists interested in western exploration, settlement, or land speculation. In fact, however, the proclamation scarcely deterred the westward movement. Prominent colonists, even resident British officials, organized land companies and petitioned the crown for immense estates in the valley of the Ohio. Virginia's Governor Dunmore, himself a speculator in western land, sent surveyors into Kentucky and eventually led troops against the Indians who had become aroused at the apparent violation of the proclamation of 1763.

Small bands of settlers as early as 1769 hacked their way through the heavily wooded ridge and valley region of western Carolina and eastern Tennessee to establish rude communities on the Wautauga River. Many of these pioneers had lived in western Carolina where they had become resentful of the colonial government because of its domination by the seaboard communities. At Wautauga they established a primitive government of their own, although technically they remained under the jurisdiction of North Carolina. Population gradually increased, and among the early arrivals was Daniel Boone, who had already explored much of the back country. From Wautauga, Boone resumed his earlier explorations of Kentucky, and his stories of fertile river valleys of the Kentucky, Cumberland, and the Licking Rivers soon led to attempts at settlement in Kentucky.

Late in 1774 Judge Richard Henderson of North Carolina formed the Transylvania Company to purchase land from the Indians and sell it for white settlement. The action was certainly a violation of the proclamation of 1763, but Henderson made no effort to conceal his project from the authorities. He announced his plans on Christmas of 1774, and, with Boone's help, a meeting with the Cherokees was arranged early in the following year. By treaty the company purchased about half of the present state of Kentucky for £10,000. Immediately this was denounced by the governor of North Carolina as unlawful, and he threatened the company "with the pain of His Majesty's displeasure and the most rigorous penalties of the law."[6] Governor Dunmore of Virginia, which claimed the Kentucky region, joined in the condemnation of Henderson and his associates.

[6] As quoted in George W. Ranck's invaluable *Boonesborough*, Filson Club Publications No. 16, Louisville, 1901, p. 6.

Boone and an advance party set out through the Cumberland Gap for a site on the Kentucky River that he had previously noted. On April 1 his group reached the site and erected a few temporary log huts. When Henderson arrived three weeks later, he chose a location a few hundred yards away and on somewhat higher ground for the permanent settlement. The name Fort Boone, and later Boonesborough, was one indication of the value Henderson placed on Boone's services to the company. A more tangible reward was a grant of 2,000 acres of land.

Although Boonesborough was not completed in 1775, a copy exists of a plan drawn by Henderson in that year. From this plan a sketch of the settlement has been prepared and is shown in Figure 123. Twenty-six cabins were arranged in a rectangle, the rear walls of the cabins forming a stockade about 260 feet long by 180 feet wide. Two-story block houses with overhanging upper floors formed the corners of the fort. Not everyone in the settlement lived in the enclosure. There were isolated cabins on farmsteads located in forest clearings, and some settlers continued to live on the site of the temporary settlement in the hollow below. But here was the store, here families gathered for social or religious occasions or at times of Indian raids, here new settlers first arrived and found temporary housing, here was the land office of the Transylvania Company, and here was the "capital" of the newly proclaimed government of Transylvania. In short, this rough, log-enclosed quadrangle performed the historic functions for which towns throughout the world have always been founded.

Transylvania ceased to exist as a separate government when Virginia created the County of Kentucky and asserted political jurisdiction. Henderson's purchase was likewise declared void. But Boonesborough was not abandoned in spite of the Indian raids that began in 1776 and increased in frequency and violence. The famous siege in the fall of 1778 marked the high point of the Indian effort, but this too the settlers survived. Other frontier stations, as these stockade forts were called, were not so fortunate; many were destroyed by the Indians and were never rebuilt. Although Boonesborough was finally created a town by the Virginia legislature in 1779, the community that survived the war could not endure in peace. Kentucky was made a state in 1792, and Boonesborough was one of the chief towns, but by 1810 it had decreased in size and in a few years disappeared altogether.

Figure 123. View of Boonesborough, Kentucky as it Existed in 1778

By 1784, when John Filson's famous map of Kentucky appeared, many settlements had been established. A reproduction of this first map of the area is shown in Figure 124, on which the cluster of communities along the Kentucky River and lesser streams can be noted. Filson designates some of these as towns, others as stations or forts, although the latter predominate. Generally, these resembled closely the stockaded quadrangle form used at Boonesborough. Because of the importance of this fortress town plan in Kentucky, Tennessee, and Ohio it is worth exploring the origins of the frontier station settlement pattern.

This was, of course, no new plan devised especially for the Kentucky territory. In one form or another, closely built stockaded communities were constructed wherever enemy attack might be expected. At Jamestown, Plymouth, New Amsterdam, the Swedish settlements along the Delaware, and other early towns this pattern was used. No doubt the early colonists may have adopted the idea from some of the Indian tribes who had established fairly elaborate protected communities. But as early as the beginning of the eighteenth century formalized systems of such community settlements had developed.

Immediately prior to the Kentucky colonization a proposed plan for a system of land division, similar in many respects to the frontier stations, appeared in an appendix to the account of Henry Bouquet's expedition against the Indians. This work was published in 1765. The author of the scheme is unknown, being identified merely as "an officer of great abilities and long experience, in our wars with the Indians." The explanation accompanying the plan reads as follows:

"Let us suppose a settlement to be formed for one hundred families, composed of five persons each, upon an average.

"Lay out upon a river or creek, if it can be found conveniently, a Square of one thousand seven hundred and sixty yards, or a mile for each side.

"That Square will contain   -   640 acres
Allowing for streets and public uses 40)
To half an acre for every house - 50)
To one hundred lots at five and   )   640 acres
half acres - - - - - - - 550)

"The four sides of the square measure 7040 yards, which gives

to each house about 70 yards front to stockade, and the ground allowed for building will be 210 feet front, and about 100 feet deep. . . .

"Round the town are the commons, of three miles square, containing, exclusive of the lots abovementioned, 5120 acres. On three sides of the town, five other Squares will be laid out of three square miles, containing 5760 acres each, one of which is reserved for wood for the use of the Settlement; the other four to be divided into 25 out-lotts or plantations, of about 230 acres each, so that in the four Squares, there will be one hundred such plantations, for the 100 families.

"Another township may be laid out joining this, upon the same plan, and as many more as you please upon the same line, without losing any ground."[7]

While the linear dimensions and the acreages mentioned in this scheme do not seem to work out correctly, the chief elements of the plan are clear enough. The stockaded village, nearby garden lots, and more distant farms form a pattern essentially the same as the frontier settlements later developed in Kentucky.

An even earlier plan for settlement along the same lines originated in colonial Virginia. Since many of the Kentucky pioneers came from Virginia and the area lay under the governmental jurisdiction of that state, it seems likely that the settlers looked back to the pattern established when the frontier ran farther to the east. In 1701 the Virginia General Assembly enacted a law entitled "An Act for the Better Strengthening the Frontiers and Discovering the Approaches of an Enemy."[8] The law established a system of "settling in cohabitations," groups of not less than twenty families. Land grants of between ten and thirty thousand acres could be made to any society undertaking to settle the frontier lands, provided

". . . that for every five hundred acres of land to be granted . . . there shall be and shall continually be kept upon the said land one christian man between sixteen and sixty years of age perfect of limb, able and fit for service who shall alsoe be continually pro-

[7] *Historical Account of the Expedition Against the Ohio Indians in the Year MDCCLXIV Under the Command of Henry Bouquet, Esq.* (Philadelphia, 1765), Ohio Valley Historical Series, Cincinnati, 1868, pp. 119-20.

[8] William Hening, *Virginia Statutes at Large*, Philadelphia, 1823, III, 204-209.

Figure 124. John Filson's Map of Kentucky: 1784

vided with a well fixt musquett or fuzee, a good pistoll, sharp simeter, tomahauk and five pounds of good clean pistoll powder and twenty pounds of sizable leaden bulletts or swan or goose shott."[9]

Each settler was to be given 200 acres of land for a farm, "together with halfe an acre to seat upon and live." The law also specified how the "cohabitation" was to be planned. An area of 200 acres was to "be laid out in a geomitricall square or neare that figure as conveniency will admitt." The half-acre grants for house lots were to be located within this square, and the law then required the society to

". . . palesado in or cause to be pallisadoed in for a fort one half acre of land to be laid out in the middle of the said two hundred acres appointed for the cohabitation with good sound pallisadoes at least thirteen foot long and six inches diameter in the middle of the length thereof, and set double and at least three foot within the ground."[10]

Possibly some settlements in western Virginia were made under this colonization scheme, although the extent to which colonization societies made use of these authorized land grants is not known. For the frontier stations of pioneer Kentucky and Ohio there were thus ample precedents.

The City at the Ohio Rapids

One of the early visitors to Boonesborough, who ranked with Boone among America's great heroes of the west, became responsible for founding an important city on the Ohio and for giving his name to a lesser community nearby. This was George Rogers Clark, commissioned by Virginia in the Revolution with nothing less than the capture of the entire Old Northwest from the well-equipped and entrenched British troops. In the spring of 1778 Clark assembled at Wheeling and Pittsburgh a forlorn little army with the announced purpose of defending Kentucky but with secret orders to proceed against Kaskaskia. Among the volunteers were a number of men who had little interest in military expeditions but who frankly admitted they were seeking land along the

Ohio for settlement. With the families of these soldiers Clark and his men departed.

In May the party reached the great rapids of the Ohio. At Corn Island Clark established a camp and began drilling his men. The settlers in the group built some log huts, began farming, and thus established the first permanent settlement at Louisville. They were not the first to settle on the site, however. Five years earlier Captain Thomas Bullitt of Virginia had laid out a town for Dr. John Connolly, a surgeon in the British army who had been awarded 2,000 acres of land at the site in reward for his services. In the following year Connolly had advertised in Williamsburg that town lots and outlots were available for long lease. The war caused the abandonment of the town promotion scheme, however, and the area remained unoccupied until Clark's arrival.

The first settlement on the island took the form of a typical Kentucky frontier station as previously described. Later, after Clark had achieved his military victories over the British in Indiana and Illinois, the settlers moved to the south bank of the river and erected a similar stockaded village surrounded by farms and gardens. This was located near the end of what is now Twelfth Street in Louisville. In April 1779 the inhabitants formally organized a town government, agreed on a town plan for the land east of the fort along the river, and, at the suggestion of Clark, adopted the name of Louisville in honor of the French king. Among the minutes of that first meeting appears the following resolution governing the distribution of land:

". . . that a number of lots, not exceeding 200 for the present, be laid off, to contain half an acre each, 35 yards by 70 where the ground will admit of it, with some public lots and streets.

"That each adventurer draw for only one lot by chance. That every such person be obliged to clear off the undergrowth and begin to cultivate part thereof by the 10th of June, and build thereon a good covered house, 16 feet by 20, by the 25th of December. That no person sell his lot unless to some person without one, but that it be given up to the Trustees to dispose of to some new adventurer on pain of forfeiture thereof."[11]

A plan of the town attributed to George Rogers Clark is reproduced in Figure 125. According to this plan all the land between

[9] ibid., 206-07.
[10] ibid., 207.

[11] Quoted in Ruben T. Durrett, The Centenary of Louisville, Filson Club Publication No. 8, Louisville, 1893, p. 34n.

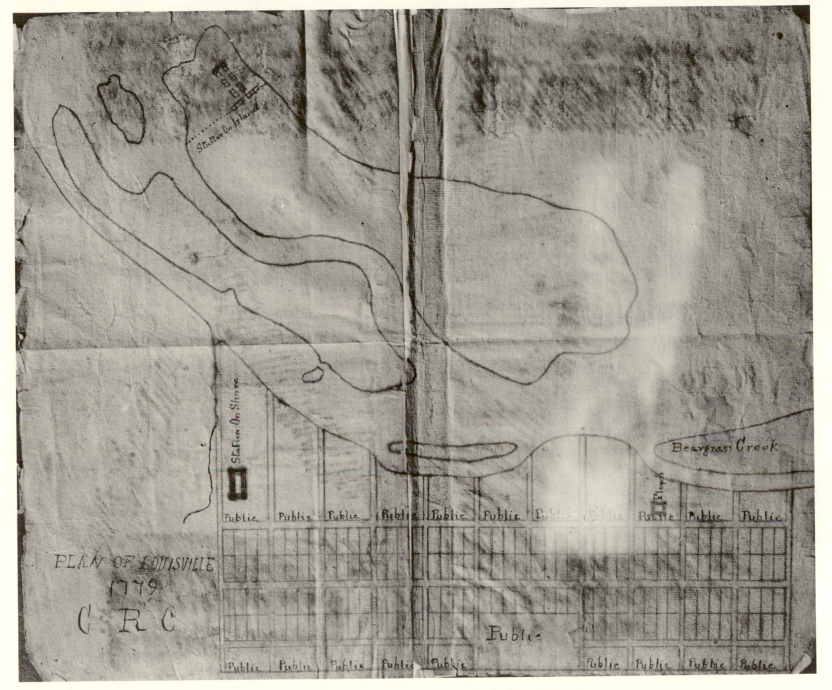

Figure 125. George Rogers Clark's Plan of Louisville, Kentucky: 1779

the present Main Street and the river was to be public property, as well as a strip of land the entire length of the town along its southern boundary. Whether this map represents the town as actually laid out or an alteration in the original plan proposed by Clark remains a matter of conjecture. A local legend is that Clark intended to repeat this strip of common land after every third street as the town was extended to the south. What is a matter of record, however, is that the town was forced to sell its common lands to satisfy a debt which Connolly, the earliest owner, owed to one of his associates, John Campbell. Campbell exercised his influence with the Virginia legislature to secure the passage of a series of curious laws which in effect made the town of Louisville liable for Connolly's obligations. For $3,300 the town disposed of its lands and lost an opportunity to retain a feature in its plan which would have been as attractive and functional as it would have been unique. That some attempt was made to salvage the strip common feature of the original plan is indicated in Figure 126, which shows in 1836 the remnants of the old common or a start on a new one located one tier of lots south of the first location. Also of interest are the regular parallel strips of outlots of 5, 10, and 20 acres. Like the common, these agricultural field divisions have given way with the growth of the city far beyond the boundaries ever contemplated by Clark.

When Francis Baily, Fellow of the Royal Society, visited Louisville in 1797, he noted the favorable location of Louisville and also another community on the Indiana side of the falls:

"Louisville, which may contain about 200 houses, chiefly frame-built, is pleasantly situated on the second bank of the river, which is about fifty feet higher than the bed. . . . The prospect from Louisville is truly delightful. The Ohio here is near a mile wide, and is bounded on the opposite side by an open champaign country. . . . About two miles lower down on the opposite shore is Clarkesville, a little village consisting of about twenty houses. This settlement was formed by General George Rogers Clarke, who had a share of the 150,000 acres of land which was given to him and other officers who were at the reduction of Kaskaskias and St. Vincent's, and which was laid out in the part of the northwestern territory immediately opposite Louisville."[12]

[12] Francis Baily, *Journal of a Tour in Unsettled Parts of North America in 1796 & 1797*, London, 1856, pp. 239-40.

Other cities were built at the falls of the Ohio River on both shores. Among them was Jeffersonville, Indiana, planned in 1802 on a pattern so unusual, both because of its form and because of the source of its design, that it is given extended treatment in a later chapter.

Public policy affecting land received early attention by the nation's leaders. The growth and development of Louisville and its neighboring cities during the early nineteenth century was stimulated by the formulation of a national land policy and the first efforts at mass colonization beyond the mountain frontier. A review of these activities is essential for an understanding of urban planning in America.

The Continental Checkerboard of the Continental Congress

At the conclusion of the Revolutionary War the now independent states, only loosely bound together by the Articles of Confederation, advanced their separate claims to ownership and political jurisdiction in the western lands. Virginia had already organized Kentucky and a portion of the territory north of the Ohio into counties. North Carolina and Georgia claimed all the land west of their boundaries to the Mississippi River. Massachusetts pressed its rights to most of western New York and a wide strip of land running through lower Michigan and Wisconsin. Little Connecticut claimed a continuation of its northern and southern boundaries running west through northern Pennsylvania, Ohio, Indiana, and Illinois. So intense were feelings that the Articles of Confederation, approved by the Continental Congress in 1778, did not go into effect until 1781 because Maryland refused ratification due to Virginia claims of land west of her territory. Maryland's final approval came only after New York offered to cede to the Congress all western lands claimed by her.

The debates and resolutions and petitions in Congress on the question of western land cession were almost endless, but eventually satisfactory agreements were reached. In 1783 Virginia surrendered her claims to the Ohio country, retaining only the ownership of a tract known as the Virginia Military District to be used by the state in granting land bounties to veterans of the Virginia militia. Massachusetts in 1785 and Connecticut in 1786 waived

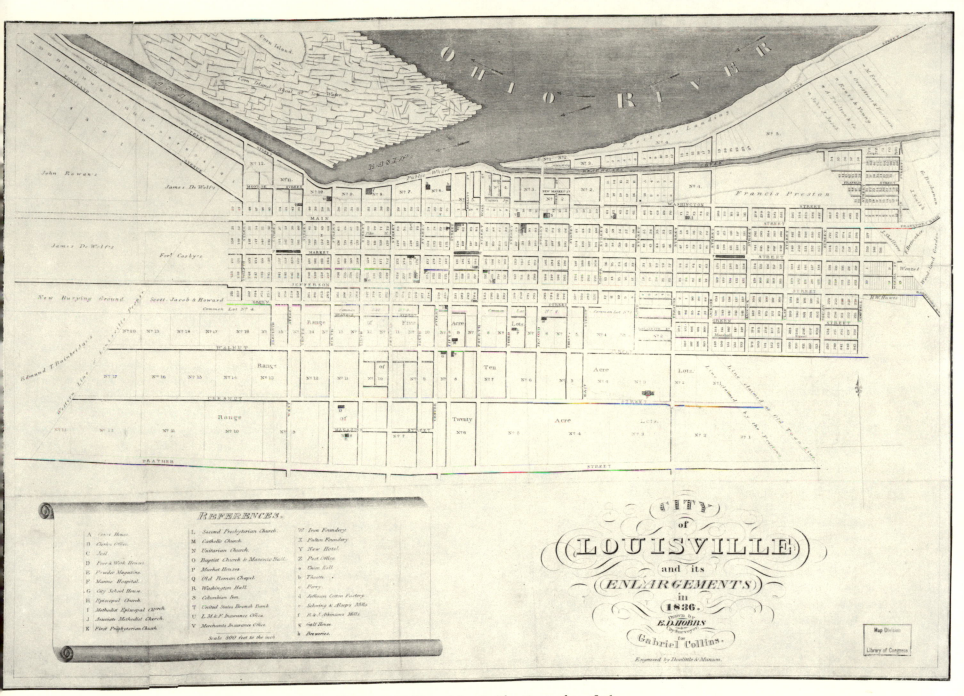

Figure 126. Plan of Louisville, Kentucky: 1836

their western claims and thus cleared the way for Congress to establish a national land policy for settlement of the region north of the Ohio River. Connecticut did retain both ownership and governmental authority over the northeastern part of Ohio, an area designated as the Connecticut Reserve, but in 1800 it ceded to Congress its political jurisdiction. Not until 1802, with the Georgia cession, did the national government come into full control of the western lands.

Along with the questions of ownership and sovereignty went the problem of establishing a national land policy. The desire for western land had always been strong; now, with the end of war and the removal of colonial restraints on western settlement, the demands for land across the Appalachian frontier mounted. On the one hand the great land companies, organized before the Revolution but unable to win crown approval, renewed their claims before Congress for large land grants. On the other were thousands of individuals, for the most part poor although not lacking in energy or courage, who clamored for just enough land in the west for a farm—preferably as a grant, but, if offered for sale, then at a low price and with liberal credit. To some extent opposed to these demands of the small farmers were members of Congress who looked to the sale of public lands as the easiest method of raising funds necessary to carry on the work of government.

The Land Ordinance of 1785 resulted from the attempts by the Continental Congress to balance the conflicting wishes of all parties interested in disposal of the public domain. The background of this legislation has been fully treated by a number of authorities and need not be repeated here.[13] The main provisions of the law, however, are important to an understanding of its effects on settlement patterns in rural sections, in the planning of towns and cities, and its stimulation of land speculation.

Prior to its sale, land was to be laid out in rectangular townships 6 miles square. Each township was to be divided into 36 square sections of 1 square mile or 640 acres. Half of the land was to be sold by townships, the other half by sections. Sales were to be by auction in the eastern states, and a minimum price was established of $1 per acre plus survey costs of $1 per section or $36 per township. Terms of sale were cash at the time of purchase. The ordinance specified that the first seven ranges of townships should be laid out west of a line running directly north from the termination of the southern boundary line of Pennsylvania. From these townships one-seventh of the area was to be reserved by the Secretary of War to be exchanged for land certificates given in part payment for military service during the Revolution. Further, township sections 8, 11, 26, and 29 were to be reserved to the national government, and section 16 in every township was to be set aside for the maintenance of public schools.

The survey of the first seven ranges is shown in Figure 127. This was completed by 1786, and the first sales of land were begun. The response was disappointing to those hoping for vast revenues for the national treasury. There were a number of reasons. The Indian menace had not yet been removed, and settlers were reluctant to venture far beyond the established line of the frontier. Most of the land indicated as sold in Figure 127 was located in the safer eastern tier of townships close to the Ohio River. Because no credit could be extended and since the minimum sale was for an entire section, many persons desiring land could not afford to purchase. Settlers already squatting illegally on western lands could hardly afford the trip to an eastern city to bid at an auction. And, finally, most of the persons with money to buy land for later speculation felt they could convince Congress to grant them large tracts of land in some favored location either without payment or at low cost with liberal credit terms.[14] In this they were not mistaken.

The survey system adopted by the Continental Congress and the policies for disposal of western lands established in 1785 governed the settlement of America during the next century until the closing of the frontier. Today, as one flies over the last mountain ridges from the east, one sees stretching ahead to the horizon a vast checkerboard of fields and roads. With military precision, modified only on occasion by some severe topographic break, or some earlier system of land distribution, this rectangular grid persists to the shores of the Pacific. America thus lives on a giant

---

[13] Among others the following studies are valuable: Shosuke Sato, *The Land Question in the United States*, Johns Hopkins University Studies in Historical and Political Science, IV, Baltimore, 1886; Payson Jackson Treat, *The National Land System, 1785-1820*, New York, 1910; and Amelia C. Ford, *Colonial Precedents of our National Land System as it Existed in 1800*, Wisconsin University Bulletin, History Series, II, No. 2, Madison, 1910.

[14] For an excellent description of the first surveys see Walter Havighurst, *Wilderness for Sale*, New York, 1956, pp. 62-88.

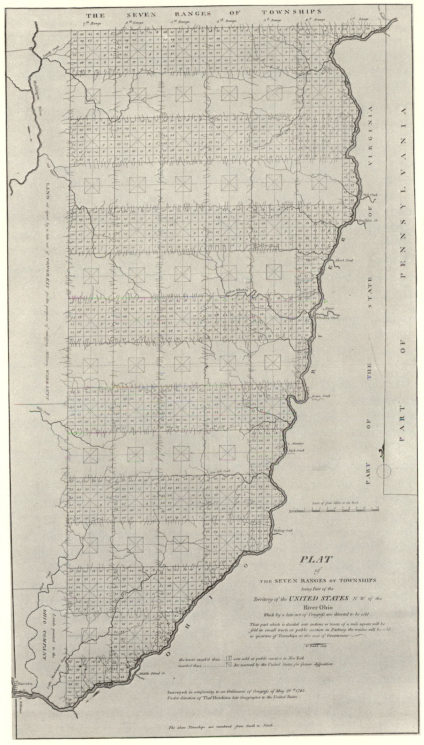

Figure 127. Map of the First Townships Surveyed in Ohio: 1796

gridiron imposed on the natural landscape by the early surveyors carrying out the mandate of the Continental Congress expressed in the Land Ordinance of 1785.

The effect on city planning was to reinforce the natural inclination for the gridiron street system, the easiest of all to lay out when speed or the desire for land speculation guide the hand of the surveyor. Section lines became rural roads. Where they intersected small hamlets grew up slowly or were laid out with an eye to quick development stimulated by clever promotion and exaggerated claims of their advantageous locations. The original right angle crossing served as base lines for new streets parallel and perpendicular to the section line roads. Later federal legislation establishing half-section townsites of 320 acres perpetuated the rectangular street system for the overwhelming majority of American cities. Perhaps the rectangular survey pattern for the west was the only system that could have resulted in speedy settlement and the capture of a continent for the new nation, but its results in city planning were dullness and mediocrity.

Marietta on the Muskingum

The ordinance of 1785 providing for sale of western lands by townships and sections was scarcely printed before Congress was confronted with offers to purchase land in the territory northwest of the Ohio in wholesale quantities. One of these proposals came from the Ohio Company of Associates, a group of army veterans chiefly from Massachusetts but including persons from Rhode Island and Connecticut, organized in 1786. This organization stemmed from an earlier attempt by a number of army officers who, in 1783 under the leadership of Colonel Rufus Putnam, petitioned Congress to establish a new territory in Ohio where lands would be granted soldiers in fulfillment of earlier promises of land bounties for military service. The Ohio Company sent the Reverend Manasseh Cutler as its agent to negotiate the terms of the proposed land purchase with Congress. By the fall of 1787 Cutler had secured congressional approval for the purchase of 1½ million acres by the Ohio Company at $1 an acre, with a portion of the purchase price to be paid within three months and the remainder at later times.

In order to gain congressional sanction for this departure from the land policy established in 1785, Cutler was forced to enter privately into an agreement with Colonel William Duer, secretary of the Board of the Treasury. Duer pointed out to Cutler that Congress was badly in need of funds and would be more likely to approve a request for a much larger tract than the 1½ million acres acquired by the Ohio Company. Cutler and Duer reached an agreement, the exact nature of which remains obscure, for the Ohio Company to petition for some 5 million acres of land, and it was this request that Congress approved and directed the Board of Treasury to conclude. Duer and his associates, usually referred to as the Scioto Company, then took over 3½ million acres for their own purposes.[15]

The Scioto scheme was an out-and-out land speculation. The Ohio Company project, on the other hand, was as nearly divorced from speculative influence as any colonization enterprise in North America. True, some of the purchasers of shares in the company did so in hopes of enriching themselves by later land sales. Most of the members, however, intended to take up land in the purchase and to establish a new life in the west. The plan for settlement coincided with the ordinance of 1787 establishing the framework of government in the Northwest Territory, and the early history of the company's activities in Ohio is closely related to the first establishment of civil government under United States jurisdiction beyond the Appalachians. It would have been difficult for either enterprise to succeed without the other, and the speedy settlement of the west with the orderly formation of territorial and then state governments was due in considerable measure to the Ohio Company and its leaders.

The planning of the chief city in the territory received early attention. The map of Ohio shown in Figure 128, attributed to Manasseh Cutler and probably dating from 1788, shows an inset plan of the "City to be built on the Muskingum River." This map also shows the division of Ohio lands into townships with the five reserved sections in each township specified in the ordinance of 1785. The city plan is somewhat different from that described in the proceedings of the Ohio Company. At its meeting on August 30, 1787, the day after they learned from Cutler that the purchase had been approved, the directors resolved to set aside nearly 6,000 acres at the mouth of the Muskingum for "a City & Commons," and

"That within the said Tract and in the most eligible situation there be appropriated for a City, sixty squares of three hundred & sixty feet by three hundred & sixty feet each, in an oblong form. . . .

"That four of said squares, be reserved for public uses, and the remaining fifty six divided into house Lots. That each square contain twelve house lots of sixty feet front, and One hundred feet depth. . . .

"That contiguous to, and in the vicinity of the above tract there be laid off one Thousand Lots of Sixty-four acres each . . . which as the city lots, shall be considered a part of each proprietary share."[16]

At a later meeting the size of the city lots was increased to 90 by 180 feet, provision was made for 10-foot alleys through each block, and the central street was directed to be laid out with a width of 150 feet.

Early in April 1788 an advance party led by Rufus Putnam arrived at the site selected for the city. Like many other similar locations throughout Ohio, the spot had previously been occupied by the early mound-building Indians. Along the high ground parallel to the Muskingum River stretched two great quadrangles and other geometrical earthworks, including a high circular mound. Connecting the largest of the rectangular enclosures with the river ran a broad, straight, avenue-like processional way. These features of the site appear on the map reproduced in Figure 129.

In designing the city, Putnam incorporated some of the mound constructions in a most interesting manner. Figure 130 shows the plan of Marietta as prepared by Putnam and his helpers following the directions of the company but adapted to the peculiarities of the site. Classical names were given to the open spaces: Quadranaou, Capitolium, and Cecelia. The conical mound became known as Conus, and the processional path was named Sacra Via.

This ambitious plan could not be realized immediately. For the protection of the first settlers, Putnam's party set about the construction of a fortified enclosure. At the top of the river bank, a

---

[15] The best treatment of the fascinating background of the Ohio Company and Cutler's negotiations is the long editorial introduction by Archer B. Hulbert in *The Records of the Original Proceedings of the Ohio Company*, Ohio Company Series, I, Marietta, 1917.

[16] *ibid.*, 15-16.

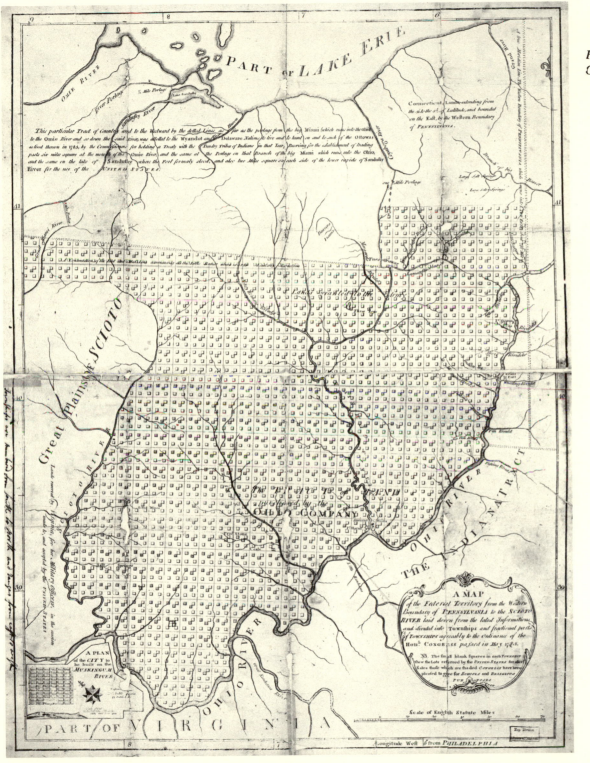

Figure 128. Manassah Cutler's Map of Ohio: ca. 1787

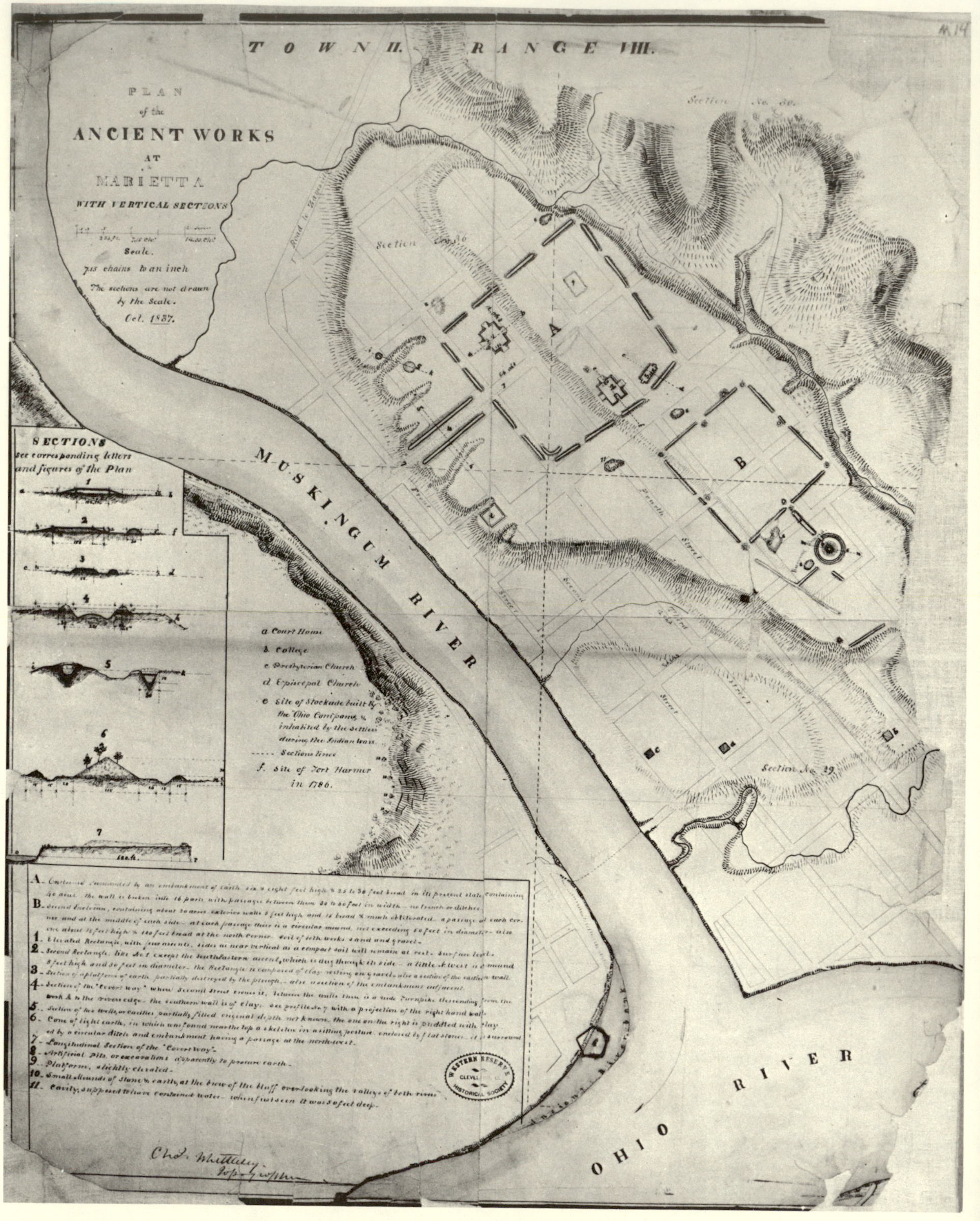

Figure 129. Plan of Marietta, Ohio and the Indian Earthworks: 1837

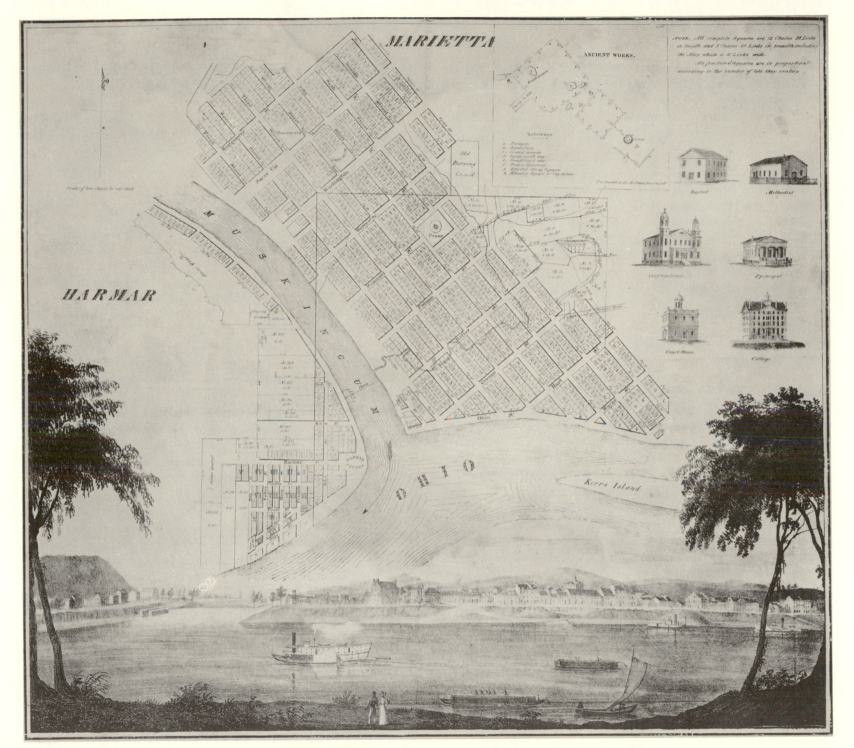

Figure 130. Plan of Marietta, Ohio: ca. 1837

block southeast of the Sacra Via, they built a stockade similar to the Kentucky stations. Following the classical pattern in names for other parts of the town, this structure was termed the Campus Martius. A view showing its appearance is reproduced in Figure 131. Putnam described this fortified village in his memoirs:

"Campus Martius . . . consisted of four block houses of hewed or sawed timber, two story high (erected at the expense of the Company) the upper stories on two sides projected two feet with loop holes in the projection to rake the sides of the lower stories. Two of the block houses had two rooms on a floor, & the other two three rooms. The block houses were so placed as to form bastions of a regular square and flank the curtains of the work, which was proposed to consist of private houses, also to be made of hewed or sawed timber and two story high—leaving a clean area within of 144 feet square."[17]

On two sides of the Campus Martius and in the adjacent block, gardens were laid out for the use of those living within the stockade. The company assigned lots within the enclosure for 20 years only and specified that in the event of attack all persons in the community were to be given shelter in these dwellings. Putnam's own house was located here adjacent to one of the corner blockhouses, and it still stands on its original site, now enclosed by the Marietta Historical Museum.

Most of the land reserved for public use in the original plan still remains, including a broad stretch of park extending along the banks of the Muskingum. The common land mentioned in the early records of the company no longer surrounds the town. This was apparently regarded, as were many of the New England common lands, as fields to be farmed in common and later distributed to original settlers and later arrivals. Part of the common land was surveyed almost immediately into garden and farm parcels and distributed by lot when it was discovered that in the earlier drawings for land some of the company's officials had been allocated plots some distance from the town. Putnam opposed this action, but others overruled him and he was directed to divide 3,000 acres of the common land into lots of 3 acres.

While Marietta grew and other settlements were laid out under the Ohio Company, Duer and his friends of the Scioto speculation were attempting to unload their vast holdings at a profit. Actually their "title" to the land consisted of a contract to take over a portion of what amounted to a land option held by the Ohio Company on 5 million acres of land. Their plan seems to have been to make sales of large tracts abroad for cash and to use the funds in exercising their rights under the contract. Joel Barlow was sent to Europe as their agent and centered his operations in France. Unable to find buyers for large tracts of land, he established a French subsidiary to "buy" land from the parent company on installments. To persons buying shares in the French company he guaranteed land titles and the right to immediate settlement of Ohio land in proportion to their share holdings. Barlow met with considerable success in this venture, and in 1790 some 500 Frenchmen arrived in Alexandria, Virginia, believing that they would be transported to Ohio by the Scioto Company and there would find a great city in which to live.

Barlow's claims for the state of civilization in Ohio were highly exaggerated, and Duer and his friends, who were not prepared to spend a penny on improvements in their domain, made almost no arrangements to care for these new settlers. Nor were the French at all suited to life on the American frontier. The group included such oddly assorted persons as a dancing master, doctors, lawyers, jewelers, and exiled nobility. As a final touch to this fiasco, Barlow, through error or design, had sold land for the settlement in territory belonging to the Ohio Company. Duer finally contracted with the company to lay out a town for the French, and Major John Burnham was sent down the Ohio to clear some land, plan a town and construct some cabins for the settlers. Gallipolis was the result, with a great square opening to the river much like the earlier French colonial towns.[18] The first houses were small huts built in compact rows in the square, as depicted in Figure 132. When a countryman, C. F. Volney, visited the city in 1796 he described the unfortunate condition of the community:

"Next day I took a view of the place, and was struck with its forlorn appearance; with the thin pale faces, sickly looks, and

---

[17] Rufus Putnam, *Memoirs*, Boston, 1903, p. 105. Spelling and punctuation modernized.

[18] A plan of Gallipolis is reproduced, without identification of the source, in Antoine Saugrain, *L'Odyssee Americaine d'une Famille Française*, Baltimore, 1936, following p. 22.

Figure 131. View of the Campus Martius at Marietta, Ohio in 1791

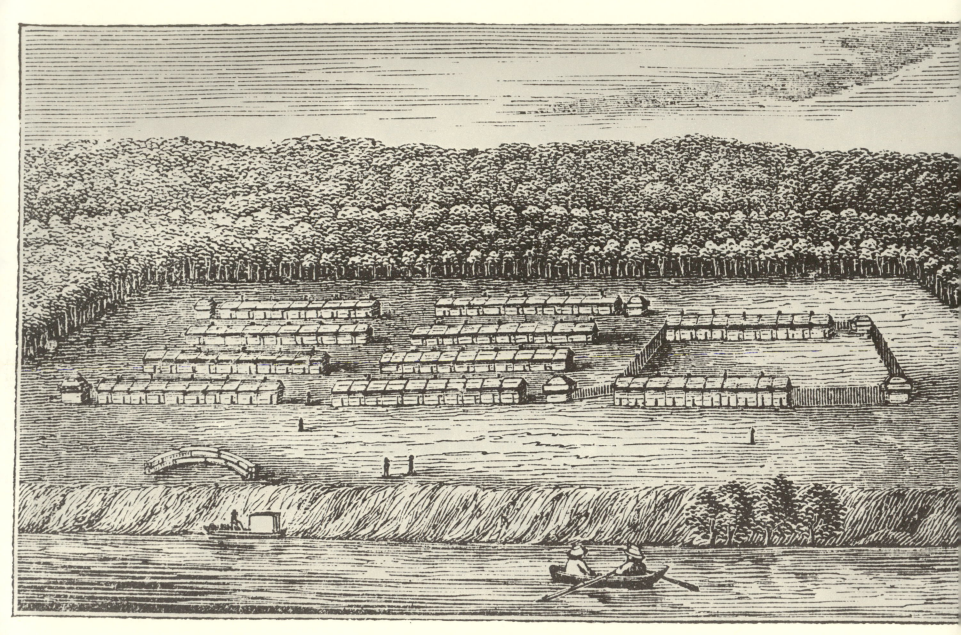

Figure 132. View of Gallipolis, Ohio in 1791

anxious air of its inhabitants. . . . Their dwellings, though made externally cheerful by whitewash, were only log huts, patched with clay, and roofed with shingles, consequently damp, unwholesome, and uncomfortable. The village forms an oblong quadrangle of two rows of contiguous buildings, which a spark would consume altogether."[19]

Many of the original settlers drifted away from Gallipolis when it became evident, after the collapse of the Scioto Company, that they had no legal title to the lands they occupied. In 1795 Congress recognized the plight of the French and granted 24,000 acres of land near the mouth of the Scioto for distribution to the Gallipolis residents. In that same year the Ohio Company agreed to sell the land occupied by the community for a nominal amount, donating the cost of the improvements made at company expense.

Meanwhile Marietta continued to grow as additional shareholders of the Ohio Company and other western pioneers came down the Ohio. The town became the seat of government for the Northwest Territory, and in 1800, following a change in sales policy for the public lands, a government land office was established there. As the Indians were pushed farther west the danger of attack subsided, and the Campus Martius was dismantled. The owners of houses forming the sides of the enclosure moved them to their town lots, and Marietta began to assume the air of an older community in the east. With its wide streets, generous open spaces, the riverbank promenade, the Academy (later Marietta College), and the territorial offices, the community must have had some of the sophistication and elegance of a Williamsburg or an Annapolis. Marietta today retains some of this early charm and stands as an excellent example of the benefits of sound community planning.

The Towns of Southern and Central Ohio

In the same year that saw the establishment of the Ohio Company and the planning of Marietta near the eastern border of the Northwest Territory, Congress approved another wholesale land purchase. This lay between the Little and Great Miami Rivers in

what is now southwestern Ohio. The purchaser was John Cleves Symmes, a member of Congress from New Jersey, who obtained terms similar to those granted the Ohio Company. Asking first for 2 million acres, he later reduced his proposal to 1 million and paid down $82,000, with the remainder to follow in seven installments. Even before the conclusion of the contract with the Board of the Treasury, Symmes departed for the west leaving his associates, Elias Boudinot, formerly President of the Continental Congress, and Jonathan Dayton, later to become Speaker of the House of Representatives, to work out the details. Symmes' later financial difficulties caused him to forfeit all but 300,000 acres of his purchase, and later he was to lose everything. Before this occurred, however, he and his associates were responsible for the founding of several settlements, two of which became important cities in southwestern Ohio.

The first of these was called Columbia, located just west of the mouth of the Little Miami, now a part of Cincinnati. Here, in November 1788, Benjamin Stites laid out a little town on land purchased from Symmes. Two months later Symmes himself established the settlement of North Bend near the mouth of the Great Miami at the western end of his purchase.

Both of these towns were soon outstripped by a third community on the north bank of the Ohio, opposite the mouth of the Licking River. Symmes had sold this site to Matthias Denman, a New Jersey land speculator, who in turn sold equal interests to Robert Patterson and John Filson of Kentucky. Filson and Israel Ludlow planned the town in December 1788, giving it the name Losantiville. The name was the verbal patchwork of Filson to indicate that it was the city (*ville*) opposite (*anti*) the mouth (*os*) of the Licking (*L*). Governor Arthur St. Clair soon renamed the community in honor of the military order formed after the Revolution, and Cincinnati it became. With the establishment of Hamilton County and the designation of Cincinnati as the county seat and the location of Fort Washington, the future of the town was assured.

The plan of Cincinnati appears in Figure 133, which shows the town as it existed in 1815. There is nothing remarkable about the plan; indeed, it shows every indication of being laid out by its proprietors as a speculative investment. In its design it resembled hundreds of other similar towns that were soon to spring

[19] C. F. C., comte de Volney, *A View of the Soil and Climate of the United States of America*, Philadelphia, 1804, Appendix IV, "Gallipolis, or the French colony at Scioto," p. 327.

Figure 133. Plan of Cincinnati, Ohio: 1815

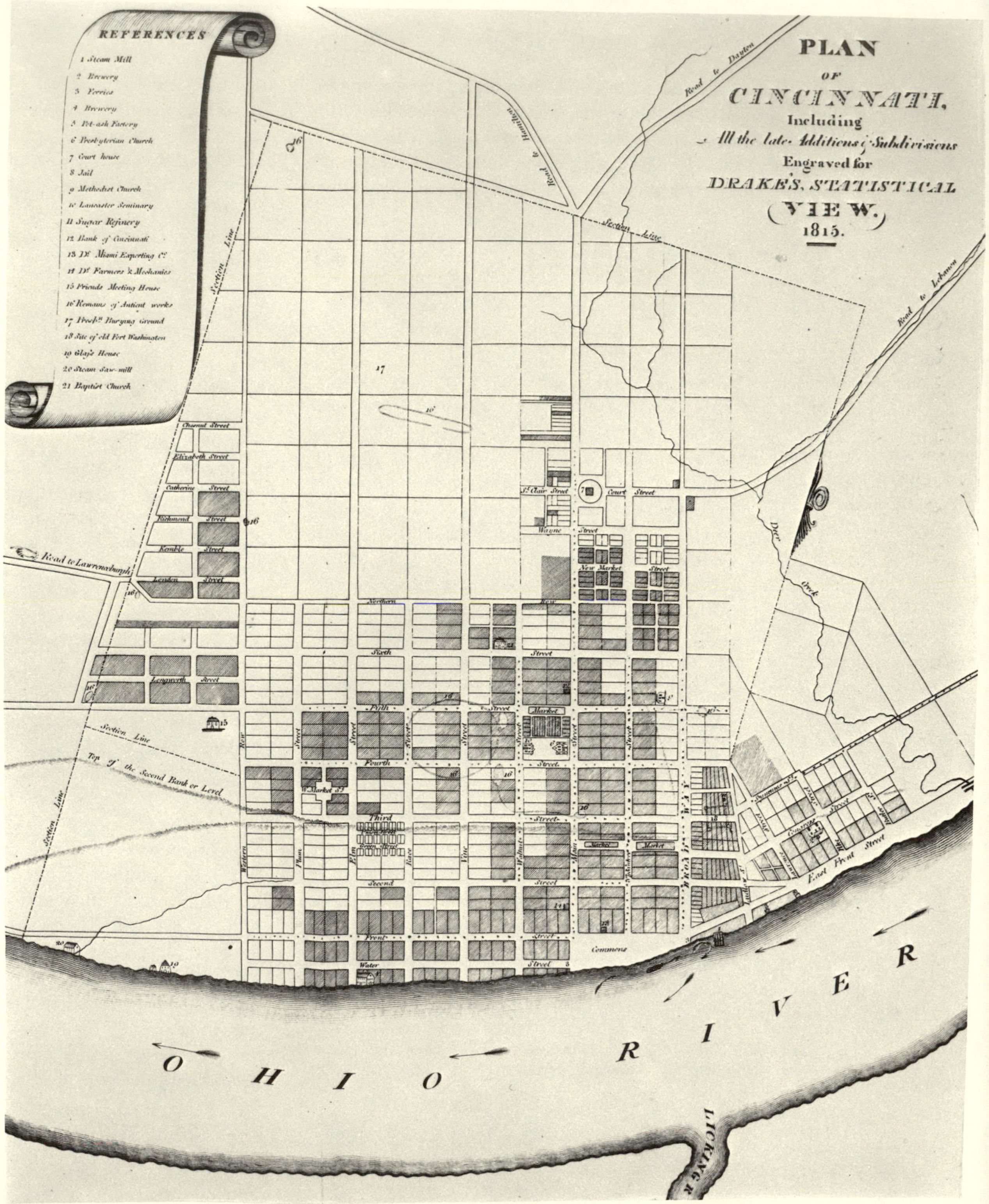
REFERENCES
1 Steam Mill
2 Brewery
3 Ferries
4 Brewery
5 Pot-ash Factory
6 Presbyterian Church
7 Court house
8 Jail
9 Methodist Church
10 Lancaster Seminary
11 Sugar Refinery
12 Bank of Cincinnati
13 Do. Miami Exporting Co.
14 Do. Farmers & Mechanics
15 Friends Meeting House
16 Remains of Antient works
17 Presbn. Burying Ground
18 Site of old Fort Washington
19 Glass House
20 Steam Saw-mill
21 Baptist Church
PLAN
OF
CINCINNATI,
Including
All the late Additions & Subdivisions
Engraved for
DRAKE'S, STATISTICAL
(VIEW,)
1815.
Road to Dayton
Road to Hamilton
Section Line
Road to Lebanon
Road to Lawrenceburgh
Chesnut Street
Elizabeth Street
Catherine Street
Richmond Street
Kemble Street
Lenton Street
Longworth Street
Court Street
Wayne Street
New Market Street
Northern Row
Sixth Street
Fifth Street
Fourth Street
Third Street
Second Street
Front Street
Water Street
Market
Commons
East Front Street
Top of the Second Bank or Level
Deer Creek
OHIO RIVER
LICKING R.

up throughout southern and central Ohio as the region began to attract land-hungry settlers from the east. Soon a brisk trade developed in Cincinnati town lots and adjacent outlots. Symmes, realizing that the town was destined to grow, platted in 1790 a small addition to the city on land owned by him at its eastern boundary. This addition can be seen in Figure 133.

The other major city to be founded in Symmes' purchase was Dayton, planned in 1795 on land purchased from him by St. Clair, Jonathan Dayton, Israel Ludlow, and James Wilkinson. While Symmes had represented himself as the owner of this land, he did not in fact have clear title. Eventually the new residents were forced to repurchase their property at standard land office prices, but the city of Dayton grew nonetheless as the fertile valleys of the new territory began to fill with settlers and the need developed for trading and governmental centers.

The development of towns in central Ohio lagged somewhat behind the Ohio River communities because of the difficulties in interior transportation. Recognizing this problem, Congress in 1796 authorized Ebenezer Zane to develop a road from Wheeling, West Virginia, through a portion of central and southern Ohio. Zane's payment consisted of the right to use his military land warrants to locate land not otherwise patented by others. On one of these sites, near the falls of the Muskingum at its confluence with the Licking River, he planned a town in 1799. Zanesville, shown in Figure 134, became a thriving community and for a time was the state capital. With its wide streets, riverside common land, and unique Y-shaped bridge, the town received many favorable comments from early visitors. Nearby, Newark was laid out by General William Schenck in 1802 and named for his home town in New Jersey. Streets were so wide and in rainy weather so muddy that some of the local citizens claimed that strangers sometimes were swallowed up in the mud and never seen again.

Other cities on Zane's Trace included Lancaster and Chillicothe, which became important communities in the development of Ohio. Chillicothe was designated as the seat of government of the Northwest Territory in 1800, and a government land office also was located there. During the early years of statehood it was the capital of Ohio. In 1812 the state legislature directed Joel Wright to plan a new capital city on the site of the present Columbus. At a bend in the Scioto River Wright platted a gridiron town with squares of 10 acres each reserved for the capital buildings and a penitentiary. His plan is shown in Figure 135. The broad strip of open land beyond the capital square was reserved for the original owners of the site who were induced to give up their land so that the town might be laid out.[20]

In most of these southern Ohio communities the influence of land speculation is reflected in their plans. With little of the imagination or respect for site conditions shown by the planners of Marietta, these communities added nothing to the art of town planning in western America. In the northeastern part of the Territory, however, a more interesting venture in town development took place during this period. Like Marietta, these towns of Northern Ohio were built by New Englanders who placed a high value on beauty and order along with due regard for possible speculative profits from the sale of town lots.

New England Recreated in Frontier Ohio

When Congress accepted Connecticut's waiver of claims to western lands except for a Reserve in northeastern Ohio, this small New England state became the recognized owner of 3½ million acres of land. The actual boundaries were established between the 41st parallel and Lake Erie and a north-south line 120 miles west of the Pennsylvania boundary. For a time the state government took no action to dispose of this enormous holding, but with the defeat of the Indians by Anthony Wayne and the Treaty of Greenville in 1795 one of the difficulties to settlement was eliminated. The General Assembly determined to dispose of the entire tract at once rather than become involved in piecemeal sales or face the complications of awarding lands as bounties to its militia veterans. The western 12 miles of the reserve, called the Firelands, were set aside to be granted to residents of certain Connecticut shore towns whose property had been destroyed during the war. Under the legislation, proceeds from the sale of the Reserve were to constitute a perpetual fund with the interest devoted to support the public schools of the state.[21]

[20] Alfred J. Wright, "Joel Wright, City Planner," *Ohio Archaeological and Historical Quarterly*, LVI (1947), 287-94.

[21] The best brief history of the Western Reserve is the scholarly and interesting work by Harlan Hatcher, *The Western Reserve*, Indianapolis, 1949, on which I have relied for much of the material in this section.

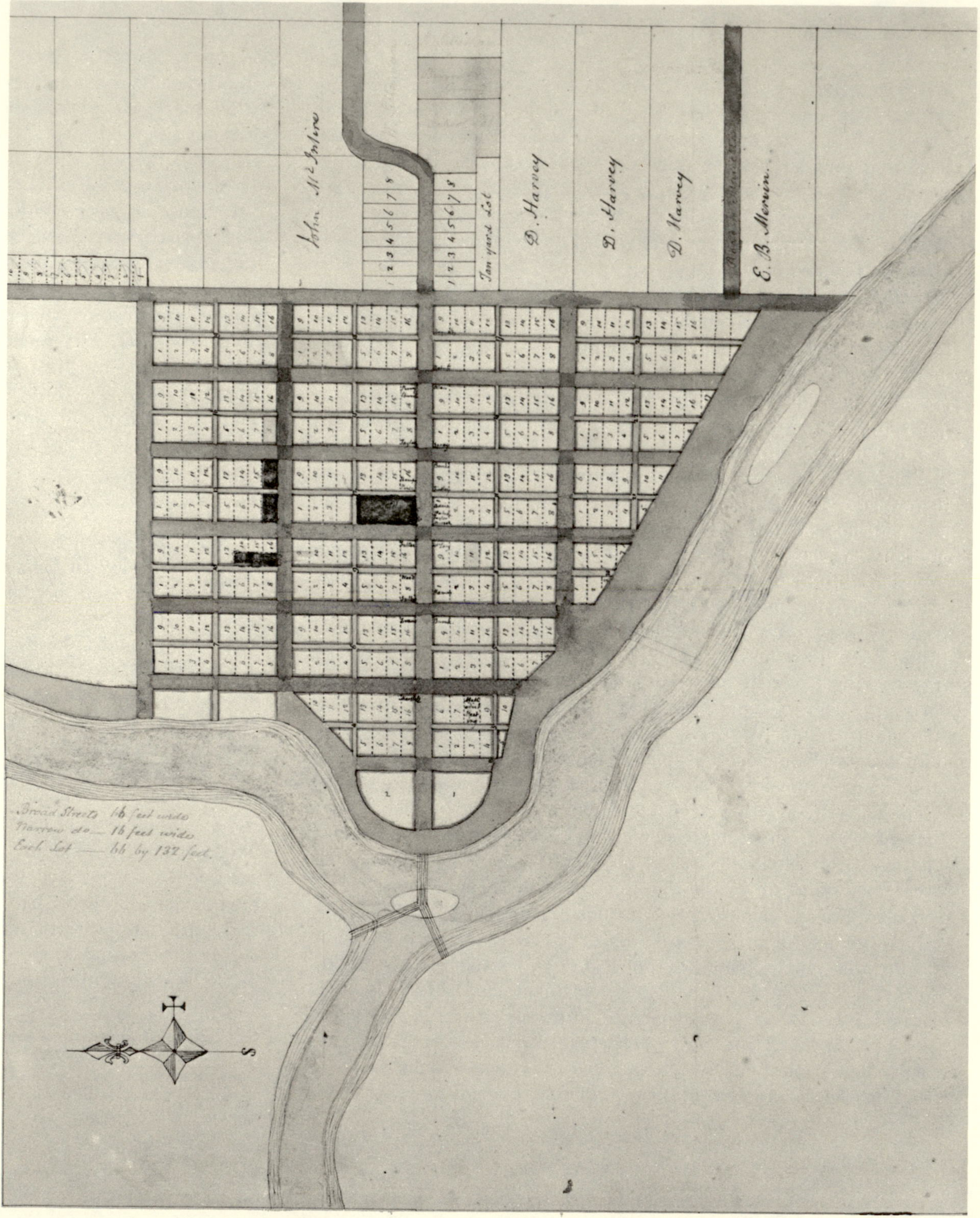

Figure 134. Plan of Zanesville,
Ohio: ca. 1815

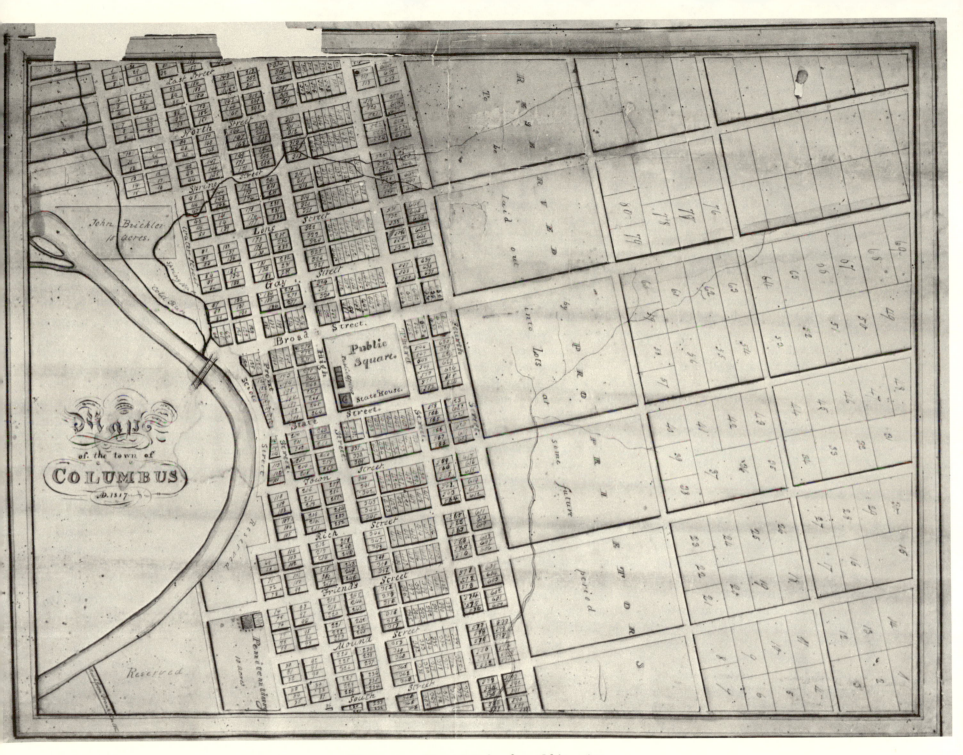

Figure 135. Plan of Columbus, Ohio: 1817

In the fall of 1795 a sale agreement for $1,200,000 was concluded with an association of some 50 speculators. Shares ranged from $1,683 to the $168,185 pledged by Oliver Phelps. A syndicate called the Connecticut Land Company received a deed to this still unsurveyed wilderness, putting up a bond and a mortgage on the land with the state treasurer. The company transferred its property in trust to three persons to hold title until the tract could be surveyed. When the survey was completed and the Indian title extinguished, the members of the syndicate would then receive land in proportion to their financial contributions, and the location of the land so received was to be decided by lot. The land was to be divided into townships 5 miles square, similar to although smaller than the congressional townships provided for by the ordinance of 1785.

A survey party under the direction of General Moses Cleaveland set out for Ohio and on the 4th of July, 1796, located the stone monument marking the northwest corner of Pennsylvania set there by Andrew Ellicott, who had run the western boundary of the state in 1786. The initial task for the surveyors was to lay out the township grid as far west as the mouth of the Cuyahoga River and to select a site for and plan a city as the "capital" of the Reserve. While some of his surveyors followed the Pennsylvania line south to the other corner of the Reserve, Cleaveland moved westward along the shore of Lake Erie. When he reached the mouth of the Cuyahoga River, roughly in the center of the Reserve, he selected a site on the bluff overlooking the lake and marked out the town.

One of two virtually identical original plans of the town appears in Figure 136, the Seth Pease survey in 1796. The public square, a characteristic of most of the settlements in the Reserve, included some 10 acres of ground. From the sides of the square ran streets 99 and 132 feet wide. Other streets parallel and perpendicular to these formed a familiar grid pattern except for the irregular roads leading down the bluff to the river's bank. Town lots of 2 acres and outlots up to 100 acres were surveyed. Certainly Cleaveland, who thought that his city might someday be "as large as Old Windham" in his native Connecticut, never envisaged the true future of the city. The Cleveland plan of 1796 is simply a New England village transplanted to northern Ohio and in the process

gaining something in regularity but perhaps losing part of its charm.

For the first half-century of its existence this present industrial metropolis had the peaceful atmosphere of a remote country village. Figure 137, a view of the city in 1834, shows the community just before the canals and then the railroads began transforming it into a bustling transportation and industrial center.

Cleveland began under company sponsorship; the other communities in the Western Reserve owe their origins to individual proprietors who received their shares of land when the surveys were complete and townships and fractional townships were distributed by lot. Almost every landowner, whether one of the original proprietors or a purchaser from one, seemed to interest himself in town planning. Because of the diverse backgrounds, resources, and intentions of the owners, the towns varied in form and size. Yet if there was variation in details there was a common pattern of atmosphere pervading these communities. Most towns in the Reserve share general characteristics: a system of outlots and town lots of ample size, one or more central greens, wide streets, moderate size, and a general air of order and repose. The resemblance to New England communities is as unmistakable as it is understandable. The settlers came mainly from Connecticut and the other New England states, and in this wilderness they attempted to recreate the community pattern they knew best.

A sampling from the rich treasure of town planning experience in this area may serve to demonstrate the wealth of material that may be found. One of the earliest and most ambitious plans was for Jefferson, laid out by Gideon Granger, Postmaster General of the United States, which is shown as it existed in 1874 in Figure 138. Granger's plan is summarized in the following passage from a county history roughly contemporary with this illustration:

"Mr. Granger prepared a draft (1805) of his townsite and designated streets, which as yet had an existence only on paper. Nine large avenues running east and west and crossing at right angles, seven others running north and south, with several squares at the crossing of the streets, one of these in the center of the plat being 38 rods from east to west by 22 rods from north to south. . . . It required only a vivid imagination, and lo! here was a magnificent city of palatial residences and churches whose spires

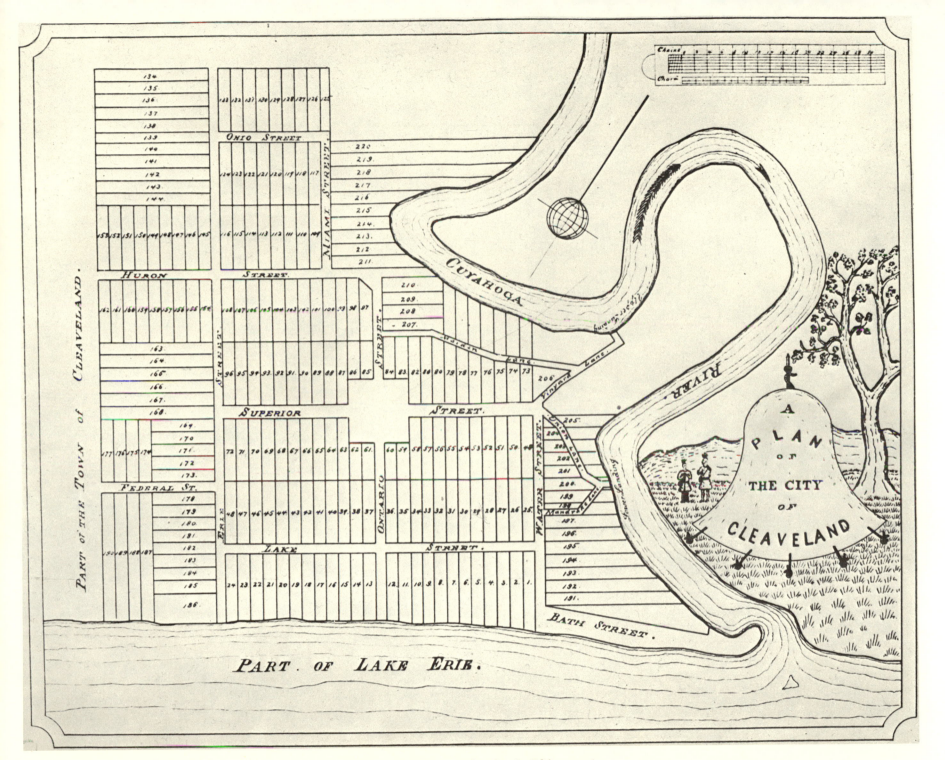

Figure 136. Plan of Cleveland, Ohio: 1796

CLEVELAND, OHIO.

FROM THE BUFFALO ROAD, EAST OF THE COURT HOUSE.

Published, N.York 1834, by Thos. Whelpley, of Cleveland.

Figure 137. View of Cleveland, Ohio: 1833

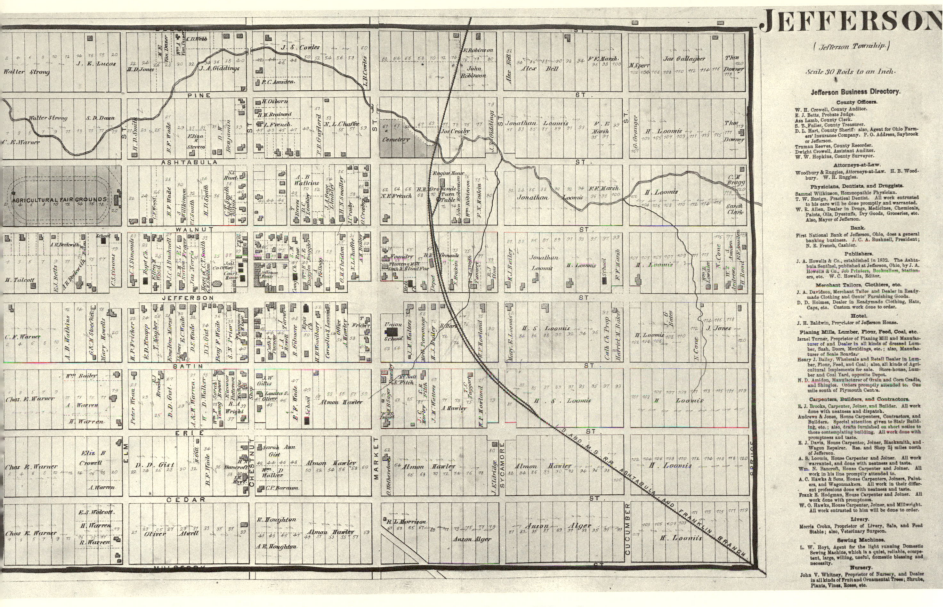

Figure 138. Plan of Jefferson, Ohio: 1874

pointed heavenward, but the sober fact is that the town plat was recorded when only a solitary cabin occupied the townsite. . . ."[22]

The central square and portions of three others have survived, but the remainder were used as building sites when Jefferson failed to live up to the glorious expectations of its proprietor.

Canfield is located near the southeastern corner of the Western Reserve. The plan, reproduced in Figure 139, does not convey the beauty and serenity of this lovely village. The great central green measures 600 by 2,200 feet, sloping gently upwards to the south. Facing it on lots of generous size stand some of the most elegant houses in the Reserve. As in New England, the plan forms are deceptive and fail to reveal the true quality in the third dimension of architecture. Chardon, planned in 1808 by Peter Chardon Brooks and offered by him as the seat of Geauga County on condition that it be given his middle name, is of similar charm and scale. The rectangular green occupies the crest of a modest hill. Streets enter at the center and the ends of its shorter sides. Around the village a kind of ring road serves as a link between village and the surrounding farmlands.

Twenty miles west of Cleveland, where the two forks of the Black River come together, Herman Ely, son of one of the original company shareholders, planned his town of Elyria in 1817. The attractive site was a narrow strip of high ground formed by the looping rivers. At the highest point above the river Ely placed an open space in the form of an elongated rectangle. He laid out the main street to run southward from one corner of the central "square." Other streets were surveyed parallel and at right angles to this principal axis. The plan of the town appears in Figure 140, and a view is reproduced in Figure 141. The design of Elyria was one of the most successful of all the Reserve towns in its adaption to natural site conditions and its adaptability to modern requirements.

Treatment of the green or public square received the greatest attention from the planners of the Reserve's communities. The rectangle at Sharon Center, the ellipse at Leroy, the parallelogram at Madison, and the variations on these shapes in other communities probably represent attempts by the proprietors to be a bit different from then existing nearby towns, or, it may simply have resulted from imitations of the home communities of the planners in New England. But to a considerable extent these diverse patterns indicate efforts to experiment with different forms in the search for a better plan, a more livable town, a more attractive and impressive site for a church or a town hall or a county courthouse.

Of great interest because of its break with the gridiron pattern is Tallmadge, now a suburb of and almost engulfed by the city of Akron. The Reverend David Bacon purchased the township in 1807 with the idea of establishing a kind of religious commonwealth. Although this aspect of the community was never fully carried out, Bacon's plan for the township and the village at its center was evidently based on his belief that all settlers should be in close communication and that the church in the village should be the focus of the entire settlement.

He had the township divided into 16 squares of 1,000 acres each with 66-foot wide roads at the boundaries of these mile and a quarter square sections. Then he boldly ran four roads diagonally from the corners of the township toward the center, where they met at the village. From the rectangular village square, four other roads ran north, south, east, and west. Town hall and church inside the oval green in the center of the square completed the composition. The village plan and a view of the central green are shown in Figures 142 and 143.[23]

Thus, gradually, the northern part of Ohio filled with settlers from the New England states who planned for the future of their communities with intelligence and skill. The difficulties were many and the hardships great. These courageous pioneers and their predecessors throughout Kentucky and Ohio left a rich legacy of planning experience. The communities which they built—where some of the original grace and charm still remains—deserve the utmost efforts by their present residents in protecting and preserving this unique heritage.

[22] Williams Brothers, *History of Ashtabula County, Ohio*, Philadelphia, 1878, p. 147.

[23] More extended treatment of Tallmadge can be found in the following: Carl Feiss, "Tallmadge, Township No. 2, Range 10, Connecticut Fire Lands: An Early Ohio Planned Community," *Journal of The Society of Architectural Historians*, XII (1953), 25-26; Henry Howe, *Historical Collections of Ohio*, Cincinnati, 1900, II, 637-40; T. C. Mendenhall, "The Town of Tallmadge—The Bacons and Shakespeare," Ohio Archaeological and Historical Society, *Publications*, XXXII, 590-612; and E. O. Randall, "Tallmadge Township," Ohio Archaeological and Historical Society, *Publications*, XVII, 275-306.

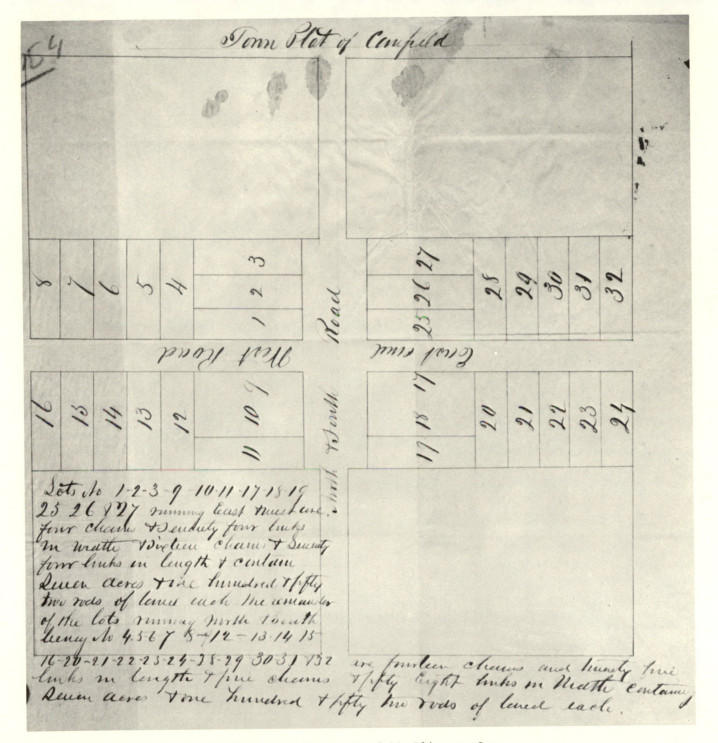

Figure 139. Plan of Canfield, Ohio: ca. 1800

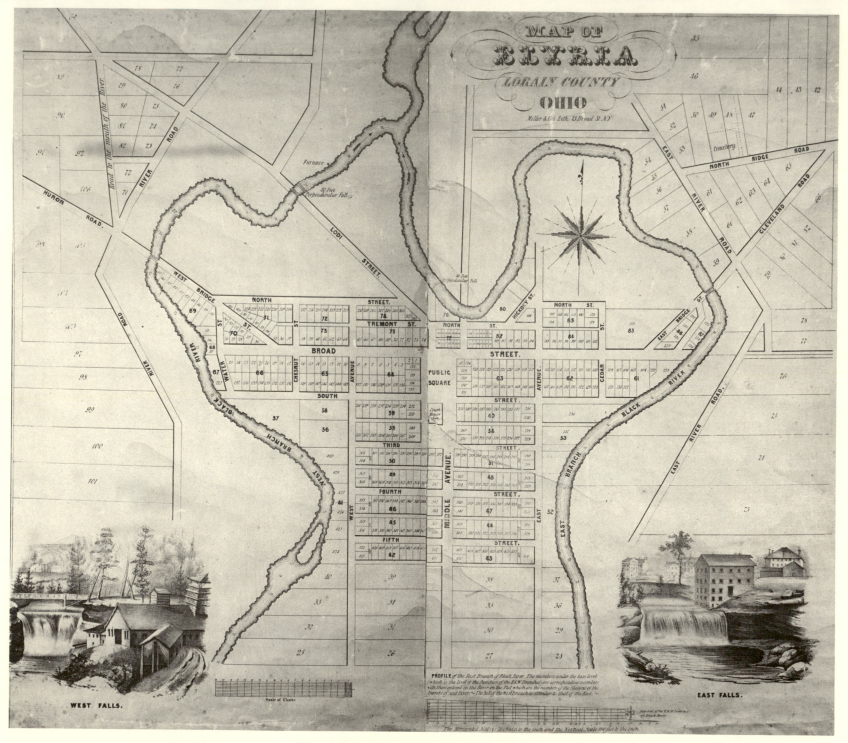

Figure 140. Plan of Elyria, Ohio: ca. 1850

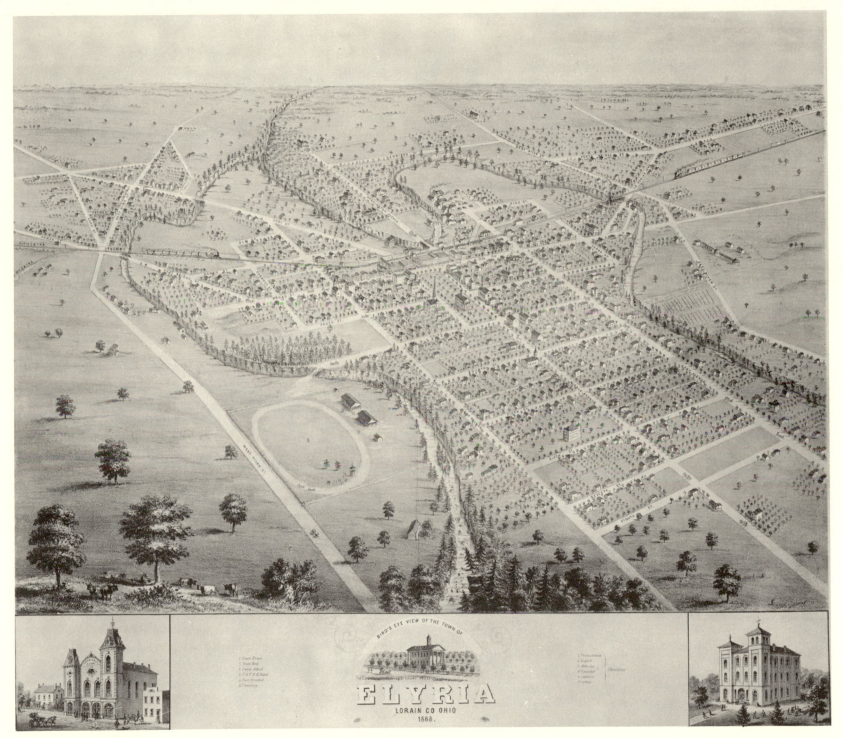

Figure 141. View of Elyria, Ohio: 1868

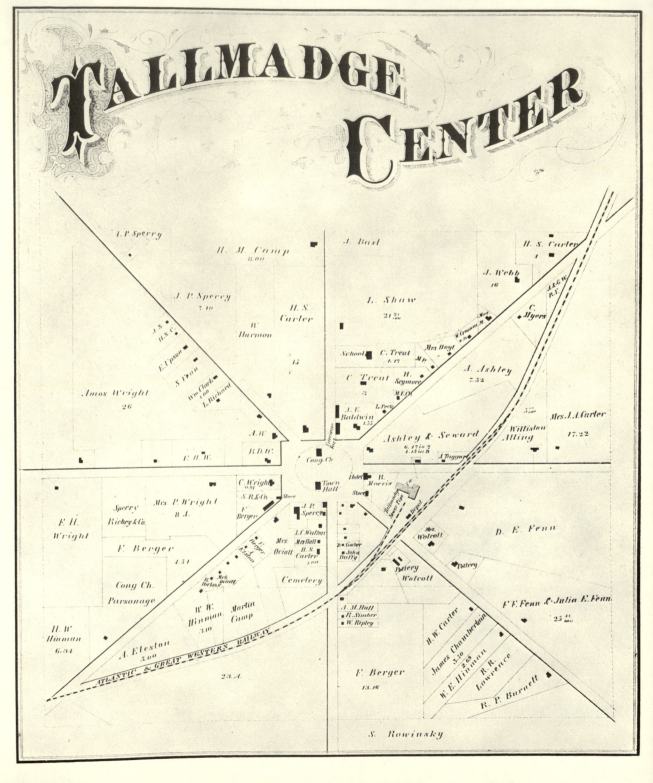

Figure 142. Plan of Tallmadge Center, Ohio: 1874

TALLMADGE CENTER PARK   TOWN HALL

Figure 143. View of the Central Green in Tallmadge, Ohio: 1874

CHAPTER 9

Planning the National Capital

WITH the end of their war of revolution Americans resumed the settlement of a continent and the building of towns. While the planning of most new towns took place on the frontier, other towns were laid out along the Atlantic coast in older sections of the country. Typically, the promoters of such towns chose a suitable site, reached some kind of agreement with the land owners if they did not acquire title themselves, had the site surveyed into streets, blocks and lots, and with a handsomely printed map and brochure describing the advantages of the town proceeded to sell lots to anyone with cash for a down payment.

In 1791 just such a town was planned by an enterprising group on the banks of the river dividing Virginia from Maryland. While in broad outline the birth of this town may have resembled that of scores of others, it was unique in a number of respects. In size the new town dwarfed all others that had heretofore been projected in America. Its highly unusual plan introduced to America new concepts of city design and influenced the layouts of many later cities. It was a city designed as the center of a great enterprise, the eventual scope of which could not be foreseen even by its founders. Finally, its promoters were no mere real estate speculators interested in private enrichment but included such towering figures as Washington and Jefferson, who in this capacity acted as trustees for an entire nation. For this city was Washington on the Potomac, the future capital of an ambitious and confident government, intended to express the glory and power that the new nation would surely acquire. Taken singly, any one of these elements present would arouse interest in the plan of the city; together, they account for the intense fascination that the development of the city of Washington has always created in anyone familiar with even the most superficial aspects of its history.

Compromise on the Potomac

During the long years of the war, the Continental Congress conducted its affairs mainly from Philadelphia, but military reverses caused its removal to Baltimore, Lancaster, and York during a two-year period before Philadelphia became the capital once again. The peace of 1783 did not result in less movement, but in more. From Philadelphia Congress moved to Princeton, Annapolis, Trenton, and finally New York, where it met until succeeded by the new Congress under the Constitution.

The prospect of a permanent home for the infant government seemed elusive. During the war apparently some consideration was given to the purchase of a site near Princeton, but nothing came of this proposal. With the cessation of hostilities the question was again raised. Dozens of sites were considered, most of them being brought to the attention of Congress by petitions from existing communities proposing their location as a permanent seat of government. In 1783, for example, Kingston, N.Y.; Nottingham Township in Burlington County, N.J.; and Annapolis, Md., all invited Congress to take up residence within their boundaries. In that same year the state of New Jersey offered to cede any site of up to 20 square miles within its limits for governmental purposes. The Virginia legislature similarly offered Williamsburg, or any site located on the Potomac River. Over the years the list grew: Newport, Wilmington, Reading, Lancaster, Germantown, New York, Philadelphia, Princeton, and others.

One major difficulty was the reluctance of the southern states to agree to a location in the north, while the northern states were equally unwilling to approve a southern site. In the fall of 1783

Congress, in desperation, approved a plan for two capitals—one at Georgetown in Virginia and the other just below the falls of the Delaware. Although this plan was revoked the following year, it inspired one wit to suggest that there should be but one town for the two sites, a town on a wheeled platform that could be accompanied by a portable statue of General Washington, a monument to whom had been recently authorized, and that both could be moved between the two sites as needed.[1]

Apparently the double capital scheme exhausted the efforts of the Congress in seeking an acceptable solution to the problem, and in the next two or three years the subject was given only occasional attention. Finally, in 1787 the Constitutional Convention reopened the matter when it adopted, without debate, the following clause in Article I of the proposed constitution giving Congress the power:

"To exercise exclusive legislation in all cases whatsoever over such district (not exceeding ten miles square) as may, by cession of particular States and the acceptance of Congress, become the seat of Government of the United States, and to exercise like authority over all places purchased by the consent of the Legislature of the State in which the same shall be, for the erection of forts, magazines, arsenals, dry-docks, and other needful buildings."

When the first constitutional congress met in 1789 the debate over a permanent location was reopened. It soon became apparent that two sites were generally favored—one by the southern delegates at or near Georgetown on the Potomac, and the other by the northern states at Wrights Ferry, Pennsylvania, near the falls of the Susquehanna. In September the House approved the Susquehanna site, but the Senate substituted a location at Germantown. Before agreement could be reached, however, the session adjourned. In the summer of 1790 debate resumed, and at last a decision was reached. The result was a compromise favoring the southern view made possible by an agreement of southern legislators to support the measure proposed by Secretary of the Treasury Hamilton for funding the public debt and assuming state obligations. In return, the New York delegates threw their support to a southern location for the capital.

The Residence Act of 1790 did not define the exact site. Instead it authorized the President to select a site not exceeding 10 miles square on the Potomac River "at some place between the mouths of the Eastern Branch and the Connogocheague," a distance of some 80 miles. Three commissioners appointed by the President were to "survey and define said district" under his direction, and by the first Monday in December 1800 were "to provide suitable buildings for the accommodation of Congress and of the President and for the public offices of the United States." During the intervening ten years the capital would be located in Philadelphia.

Although the Residence Act itself was vague as to the exact location of the future capital, it is obvious that the Georgetown site was what the southern delegates, at least, had in mind. Even before the President signed the bill on July 16, Jefferson was writing to Monroe and Randolph that the bill had passed and that, after ten years in Philadelphia, the capital would move to Georgetown. Washington, of course, was familiar with this area, having surveyed the original plat of nearby Alexandria, and since it had been the site selected previously in the abortive twin capital resolution, it seemed favored from the beginning.

In the middle of October 1790 Washington began his inspection of the territory specified in the act. From Georgetown he rode to look at the land to the southeast along the Eastern Branch, or Anacostia. On his visit he received from some of the property owners in the vicinity an offer to sell necessary land on terms the President determined to be reasonable. He then set out to look at other possible sites up the Potomac. At each town and village he was welcomed and handed statements and petitions advocating that particular location as the most desirable for the seat of government. Apparently Washington directed that two or three possible sites should be surveyed to determine the extent and ownership of the land. By the end of October he was back in Mount Vernon,

[1] Wilhelmus Bogart Bryan, A History of the National Capital, New York, 1914-16, I, 18. Much of the material in this section and other valuable information about the planning of Washington has been obtained from Bryan's indispensable work. Other sources include: William Tindall, Origin and Government of The District of Columbia, Washington, 1908; Tindall, Standard History of the City of Washington, Knoxville, 1914; and W. B. Webb and John Wooldridge, Centennial History of the City of Washington, D.C.

and a month later he journeyed to Philadelphia, where Congress was scheduled to meet early in December.

There Washington conferred with Jefferson, who, no doubt at the request of the President, had prepared a memorandum setting forth his views on how the Residence Act should be implemented. Jefferson pointed out that while the law did not expressly authorize a town to be planned on the site selected, he had "no doubt it is the wish, & perhaps expectation . . . that . . . it will . . . be laid out in lots & streets." He made suggestions also for the selection of commissioners, acquisition of land, and financing of the required improvements through sale of lots in the new town. Also, Jefferson put down his thoughts on the size of the town, the amount of land necessary for public buildings and open space, and the manner in which it should be laid out. Running through this document are references to Georgetown or the area adjacent, and we can safely assume that by this time Washington had chosen the site on which the city was eventually to be built.

By January 1791 the President was ready to act. Daniel Carroll, Thomas Johnson, and David Stuart were appointed commissioners for the federal district. On January 24 Washington informed Congress that, after "mature consideration of the advantages and disadvantages of the several positions," he had selected a site at the southern end of the prescribed territory and had directed the commissioners to survey its boundaries. However, he suggested that Congress might wish to amend the Residence Act to permit the inclusion of land south of the East Branch in Maryland, and also the town of Alexandria in Virginia. Congress adopted this suggestion and passed the necessary amendment on March 3.

The Site and Its Surveyors

Two men were quickly appointed by the President to direct the surveys of the new district. Andrew Ellicott, a professional surveyor of repute and a member of the American Philosophical Society, was employed to run the bounds of the district. By February 14 he reported to Jefferson the results of the first few days of surveying and made certain suggestions about minor changes in the boundaries as a result of his preliminary work.

On March 9 Ellicott was joined by Major Pierre Charles

L'Enfant, whose letter of appointment from Jefferson clearly specified the nature of his work:

"The special object of asking your aid is to have drawings of the particular grounds most likely to be approved for the site of the federal town and buildings. You will therefore be pleased to begin on the eastern branch, and proceed from thence upwards, laying down the hills, valleys, morasses, and waters between that, the Potomac, the Tyber, and the road leading from Georgetown to the eastern branch, and connecting the whole with certain fixed points of the map Mr. Ellicott is preparing. Some idea of the height of the hills above the base on which they stand, would be desirable."[2]

There is in this letter no indication that L'Enfant would be engaged to prepare the plan for the new city; yet this may have been understood, and it seems likely that Washington or some emissary must have conferred with L'Enfant prior to his appointment. A year and a half earlier L'Enfant had written to Washington offering his services in planning the capital city, and, as the architect in charge of remodeling the New York city hall for use by the Congress in 1789, he would have had ample opportunity to discuss this matter with federal officials. As a French volunteer who had become an American officer under Washington in the Revolution, as the designer of the insignia for the Society of the Cincinnati, of which Washington was President-General, and as one for whom Washington evidently felt affection and admiration, L'Enfant, with his training as an artist and military experience as an engineer, was a natural choice.

While Ellicott continued his surveys of the district's boundaries, L'Enfant, as directed, began to explore the territory along the East Branch and later the land to the northwest in the direction of Georgetown. This was done in an effort to obtain lower prices for land immediately adjacent to that existing town. For on the day of his proclamation of the federal district the President entered into confidential correspondence with friends of his in George-

[2] Letter from Jefferson to L'Enfant, dated March 1791 (no day given) in Saul Padover, *Thomas Jefferson and the National Capital*, Washington, 1946, pp. 42-43. Padover's collection of correspondence and public papers relating to the selection of the site, the planning, and the development of the capital is invaluable.

town asking them to begin negotiations for land in the vicinity.[3] He shrewdly reasoned that the sight of L'Enfant working along the Anacostia would persuade the owners of land along the Potomac to be more reasonable in their demands.

It was obvious to all that the city would be located along one of the rivers. Jefferson thought that about 1,500 acres would be sufficient, and his view of the amount of land required was probably more generous than most. So, it appeared that any of three or four possible locations might be chosen. Two small towns already had been platted below Georgetown—Hamburg, half way between Georgetown and Goose or Tyber Creek, and Carrollsburg on the East Branch at its juncture with the Potomac. These towns, largely paper communities with but a few houses, and the divisions of property elsewhere in the vicinity, are shown in Figure 144.[4]

Among the property owners on the site there developed an intense rivalry over the location of the city and the exact lands to be purchased for government use. Jefferson despaired of achieving any agreement with the Carrollsburg interests and, as will be seen, recommended development of the land between Goose Creek and Georgetown. The owner of much of this land, David Burnes, soon became the chief stumbling block in the way of speedy agreement over land prices and terms of sale. But even "the obstinate Mr. Burns," as Washington referred to him, was not to block the President's determination for a site of ample size.

On March 28 Washington arrived in Georgetown, where he met with the commissioners and reviewed the surveys and reports of Ellicott and L'Enfant. His diary records that on the evening of the 29th he called the proprietors of land to his rooms and discussed with them his requirements. The following day the proprietors returned and agreed to his terms. From Mount Vernon on the last day of the month Washington jubilantly wrote Jefferson the details of this agreement:

[3] The text of some of these letters and other valuable material on the early development of Washington can be found in Allen C. Clark, "Origin of the Federal City," Columbia Historical Society *Records*, XXXV-XXXVI (1935), 1-97.
[4] Manuscript plans of Hamburg and Carrollsburg are in the Map Division of the Library of Congress. They are reproduced in U. S. Library of Congress, *District of Columbia Sesquicentennial*, Washington, 1950.

"The terms . . . are That all the land from Rock-creek along the river to the eastern-branch and so upwards to or above the ferry including a breadth of about a mile and a half, the whole containing from three to five thousand acres, is ceded to the public, on condition that, when the whole shall be surveyed and laid off as a city, (which Major L'Enfant is now directed to do) the present Proprietors shall retain every other lot, and for such part of the land as may be taken for public use . . . they shall be allowed at the rate of Twenty five pounds per acre. . . . No compensation is to be made for the ground that may be occupied as streets or alleys."[5]

Thus, not only did Washington settle the difficulties with the landowners, at least temporarily, but he also effectively increased the area which could be occupied by the city, and he engaged L'Enfant to prepare a plan for its development. His selection of the Frenchman may well have been decided in advance of this date, but any doubts he might have had about this appointment were evidently removed after talking with L'Enfant and reading his report on the potential development of the site.

L'Enfant's site analysis was submitted to the President on his arrival at Georgetown. It was a document of considerable length, written in L'Enfant's own version of English and typically enthusiastic about what might be accomplished. In it he identifies Jenkin's Hill, now the location of the Capitol, as the most advantageous site for public buildings and describes the general topography and site possibilities elsewhere. Then, turning to the point obviously of most immediate interest to him, he states:

"In viewing the intended establishment . . . and considering how in process of time a city so happily situated will extend over a large surface of ground, much deliberation is necessary for to determine on a plan for the total distribution and . . . that plan [should be conceived] on [such] a system . . . as to render the place commodious and agreeable to the first settler, [while] it may be capable of . . . being enlarged by progressive improve-

[5] Letter from Washington to Jefferson, March 31, 1791, Padover, *Thomas Jefferson*, 54. The full text of the agreement may be found in H. P. Caemmerer, *Washington*: *The National Capital*, Senate Document No. 332, 71st Congress, 3rd Session, Washington, 1932, pp. 19-21.

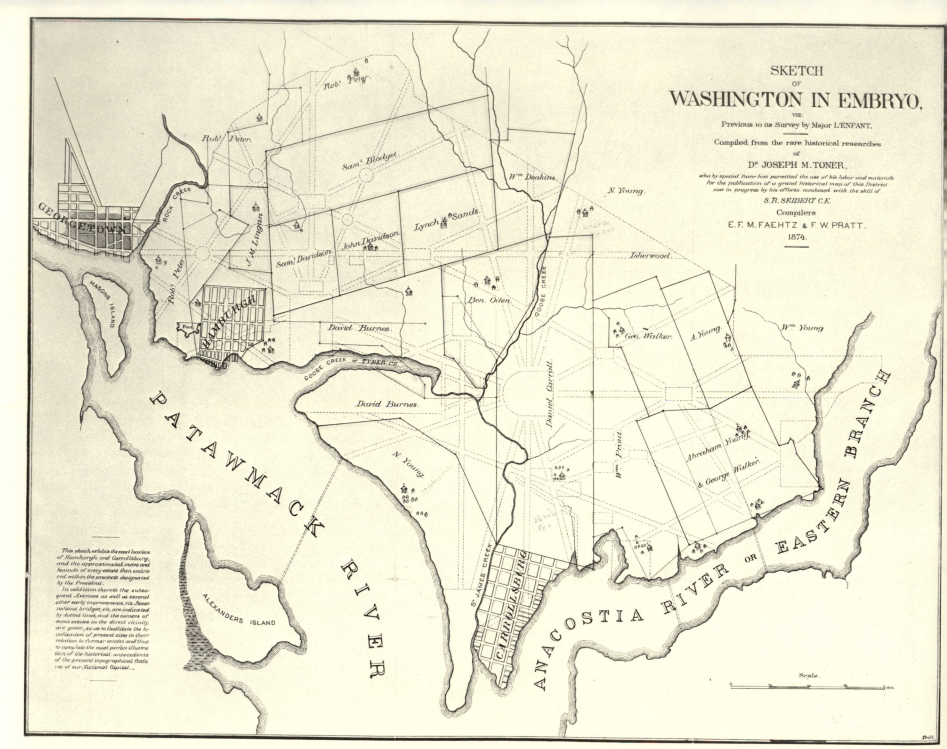

GEORGETOWN

Rob.ᵗ Peter.

Rob.ᵗ Peter.

Rob.ᵗ Peter.

ROCK CREEK

MASONS ISLAND

Sam.ˡ Blodget.

Wᵐ Deakins.

N. Young.

J. M. Lingan.

Sam.ˡ Davidson.

John Davidson.

Lynch & Sands.

Isherwood.

Rob.ᵗ Peter.

HAMBURGH

Fort

Ben. Oden.

GOOSE CREEK

Geo. Walker.

A. Young.

Wᵐ Young.

David Burnes.

GOOSE CREEK or TYBER CR.

David Burnes.

Daniel Carroll.

Wᵐ Prout.

N. Young.

Abraham Young.

& George Walker.

PATAWMACK RIVER

ALEXANDERS ISLAND

St JAMES CREEK

CARROLLSBURG

ANACOSTIA RIVER OR EASTERN BRANCH

Scale.

Figure 144. Division of Land on the Site of the National Capital: 1791

ment . . . [all] which should be foreseen in the first delineation in a grand plan of the whole city. . . ."[6]

These views must have coincided with those of Washington, and L'Enfant was directed to proceed with "a grand plan" for the site, the size of which was now greatly enlarged thanks to Washington's conference with the proprietors. Washington may not then have specified the terms of the appointment, or, equally likely, L'Enfant may have been too animated to understand that he was to be subordinate to the commissioners of the federal district while undertaking his task. His lack of comprehension of this was to result in difficulties for the commissioners, embarrassment to the administration, and the final dismissal of L'Enfant from his post. But in March 1791 there were no signs of these problems that lay ahead, and L'Enfant's appointment was regarded as an excellent, almost inevitable, choice. It was with high hopes and every expectation of success that Washington left L'Enfant to proceed with the task he had so ardently desired.

Jefferson's Plan for the Federal City

In examining the site, L'Enfant's agile mind had undoubtedly begun to conceive the broad pattern of his eventual plan. He was, however, not the first to project a scheme for a capital city layout on the Potomac site. That honor belongs to Jefferson, and his ideas for a capital city are not only of intrinsic interest but illuminate some of L'Enfant's contributions to planning in America. Jefferson's concept of the city must be pieced together from his rough drawing, a marginal sketch in one of his letters, scattered comments in various communications to Washington and L'Enfant, and his draft of a Presidential proclamation.

The first mention by Jefferson of his thinking on the plan of the capital appears in a note dated November 29, 1790, doubtless prepared to guide his discussion with Washington concerning the implementation of the Residence Act. After mentioning that the apparent intention of the act was to have the purchased land laid out in lots and streets, he continued:

[6] The complete text of L'Enfant's report with omitted words supplied in brackets as in the passage quoted appears in Elizabeth S. Kite, *L'Enfant and Washington 1791-1792*, Baltimore, 1929, pp. 43-48.

"I should propose these to be at right angles as in Philadelphia, & that no street be narrower than 100. feet, with foot-ways of 15. feet. where a street is long & level, it might be 120. feet wide. I should prefer squares of at least 200. yards every way, which will be of about 8. acres each."[7]

Jefferson suggested that the "squares" or city blocks be divided into lots 50 feet wide and that their depth extend to the diagonals connecting the corners of the square. He appended a little marginal sketch, reproduced in Figure 145, showing a block divided into 32 lots. The purpose of this odd method of subdivision is not explained, but it may have been intended to equalize the value of lots by reducing the size of corner locations while allowing interior lots to have progressively greater depth from corners to the midpoint of the boundary street lines.

Figure 145. Thomas Jefferson's Suggested City Block Division: 1790

In this memorandum he listed the sites that would be required for public purposes, including the capitol building, federal offices, the president's house and gardens, a city hall, market, public walks, and a hospital. For the presidential residence and gardens, he suggested consolidating two blocks, for the public walks, nine blocks, with the capitol building and offices to occupy one block, and another block for the market.

His later concern for building regulations of various sorts was anticipated in this same document. Commenting on building setbacks and height restrictions, he observed:

"I doubt much whether the obligation to build the houses at a given distance from the street, contributes to its beauty, it pro-

[7] Jefferson Note, "Proceedings to be had under the Residence Act," November 29, 1790, Padover, *Thomas Jefferson*, 31.

duces a disgusting monotony, all persons make this complaint against Philadelphia, the contrary practice varies the appearance, & is much more convenient to the inhabitants.

"In Paris it is forbidden to build a house beyond a given height, & it is admitted to be a good restriction, it keeps the houses low & convenient, & the streets light and airy, fires are much more managable where houses are low. This however is an object of Legislation."[8]

At this time Jefferson was thinking of the site then occupied by Carrollsburg along the Anacostia. In a second sketch at the end of the memorandum, reproduced in Figure 146, he showed a little gridiron layout 4 blocks deep by 13 blocks long, with the 5 major streets running parallel to the banks of the Anacostia and the less important frontage on the Potomac. Jefferson explained that the Potomac end of the town would be for governmental use, with commercial development along the Anacostia. It is evident that at this time his ideas about the size of the town and its other features were not clearly fixed, for he mentioned that 1,500 acres of land might be the total requirement, of which 300 acres would be used for "public buildings, walks, &c and 1200 Acres to be divided into quarter acre lots." These last figures cannot be reconciled with his proposals earlier in the same memorandum.

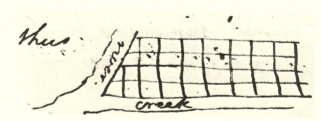

Figure 146. Thomas Jefferson's Plan for a Capital City on the Site of Carrollsburg, District of Columbia: 1790

When it seemed that the attitude of the Carrollsburg proprietors would block purchase of their land at reasonable prices, Jefferson shifted his attention to the land along Tyber Creek including the

[8] *ibid.*

site of Hamburg. In his papers may be found the draft for a presidential proclamation that would have appropriated,

". . . the highest summit of lands in the town heretofore called Hamburg . . . with a convenient extent of grounds circumjacent . . . for the accommodation of Congress, & such other lands between Georgetown & the stream heretofore called the Tyber, as shall on due examination be found convenient & Sufficient . . . for the accommodation of the President of the U.S. for the time being, & for the public offices of the government of the U.S."[9]

With this draft was apparently included the map shown in Figure 147, and both were probably given to Washington the end of March before he left for his meeting in Georgetown with the commissioners, Ellicott, L'Enfant, and the proprietors. Jefferson's plan shows many of the features first put forward in his memorandum three months previously, but now transferred to the site along the Tyber. The little gridiron town appears 3 blocks deep and 11 blocks long, with 3 blocks consolidated for the president's house and gardens and an equal area for the capitol to the east. Connecting these two sites Jefferson showed a stretch along the Tyber as a public walk. Here, perhaps is the genesis of the present mall as well as the eventual relationship of the White House and capitol building.

Jefferson's notes on the map indicate that the squares shown around the public buildings would be platted immediately and "sold in the first instance." Surrounding this area of initial settlement are dots showing the intersections of streets, with the notation, "to be laid off in future." Jefferson has sometimes been accused of limited vision in his concept of a capital city, but his sketch, if fairly interpreted, disproves any such contention. The area for immediate and eventual development amounted to roughly 2,000 acres, measuring about 1¼ by 2½ miles. This is somewhat larger than the original plat for Philadelphia and well over twice the amount of land actually developed for urban use in that city, then the largest in the nation. In his advocacy of initial settlement

[9] Jefferson draft, "A Proclamation," March 30, 1791, Padover, *Thomas Jefferson*, 53. The portion quoted was placed in brackets, with a footnote by Jefferson reading: "the part within [ ] being conjectural will be to be rendered conformable to the ground when more accurately examined." Both the portion quoted and the footnote are lined through on the original manuscript.

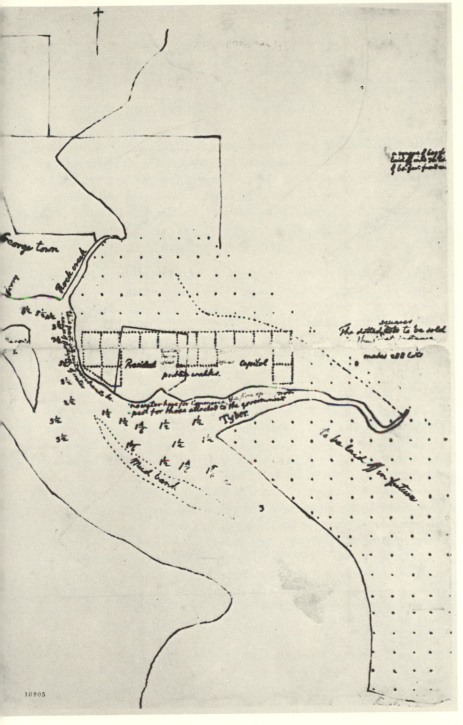

Figure 147. Thomas Jefferson's Plan for Washington, D.C.: 1791

within a fairly restricted area containing essential governmental buildings, Jefferson would have avoided the scattered, piecemeal growth that L'Enfant's Washington was to encounter.

The Jefferson plan for the city on the Tyber was prepared on the assumption that land elsewhere in the district could not be acquired on reasonable terms. When he learned of the agreement concluded by Washington at Georgetown under which from three to five thousand acres would become available if needed, he may have felt that even his original generous plan could have been enlarged. We do not know what he might have devised for the augmented site. He did suggest both to Washington and L'Enfant that "very liberal" reservations should be made for public use. To Washington he mentioned that he had sent to L'Enfant, at the latter's request, his plans of Frankfurt, Karlsruhe, Paris, Orleans, Milan, Amsterdam and half a dozen other cities, "they are none of them however comparable to the old Babylon, revived in Philadelphia, & exemplified."

We see Jefferson, then, a faithful adherent to the gridiron or checkerboard plan. In this his ideas clashed with those of L'Enfant. Washington on April 4 sent Jefferson's sketch plan for the city to L'Enfant, saying:

"Although I do not conceive that you will derive any material advantage from an examination of the enclosed papers, yet, as they have been drawn under different circumstances, and by different persons, they may be compared with your own ideas of a proper plan for the Federal City, under the prospect which now presents itself. For this purpose I commit them to your private inspection. . . . The rough sketch by Mr. Jefferson was done under an idea that *no* offer, worthy of consideration, would come from the Land holders in the vicinity of Carrollsburg . . . and therefore was accommodated to the grounds about George Town. The *other* is taken upon a larger scale, without reference to any described spot."[10]

This second plan remains a mystery, for the drawing has not survived. It may have been another drawing by Jefferson, but from the wording of the letter it seems more likely it had come to Washington from a different person.

[10] Letter from Washington to L'Enfant, April 4, 1791, H. P. Caemmerer, *The Life of Pierre Charles L'Enfant Planner of the City Beautiful: The City of Washington*, Washington, 1950, p. 144.

L'Enfant's reaction to Jefferson's plan was certainly unfavorable, for in his site analysis report to the President only a few days earlier he had roundly condemned the rectangular plan in a typically emotional outburst of criticism, asserting:

". . . it is not the regular assemblage of houses laid out in squares and forming streets all parallel and uniform that . . . is so necessary, for such a plan could only do on a level plain and where no surrounding object being interesting it becomes indifferent which way the opening of streets may be directed.

"But on any other ground, a plan of this sort must be defective, and it never would answer for any of the spots proposed for the Federal City, and on that held here as the most eligible it would absolutely annihilate every of the advantages enumerated and . . . alone injure the success of the undertaking.

"Such regular plans indeed, however answerable they may appear upon paper or seducing as they may be on the first aspect to the eyes of some people must even when applyed upon the ground the best calculated to admit of it become at last tiresome and insipid and it never could be in its origin but a mean continuance of some cool imagination wanting a sense of the real grand and truly beautiful only to be met with where nature contributes with art and diversifies the objects."[11]

Although Jefferson read this report and could hardly escape the conclusion that he and the capital planner were at opposite poles in their concepts of planning, he did not allow this to affect his relationship with L'Enfant. Thus on April 10 in a letter accompanying the maps sent to him, Jefferson wrote: "I am happy that the President has left the planning of the Town in such good hands, and have no doubt it will be done to general satisfaction."[12] And, then, in a reference to his earlier suggestions about the planning of the town, Jefferson continued:

"Having communicated to the President, before he went away, such general ideas on the subject of the Town, as occurred to me, I make no doubt that, in explaining himself to you on the subject,

he has interwoven with his own ideas, such of mine as he approved: for fear of repeating therefore, what he did not approve, and having more confidence in the unbiassed state of his mind, than in my own, I avoid interfering with what he may have expressed to you."[13]

So L'Enfant was left with complete freedom to develop his own ideas of a plan for the capital city. During the following three months he was busy with his surveys and designs, spurred on by the confidence shown in his abilities by Washington and Jefferson and excited by the unique opportunity that lay before him.

The Grand Plan for the Capital City

As has already been suggested, L'Enfant had probably conceived of the main elements of his plan while making his site surveys. As early as the third week in April these ideas had been refined, and tentative locations were selected for some of the features that would appear on his later plans. We have one account by a visitor to the area as evidence that L'Enfant had proceeded with such speed—the journal entry of William Loughton Smith for April 22, 1791:

"As soon as I arrived at Georgetown, I rode with Major L'Enfant, appointed . . . to make plans, surveys, etc., of the Federal city, to survey the land laid out for that purpose . . . I rode over the greatest part of the ground; the Major pointed out to me all the eminences, plains, commanding spots, projects of canals by means of Rock Creek, Eastern Branch, and a fine creek called Goose Creek, which intersects the plan of the city along the Eastern Branch, quays, bridges, etc., magnificent public walks, and other projects. . . .

"The ground pleased me much; the Major is enraptured with it; 'nothing,' he says, 'can be more admirably adapted for the purpose; nature has done much for it, and with the aid of art it will become the wonder of the world.' I proposed calling this new Seat of Empire Washingtonople. . . . The Major showed me all his plans and surveys . . . ; they are to be all ready for the President on his return from his tour."[14]

[11] Undated communication by L'Enfant entitled "Note relative to the ground lying on the eastern branch of the river Potomac and being intended to parallel the several positions proposed within the limits between the branch and Georgetown for the seat of the Federal City," Kite, *L'Enfant*, 47-48.

[12] Letter from Jefferson to L'Enfant, April 10, 1791, Padover, *Thomas Jefferson*, 59.

[13] *ibid*.

[14] *Journal of William Loughton Smith* (1790-1791), Massachusetts Historical Society, *Proceedings*, LI, Boston, 1918, 60-62.

Washington's presence was needed in Georgetown again. During his absence while visiting North and South Carolina and Georgia some of the proprietors of land evidently reconsidered their agreement of March and protested to the commissioners that too much land was being taken for the city. When they refused to deed their land in trust as provided in the agreement the project once more appeared to be in difficulty, but the persuasive powers of the President again proved adequate. During the days of June 27, 28, and 29, while in Georgetown, Washington met with the proprietors and also conferred with the commissioners, L'Enfant, and Ellicott on matters affecting the city. While the deeds were being prepared on the 28th, the President, as he records in his diary, "went out with Major L'Enfant and Mr. Ellicott to take more perfect view of the ground in order to decide finally on the spot on which to place the public buildings. . . ." Then, the following day, when all the deeds had been signed, he called the proprietors together and informed them of the sites for the executive and legislative buildings. The diary then records this significant passage:

"A plan was also laid before them of the city; but they were told that some alterations, deviations from it, would take place, particularly in the diagonal streets or avenues, which would not be so numerous, and in the removal of the President's house more westerly, for the advantage of higher ground. They were also told that a Townhouse or Exchange would be placed on some convenient ground between the spots designed for the public buildings before mentioned, and it was with much pleasure that a general approbation of the measure seemed to pervade the whole."[15]

The plan revealed by the President at this meeting was one that L'Enfant had submitted with a memorandum dated June 22. It probably reached Washington sometime during the period June 13-27, while he was at Mount Vernon. This first plan of L'Enfant has, unfortunately, never been discovered, although one scholarly attempt has been made to reconstruct its details from the internal evidence of L'Enfant's second and later plan as well as through an examination of pertinent documents.[16]

[15] Joseph A. Hoskins, ed., *President Washington's Diaries, 1791 to 1799*, Summerfield, N.C., 1921. Entry for June 29, 1791, p. 52.
[16] See William T. Partridge, "L'Enfant's Methods and Features of his Plan for the Federal City," National Capital Park and Planning Commission,

The plan submitted by L'Enfant at the June meeting in Georgetown probably showed all the streets as then proposed as well as the other features of the city. But this was plainly intended as a draft plan, subject to such changes as Washington and others might suggest, and with the understanding that any new features as well as those retained would be studied in more detail. As L'Enfant stated in his explanatory memorandum to the President,

"My whole attention was directed to a combination of the general distribution of the several situations . . . in submitting to your judgment . . . and in presenting to you a first drawing, correct only as it respects the situation and distance of objects."[17]

L'Enfant fully described his methods of planning and the objectives he hoped to achieve in this report to Washington. In somewhat better English and considerably abridged, much of the same material appeared on the second and revised plan, work on which began as soon as Washington left Georgetown the last day of June. This first statement by the planner explaining his grand design is an extremely important and interesting document. Both L'Enfant's enthusiasm for and technical understanding of his unique assignment are apparent as he began the explanation for his illustrious client:

"Having determined some principal points to which I wished to make the other subordinate, I made the distribution regular with every street at right angles, North and South, east and west, and afterwards opened some in different directions, as avenues to and from every principal place, wishing thereby not merely to contract [contrast] with the general regularity, nor to afford a greater variety of seats with pleasant prospects, which will be obtained from the advantageous ground over which these avenues are chiefly directed, but principally to connect each part of the city, if I may so express it, by making the real distance less from place to place, by giving to them reciprocity of sight and by making them thus seemingly connected, promote a rapid settlement over the whole

Reports and Plans, Washington Region, Supplementary Technical Data to Accompany Annual Report, Washington, 1930, pp. 21-38. Partridge's penetrating analysis of the changes made in L'Enfant's first plan is a remarkable piece of scholarship.
[17] Undated report by L'Enfant to Washington, the text of which appears in Kite, *L'Enfant*, 52-58.

extent, rendering those even of the most remote parts an addition to the principal. . . ."[18]

The avenues were to be extremely broad. L'Enfant stated that roadways would be 80 feet, with 30 feet on each side "for a walk under a double row of trees," and with 10 feet on each side between the trees and the houses. The widths of the other streets were not specified, although that may have been indicated on the map. L'Enfant described the principal avenue that would lead from the crossing of the East Branch directly to Georgetown; this is the present Pennsylvania Avenue. The two chief features of the city, the "Presidential palace" and the "Federal House" were planned to lie in the path of this great thoroughfare. The house for the President with its "garden park and other improvements" L'Enfant placed facing the Tyber and toward the western end of the city. About halfway between the president's residence and the East Branch along the main avenue lay Jenkin's Hill, which L'Enfant had already previously remarked as the best site for the Capitol. Here, said L'Enfant, was a spot that "stands really as a pedestal waiting for a superstructure," and no other location "could bear a competition with this."

The memorandum took up one by one many of the other features that we now see in contemporary Washington. There were the "public walks" that would connect the presidential gardens with the grounds of the Capitol; a monument at the intersection of the axis of presidential grounds and the mall; and the executive buildings close to the house of the president. One ambitious proposal made by L'Enfant, however, was never to be developed. This was the channelization of the Tyber from its headwaters so as to flow toward the Capitol where L'Enfant suggested ". . . letting the Tiber return to its proper channel by a fall, which issuing from under the base of the Congress building, may there form a cascade of forty feet high, or more than one hundred wide, which would produce the most happy effect in rolling down to fill up the canal and discharge itself in the Potomac. . . ."[19]

An important feature of L'Enfant's plan as described in his memorandum was a canal connecting the Potomac and the East Branch. Tyber Creek was to form the basis for this canal. Its course was to be straightened, deepened and confined to an east-west channel running along the north side of the public walks, or mall, then to turn south and cross in front of the Capitol and its cascade. It was along this canal that L'Enfant proposed the initial development of the city. It is worth noting that even at this early stage in planning he was looking beyond the mere physical plan for the city to a land development policy that would result in rapid growth. He suggested that building ". . . should be begun at various points equi-distant as possible from the center; not merely because settlements of this sort are likely to diffuse an equality of advantages over the whole territory allotted, and consequently to reflect benefit from an increase of the value of property, but because each of these settlements by a natural jealousy will most tend to stimulate establishment on each of the opposed extremes. . . ."[20] In this manner, according to L'Enfant, these individual nodes of settlement would quickly become joined, and the city would soon begin to take form. The canal was intended to provide lateral communication between these points, guide development in the proper direction, and speed the rate of growth.

After Washington's departure, L'Enfant began work on the revisions suggested by the President. These were completed during the next six weeks, and on August 19 L'Enfant sent a drawing to Washington indicating that the desired changes had been made. Later in the month L'Enfant came to Philadelphia, where, as Jefferson mentions in a letter to the commissioners dated August 28, "Major L'Enfant . . . laid his plan of the federal city before the President. . . ." That plan is reproduced in Figure 148, from a copy made in 1887 of the L'Enfant manuscript drawing, then badly faded and with some of its details missing.[21]

Here we see L'Enfant's plan as modified by Washington and with additional details worked out by the planner during July and August and described in his marginal comments. The major elements of central Washington as it now exists all appear, although there have been many changes in the shapes and sizes of

[18] *ibid.*   [19] *ibid.*

[20] *ibid.*

[21] The evidence indicates that this map or a close copy was the one L'Enfant took to Philadelphia in August. In his August 19 memorandum L'Enfant mentions another map—an "annexed map of dotted lines . . . explanatory of the progress made in the work. . . ." This doubtless refers to the "Map of Dotted Lines" reproduced in Caemmerer, *Washington* on page 26 and described in the *Report of the Librarian of Congress, 1930*, pp. 164-67. This description may also be found in Appendix D of Caemmerer, *L'Enfant*, 428-31.

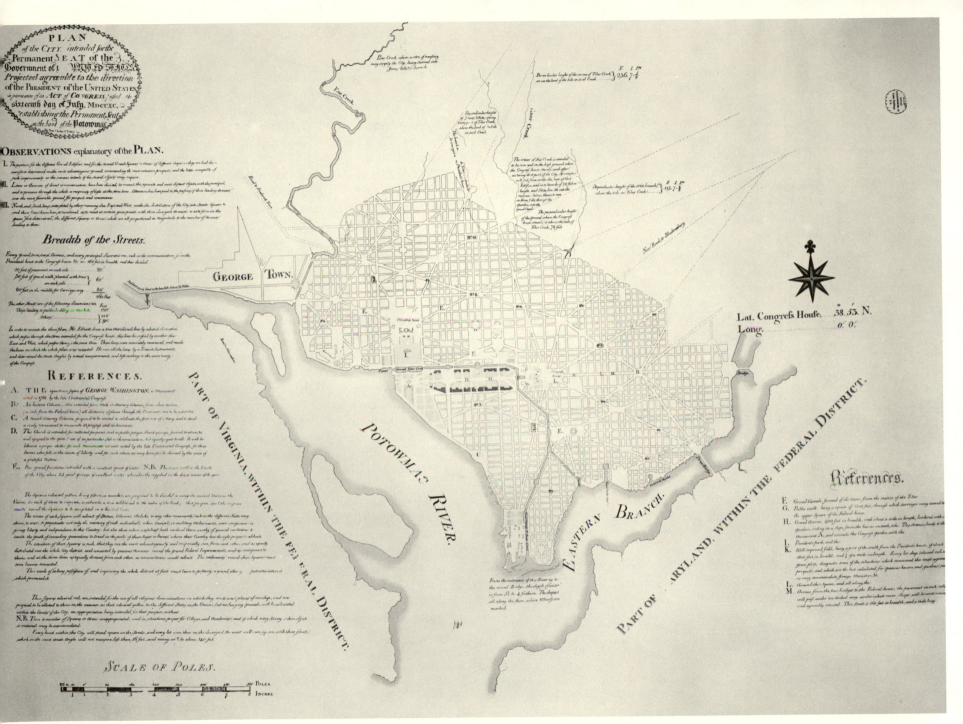

Figure 148. L'Enfant's Plan for Washington, D.C.: 1791

the squares and several major modifications in portions of the street pattern.

L'Enfant's plan shows many features other than those previously described in his August memorandum. Fifteen **squares were** designated, one for each of the states of the union to embellish with "Statues, Columns, Obelisks, or any other ornament." These squares were part of L'Enfant's proposals for nodal development, since each state was expected to make "improvements around the Square to be completed in a limited time," and he expected that "The Settlements round those Squares must soon become connected." Another square was to be occupied by a church, "intended for national purposes, such as public prayer, thanksgiving, funeral orations, etc." While this was to be a nondenominational church, other church sites were marked out to be distributed on the same basis as the squares of the states. The remaining undesignated squares were to be used as sites for "Colleges and Academies" or societies "whose object is national."

The new capital was to be a city of beauty. In addition to the cascade issuing from the base of the Capitol, "Five grand fountains intended with a constant spout of water" appear on the plan. The concept of the public walks was further refined. For what we now know as the mall L'Enfant proposed a "Grand Avenue" 400 feet wide with gardens on each side leading from the Capitol to the Potomac. Three important monuments were described: an equestrian statue of Washington at the intersection of the axes of mall and president's gardens; a column in what is now Lincoln Square one mile east of the Capitol, from which all distances on the continent were to be measured; and a column in honor of the navy on a line directly south of the national church and located on the Potomac.

The general arrangement of principal uses of land was also indicated in L'Enfant's memorandum and in the marginal comments on the plan. "Mercantile interests should be pushed with the greatest activity" along the banks of the canal connecting the two rivers. Shops were to be located in two areas: one along "the streets from the grand avenue to the palace and towards the canal"; and the other along the street running directly east from the Capitol. In this latter area we are told that the sidewalk "on each side will pass under an Arched way, under whose cover Shops will be most conveniently and agreeably situated."[22]

In his memorandum to the President, L'Enfant stated, "It was my wish to delineate a plan wholly new." Certainly in its magnitude, its clever fitting of a generally symmetrical design to irregular topography, and its generous provision of a variety of open spaces, the plan for Washington must stand as one of the great city planning efforts of all time. At least as remarkable as the plan itself is the speed with which L'Enfant prepared and revised it. Site surveys, first draft, and revised version—all were carried out in less than six months. Clearly this would have been impossible for anyone less a genius than L'Enfant or less familiar with the design idioms that make up this vast essay in civic development. In this respect, then, the plan is not "wholly new"—no city plan except the first has ever been—for L'Enfant used the familiar devices of the baroque designers in devising his grand plan. To say this is not to minimize L'Enfant's accomplishment but merely to assert the obvious, that he was a product of his age and the instrument through which certain principles of civic design that had been developed in western Europe found expression on the Potomac River.

As a young lad L'Enfant knew at first hand the gardens of Versailles, that great composition by LeNôtre, where his father was a court painter. And later, as a student in the Royal Academy of Painting and Sculpture, he could observe the Garden of the Tuilleries, the Place de la Concorde, and the beginnings of today's Avenue des Champs Elysées, which then was a track through the woods and fields ending at a *rond point* in an apple orchard, the modern Place de l'Etoile. In the works of LeNôtre, his contemporaries, and their followers we can see the same concern with axial treatment of building masses and open spaces, the same delight in sweeping diagonal avenues, the same studied use of monuments or important buildings as terminal vistas to close street views that L'Enfant employed in his plan of Washington. This was the language of civic design that came most naturally to him, and he spoke it fluently and with conviction.

[22] It is possible that L'Enfant got the idea for an arcaded shopping street from the arrangement of shops facing the gardens of the Palais-Royale in Paris. L'Enfant had visited Paris after the Revolutionary War and doubtless saw this project under construction. The arcaded street, of course, dates from a much earlier time. The arrangement would have been ideal for the Washington climate.

L'Enfant Terrible

When L'Enfant journeyed to Philadelphia with his revised plan he was concerned not only with submitting the design to the President but with presenting his ideas on the development policy that should be followed in carrying out the plan. These ideas were stated in his memorandum of August 19 and were doubtless the subject of much discussion during his meeting with Washington, Jefferson, and Madison. In brief, L'Enfant strongly opposed the early sale of lots in the new city which everyone else concerned with the project had anticipated. About 15,000 lots would come into public ownership for disposal under the agreement negotiated by the President. L'Enfant pointed out that if lots of greatest potential value—those near the President's mansion—were put up for sale first, as was evidently the intention, they would fail to bring their true value. It would be far better, he maintained, to complete many of the streets and public buildings first, since then the lots would appear more attractive and yield greater revenue. He advocated borrowing a large sum of money by mortgaging property located toward the edge of the city, completing the improvements, and only then placing a limited number of lots on the market. With the proceeds, the loan could be repaid and decisions on the timing and location of development could be made independently of immediate concern with raising funds.

To this suggested method of finance Washington could not agree, nor did Jefferson or the commissioners support L'Enfant. While in other circumstances they might have consented to this procedure, which had considerable merit, they were under extreme pressure to show immediate results in the development of the capital city. For at this time, before any plan of the city had been published and when many weightier problems faced the new nation, many persons were skeptical that a suitable city could be created, while others favored the retention of the capital in Philadelphia. Moreover, Washington and Jefferson were already reporting that the first lands would be available for sale soon, and to abandon this policy in favor of long negotiations over loans would simply give the enemies of the new city additional grounds for criticism. Finally, there was an additional reason which L'Enfant apparently had overlooked. Half of the lots in the city belonged to the original proprietors, who would be able to meet any foreseeable demand for building sites, thus obtaining for private landowners the profits that might otherwise accrue to the government.

On September 8, following the conference in Philadelphia, Jefferson and Madison met with the commissioners in Georgetown. At that meeting the details of the first sale were agreed on, building regulations were discussed, and the system for numbering and lettering streets was established. The date of October 17 was fixed as the date for the sale of lots at public auction. The next day the commissioners wrote to L'Enfant, still in Philadelphia, telling him of the street designations, their decision to call the district "The Territory of Columbia" and the town "The City of Washington," and requesting him to have 10,000 copies of the city map printed for distribution.

Whether through L'Enfant's own action or, as he stated to Tobias Lear, Washington's secretary, because the printer could not obtain a suitable piece of copper for the plate, no copies of the map were printed. This naturally distressed Washington and the commissioners, but they were even more dismayed when L'Enfant refused to permit the display of his drawing at the sale itself. The only maps available were the plats of individual blocks, and the purchasers were unable to determine their exact location within the city. L'Enfant explained his strange behavior to Lear in a letter written two days after the sale:

"The advantageous price obtained for a number of lots, the less advantage in their local [location] being wholly owing to the care I took to prevent the exhibition of the general plan at the spot where the sale is made must convince that enabling individuals to then compare the situation offered for sale with many others apparently more advantageous would have depreciated the value of those lots that sold the most high."[23]

This was the first of a series of actions that led to L'Enfant's replacement. The President wrote to one of the commissioners, David Stuart, that he had informed L'Enfant that hereafter "he must . . . look to the commissioners for directions," and expressing his displeasure at the lack of a printed map. "There has been something very unaccountable in the conduct of the engraver, yet I cannot be of opinion the delays were occasioned by L'Enfant," wrote

[23] Letter from L'Enfant to Lear, October 19, 1791, Caemmerer, *L'Enfant*, 174.

Washington, evidently not wishing to condemn him on evidence only circumstantial.

The next incident was more serious. One of the proprietors, Daniel Carroll of Duddington had begun the construction of his house south of the site of the Capitol. When the surveys of New Jersey Avenue were run in August it was found that the house extended into the avenue and block bounded by that avenue and E, F, and 2nd Streets, S.E., by some 7 feet. According to L'Enfant, he directed Carroll to remove the house, and when this was not done he ordered his workmen to demolish it. He did not consult the commissioners on the matter, although he did report to them the action he had taken. Then followed a series of letters between L'Enfant, the commissioners, Washington, Carroll, and Jefferson. Washington was anxious to avoid any scandal that might hinder progress in the city, and he advised the commissioners to have patience with the Major. But to L'Enfant he sent a stern warning:

"In future I must strictly enjoin you to touch no man's property without his consent, or the previous order of the Commissioners. I wished you to be employed in the arrangements of the Federal City. I still wish it: but only on condition that you can conduct yourself in subordination to the authority of the Commissioners, to whom by law the business is entrusted, and who stand between you and the President of the United States—to the laws of the land—and to the rights of its citizens."[24]

The commissioners accepted the President's advice to continue with L'Enfant, and for a time things went smoothly in surveying streets, felling trees, and in construction activities. But in December new difficulties arose. L'Enfant had gone to Philadelphia to see about the engraving of his map and had left orders with his assistant, Isaac Roberdeau, to begin the quarrying of stone. The commissioners, on the other hand, directed Roberdeau to continue the brickmaking. When he ignored this order on the grounds that he was responsible to L'Enfant, Roberdeau was then arrested. On learning of this L'Enfant immediately appealed to the President, stating flatly that he would "renounce the pursuit unless the power of effecting the work with advantage to the public and credit to myself is left me." The commissioners had already reported the events to the President and indicated that they would "truly lament if it so happens the loss of Major L'Enfant's taste and abilities; but we owe something to ourselves and to others which cannot be given up."

Meanwhile Washington and Jefferson had been pressing L'Enfant to produce the engraved map so that copies could be distributed throughout the country and abroad. When L'Enfant still delayed, Washington directed Ellicott to take over this assignment. Here again, L'Enfant attempted to assert his independence of authority, for toward the end of February 1792 we find Ellicott complaining to the commissioners that L'Enfant had refused to let him have the original drawing, adding, "what his motives were, God knows." But Ellicott informed the commissioners that he would use the survey data in his possession for the engraving and stated his belief that "The plan which we have furnished . . . will be found to answer the ground better than the large one in the Major's hands."

Two engravings were finally made, one printed in Boston and the other, shown in Figure 149, by Thackara and Vallance in Philadelphia. They are substantially identical and both show changes from the revised L'Enfant plan of the previous fall. The changes may have originated with Jefferson, since he proposed certain modifications to Washington and there were pencil notations by him on a drawing sent to the engraver indicating details that should be omitted.[25] Ellicott on his own initiative may have modified the L'Enfant plan, and since he lacked survey information withheld by L'Enfant some of the modifications may have resulted from his attempt to reconstruct from memory the details of the original.

[24] Letter from Washington to L'Enfant, December 2, 1791. Caemmerer, *L'Enfant*, 182. The mass of correspondence on this issue may be found in Kite and Padover. Padover includes the opinion by Jefferson on the legality of L'Enfant's action. Kite defends L'Enfant as acting within the law. While this position might be technically correct L'Enfant's action appears as an act of defiance aimed at the commissioners and an assertion of power scarcely compatible with the previous orders to L'Enfant to "look to the commissioners for directions."

[25] Letter from Washington to Jefferson, February 15, 1792: "Before I give any decided opinion upon . . . the alternations proposed for the engraved plan. . . ." Padover, *Thomas Jefferson*, 91; letter from Washington to commissioners, December, 1796: "In it [the plan] you may discover (Though almost obliterated) the directions given to the engraver by Mr. Jefferson with a pencil of the parts to omit. . . ." As quoted by Partridge, "L'Enfant's Methods," 25.

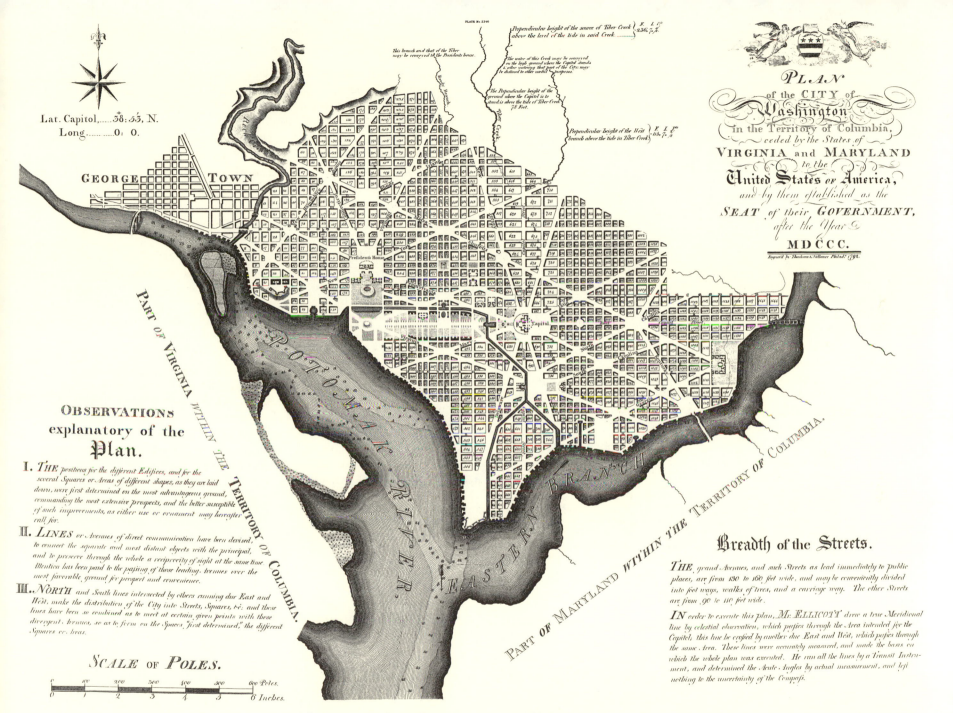

Figure 149. The Ellicott Plan for Washington, D.C.: 1792

The most obvious difference is the change in direction and alignment of Massachusetts Avenue, which was straightened. Because it was tilted from its original axis, its eastern end terminated not at the bridge at the foot of East Capitol Street, as L'Enfant originally intended, but at the Marine Hospital. Other changes were less drastic and may have resulted in fitting L'Enfant's plan to the more accurate boundary and topographic surveys completed by Ellicott after August of the preceding year. One feature suppressed from the original drawing which justifiably angered L'Enfant was any mention of the designer's name. Only Ellicott's appears on the printed version. Whether this deletion was deliberate or an unfortunate oversight is not known.

At the time L'Enfant charged that his plan had been "most unmercifully spoiled and altered . . . to a degree indeed evidently tending to disgrace me and ridicule the very undertaking," and he placed the blame squarely on Ellicott in a bitter letter written to the President's secretary.[26] Matters now drew quickly to a conclusion. On February 22 Jefferson wrote to L'Enfant on behalf of the President stating that he might continue if he were willing to accept the general direction of the commissioners. L'Enfant replied with a long tirade against the commissioners, accusing them of incompetence, laxity, and favoritism and declining to submit himself to their control. Washington made one last attempt to retain L'Enfant's services by sending his secretary, Tobias Lear, to talk with him. L'Enfant brusquely dismissed Lear, saying, "that he had already heard enough of this matter." The next day Washington, Jefferson and Madison met and determined that L'Enfant should be notified that his appointment was terminated.

So ended L'Enfant's brief career as planner of the city of Washington. For many years, however, he was to be seen about the city observing the progress of construction and, no doubt, offering his observations to anyone who might listen. In typical fashion he had rejected the payment "of 500 guineas and a lot in a good part of the city" offered him by the commissioners at Washington's suggestion in March 1792, but in 1800 he sent to Congress the first of three memorials requesting compensation for his services, claiming $95,500. This was not approved, but in 1804 Congress passed a bill authorizing settlement on the same basis as offered in 1792.

Apparently a creditor secured a judgment against this sum, and there is no record that L'Enfant received any payment. Finally, in 1810 another payment was authorized, totaling $1,394.20. Most of this, too, went to his creditors.

L'Enfant died in 1825 at the Maryland estate of William Dudley Digges, who had given him, then an old man of 70, a home the previous year. By an ironic coincidence Digges had married Eleanor Carroll, whose father's house L'Enfant had earlier ordered destroyed. A kinder fate ordained that L'Enfant's final resting place should be on a spot overlooking the city he had planned. In 1909 his body was moved from the grave at the Digges home to the Capitol Rotunda. There a memorial service was held, with the French Ambassador, the President of the District commissioners and the Vice-President as speakers. Then a funeral procession led to the National Cemetery at Arlington, where L'Enfant was reburied. From the tomb the city of Washington can be seen across the Potomac, and on the slab of Tennessee marble is carved the plan that L'Enfant devised for his beloved capital city.

The City of Magnificent Distances

During the early years the city grew so slowly that there were renewed doubts about the transfer of the capital from Philadelphia. The site of the city must have presented a strange picture during the early years of construction. When Thomas Twining visited the Federal District the end of April 1796, he says that he

". . . entered a large wood through which a very imperfect road had been made, principally by removing the trees, or rather the upper parts of them in the usual manner. After some time this indistinct way assumed more the appearance of a regular avenue, the trees here having been cut down in a straight line. Although no habitation of any kind was visible, I had no doubt but I was now riding along one of the streets of the metropolitan city. I continued in this spacious avenue for half a mile, and then came out upon a large spot, cleared of wood, in the centre of which I saw two buildings on an extensive scale. . . ."[27]

These buildings were the Capitol and a tavern. From the hills

[26] Letter from L'Enfant to Lear, February 17, 1792, Caemmerer, *L'Enfant*, 205-208.

[27] Thomas Twining, *Travels in America 100 Years Ago*, New York, 1894, p. 100.

Twining could see "on every side a thick wood pierced with avenues in a more or less perfect state." Twining was somewhat surprised to see the city in such a "sylvan state," since maps and descriptions of the city had led him to believe that more progress had been made. He had been deceived by one of the broadsides that the original proprietors and later speculators were issuing in an effort to speed the sales of lots. As was usual in the real estate promotional literature of the time, the wildest claims were advanced of the advantages of the site and the great progress that had been made.[28]

In the fall of 1796 Francis Baily also recorded his impressions of the embryonic city. He admired the President's house, the Capitol, and the view from the point where the Potomac and Anacostia join. However, very little in the way of a city was to be seen, as Baily soon discovered:

"The private buildings go on but slowly. There are about twenty or thirty houses built near the Point, as well as a few in South Capitol Street and about a hundred others scattered over in other places: in all I suppose about two hundred: and these constitute the great city of Washington. The truth is, that not much more than one-half the city is *cleared*:—the rest is *in woods*; and most of the streets which are laid out are cut through these woods, and have a much more pleasing effect now than I think they will have when they shall be built; for *now* they appear like broad avenues in a park, bounded on each side by thick woods; and there being so many of them, and proceeding in so many various directions, they have a certain wild, yet uniform and regular appearance, which they will lose when confined on each side by brick walls."[29]

It was a long time before brick walls were to confine the avenues through the woods. Morris Birkbeck, who had come to America from England to establish a colony in the Illinois country, visited Washington in May 1817. He mentions that most of the streets could be distinguished only with difficulty, mainly by the rows of poplars that had been planted along their borders. He was disdainful of the marble capitals brought over from Italy to be used on the columns of the Capitol, which showed "how *un*-American is the whole plan." Then he sourly commented:

"This embryo metropolis, with its foreign decorations, should have set a better example to the young republic, by surrounding itself first with good roads and substantial bridges, in lieu of those inconvenient wooden structures and dangerous roads, over which the legislators must now pass to their duty. I think too, that good taste would have preferred native decoration for the seat of the legislature."[30]

Birkbeck was one of the first in a long succession of Europeans, chiefly English, who dutifully visited the capital and almost invariably published derisive accounts of the town with predictions that its ambitious street system would never be lined by buildings. "The City of Magnificent Intentions," "The City of Magnificent Distances," were but two of the titles invented by visitors and residents alike. Nor were these epithets inaccurate. Part of the mall had been enclosed and was used for cattle grazing, many of the squares were used as vegetable gardens, and crops were planted within the street lines beyond the little groups of houses clustered here and there around the principal buildings. The bucolic appearance of the city moved the Irish poet, Thomas Moore, to write these lines following his visit in 1804:

> This embryo capital, where fancy sees
> Squares in morasses, obelisks in trees;
> Which second-sighted seers, ev'n now, adorn
> With shrines unbuilt, and heroes yet unborn,
> Though naught but woods and Jefferson they see,
> Where streets should run and sages ought to be.

Slowly the city began to grow. By 1834 Washington presented a rather handsome sight as viewed from the south bank of the Anacostia. Figure 150 shows the city in that year with the Capitol dominating the skyline from the top of Jenkin's Hill, which L'En-

[28] One of the earliest of these broadsides was issued by Washington's friend, George Walker, who had acquired an interest in some land after the location of the District was announced. The full text of Walker's description distributed in England during the spring of 1793 appears in P. Lee Phillips, *The Beginnings of Washington as Described in Books, Maps and Views*, Washington, 1917, pp. 18-26.

[29] Francis Baily, *Journal of a Tour in Unsettled Parts of North America in 1796 & 1797*, London, 1856, pp. 127-28.

[30] Morris Birkbeck, *Notes on a Journey in America from the Coast of Virginia to the Territory of Illinois*, 3rd ed., London, 1818, p. 29.

Figure 150. View of Washington, D.C. from the South Bank of the Anacostia River: 1834

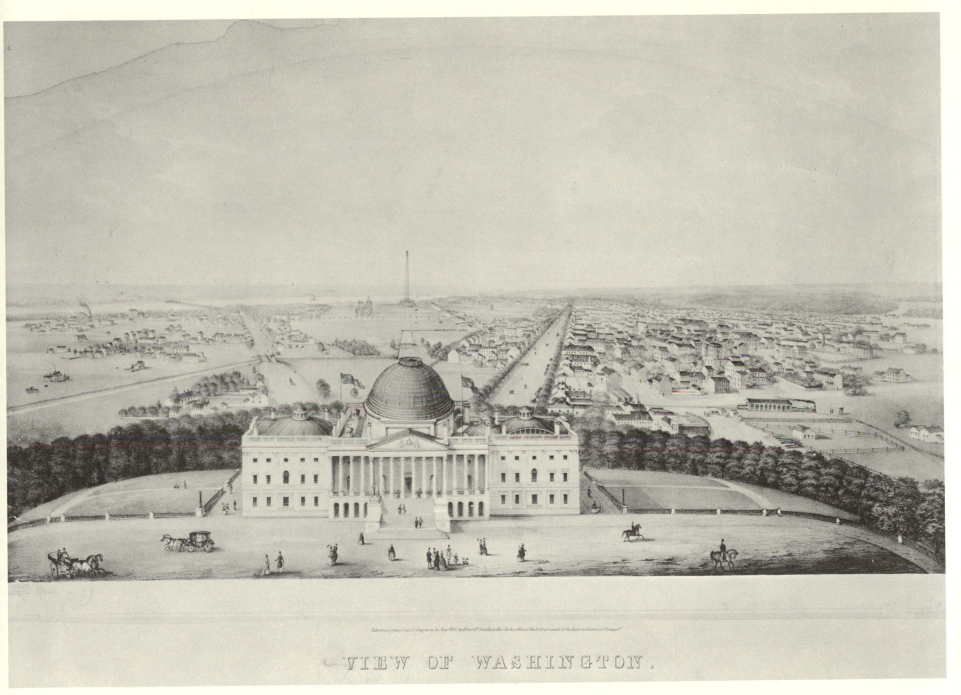

VIEW OF WASHINGTON.

Figure 151. View of Washington, D.C. from the Capitol to the White House: 1850

The Corcoran Art Building.   Franklin School.   War Department.   Treasury Department.   Patent Office.   Post Office.   Winder Building.   Navy Department.   Smithsonian Institute.   General Grant's Headquarters.   Washington Monument.
White House.   Agricultural Bureau.   Navy Yard.

WASHINGTON CITY, D. C.—SKETCHED BY THEO. R. DAVIS.—[SEE PAGE 170.]

Figure 152. View of Washington, D.C. from the White House to the Capitol: 1869

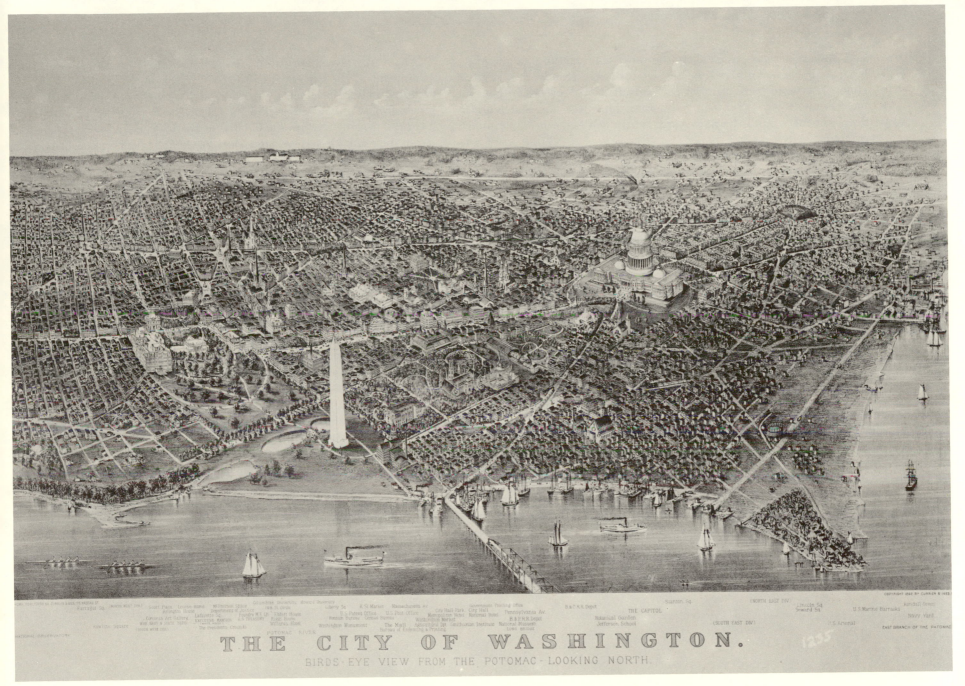

THE CITY OF WASHINGTON.
BIRDS-EYE VIEW FROM THE POTOMAC - LOOKING NORTH.

Figure 153. View of Washington, D.C. from the Potomac River: 1892

fant had at once recognized as the most commanding site in the federal district. To the left, in the distance, stands the White House. Between these symbols of legislative and executive power most of the town had grown, although there was also substantial development around the navy yard, which can be seen in the foreground.

L'Enfant's great formal composition was only imperfectly expressed, however. The view from the Capitol to the White House and the Potomac in 1850, reproduced in Figure 151, reveals how little the central area of the city resembled his vision of baroque magnificence. In the vast stretch of the mall westward from the Capitol only the Smithsonian Institution appears. The Washington Monument in the distance is a vision of the artist; only the lower courses of this imposing obelisk had then been completed. The canal winding its way from the Potomac to the Anacostia is the old Tyber Creek, utilized as L'Enfant suggested. However, its warehouse-lined banks scarcely added to the beauty of the city. South of the "mall" appear scattered dwellings on the few streets that had been surveyed in this portion of Washington. Only to the north of Pennsylvania Avenue, the broad boulevard leading to the White House, can one discern anything resembling a city.

With the Civil War and the reestablishment of the Union, the importance of the central government increased. It was then that Washington began to develop the economic base that sustains it today—the vast bureaucracy of governmental employees. By 1869, as the view in Figure 152 indicates, modern Washington had begun to take shape. In the foreground stands the White House in its spacious grounds with Lafayette Square to the left. Just beyond is the Treasury Building, the beginning of the neo-classic structures erected for administrative departments that now dominate the central part of the city. Some of the handsome town houses can be seen in the distance, along with several in the foreground that appear less substantial.

The mall, stretching from the still uncompleted Washington Monument at the center right to the Capitol on the horizon, had acquired only a little sense of order, and even that was quite different from the kind envisaged by L'Enfant. Portions of the mall had been designed before the Civil War by Andrew Jackson Downing in the romantic style of landscape gardening, each section being treated as a unit. Only a part of Downing's plan was executed. The monument itself was erected off the axes of both the White House and the Capitol because of the unsuitability of the soil on the spot selected by L'Enfant as a memorial to Washington.

Far more serious damage had been done to the L'Enfant plan when Congress approved a railroad station on the north side of the mall to be reached by tracks running across the mall from the south almost in the shadow of the Capitol itself. The effect of this legislative folly can be seen in the view of Washington in 1892 shown in Figure 153. This somewhat distorted and romanticized view of the city fails to reveal all the encroachments on and changes in the L'Enfant plan made through the years. They were many in number and serious in nature.

As Washington approached the centennial year of its location as the seat of government, thoughtful persons in the capital and elsewhere in the nation began to think about appropriate ways to mark this historic date. Many legislators advanced suggestions for the construction of buildings, parks, or monuments to commemorate the occasion. In the end, no specific project resulted. Much more important, however, the L'Enfant plan itself was revived and given fresh meaning as a guide to urban growth and change. Those activities are reviewed in Chapter 18, which describes the rebirth of city planning in America under a philosophy of design which L'Enfant himself would have supported. That period of urban development—the City Beautiful movement of the early 1900's—thus had its spiritual roots in the Washington of Pierre Charles L'Enfant.

CHAPTER 10

Boulevard Baroque and Diagonal Designs

L'ENFANT'S grandiose plan for Washington seldom escaped the taunts of visiting Europeans. It was not only the scale of the scheme which appeared so ridiculous but the concept of the grand plan with its squares and circles, its mall, and its wide boulevards radiating outward from the sites for major buildings. For a republic so often proclaiming the equality of men and the virtues of democracy, there appeared something incongruous in adopting as a plan for its capital the architectural and landscape forms brought to perfection first in ancient Rome and then in eighteenth-century France under the most autocratic of regimes.

But while European critics and native skeptics might scoff at Washington, to most Americans the Federal City stood as a symbol of what the future promised for the entire country, which, like the capital city, remained unfinished but which boasted of boundless energy, optimism, and natural resources.

As an influence on the plans of other cities Washington exercised greater force than is generally believed. Two major metropolitan cities, three substantial communities which are, in addition, state capitals, a number of locally important resort or trading centers, and a host of minor communities all owe their original plans to the direct or indirect influence of the Washington pattern. Extensions to many other cities, either executed or proposed, all stem from L'Enfant's design or from cities laid out in imitation of Washington and themselves becoming the models for subsequent communities.

The most imitated feature, probably because it was the most noticeable and the easiest to duplicate, was the system of diagonal streets. Open squares or circles also appear, although usually not in such abundance nor so elaborately conceived as those of the original. A few of these plans show considerable skill in planning and an understanding of the use of diagonals and open spaces in focusing attention on some prominent feature of the community. Many of the designs, on the other hand, are purely mechanical—mere exercises in plane geometry—in which the forms of the grand plan were employed at the whim of some town promoter without any real comprehension of their meaning.

The first such scheme was not an imitation of Washington, since it was conceived by L'Enfant himself. Unfortunately the drawings of the plan were destroyed more than a hundred years ago, and apparently no copies were made. It can only be inferred from the surviving evidence that L'Enfant incorporated diagonal streets in his proposed layout. The town was Paterson, New Jersey, the site for which was purchased in 1791 by Alexander Hamilton and his Society for Establishing Useful Manufactures. L'Enfant and Nehemiah Hubbard were commissioned to prepare a plan for the rugged site. The proceedings of the society for August 19, 1792, include a statement by L'Enfant on how the city should be laid out. After discussing the problem of bringing water to the wheels of the cotton factory, he reviews some of the problems of street planning due to the broken topography:

"I considered it was not material to observe a regular North and South, and East and West direction for the Streets. . . . I have taken advantage of a rising ground to reserve the summit of it for the erection of some Public Building, carrying the streets from thence according as the accidental opening may admit prolonging them at a distance in measure as the town will enlarge. . . ."[1]

The similarity of L'Enfant's reasoning here to his explanation of the basis for his plan of Washington is apparent. We can assume that the physical results would also have some resemblance, although the diagonal streets proposed for Paterson undoubtedly were less symmetrical than those for Washington.

Two other early imitations of the Washington plan are the paper city of Esperanza on the Hudson, planned before 1800, and Buffalo,

[1] Quoted by Henry James, "A Review of Earlier Planning Efforts," Regional Plan of New York and its Environs, *Physical Conditions and Public Services*, Regional Survey, VIII, New York, 1929, p. 173.

laid out by Joseph Ellicott, the brother of L'Enfant's successor, in 1802. Because these two town plans were linked so closely with land speculation activities they will be discussed in a later chapter. About the same time and under circumstances that are obscure, P. C. Verlé proposed an extension to Philadelphia in 1802 on the west side of the Schuylkill River with a system of squares, diagonal streets, and an oval open space. This formal plan, shown in Figure 154, was never carried through, as the city was expanded on the original grid pattern but without the open spaces provided by Penn in his plan of 1682. Verlé's scheme would have provided a magnificent entrance to the city from the west and an interesting contrast to the rectangular block pattern of the old city.

In point of time the next city planning project to employ the diagonal plan was Detroit, the largest of all and unquestionably the most interesting after Washington because of both plan and personalities involved.

Honeycomb in the Hinterland: Detroit, 1805-1830

On June 11, 1805, a fire swept through the frontier outpost of Detroit destroying the fort, barracks, and 300 dwellings in the tightly packed village that had grown up from the French settlement originally established in 1701. By one of those accidents of history Detroit's fire coincided with a change in government and the introduction of new personalities into the community. In the preceding January, Congress had established Michigan as a separate territory effective on July 1, and the President had designated the new officials of the government who were to take office in Detroit as the capital of the Territory. President Jefferson appointed General William Hull, a veteran of the Revolution, as governor. Under the system of territorial government three judges formed the judiciary, and the governor and judges sitting together constituted the legislative board. Frederick Bates, a local resident, received one of the judicial appointments. John Griffin of Indiana was also appointed, but he did not actually take office until the fall of the following year. The other judge was Augustus Brevoort Woodward.

Woodward was a young man of thirty-one at the time of his appointment, but his age was no indication of his accomplishments. At fifteen he had entered Columbia College. In 1797 he came to

Washington and four years later was admitted to the practice of law in that city. In 1802 he was elected as one of the twelve councilmen in Washington. Like most Washingtonians he dabbled in land speculation, and among his possessions when he came to Detroit was a small notebook in which were pasted sections of a Washington map with symbols in ink that perhaps indicated property he owned or had sold. He evidently knew Major L'Enfant, since there is some evidence that he performed legal services for him. He became a friend of Jefferson and shared the older man's love of philosophic and scientific speculation. In 1801, for example, Woodward published a booklet entitled *Considerations on the Substance of the Sun*. It was this man—learned, precocious and a little eccentric—who was shortly to focus his numerous talents on the exciting task of creating a metropolis in the west.[2]

Woodward arrived in Detroit on July 1, 1805, just three weeks after the fire. He found the citizens of Detroit preparing to rebuild the old town, but he persuaded them to postpone this action until the new officials had an opportunity to review the problem. Hull arrived the next day and called a meeting of officials and citizens. For three days talks continued; then, as Hull and Woodward summarized the situation in a report to Congress:

"The result of these discussions was, to proceed to lay out a new town, embracing the whole of the old town and the public lands adjacent; to state to the people that nothing in the nature of a title could be given under any authorities then possessed by the Government . . . but that every personal exertion would be used to obtain a confirmation of the arrangements about to be made, and to obtain the liberal attention of the Government of the United States to their distresses."[3]

Woodward was appointed a committee of one to lay out the new town. Thomas Smith, a Canadian surveyor, was engaged to furnish technical assistance. No copy of that plan has survived, and little wonder, since according to one account, ". . . the original plan fell into the hands of Aaron Greely, surveyor, in whose house it was seen in a broken window, keeping out the weather, and in

[2] The only biography of Woodward is Frank B. Woodford, *Mr. Jefferson's Disciple, A Life of Justice Woodward*, East Lansing, 1953.
[3] Report to Congress by Hull and Woodward, October 10, 1805, Michigan Pioneer and Historical Society, *Historical Collections*, Lansing, 1908, XXXVI, 103-105.

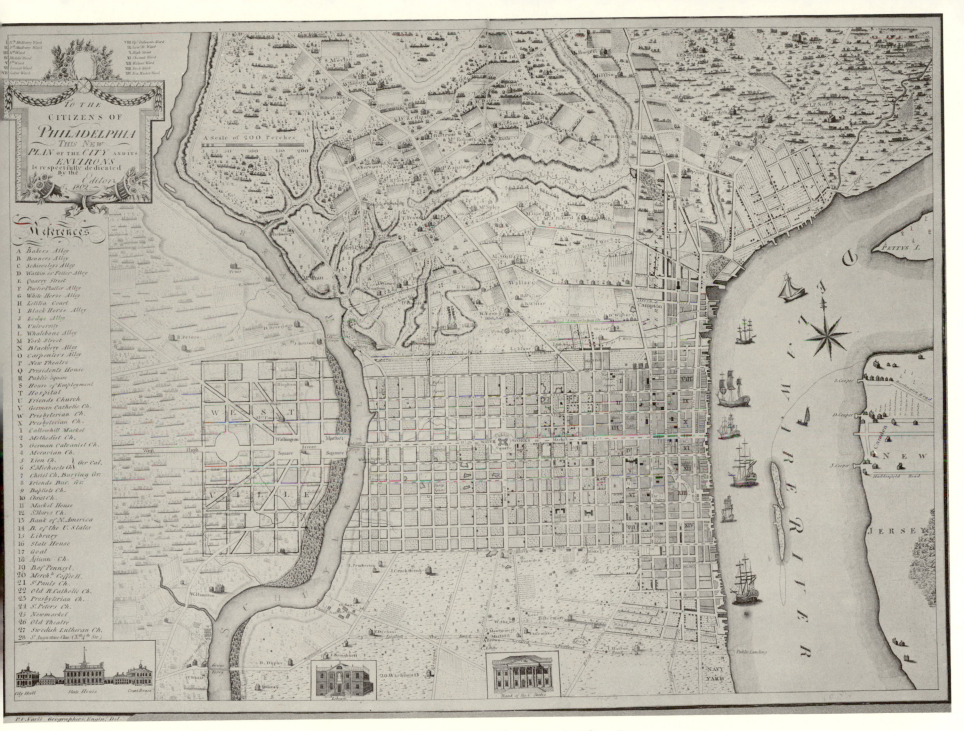

Figure 154. Plan of Philadelphia, Pennsylvania: 1802

whose hands it disappeared. . . ."⁴ But it is known that it was based on a novel triangular system of land division and that Woodward was the originator of the scheme.

Lots in the new town were then put up for sale. Owners of land in the old town were entitled to equal amounts of land under the new plan. Most of the new lots, however, were larger, and the owner was required to pay for the extra area. No money was actually accepted pending the approval by Congress of the action taken by the new government.

That winter both Hull and Woodward traveled to Washington seeking congressional sanction for the plan and the method of land allotment. The governor continued on to his former home in Massachusetts, leaving Woodward in the capital to look after territorial legislative matters. In April 1806 the President approved "An Act to Provide for the Adjustment of Title of Land in the Town of Detroit and Territory of Michigan and for Other Purposes."⁵ This early example of planning enabling legislation authorized the governor and judges "to lay out a town, including the whole of the old Town of Detroit, and ten thousand acres adjacent" and to adjust all claims for land under a provision granting a lot of not more than 5,000 square feet to every resident of the city over seventeen at the time of the fire.

During the summer a new plan was prepared, taking in more land than the original survey of Smith's and probably modifying the original design. This time the survey work was carried out by Abijah Hull, a relative of the governor's, working under Woodward's close supervision. By September the surveys were complete, and the legislative board gave official approval to one of the most unusual city plans ever devised. The law adopted by the board specified ". . . that the bases of the town of Detroit shall be an equilateral triangle, having each side of the length of four thousand feet, and having every angle bisected by a perpendicular line upon the opposite side, such parts being excepted, as from the approximation of . . . [the] . . . river Detroit, or other unavoidable circumstances, may require partial deviation."⁶

⁴ Letter from Thomas Smith to the Governor and Judges of Michigan, May 10, 1821, *American State Papers*, Public Lands Series, VI, 274-75.
⁵ Chapter 43, Laws of 1806, Ninth Congress, Session I.
⁶ An Act Concerning the Town of Detroit, *Laws of the Territory of Michigan*, 1807.

The "perpendicular lines" divided each equilateral triangle into six right-angle triangles. Each of these was to be known as a "section." Section 1 was described by metes and bounds in the act, which then specified that other sections of identical size were to be laid out from time to time as the plan was extended. Late in 1806 the governor and judges sent the new plan to Congress, at which time they reported that land allotments had begun.

The plan submitted at this time was probably that shown in Figure 155, which includes an area of about 3,000 acres, almost one-third of the district over which the board had been given jurisdiction. It seems likely that the governor and judges also submitted one or more detailed plats of individual triangular sections showing the division of land into lots. The original drawing of one of these has survived and is reproduced in Figure 156. The Board may also have included a plan showing streets and lots in the central portion of the general plan. Figure 157 is from a copy of this map prepared after the War of 1812 to replace a similar drawing evidently destroyed during the British occupation of the city. An area of almost 400 acres, comprising 14 sections of land, is shown in this detailed plan.

Woodward's Detroit was no mere copy of the Washington plan, to which it has been frequently compared. It is true that both plans were on a grand scale, both utilized diagonal streets, and both made frequent use of symmetrical open spaces as terminal features for broad avenues. The underlying concepts, however, were different.

Washington as planned by Major L'Enfant combined two types of street systems. The basic pattern was a grid of straight streets with right-angle intersections. Superimposed on this system was another, consisting of diagonal avenues directly connecting the principal points of the new city. Aside from certain visual defects resulting from the rolling terrain, there were other shortcomings in the Washington plan. Acute-angle street intersections, irregular shaped lots, and unusable remnants of land all owe their origins to L'Enfant's attempt to combine rather than integrate two different street systems.

In the plan of Detroit these faults were largely overcome. A single integrated pattern was used, a pattern as suitable to the level topography as any other abstract system of land subdivision, including the gridiron. Unlike the typical block plan so familiar

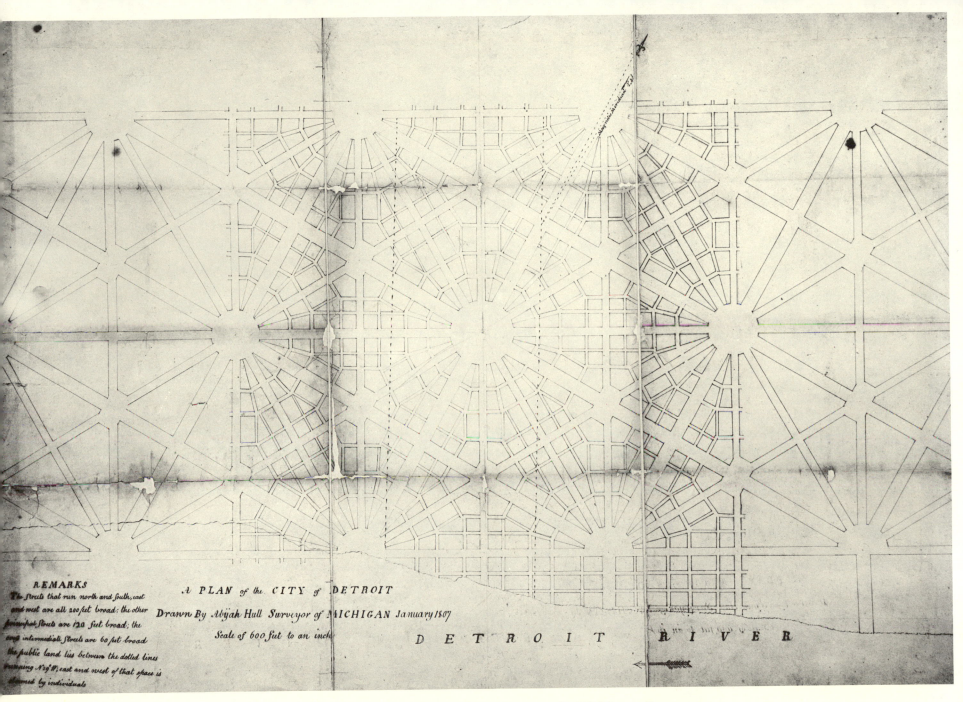

REMARKS
The streets that run north and south, east
and west are all 200 feet broad: the other
principal streets are 120 feet broad; the
smaller intermediate streets are 60 feet broad
the public land lies between the dotted lines
running N. & W.; east and west of that space is
claimed by individuals

A PLAN of the CITY of DETROIT
Drawn By Abijah Hull Surveyor of MICHIGAN January 1807
Scale of 600 feet to an inch

DETROIT RIVER

Figure 155. Judge Woodward's Plan for Detroit, Michigan: 1807

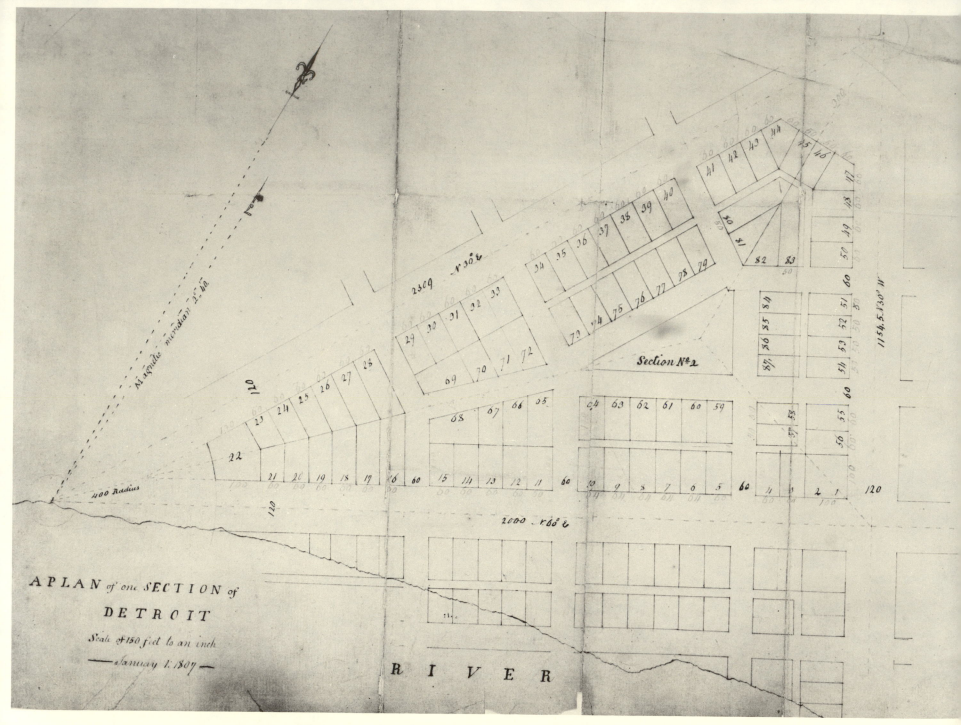

Figure 156. A Section of Judge Woodward's Detroit Plan: 1807

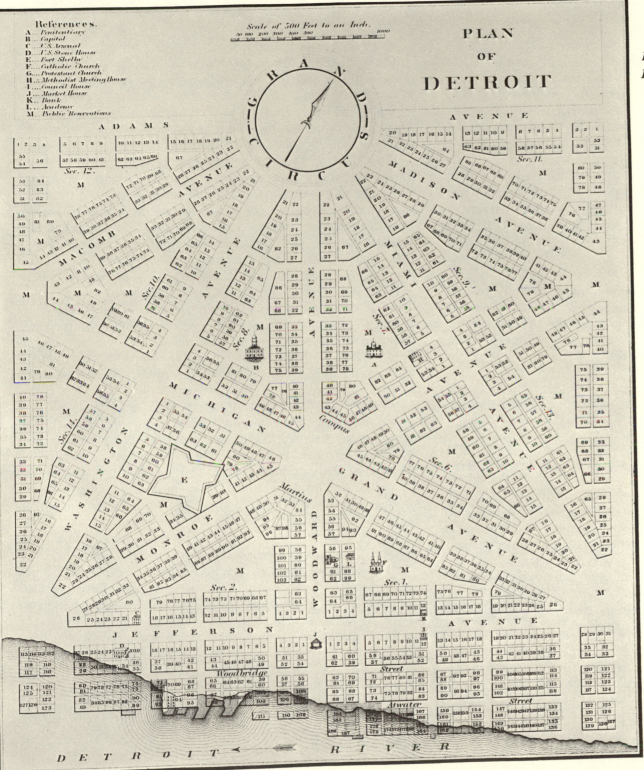

Figure 157. Plan of the Central Portion of Detroit, Michigan: 1807

throughout most of America, the plan of Detroit, like that of Washington, provided for streets of different widths. Principal avenues were laid out north-south and east-west with a width of 200 feet. Other main streets were platted 120 feet wide, while minor streets were given the generous width of 60 feet. Every lot was afforded rear access from an ingenious system of alleys.

Two units of open space were employed at regular intervals. At the intersection of 12 avenues Woodward designed a "Grand Circus" of 5½ acres. To avoid sharp points at these intersections, he cut back the blocks to provide for lots of more normal shape. Smaller rectangular open spaces at every intersection of 6 avenues were treated in similar fashion. The "Campus Martius" between Grand Circus and the river is an example of this second type of public open space.

Woodward did not lose sight of the importance of river traffic in his vision of a baroque city. Streets along the riverfront were laid out on a grid system, probably the most satisfactory pattern for warehouses, industry, and dockside activities. Broad streets from the waterfront provided connections with the triangular street system at convenient points.

The central portion of each triangular section of land was left open. An Act of the Governor and Judges in May 1807 makes the reason clear.

". . . the internal space of ground, in the middle of every section, shall be reserved for public wells and pumps, for markets, for public schools, for houses for the reception of engines or other articles for the extinction of fires, and the preservation of the property of the inhabitants, for houses for the meeting of religious, moral, literary, or political societies, or other useful associations, and generally, for such purposes of utility or ornament, as the city council of Detroit may, at any time, by law, provide; or as, otherwise, the inclination and taste of the proprietors of the lots in such section, or that of the major part of them, may direct; and in the same manner shall be paved, gravelled,[7] planted with trees, or otherwise improved and ornamented."

Here was another unique feature in American town planning—the equivalent of London's Bloomsbury squares, but oriented inward toward a central neighborhood building or park.

[7] An additional Act Concerning the Town of Detroit, *Laws of the Territory of Michigan*, 1807.

The same law provided for double lines of trees on both sides of the 120-foot avenues, and for trees in "clumps or groves to be of an elliptical shape" on both sides of the 200-foot avenues. Spaces for walks and front yards and porches were also defined in this law. Judge Woodward and his colleagues were clearly concerned with beauty as well as utility.

The citizens of Detroit appeared much less interested in Woodward's vision of a great metropolis than in obtaining clear and immediate title to property in the new town. As soon as the terms of the congressional act of 1806 became known, demands for "donation" lots were presented to the board. Those who had purchased lots under the scheme devised by Hull and Woodward in 1805 understandably felt that such lots now should be awarded them without payment, since Congress had authorized a free lot to every adult resident of Detroit before the fire.

What should have been a straightforward and speedy procedure of land allocation became mired in a bog of conflict and dissension. Not only were the Detroiters dissatisfied with the various suggestions for land distribution put forward by the land board, but the members of the board frequently disagreed violently among themselves.

Whatever Hull's original attitude was toward Woodward as a person and town planner, he soon came to regard the judge with suspicion and hostility. These two men of opposite temperament and interests were often at odds. Their first serious clash affecting the plan of the city came late in 1807, when Hull proposed to strengthen the fortifications of Detroit. In a letter to the Secretary of War, Hull revealed his mistrust of Woodward's visionary mind.

"Judge Woodward . . . condemns the fortification of the Town of Detroit, as a *useless*, *expensive*, and *prejudicial* measure. . . .

"It was my own opinion, to have built the Stockade on a much smaller scale. . . . Those Inhabitants, that would have been left out complained, promised all the aid in their power, and I found it was the general wish to include the whole of the Town—The fortifications, however, are on too small a scale, for the expanded Ideas of the learned Judge. Had an attempt been made to have built a solid wall around the Territory, or indeed from the Earth to the Sun it would have met his cordial approbation. . . . He considers the Man destitute of talents, who will tread in paths, which have before been trod. He despises every thing tinged with the rust of antiquity, and is enamoured with modern improvements and speculations, whether on the Earth or in the Sun. Unfortunate it is indeed, that a Man of his fine talents, cannot level them to useful and practical purposes. . . ."[8]

From June 1807 to October 1808 no meetings of the land board were held. In the fall of 1808 Woodward left for Washington to arrange for the publication of his study, *The Executive Government of the United States*. Before his departure he introduced 13 resolutions at a meeting of the legislative board, many of which condemned the actions of Governor Hull in fortifying the town. Hull, appointed as a committee of one to report on these resolutions, reacted in characteristic fashion by roundly condemning the judge and his town plan.

"The second resolution states that . . . the government of the United States have been induced to defray the expenses of unauthorized fortifications for the defence of the town of Detroit. . . .

"Without imputing it to any malignity of heart, your committee is willing it should be considered as having arisen from his devotion to his darling child, the plan of the city of Detroit. It is deeply to be regretted that he ever had influence sufficient to have brought that plan into existence. It is certainly the most unfortunate act of the administration of this government. In experiment it is found to be ill adapted to the situation and circumstances of the town."[9]

The governor lost no time in attempting to scrap the new plan. In November 1808 James McCloskey, a surveyor, was retained to prepare a revised plan for Detroit using the traditional gridiron pattern. And on February 24, 1809, the legislative board repealed the territorial act of 1806, which had established the triangular section as the basis of land subdivision in Detroit. In addition, the governor and Judge Witherell, who had arrived in October of 1808 and who had apparently taken an immediate dislike to Woodward, proceeded to repeal virtually all of the statutes in the so-called "Woodward Code." While this action was later held to be illegal by Judges Woodward and Griffin, and the Woodward Code was reenacted in 1810, the territorial government was split by conflict,

and the people of Detroit became increasingly dissatisfied under its rule.

In the autumn of 1813 Hull was succeeded by Lewis Cass. For a time the affairs of Detroit seemed to move more smoothly, the new governor declining to join either the Woodward or the Witherell faction. However, with the increase in Detroit's population following the war, mounting opposition developed to the extension of the triangular system of land subdivision throughout the 10,000 acres surrounding the original settlement. The legislative board was requested to sell this reserve land in rectangular farms of 160 acres. To prevent such action from interfering with the city plan, Woodward introduced the following resolution at a meeting of the land board on October 15, 1816:

"That no future deviation shall be made from the original plan of the City of Detroit. . . . All ground hereafter disposed of in quantities exceeding one lot, a five thousand square feet, shall be sold upon this express condition, that the City of Detroit may extend over them, without the purchaser expecting or claiming any compensation, for the avenues, streets, roads, lanes, alleys, squares, circuses and other public spaces and reservation of ground of the said City of Detroit, according to the original plan thereof."[10]

Despite this resolution, Woodward was soon to witness the final abandonment of his novel plan. In the fall of 1817 the judge was again absent in Washington. Judge Witherell persuaded Cass and Griffin to begin the sale of rectangular 160-acre farms in the tract of reserve land. As a personal affront to their absent colleague, the name of Woodward Avenue below the Grand Circus was changed to Market Street, its extension to the northwest was narrowed from 120 feet to 66 feet, and it was renamed Witherell Avenue.

Land sales under this revised plan were scheduled to begin on the first of June 1818. On that day Woodward submitted to the governor and judges a truly remarkable document attacking the new proposal as illegal on a number of grounds. He did not confine his arguments to the legal issues involved but continued with a number of persuasive statements on the necessity of planning as an essential element of policy to be followed in a rapidly developing nation. Moreover, he envisaged Detroit as the great metropolis it has since become:

[8] Letter from Hull to Secretary of War Dearborn, December 29, 1807, Michigan Historical Commission, *Michigan Historical Collections*, Lansing, 1929, XL, 242-44.
[9] Governor Hull's report, December 23, 1808, Michigan Pioneer and Historical Society, *Historical Collections*, Lansing, 1888, XII, 468.

[10] Governor and Judges Journal, *Proceedings of the Land Board of Detroit*, Detroit, 1915, p. 62.

"Nature had destined the city of Detroit to be a great interior emporium, equal, if not superior, to any other on the surface of the . . . globe. . . . In such a case the art of man should aid the benevolence of the Creator, and no restricted attachment to the present day or to present interests should induce a permanent sacrifice of ulterior and brilliant prospects."[11]

Woodward's forceful appeal was of no avail. Land sales were begun, and the opportunity to extend the original plan was lost for all time. The judge was soon to leave the territory, for in 1824 his term of office expired, and he was not reappointed.

During the 1820's Detroit grew on the familiar gridiron pattern. Figure 158, "Plan of Detroit," drawn in 1830 by John Mullett, shows what remained of the Woodward plan in that year. Some of the diagonal streets were narrowed; many were abandoned completely. The military tract where the fort had stood was turned over to city authorities and promptly platted in checkerboard fashion. Only a few of the original streets, the Campus Martius, and half of the Grand Circus were retained. Planning was forgotten in the haste for expansion and land speculation.

What would Detroit be like if Woodward's vision had been followed? Would it have been a workable plan for a modern city? Perhaps the plan with its intricate triangular pattern was too abstract and complicated. Modern planners might shudder at the maze of diagonal streets and confusing intersections. One thing is certain. If Detroit's growth through the years had been guided by men approaching Woodward in vision, determination, and wisdom, and with the additional ability of intelligent compromise and flexibility which he perhaps lacked, Detroit's planners of today would be facing an easier and more enviable task of adjusting the pattern of a complicated metropolis to meet the demands of contemporary life.

The Diagonal Capitals of Indiana, Wisconsin, and Louisiana

In 1816 Congress approved the creation of the new state of Indiana. One section of the act passed in that year authorized the state to select as a site for its capital four sections of public land anywhere in the state not already sold by the government land office. In 1820 the state legislature appointed a commission of ten men to locate a suitable site. After a series of preliminary surveys the commission reported favorably on a central location near the junction of the White River and Fall Creek. The legislature accepted the recommendation and appointed a second commission to prepare the town plan. Alexander Ralston, who had been one of the surveyors under L'Enfant and Ellicott at Washington, was retained by the commission as its planner.[12]

Ralston's plan for Indianapolis in 1821 appears in Figure 159. From the corners of the mile-square gridiron Ralston laid out four diagonals which converged to the intersections of four streets near the center of the city. Within this smaller square Ralston established the site for the governor's house in a circle some 300 feet in diameter. Three squares lying in the path of the diagonals were set aside for religious purposes, market places were reserved, and two complete blocks were retained for a capitol building and the courthouse. The influence of the Washington plan shows not only in the plan of streets but in the names given to them honoring other states in the union.

Ralston had the good sense not to bring the diagonals together at the center but to terminate them some distance apart. Nor was his plan surveyed with complete disregard for topography. Along Fall Creek in the southeastern part of the city Ralston departed from the otherwise symmetrical pattern and planned two streets paralleling the creek, no doubt as sites for mills and other industries requiring water power or a place for waste disposal.

His plan was less satisfactory where the diagonals crossed the intersections of the gridiron streets. Instead of cutting back the acute angled lots at this point or providing smaller circles or squares as L'Enfant and Woodward had done, Ralston retained the precise corners resulting from the geometrical pattern. Some of the city's present traffic problems stem from this failure to modify the scheme at these points of intersection. It might have been more in keeping also with the concept of the grand plan to leave open at least a portion of the blocks surrounding the central circle. The

[11] The full text of Woodward's appeal may be found in Michigan Pioneer and Historical Society, *Historical Collections*, XIII, 473-83.

[12] For material on the background of the planning of Indianapolis see Donald F. Carmony, "Genesis and Early History of the Indianapolis Fund, 1816-1826," *Indiana Magazine of History*, XXXVIII (1942), 17-30; and Nathaniel Bolton, *Early History of Indianapolis and Central Indiana*, Indianapolis, 1897.

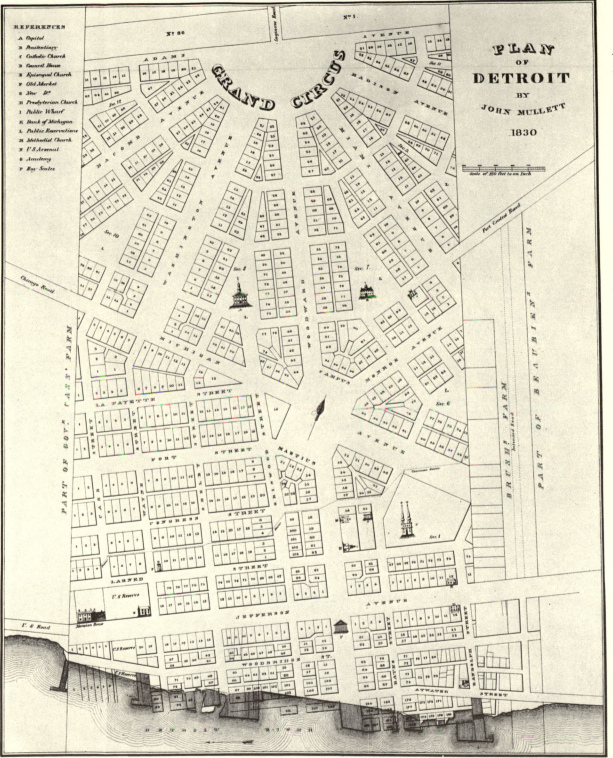

Figure 158. Plan of Detroit, Michigan: 1830

Figure 159. Plan of Indianapolis,
Indiana: 1821

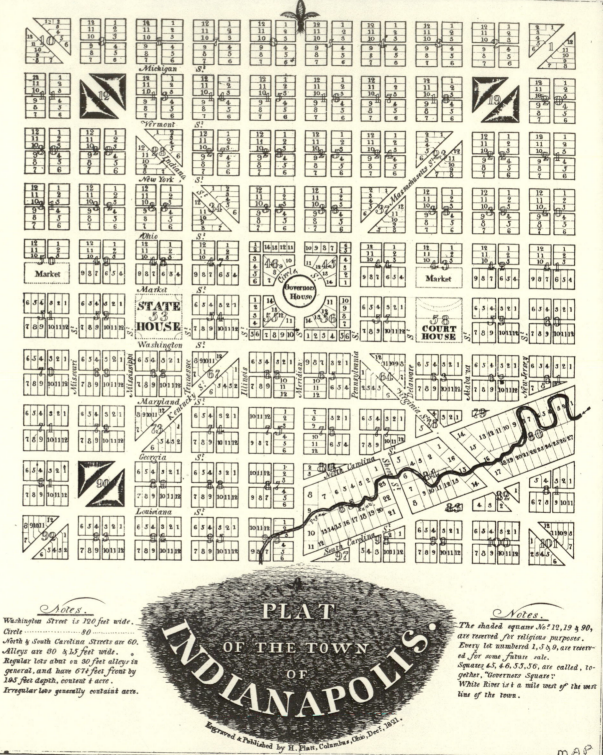

Engraved & Published by H. Platt, Columbus, Ohio, Dec.r 1821.

Notes.
Washington Street is 120 feet wide.
Circle ··········· 80 ···········
North & South Carolina Streets are 60.
Alleys are 30 & 15 feet wide.
Regular lots abut on 30 feet alleys in
general, and have 67½ feet front by
195 feet depth, content ¼ acre.
Irregular lots generally contain acres.

Notes.
The shaded square No.s 12, 19 & 90,
are reserved for religious purposes.
Every lot numbered 1, 5 & 9, are reserved for some future sale.
Squares 45, 46, 55, 56, are called, together, "Governors Square."
White River is ½ a mile west of the west
line of the town.

PLAT
OF THE TOWN
OF
INDIANAPOLIS.

governor's mansion, started in 1827, must have been invisible from the diagonal approaches as the lots surrounding the circle were built on. A more satisfactory solution from the visual standpoint has resulted from the erection of the present Soldiers' and Sailors' Monument standing over 300-feet high on the site of the old governor's residence. Here at least is a visual exclamation point marking the center of the city and, very nearly, the state itself.

The orderly approach to the location of the Indiana capital city stands in sharp contrast to the squabble over sites that occupied the Wisconsin legislature when it met in 1836 to select a permanent seat of government. At least a dozen cities were advanced by their supporters as having advantages so unique and outstanding that no other community could be seriously considered. One participant in this contest with more than ordinary interest in its outcome was James Duane Doty, already with considerable experience in townsite promotion and with strong and rather eccentric ideas about how cities should be laid out. Much of his youth had been spent in Detroit, and perhaps he had absorbed some of Woodward's enthusiasm for town planning as he walked the streets of Detroit or listened to the older residents recount the controversies between Woodward and Witherell and Hull.

As the debate on a capital site dragged on inconclusively Doty and his surveyor, John V. Suydam, left Belmont and started for an unannounced destination. On the way they laid out Cliffton and Wisconsinapolis on land owned by Doty and perhaps to be used by him as alternative sites for the capital city if the occasion demanded. But Doty had in mind a site of unusual beauty and topography located on a narrow neck of land separating two lakes. Doty and Suydam arrived there after eight days on horseback and quickly surveyed the boundaries of the site. Then, as Suydam recalls,

"We went directly to Belmont, where the Legislature was in session. On arriving there, I immediately set about drawing the plat of Madison, the Governor, in the mean time, giving me minute directions as to its whole plan, every item of which having originated with him while on the ground, as being the most suitable, and best calculated, to develop the peculiar topography of the place."[13]

[13] Recollections of John V. Suydam, Wisconsin State Historical Society, *Report and Collections*, Madison, 1872, VI, 390-92.

Doty tirelessly advanced his new city as the most eligible spot for the new capital. There exists fairly good evidence that he supplemented his verbal appeals to the members of the legislature with persuasion of another kind. One member of the body recalled that as Madison slowly appeared to be gaining favor, stories began to circulate ". . . of a certain stock company, owners of the city of Madison, with thirty-six shares in all—just the number of the two Houses of the Legislative Council; and that most of the members, and particularly those west of the Mississippi, were stockholders."[14]

Suydam is even more specific about Doty's promotional methods and their success: "On the adjournment of the Legislature, quite a number of gentlemen, I never learned how many, belonging to that body, went to their homes the owners of sundry corner lots in a new town, and the seat of Government of Wisconsin was permanently located at Madison. . . ."[15]

Madison's superb site is shown in the lower half of Figure 160, with the plan itself above. The diagonal streets are extensions of section lines of the rectangular township surveys. By coincidence, the point of intersection of two of these lines fell close to the highest point of land on the narrow neck between the two lakes. Possibly this suggested to Doty the opportunity of combining diagonal streets and a grid pattern oriented northeast-southwest to fit the long rectangular site. His plan is an interesting one and shows considerable care in its adaption to the site despite the haste with which it was prepared.

Near the high point of the site Doty reserved a square 900 feet on the side for the capitol and other state buildings. North, east, and south diagonals lead from the square to the lake shores. The western diagonal runs parallel with the shore of Lake Mendota and is now the principal connection to the University of Wisconsin. From the sides of the square, four broad avenues extend across the neck of land and through its length. Doty also planned two other diagonal streets at the northeastern entrance to the city, but these, like the mill race connecting the two lakes across the narrowest point of land, were never constructed. One curious feature can be noticed: the extra streets close to and parallel with the northeast and southwest sides of the square. One is tempted to con-

[14] Recollections of General Albert G. Ellis, Wisconsin State Historical Society, *Report and Collections*, VI, 389-90.
[15] Suydam Recollections, 392.

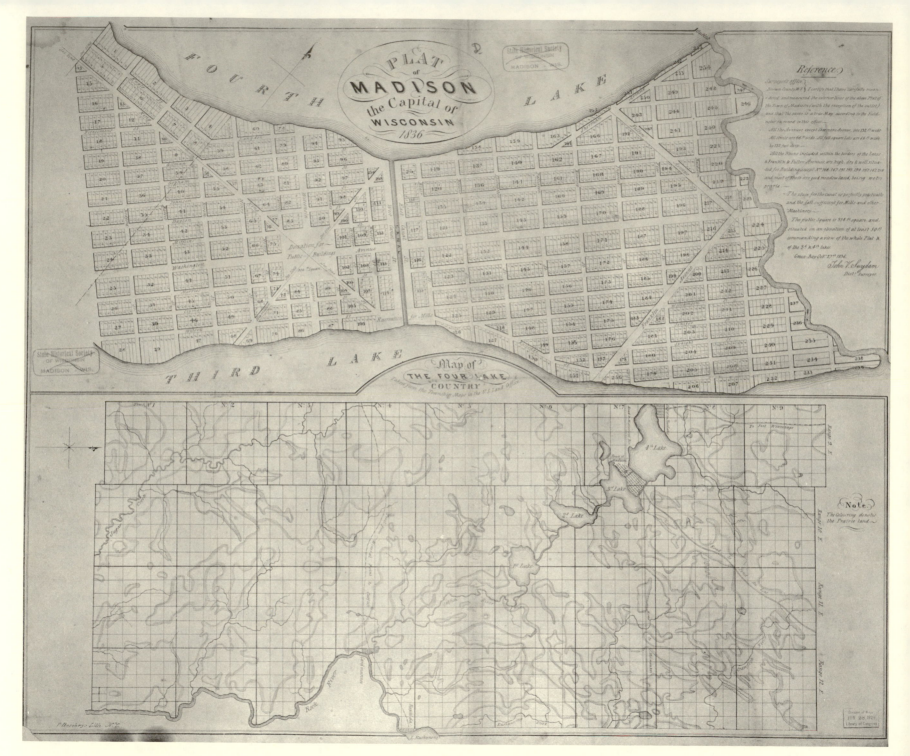

Figure 160. Plan of Madison, Wisconsin: 1836

clude that this was a device used by Doty to provide additional "sundry corner lots" for bribery purposes without depriving the proprietor of all such choice locations.

Madison has become a thriving university, manufacturing, and mercantile city in addition to continuing its important role as a center of government. Because of the character of its site and its intelligent plan it has retained much of the beauty and charm shown in the accompanying view in Figure 161 of the city more than one hundred years ago.

In a third capital city, Baton Rouge, Louisiana, the diagonal plan was adopted for a section of the community sometime prior to the Civil War. The map in Figure 162 shows this interesting layout in what was then the southern portion of the town. One unusual feature of this plan is that the diagonals leading from Royal Square toward the Mississippi diverge at a different angle from those on the western side. Unlike Indianapolis or Madison the diagonal portion of Baton Rouge apparently never dominated the plan of the entire community and today constitutes but a small portion of the entire city.

Diagonals by the Dozen

In the development of Cleveland, sketched in an earlier chapter, mention was made of the platting of outlots beyond the original village area. Major division lines between tiers of outlots formed a kind of fan pattern to the east of the built-up portion of the community. Roads naturally followed these field divisions, and as early as 1825 one of them, now Euclid Avenue, was extended into the village proper, entering the public square at its eastern corner. Prospect Street, parallel to Euclid, was opened a few years later. But it was during the land boom of the 1830's that Cleveland saw its first coordinated diagonal planning involving an entire section of the city. Southwest of the old town in a great loop of the Cuyahoga River was an area that in 1833 was platted with no less than ten streets radiating from an open square known as Gravity Place. This development and a later bit of radial planning farther to the southeast appear in Figure 163 which shows the city and its surrounding territory in 1835. Only a few of these diagonal streets exist today; many were eliminated as the river bottoms were developed for warehousing and industry during the last century.[16]

[16] A reproduction of this and other maps and views of Cleveland illus-

Even before this period, radial plans appeared in other parts of Ohio. In Stark County, near Massillon, Amos Janney platted the little town of Sparta in 1815. Its plan with four wide streets, four squares and diagonal alleys, is shown in Figure 164. The bizarre plan had equally peculiar street names: Wolf, Bear, Elk, and Buffalo. Either from admiration of this strange layout or simply to save planning costs, Peter Dickerhoof and Henry Wise laid out an identical town, Greentown, just ten months later in the same county.[17]

Washington was not the only diagonal city planned under the sponsorship of the federal government. As a result of Indian treaties the government controlled an area 12 miles square at the falls of the Maumee River above Toledo. Congress, by an act of April 27, 1816, directed the surveyor general to plan a town on this site. Perrysburg, shown in Figure 165, was the result. The spiderweb pattern of outlots resembles that of Cleveland, but the two diagonal streets are not a very important element in the over-all plan.

Midway between Perrysburg and Cleveland in the old Connecticut Firelands the most interesting of the Ohio radial cities was planned in 1818. A settlement of sorts had existed on Sandusky Bay for some years before. One Isaac Mills became owner of a portion of the site and had it laid out by Major Hector Kilbourn. A copy of his extraordinary plat is reproduced in Figure 166. A local legend has it that Washington Square in the center of town, with its reserved sites for public buildings, and the interlocking diagonal streets of the city were intended to represent the Masonic emblem of an open bible, mason's square, and open compass. This has never been verified, but certainly it is a possible explanation of the strange pattern of streets and open spaces. It is known that Kilbourn was an avid Mason and the master of the first Masonic lodge in Sandusky.[18]

trating the development in the city may be found in Edmund H. Chapman, "City Planning Under Mercantile Expansion: The Case of Cleveland, Ohio," *Journal of the Society of Architectural Historians*, x (December 1951), 10-17.

[17] The plan of Greentown appears in F. W. Beers, *Atlas of Stark County, Ohio*, New York, 1870. For a description of these and other unusual towns in Stark County, Ohio, see Edward Thornton Heald, *The Stark County Story*, Canton, 1949, I.

[18] See Charles Merz, "Masonic Plat of Sandusky," *Sandusky Masonic Bulletin*, xxv (1944).

VIEW of MADISON the CAPITAL of WISCONSIN.

TAKEN FROM THE WATER CURE,

SOUTH SIDE OF LAKE MENONA, 1855.

Figure 161. View of Madison, Wisconsin: 1855

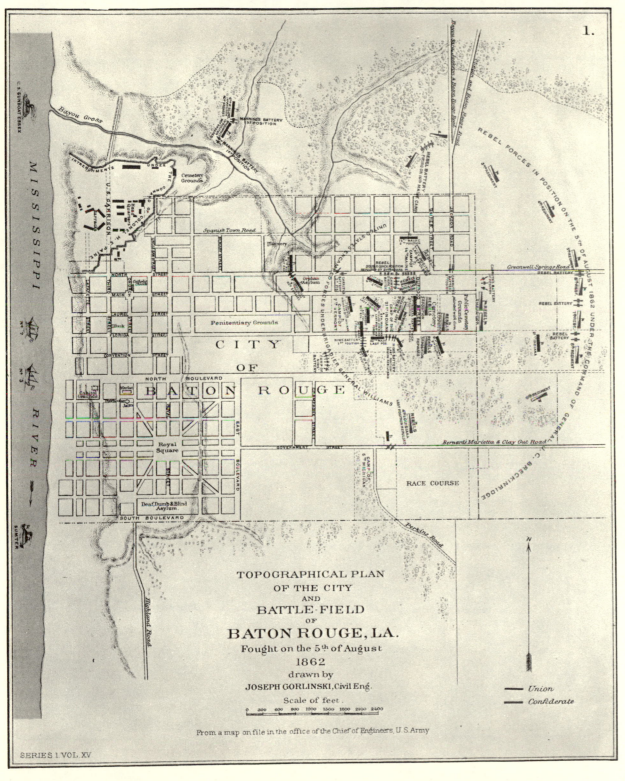

Figure 162. Plan of Baton Rouge, Louisiana: 1862

Figure 163. Plan of Cleveland, Ohio: 1835

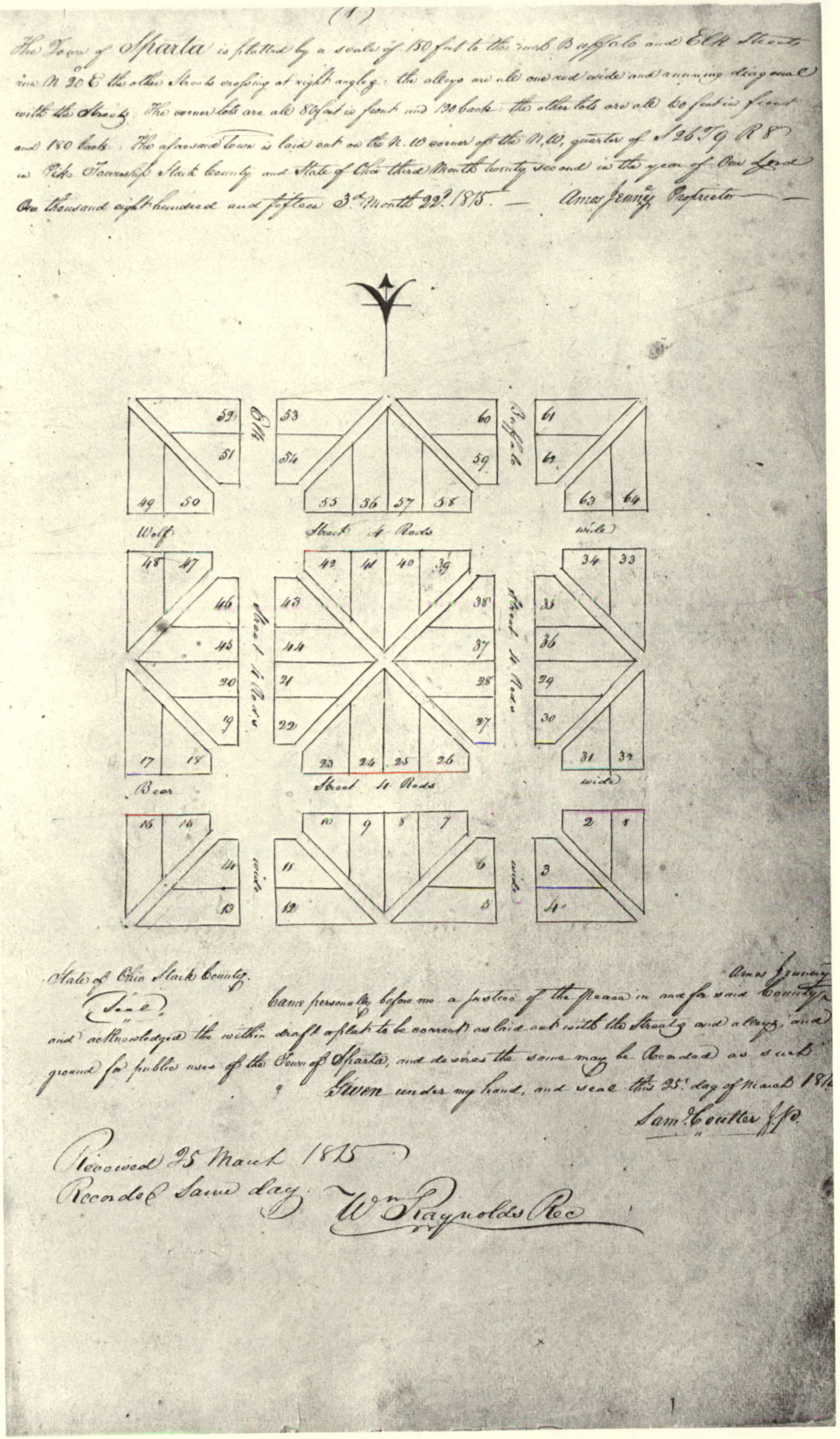

Figure 164. Plan of Sparta, Ohio: 1815

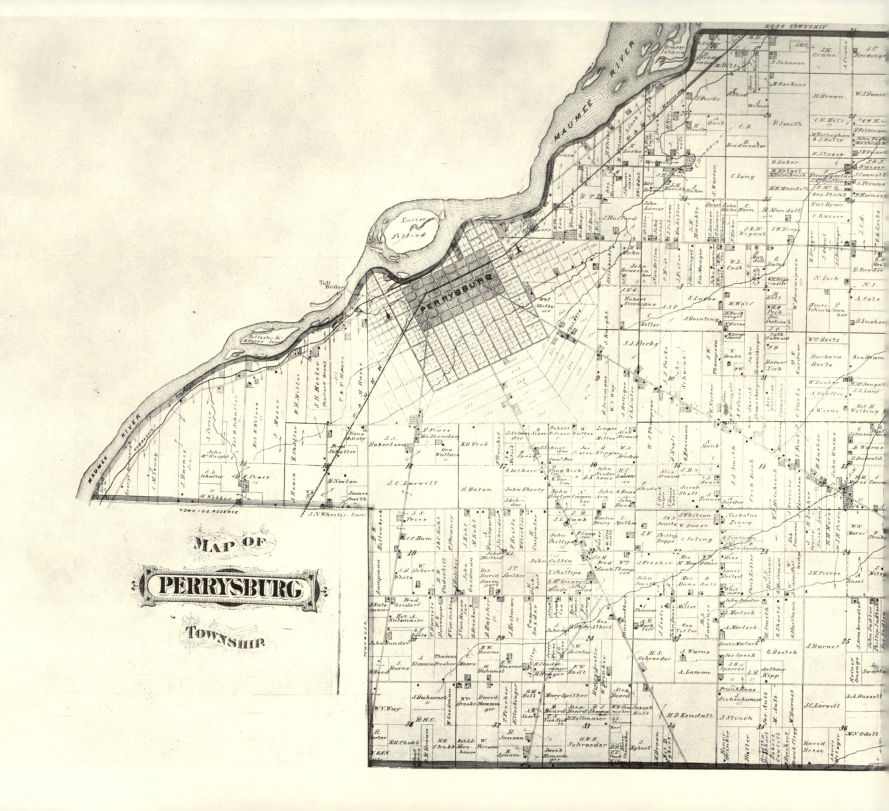

MAP OF
PERRYSBURG
TOWNSHIP

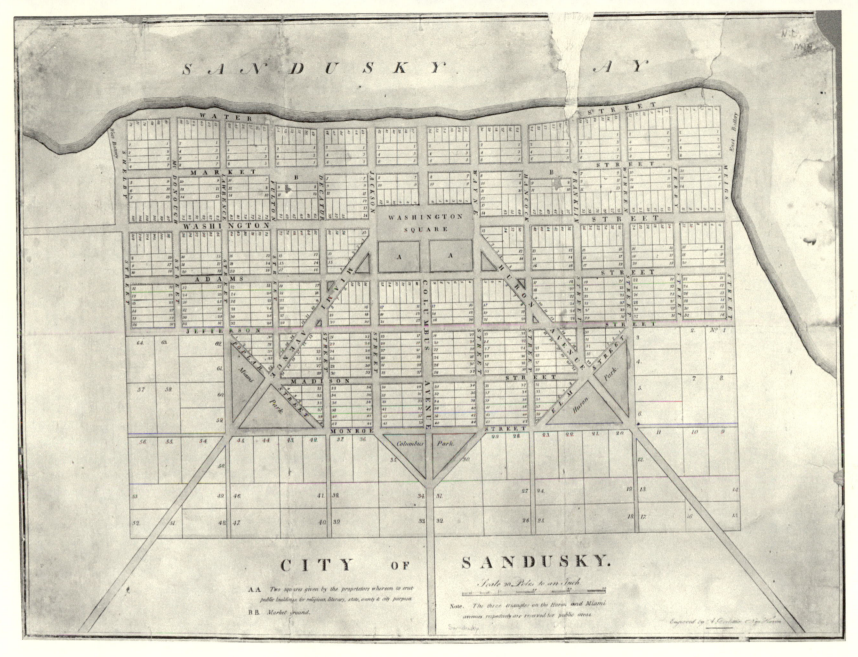

Figure 166. Plan of Sandusky, Ohio: 1818

Figure 165. Plan of Perrysburg, Ohio: 1875

Whatever the inspiration for the plan, it has resulted in a generous allotment of open spaces in the central portion of the modern city. These can be seen in the view of Sandusky drawn in 1883 shown in Figure 167. The three large triangular parks and the smaller triangles along the main diagonals are visible, as well as the widened sections along Market Street intended for street markets. Although when Dickens visited the city in the 1840's he said it looked "something like the back of an English watering-place, out of season," Sandusky later developed an air of quiet prosperity and openness. The essential failure of its plan as an essay in grand design must, however, be noted. The two chief diagonals were planned, strangely enough, to terminate at open spaces rather than at the sites designated for public buildings. Here was lost a splendid opportunity to create a little regional capital with something of the elegance of a Williamsburg. Instead, mere eccentricity of design resulted from the use of the motifs of the grand plan without a clear concept of their function in urban aesthetics.

The Grand Plan on the Great Plains

On the western plains hundreds of towns sprang into existence with the coming of the railroad and the beginning of permanent settlement on land available for agriculture. It was not surprising that some of these towns were planned on the radial pattern. Perhaps their proprietors hoped to differentiate them from neighboring communities invariably laid out on some gridiron scheme and differing from one another only in trifling details like the dimensions of blocks or the width of streets. Or, equally likely, the founder of the town, venturing onto the trackless prairies into a friendless territory, summoned up some remembrance of an eastern community of his youth and attempted to recreate its pattern in the west.

Consider, for example, Hatfield, Kansas, the plan of which is shown in Figure 168. Here on a somewhat reduced scale is the plan of Indianapolis, duplicated on the western plains almost to the last alley and lot line. Hugoton and Montezuma, shown in Figures 169 and 170, reveal the enduring appeal of a symmetrical geometric design exhibited earlier in the Ohio communities of Sparta and Greentown or the more ambitious plan of Detroit. At

Palmyra in Nebraska, shown in Figure 171, the designer introduced a new but hardly effective device: two little grids turned inward forty-five degrees from the main axis of the town.

In all of these communities, and even in the much grander city of Colorado Springs, described in Chapter 14, which was deliberately laid out as a luxurious resort town, the potentially powerful impact of the radial streets seems almost deliberately blunted by the failure to provide terminal features or even sites for them which might enhance the formal character of the plan. A long radial terminating in a park or merely ending at another street is devoid of interest; while it may arouse the curiosity of the beholder, it never fully satisfies it. The failure of these radial planners lay in their inability to match the sweep of certain monumental street patterns with architecture or at least building sites of similar character. Few persons in America possessed the understanding and talent necessary to apply the principles of the grand plan to urban design. There were, however, at least two advocates of this style of planning whose ideas are worth reviewing.

An American Alberti

In 1830 the *American Journal of Science and Arts* published a series of articles under the title, "Architecture in the United States." They were unsigned, and there is no clue to the author's identity. His observations extended beyond the criticism of individual buildings, for, as the author stated at the outset, "My remarks will also take a wider range, and embrace a science, for which I cannot find a name, for the good reason, that among the nations from which we draw our language, no such science could be known. I mean the choice of position, and the planning of towns, with the grounds and appurtenances connected with them."[19]

This anonymous critic also pointed out the great opportunity then available to the nation whose greatest population growth and urban development lay ahead:

"We have yet to choose the sites of what are to be large towns and cities, in a generation or two: we have to plan them, with full choice as to convenience or beauty in these things. . . .

[19] "Architecture in the United States," *American Journal of Science and Arts* (New Haven, 1830), XVII, 101.

CITY OF SANDUSKY, O.

MILLS CREEK

SCHOOLS AND CHURCHES.

REFERENCES.

Figure 167. View of Sandusky, Ohio: 1883

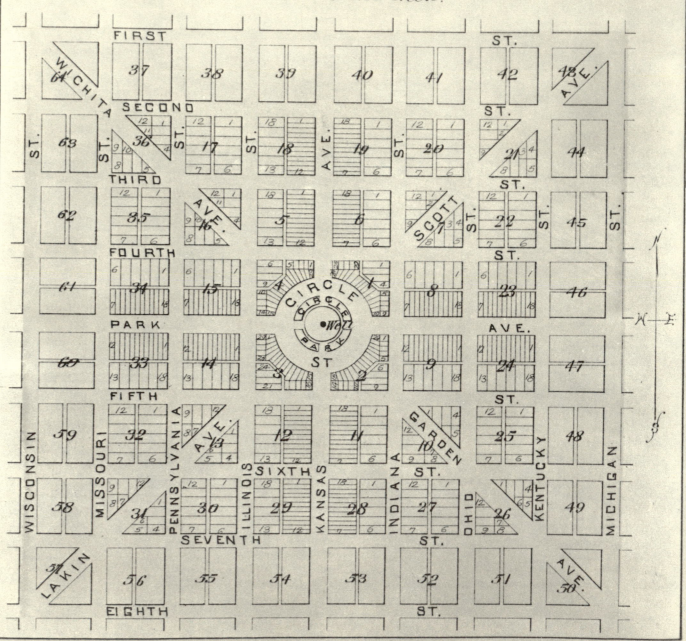

Figure 168. Plan of Hatfield,
Kansas: 1887

HUGOTON
STEVENS CO.
Scale 600 ft.

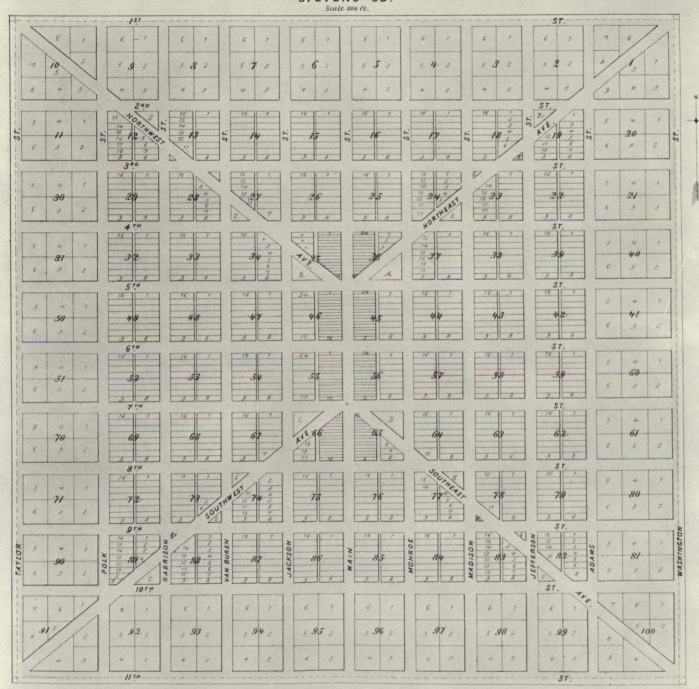

Figure 169. Plan of Hugoton, Kansas: 1887

Figure 170. Plan of Montezuma,
Kansas: 1887

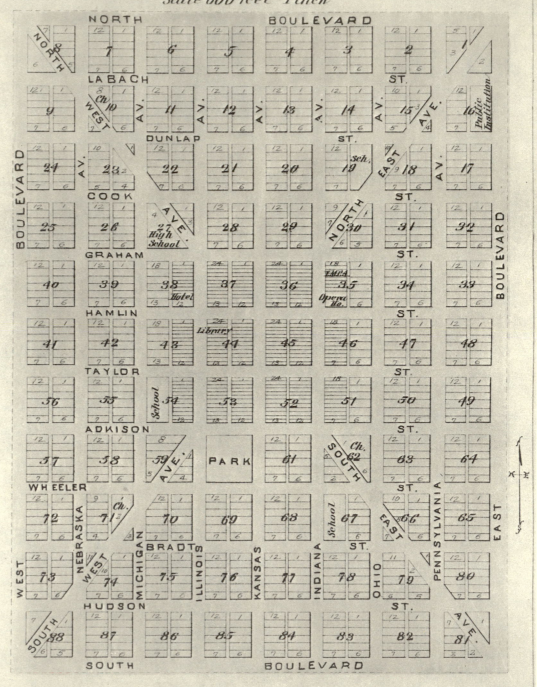

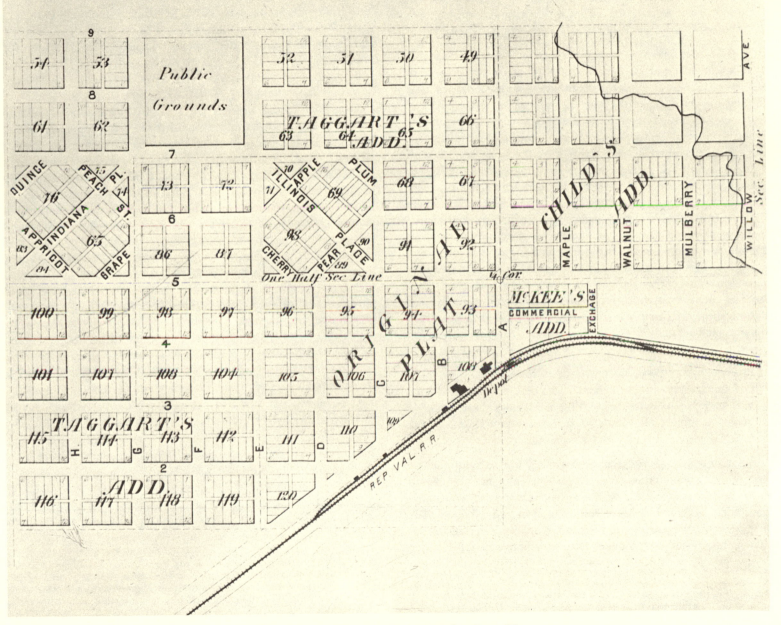

Figure 171. Plan of Palmyra, Nebraska: 1885

"Let no one urge that we are not prepared for these things; that they require wealth and leisure, which we have not for them; and that business, not taste, must engross the attention of a young nation. We *are* prepared for them. It is as easy in planning a town to consult good taste and beauty as not to do it, and unless this is done now, the odds are greatly against its ever being done."[20]

Starting from this premise that planning for towns is possible and even essential, the author examines the gridiron street system, catalogues its advantages and disadvantages, and concludes that while rectangular building sites may be advisable, some planned irregularity in our cities would be desirable. Certain principles are laid down: special features of the site should be emphasized; fountains and parks should be provided; squares or plazas with several streets terminating there with a view of some building or monument are advocated. To illustrate his precepts the author included a prototype plan, reproduced in Figure 172. The street pattern, the statues, obelisks, and arches serving as terminal vistas, the tree-lined avenues, the off-set street intersections providing advantageous sites for public buildings and churches, the oval open space, all show the obvious influence of the baroque philosophy. He acknowledges his debt to the plan of Washington, with which he may have been familiar at first hand, and to other examples from the past. Summarizing his proposals, he concludes with this statement:

"I think regularity will be found combined with variety, simplicity with beauty, and symmetry with a sufficient attention to the multifarious circumstances of man. . . . There is scarcely a turn that will not surprise us with something unexpected, and it is at the same time of such a character as to be accommodated to the circumstances of almost every town in our country."[21]

With what anguish he must have watched the subsequent development of American cities, the excesses of the land boom in the 1830's and the senseless gridiron planning that continued throughout the century. Whoever this man was and whatever his practical talents may have been, his words are as meaningful today as when they were first penned a century and a quarter ago.[22]

[20] *ibid.*, 103.
[21] *ibid.*, 262.
[22] Much of the preceding section follows closely material first used in my *Ideal Cities*, unpublished Master's Thesis, Cornell University, 1947.

Boston Baroque

Nineteenth century Boston was the setting for two proposals similar in spirit to the type of urban design advocated in 1830. The first, put forward in 1844 by Robert Fleming Gourlay, lay squarely in the baroque tradition. The second, described by the landscape designer Robert Morris Copeland in 1872, a former partner of H. W. S. Cleveland who was himself to write on the principles of city planning a year later, was more restrained and of rather less interest.

Gourlay's plan is reproduced in Figure 173, and his debt to the baroque planners of the past will at once be apparent. His plan, however, was no mere abstract design for a vacant site but a serious and clearly thought-out proposal for the redevelopment and expansion of a great city. Gourlay, a Scotsman who had earlier prepared plans for projects in Edinburgh, was no stranger to the United States. Indeed, he states that it was while inspecting the plan of Detroit in 1817 that ". . . it first dawned on my mind, that City-building might and should be reduced to a science of incalculable value in America, where thousands of cities are yet to be founded. This idea has been cherished ever since; and, in London, Edinburgh, New York, Cleveland, and Kingston, I have been employed spare time in drawing plans, with a view, ultimately, of illustrating the science. . . ."[23]

Although this larger work was apparently never completed, Gourlay did develop in some detail a plan for Boston. His scheme of 1844 included not only the city as it then existed but a large area to the south and west. This plan featured a regional highway pattern of concentric circles crossed by radial routes converging on a great boulevard following the banks of the Charles River.[24]

The details of the central part of this plan are fascinating. Among other proposals, Gourlay urged the creation of a great circus around the State House, from which six imposing radial boulevards would lead to all sectors of the city. The Charles River basin would be enlarged and transformed into an enormous lagoon within which two islands, Circus Island and the Elysian Fields, would be located. Following the sweep of the basin would be a

[23] Robert Fleming Gourlay, *Plans for Beautifying New York*, and for Enlarging and Improving the City of Boston, Boston, 1844, p. 14.
[24] The regional plan is reproduced in Fletcher Steele's useful article, "Robert Fleming Gourlay, City Planner," *Landscape Architecture*, VI (1915), pp. 1-13.

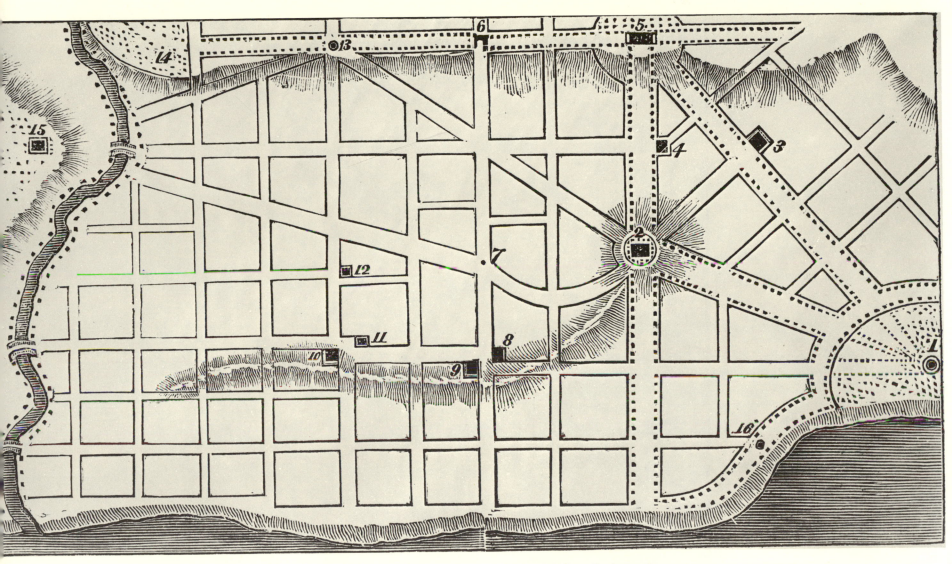

Figure 172. Town Plan Showing Principles of Urban Design: 1830

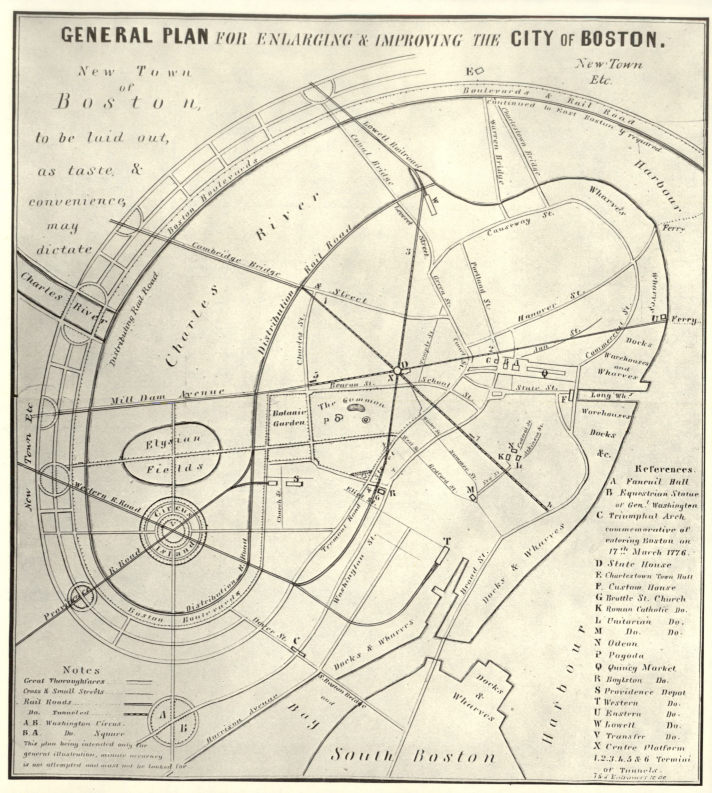

Figure 173.
Robert Fleming Gourlay's Plan
for Boston,
Massachusetts: 1844

railroad and parallel boulevards with crescent and circular elements for variety. Gourlay also proposed a greatly augmented system of park lands to supplement the existing Common and Public Garden, including a plan to landscape the islands in the harbor. He also advocated construction of a subway system with lines connecting at a central point near the State House. Gourlay mentioned that the propulsive power might be "atmospheric pressure" by which passengers would "be conveyed by the distributing cars in five minutes to any quarter of the city, without the slightest disturbance, even of the ladies' furbelows."

"Imagine yourselves," he wrote to Governor George Briggs in 1844, "at the top of the State House surveying the finished work. Behold the crescent of three miles in length, with pleasure grounds in front, and these embracing the outspread waters of Charles River. See the city around, and that embossomed in an amphitheatre of surpassing beauty,—'with hills, and dales, and woods, and glittering spires.' Next, turn sea-ward, and refresh the eye among the green islands of the harbor, with old ocean bearing toward it ships from every clime. Then, estimate the glory of Boston!!"[25]

But this heady exhortation was lost on mercantile Boston whose political and business leaders regarded Gourlay as little more than a crank. Nevertheless, his place as one of the spiritual fathers of the planning movement in America should be recognized, whatever we may think of his vision for a new Boston with the bold diagonals that would surely have altered the picturesque character of the old city. His plan for Boston and the closely reasoned supporting document that accompanied it might be regarded as the first modern city planning study, a forerunner of the thousands to come later and the superior of most in literary quality and inspirational character.

Copeland's plan a generation later was far more realistic, perhaps, but it too was disregarded. Yet Copeland's eloquent plea for advance planning of urban expansion may have helped to open the minds of Boston's elite and possibly made easier the later development of the superb metropolitan park system which girds the city:

"If the group . . . [of private buildings] . . . can be planned for, why not the town or city? If Boston has a present area of a definite number of square miles, with its destiny plainly marked out as a commercial and manufacturing city, why should the city's progress

[25] Gourlay, *ibid.*, p. 17.

be haphazard and halting, sometimes making one, sometimes another advance with no apparent relation to each other, or the future improvements which must be required? How best to use Boston's area must be a problem which admits of division into parts, of discussion and measurement, and a plan can be as well digested for its future progress so as to do full justice to the wants of a future population as for the laying out and construction of a building for public or domestic use. . . .

"The city whose area is carefully studied, which shows by plan where wharves may be built, where new avenues are to be laid out, and where factories may congregate; where parks, gardens, and palaces, if desired, may be made, will grow in a sure, orderly, and progressive way."[26]

There were, of course, plans for other cities using or incorporating in part diagonal boulevards and other features of baroque planning. Some of these are mentioned in other contexts: Coronado, Brawley, and Cotati in California; Perryopolis and Marienville in Pennsylvania; Circleville, Ohio; and Hygeia, Kentucky. But even when faced with this reasonably long list of diagonal cities, and with the realization that it is undoubtedly incomplete, one must still acknowledge that the radial plan in America never rivaled in popularity the more conventional grid.

Nor can one escape the conclusion that the concepts of baroque planning were never fully grasped by American town planners. With the possible exception of the plan of Washington, the imitation baroque plans of the United States lack assurance, polish, and grandeur.

Not until the Chicago Fair of 1893 did interest in the grand plan become widespread in this country. At first limited mainly to efforts at achieving formal groupings of public buildings in civic centers, this movement soon embraced the concept of great diagonal boulevards and parkways. The reawakening of interest in the plan of Washington following the work of the McMillan Commission in 1901 hastened recognition of the monumental effects that might be obtained by this type of street pattern. Many new communities, mainly company towns or real estate promotions, planned after the turn of the century incorporated diagonal streets in their plans. In the concluding chapter we shall examine the background and results of this period of American planning, the beginning of the modern era.

[26] Robert Morris Copeland, *The Most Beautiful City in America: Essay and Plan for the Improvement of the City of Boston*, Boston, 1872, pp. 10-11.

CHAPTER 11

Checkerboard Plans and Gridiron Cities

AS Francis Baily passed through the northeastern United States in the last years of the eighteenth century, his admiration for the orderly plans of the cities he visited was almost limitless. Philadelphia, he noted, was laid out with "perfect regularity," and he added that this feature of American towns was what he most admired. Baltimore, too, he found was planned with straight streets intersecting at right angles, and Baily commented: "This is a plan of which the Americans are very fond, and I think with reason, as it is by far the best way of laying out a city. All the modern-built towns in America are on this principle."[1]

Foreigners visiting America rarely failed to remark on this feature of the cities. Most of them, like Baily, found in this regularity and geometric order much to admire. One is tempted to think that this attitude may have resulted from the ease with which they, as strangers, could find their way about in contrast to the difficulties encountered in the older cities of Europe with their winding streets of uneven width and random intersections. But there must have been an appeal as well to the spirit of rationalism and scientific method to which many of these travelers had become attracted.

However, what may have first seemed like a vision of a new urban world of order, regularity, and simplicity all too quickly blurred into an impression of dullness and rigidity. Thus, by the time Baily arrived in Cincinnati, the sight of regular gridiron towns was no longer a novelty, and the lack of imagination in American planning had become apparent. His comments at that time show his realization of both the aesthetic and the functional shortcomings of the grid plan as typically applied to an American townsite:

"I have taken occasion to express my approbation of the American mode of laying out their new towns, in a general way, in straight lines; but I think that oftentimes it is a sacrifice of beauty to prejudice, particularly when they persevere in making all their streets cross each other at right angles, *without any regard to the situation of the ground*, or the face of the surrounding country: whereas, these ought certainly to be taken into consideration, in order that a town may unite both utility and beauty; and, with a little attention to this, a town might still preserve the straight line, and yet avoid that disgusting appearance which many of the new towns in America make. For it not unfrequently happens that a hill opposes itself in the middle of a street, or that a rivulet crosses it three or four times, thereby rendering its passage very inconvenient. . . ."[2]

Baily's solution to this problem was to adopt the mixed radial and grid pattern as used in Washington, which he had just seen and whose plan he had admired. Although this was done in a number of cities, the overwhelming majority of American towns were begun and extended on the gridiron plan. Much of the early impetus to the grid plan, aside from its intrinsic ease in surveying, its adaptability to speculative activities, and its simple appeal to unsophisticated minds, stemmed from the position and influence of Philadelphia. As the most important city on the continent, and as a much used point of departure for westward migrations to the interior, Philadelphia lent its plan as well as its capital to aid in the establishment of new towns beyond the Appalachians.

For a century or more this city served as a model for the planning of other towns, at least with respect to its gridiron street system and its provision for public squares. By a curious and on the whole unfortunate coincidence, as political power and economic dominance became centered in Washington and New York City at the beginning of the nineteenth century, a new and more ambitious gridiron plan was fashioned in the rival city to the north. Here at New York, which soon developed into the great entrepôt

[1] Francis Baily, *Journal of a Tour in Unsettled Parts of North America in 1796 & 1797*, London, 1856, p. 105.

[2] *ibid.*, 226-227.

Figure 174. Plan of New York City: 1797

for the continent, the apotheosis of the gridiron took form. And as hundreds and thousands of west-bound settlers passed through New York bound for the west via the Mohawk Valley they observed and remembered this supergrid throughout the frontier. Because the influence of this extension plan for New York City was so important, it deserves more than passing examination.

One Hundred and Fifty-Five Streets

New York City had suffered grievously during the Revolution. In 1776, the first year of British occupation, and again in 1778 fire swept the city and destroyed many of its buildings. The early years of the peace that followed proved difficult ones for the merchants of the city, as many of the old shipping and importing connections had been severed at the time hostilities began. By 1789, when New York became the temporary capital, trade once more began to flourish; and by the beginning of the nineteenth century New York had become the economic capital of the nation. This position of dominance resulted in new population growth and the extension of the city. Figure 174 shows the city as it appeared in 1797, the shaded portions indicating generally the limits of the built-up area. At this time no marked changes from the prewar layout can be noted. The Great Square of the Delancey subdivision no longer appears, but along the Hudson River side of the city Hudson Square is shown. This was one of the few residential squares in New York laid out on the pattern of the Bloomsbury Squares in London.

Substantial tracts of land had come into public ownership under the 1782 Act of Confiscation by which land owned by loyalists was declared forfeit. In addition, under the early English charters the city had been given ownership of all of the common lands not previously granted to individuals. In 1785 these common lands were surveyed by Casimir Goerck, the city surveyor, who laid them off in rectangular parcels. In 1796 a second survey was made of these lands stretching northward in a long strip up central Manhattan. This time streets were platted, with north-south streets 100 feet wide, and cross streets every 200 feet with a width of 60 feet. Reproductions of these two surveys are shown in Figure 175. They represent the beginning of a series of events that were to culminate in a street plan for most of the Island of Manhattan.

· 296 ·

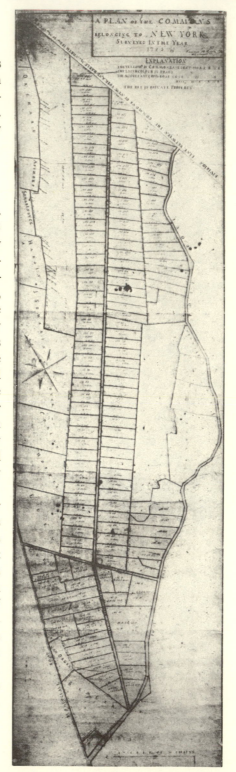

The city's power to control street width and alignments was by no means clear. In addition, new surveys of the city failed to agree with the descriptions of properties in private deeds. By 1804 the mayor and aldermen resolved to take advantage of the power granted them by the legislature in 1801 to regulate buildings and street lines. At first they apparently considered only the preparation of a new and accurate map of all streets and public and private properties, but by 1806 they came to the conclusion that a commission should be created with power to lay out new streets. Uncertain of their authority, they requested the legislature to grant them the necessary powers and presented a draft of a bill that would accomplish the desired ends. Then, in an effort to detach this important task from the conflicts of local politics and the conflicting claims of property owners, the city, in 1807, asked that the commission be appointed by the State, suggesting the names of Simeon DeWitt, Gouverneur Morris, and John Rutherford for the positions. On April 3 the legislature passed the measure and conferred on the three commissioners the following duties: ". . . to lay out . . . the leading streets and great avenues, of a width not less than 60 feet, and in general to lay out said streets, roads and public squares of such ample width as they may deem sufficient to secure a free and abundant circulation of air among said streets and public squares when the same shall be built on. . . ."[3] The map, according to the law, was to be "final and conclusive" in governing the extension of the city into the area north of the then developed portion of the city. A line across Manhattan running east and west from the present Washington Square would mark the starting point for this new survey and plan.

The commissioners faced all the normal difficulties in working out a suitable plan for a large area, but in addition they were confronted with general hostility by property owners who already held land in the area to be studied. According to one account, their surveyors were sometimes driven off property they were attempting to survey, in one case being pelted with artichokes and cabbages by an irate woman who had made a living by selling vegetables for 20 years and who did not intend to have her property divided by strangers.

The appointment of the commissioners started a flurry of land speculation. Owners hurried to plat their property into blocks and streets, believing that in this manner they could establish a street pattern for their land that the commissioners would be forced to observe. In their report, which was not submitted until 1811, the commissioners referred to this problem:

". . . [An] important consideration was so to amalgamate it [the plan] with the plans already adopted by individuals as not to make any important change in their dispositions. This, if it could have been effected, consistently with the public interest, was desirable, not only as it might render work more generally acceptable, but also as it might be the means of avoiding expense. It was therefore a favourite object with the Commissioners, and pursued until after various unfruitful attempts had proved the extreme difficulty; nor was it abandoned at last but from necessity."[4]

The commissioners found it impossible to adjust their plan to the irregular property boundaries and the random streets that already existed in the vast territory under their jurisdiction. Perhaps this is one reason their report has a curiously defensive tone; or it may be that they realized the plan they had prepared was inadequate in several respects. The report of their four years of study was finally made public in 1811, accompanied by the plan reproduced in Figure 176.

The explanation of the plan supplied by the commissioners is of considerable interest since it provides an understanding of their basic concepts and assumptions. They begin by stating their reasons for adopting the gridiron system, a patent attempt to establish themselves as practical men of the world:

"That one of the first objects which claimed their attention, was the form and manner in which the business should be conducted; that is to say, whether they should confine themselves to rectilinear and rectangular streets, or whether they should adopt some of those supposed improvements, by circles, ovals, and stars, which certainly embellish a plan, whatever may be their effects as to convenience and utility. In considering that subject, they could not but bear in mind that a city is to be composed principally of the habitations of men, and that strait sided, and right angled houses are the most cheap to build, and the most convenient to live in. The effect of these plain and simple reflections was decisive."[5]

[4] "Commissioners' Remarks," in William Bridges, *Map of the City of New York and Island of Manhattan*, New York, 1811, pp. 24-5.
[5] *ibid.*, p. 24.

[3] Acts of New York, 1807.

Figure 175. Map of the Common Lands of New York City: 1785 and 1796

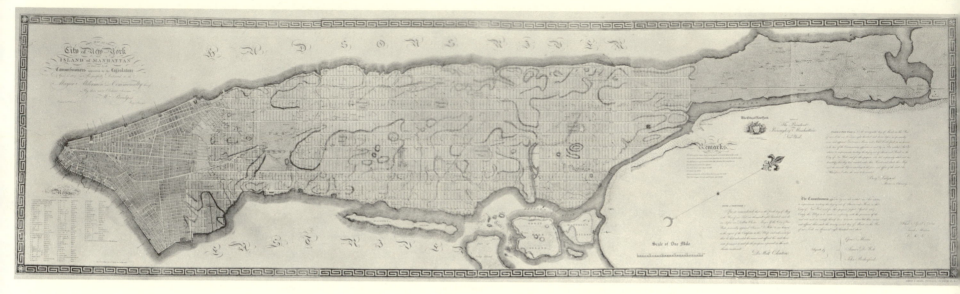

Figure 176. The Commissioners' Plan of New York City: 1811

Giving effect to this decision was comparatively simple. A dozen north-south avenues, each 100 feet wide, were laid out. Crossing these at right angles every 200 feet were 155 streets 60 feet in width running east-west between the two rivers. The similarity to the earlier Goerck plan for the common lands in central Manhattan is obvious. Not only are the street widths and intervals identical but the location of the streets between 23rd and 93rd Streets and 5th and 6th Avenues coincided exactly with the Goerck survey of 1796. The commissioners do not refer to this earlier survey, but there can be no doubt that they were guided by it and simply extended the Goerck plan throughout the land under their control.

In one respect the commissioners were farsighted. They established a plan for an area far in excess of what anyone believed would be needed even in the distant future. The report explains the reasons for extending the proposed street pattern as far north as 155th Street:

"To some it may be manner of surprise, that the whole Island has not been laid out as a City; to others, it may be a subject of merriment, that the Commissioners have provided space for a greater population than is collected at any spot on this side of China. They have in this respect been governed by the shape of the ground. It is not improbable that considerable numbers may be collected at Haerlem before the high hills to the southward of it shall be built upon as a City; and it is improbable, that (for centuries to come) the grounds north of Haerlem Flat will be covered with houses. To have come short of the extent laid out, might therefore have defeated just expectation and to have gone further, might have furnished· materials to the pernicious spirit of speculation."[6]

The reference to topography in the preceding passage is the only indication that the commissioners took any notice whatsoever of the marked and often sharp changes in elevations on the island. Certainly the street system they established is totally unrelated to the contours of the land. Along with the general mechanical dullness produced by their gridiron pattern, this is one of the outstanding defects of the commissioners' plan. Not only was topog-

[6] *ibid.*, p. 30.

· 298 ·

raphy overlooked but important existing roads were ignored. One or two of these, notably Broadway, did manage to survive the rigid grid as development took place, but the others gave way under the subsequent relentless expansion.

A final problem of the commissioners was to decide on the amount and location of the open spaces mentioned in the act of the legislature from which they derived their powers. Slightly less than 500 acres were set aside for various purposes, the largest site being the Parade bounded by 14th and 34th Streets and 3rd and 7th Avenues. This was to be used "for Military Exercise" and as a place to "assemble, in case of need, the force destined to defend the City." Several small parks occupying the space normally used for four blocks may be seen on the plan, a slightly larger site between 4th and 5th Avenues at 90th Street was designated as the location of a future reservoir, but until needed for this purpose the site was to be "consecrated to the purposes of science, when public spirit shall dictate the building of an observatory." The other reserved area was the site for a public market located between 6th and 10th Streets and extending back from the East River to First Avenue.

Although these provisions for open spaces seem parsimonious by modern standards, if followed, they would have been an improvement over conditions which then existed. The commissioners were aware, however, that their plan might be criticized on the grounds that sufficient space had not been provided, and they were ready with the following explanation:

"It may, to many, be matter of surprise, that so few vacant spaces have been left, and those so small, for the benefit of fresh air, and consequent preservation of health. Certainly, if the City of New York were destined to stand on the side of a small stream, such as the Seine or the Thames, a great number of ample spaces might be needful; but those large arms of the sea which embrace Manhattan Island, render its situation, in regard to health and pleasure, as well as to convenience of commerce, peculiarly felicitous; when, therefore, from the same causes, the price of land is so uncommonly great, it seemed proper to admit the principles of economy to greater influence than might, under circumstances of a different kind, have consisted with the dictates of prudence and the sense of duty."[7]

[7] ibid., p. 26.

How should the commissioners' plan for New York be judged—by modern standards or by those of the time? The unfortunate results of the prejudices and mistakes of the planners of 1811 are well known today. The lack of suitable sites for public buildings, the traffic congestion at the frequent intersections, the lack of enough north-south arteries, the overbuilding on narrow lots that inevitably resulted from the shallow blocks—these are but a few of the shortcomings. But even by the standards of the early nineteenth century the plan was inadequate. In an effort to escape criticism on the grounds of economy and practicality the commissioners ignored well-known principles of civic design that would have brought variety in street vistas and resulted in focal points for sites for important buildings and uses. True enough, no one could have foreseen the rapid growth of the city and the changes in transportation and population that lessened the importance of the river-to-river cross streets while placing an intolerable load on the less numerous north-south avenues. But one cannot avoid the conclusion that the commissioners, in fixing upon their plan, were motivated mainly by narrow considerations of economic gain. Their surveyor, Randel, was later to defend the plan by steadfastly maintaining its utility for the "buying, selling and improving of real estate." As an aid to speculation the commissioners' plan was perhaps unequalled, but only on this ground can it be justifiably called a great achievement. The fact that it was this gridiron New York that served as a model for later cities was a disaster whose consequences have barely been mitigated by more modern city planners.[8]

Section 9, Township 39, Range 14

New York was a city of 200,000 and had already filled in a good part of the commissioners' grid when civil engineer James Thompson filed his plat of Chicago in 1830. Here on the shore of Lake Michigan another of America's numerous gridiron cities began its development. Although the original plan has very little to interest us, the circumstances of the city's founding and of its first few years of growth are instructive.

[8] I. N. Phelps Stokes, *Iconography of Manhattan Island*, New York, 1895-1928, and Fred Roy Frank, *The Development of New York City; 1600-1900*, unpublished Master's Thesis, Cornell University, 1955, have been my chief sources for this section.

Chicago owes its origins, its growth, and its future prospects to transportation. Where now it is the railroads, the airlines, and the St. Lawrence Seaway, in the beginning a canal that was to connect the Great Lakes with the Mississippi furnished the main impetus to growth. The canal had long been a subject of comment. Joliet, after his visit to the site in 1673 mentioned the possibility of the project in his reports to his superiors. In 1808 Gallatin recommended its construction in his program of internal improvements. Finally, in 1822 Congress authorized the young state of Illinois to survey and acquire a 90-foot swath of land for a canal.

There were conflicts over the exact location for the canal, and the state faced serious difficulties over financing such an improvement as it might be. In 1826 the Illinois legislature requested, and Congress a year later approved, federal aid in the form of a land grant. Under the act the state was to receive title to alternate sections of land for five miles on each side of the canal's route. By 1829 three canal commissioners were appointed, a route was selected, and in the following year the commissioners had Thompson lay out a town in Section 9, Township 39, Range 14, so that a few lots might be sold in order to meet current expenses. Chicago thus had its origins in a speculative real estate transaction, an event to be endlessly repeated in the early years of the growth of the second largest metropolis.[9]

Until 1832 Chicago consisted of little more than a dozen or so log cabins, a store, two taverns, and Fort Dearborn, which had been established in 1803. While the general location of the infant city held much promise for future development, the site itself was a miserable, mosquito-ridden bog of soft mud, ill-suited for buildings. Historians still argue over the origin of the name, some maintaining it comes from the Indian *Chickagou*, "garlic," while others hold that it was derived from *Shegagh*, or "skunk." There is general agreement, however, that the odors of the place were dreadful and that the Indians were correct in referring to it as "the place of the evil smell." Some would assert that the earlier names are still valid; the mud, at least, was overcome when under the leadership of young George Pullman, who was later to found his

own town nearby, wholesale filling of streets and building sites was carried out in the mid 1850's.

Construction on the canal did not begin until 1836 and was not completed for a dozen years, but the promise of this project was enough to draw settlers and to stimulate a lively speculation in city lots. Evidently Chicago has always been a city of optimists, for it must have required a sturdy faith in the future to survive the discomforts in this pioneer city. That faith was strengthened by the knowledge of what the Grand Erie Canal had brought to the cities of upstate New York, and it was with the expectations that similar prosperity would soon be enjoyed by Chicago that speculators shortly began to flock to the city.

The boom began in 1833, and in that year 200 houses were built. The population then was under 400. In 1834 this had increased to 1,800, and at the height of the boom in 1836 there were about 4,000 persons living in the city. A map of the city in 1834 is reproduced in Figure 177. The original "canal lots" of the 1830 survey can be seen in the 6 by 10 block grid at the forks of the Chicago River. The other streets and blocks, including those in the land set aside to be sold for the support of schools, had been laid out in the intervening 6 years. Although in 1839 the town council purchased 2 acres of land for park purposes, at the time of this map the only public reservation was the land at the mouth of the river where Fort Dearborn was located. Land for the present Grant Park along the Lake was, however, set aside at about this time, an example of foresight all the more commendable because of the pressure to subdivide all available building sites.

The beginnings of the vast gridiron that is modern Chicago are clearly to be seen. With each succeeding addition to the town new streets were laid out connecting with or parallel to Thompson's original grid system.

For land speculation this was, of course, the ideal pattern. The mania for buying and selling town lots that swept the country was nowhere wilder than at Chicago. Harriet Martineau described some of the events she observed when she visited the city in 1836:

"I never saw a busier place than Chicago was at the time of our arrival. The streets were crowded with land speculators, hurrying from one sale to another. A negro dressed up in scarlet bearing a scarlet flag and riding a white horse with housings of

[9] For the early planning and growth of Chicago see: Homer Hoyt, *One Hundred Years of Land Values in Chicago*, Chicago, 1933; Bessie Louise Pierce, *A History of Chicago*, New York, 1937; and Joseph N. Balestier, *The Annals of Chicago: A Lecture Delivered Before the Chicago Lyceum, January 21, 1840*, Chicago, 1876.

Figure 177. Plan of Chicago, Illinois: 1834

scarlet announced the time of sale. At every street corner where he stopped the crowd gathered around him; and it seemed as if some prevalent mania infected the whole people. As the gentlemen of our party walked the streets, storekeepers hailed them from their doors with offers of farms and all manner of land lots, advising them to speculate before the price of land rose higher."[10]

Land prices soared. Buckingham may have exaggerated, but he reported that some lots changed hands ten times in a single day and that the "evening purchaser" paid at least "ten times as much as the price paid by the morning buyer for the same spot!"[11] The school section, which in 1833 had been sold for $38,000, was valued at $1,200,000 in 1836. Land in the present city limits which was worth $168,800 in 1830 had risen in value to more than $10,000,000 at the peak of the boom. Most of this value was fictitious since it was not based on cash sales but on purchases with extremely liberal credit. Of course this did not prevent everyone who owned land from imagining himself a millionaire.

In the rush to lay out new subdivisions, sites beyond the immediate area of Chicago were not overlooked. As one participant later recalled,

"The prairies of Illinois, the forests of Wisconsin, and the sandhills of Michigan, presented a chain almost unbroken of supposititious villages and cities. The whole land seemed staked out and peopled on paper. . . . Often was a fictitious streamlet seen to wind its romantic course through the heart of an ideal city, thus creating water lots, and water privileges. But where a *real* stream, however diminutive, did find its way to the shore of the lake . . . the miserable waste of sand and fens which lay unconscious of its glory on the shore of the lake, was suddenly elevated into a mighty city, with a projected harbor and lighthouse, railroads and canals. . . . Not the puniest brook on the shore of Lake Michigan was suffered to remain without a city at its mouth. . . ."[12]

The Chicago land boom collapsed, as it did in every other American city, with the panic of 1837. But by the early 1840's growth began anew, and by the opening of the long delayed canal in 1848

[10] As quoted in Hoyt, *Land Values*, 30.
[11] James Silk Buckingham, *The Eastern and Western States of America*, London, 1842, III, 261.
[12] Balestier, *Annals of Chicago*, 27-29.

the city had a population of 20,000. In a sense the canal was already obsolete at its completion, for railroads soon outstripped it in importance. Yet the canal, or rather the promise of the canal, had served the purpose of stimulating the growth of the city and establishing the city's importance as a place to which railroads had to run. The first rail line opened in 1848, and by the end of the next decade the basic fabric of Chicago's existing railroad network had been woven. Thus a few years before the Civil War the city was the focal point of ten rail lines, its population was approaching 100,000, and its rate of growth was steadily increasing. The next years were to witness perhaps the most rapid increase in population of any large American city. In 1865 the population was about 180,000. This had doubled by 1872 and quadrupled by 1885.

In the vast extensions required to accommodate this remarkable increase the gridiron plan predominated. Such experiments as Lake Forest and Riverside, discussed in another chapter, were but tiny spots on the otherwise almost unbroken grid. A few of the old trails and rural roads leading into the city on radial lines did manage to survive and are important and useful elements in the modern street system. The view of the city in 1892 shown in Figure 178 illustrates the rapid growth of the city in its first 60 years. While the absence of many pronounced changes in topography make the gridiron pattern of Chicago less objectionable on functional grounds than in Manhattan, its greater extent is all the drearier. Only in its newer suburbs can one find relief from the relentless patterns of Chicago's oppressive grid, magnificent only because of its scale and because of the tenacity with which the original village plan was extended. Modern attempts to reshape Chicago stem from the World's Fair of 1893 and Daniel Burnham's monumental plan for the city in 1909. These events are reviewed in Chapter 18.

The Grid by the Golden Gate

The gridiron spread across the country as the natural tool of the land speculator. No other plan was so easy to survey, and no other system of planning yielded so many uniform lots, easy to describe in deeds or to sell from the auctioneer's block. Everywhere there was gold in the land if it could be bought, subdivided, and sold, even in the hills, if promoted by a skillful operator. What

THE CITY OF CHICAGO.

Figure 178. View of Chicago from Lake Michigan: 1892

more natural development then than the use of the gridiron in laying out the cities of the California goldrush, itself a mad speculative scramble that for a time even eclipsed the mania for speculation in town lots.

As the great port of entry for those arriving in California by sea and as the base from which to outfit expeditions to the goldfields, San Francisco felt the full impact of the boom. Literally almost overnight the gridiron spread over the steep hills that formed one of the world's most spectacular sites for a city. On the eve of the goldrush San Francisco was confined to the boundaries of the little grid plan shown in Figure 179. From the bay this little town could be seen commanding the natural harbor two miles or so from the old Spanish *presidio*. Figure 180 gives a reasonably accurate view of the city and the harbor before the city was swamped by the treasure seekers a century ago.[13]

The first survey of the little town, then called Yerba Buena, was made in 1839 by a Swiss surveyor, Jean Jacques Vioget. He platted the blocks between Pacific, California, Montgomery, and Dupont (now Grant) Streets. This brought some order to the settlement, which then consisted of perhaps a dozen houses and some fifty residents. For some reason the streets as then platted intersected at two and one-half degrees off a true right angle. In 1845 this little gridiron was extended, and two years later Jasper O'Farrell resurveyed the town, extended its limits again, and corrected the angular error in the Vioget plat. The plaza on Kearney Street between Clay and Washington was the only open space, and here, on what is the modern Portsmouth Square in front of the old custom house, the Americans took possession of the city in 1846.

It was from this little grid as extended and rectified by O'Farrell that the modern San Francisco was to grow with such amazing speed. The population at the time the gold rush began has been estimated at 850; by the end of 1849 the population was nearly 6,000, and in another year this had more than doubled. In addition to the resident population many thousands more passed through San Francisco on the way to the gold fields and returned to the city during the winter.

When news of the discovery of gold near Sutter's Mill reached San Francisco in 1848 the immediate effect on land values and speculation in town lots was depressing. Many of the residents left for the gold region, and it appeared likely that other cities would become more important. With the return of the miners in the late fall and the arrival of new immigrants, however, the land boom got underway in earnest. Land prices soared to eight and ten times what they had been just a few months before. New surveys were quickly run, and the size of the town was greatly increased. The plan of the city in 1849, shown in Figure 181, reveals the vast extensions that were made in response to the demand for building sites. The easiest and quickest method of expansion was followed, and the original grid of modest size was enlarged to immense proportions by street extensions and surveys for additional parallel streets. At a forty-five degree angle from the streets in the area of first settlement another gridiron section had already been started. Market Street served as the dividing line between these two sections of the city. Today that broad street and the large blocks to the southeast confine the business district centering on Union Square to the older portion of the city. The compactness and convenience of the San Francisco business district is largely due to this happy accident originating in the scramble to lay out streets and blocks in the competition for real estate development.

Among the early arrivals in San Francisco was Bayard Taylor, whose description of the city and the towns of the mining area are particularly vivid. His first view of the city was from the harbor:

"Around the curving shore of the Bay and upon the sides of three hills which rise steeply from the water, the middle one receding so as to form a bold amphitheatre, the town is planted and seems scarcely yet to have taken root, for tents, canvas, plank, mud and adobe houses are mingled together with the least apparent attempt at order and durability."[14]

Then, as he came ashore and looked along the curve of the bay, Taylor saw at close view the strange appearance of this boom city:

"On every side stood buildings of all kinds, begun or half-finished, and the greater part of them mere canvas sheds, open in front, and covered with all kinds of signs, in all languages. Great

---

[13] The full story of the planning of San Francisco from Spanish to modern times is told in the exhaustive and fascinating work by Mel Scott, *The San Francisco Bay Area*, Berkeley, 1959.

[14] Bayard Taylor, *El Darado*, New York, 1850, as quoted in Warren S. Tryon, *A Mirror for Americans*, Chicago, 1952, III, 692.

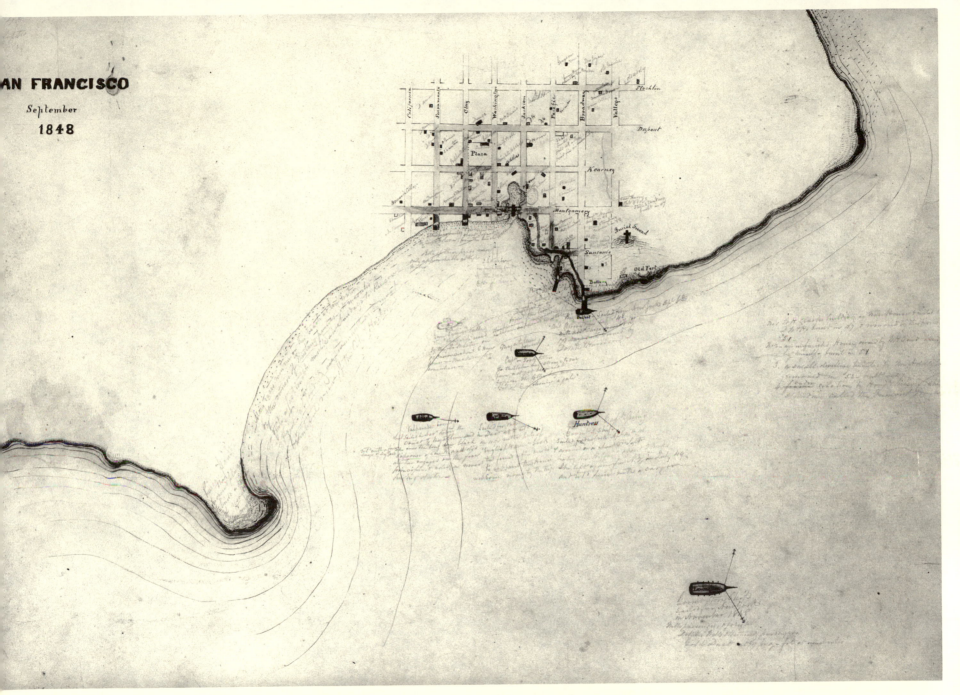

Figure 179. Plan of San Francisco, California: 1848

Figure 180. View of San Francisco, California: 1847

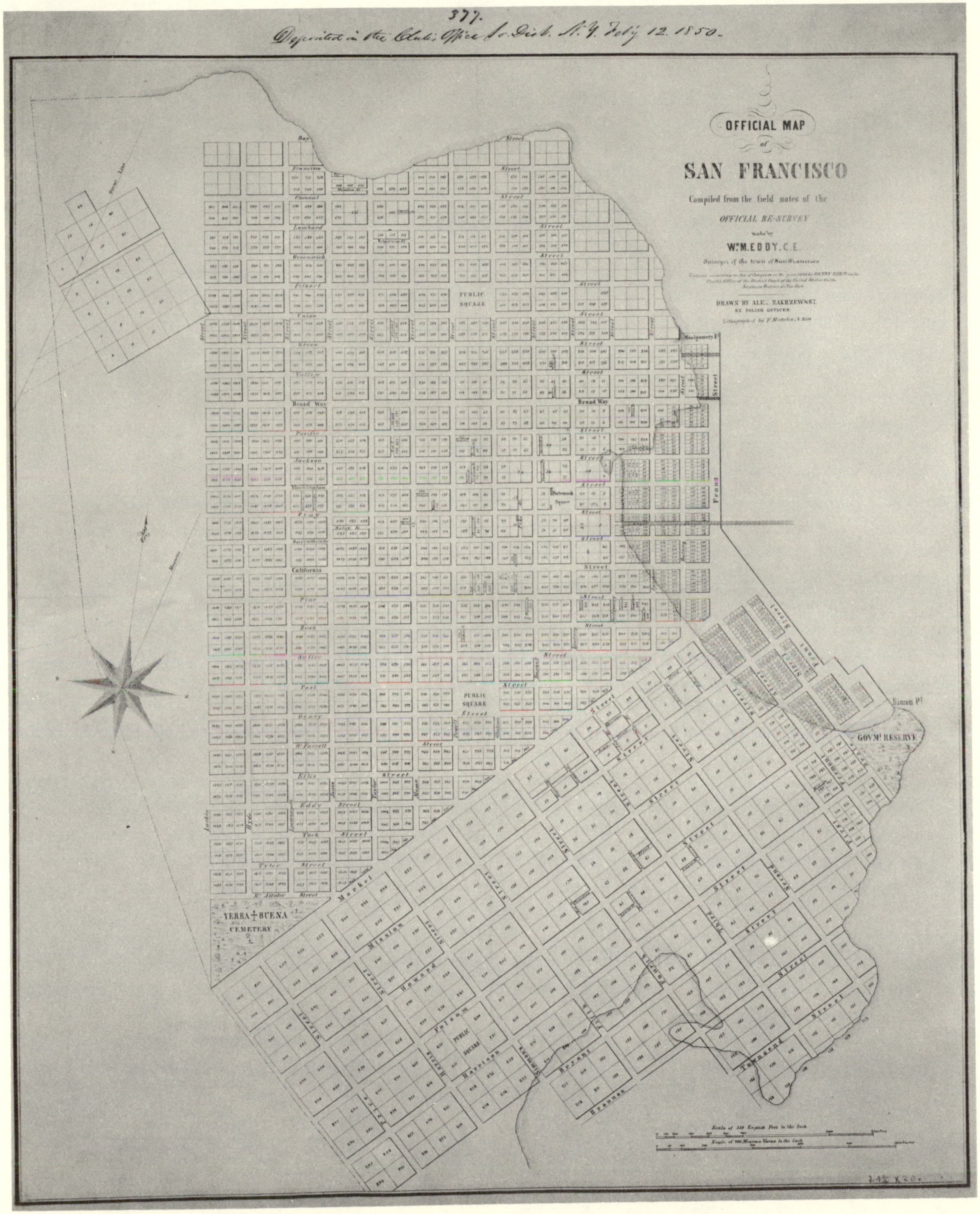

Figure 181. Plan of
San Francisco, California: 1849

quantities of goods were piled up in the open air, for want of a place to store them. The streets were full of people, hurrying to and fro, and of as diverse and bizarre a character as the houses: Yankees of every possible variety, Sonorians, native Californians in *sarapes* and sombreros, Chilians, Kanakas from Hawaii, Chinese with long tails, Malays armed with their everlasting creeses, and others. . . ."[15]

Three weeks later Taylor returned from his visit to the mining areas and recorded the changes which had taken place in the city during that brief interval:

"The town had not only greatly extended its limits, but actually seemed to have doubled its number of dwellings since I left. High up on the hills, where I had seen only sand and chapparal, stood clusters of houses; streets which had been merely laid out, were hemmed in with buildings and thronged with people; new warehouses had sprung up on the water side, and new piers were creeping out toward the shipping; the forest of masts had greatly thickened; and the noise, motion and bustle of business and labor on all sides were incessant."[16]

The new piers mentioned by Taylor included, among others, those at the foot of California, Sacramento, Clay, and Washington Streets. Within a short time these were converted into streets, cross streets were added, and the gridiron was thus extended into what once had been the bay. And, as Taylor states, the slopes of the steep hills that rise almost from the water's edge quickly became covered first with tents and shacks and then with more substantial dwellings as the city took form. In these extensions inland the topography was ignored, and the gridiron plan was merely tilted on its side as new streets were laid out running perpendicular and parallel with the natural slopes.

The great gold migration to California stimulated the growth of many other cities. Of these, the earliest to develop was Sacramento near the site of the first discovery of gold. A view of the town in 1849 is shown in Figure 182. At the time the view was drawn, the land boom was just getting under way, and within a

few months the site was surveyed into an enormous gridiron, the plan of which is reproduced in Figure 183. Here is the standardized grid town *par excellence*, the hundreds of identical blocks and streets being relieved only by a few open squares and one street slightly wider than the rest. Taylor again provides a verbal picture of the city at this time:

"The limits of the town extended to nearly one square mile, and the number of inhabitants, in tents and houses, fell little short of ten thousand. The previous April there were just four houses in the place! Can the world match a growth like this?

"The original forest-trees, standing in all parts of the town, give it a very picturesque appearance. Many of the streets are lined with oaks and sycamores, six feet in diameter, and spreading ample boughs on every side. The emigrants have ruined the finest of them by building camp-fires at their bases, which, in some instances, have burned completely through, leaving a charred and blackened arch for the superb tree to rest upon. . . .

"The value of real estate in Sacramento City is only exceeded by that of San Francisco. Lots twenty by seventy-five feet, in the best locations, brought from $3,000 to $3,500. Rents were on a scale equally enormous. The City Hotel, which was formerly a saw-mill, erected by Capt. Sutter, paid $30,000 per annum."[17]

Two other cities in the San Francisco Bay area deserve brief mention. Vallejo and Benicia, shown in Figures 184 and 185, both were platted by General Vallejo, the former Mexican officer who had planned the *pueblo* of Sonoma. Benicia was created in 1847 and was thus in a position to capitalize quickly on the land boom created by the goldrush. With its central park, four additional open squares, and its cemetery reservation, the plan shows some consideration for community needs. Vallejo was hastily laid out to take advantage of the land boom. Both towns served briefly as the capital city of the new state of California before the legislators made their decision to locate permanently in Sacramento. At that time the plan of Sacramento was modified to permit sufficient land to be assembled for the capitol grounds.

The growth of San Francisco continued unabated. Figure 186 shows the new addition that had been laid out by the middle 1850's

[15] *ibid.*, 693.
[16] *ibid.*, 705-706.

[17] *ibid.*, 698-99.

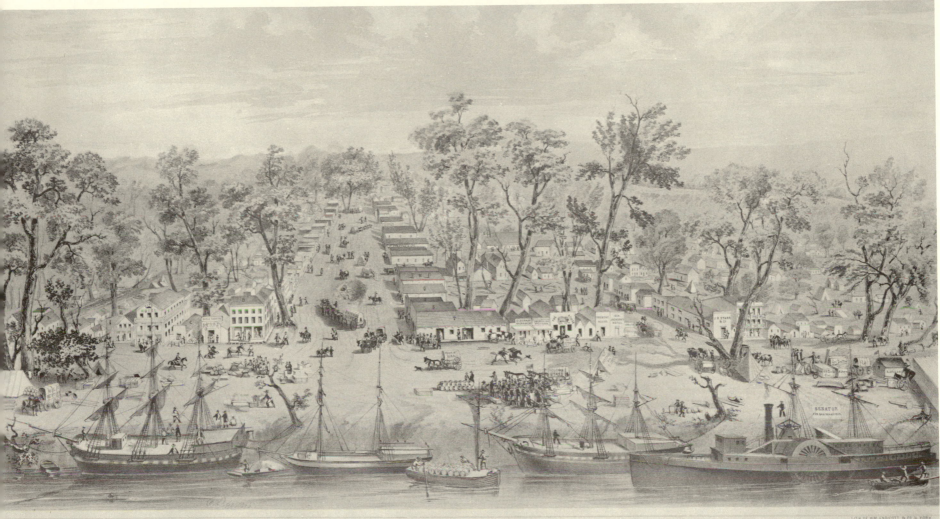

DRAWN DEC. 20TH 1849 BY G.V. COOPER.

LITH OF WM. ENDICOTT & C? N.YORK

A Hensley, Redding & C?
B Peoples Market
C T.M? Dowell & C?
D S Taylor
E Rental tent (S. Weeks)
F Montgomery & Warbour Zinc Store
G Myrick Nelson & C?
H The Gem
I Depeyker Brothers
J Mechanikus
K Oregon Bowling Saloon
L Cotton Boxie & C?

M R M Gorup & C?
N Robert M Folger
O Barron Hotel
P Van Bowres Hotel
Q Gordolds
R H.E. Robinson & C? Post Office
S Empire
T Mountain House Barnes, Skrener's Store
U United States Hotel
V J.B Starr & C?
W Auction Hotel
X Luont & C? Express Office

S A C R A M E N T O   C I T Y C?

FROM THE FOOT OF J. STREET,

SHOWING I. J. & K. ST? WITH THE SIERRA NEVADA IN THE DISTANCE.

NEW YORK PUBLISHED BY STRINGER & TOWNSEND 222 BROADWAY.

425.
Deposited in the Clerks' Office So. Dist. of NewYork March 2. 1850.

Figure 182. View of Sacramento, California: 1849

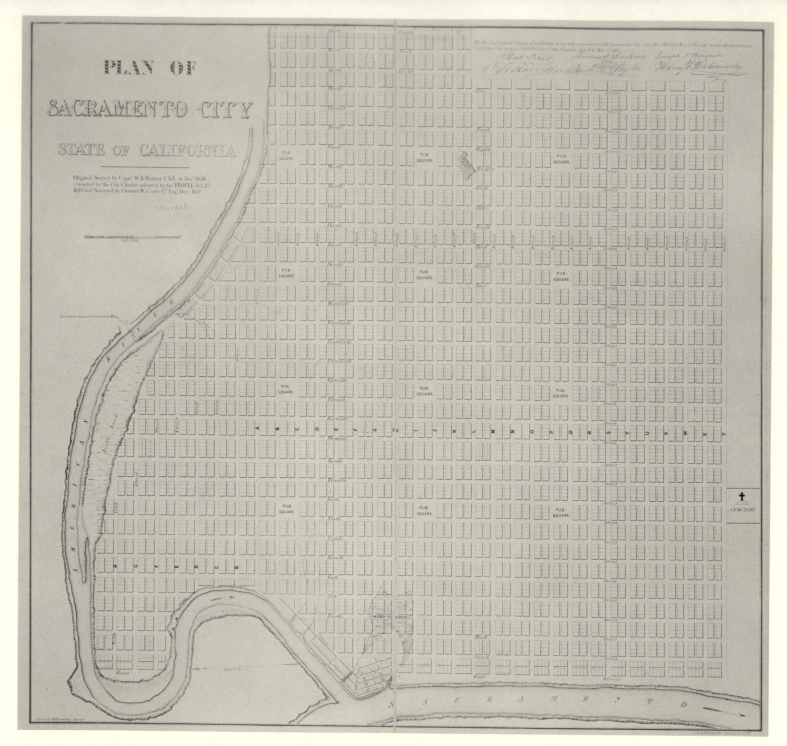

Figure 183. Plan of Sacramento, California: 1849

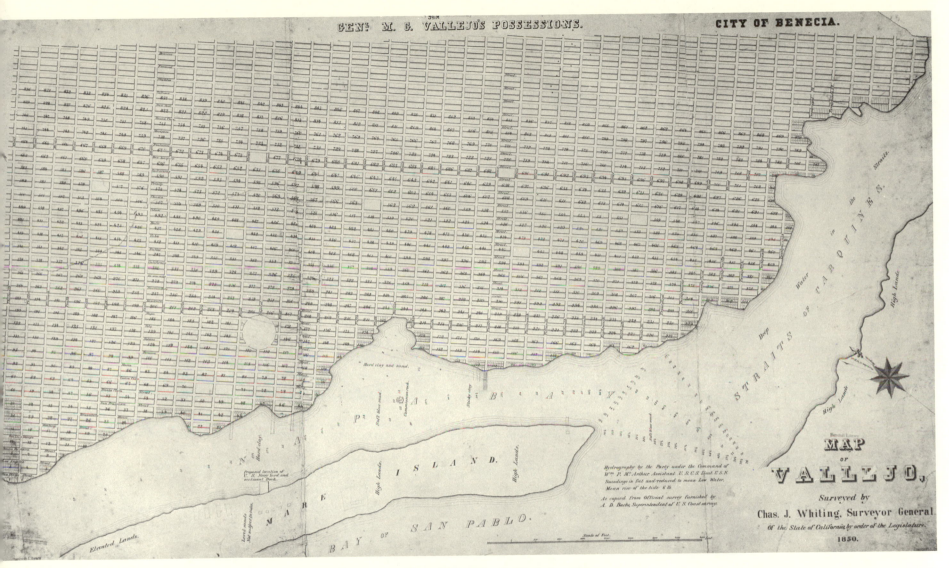

Figure 184. Plan of Vallejo, California: 1850

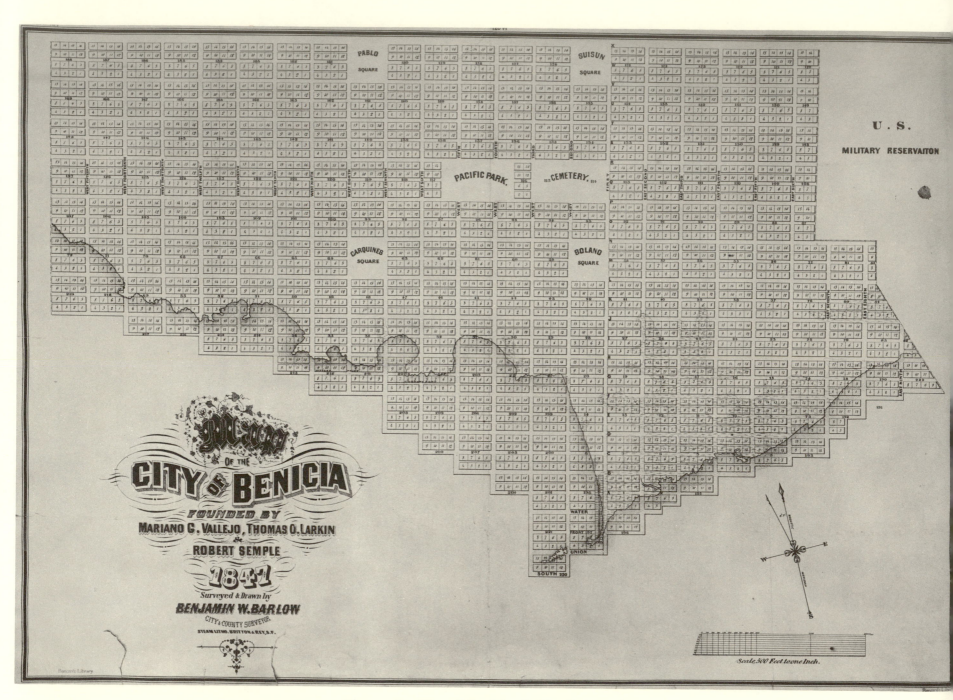

Figure 185. Plan of Benicia, California: ca. 1850

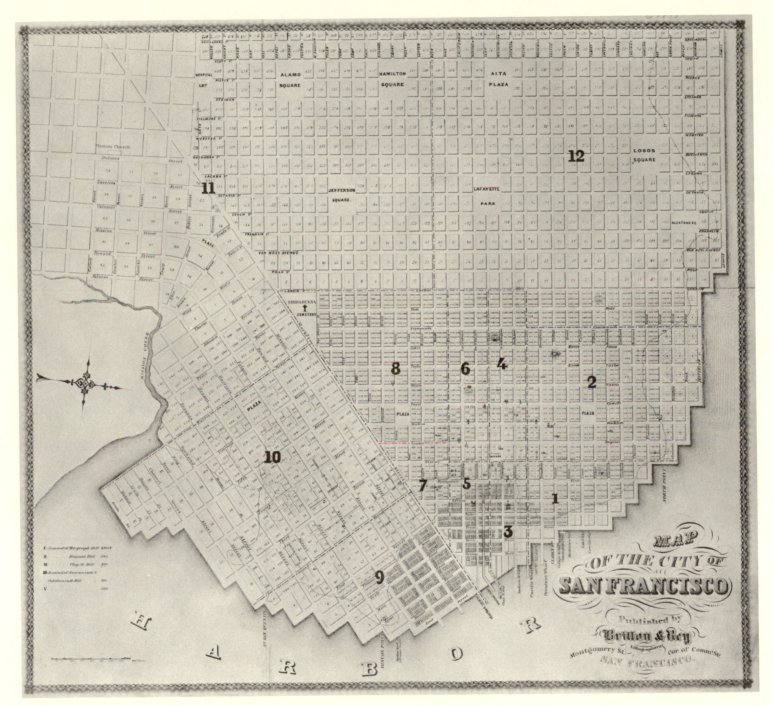

Figure 186. Plan of San Francisco, California: 1856

west of the original settlement. Unlike the other sections, here reasonably adequate provision was made for open spaces. Six large squares each the size of four normal blocks, one smaller square, and a hospital site were set aside. This area did not develop immediately, as can be seen by comparing the preceding map of 1856 with the view of the city in 1868, reproduced in Figure 187. The rugged topography of the city is apparent, and the highest hills in the foreground blocked development in that direction for many years.

Even by 1878, as the view of San Francisco from the bay in Figure 188 indicates, the western addition was only sparsely settled. The older sections of San Francisco, however, had become almost fully developed. The lack of a large park in the growing city had led to the planning of what is now the magnificent Golden Gate Park. The beginning of this important addition to the city can be seen at the top of the view in Figure 188 stretching back from the Pacific Ocean.

While the folly of using a gridiron street system on the hills of San Francisco should have been apparent, the view shows few deviations from that type of plan. Much like the parquet-like appearance of Manhattan before the commissioners' plan of 1811, San Francisco today retains the pattern of interconnected grid street systems laid out from time to time during the past century. The city should be dull and monotonous like virtually all the other large grid cities in the country. San Francisco, however, with its magnificent hills and spectacular views of the ocean and bay, rises above the limitations of its street system.

The "plaza," bounded by Powell, Post, Stockton, and Geary Streets, appears on the early maps to be no different from thousands of other public squares platted in towns across the nation. Yet, as the modern Union Square, it is equalled by only a dozen other such spaces in America in urbanity and charm. The hilly streets provide excitement for both driver and pedestrian; they also offer an excuse to retain at least portions of the once extensive cable car system which furnishes the country's most unusual public transit ride. San Francisco is a glorious exception to the otherwise gloomy record of the grid. On no site less superb could this have happened, nor is this, visually the greatest of America's cities, likely to be duplicated.

Thomas Jefferson and the Checkerboard Plan

The gridiron plan stamped an identical brand of uniformity and mediocrity on American cities from coast to coast. From the early seaboard settlements of New Haven, Philadelphia, Savannah, and St. Augustine to the platting of more recent communities on the Pacific coast, the rectilinear street system predominated. Cities with other types of plans always constituted a distinct minority. We now view most of these gridiron plans with distaste. Their lack of beauty, their functional shortcomings, their overwhelming dullness and monotony, cause us to despair. Although new patterns are beginning to emerge in our burgeoning suburbs, the great grids of the central cities remain virtually unaltered even under the impact of our growing modern redevelopment projects.

The original plans of many gridiron cities avoided some of the later errors committed by those who seized upon this pattern of development as apparently the most effective and certainly the quickest system for laying out towns. New Haven, for example, was planned with one-ninth of the land within its boundaries intended as permanent open space. Savannah developed by the gradual addition of new little neighborhood units, each with its central square. And William Penn's "green country town" of Philadelphia was planned with a civic focal point at its central square and with the provision of four other open spaces for recreational purposes. We do not condemn these and similar early uses of the grid plan, but the hasty use of the rectangular plan by the land speculator and his unimaginative land surveyor, who adopted the street system of the early grid planners without the other features that served to relieve its monotony with points of interest and beauty.

How could those gridiron cities have been planned so as to avoid the characteristics that now make them so unattractive? The keenest mind in America furnished one answer to this question. That hundreds of new cities would be built beyond the Appalachians there could be no doubt, and Thomas Jefferson had devised a system for their planning which, had it been followed on any large scale, would have brought to them the admirable qualities of the best of America's earlier communities.

Thomas Jefferson's interest in city planning during his presi-

CITY OF SAN FRANCISCO

Figure 187. View of San Francisco, California: 1868

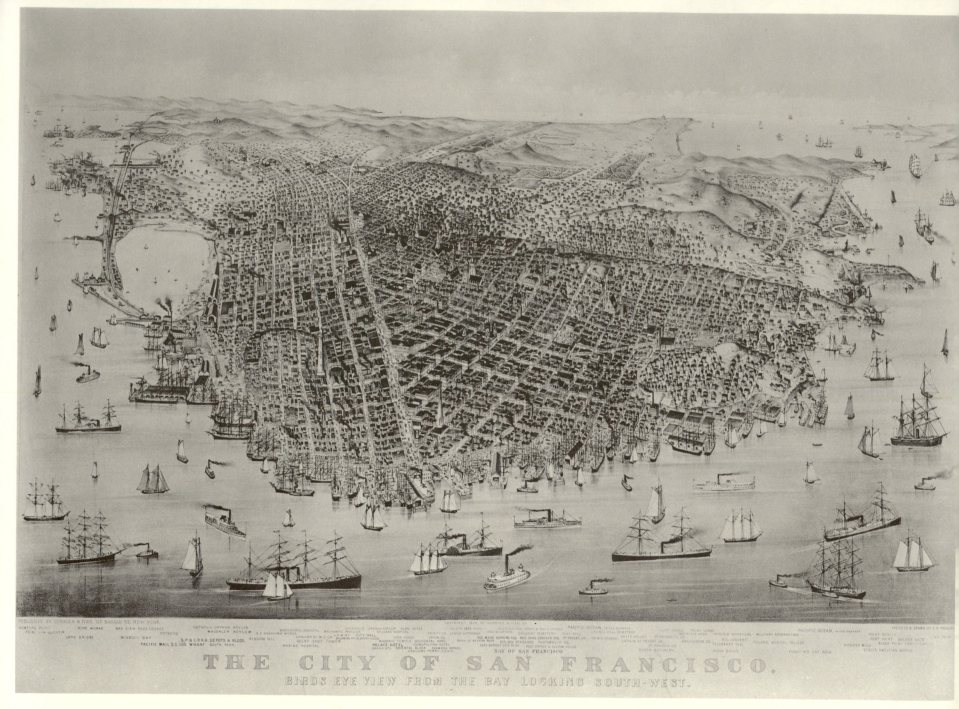

Figure 188. View of San Francisco, California: 1878

dency was no sudden development. We have already seen how deeply he was concerned with the planning of Washington. Even before that time he had been involved in the drafting of the Ordinance of 1785 which established the basic system of land surveys in the Northwest Territory. He knew the details of the first city planned in that area by Rufus Putnam and his Ohio Company associates. He had systematically collected maps of European cities, some of which he passed on to L'Enfant for his studies of Washington. From abroad came letters from such people as Granville Sharp and Sir John Sinclair containing plans for building new towns on novel and improved lands.

The first reference to Jefferson's new planning system is in a letter written to him by William Henry Harrison, the governor of Indiana Territory early in August 1802. From Vincennes, the territorial capital, Harrison wrote:

"When I had the honour to see you in Philadelphia in the Spring of the year 1800 you were pleased to recommend to me a plan for a Town which you supposed would exempt its inhabitants in a great degree from those dreadful pestilences which have become so common in the large Cities of the United States. As the laws of this Territory have given to the Governor the power to designate the seats of Justice for the Counties, and as the choice . . . was fixed upon a spot where there had been no town laid out, I had an opportunity at once of gratifying them—of paying respect to your recommendation, and of conforming to my own inclinations—The proprietor of the land having acceded to my proposals a Town has been laid out with each alternate square to remain vacant forever (excepting one Range of squares upon the River)—and I have taken the liberty to call it Jeffersonville. . . .

"I have done myself the Honour to enclose a plan of the Town of Jeffersonville and one which shows its situation with Regard to Louisville and Clarksville."[18]

The town would be an important one, Harrison assured the President, and, as evidence of its desirable location near the falls of the Ohio, he mentioned that at the first sale of lots several had

sold for as high as two hundred dollars. A proposed canal around the rapids would provide the impetus for commercial and industrial development, and Harrison added that he had "very little doubt of its flourishing." As will be seen, Harrison's optimism was not well founded.

The two plans enclosed with this letter have not survived, but a copy of the original town plat exists in the county records, and it was no doubt a similar drawing that the President received. That unusual plan is reproduced in Figure 189. The chief feature of the plan, as Harrison mentioned, is the alternating pattern of open squares and subdivided blocks. This is the basis of the Jeffersonian grid system. Jefferson explained his reasons for proposing this pattern in a letter to the Comte de Volney, where, after discussing the outbreaks of yellow fever then plaguing American cities, he continues:

"Such a constitution of atmosphere being requisite to originate this disease as is generated only in low, close, and ill-cleansed parts of a town, I have supposed it practicable to prevent its generation by building our cities on a more open plan. Take, for instance, the chequer board for a plan. Let the black squares only be building squares, and the white ones be left open, in turf and trees. Every square of houses will be surrounded by four open squares, and every house will front an open square. The atmosphere of such a town would be like that of the country, insusceptible of the miasmata which produce yellow fever. I have accordingly proposed that the enlargements of the city of New Orleans, which must immediately take place, shall be on this plan. But it is only in case of enlargements to be made, or of cities to be built, that this means of prevention can be employed."[19]

The plan of Jeffersonville departed from the ideas of the President in one respect. This was in the curious use of diagonal streets in the open checkerboard portion of the town. The reason for incorporating the diagonal street pattern in Jefferson's scheme remains a mystery. Perhaps John Gwathmey, who laid out the town, fancied himself something of a L'Enfant and wished to employ the most up-to-date features of civic design, presumably as then

---

[18] Letter from Harrison to Jefferson, August 6, 1802, U.S. Department of State, *The Territorial Papers of the United States*, Washington, 1939, VII, "The Territory of Indiana, 1800-1810," pp. 66-67.

[19] Letter from Jefferson to C. F. C. de Volney, February 8, 1805, in A. A. Liscomb and A. L. Bergh, eds., *The Writings of Thomas Jefferson*, XI, 66-67.

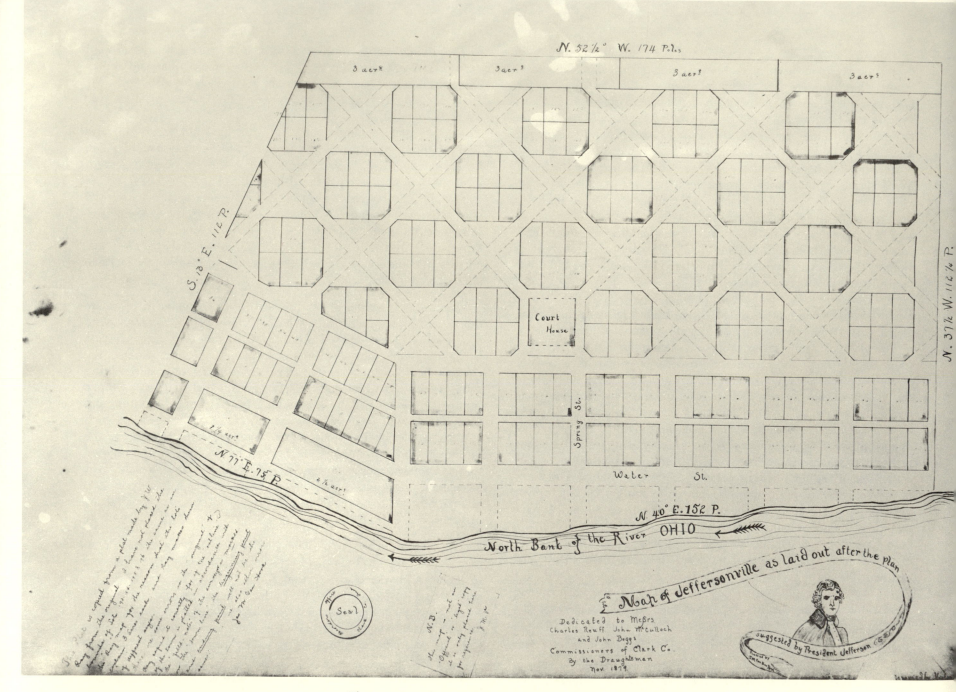

Figure 189. Plan of Jeffersonville, Indiana: 1802

embodied in the radial plan for Washington. Certainly the combination of the two plans was unfortunate. The open squares were each cut into four small triangles, the exterior lots had to be clipped at their corners, and the interior lots had no street frontage at all.

The subsequent correspondence of Jefferson and Harrison fails to explain this peculiar circumstance. When the President acknowledged the governor's letter early in 1803, he commented that he thought "the plan of the town . . . handsome and pleasant," but he added: "I cannot decide from the drawing you sent me, whether you have laid off streets round the squares . . . or only the diagonal streets therein marked. The former was my idea, and is, I imagine, more convenient."[20]

Harrison's reply is more confusing than illuminating, for there is only the following explanation: "The Streets of the town of Jeffersonville are made to pass diagonally through the Squares and not parallel with them as I knew to be your intention—but the proprietor was so parsimonious that he would not suffer it to be laid out in that manner. . . ."[21]

The only logical interpretation of this seems to be that Harrison was unable to persuade the land owners to use the more conventional grid street system in addition to and in combination with the diagonals. Such a combined street layout would have been perhaps even more undesirable, since the open squares would have been reduced still further in size, and the street intersections would have been extremely awkward.

Even with the diagonal streets destroying the effectiveness of the open spaces, the plan of Jeffersonville was a remarkable achievement. Whether it would have had the results that Jefferson hoped cannot be known, but its openness and refreshing break with the traditional grid pattern would have provided an atmosphere of distinctive charm. All this, however, can be only conjecture; within fifteen years of the founding of the town, its plan would be changed, and it would become indistinguishable from hundreds of others.

The proprietors of the town doubtless soon regretted their generosity in allotting the eighteen open squares for public use. At a time when a brisk trade in town lots had developed in the vicinity and when Jeffersonville seemed a likely candidate for the chief metropolis at the Ohio falls, these squares lying idle and unimproved became too tempting to resist. A petition was prepared, proper political contacts established, and representations made to the legislature. In 1816 the necessary legislation was finally secured. In "An Act to Change the Plan of the Town of Jeffersonville" the legislators recited the reasons for permitting modification of the original plan: "Great inconvenience arises from the manner in which that part of the town of Jeffersonville lying north of Market street is laid out partly on account of there being no street in said section of said town, and partly because every other square thereof is left vacant. . . ."[22]

The law provided that all the land north of Market Street should be consolidated, "as if the same had never been laid off into town lots," and then replanned as the trustees of the town might direct. In making the new plan the trustees were to provide lots of the same size as those south of Market Street. Existing owners of lots in the area were to receive lots of equal size and value in the re-platted portion, or to pay or receive in cash any difference in value. Provision was made for arbitration if dissatisfaction arose from the distribution of land. All lots remaining after the exchange were to be sold at auction, with the proceeds to be used for town purposes. As an early example, possibly the first, of compulsory land pooling for urban redevelopment purposes this law is of more than passing interest. Its effects on the Jeffersonian plan, however, were disastrous.

The law received the governor's approval on January 3, 1817. By July 1 the new plan, shown in Figure 190, had been surveyed and recorded. With the exception of the court house square in the old plan, which with its surrounding streets became the public square, all traces of the original scheme were obliterated. One new

[20] Letter from Jefferson to Harrison, February 27, 1803, U.S. Department of State, *Territorial Papers*, 89. The same letter contains some additional observations about his plan: "I do believe it to be the best means of preserving the cities of America from the scourge of the Yellow fever which being peculiar to our country must be derived from some peculiarity in it. That peculiarity I take to be our cloudless skies. In Europe where the sun does not shine more than half the number of days in the year which it does in America, they can build their towns in a solid block with impunity. But here a constant sun produces too great an accumulation of heat to admit that. Ventilation is indispensably necessary. Experience has taught us that in the open air of the country the yellow fever is not only not generated, but ceases to be infectious."

[21] Letter from Harrison to Jefferson, October 29, 1803, *ibid.*, 147.

[22] Laws of the State of Indiana, 1816, Chap. LIV.

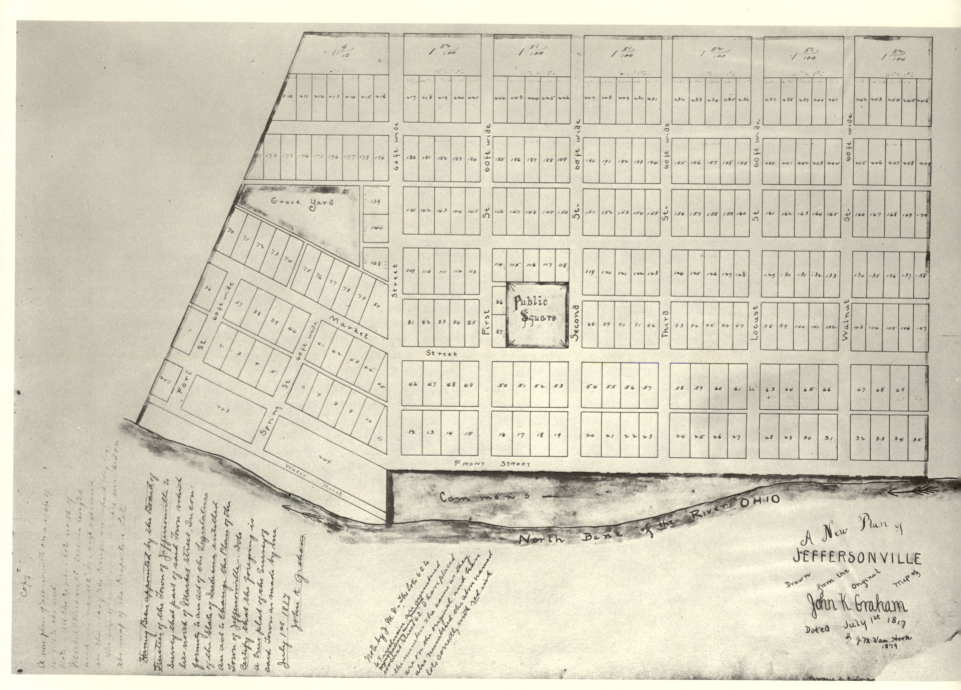

Figure 190. Plan of Jeffersonville, Indiana: 1817

feature was added—the designation of the land lying between Front Street and the Ohio River as a town common—but the unique aspects of the Jefferson plan had vanished.

Jeffersonville's ambition to become the leading city of the area was not realized. The canal around the rapids was built on the Louisville side of the river, and Jeffersonville today has neither the prosperity it desired nor the unique plan it did not appreciate.

Jeffersonville was not the only city for which the Jeffersonian checkerboard plan was considered or used. Jefferson had advocated the use of his system in the extensions of New Orleans, and had communicated this to Governor Claiborne of Orleans Territory. In August 1804, the governor replied to the President:

"It is impossible to dwell for one moment on the plan you propose, without receiving an Impression of the preference to which it is entitled as well on the score of elegance and comfort as of health. I should esteem it a great happiness should I be yet enabled to introduce such a plan into the parts of this City, that yet remain to be built. As this City promises to have a rapid increase (& the havoc of Disease is at present so evident) I must confess, I entertain sanguine hopes of introducing this favourite Scheme, and with that view shall spare no pains to impress its excellencies on the minds of those Citizens, whose influence will be serviceable."[23]

Possibly the governor's powers of persuasion proved inadequate. At least there is no record that the alternate open square pattern was employed in the expansion of New Orleans. The detailed map of the city in 1815 reproduced in Figure 50 shows no trace of the Jefferson plan, although there is a fairly generous distribution of open squares. The New Orleans extension plan, however, plainly derived from other sources.

Yet Governor Claiborne's interest in the Jeffersonian checkerboard was to result in the use of this pattern in the planning of another city. In 1821 the General Assembly of the newly created state of Mississippi appointed three commissioners to select a site for a permanent capital near the center of the state. Two of the commissioners, Colonel Thomas Hinds and Dr. William Lattimore, investigated a number of possible locations. They finally selected a spot on the western bank of the Pearl River where a high bluff provided a commanding location. One of their major considerations was that the site prove healthy, a motive no doubt emphasized by Dr. Lattimore. In their report to the legislature, submitted in November, they took up this question after describing the other desirable features that had led them to recommend the site:

"The General Assembly will appreciate the peculiar interest which their Commissioners evince, and indulge the latitude which they take, in their remarks under this head. Cherishing this persuasion, and availing themselves of the protection of a great name, they venture further to suggest, that the present occasion would be a favorable one for the experiment of a town upon the Checkerboard plan, as suggested by President Jefferson, in a letter to Governor Claiborne, about seventeen years ago. Although there would not be the same necessity for such a plan, in a small interior town, as in a populous maritime city, yet it might be pursued with more propriety in the former, as it respects the value and extent of the ground."[24]

In this passage there is perhaps a clue to the reason why the plan was not adopted in New Orleans. It also suggests that Dr. Lattimore, with his natural interest in public health, was the person who was aware of Jefferson's plan and who suggested its adoption for the capital of the new state.

The report then continued with the following additional observations on the merits of the plan:

"And even in a small town (to say nothing of the novelty) there would be a comfort, convenience and greater security against fire, as well as a fairer promise of health, all combined, by having every other square unoccupied by anything except the native trees of the forest, or artificial groves."[25]

And, obviously not aware of the previous experiment at Jeffersonville, the commissioners concluded:

"As yet, probably, this plan has not been adopted in any coun-

[23] Letter from Claiborne to Jefferson, August 30, 1804, U.S. Department of State, *The Territorial Papers*, 1940, IX, "The Territory of Orleans, 1803-1812," p. 287.

[24] Report of the Commissioners appointed by the Legislature, for Locating and Establishing a Permanent Site, for the Seat of Government of the State of Mississippi, Dunbar Rowland, *History of Mississippi*, Chicago, 1925, I, 516-22.
[25] *ibid.*

try; and if first adopted in this, our State would have the merit of being foremost in an improvement recommended by an eminent American philosopher, an illustrious benefactor of his country, and a friend to mankind."[26]

Eight days later the legislature authorized Hinds, Lattimore, and Peter Van Dorn to establish the exact boundaries of the capital site and to lay out the town, which was to be named in honor of General Andrew Jackson. The original plat of Jackson is reproduced in Figure 191 and shows the alternating open square pattern exactly as Jefferson had originally proposed. As suggested by the commissioners, the land between the town and the river was reserved as a common. Additional features which Jefferson surely would have approved were the sites for the capitol building, a college, and the courthouse. The three sites were connected by the gentle curve of Crescent Street bordering the common. College, Capitol, and Court Streets leading to these important sites were platted 100 feet wide. By varying street widths, reserving large sites for important buildings, and providing a connecting street to link these locations, the planners of Jackson improved markedly on the layout of Jeffersonville.

But again, as in the Indiana town, the open squares offered too great a temptation as building sites, and most of them were diverted from their original purpose of providing light, air, and beauty. The official map of Jackson in 1875 reveals that in that year the city hall and the gas works occupied one of the original open squares. On another was located the penitentiary. Only one of the others had not been divided into lots. The effect of the original pattern had been totally and irretrievably lost.

Open Squares in the Missouri Ozarks

Perhaps the account of the Jeffersonian checkerboard should end at this point, since so far as is known it inspired no other city plan. Yet at least one town was planned with a system of alternating open squares. Whether its promoters consciously followed the Jefferson model, merely imitated with some variations the earlier

plans of Jeffersonville or Jackson, or arrived at the pattern independently can be only a matter of conjecture. Considering all the circumstances it seems most probable that this plan evolved simply as an abstract pattern designed to startle the beholder and attract his attention to the accompanying proposals for speculation in a combined railroad, mining, and town lot booming enterprise.

The plan was for a town to be known as Missouri City, 90 miles south of St. Louis and 40 miles west of the Mississippi River in what is now St. François County. The map circulated in 1836 to arouse public interest in the scheme appears in Figure 192. Certainly no more bizarre town plan was ever devised, and it is something of a minor tragedy for the connoisseurs of civic eccentricities that the panic of 1837 forced its promoters to abandon it.

The Messrs. Van Doren and Pease, joint proprietors, intended nothing less than the construction of a network of rail lines, the exploitation of the mineral resources of Iron Mountain by a mining and smelting company of their creation, the establishment of two towns, the other being the manufacturing and river port community of Iron Mountain City on the Mississippi, and the founding of a great university. This latter project explains the use of land proposed for the central ranges of blocks shown in the city plan. Among the benefits of living in Missouri City was to be the privilege of attending the university without payment of tuition. This was to be made possible by the annual contribution to the university endowment of $75,000 from the profits of the mining operations. In the remaining blocks, except for those in the commercial sections along the railroad, the plan follows the Jeffersonian pattern.[27]

This paper city scheme exhibits all the characteristics of a typical nineteenth-century American town jobbing promotion. While the proposed allocation of land for open space and institutional purposes was unusually generous, the similarity of its plan to the ideal system put forward by Thomas Jefferson was more than likely mere coincidence. In its other aspects—the carefully

[26] *ibid.*

[27] Adequate information on the Missouri City scheme is lacking. The only material I have been able to find, aside from the two towns plans is an article by Henry C. Thompson which appeared in the Farmington, Missouri *News* for December 16, 1938. This is reprinted in the *Missouri Historical Review*, XXXIII (1939), 466-68.

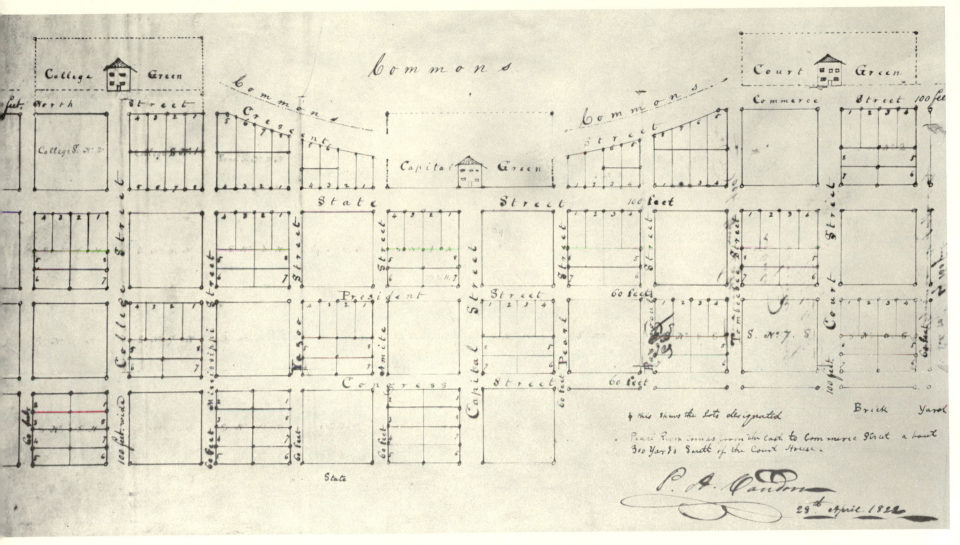

Figure 191. Plan of Jackson, Mississippi: 1822

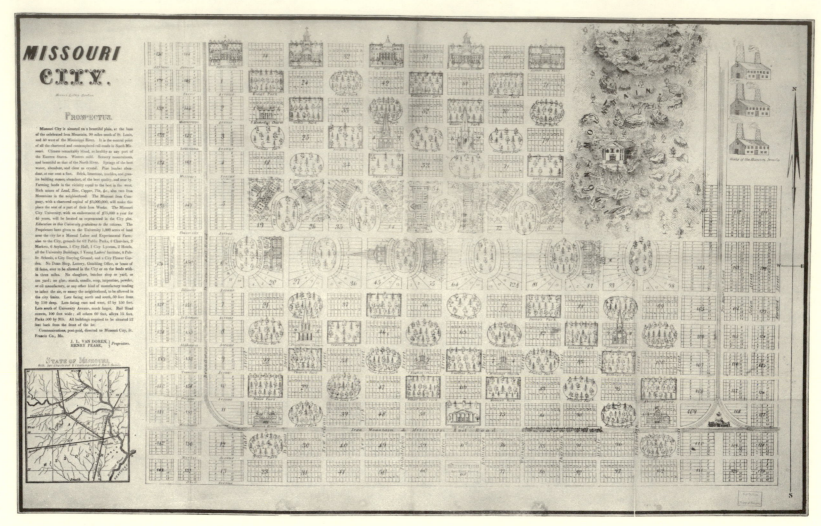

Figure 192. Plan of Missouri City, Missouri: 1836

delineated asylums for lunatics, orphans, the deaf and the blind; the city hall; the "Young Ladies' Institute"; and the several magnificent churches—the plan displays that curious mixture of appeals to realism with the patently impossible that marked so many of these attempts to separate the gullible frontiersman from his gold.

Jefferson's vision of planned cities that incorporated his system of open squares was never realized. In the frenzy for trading in town sites that characterized so much of the nineteenth century the standardized grid became the playing board of the clever and the unscrupulous land speculator. Always he seemed one move ahead of his unknowing and unwary opponent. It is one of the tragedies of America's urban history that the game was not played out under proper rules on the checkerboard of Thomas Jefferson.

CHAPTER 12

Cemeteries, Parks and Suburbs: Picturesque Planning in the Romantic Style

L'ENFANT'S plan for Washington established in America a brief vogue for the grand plan on an heroic scale. Buffalo, Detroit, Indianapolis, Madison, and two dozen and more lesser known cities were laid out under this influence. In architecture, too, it was the period of imitation Greek and Roman buildings and building groups. Jefferson's designs for the Virginia capital at Richmond and for the University of Virginia at Charlottesville were examples of the formal, classical revival mode that dominated the country during the early years of the eighteenth century. Little Greek temples dotted the countryside, occupied by the wealthy on large country estates or by the farmer on land used for agriculture. Town houses, banks, offices, and even industrial or warehouse structures used classical details. The fashion spread westward from the centers of taste in Boston, New York, and Philadelphia, and duplicates or close imitations of eastern buildings sprang up in Ohio, Kentucky, Illinois, and Michigan as the first crude frontier cabins gave way to more elegant houses in the Graecian manner.

As early as the 1830's, however, newer design concepts gained favor. This resulted at first in experimentation within the prescribed classical motifs, then a general questioning of the applicability of classical design to American life, and finally, its virtual abandonment. Supplanting the rigid formal design concepts, new theories based on informality, naturalism, romanticism, and the picturesque became accepted. In architecture the Gothic, English cottage, Swiss chalet, and other rustic styles predominated. In land planning, the new concepts took the form of English garden layouts with curving streets or paths, informal or picturesque landscape planting, rustic gates and out-buildings, irregular pools, quaint bridges, grottos, bowers, and other devices popularized by Repton, Brown, Louden, and others in England.

American designers, in fact, simply adopted a body of design principles developed during the previous century in England and, to a lesser extent, elsewhere in Europe. That this should occur during a period of intense nationalism and local pride demonstrates the continuing influence of European tradition and culture in the United States.

Romantic theories were not immediately applied to the layout of towns. Curiously, the first application of these new design concepts, except in the landscaping of private estates, was apparently in the layout of cemeteries. Cemetery design, in turn, influenced both the movement for public parks and the designs of the parks themselves. And, finally, the romantic concept found favor with the promoters of suburban communities.

Cemeteries for the Living

In 1849, writing in *The Horticulturist*, the influential Andrew Jackson Downing observed:

"One of the most remarkable illustrations of the popular taste, in this country, is to be found in the rise and progress of our rural cemeteries.

"Twenty years ago, nothing better than a common grave-yard, filled with high grass, and a chance sprinkling of weeds and thistles, was to be found in the Union. If there were one or two exceptions . . . they existed only to prove the rule more completely. . . .

"At the present moment, there is scarcely a city of note in the whole country that has not its rural cemetery. The three leading cities of the north, New-York, Philadelphia, Boston, have, each of them, besides their great cemeteries,—Greenwood, Laurel Hill, Mount Auburn,—many others of less note; but any of which would have astonished and delighted their inhabitants twenty years ago."[1]

[1] A. J. Downing, "Public Cemeteries and Public Gardens," *The Horticulturist* (July 1849), collected with other essays in A. J. Downing, *Rural Essays*, New York, 1853, pp. 154-55.

Mount Auburn, in Cambridge, Massachusetts, was the first of these "rural cemeteries." Dr. Jacob Bigelow of Boston conceived the idea in 1825, but not until five years later was a site acquired. Meanwhile the Massachusetts Horticultural Society had been established in 1829 and had joined in the sponsorship of the enterprise, with the understanding that an experimental garden would also be developed in the site. This combined plan came to nothing, but it indicates the early intention of laying out a burial ground different in concept from the usual crowded church yard type then common in cities.

The enterprise, as ultimately planned, was evidently well financed, and little expense was spared in the landscaping and embellishment of the grounds. The results, in the eyes of one observer, fell little short of paradise:

"The avenues are winding in their course and exceedingly beautiful in their gentle circuits, adapted picturesquely to the inequalities of the surface of the ground, and producing charming landscape effects from this natural arrangement, such as could never be had from straightness or regularity. Various small lakes, or ponds of different size and shape, embellish the grounds; and some of these have been so cleansed, deepened, and banked, as to present a pleasant feature in this widespread extent of forest loveliness—this ground of hallowed purpose. The gates of the enclosure are opened at sunrise and closed at sunset, and thither crowds go up to meditate, and to wander in a field of peace; to twine the votive garland around the simple headstone, or to sow the seed of floral life over the new-made grave—fit emblems of our own growth, decay, and death."[2]

The plan of Mount Auburn in 1831 is reproduced in Figure 193. Here can be seen all the physical characteristics of the romantic movement: winding drives, naturalistic pools, secluded groves, and other typical landscape features. Mount Auburn established the pattern for similar developments. Laurel Hill Cemetery in Philadelphia was planned in 1836. Greenwood Cemetery in New York opened in 1838. The designers of both employed the romantic landscape devices used so effectively at Mount Auburn. The view of Greenwood Cemetery which appears in Figure 194 reveals the picturesque effect.

[2] Cornelia W. Walter, *Mount Auburn*, New York, 1847, p. 14.

The popularity of these rural cemeteries for uses other than as burial places must have astounded and perhaps horrified their sponsors. On fine spring or summer days visitors by the hundreds flocked to their park-like enclosures. True, some may have gone "to twine the votive garland," but the plain fact was that most of the visitors were simply out for a good time. Downing reported that between April and December, 1848, nearly 30,000 persons visited Laurel Hill Cemetery at Philadelphia. He commented that from his own observations twice as many persons visited Greenwood and at least as many came to Mount Auburn.

Handsome books with engraved plans and views of these cemetery-parks proved popular and brought visitors from distant communities to inspect in person the marvels of gardener and sculptor. So attractive did the cemeteries become as sight-seeing spots that guide books appeared containing suggested routes to follow and descriptions of outstanding monuments. These guide books usually contained the rules for visitors, and one of the Mount Auburn guides included prohibitions against carrying refreshments into the grounds or discharging firearms.[3] It can thus be safely inferred that at some earlier time Mount Auburn served as a picnic and shooting ground for the especially irreverent.

By the 1870's practically every town of any size could boast of its rural cemetery laid out on the lines of Mount Auburn, Greenwood, or Laurel Hill. While many of these show at least some elementary skill and understanding of the design elements involved, others were extremely clumsy. The Maple Grove Cemetery in Mechanicsburg, Ohio, shown in Figure 195 demonstrates what an unskilled designer could do to romantic planning motifs. The name of the town is perhaps symbolic. In looking through the city maps appearing in the county atlases of the midwest that were published in such quantity during the post-Civil War years, one is struck by the contrast in land layout between the cities themselves and the cemeteries at their edges. City streets stretched grid-like into the countryside catching the landscape in a geometric web. But here and there, bounded by four lines of the grid, appear the fanciful, flowing lines of a cemetery's drives and lanes.

One wonders why it did not occur to some daring mind that the picturesque curving drives of the local cemetery might serve as a

[3] Nathaniel Dearborn, *Dearborn's Guide Through Mount Auburn*, Boston, 1850, p. 4.

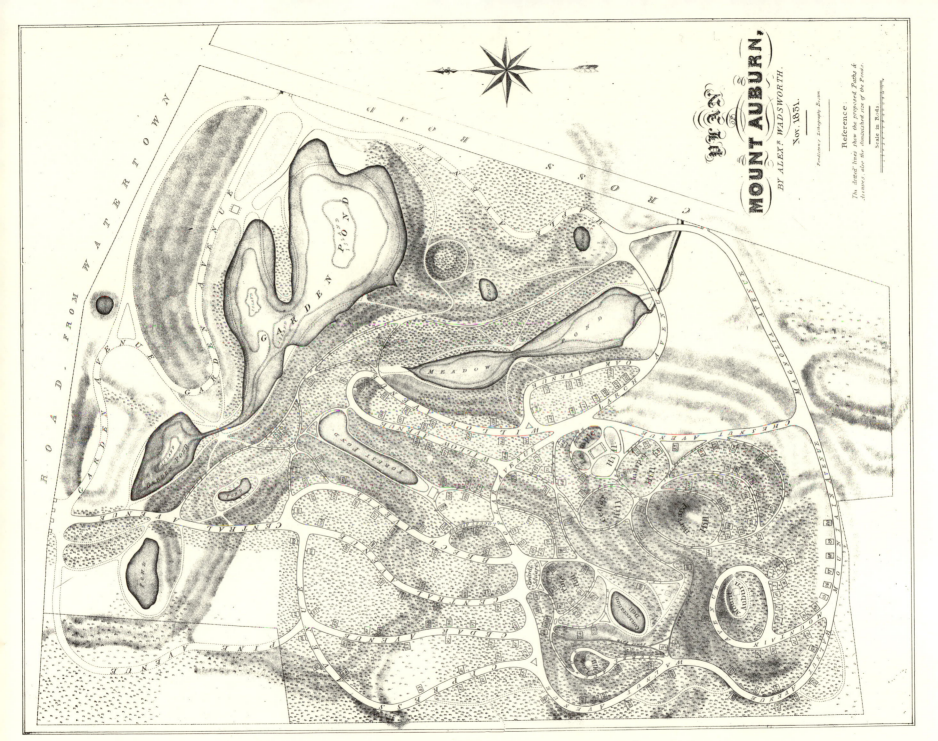

Figure 193. Plan of Mount Auburn Cemetery in Cambridge, Massachusetts: 1831

BIRDS EYE VIEW
OF
GREENWOOD CEMETERY.
NEAR NEW-YORK.

Figure 194. View of Greenwood Cemetery, New York City: 1852

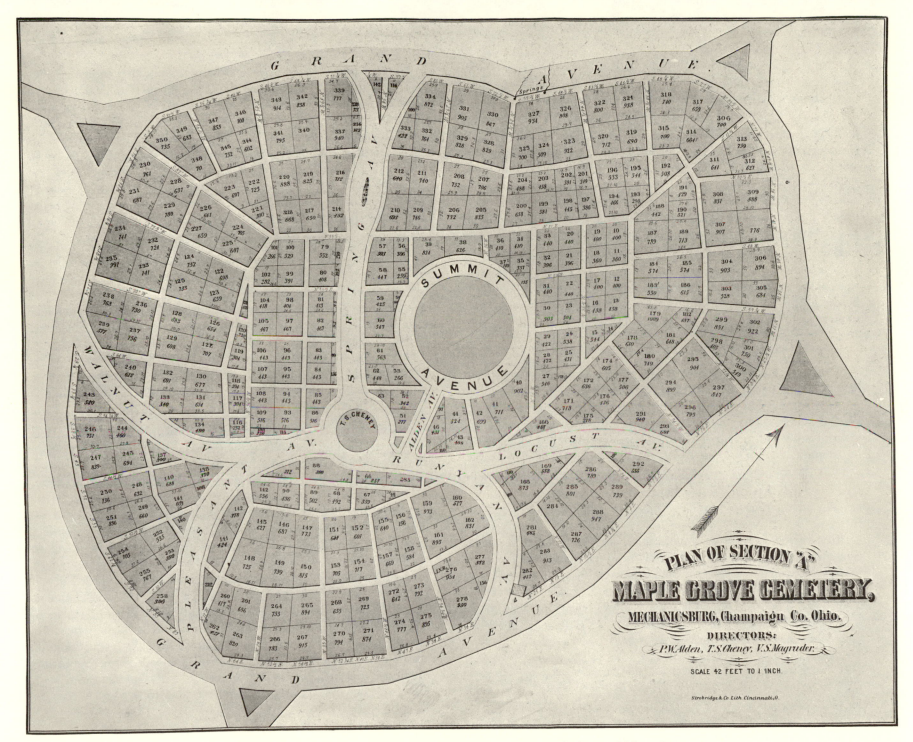

Figure 195. Plan of Maple Grove Cemetery, Mechanicsburg, Ohio: 1874

pattern for a successful residential subdivision. A writer, in stating the principles of good cemetery planning, did remark on one aspect of the similarity between cemetery and city layout:

"Avenues should have an easy grade, graceful curves, and be so located as to give to each section a natural outline. In regard to the necessity of every burial lot fronting on an avenue, I will merely state that seclusion is more in unison with the feelings of many friends of the dead than publicity, glare, and notoriety. While persons engaged in the ordinary business of life might prefer front or corner lots, it may be questioned whether a cultivated and refined taste would prefer a more secluded spot for a final repose."[4]

But while romantic planning was accepted for cemetery design with astonishing rapidity, the use of the same landscape principles for suburban residential districts lagged some twenty-five years behind. These concepts of large-scale planning were to be used next in a different aspect of the urban scene.

Making Livable the Cities for the Dead

A major influence of cemetery planning was on the development of municipal parks in America. Downing, in the essay already quoted, pointed out that "in the absence of great public gardens" rural cemetery design had accomplished a great deal in acquainting visitors with the principles of landscape architecture and in raising popular taste. He then argued:

"But does not this general interest, manifested in these cemeteries, prove that public gardens, established in a liberal and suitable manner, near our large cities, would be equally successful? . . .

"It is only necessary for one of the three cities which first opened cemeteries, to set the example, and the thing once fairly seen, it becomes universal. The true policy of republics, is to foster the taste for great public libraries, sculpture and picture galleries, parks, and gardens, which *all* may enjoy, since our institutions wisely forbid the growth of private fortunes sufficient to achieve these desirable results in any other way."[5]

[4] Robert Clarke & Co., *Spring Grove Cemetery*, Cincinnati, 1869, p. 9. This description of the rural cemetery in Cincinnati also contains brief comments on the most famous cemeteries in other American cities, pp. 129-33.

[5] Downing, *Rural Essays*, 156, 159.

In other essays in *The Horticulturist*, particularly in one appearing in October 1848, entitled "A Talk About Public Parks and Gardens," Downing pointed out the general lack of parks in American cities. Contrasting London, Paris, Frankfort, and other European cities having large parks and promenades with American cities then almost devoid of such facilities, Downing advanced the revolutionary idea that city parks be maintained at the expense of taxpayers. Land for such parks, he believed, could be obtained through the generosity of wealthy men. In concluding, he stated his belief that public parks, once started, would rival cemeteries in popularity:

"Get some country town of the first class to set the example by making a public park or garden of this kind. Let our people once see for themselves the influence for good which it would effect, no less than the healthful enjoyment it will afford, and I feel confident that the taste for public pleasure-grounds, in the United States, will spread as rapidly as that for cemeteries has done. . . . In short, I am in earnest about the matter, and must therefore talk, write, preach, do all I can about it, and beg the assistance of all those who have public influence, till some good experiment of the kind is fairly tried in this country."[6]

If the rural cemeteries admired by Downing were of greatest use to the living, then the growing industrial cities of America were fit only for the dead or the dying. It is difficult to imagine now the crowding and congestion prevailing in the great cities. These conditions were particularly acute in the cities along the Atlantic coast. The steady flow of immigrants from Europe during the early part of the century became a flood when political unrest in many European countries during the 1840's added to the forces stimulating emigration. While many immigrants moved westward to farms and smaller towns, most of them settled in the seaboard cities. Steady and rapid extension of urban development into the countryside and an upward growth in taller and taller tenements and office buildings resulted. Almost without exception this urban sprawl took place unaccompanied by any acquisition of open spaces for public use. Such open land in squares appearing in the original plan for these cities, like the central square in New Haven or the five squares in Penn's Philadelphia, was forced to

[6] *ibid.*, 146.

serve a population far greater than anticipated by the early planners of these communities. Only a rare city like Savannah, and there only until the 1850's, provided new parks and squares on a scale sufficient to meet the needs of an expanding population.

In 1844 William Cullen Bryant, writing in the *New York Evening Post*, began the campaign for additional park space in New York City. Bryant proposed the acquisition of a site between Sixty-eighth and Seventy-seventh Streets and bounded east and west by Third Avenue and the East River. The following year Bryant, then writing from England, renewed his plea, saying,

"The population of your city, increasing with such prodigious rapidity; your sultry summers, and the corrupt atmosphere generated in hot and crowded streets, make it a cause of regret that in laying out New York, no preparation was made, while it was yet practicable, for a range of parks and public gardens. . . . There are yet unoccupied lands on the island which might, I suppose, be procured for the purpose, and which, on account of their rocky and uneven surfaces, might be laid out into surpassingly beautiful pleasure-grounds; but while we are discussing the subject the advancing population of the city is sweeping over them and covering them from our reach."[7]

Bryant found many supporters, including Washington Irving and, of course, Downing. He, too, came away from England more convinced than ever of the need for public urban parks in his own country. Writing in *The Horticulturist* in 1850, he complained

"I will merely say . . . that every American who visits London, whether for the first or the fiftieth time, feels mortified that no city in the United States has a public park—here so justly considered both the highest luxury and necessity in a great city. What are called parks in New York, are not even apologies for the thing; they are only squares or paddocks."[8]

By 1851 the subject of a large park for New York City had become a major political issue. The newly elected Mayor Kingsland sent a message to the Common Council that year recommending

that the park question be studied, and a council committee subsequently issued a favorable report suggesting the site proposed by Bryant. The state legislature authorized the city to acquire land for such a purpose, and the project appeared to have started. Opposition developed almost immediately, however, some of it directed against the specific site and some at the very idea of the park itself. Downing, while delighted at the prospect of seeing his ideas accepted, criticized the 160-acre site as being much too small, and advocated that at least 500 acres be acquired. The advocates of a more central location and of a larger site prevailed, and the legislature was asked to grant authority for the purchase of what is now Central Park. For a time it appeared that both sites might be acquired, but the opposition was too strong, and the splendid riverside location was rejected. On November 17, 1853, with the appointment of the Commissioners of Estimate and Assessment to appraise and acquire the land, work began on Central Park.

An Oasis in the Urban Desert

For three years the Commissioners of Estimate and Assessment acquired land for the project. In 1856 this phase had been accomplished, and a Board of Commissioners was appointed to prepare plans and carry out construction. A consulting board of prominent citizens to advise the commissioners was created, with Washington Irving as its first president. As to staff, the commissioners appointed Egbert Viele as chief engineer. Viele, at his own expense and apparently in reliance on this appointment, had been preparing a topographic survey of the site and had also prepared a general plan for its development. Viele's survey and plan appeared in the first report of the commissioners and is shown in Figure 196. The note on the plan, "Adopted by the Commissioners, June 3rd 1856," was apparently intended to signify that Viele's scheme would be used to guide any preliminary construction. Later this plan was used by Viele in his successful lawsuit claiming payment from the commissioners in which he also maintained that his plan had been copied by other designers.[9]

For superintendent the commissioners appointed young Frederick Law Olmsted, then 34 years old. As a boy Olmsted had exhibited an interest in nature and had traveled widely with his family. Be-

[7] As quoted in Frederick Law Olmsted, Jr., and Theodora Kimball, *Frederick Law Olmsted*, New York, 1928, II, 23. Much of the basic source material relating to the planning and early development of Central Park is reprinted in this volume.

[8] *ibid.*, 23-24.

[9] For an account of this suit and excerpts from the testimony see Olmsted and Kimball, *ibid.*, Appendix III.

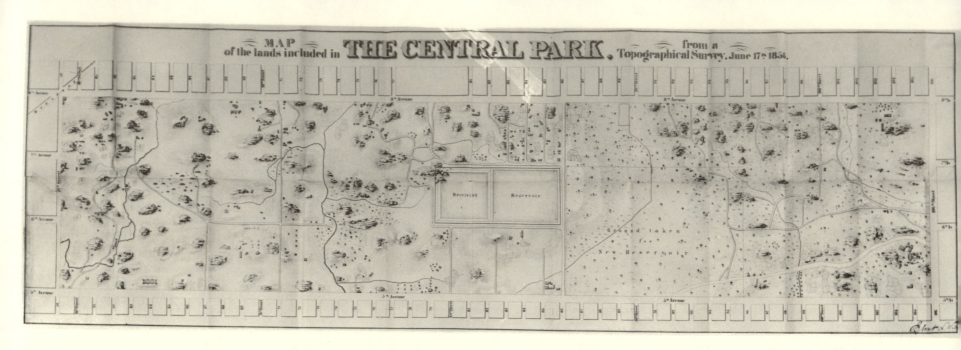

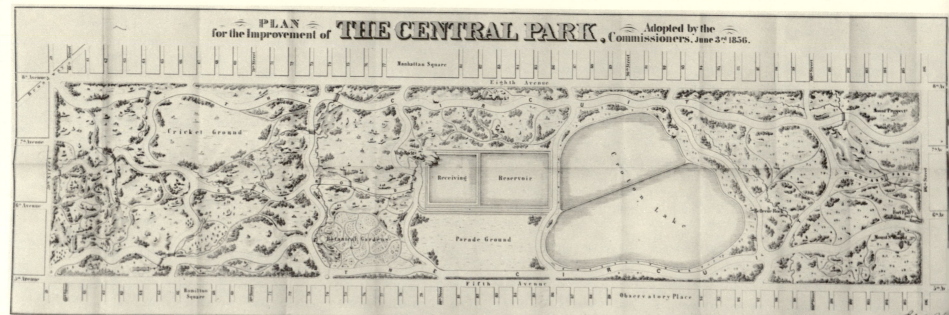

Figure 196. Viele's Survey and Plan for Central Park, New York City: 1856

cause of weak eyesight his college education was brief, and he began farming on Staten Island. Here he operated a nursery and wrote on farming and horticulture for several magazines. In 1850 he visited England, where he was impressed with the English parks and gardens, and two years later he published his *Walks and Talks of An American Farmer in England*. Later he published several works on his travels in the southern and western states. If his qualifications for the position of superintendent were not readily apparent at the time of his appointment, his true genius soon became evident.

On the day of Olmsted's appointment—September 11, 1857—the commissioners decided to open the design of the park to a competition. Two thousand dollars was offered to the winner, with the next three places also to receive premiums. This action of the commissioners, of course, amounted to a rejection of the Viele plan. Since Viele was known to be one of the competitors and was Olmsted's superior, Olmsted felt that he should not enter the competition. Calvert Vaux, an English architect who had come to America to form a partnership with Downing and who had practiced by himself after Downing's death in 1852, persuaded Olmsted to join him in preparing a design.

Thirty-five drawings were submitted to the commissioners, including the one by Olmsted and Vaux signed "Greensward." In April 1858 the commissioners reached their decision, with seven of the eleven commissioners voting in favor of the Olmsted and Vaux plan. The following month Olmsted was appointed architect-in-chief, a new office combining the duties of superintendent and engineer, and completion of the park on the new plan was authorized.

In any era and under any circumstances the Olmsted and Vaux plan for Central Park would have been remarkable. It must be regarded as all the more outstanding because of the lack of American precedents on which its authors could rely. The opportunity was magnificent; their response was equally so. Coming as it did for the first large public park in America, the design of Central Park excited intense interest and exerted widespread influence.

Figure 197 shows the plan of Central Park in 1871, when most of the original proposals had been carried out. The plan includes the extension of the park to the north beyond its original boundary at 106th Street. Along with the drawings illustrating their proposals, Olmsted and Vaux submitted a comprehensive statement describing and analyzing its design principles and details.

They first of all pointed out that the site divided itself into two nearly equal portions because of topography and the location of the reservoir. The upper or northern half exhibited "bold and sweeping" horizon lines, and the designers recommended as little change in this rugged character as possible. The lower portion was much different, with varied topography ranging from flat meadow to rock cliffs. Because of these variations and the location nearer to the built-up portion of the city, this section of the park received the greatest attention. Here the designers proposed the widest range of recreation facilities.

Instructions to competitors required that designs include four transverse roads. For this feature Olmsted and Vaux demonstrated their ability to solve complex problems with skill and imagination. Their solution was as bold as it was practical. Rejecting crossings of the park at grade because of the disruption to crosstown traffic and the adverse effects on the unity of the park design, they proposed that the transverse roads ". . . be sunk so far below the general surface that the park drives may, at every necessary point of intersection, be carried entirely over it, without any obvious elevation or divergence from their most attractive routes. The banks on each side will be walled up to the height of about seven feet . . . and a little judicious planting on the tops or slopes of the banks above these walls will, in most cases, entirely conceal both the roads and the vehicles moving in them, from the view of those walking or driving in the park."[10]

The location of the four chief crossroads divided the park into five separate but related areas. Supplementing the depressed roadways were three additional crossings at grade which could be used by private carriages, although not by commercial traffic. Inside the park ran a great winding loop road which could be entered at convenient points along the boundary. Complete separation of various kinds of traffic was achieved by a system of bridges and archways so that pedestrians, horseback riders, and carriages would each be provided with paths and drives at different levels. These features

[10] Olmsted and Vaux, "Description of a Plan for the Improvement of the Central Park, 'Greensward,' 1858." The complete text of this explanation as reprinted in 1868 may be found in Olmsted and Kimball, *ibid.*, 214-232.

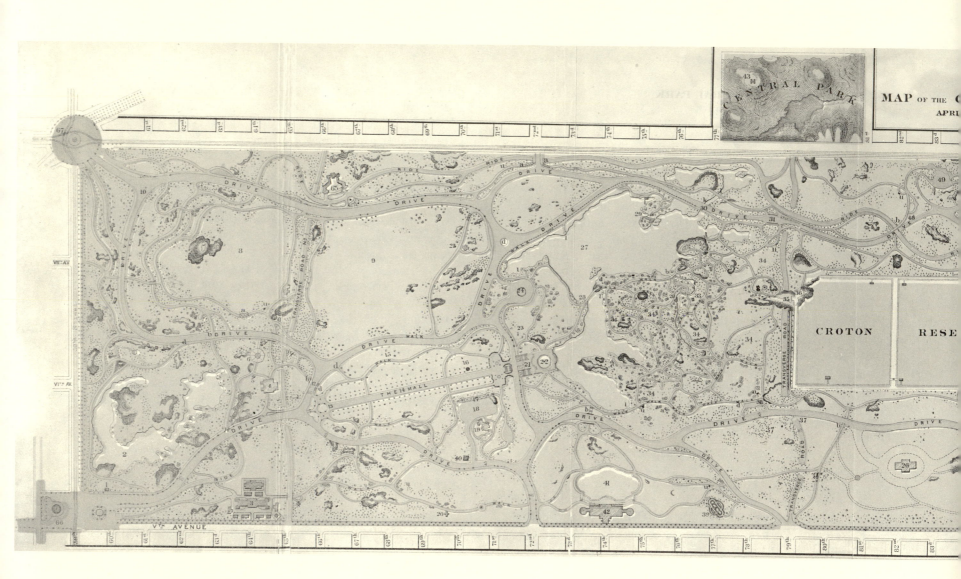

CROTON   RESE

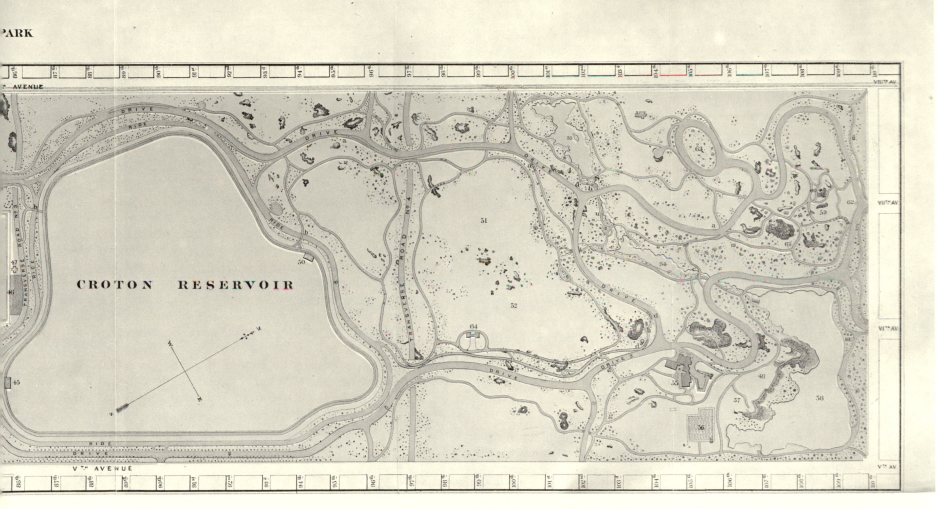

Figure 197. Plan of Central Park in New York City: 1871

can be seen in Figure 198, a view of Central Park from the south in 1863.

The main entrance was designed at the corner of Fifty-ninth Street, the southern boundary, and Fifth Avenue, which ran along the eastern edge of the park. From here the drive led diagonally toward the interior to a point where prominent topographical features served to attract attention still further. As Olmsted and Vaux then explain, "We therefore accept this line of view as affording an all-sufficient motive to our further procedure. Although averse on general principles to a symmetrical arrangement of trees, we consider it an essential feature of a metropolitan park that it should contain a grand promenade, level, spacious, and thoroughly shaded."[11]

This single formal element was designed as a mall a quarter of a mile in length flanked on each side by double rows of elms. At the terminus of the mall, very nearly in the center of the lower park, a terrace and esplanade looking out on an irregular pond was proposed by the designers. North of the pond on a rocky and irregular slope Olmsted and Vaux suggested an intricate pattern of paths amidst a generally wild background of plant materials. From the lower end of this area, now called The Ramble, the terrace and mall could be seen. Figure 199 shows the splendid scene envisaged by the planners in their design and as it eventually appeared.

Large open spaces to the west of the mall were intended for a parade ground, which was a requirement of the competition rules, and a cricket field. In the southeastern corner of the park, where the ground was naturally low and marshy, a lake was proposed. There were many other features, including a music hall, flower garden, police station, arboretum, towers, and fountains. Most of these can be identified on the plan and the two views reproduced in Figures 197, 198, and 199.

While one might object to certain of the details or the wisdom of introducing the formal mall into an essentially naturalistic composition, taken as a whole the park design was a magnificent contribution to urban planning and landscape design. More than that, it has become the great humanizing element in an inhuman megalopolis; to conceive of New York without the park is to imagine the

intolerable. Olmsted and Vaux once wrote of the justification for the park and of their design in these words:

"The time will come when New York will be built up, when all the grading and filling will be done, and the picturesquely-varied, rocky formation of the Island will have been converted into formations for rows of monotonous straight streets, and piles of erect buildings. There will be no suggestion left of its present varied surface, with the single exception of the few acres contained in the Park. Then the priceless value of the present picturesque outlines of the ground will be more distinctly perceived, and its adaptability for its purpose more fully recognized. It therefore seems desirable to interfere with its easy, undulating outlines, and picturesque, rocky scenery as little as possible, and, on the other hand, to endeavor rapidly, and by every legitimate means, to increase and judiciously develop these particularly individual and characteristic sources of landscape effects."[12]

Olmsted and Vaux were to spend a good part of their time defending these principles and resisting the efforts of well-meaning but poorly informed citizens and officials to use the park as a site for almost every conceivable recreational building or facility. Although their efforts did not always meet with success, the park remains as a monument to their genius, the intelligence of the commissioners who recognized the unique merits of their plan, and the citizens who through the years have rallied to defend the park from those who wished to destroy its artistic integrity.

Central Park was not only of incalculable benefit to New York City it also became the great example for other cities. The commissioners must have been proud and not a little astonished at how eagerly other communities busied themselves in similar projects. In their report for 1868, a scant ten years after work had begun on the new plan, they observed:

"There is scarcely a city of magnitude in this country that has not provided, or taken measures to provide a Park for the pleasure of its citizens. . . .

"Baltimore has laid out and improved its Park under the en-

[11] *ibid.*, 221.

[12] Commissioners of Central Park, Document No. 5 of 1858, as quoted in Olmsted and Kimball, *ibid.*, 46.

CENTRAL PARK.

Published by JOHN BACHMANN 76 Nassau St New York

Figure 198. View of Central Park, New York City, Looking North: 1863

Figure 199. View of the Ramble, Lake, Terrace, and Mall in Central Park, New York City: ca. 1870

lightened action of its Commissioners. Philadelphia has already secured grounds of great extent; enlightened citizens throughout the country already perceive the desirability of procuring conveniently situated pleasure grounds that will accommodate present and future generations, while the necessary space can be acquired within the limits at a reasonable cost; and the subject is under discussion in Providence, Albany, Troy, Cincinnati, Pittsburgh, Chicago, St. Louis and Louisville."[13]

Many of these parks were designed by Olmsted alone or by him and Vaux. The list is a long one: Buffalo, Chicago, Montreal, Detroit, Boston, Brooklyn, Bridgeport, Rochester, Knoxville, Louisville are some of the cities in which Olmsted's work may be found. Where he was not the designer, his work served as the inspiration and the standard by which the designs of others were judged.

Romantic Planning in the American Suburb

Downing's teachings of naturalistic landscaping for the individual home, the attractiveness of the rural cemeteries planned in the romantic manner, and the new popularity of the picturesque park led to the use of these design elements in the expanding suburbs of American cities. Possibly the earliest and without question one of the most skillfully handled developments of this sort was Llewellyn Park at Orange, New Jersey. Developed by Llewellyn Haskell, a New York businessman who professed the religious doctrines of the Perfectionists, the development was planned for fellow believers in 1853. The architect Alexander Davis, a friend of Downing, was the designer of both the park and many of the houses built between 1853 and 1869. The site itself was wild and romantic, located on the eastern slope of a mountain capped by a rocky cliff. Haskell acquired nearly 400 acres of land extending up the hill from which views of New York and hills along the Hudson could be seen. One section of Llewellyn Park is shown in Figure 200, and a view of the entrance appears in Figure 201. A contemporary description of the park and surrounding houses provides some of the details:

"That portion of the grounds selected for the Park proper is centrally situated . . . and in form it is irregular, following the

[13] As quoted in Olmsted and Kimball, *ibid.*, 178.

natural indications of the surface—being traversed by a finely wooded ravine, through which flows a brook. . . . It comprises nearly sixty acres—its greatest length measuring one mile—the entire tract being encompassed by a road which gives access to the surrounding residences. . . . The walks . . . lead from the entrance, to the summit of the cliff, and to other interesting parts of the grounds; while at suitable points are kiosks, seats, and bridges, constructed in rustic-work, to be in keeping with the natural character of the surrounding forests."[14]

Around the park, sites for about 50 houses were laid out, ranging in size from 3 to 10 acres. Property owners were assessed for the cost of maintaining the central park strip and, by general agreement, no fences were erected so that park and house sites could be treated as a single design. Only a few of the original structures remain today, but so attractive was the subdivision layout that instead of being cut up into smaller plots or the large villas converted to apartments, the older houses were replaced. Today the character remains much as it was first established. Only the surroundings have changed, as adjacent tracts were developed on more conventional plans. Llewellyn Park demonstrates as forcefully as is possible the value of sound planning on a spacious scale.

At about the same time near Chicago another experiment in neighborhood planning began in 1855. The sponsors of this scheme, too, were motivated by religious desires rather than speculative profit. These divines of the Presbyterian Church set out from Chicago to locate a site for a Presbyterian college. North of Chicago along Lake Michigan they found a suitable spot. They called a meeting of those members of their congregations who might help the enterprise, and early in 1856 five trustees of the newly formed Lake Forest Association were instructed to purchase the necessary land. Fifty acres were to be reserved for the college site, with the remaining land to be divided equally between the association and the college. The trustees purchased nearly 1,400 acres of land and retained David Hotchkiss, a St. Louis surveyor and landscape gardener, to design the community.

[14] A. J. Downing, *A Treatise on the Theory and Practice of Landscape Gardening*, New York, 8th ed., with a supplement by Henry Winthrop Sargent, 1859. Sargent's supplement contains a description of Llewellyn Park from which the above quotation is taken.

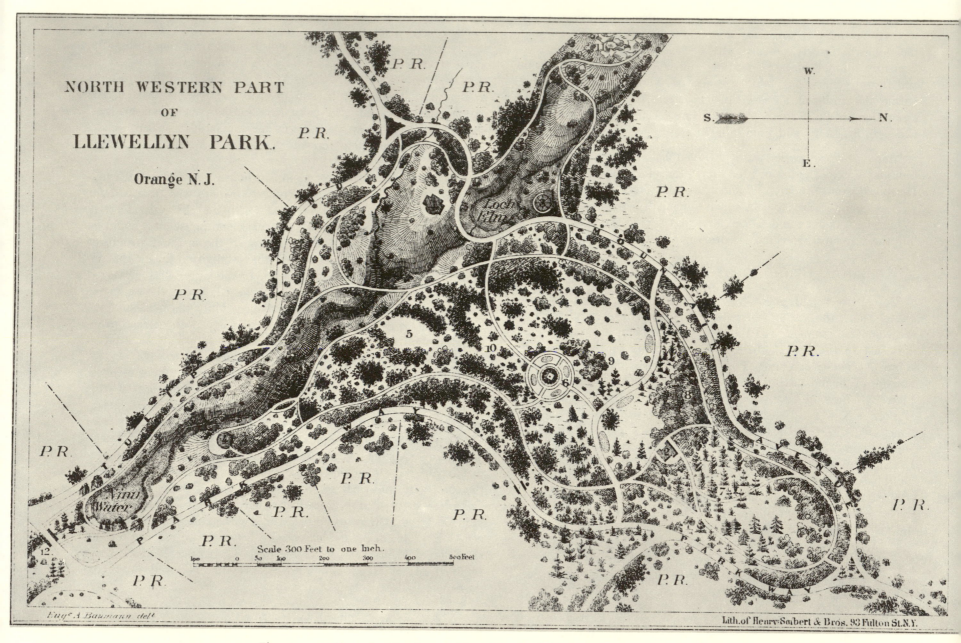

Figure 200. Plan of a Portion of Llewellyn Park in Orange, New Jersey: 1859

ENTRANCE TO LLEWELLYN PARK, ORANGE, N.J.

Engraved for H.W. Sargent's edition of Downing's Landscape Gardening

Figure 201. View of the Entrance of Llewellyn Park in Orange, New Jersey: 1859

In July 1857 there was a public sale of the 650 acres retained by the association. Lots were bought by members and friends of the association, with the remaining 650 acres set aside for the college in lots scattered through the development. Sale of these college properties as the community grew was to provide endowment funds for the institution. Construction of a hotel and a number of country estates began almost immediately, and Lake Forest soon became a suburban community of great distinction for the well-to-do, a quality which it has retained through the years.

The Hotchkiss plan was another early essay in romantic town planning. With building sites of generous size, winding streets conforming to the topography, and its interior and lakeside parks, Lake Forest ranks with the finest examples of curvilinear planning in America. The plan, shown in Figure 202, reveals the mastery with which Hotchkiss adapted the motifs of garden design to the larger problem of town planning. The market square, now such a prominent feature of Lake Forest, was a later development designed by Howard V. Shaw. Laid out with a tree-planted common in the center and with surrounding shop buildings with arcaded walks and punctuated by two towers, this composition is a harmonious addition to the original design.

Another community design which grew out of the founding of an educational institution was Olmsted's plan for what is now the University of California at Berkeley. He was retained in 1866 to advise on the development of the College of California, already located on a sloping site overlooking San Francisco Bay. His plan for the institution and the surrounding lands is shown in Figure 203. In his report to the site development committee Olmsted urged the creation of attractive surroundings for the college and suggested that the most appropriate way to achieve this would be to lay out and sell land for residential lots. Olmsted proposed several areas for this purpose, saying that each one ". . . could be easily subdivided by simple lines into lots, each of one to five acres in extent, of suitable shape and favorably situated in all respects for a family home. . . . The divisions are separated one from the other by lanes bordered . . . on each side by continuous thick groves, and access to each private lot from these lanes is arranged by short approaches branching from them."[15]

A small village had already been laid out on a gridiron pattern

[15] Olmsted, Vaux & Co., *Report Upon a Projected Improvement of the Estate of The College of California*, New York, 1866, p. 19.

Figure 202. Plan of Lake Forest, Illinois: 1857

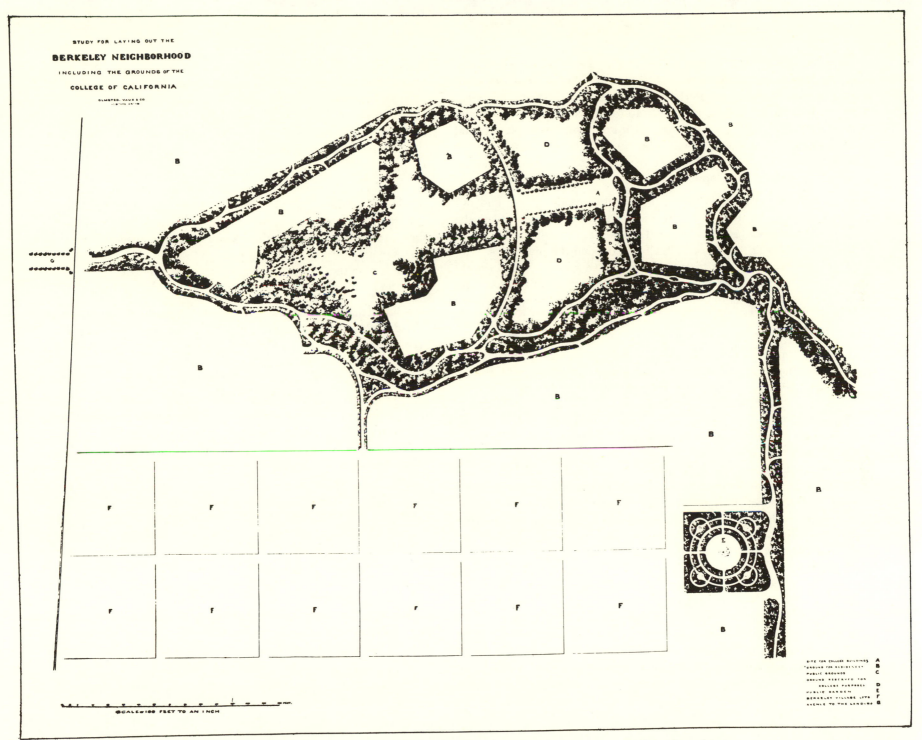

STUDY FOR LAYING OUT THE

BERKELEY NEIGHBORHOOD

INCLUDING THE GROUNDS OF THE

COLLEGE OF CALIFORNIA

OLMSTED. VAUX & CO

SCALE 100 FEET TO AN INCH

Figure 203. Olmsted's Plan for Berkeley, California and the College of California: 1866

down the slope, but Olmsted, of course, proposed a curvilinear street system for the college tract. As a transition from the rigid grid of the village to the Berkeley community he suggested widening one of the existing streets "so as to form a small plaza or village market-place," with a public garden and children's playground adjoining. Olmsted pointed out what many later planners have repeated endlessly as an advantage of the curvilinear street system for neighborhood development:

"It will be observed, that . . . while the roads are so laid out as to afford moderately direct routes of communication between the different parts of the neighborhood, they would be inconvenient to be followed for any purpose of business beyond the mere supplying of the wants of the neighborhood itself,—that is to say, it would be easier for any man wishing to convey merchandise from any point a short distance on one side of your neighborhood to a point a short distance on the other side, to go around it rather than go through it."[16]

This statement reveals one of Olmsted's most interesting characteristics—that of justifying the naturalistic style on logical as well as artistic grounds. Earlier, in his explanations of the Central Park design, he had remarked on the savings in construction cost that could be achieved by contour street planning and the reduced landscaping and grading expenses possible by preserving the natural topography and planting of the site.

The dynamic growth of the University of California has all but obliterated Olmsted's plan for Berkeley, but time has treated more kindly another and larger suburban plan of the same period. This is Riverside, Illinois, now surrounded by the relentless flow from Chicago's limitless well of population, but which in 1868 lay far beyond the outer boundaries of the urbanized area. The Riverside Improvement Company, headed by E. E. Childs, had purchased about 1,600 acres of land along the Des Plaines River at the crossing of the main line of the Burlington Railroad, and Olmsted and Vaux were retained to prepare the plan for its development.

In the preliminary report to the owner, submitted in September 1868, Olmsted discussed the general principles that should govern the development of the tract. He recommended that a distinctly rural and open atmosphere be aimed for, ". . . and, in regard to those special features whereby the town is distinguished from the country, there should be the greatest possible contrast which is compatible with the convenient communication and pleasant abode of a community."[17]

As to street alignment, Olmsted once again used both logical and artistic arguments to justify his naturalistic design even where, as here, topography did not demand it:

"In the highways, celerity will be of less importance than comfort and convenience of movement, and as the ordinary directness of line in town-streets, with its resultant regularity of plan would suggest eagerness to press forward, without looking to the right hand or the left, we should recommend the general adoption, in the design of your roads, of gracefully-curved lines, generous spaces, and the absence of sharp corners, the idea being to suggest and imply leisure, contemplativeness and happy tranquility."[18]

Olmsted pointed out that, while no control over the design of individual houses should be attempted, it would be appropriate to require each dwelling to be set back from the street and to specify that each owner maintain "one or two living trees between his house and his highway-line." Then Olmsted, in a passage that might be considered a credo of the romantic planners, described the qualities he believed such a development should possess:

"A few simple precautions of this kind, added to a tasteful and convenient disposition of shade trees, and other planting along the road-sides and public places, will, in a few years, cause the whole locality, no matter how far the plan may be extended, to possess, not only the attraction of neatness and convenience, and the charm of refined sylvan beauty and grateful umbrageousness, but an aspect of secluded peacefulness and tranquility more general and pervading than can possibly be found in suburbs which have grown up in a desultory hap-hazard way. If the general plan of such a suburb is properly designed on the principles which have been suggested, its character will inevitably also, notwithstanding its tidiness, be not only informal, but, in a moderate way, positively picturesque, and when contrasted with the constantly repeated right angles, straight lines, and flat surfaces which characterize our large modern towns, thoroughly refreshing."[19]

[17] Olmsted, Vaux & Co., *Preliminary Report upon the Proposed Suburban Village at Riverside, Near Chicago*, New York, 1868, pp. 16-17.
[18] *ibid.*, 17.
[19] *ibid.*, 25.

[16] *ibid.*, 23-24.

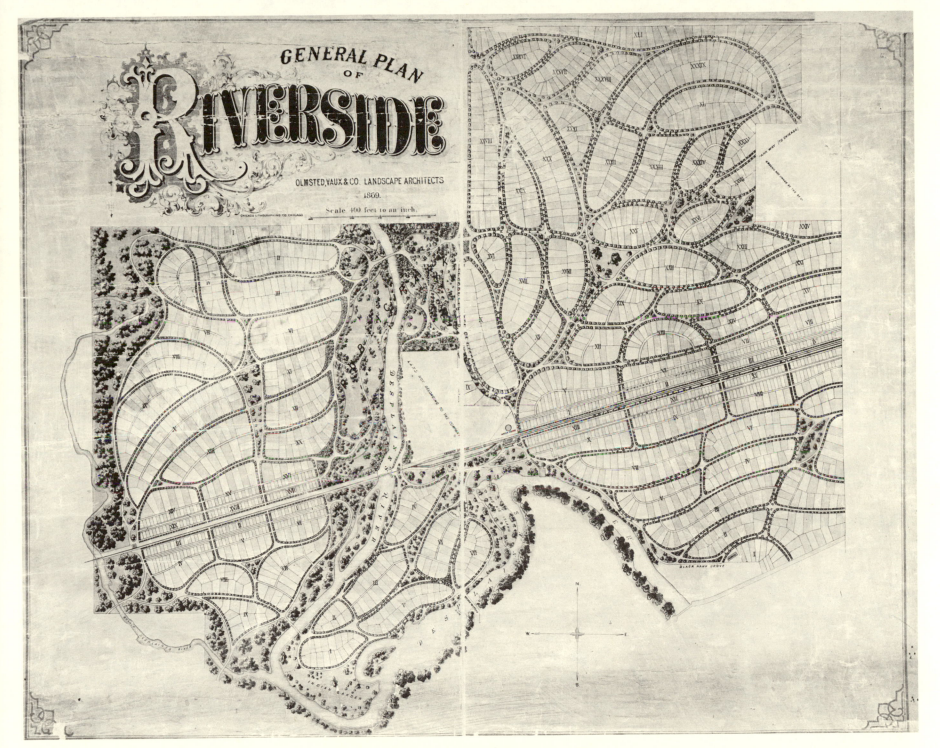

Figure 204. Plan of Riverside Illinois: 1869

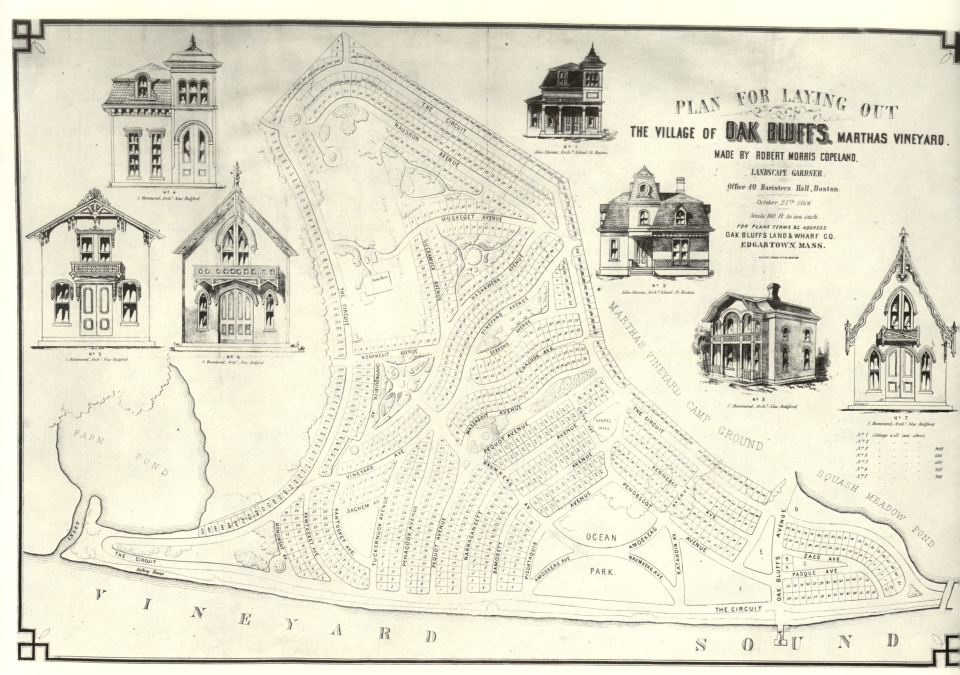

Figure 205. Plan of Oak Bluffs, Martha's Vineyard, Massachusetts: 1866

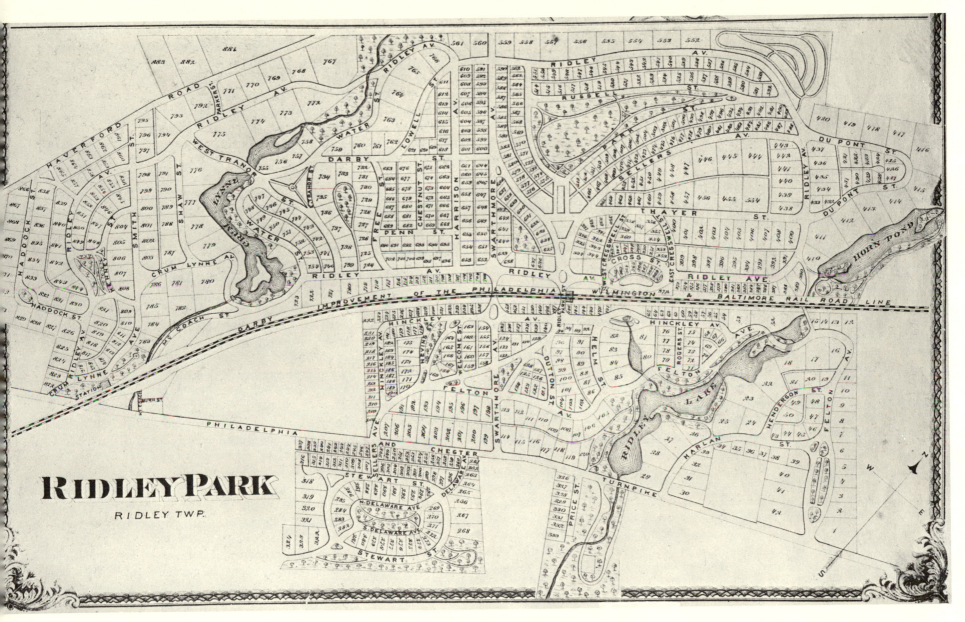

Figure 206. Plan of Ridley Park, Pennsylvania: 1875

The plan of Riverside prepared by Olmsted and Vaux the following year is shown in Figure 204. Along the river on both sides an irregular park was planned. Supplementing this recreational area were several smaller informal open spaces at important road junctions. In the northeast section of the community a long, irregular common led to the railway station. And throughout ran Olmsted's gracefully curving roadways.

Riverside was constructed on this plan, although the portion of the tract west of the river was built up later and on a different pattern. Vaux designed many of the houses and established an architectural character to complement the romantic layout established by Olmsted. As at Lake Forest, the quality of the original plan has remained. Old houses have been torn down and new ones built without changes in the features of spaciousness and quiet that Olmsted intended.

Two other projects which Olmsted designed are worth a brief note. The Tarrytown Heights project in upper Westchester County was planned in 1871. Because of the irregular boundary of the site, this design lacks the unity of Riverside. Estate lots averaged 5 acres or so, but some were much larger, ranging up to 17 acres. At two spots along the railroad line that curved through the site Olmsted planned villages, doubtless to house domestic servants, tradesmen, and laborers who would work at the estates.[20]

Roland Park in Baltimore dates from 1891, when the first unit of what grew to be a much larger development was planned by Olmsted. A series of ridges and valleys along one end of the tract presented a major problem for the designer. He used a series of cul-de-sacs to penetrate this area in a brilliant demonstration of his skill in mastering almost any kind of topography. Olmsted and the developer also devised a set of deed restrictions governing the use of property, maintenance, and common responsibilities for the operation of a community organization. This pioneering effort was imitated by later land developers.[21] The Olmsted firm also planned the town of Vandergrift, Pennsylvania, a company town, using the design techniques employed in these earlier ventures. The town plan is reproduced in Figure 252 and discussed in Chapter 15.

Olmsted was not, of course, the only designer of such picturesque residential developments. Robert Morris Copeland, whose grand plan for Boston has already been discussed, also was responsible for at least one plan of the romantic mode. Figure 205 shows his plan for Oak Bluffs on Martha's Vineyard off the Massachusetts coast. Copeland's plan reveals his skill in the handling of curvilinear design forms. The inclusion of the several interior block parks is an interesting feature. The drawings of the "gothic" cottages which decorate the plan are typical of many of the older houses still existing in the village.[22]

By the latter part of the nineteenth century most large cities could boast of one or more suburban communities or outlying subdivisions planned in curvilinear fashion. While many of these were done with skill and understanding by facile designers, others, like Ridley Park, Pennsylvania, shown in Figure 206, had a mechanical quality resulting from mere imitation of the superficial features of the romantic plan without real comprehension of the over-all effect that was essential.

In most cases the curvilinear plan was used in subdivisions for the fairly well-to-do. It became a mark of fashion and distinction to live in such areas, although they never entirely superseded the old, straight, tree-lined drive or boulevard in older sections of cities. Even at the height of enthusiasm for the romantic and picturesque suburb, the gridiron plan remained predominant. In such unsophisticated communities as Tacoma, Washington, busy with its railroad and port construction, a curvilinear plan for the entire city, such as the one submitted by Olmsted in 1873 and discussed in Chapter 14, was certain to be rejected.

Not until the 1930's, with the educational and promotional campaign of the Federal Housing Administration, did curvilinear plans reappear in great numbers. By that time the demand for new housing arose from middle and lower income groups. A few curves, a few cul-de-sacs amidst the 60-foot lots proved insufficient to recreate the romantic elements that Olmsted, Davis, Downing, and Copeland created. Whatever merits modern curvilinear plans may now have on grounds of safety, cost, and creation of visual relief from grid monotony, most of them are but feeble reminders of the great designs of the last century.

[20] A plan of Tarrytown Heights may be found in J. B. Beers & Co., *County Atlas of Westchester, New York*, New York, 1872.

[21] A description and plan of Roland Park appear in Arthur C. Comey and Max S. Wehrly, *Planned Communities*, Washington, 1939, pp. 89-92.

[22] Another plan for a community on Martha's Vineyard, similar in concept but much less skillful in execution, was for the Highlands Development. An undated plan is in the collection of The New-York Historical Society.

CHAPTER 13

Cities for Sale: Land Speculation in American Planning

"GAIN! Gain! Gain! is the beginning, the middle and the end, the *alpha* and *omega* of the founders of American towns. . . ."[1]

In one form or another this lament was echoed by critics of land speculation in every era of development and in all parts of North America. But louder—much louder—rose the huckster voices of the land boomers, the townsite promoters, and the wholesalers and retailers of frontier land. To some extent an element of speculation was present in almost every venture in American town planning. Even the communities formed by religious or utopian groups were sometimes developed with an eye to possible financial profits along with the presumed benefits to mind and spirit. Philanthropic colonization or settlement projects, whether the Georgia of 1733 or the Russell Sage Foundation model suburb of Forest Hills Gardens 175 years later, rarely overlooked the possibility of financial gain, however regulated or controlled.

This chapter will explore those communities founded primarily as commercial ventures. Some of the effects of speculation in urban land on communities originally laid out with other goals in mind will also be considered. The effects of railroads on land speculation and the towns laid out and promoted by the railroads themselves are treated in a separate chapter.

Early Land Companies and Town Promotion Schemes

For the first hundred years or so after the settlement of Virginia, New England, and the other colonies along the Atlantic coast, speculation in urban land, as a dominant motif of town planning, was not widespread. Early settlements were small and were based primarily on agriculture. Hostile Indians and topographic difficul-

ties restricted settlements to a narrow band along the coast. The shortage of capital for vast land ventures and the relatively sparse and immobile population limited opportunities for land promotion schemes. Moreover, in New England at least, the system of land tenure on a modified communal basis, with land available at moderate cost for all comers, satisfied most settlers and prevented the land hunger that was to characterize the post-revolutionary period.

In one sense, of course, both the corporate and the proprietary colonies existed to make money from land distribution and improvement. But profit-making was secondary to considerations of religious freedom, rehabilitation of debtors, establishment of sovereignty over portions of North America, or the promotion of trade and commerce and development of raw material sources for the mother country. To be sure certain individuals enriched themselves at the expense of others less clever or wealthy through speculation in town and rural land, but wholesale town jobbing and promotion had not yet been seized upon as a device leading to quick and substantial wealth.

With the filling up of seaboard settlements, the accumulation of wealth by local merchants and traders, and the subjection of the Indians along the frontier, land speculation projects became feasible. Wealthy merchants or planters began to dream of acquiring large land holdings beyond the Alleghenies. In 1748 a group from Virginia formed the Ohio Company and received from the governor and council of Virginia a grant of half a million acres west of the mountains. Christopher Gist visited the area in 1750 as agent for the company to report on its prospects. Among other plans, the Ohio Company proposed to lay out a town with blocks of two acres of land adjacent to a square fort needed for protection against the Indians.[2] Other land companies were formed, and some succeeded

[1] Morris Birkbeck, *Notes on a Journey in America from the Coast of Virginia to the Territory of Illinois*, London, 3rd ed., 1818, p. 69.

[2] W. M. Dalington, ed., Christopher Gist's *Journals*, Cleveland, 1893, pp. 236-37.

in receiving grants from the colonial authorities. However, it was necessary for them to secure approval of the grants from the crown. London was besieged by agents of American companies, and this served to stimulate the interest of Englishmen seeking investment outlets, but in 1763 the King issued a proclamation prohibiting land grants by colonial governors beyond the headwaters of rivers flowing into the Atlantic.

The proclamation was clear enough, but it hardly slowed the applications for western land grants or the formation of companies to treat directly with the Indians in arranging purchases of land from them. The Loyal Company, the Transylvania Company, the Vandalia Company, and the Indiana Land Company were the most important. Participants included such notables as George Washington, Benjamin Franklin, Patrick Henry, Richard Henderson, and Sir William Johnson. Two land companies, both promoted by one William Murray, were merged under the title, The United Illinois and Wabash Land Companies. Judge James Wilson, later appointed a justice of the Supreme Court, became the head of the company. Among the documents of this project is the draft of a prospectus setting forth the following terms of settlement which include proposals for town development:

"1. There shall be laid out by the Companies . . . Two Towns and Convenient Districts Adjacent. One of which towns to be . . . as near the Junction of the Ohio and Mississippi as the nature of the ground will admit, the other town to be . . . as near the junction of the Illinois and the Mississippi as the nature of the ground will admit.

"Secondly; Each town shall consist of at least Six hundred and seventy-two Lotts of half an acre each Lot and the district adjacent to each town of Six hundred and seventy-two out lotts of Twenty Acres each and beyond these of Six hundred and Seventy two plantations of three hundred acres each agreeable to annexed plan with a convenient allowance in the towns for Streets and publick Buildings and of six per cent for roads in the plantations."[3]

Unfortunately the "annexed plan" referred to has not survived, so that the details of the plan must remain unknown. The com-

[3] C. W. Alvord, ed., *The Illinois Wabash Land Company Manuscript*, privately printed by Cyrus H. McCormick, 1915. The quotation is from a slightly edited version in Ina Faye Woestemeyer and J. Montgomery Gambrill, *The Westward Movement*, New York 1939, p. 44.

bination of town lots, outlots and "plantations" is quite similar to the original plan for Savannah. This general system of land subdivision into town lots and one or two types of outlots, garden lots, or farm lots became fairly widespread. It shows the influence of the New England agricultural village concept, a pattern of settlement that was to break down in the middle west with the development of the isolated farm homestead for agricultural purposes and the nearby village functioning as the home of a new class of merchants, craftsmen, and members of the professions.

The Revolutionary War put a stop to the activities of these land companies. Many potential settlers became soldiers, and British support of the Indians made settlement extremely hazardous if not impossible. After the war some of these companies pressed their claims with the Continental Congress, but without success. While their effect on actual settlement was negligible, they did carry out the first reconnaissance surveys of western lands, and their abortive promotional activities served to stimulate interest in western settlement after hostilities ceased.

Two land companies involved in town planning commenced operations in western New York shortly after the Revolution. This was territory claimed by Massachusetts, and in 1786 the two states agreed that New York would acquire sovereignty but that Massachusetts would retain ownership of land lying west of a north-south line running through Seneca Lake. Massachusetts sold these lands, some six million acres, to Oliver Phelps and Nathaniel Gorham in 1787, subject to acquisition of the title from the Indians. Phelps and Gorham were able to buy only the eastern one-third of this vast tract, and the remainder reverted to Massachusetts. In 1791 Robert Morris purchased this reverted land, and in turn sold it and over one million acres bought from Phelps and Gorham to two land companies. The largest portion, about three and a half million acres of the western part of the Morris Purchase, was bought by a group of Dutch bankers who formed the Holland Land Company in 1793. The remaining tract Morris sold to a group of English speculators headed by Sir William Pulteney.[4]

Development of the Pulteney Purchase was entrusted to Captain Charles Williamson, who opened his land office at Bath in 1793. Williamson was lavish in his expenditures aimed at developing

[4] Ulysses P. Hedrick, *A History of Agriculture in the State of New York*, Albany, 1933, 59-60.

the land and attracting new settlers. He built a road connecting Williamsport, Pennsylvania, with Williamsburg, New York, on the Genesee River to improve transportation. A number of town sites were surveyed, including Williamsburg, Geneva, and Great Sodus.

But it was at Bath that Williamson laid out "a handsome progressive city" designed to be the great metropolis of western New York. He built a theater and a hotel, started a weekly newspaper, and laid out a race track. In order to promote land sales in the town he held a series of fairs, with horse races, dances, and theatrical performances. The enterprise attracted a good deal of attention, and when Rochefoucauld visited Bath in June 1795 he reported its progress with obvious admiration:

"Mr. Williamson is, at present, building a school, in Bath. This he intends to endow with some hundred acres of land, and to take upon himself the maintenance of the master. . . . He is also building a sessions-house and a prison. The present inn was likewise built by him. . . . Near Bath . . . he has erected a cornmill, and two saw-mills."[5]

However, he added, only "about twenty houses compose, as yet, the whole of the town of Bath."

The following year "A Farmer," in a letter to the *Wilkesbarre Gazette* described the fever of speculation with which his son had become afflicted at Bath:

"He has been to Bath, the celebrated Bath, and has returned both a speculator and a gentleman, having spent his money, swapped away my horse, caught the fever and ague, and, what is infinitely worse, that horrid disorder which some call the 'terra-phobia.'

"We hear nothing from the poor creature now (in his ravings) but . . . of ranges, of townships, numbers, thousands, hundreds, acres, Bath, fairs, races, heats . . . etc., etc. My son has part of a township for sale, and it's diverting enough to hear him narrate its pedigree, qualities, and situation. In fine, it lies near Bath. . . . It cost my son but five dollars per acre. . . . One thing is very much in my boy's favor—he has six years' credit. Another thing is

still more so—he is not worth a sou, and never will be, at this rate. . . ."[6]

Bath was an elegant little town with its two squares connected by a short, wide street. The squares were perhaps intended to resemble those laid out in its Georgian namesake in western England. But the location of Bath was unfavorable for any large development, and the wave of western settlement washed on beyond to more advantageous sites in the Ohio Valley or along the shores of the Great Lakes.

The city planning activities of the Holland Land Company are of greater interest. Not only did its chief town become one of America's great cities but the planning concepts used there reflect the influence of L'Enfant's plan for Washington. There was, in fact, a direct connection between the Washington plan and that used for New Amsterdam, later renamed Buffalo. The land agent for the Holland Land Company in Western New York was Joseph Ellicott, the brother of Andrew Ellicott, who succeeded L'Enfant as planner for the federal city. Joseph Ellicott obviously was familiar with his brother's work and set out to duplicate it at the eastern end of Lake Erie.

Ellicott liked the future site of New Amsterdam from the beginning. As early as 1798 he described its beauty and strategic location to his superiors.[7] But it was not until 1802 that authorization was granted to lay out a city. The delay was chiefly due to the difficulties encountered in extinguishing the Indian titles to the site.

Site surveys began in the summer of 1803, and a few land sales were made. Finally, in July 1804, Ellicott could report to the general agent of the company in Philadelphia that the survey work was "in such a state for forwardnesss as to enable me to forward to you in the course of 10 or 15 days a complete plan of this Village. . . ."[8] Ellicott's plan, shown in Figure 207, reveals to what extent he followed the diagonal street pattern established in Washington. It also shows the pattern of outlots varying in size from

[5] Duke de La Rochefoucauld-Liancourt, *Travels Through the United States of North America*, London, 2nd ed., 1800, I, 233.

[6] As quoted in Isaac Weld, *Travels Through North America and Canada*, London, 4th ed., 1799, II, 336-37.

[7] See letter from Ellicott to Cazenove, September 25, 1798, in R. W. Bingham, ed., Holland Land Company Papers, *Reports of Joseph Ellicott*, I, Buffalo Historical Society, *Publications*, XXXII, Buffalo, 1937, 42-44.

[8] Letter from Ellicott to Paul Busti, July 27, 1804, as quoted in R. W. Bingham, *Cradle of the Queen City*, Buffalo, 1931, pp. 192-93.

5 to 20 acres or more. In this respect the plan resembles the proposal advanced by the proprietors of the Illinois Wabash Company and anticipates many of the later towns farther west.

Ellicott followed the practice usual in these speculative towns of reserving choice lots for the company. This was an obvious device to increase land values and thus maximize profits when the reserved lots were later put up for sale. Ellicott was paid partly in land, and for himself he chose perhaps the most desirable property. On the large plan in Figure 207 his land included out lot 104 and the extension of its boundaries east to Van Staphorst Avenue. Originally, as is shown on the small insert map, this property included a small semicircular projection into the avenue. Here Ellicott proposed to erect his residence. The municipal highway commission, however, resented such an obvious act of self-favoritism, and in 1809 cut through the projection in order to straighten the street.

Many other cities were planned by the Holland Land Company. They include Cazenovia in 1793, Batavia in 1801, and Mayvil in 1804. The company also acted as a wholesaler of land. In 1804, after protracted negotiations, Ellicott sold some 20,000 acres at the head of navigation on the Allegheny River to Adam Hoops, a protégé of Robert Morris and former *aide de camp* to Alexander Hamilton. Hoops, in 1793, had been assigned by Morris to accompany and help plan a town for a group of French refugees in northern Pennsylvania on land owned by Morris. Hoops laid out a town on the New York site, calling it first Hamilton and then Olean. Olean, like Bath, was never successful as a large-scale promotion, and Hoops was forced to relinquish the land.

Backwoods Baroque

Two other eighteenth-century and one slightly later town promotion are worth brief consideration. All exhibit some of the fanciful design elements that entered into many of the speculative town projects of this era. The first of these was literally a city built of hope, since nothing but its name, Esperanza, survives. Esperanza was founded by a distinguished group of New Yorkers headed by Edward Livingston, whose career later included service as a congressman, mayor of New York, senator from Louisiana, U. S. Secretary of State, and finally minister to France. The site of this extraordinary community was on the west bank of the Hudson almost directly opposite the thriving east-bank community bearing the name of that river.

Hudson's rival-to-be was intended to tap the trade from the western part of the state, first by a land route and ultimately by a canal. The proprietors hoped that eventually the capitol would be moved to their city. Land was purchased in 1794, and, shortly after, the plan shown in Figure 208 was prepared and circulated to prospective settlers. Beneath the title block appeared the following words in lettering now faded with age:

"This Place is situated nearly at the head of Deep Navigation of the Hudson River. It is directly East from the Military lands, & is supposed to possess more important Commercial and local advantages than any other point on the River, the road for some hundred miles west passing through a very fine and improving Country, to which this is the nearest Port."[9]

The street pattern and the names given the streets are curious. Liberty and Equality Streets suggest the influence of the late French Revolution, and the portion of the town to the northwest, with its circular and radial boulevards, also calls to mind the grand plan of a French hunting park or the grounds of a royal chateau. Of course, this was the time when the new Washington plan was widely circulated and well known. There were other interesting paired streets: Love and Happiness; Beer and Cider; Meal and Bread; Art and Science; Wheat and Rice, with Corn, in addition. With squares for a market, churches, court house, and with reserved common land and sites for "groves," Esperanza seemingly was equipped for any eventuality. But despite the prediction that ". . . this infant town, will beyond all doubt, experience a considerable increase . . ." Esperanza, like other hopes, failed to materialize. As late as 1867 a map of the township in which it was located showed the paper streets and squares in all their elegance, but this was probably the last monument to a speculation that had failed.

At about the same time in central Kentucky a group of speculators, probably English, set about promoting land sales in two or

[9] The text of this explanation and a brief description of the founding of the town appears in J. B. Beers & Co., *History of Greene County, New York*, New York, 1884, pp. 164-66.

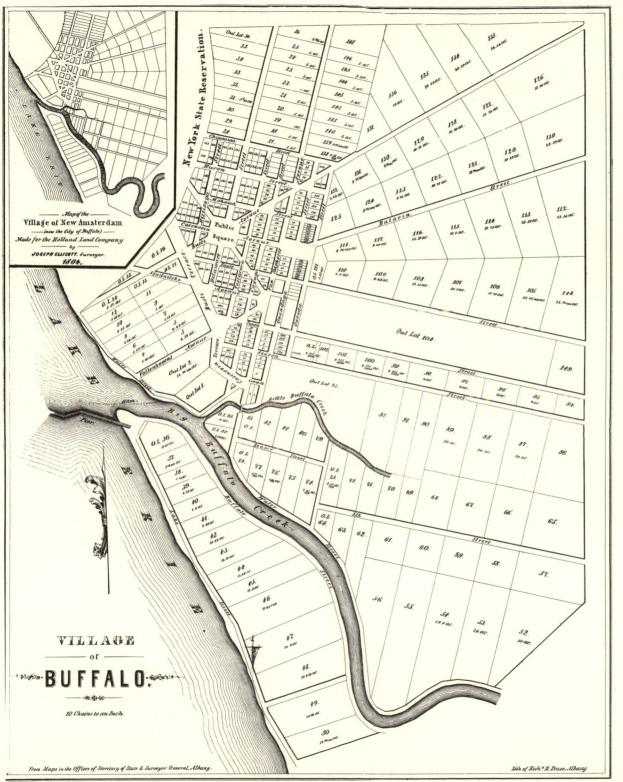

Figure 207. Plan of Buffalo, New York: 1804

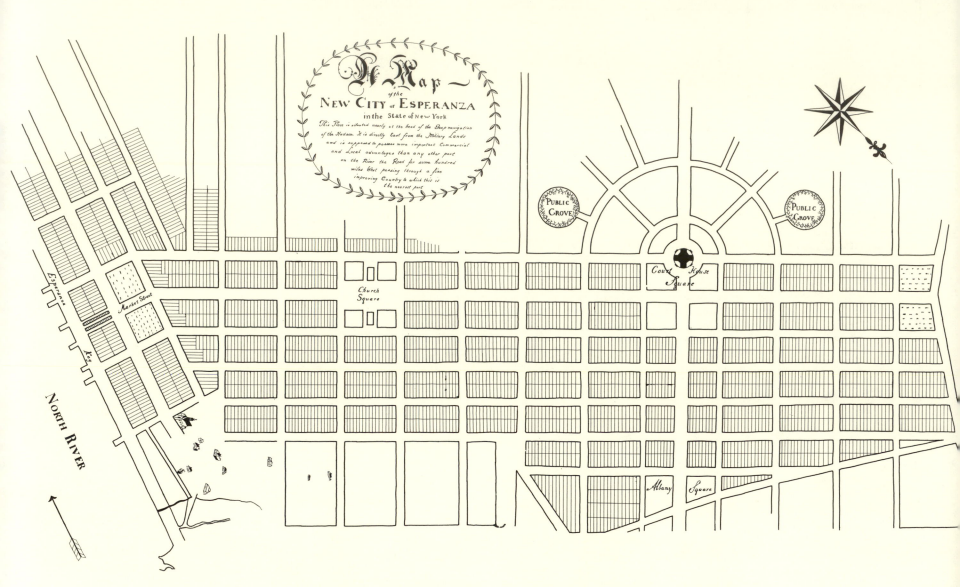

A Map
of the
NEW CITY of ESPERANZA
in the State of New York

This Place is situated nearly at the head of the Deep navigation
of the Hudson. It is directly East from the Military Lands
and is supposed to possess more important Commercial
and Local advantages than any other port
on the River the Road for some hundred
miles West passing through a fine
improving Country to which this is
the nearest port

PUBLIC GROVE

PUBLIC GROVE

Court House Square

Church Square

Market Street

Esperanza Key

NORTH RIVER

Albany Square

Figure 208. Plan of Esperanza, New York: ca. 1794

three towns which were laid out on "very eligible" plans, "combining every thing necessary for utility and ornament." The chief publicist was one William Winterbotham, who, in 1796, published a monumental work in four volumes with an accompanying atlas bearing the equally monumental title, *An Historical, Geographical, Commercial, and Philosophical View of the United States of America, and of the European Settlements in America and the West-Indies.*[10] Perhaps Winterbotham's description of the United States is reasonably accurate. One suspects, however, that he may well have had an interest in the Kentucky town promotion scheme, since the only town maps appearing were those of Kentucky cities, and his descriptions of Kentucky as a place for settlement bordered on the lyrical. Clothing the speculative wolf in the respectability of sheep's clothing is, of course, no new trick to trap the unwary.

The proposed plans are reproduced in Figures 209 and 210. Both Franklinville and Lystra show some of the same qualities as Esperanza, derived perhaps from the plan of Washington, or, more probably, from the experience in London, Bath, Exeter, and other English cities with the crescent and the circus as urban housing forms. Winterbotham provides complete details on the layout of these cities and how they were to be developed. He lists, for example, the persons to whom free lots would be provided, including the first schoolmaster, the president of a college, the first judge, representative, and senator, the first minister, the first hotel keeper, and so on. This was standard practice in town promotion.

Whether from a sincere desire to promote beauty and order or merely to lend an air of sophistication to their promotional literature, the proposals did not overlook some of the aspects of urban design. Winterbotham explains that houses were "to be built regularly" and were to be set back "upon the streets running north and south, on a line twenty-five feet distant from the street." He also describes the town hall, church, college, and theatre as "edifices to be handsome and uniform, to be built with wings fronting the curve line which forms the circus; the church to be adorned with a steeple, and the other buildings with cupolas."[11]

Another proposed city, apparently sponsored by the same promoters, was to be given the lyrical name of Ohiopiomingo. Of it Winterbotham says:

"The town is to contain upwards of a thousand houses, forty-three streets, a circus and several capital squares, which will be embellished with various suitable and handsome structures: each settler in the township will be entitled, in fee simple, to one town lot of an hundred feet in width, and three hundred feet in length: a field of five acres, and another of twenty acres, will also be allotted to each of them, and their farms will consist of five hundred acres each, which will be granted on lease for nine hundred and ninety-nine years. . . ."[12]

Like its companion cities of Lystra and Franklinville, Ohiopiomingo never existed except on paper.

An even more involved plan was put forward by William Bullock in 1827 for his proposed city of Hygeia opposite Cincinnati on the Kentucky side of the Ohio River. Bullock was an English traveler and lecturer, and his *Sketch of a Journey Through the Western States of North America*, published in London in 1827, was something of a promotional tract for the Ohio Valley in general and the Cincinnati area in particular. Mrs. Frances Trollope, then in Cincinnati, may have found little else to her liking in America but she was impressed by Mr. and Mrs. Bullock. About them she observed:

"About two miles below Cincinnati, on the Kentucky side of the river, Mr. Bullock . . . has bought a large estate, with a noble house upon it. He and his amiable wife were devoting themselves to the embellishment of the house and grounds; and certainly there is more taste and art lavished on one of their beautiful saloons, than all Western America can shew elsewhere."[13]

Bullock had purchased the land from a wealthy Kentuckian after visiting his house and grounds and being struck with the possibility of "building a small town of retirement, in the vicinity of a populous manufacturing city." Then Bullock ". . . made a little model of the land, and determined to have it laid out to the best possible advantage, with professional assistance, on my arrival in England."[14]

John Buonarotti Papworth, self-styled "Architect to the King of Wirtemburg," was engaged as town planner. Papworth was an

[10] New York, 1796.
[11] Winterbotham, *View of the United States*, III, 145.

[12] *ibid.*, 149.
[13] Donald Smalley, ed., Frances Trollope, *Domestic Manners of the Americans* (London, 1832), New York, 1949.
[14] William Bullock, *Sketch*, in R. G. Thwaites, ed., *Early Western Travels, 1748-1846*, Cleveland, 1904-07, XIX, 140.

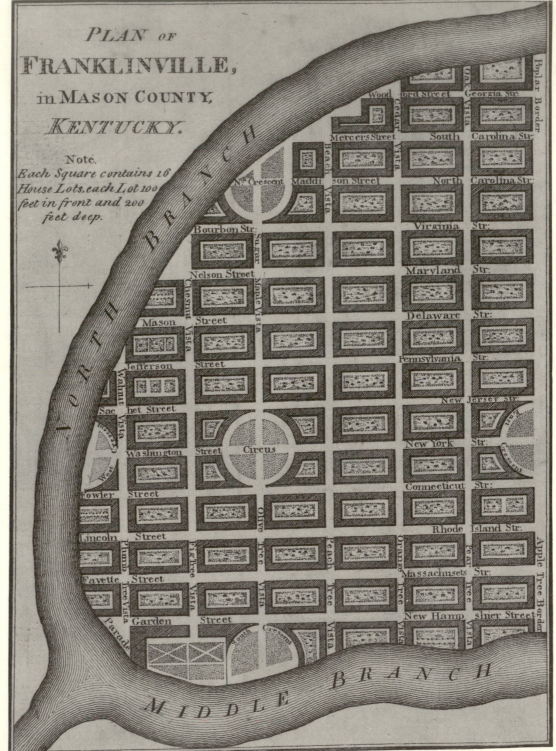

Figure 209. Plan of Franklinville, Kentucky: 1796

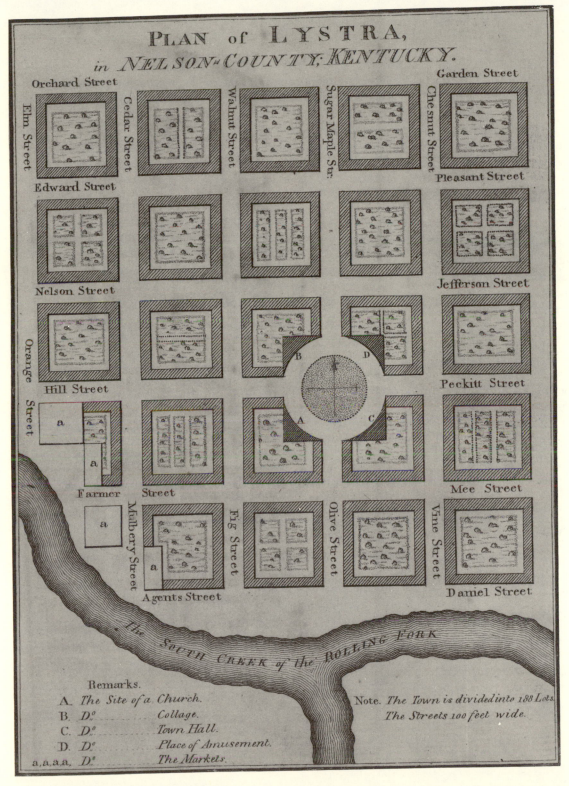

PLAN of LYSTRA,
in NELSON COUNTY, KENTUCKY.

Orchard Street
Garden Street
Elm Street
Cedar Street
Walnut Street
Sugar Maple Str:
Chesnut Street
Edward Street
Pleasant Street
Orange Street
Nelson Street
Jefferson Street
Hill Street
Peckitt Street
Farmer Street
Mee Street
Mulbery Street
Fig Street
Olive Street
Vine Street
Agents Street
Daniel Street

The SOUTH CREEK of the ROLLING FORK

Remarks.
A. The Site of a Church.
B. D.º .... Collage.
C. D.º .... Town Hall.
D. D.º .... Place of Amusement.
a,a,a,a. D.º .... The Markets.

Note. *The Town is divided into 188 Lots.*
The Streets 100 feet wide.

Figure 210. Plan of Lystra, Kentucky: 1796

architect of some reputation and had recently completed the layout of country estates in and around Cheltenham. Papworth's plan for Hygeia, reproduced in Figure 211, shows in considerable detail a proposed town incorporating most of the building types and plan forms developed in England during the preceding hundred years or so. Detached villas, semi-detached houses, and row houses all appear. The four small and two larger residential squares were typical planning layouts of the Georgian and Regency builders in England. While these are well handled, the street pattern appears more as an abstract design than a functional system. The four diagonals lead from the outer corners of the small squares to nowhere, and, with no real point of architectural interest at either end, these streets are largely meaningless. Nor is there any real civic focus to the town. Museum, town hall, and library seem relatively isolated at one end of the long street leading upward from the river. The market place at the eastern edge of the town is unrelated to other features of the plan.

Regardless of Mrs. Trollope's admiration for Bullock's "taste and art," his speculation was a failure. Perhaps the baroque layout was too advanced for the simple river settlers or even the more knowledgeable Cincinnatians of some wealth, or perhaps Bullock was not effective in his promotional activities. Whatever the reasons, Hygeia joined its earlier Kentucky sister towns in obscurity.

Towns for Sale in the Old Northwest

The opening of western lands for settlement by the Land Ordinance of 1785 and the establishment of government in the Northwest Territory in 1787 provided the impetus for wholesale townsite promotion throughout the Ohio Valley. Francis Baily, on his travels there in 1796 and 1797, describes how one of his companions had purchased several thousand acres on the Little Miami and intended to lay out a town to attract settlers.

"In order to found a colony at first, he holds out an encouragement to settlers by giving them a town lot and four acres of ground for nothing. . . . This he does only to the first twelve or twenty that may offer themselves. . . . In order to manage this concern to the best advantage, the landowners will always take care and not sell all their land *contiguous to each other*, but only at *certain*

distances, so that the whole face of it may be cultivated, and the intermediate uncultivated parts consequently rise in value. . . .

"The town he had laid out at right angles, nearly on Penn's plan, with a square in the middle, which he told me, with a degree of exulting pride, he intended for a court-house, or for some public building for the meeting of the legislature; for he has already fallen into that flattering idea which every founder of a new settlement entertains, that his town will at some future time be the seat of government."[15]

Another Englishman, Morris Birkbeck, writing from Illinois in 1817, mentions how widespread this practice of town speculation had become. He noted that wherever there appeared to be some natural advantage, such as good soil or a mill or a crossroads location, an enterprising landowner would lay out a town. Then, as Birkbeck describes the evolution of the community:

"The new town then assumes the name of its founder:—a storekeeper builds a little framed store, and sends for a few cases of goods; and then a tavern starts up, which becomes the residence of a doctor and a lawyer, and the boarding-house of the storekeeper, as well as the resort of the weary traveller: soon follow a blacksmith and other handicraftsmen in useful succession: a schoolmaster, who is also the minister of religion becomes an important accession to this rising community. Thus the town proceeds, if it proceeds at all, with accumulating force, until it becomes the metropolis of the neighborhood. Hundreds of these speculations may have failed, but hundreds prosper; and thus trade begins and thrives, as population grows around these lucky spots; imports and exports maintaining their just proportion. One year ago the neighborhood of this very town of Princeton, was clad in 'buckskin;' now the men appear at church in good blue cloth, and the women in fine calicoes and straw bonnets."[16]

Still another English observer, Joseph Briggs, emphasized the more fraudulent aspects of speculating town planning:

"A speculator makes out a plan of a city with its streets, squares, and avenues, quays and wharves, public buildings and monuments. The streets are lotted, the houses numbered, and the squares called

[15] Francis Baily, *Journal of a Tour in Unsettled Parts of North America in 1796 & 1797*, London, 1856, pp. 196, 215.
[16] Birkbeck, *Notes*, 104.

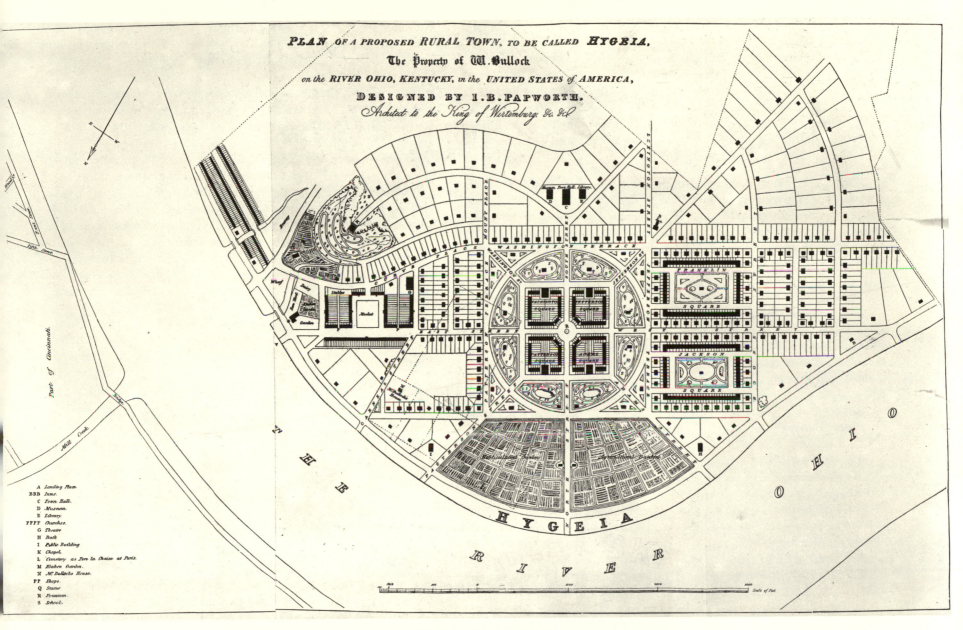

Figure 211. Plan of the Proposed Town of Hygeia, Kentucky: 1827

after Franklin or Washington. The city itself has some fine name, perhaps Troy or Antioch. This is engraved and forthwith hung up in as many steamboats and hotels as the speculator's interest may command. All this time the city is a mere vision. Its very site is on the fork of some river in the far West, five hundred miles beyond civilization, probably under water or surrounded by dense forests and impassable swamps. Emigrants have been repeatedly defrauded out of their money by transactions so extremely gross as hardly to be credited."[17]

Land speculation produced unnumbered tragedies. Families lured from the comparative comfort of some seaboard community by the siren songs of the town promoter frequently found themselves suddenly stripped of their savings and faced with the crude life of the frontier. Many could not adjust to these raw circumstances and returned to their former homes. Some drifted westward, perhaps to become speculators themselves and recoup what they had lost. Most, of course, remained at their new location, partly because further movement was difficult, partly because of stubborn determination to make the best of their new situation. Hundreds of these paper towns did, gradually, become actual settlements. In fact, so widespread was townsite promotion and speculation that most midwestern communities were once struggling hamlets of a few dozen houses scattered on lots that had first appeared on a grandiose plan displayed by some glib and convincing promoter.

But if there was tragedy, these was also humor. Somehow a swindled American is a humorous figure, especially if he tells the joke on himself. Possibly the earliest work in the substantial literature debunking the speculative activities of the frontier town developer was the *Journal of Doctor Simpleton's Tour of Ohio*, published in Boston in 1819. The narrator, seeking his destination in some town where he had purchased land, found the site occupied only by mosquitoes and and wild animals. A later work in the same style involved one Major Walter Wilkey. Wilkey invested in Illinois town lots in the 1830's, and, safely returned to his native Maine ". . . with a whole skin, (but with precious little flesh. . .) ," dramatizes his experience in first arriving in Edensburgh, where he had purchased ". . . twenty valuable house lots. . . .":

[17] As quoted by Walter Havighurst, *Wilderness for Sale*, New York, 1956. Havighurst's work is a valuable contribution to the literature on land development and speculation.

"Major—I . . . have come with my family a great way from down east, as purchasers in and actual settlers of the populous and thriving City of Edensburgh! And now, madam . . . inform us whether you ever heard of such a city in these parts or no?

"Landlady—Wha! unbelieving man, you, as sure as parsnips are parsnips, this here city is Edensburgh—so named but a-three months ago by Squire Soaper, the lucky good man who bought the land!

"Major—(Provoked, dismayed, disheartened) Soaper, indeed, and a *soft* one, no doubt! Edensburgh! . . . But where in the name of *gosh*, woman, are its public and private edifices, its increased population, its Park, College, State House, and other squares, its Broadway, Pearl, Washington, Wall, Grand, and other streets?

". . . The old lady hastily withdrew from the window, and . . . soon returned with the 'Platt' that the Squire had left with her. Here, said she, it is, in plain black and white, just as it was staked down by Squire Soaper . . . you now stand Major, (observed she) with one foot in Washington street, and the other in Grand street; your good woman between Pearl and Broadway, your house in State street, the forewheels of your waggon in Wall street, and the hind in Market street; and your black man stands in Commercial street; . . . and your dog in College Square!

"Major—My dog in College Square! and there let him remain until he becomes more wise than his master has proved himself:— Hem! . . . And pray tell me, good woman, how long was the Squire himself an inhabitant of Edensburgh, as you call it?

"Landlady—Just three half days; half a day in making the purchase and staking out the City—half a day in drawing and fixing this here Platt, and another half day, with the assistance of my old man, in logging the house we live in.

"Major—Squire Soaper was a Speculator, I suspect, and came into this country with plenty of gold and silver to buy up government lands?

"Landlady—O, no indeed, that he didn't! He came into this country a poor man . . . not worth more than five dollars in the world, and that in a few yankee notions, wooden bowls, and pewter spoons, and the like, which he swapped for this township, and which he says as good opportunities offer, he intends to swop away for good cultivated farms down east!"[18]

[18] Major Walter Wilkey, *Humorous Account of Western Life; Narrative of Major Wilkey's Tour to the West* (1839) as quoted in Woestemeyer, *Westward Movement*, pp. 316-17.

Newspapers usually were enthusiastic supporters of local efforts at town promotion. But on occasion when nearby communities threatened to attract attention or when local excesses became too pronounced, editorial condemnation resulted. A favored device was satire, although this of necessity had to be exceedingly broad to distinguish it from the exaggerated claims of the real town promoters. A St. Louis paper, with mock seriousness, announced in the 1820's the planning of the city of "Ne Plus Ultra." This town was described as having streets one mile wide, blocks of one square mile, a vast forested mall, and with its two main streets leading ". . . one from the south pole to Symnes's hole in the north, and another from Pekin to Jerusalem."[19]

Town Jobbing at the Water's Edge

Nowhere was speculation in town lots and new town development more intense than along the principal rivers, and later the canals, serving as major arteries of transportation from coastline to interior. Immediately after the opening of western lands, the Ohio River became the chief avenue to the west. Along its banks dozens of cities were laid out, some to flourish like Cincinnati, others to perish like Hygeia. The coming of the steamboat and the development or proposed development of great systems of canals added new importance to waterside locations. Although the railroads were to change the competitive positions of many of these river and canal cities, at the time they were planned their futures seemed secure.

Certain locations were favored by western speculators seeking sites for these cities: the juncture of two streams, as at Pittsburgh; at major falls, as at Louisville; or at the mouth of a river along one of the Great Lakes, as at Cleveland or Toledo. Usually, not one town was laid out, but half a dozen or more. For example, consider Louisville and its neighboring cities at the falls of the Ohio, shown as they existed in 1824 in Figure 212. Clarksville and Louisville were early arrivals. As river traffic developed and canal projects for easing the passage over the falls began to be discussed, Jeffersonville, Shippingsport, and Portland were platted. Still later came New Albany on the north bank. Each of these cities claimed to be the future metropolis of the falls area and engaged in the typical antics of town promotion.

[19] Timothy Flint, *Recollections of the Last Ten Years*, Boston, 1826, pp. 187-88.

A similar cluster of speculative towns developed on the Ohio a few miles below Pittsburgh at the mouth of Beaver Creek. Here lay the city of Beaver, a pleasant little community planned in 1791 by the state of Pennsylvania on land reserved by an act of the legislature in 1783. The plan was a simple one, quite similar to Philadelphia's, with a central open space of four squares, and with four additional reserved squares, one at each corner of the town. Until about 1830 the town grew relatively slowly. Then, as one historian, writing in 1843, put it:

"The astonishingly rapid growth of Buffalo, Rochester, Lockport, Syracuse, and other towns along the great New York canal, had insensibly created a vast *school of speculation*, the pupils of which subsequently spread themselves over all the other states. . . . The great natural resources at the mouth of Beaver did not escape their notice nor their grasp. Enlisting in their visionary plans some of the original holders of property, who too soon became apt scholars at the new science, they proceeded to purchase up the real estate and mill sites along the banks of the river. . . . Better adepts with the pen and the drawing instruments, than with the apparatus of the mill, these gentlemen preferred laying out paper cities, and trumpeting the value of their lots in overwrought puffs."[20]

Figure 213 shows the results of this feverish activity. Streets, blocks, and lots stretched along Beaver Creek for several miles from its mouth. Finally, after the usual booming and the building of grand hotels and other similar "improvements" designed to show that progress was both rapid and inevitable, "The fever subsided, and the ague succeeded—the bubble burst with the U.S. Bank, and . . . the speculators returned to more useful employments."[21]

Along the Maumee River in the vicinity of the present Toledo virtually the same events occurred. Perrysburg had been platted by the U.S. government on a federal reserve in 1817. Maumee City, on the opposite bank dates from about the same time. Then came the excitement over the terminus of the canal to connect the Maumee River with the Ohio in the 1830's. In quick succession Port Lawrence, Vistula, Manhattan, and several other towns were platted on both sides of the river one after the other. As at Beaver, the emphasis was on haste and minimum investment; consequently

[20] Sherman Day, *Historical Collections of the State of Pennsylvania*, Philadelphia, 1843, p. 107.
[21] *ibid.*, 108.

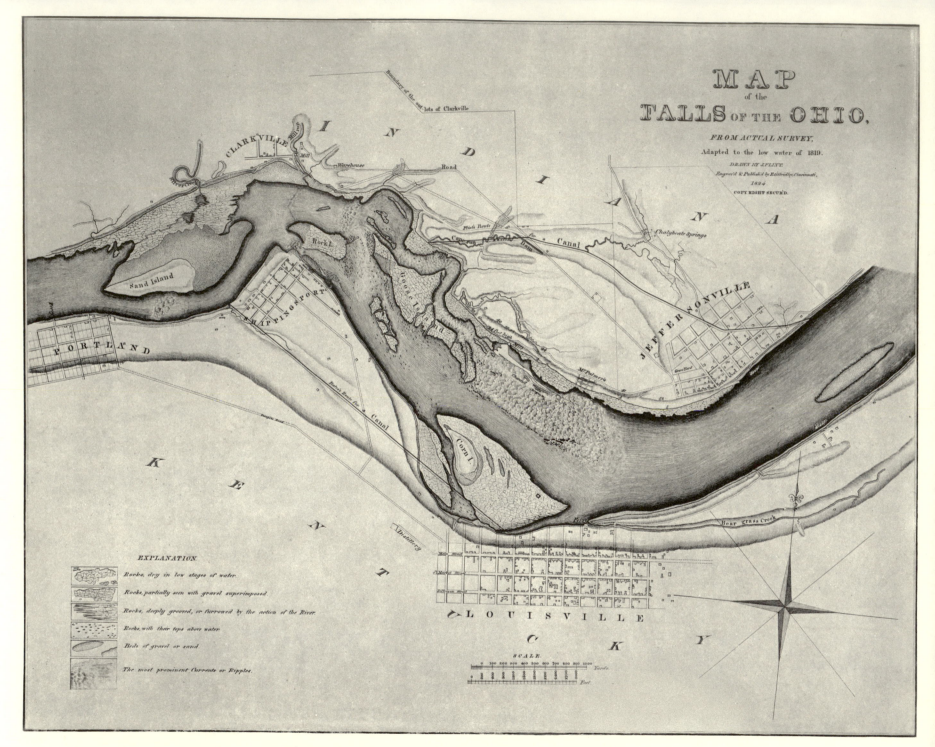

Figure 212. Map of Louisville, Kentucky and Vicinity: 1824

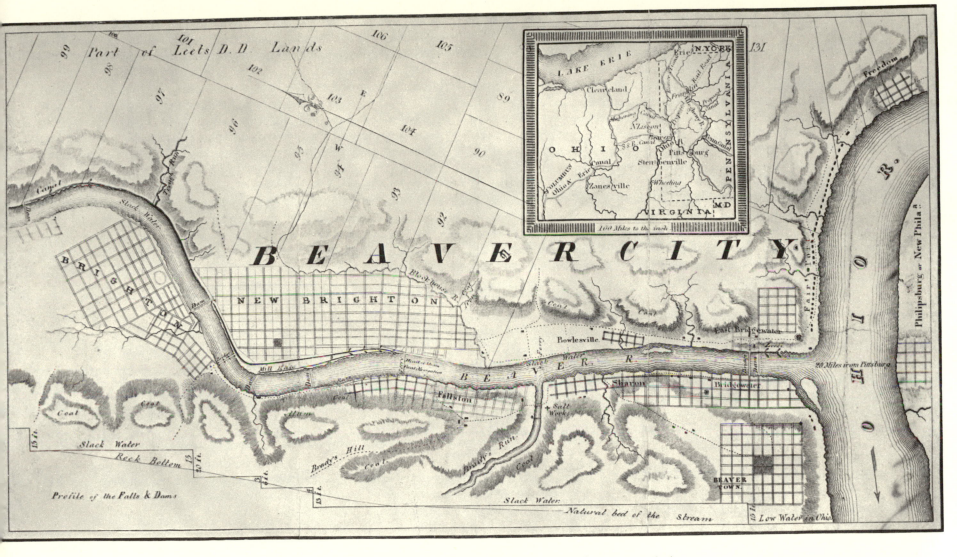

Figure 213. Plan of Beaver, Pennsylvania and Environs: ca. 1836

these cities have little to offer by way of interest or quality in their plans.[22]

Farther to the north the fever of townsite speculation also raged in Wisconsin Territory, created in 1836. Controversy over the site for a territorial capital stimulated the platting of dozens of new towns, all with impressive claims. Belmont, hurriedly laid out in 1836 for the first meeting of the territorial legislature, is shown in Figure 214. Wisconsin City, shown in Figure 215, with its two market places, three large squares with appropriate patriotic names, and its public grounds along the Wisconsin River, had its backers. But a visitor to the place the following year records only that "it was then in its glory, with the stakes all standing, or enough to show the public grounds." But the prize finally went to Madison, which James Doty laid out with a system of diagonal and gridiron streets. Doty, it will be remembered, helped the members of the legislature to reach a decision by offering them choice corner lots in the new town if it were chosen.

Doty, who later became governor of Wisconsin, operated for years as a promoter of townsites. In addition to Madison, he was responsible for Astor, now a part of Green Bay; Caramaunee; Menasha; Town of the Island; and, earlier than these, Fond du Lac. The Fond du Lac plan, shown in Figure 216, is a most curious layout. More than a dozen cross-shaped open spaces were featured in the plan, which Doty devised in 1835. These apparently were not developed as formal plazas, but later views of the town do show streets running through the spaces with houses built on the lots as platted and set back from the streets.[23]

During the 1830's speculation in town lands reached its peak in the country between the Alleghenies and the Mississippi. Twenty years later Kansas became the center of townsite promotion. There an even more furious pace was maintained. "Doing a land office business" was then a fresh and meaningful figure of speech, as the sketch of a busy Kansas Land Office in Figure 217 shows.

That perceptive and reliable observer of the early development of Kansas, Albert D. Richardson, is the best source of information.[24] He noted that along the 125 miles of the Missouri River in

Kansas no less than 14 cities had been platted by 1857. New towns appeared so rapidly that certain frontier wits proposed that Congress reserve some of the land for farming before the entire territory was cut up into building lots. As we might suspect, and as Richardson confirms, the promoters advanced extravagant claims of buildings already existing or to be constructed shortly. The New Babylons of Kansas Territory, as shown in Figure 218, were usually represented as having one or more railroads, a university, churches, parks, exchanges, and the like. In fact New Babylon, as Richardson suggests in Figure 219, was rarely more than a shack or tent and often consisted solely of an expanse of rolling prairie. Few persons bothered to visit the site of one of these "cities" before buying a lot or share. Of course many of the sales were made in the eastern states, but even Kansas residents made purchases sight unseen much as one might buy a lottery ticket. In describing how practically all Kansans took part in this craze of speculation Richardson comments, "it was not a swindle, but a mania. The speculators were quite as insane as the rest."

There were swindles by townsite speculators, however, and a good many Kansas residents were guilty of fraud and perjury. Land preemption regulations permitted the purchase, at nominal cost, of 160 acres of land if it was actually occupied and "improved" by the preemptor. A witness was required to swear that the claim had been improved with a habitable dwelling "twelve by fourteen." Richardson tells of such a claim being based on a house "whittled out with a penknife, twelve inches by fourteen." He also mentions the use of a detached window sash without glass hung on a nail in the wall so that a witness might swear that there was a window in the house, a house on wheels that rented for five dollars a day and was moved from claim to claim, and other frauds of the same type.

Kansas townsite promoters used another device to enlarge the permitted 320-acre tract for a town so as to increase their profits. Richardson tells how this was accomplished:

"In founding a city, a few speculators become corporated, by special act of the legislature, as a town company. Then, if the land is already open for preemption, they survey and stake out three hundred and twenty acres—the quantity which the Government allows set apart for a town-site—at one dollar and a quarter per acre. But the large ideas of the West will never be satisfied with

[22] Randolph C. Downes, *Canal Days*, Lucas County Historical Series, II, Toledo, 1949, pp. 55-69.

[23] Doty's interesting career, including his town speculations, is the subject of Alice Elizabeth Smith, *James Duane Doty*, Madison, 1954.

[24] Albert D. Richardson, *Beyond the Mississippi*, Hartford, 1867.

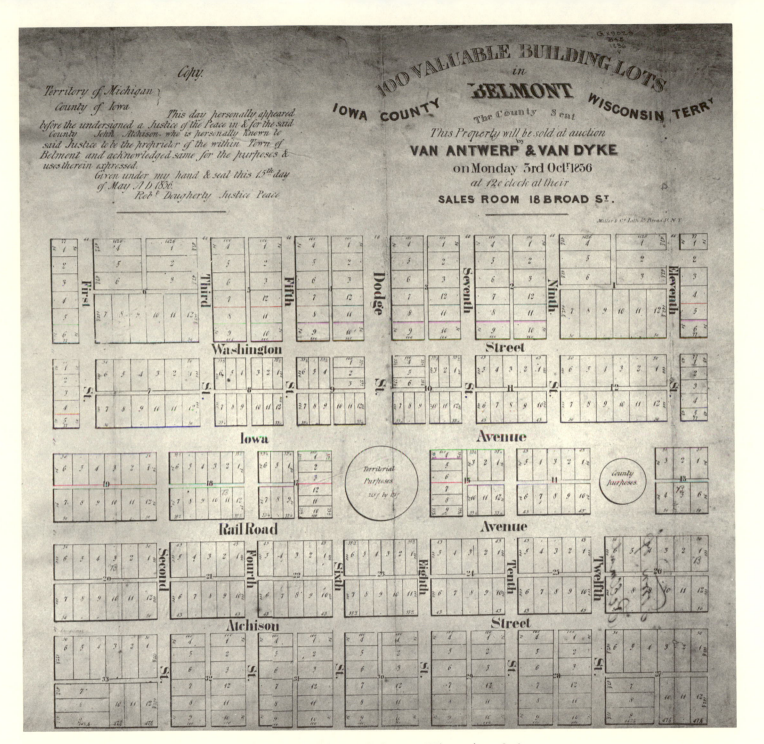

Figure 214. Plan of Belmont, Wisconsin: 1836

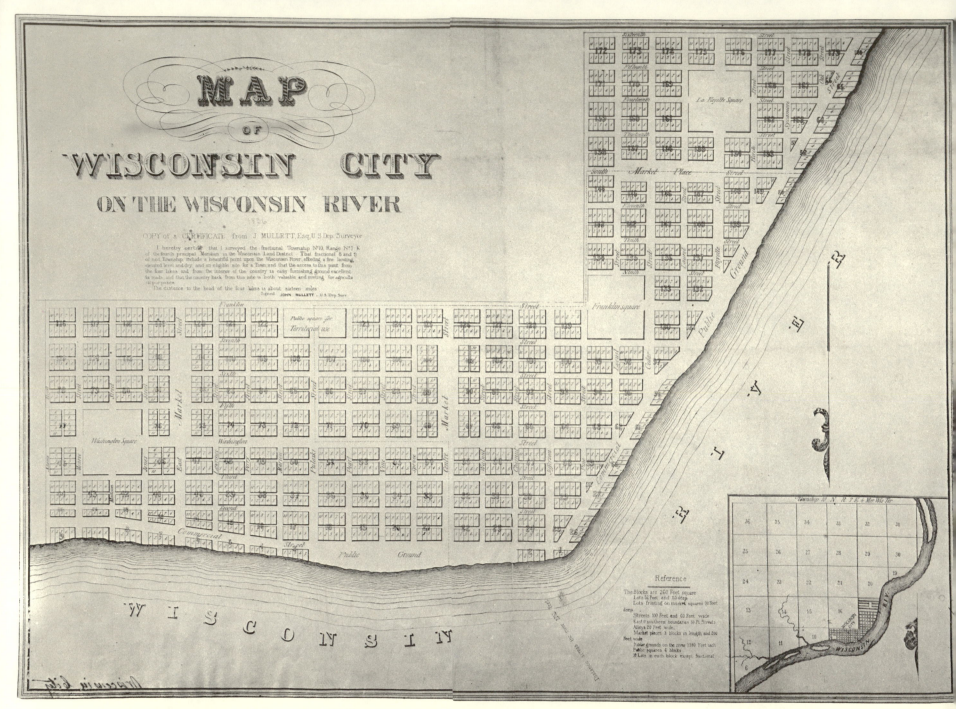

Figure 215. Plan of Wisconsin City, Wisconsin: 1836

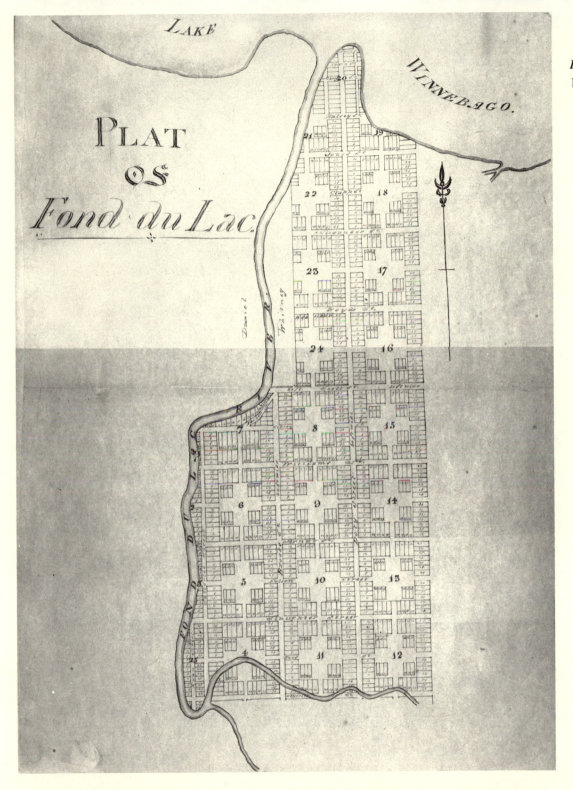

Figure 216. Plan of Fond du Lac, Wisconsin: ca. 1835

Figure 217. A Kansas Land Office in 1874

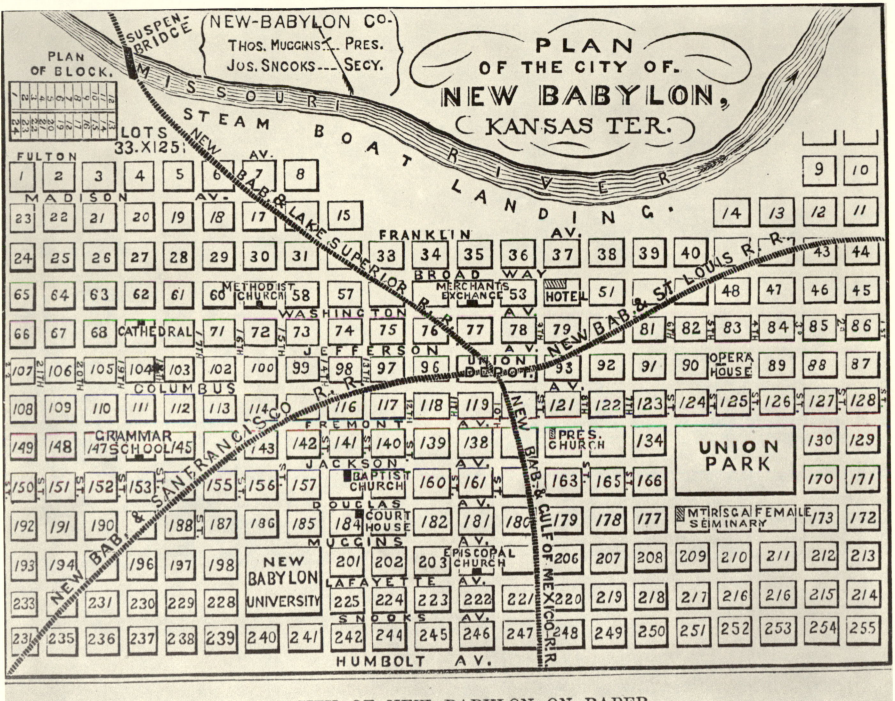

THE CITY OF NEW BABYLON ON PAPER.

Figure 218. Plan of the City of "New Babylon" on Paper

THE CITY OF NEW BABYLON IN FACT.

Figure 219. View of "New Babylon" in Fact

such a pent-up Utica. So they engage settlers each to preempt one of the adjacent quarter-sections (one hundred and sixty acres). The settler can only do this by swearing that it is for his homestead, for his own exclusive use and benefit; that he has not contracted, directly nor indirectly, to sell any portion of it. The invariable alacrity with which he commits this bit of perjury, is a marvel to strangers not yet free from eastern prejudices. When his title is perfected, he deeds his land to the corporation, and receives his money as per agreement. Thus the company secures from five hundred to a thousand acres, cutting it into building lots usually twenty-five by one hundred and twenty-five feet. . . .

"If the town succeeds, the original proprietors grow rich. If it fails, having risked little, they lose little."[25]

One of the Kansas boom towns platted along the Missouri River was Sumner. This town was widely advertised in the east, and the view reproduced in Figure 220 purported to represent the city as it actually existed in 1857. An early settler was young John James Ingalls of Boston, who reached Sumner in 1858 and whose letters to his father describing the place have been preserved. Referring to the promotional view of Sumner as a "lithographic fiction," Ingalls tells his father of the steep, stump-strewn street leading to the primitive hotel, and then continues:

"This is the only street in the place which has any pretension to a grade, the others being merely footpaths leading up and down the wild ravines to the few log huts and miserable cabins which compose the city. None of the premises are fenced. . . .

"There are no churches in the place, instead of four, as was represented to me. No respectable residences; no society; no women except a few woebegone, desolate-looking old creatures; no mechanical activity; nothing which would seem to indicate a large and intelligent energy; no schools, no children; nothing but the total reverse of the picture which was presented to me. On the engraved romance a 'college' was imagined, of which no person here . . . has even so much as heard the idea advanced."[26]

Yet in two months Ingalls helped to draft a proposed city charter and in January wrote from Lawrence of his activities as a lobbyist in behalf of the Sumner Company. By the middle of the following month he told his father that "Improvements are going on in Sumner to a considerable extent. It compares very favorably with any of the towns in the territory which I have visited, and I believe I have seen all except Topeka and Manhattan."[27]

The critical young visitor from Boston had become as much of a town boomer as the rest. Yet for all his energy and enthusiasm the town did not succeed. Richardson, who had lived in Sumner for a time in 1858, passed by the site in 1866 on a river steamer and reported sadly: "In 1858 Sumner . . . had five hundred people. Now it has about twenty-five. All the buildings save five or six have been torn down and taken away. Young oaks and cottonwoods choke its deserted streets. . . ."[28]

The Colleges Enroll in the School of Speculation

Townsite promotion touched virtually every element in the country. Colleges and universities were no exception. Two examples have been discovered, and no doubt there were many other cases where town planning and university development were connected. Perhaps most interesting is the abortive attempt by Bishop Philander Chase, head of the infant Kenyon College in Gambier, Ohio, to found a new town. The college, but a few years old, found itself in serious financial difficulties. Chase observed the widespread town promotion activities in Ohio and decided that such an activity showed promise of providing funds to complete the college buildings and to pay overdue bills.

Three miles north of Gambier, Chase fixed the site of the proposed town on land already in college ownership. Edson Harkness was employed to survey the town, and in 1829 his plat and description, along with a plea to prospective purchasers by Bishop Chase, appeared in pamphlet form in eastern cities. The plat of Cornish, named for Chase's birthplace in New Hampshire, appears in Figure 221. Chase cleverly combined the attractions of possible speculative profits with an opportunity to support a worthy cause, when he outlined his proposal:

"There being twice as many in-lots as out-lots, and it being designed to sell an out-lot and an in-lot together, the purchasers are to understand that every lot adjacent to their lots respectively, will

[25] ibid., 30-31.
[26] Ingalls' letter to his father, October 5, 1858, Kansas State Historical Society, Collections, XIV, 100.
[27] Ingalls' letter to his father, February 16, 1859, ibid., 111.
[28] Richardson, Beyond the Mississippi, 549.

VIEW OF SUMNER
KANSAS   TERRY

Figure 220. View of Sumner, Kansas: ca. 1857

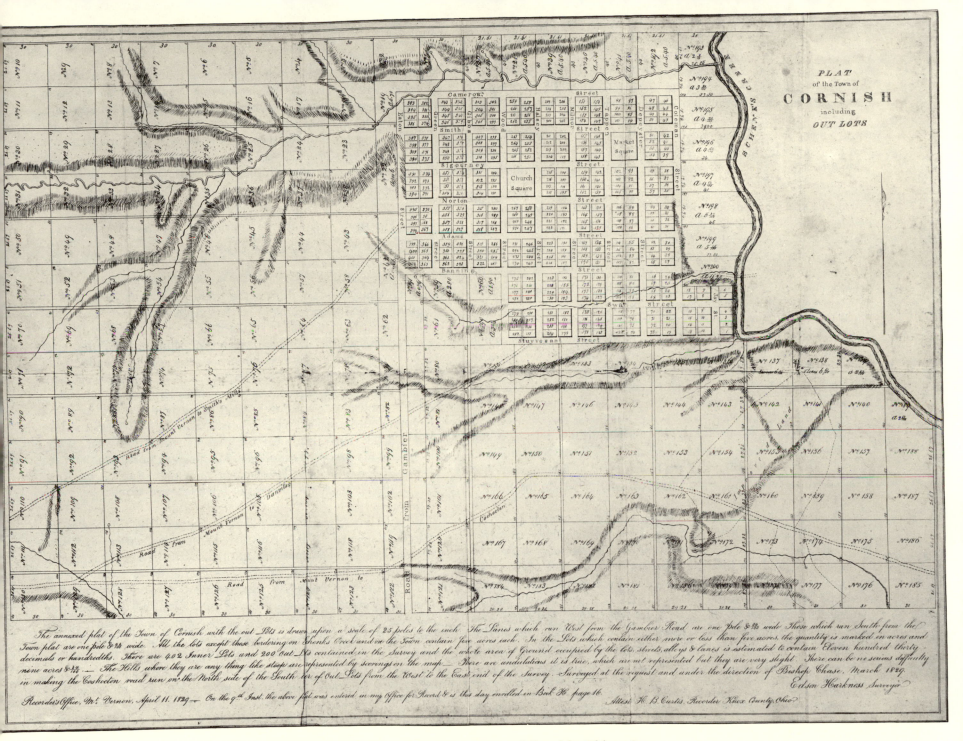

Figure 221. Plan of Proposed Town of Cornish, Ohio: 1829

be offered *gratis* to any approved settler who will build a house thereon within a given period. It is obvious that this will *surely* and *greatly* enhance the value of the contiguous property; so that on the ground of *interest* the purchaser may be confident his money could not be more advantageously invested. And when to this motive is joined that of benevolence to an institution now struggling with difficulties . . . the reasons for making this investment become irresistible."[29]

Despite the high purpose advanced by Chase, the town failed to develop, and the college was denied the speculative land profits which might have enriched its endowment.

Then there was the development of a town in Wisconsin bearing the name of a new eastern university, and whose layout and early promotion were in the hands of the university's founder, Ezra Cornell. Cornell University had been established in 1865 and designated by the New York state legislature to receive the land grant to educational institutions teaching agriculture and the mechanic arts provided by the Morrill Act passed by the U.S. Congress in 1862. This act provided scrip exchangeable for government land, then priced at $1.25 per acre, which could then be sold to finance the development of the institution. Mr. Cornell's suggestion was to use the scrip to locate land in the west, holding it for a period and then selling after prices rose. The trustees rejected this idea and sold some of the scrip at the equivalent of about 85¢ an acre. Cornell then offered to buy the remaining scrip at 50¢ an acre, use it to locate western land, and to turn over all profits to the university. This proposal was accepted, and Cornell took up land in Kansas, Minnesota, and Wisconsin as rapidly as possible.

He selected nearly half a million acres in the Chippewa River Valley in Minnesota, where there were excellent stands of pine. In 1867 he conceived the idea of laying out a town where there could be a mill to exploit the forest potential and where additional profits might be made through the sale of town lots. Cornell and some of his associates formed the New York Lumber, Manufacturing, and Improvement Company, and, typically, issued a brochure describing the new town they had laid out in Wisconsin.[30] The plan is

[29] The text of the Chase statement is given in Donald W. Ferguson, "The Proposed Town of Cornish, Ohio," *The Ohio State Archaeological and Historical Quarterly*, XLIV (April 1935), 245-49.

[30] *Prospectus of the New York Lumber, Manufacturing and Improvement Co.*, Albany, 1867.

shown in Figure 222. Certainly there was nothing particularly distinctive about the layout. The same can be said about the efforts of the corporation to attract investors. The promotion fell through, although later the university realized substantial profits from the sale of timber lands in Wisconsin, and the city of Cornell, after a slow and shaky start, did manage to survive. The university now has no real estate interests in the community, and its original association is all but forgotten.

Boomers, Sooners, and the Great Town Rush in Oklahoma

Without question the record for wholesale town promotion and town building was set during the great Oklahoma land rush of 1889. For years land-hungry settlers in Kansas and Texas had looked greedily at the lands reserved as Indian Territory by government treaty. Pressure mounted on Washington to throw open for settlement the land in Oklahoma not assigned specifically to any tribes. By 1879 the "Boomers," led by C. C. Carpenter and later by David L. Payne, announced their intention to move into Oklahoma, establish a "capital city," and claim land. Payne, in 1880, actually eluded the Federal troops endeavoring to protect the borders and laid out a city near the present site of Oklahoma City. Payne and his group were subsequently evicted, but throughout the 1880's attempts at illegal settlement increased. Finally, on April 22, 1889, at noon, the unassigned lands were thrown open for settlement.

What followed must surely rank as the most hectic days in the entire settlement of North America. Prospective settlers had lined up along the borders, mounted on horseback, or with wagonloads of household possessions, or clinging to the overcrowded special trains assigned to move into the territory. At noon the symbolic booming of cannon and the firing of guns signaled the opening of the great land rush. The number of persons who crossed the borders that day is unknown, but estimates run into the tens of thousands. By December, according to one account, 60,000 persons had entered the territory. All were seeking land, and most of them had an eye for choice lots in one of the 320-acre townsites that would be laid out. Hamilton S. Wicks leaped from the train at Guthrie the first day of the rush:

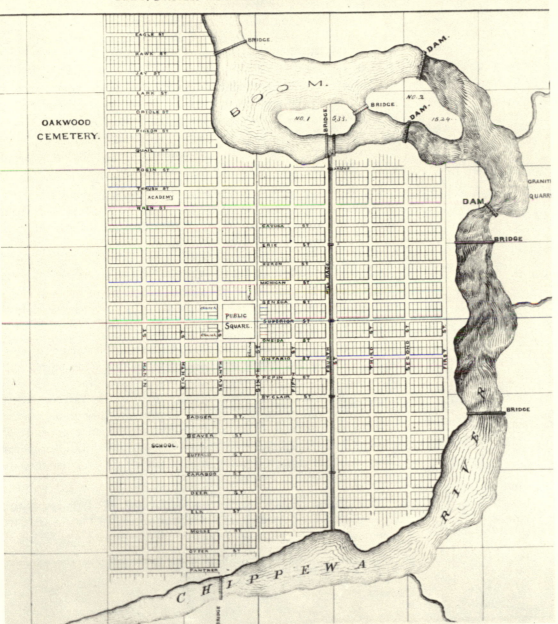

PLAN
OF PROJECTED IMPROVEMENTS IN
THE VILLAGE OF
CORNELL
AT BRUNETT'S FALLS
WISCONSIN
SHOWING THE CHIPPEWA RIVER, FALLS.
DAMS, BRIDGES, MILL RACE, STREETS, BLOCKS, LOTS & OUTLOTS.

Figure 222. Plan of Cornell,
Wisconsin: 1867

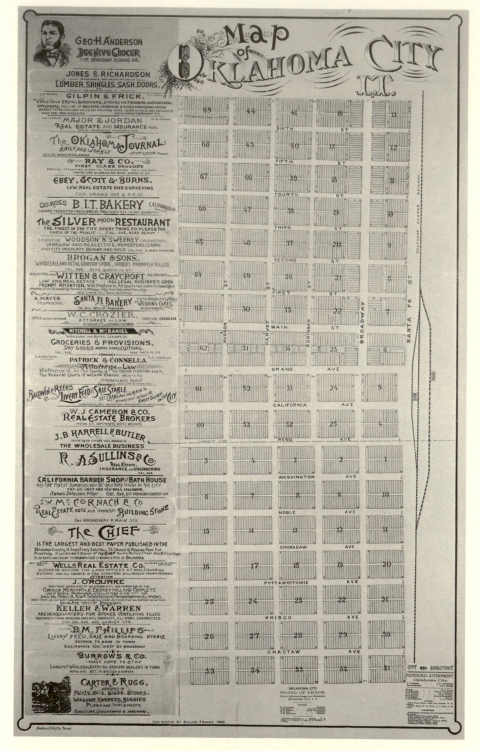

"I joined the wild scramble for a town lot up the sloping hill-side. . . . There were several thousand people converging on the same plot of ground, each eager for a town lot which was to be acquired without cost or without price. . . .

"The race was not over when you reached the particular lot you were content to select for your possession. The contest still was who should drive their stakes first, who would erect their little tents soonest, and then, who would quickest build a little wooden shanty.

"The situation was so peculiar that it is difficult to convey correct impressions of the situation. It reminded me of playing blind-man's-bluff. One did not know how far to go before stopping; it was hard to tell when it was best to stop, and it was a puzzle whether to turn to the right hand or the left. Every one appeared dazed, and all for the most part acted like a flock of stray sheep."[31]

Wicks finally located a corner lot, drove his stake and ". . . then threw a couple of my blankets over the cot, and staked them securely into the ground on either side. Thus I had a claim that was unjumpable because of substantial improvements. . . ."[32]

During the night Wicks tells of shooting, "haloos and shoutings," and imitations of Indian war cries. But the next day there were no corpses, and the pistols and rifles were put away in favor of hammers and saws. Tents gave way to shanties and later to larger houses, and in three months Wicks could write

"Guthrie presents the appearance of a model Western city, with broad and regular streets and alleys; with handsome stores and office buildings: with a system of parks and boulevards . . . with a system of water-works that furnishes hydrants at the corners of all the principal streets . . . ; with an electric-light plant on the Westinghouse system of alternating currents, capable not only of thoroughly lighting the whole city, but of furnishing the power for running an electric railway, for which the charter has already been granted by the city council. . . ."[33]

The experience at Guthrie was duplicated at other townsites. Figures 223 and 224 show the plan and a view of Oklahoma City early in 1890. Already there are six real estate offices, a Board

[31] Hamilton S. Wicks, "The Opening of Oklahoma," *The Cosmopolitan*, VII (September 1889), 466-67.
[32] *ibid.*, 467.
[33] *ibid.*, 469.

Figure 223. Plan of Oklahoma City, Oklahoma: 1889

OKLAHOMA CITY
INDIAN TERRITORY.
1890.

Figure 224. View of Oklahoma City, Oklahoma: 1890

of Trade, and the California Barber Shop and Bath House.[34] Thus civilization came to the Oklahoma plains.

Promotions in Paradise

With the westward course of empire went the town speculators. They flourished in the warm sunshine of southern California, and while many of the cities planted in this paradise grew strong and healthy others, forced too quickly, withered and died. The land boom in the Los Angeles area came later than at its rival city of San Francisco. The gold rush and the arrival of the railroad in the Bay Area had both contributed to the usual excesses of town booming, first in the 1850's and later in the 1870's. But the Los Angeles town promotions made up in fervor and eccentricities what had been lost in time.

The coming of the Southern Pacific Railroad in 1876 and the Santa Fe in 1887 touched off the first town promotion explosion. In the spring of 1887 almost 40 towns were laid out along the two rail lines in Los Angeles County, an average of about one town for each mile and a half of railroad. Wooden street markers and surveyors' stakes were so numerous that one historian suggests that the otherwise empty fields must have resembled battlefield cemeteries. Auctions proved effective in selling lots quickly. Usually they were contrived, with several agents in the crowd instructed to begin the bidding at high prices. Promoters used the time-tested tricks to attract purchasers that had worked so well through the years in Ohio, Illinois, Kansas, and Wisconsin. The town promoters in fact had an easier time of it than back east, since in California even the minimum improvements of a hotel, station, or land office seemed unnecessary. Simon Homberg in promoting his Manchester and Border City schemes in the sandy wastes bordering the Mojave Desert even skipped the expense of street and lot surveys. Armed with deeds that left a blank space to insert the name of the unlucky purchaser and with drawings of the proposed cities, Homberg hawked some 4,000 lots in eastern cities. Cost of the lots ran about 10¢, and some of them sold for $250.[35]

Even the promoters themselves could not resist poking fun at their own activities. In the midst of the boom one real estate office issued the following circular:

"BOOM! BOOM! BOOM!

The newest town out! Balderdash! Watch for it! Wait for it! Catch on to it!

To meet the great demand for another new townsite we have secured 10,000 acres of that beautiful land lying on the top of Old Baldy, and will lay out an elegant town with the above very significant and appropriate name. . . . Nine thousand acres will at once be divided into fine business lots 14 x 33 feet. All lots will front on grand avenues 17 feet wide and run back to 18 inch alleys. For the present one-tenth of the entire tract will be reserved for residences in case anyone should want to build. . . . To accommodate the inquisitive who are afraid to invest without inspecting the property a fast balloon line will be started in the near future. Parties will be permitted to return on the superb toboggan slide to be built in the sweet bye and bye. All lots will be sold at a uniform price of $1100 each. . . . All offers for lots will be refused previous to day of sale, and in order that all may have a chance no person will be permitted to buy more than 500 lots. . . ."[36]

Most of these cities of the boom followed the traditional checkerboard pattern. Santa Monica, whose plan appears in Figure 225, is an excellent example of the type. Here was an undeviating grid stretching back from Santa Monica Bay toward the coastal hills.

[34] The hectic days of the settlement of Oklahoma City are vividly related by one of the participants in the land rush in Angelo C. Scott, *The Story of Oklahoma City*, Oklahoma City, 1939. Scott's narrative explains the slight irregularity in the plan of Oklahoma City which can be seen in Figure 223. Two rival land companies had laid out different plans for the same site. The two plats were finally reconciled and settlement proceeded. Litigation over land titles occupied the frontier lawyers for years. Other useful sources include John Alley, *City Beginnings in Oklahoma Territory*, Norman, 1939; W. S. Prettyman, *Indian Territory*, Norman, 1957; and Roy Gittinger, *The Formation of the State of Oklahoma, 1803-1906*, Norman, 1939.

[35] James M. Guinn, *History of California and an Extended History of Los Angeles*, Los Angeles, 1915, I, 262-63. See also A. M. Sakolski, *The Great American Land Bubble*, New York, 1932, pp. 318-22, and especially Glenn S. Dumke, *The Boom of the Eighties in Southern California*, San Marino, 1944, for the various sales devices used by land speculators and developers.

[36] As quoted by Glenn Chesney Quiett, *They Built the West*, New York, 1934, p. 280. Quiett's Chapter 10 is an excellent treatment of the speculative growth of Los Angeles.

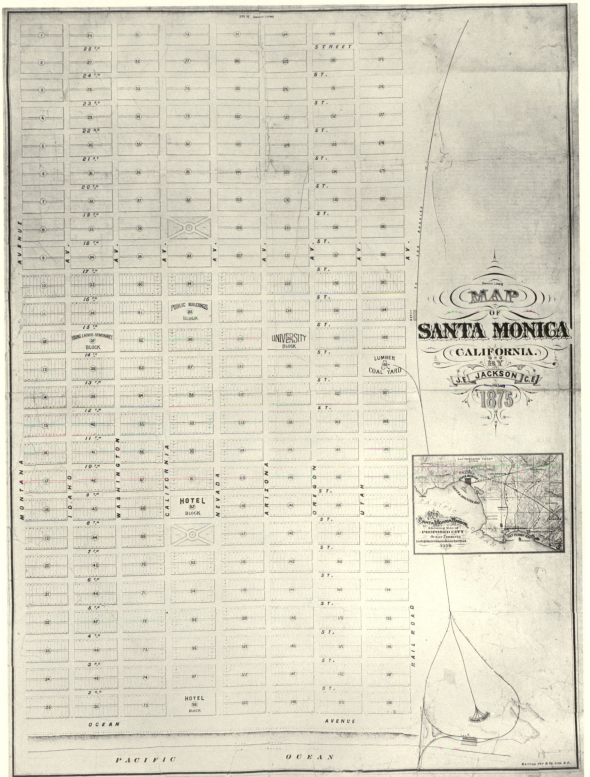

Figure 225. Plan of Santa Monica, California: 1875

The inevitable reservations for hotels, a seminary, public buildings, a university, and parks were indicated. Within nine months after Col. R. S. Baker and Senator John P. Jones platted the town it had attracted 1,000 residents. A great pier to be a mile long and worth a million dollars was begun to make the city the chief port for Los Angeles, and the possibility of great industrial and harbor development lured thousands more to the city. The bubble burst when San Pedro Bay, to the south of Los Angeles, was selected as the railroad terminus and port site in the 1890's. Yet Santa Monica shared in the growth of Greater Los Angeles and continued to exist where dozens of other boom towns completely disappeared or remained as small and unimportant villages.

Strange and exotic plans were sometimes employed. Corona, 50 miles east of Los Angeles, was laid out in 1886 with a circular boulevard exactly a mile in diameter. Brawley, in San Diego County, the plan of which appears in Figure 226, had four diagonal streets entering the sides of its diamond-shaped public square. And there was Venice, a seaside community with canals and imported gondolas; Coronado, with its combination of radial and curvilinear streets; the aptly named Ballona, which was built on a swamp but bragged of its harbor; and—but the list is endless. For the later development of Hollywood, a city of another kind of fantasy and illusion, the southern California land boom furnished ample precedent.

And so it went across the continent—cities for sale through boom and bust. Although land speculation continues to this day, we are not likely to see again such an era of wholesale humbuggery and land butchery. The stamp of the early speculator remains, however, upon most of our cities. At a pace a hundred times slower than the original development, and at enormous expense, modern city planners now are attempting to erase the worst blotches spilled across the country by the boomers, the townsite promoters, and the speculative builders of yesterday. It is an aspect of our urban history in which Americans can take little pride.

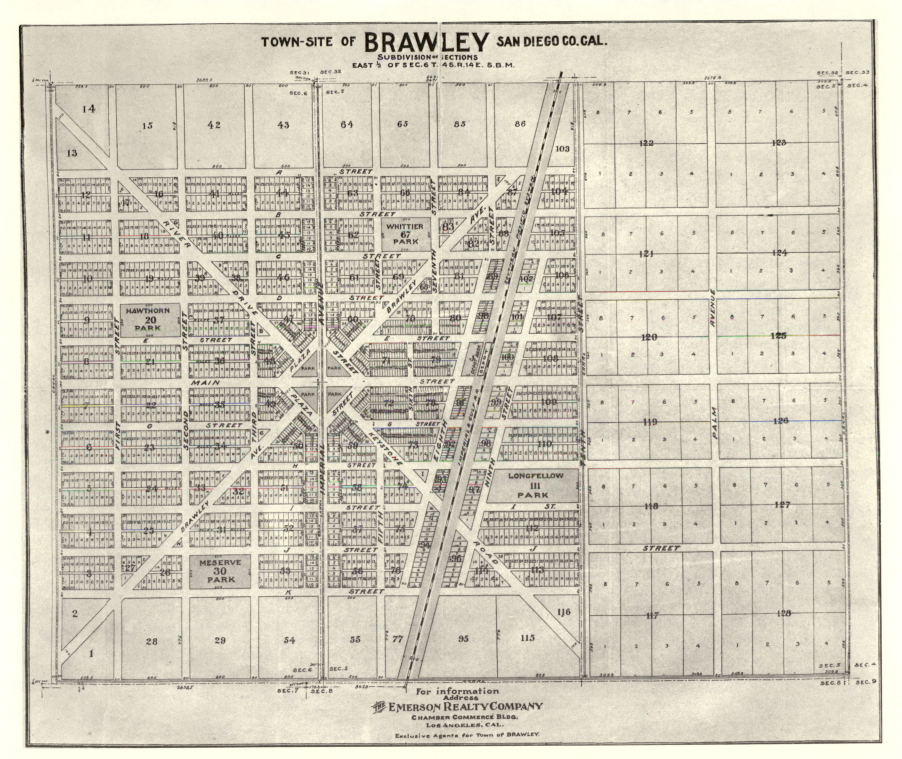

Figure 226. Plan of Brawley, California: ca. 1900

Towns by the Tracks

THE coming of the railroad opened a new era of city development and city planning in America. Railroads affected the tempo of city building, opened vast new areas for population growth, and resulted in hundreds of new towns laid out to take advantage of this more efficient means of transportation. The patterns of existing cities changed to accommodate the new stations, rail lines, yards, and shops required for railroad operation. Railroads, too, made possible the development of suburban communities for the well-to-do and thus began the phenomenon of urban sprawl which continues unabated to the present day.

Along the eastern slope of the Appalachians and on the Atlantic coastal plain the principal effect of the railroads was to stimulate the growth of existing communities. Generally the new lines followed the valley routes already exploited by the canal systems developed during the first few decades of the nineteenth century. By 1840, New York, Philadelphia, Baltimore, and Washington were linked by one or more lines. Radiating from each of these cities and from Boston were many shorter lines connecting the coastal cities with smaller centers of population in the interior. By 1850 nearly 10,000 miles of railroad had been built, and it was possible to travel from Maine to Wilmington, North Carolina, by rail if one had the money and endurance. Buffalo was connected to New York and Boston; a line from Detroit had almost reached Chicago; Harrisburg and Philadelphia had been connected; and lines from Charleston and Savannah extended to Atlanta and into Tennessee. New England had developed a vast network of rail lines connecting practically all of the important cities in that region.

Some new communities developed, of course, but most of the lines merely connected existing cities and reinforced their growth as centers of trade, shopping, and manufacturing. These cities, already the source of capital and centers of finance, eagerly sought to develop additional railroads in order to maintain or increase their commercial positions. Baltimore and Philadelphia, which had

suffered at the hands of New York when the Erie Canal had been developed, were particularly anxious to promote railroad building to the west.

Detailed studies of the effects of railroad building on these established cities would be useful. But the aim of this chapter is to trace the influence of railroads on the planning of new towns and the direct activities of the railroads and their sponsors in laying out towns and promoting town development. Since most of this activity occurred in the midwestern and western states, the focus will be shifted from the Atlantic seaboard to the less settled but rapidly developing area beyond the Appalachians. This treatment can be at best only a sampling of the more interesting episodes in this era of American planning.

Great Expectations and Hard Times: The Planning of Cairo, Illinois

The prospects of railroad development in the virgin lands of the west held out great opportunities for the planners of speculative towns. Nowhere were they pursued more relentlessly than in Cairo, Illinois, located on a seemingly advantageous site at the confluence of the Ohio and the Mississippi Rivers. In 1835 Darius B. Holbrook purchased this land and in January of the following year secured a charter from the Illinois legislature for his Illinois Central Rail Road Company. Under the terms of the charter the railroad was to begin at a point at or near the mouth of the Ohio and terminate at the end of the Illinois and Michigan Canal in Galena, then the chief city in the state. The Holbrook group obviously hoped to benefit by advancing two projects simultaneously: the railroad would stimulate growth of the town, and trade generated by the river port would contribute to profits on the railroad.[1]

[1] An earlier city plan for the same site, dating from 1818, had failed to produce results. This is described in my "Great Expectations and Hard

This scheme was partially thwarted when in 1837 the Illinois legislature passed its famous Internal Improvements Act, providing for a network of railroads to be constructed with public funds. However, since this act specified that one of the lines was to have its terminus at Cairo, Holbrook was apparently assured of railroad transportation and could focus all of his considerable energies and talents on townsite promotion.

Money was needed in substantial quantity for ·completing the land purchase, for construction of levees to protect the low-lying site from frequent floods, and for a wide range of improvements. Holbrook proceeded to London to raise the necessary capital. In February 1839 he jubilantly revealed the success of his mission in a glowing prospectus that was aimed for wide distribution. A St. Louis newspaper quoted Holbrook's statement that a million and a half dollars had been obtained from the Messrs. Wright and Co. of London for the Cairo project.

Holbrook was undoubtedly an articulate and convincing speaker, but even he could not have induced hard-headed London bankers to advance such a sum solely on his statements regarding the advantages and glorious future of his city ·of Cairo. Holbrook's claims were supported by a report and plan prepared by America's most distinguished architect, William Strickland. Strickland, the designer of the Philadelphia Exchange, the U.S. mint in the same city, and many other important buildings, was known in England and may well have been asked for advice by Holbrook's London banking contacts.

Strickland's report was prepared after he studied the site in company with Richard Taylor, an English engineer and geologist. The two planners directed their attention first to the vital matter of flood control. Extensive filling and construction of dikes were to be carried out; in addition, as an added measure of protection, all buildings were to have foundations at least 9 feet deep.

The details of the city plan probably were Strickland's responsibility. His proposals are shown in Figures 227 and 228, the plan and view of the new city. In the plan the shaded portion indicates the section to be built first, while the dashed lines indicate the eventual extent of the city. The view reveals Strickland's vision of a great commercial metropolis that would fill the peninsula between the rivers.

Strickland may have been influenced by the plan of his native Philadelphia in developing this scheme, but it seems more likely he had in mind something approaching the orderly layout in the fashionable areas of London's West End. In Bloomsbury and adjoining districts, dozens of residential squares with connecting streets on a modified grid pattern had been built. The size of Strickland's blocks and open squares—each about 500 feet on a side—was similar to the London pattern. So, too, was the vertical scale of four stories, resembling Georgian and Regency building practice.

The influence of London estate development policies may also be inferred from the terms of land tenure adopted by the company. As announced by Holbrook in his 1839 prospectus,

"When the company are prepared to dispose of their real estate, *they will offer it on lease for a certain term of years at such rent or rents, as the business of the place will justify and warrant, conditioned*, that if the consideration agreed upon is punctually paid for and during the time stipulated in the lease, the estate in question shall become bona fide the property of the lessee."[2]

Leasehold occupancy, even under terms that might culminate in a transfer of the fee, was closer to British practice than American. Only in Baltimore was leasehold development widely used. Certainly this policy, which continued for nearly twenty years, caused considerable unrest and was a factor contributing to the company's failure.

Strickland's plan apparently never achieved official status. Some construction was begun, but what projects were actually completed is a matter of controversy. According to one account written in 1841, 7½ miles of levees were built and many buildings were constructed, including a hotel, a "line of substantial brick warehouses," 100 houses for workmen, and a number of permanent homes. The same source mentions the existence of a dry dock, several saw mills, and "extensive iron foundries and machine shops."[3] But

Times: The Planning of Cairo, Illinois," *Journal of the Society of Architectural Historians*, XVI (1957), 14-21, of which the present chapter section is a condensed version. See also John M. Landsden, *A History of the City of Cairo, Illinois*, Chicago, 1910, where the plan is reproduced following p. 30.

[2] *Prospectus and Engineers' Report Relating to the City of Cairo*, February 18, 1839, as quoted in Landsden, *Cairo*, 49.
[3] J. C. Wild, *The Valley of the Mississippi, Illustrated*, No. 6, December, 1841, p. 88.

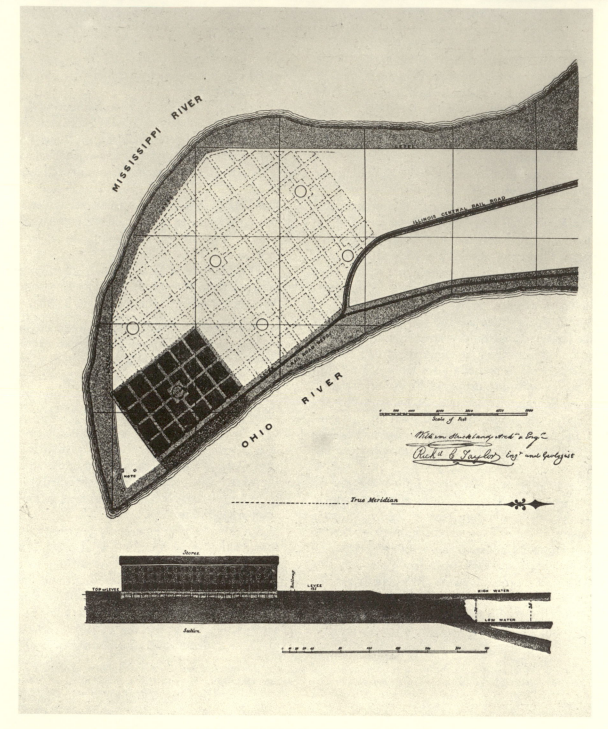

Figure 227. William Strickland's Plan for Cairo, Illinois: 1838

PROSPECTIVE VIEW OF THE CITY OF CAIRO,

at the Junction of the Ohio with the Mississippi River, *Illinois.*

Figure 228. View of Strickland's Proposed City of Cairo, Illinois: 1838

when James Buckingham visited the site about the same time he observed:

"On looking around, however, for 'the works already constructed,' which are here said to be 'considerable,' nothing is seen but a few small dwellings of the humblest class of workmen, not exceeding 20 in number, and the whole population of the spot did not appear to exceed 100. So injudiciously conducted were the first operations on the spot, that the infant settlement had already been completely submerged; and but a few weeks since, all its inhabitants were obliged to abandon it, to avoid being drowned!"[4]

Buckingham also implied, as several American and British investors directly asserted, that Holbrook and his associates had lined their own pockets at the expense of the bondholders. Indeed it is difficult to account for expenditures amounting to the one and one-half million dollars referred to previously, let alone the sum mentioned in the following account of the financial difficulties after the firm of John Wright & Company failed in November 1840:

". . . There came on that commercial crisis, which overthrew so many of the largest and wealthiest associations of both hemispheres, and completely paralyzed the business world. Thousands of merchant princes, bankers and capitalists were shipwrecked, both abroad and at home; and it . . . [was] . . . found that . . . the large outlays upon the city of Cairo, the buildings, levees and embankments, amounting, with interest, to about three and a half millions of dollars, might become unproductive, and all the unfinished works be rendered worthless. . . ."[5]

To add to the woes of the company, the Illinois internal improvements program, including the railroad to Cairo, came to a halt. Virtually all work on the town was stopped. It was at this time that Charles Dickens visited Cairo. He may well have been an investor in the enterprise. If not, he spoke for those who were in what surely ranks as the most devastating attack ever leveled at an American city. In his *American Notes* he wrote:

[4] Buckingham, *America*, 81-82.
[5] Report of a committee of stockholders, Cairo City Property, *The Past, Present and Future of the City of Cairo, in North America*, as quoted in Landsden, *Cairo*, 51.

· 386 ·

"At length . . . we arrived at a spot so much more desolate than any we had yet beheld, that the forlornest places we had passed, were, in comparison with it, full of interest. At the junction of the two rivers, on ground so flat and low and marshy, that at certain seasons of the year it is inundated to the house-tops, lies a breeding-place of fever, ague, and death; vaunted in England as a mine of Golden Hope, and speculated in, on the faith of monstrous representations, to many people's ruin. A dismal swamp on which the half-built houses rot away: cleared here and there for the space of a few yards; and teeming, then, with rank unwholesome vegetation, in whose baleful shade the wretched wanderers who are tempted hither, droop, and die, and lay their bones; the hateful Mississippi circling and eddying before it, and turning off upon its southern course a slimy monster hideous to behold; a hotbed of disease, an ugly sepulchre, a grave uncheered by any gleam of promise; a place without one single quality, in earth or air or water, to commend it: such is this dismal Cairo."[6]

Dickens heaped further scorn on the city and its promoters when, in his *Martin Chuzzlewit*, he modeled the city of Eden after Cairo. It must have been under his direction that Phiz, his illustrator, drew the two views of Eden shown in Figures 229 and 230. The city was, in fact, scarcely more imposing than the few crude huts Chuzzlewit found at Eden, when he arrived to set up his architectural practice and make his fortune.

From the early 1840's to 1850 little took place at Cairo. Holbrook concentrated his efforts at salvaging the remains of his investments. The value of the land and improvements of the Cairo City and Canal Company was—on paper and ignoring debtors' claims—three and one-half million dollars. Holbrook engineered the sale of these assets, unencumbered, to a new company for $700,000. For this purpose the Cairo City Property Trust was created in 1846, and Holbrook subscribed for half of the shares.

[6] Charles Dickens, *American Notes*, London, 1842, Ch. XII. On his return voyage Dickens could not resist a parting shot: ". . . we came again in sight of the detestable morass called Cairo; and stopping there to take in wood, lay alongside a barge, whose starting timbers scarcely held together. It was moored to the bank, and on its side was painted 'Coffee House,' that being, I suppose, the floating paradise to which the people fly for shelter when they lose their houses for a month or two beneath the hideous waters of the Mississippi," Ch. XIV.

The thriving City of Eden, as it appeared on paper.

Figure 229. Martin Chuzzlewit's City of Eden on Paper

Figure 230. Martin Chuzzlewit's
City of Eden in Fact

The thriving City of Eden, as it appeared in fact.

Still there were delays in construction and land disposal. The main reason lay in the efforts of the men active in the trust to secure federal assistance for a new railroad project so vital to the development of the site. By 1850 this grant seemed assured; at least the trustees felt confident enough to arrange for a second survey and plan for Cairo. This work was carried out by Captain Henry C. Long, who submitted his report in September.

While the bulk of Long's report concerned proposals for new levees and the engineering details and cost estimates for this work, he also put forward a new plan for the city, shown in Figure 231. As described by Long,

"The streets are 60 feet in width, with the exception of the avenues, which are 120 feet wide. From a careful study of the nature of the city site, and a comparison of most approved plans, this is considered the best arrangement that can be offered in point of economy or room, convenience for business purposes, perfect ventilation and drainage. From the direction given to the principal streets and avenues, they will generally command a fine breeze, which, during a great proportion of the year prevails from the south and west. The blocks designated by circles, are recommended as suitable positions for public squares. A commodious park may be obtained at the point, marked on the Plot "Crescent Park," by extending the line as shown on the drawing, and reclaiming a valuable portion of land, now entirely useless."[7]

This plan was apparently but the first of numerous proposals for the city considered by the trustees and exhibited to the public from 1850 to about 1853. In the latter year the first official plat was filed in December, and the first land sales were begun shortly after. The final plan is a curious patchwork, lacking the consistency of all of the earlier schemes. Looking at the view of the city in 1888, shown in Figure 232, and knowing nothing of the history of its origin, one would be convinced that Cairo was simply one more example of planless, haphazard development.

The problems of Cairo were not at an end. The city was to witness disastrous floods, there were conflicts over land titles, responsibility for maintenance of levees remained for many years a point of conflict between the city and the railroad, and there were

the normal growing pains of any infant community. But after several abortive attempts, the future pattern for the city of Cairo had finally been established. The most planned city in America had, with the arrival of its long-sought railroad, at last been started.

Cheaper by the Dozen in Illinois and Beyond

To western settlers, plagued by poor roads and lack of local markets for their agricultural products, the railroads appeared to open the path to prosperity and comfort. Nowhere was this feeling more widespread than in Illinois, and it was here that the railroads first entered the field of town planning on a broad scale.

Early western railroad promoters quickly realized that town development and railroad company profits went hand in hand. Towns were needed as shipping points where agricultural products could be made ready for transportation to eastern markets and from which manufactured goods could be distributed to local merchants and peddlers. Concentration of population in railroad towns inevitably would lead to an increase in the value of railroad-owned land, which might then be sold at substantial profits. The history of the early Illinois and midwestern railway towns is one of land speculation and profit-making on a grand scale. Business ethics commonly employed in these ventures would have shamed the most hardened grave-robber.

Consider the activities of certain worthies connected with the Illinois Central Railroad.[8] The Illinois Central received its charter in 1851, the year after Senator Stephen A. Douglas succeeded in pushing through Congress the first federal aid act to assist railroad development. Under this law, alternate square-mile sections of the public domain on each side of its line would be donated to the railroad company. Sections reserved by the government were fixed in price at $2.50 per acre. With this generous promise of free government land the Illinois Central began construction.

One slight impediment to maximum profits existed: an amendment to the company charter in 1851 prohibited the railroad from laying out towns on its line. Four of the directors of the railroad

[7] Henry C. Long, *Report on the Conditions and Prospects of Cairo City,* New York, 1850.

[8] For information on the early history of the Illinois Central line I have relied on the excellent study by Paul Gates, *The Illinois Central Railroad and Its Colonization Work*, Cambridge, 1934. Chapter VII, "Town-Site Promotion," has been particularly helpful.

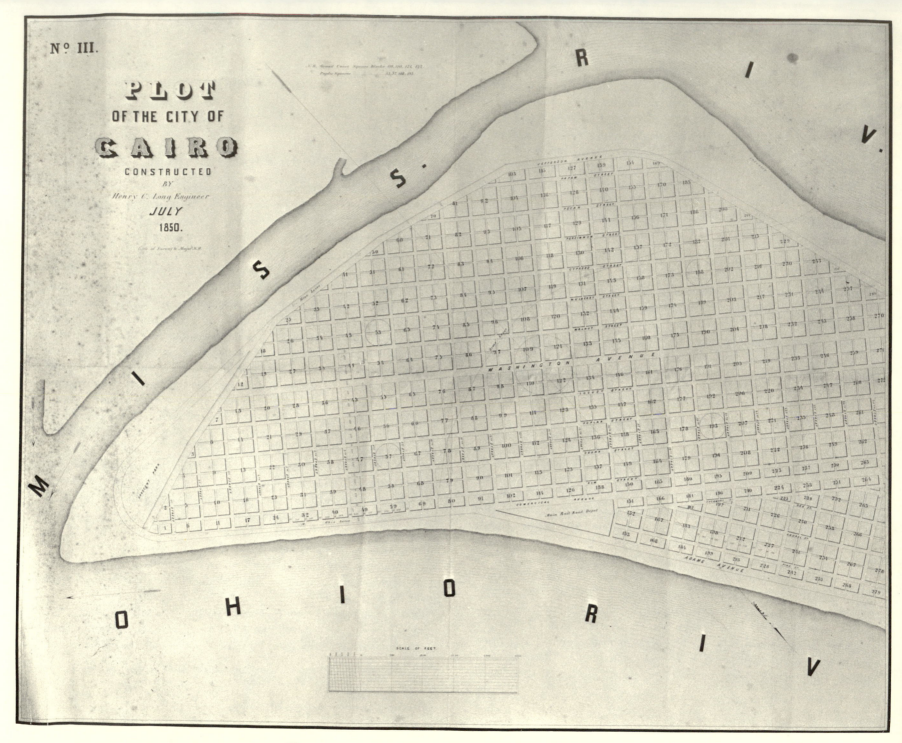

Figure 231. Henry Long's Plan for Cairo, Illinois: 1850

Figure 232. View of Cairo, Illinois: 1888

and the engineer in charge of its construction determined to circumvent this restriction and incidentally to enrich themselves in the process. Organizing themselves as "The Associates," they directed their agent to purchase government land in the alternate sections where, as directors of the railroad, they knew depots were to be located. Station sites were kept secret, of course, until land purchases were completed.

Then, after platting the land in town lots, the associates began to sell land to persons attracted by the railroad station. In what to some must have seemed a burst of generosity the associates deeded land for depots and yards to the railroad company. In some of the towns the associates donated sites for churches and public buildings and in other ways endeavored to stimulate local industry. Where these efforts succeeded, of course, higher profits from land sales resulted.

David Neal, one of the associates and until 1855 vice-president of the railroad, spent much of his time conducting the land promotion affairs of the group. Apparently it was Neal who hit upon the scheme of using a standard plat for all thirty-three of the towns developed by the associates. Figure 233 shows the plan used by Neal and his friends. In all of the towns street names and numbers were identical, as were sizes of blocks and lots and street widths. The freight and passenger stations were always located between North and South First Streets and between Chestnut and Oak Streets. Such wholesale planning reduced engineering and surveying costs, whatever might be the results in monotony and dullness.

The map reproduced in Figure 234 locates the Illinois Central stations as they existed in 1860. About half of these, including such towns as Mattoon, Manteno, Onarga, Farina, and Odin, to name but a few, were sites for speculations by the associates. Perhaps "speculation" is hardly correct, since so little risk was involved. Certainly the profits were substantial. The Kankakee development cost the associates some $18,000 to May 1855. By the end of that year the associates collected nearly $50,000 through sale of lots, and the value of the remaining property was estimated at more than $100,000. Large dividends were paid during the next ten years, and finally the Kankakee business was sold for $50,000.

After 1855 the railroad company secured a charter amendment permitting it to engage in town development on sites where stations were already located. Town lot promotions were pushed in twenty-nine towns along the line, and the company advertised its operations extensively in newspapers, and by pamphlets and posters prominently displayed in its stations. Of course other individuals and companies engaged in similar activities. The philosophy prevailed that every town could become an important metropolis. With such virtually unlimited expansion to be expected, what was more natural than to lay out a town designed to grow without causing confusion in street names? Natrona, platted by Conklin and Company in 1857 along the Chicago, Alton and St. Louis Railroad provided an ingenious solution to the problems of uninhibited expansion. Figure 235 shows the plan with Eleventh and Sixteenth and I and P as the outermost streets. With ten more streets to the east, one-third of the alphabet to exhaust north and south, and infinity to the west, the town seemed well equipped for future growth. Unfortunately for its promoters Natrona fell somewhat short of their expectations.

Many towns existed before the railroads were built. Almost without exception these had been laid out with streets running precisely north-south and east-west. All existing communities naturally vied fiercely with one another to attract the rail lines that would bring fame and prosperity. Galva, Illinois, shown in Figure 236, exhibits what often occurred when the railroad, for engineering reasons, passed through the town diagonally. The central section around the depot evidently was hurriedly replatted with little care for arranging sensible street connections with the older portion of the city. One of the two open spaces became a rail yard and right of way for the Peoria and Rock Island and the Chicago, Burlington and Quincy lines.

The Burlington Railroad, among others, carried out townsite speculation and development activities on the pattern established earlier by the Illinois Central Associates. Most of the directors of the Burlington were active in an association formed to purchase land in and near the locations where stations were to be established. Following the familiar practice developed by Neal and his friends, the Burlington associates donated town lots for mills, churches, and stores. The land agent for the railroad company, young Charles Perkins, later to become president of the road, received the modest sum of $100 per year to manage the private

PLAN OF

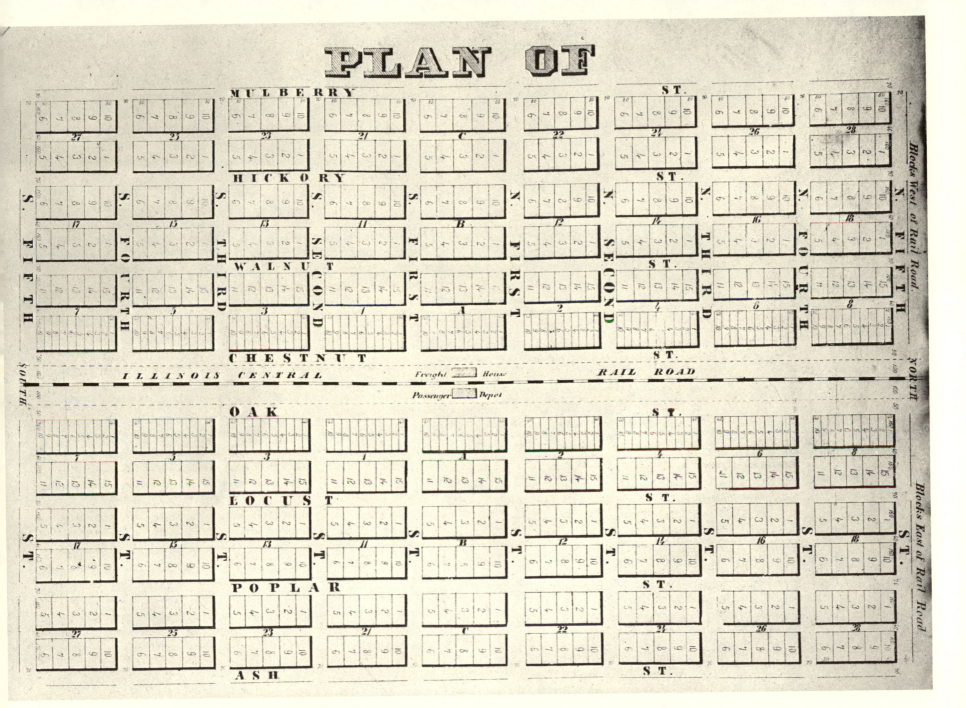

Figure 233. The Illinois Central Associates Standard Town Plat

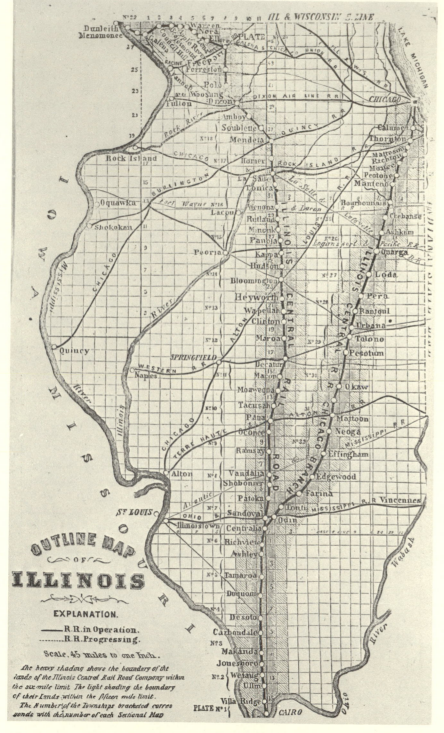

Figure 234. Lines and Stations of the Illinois Central Railroad: 1860

land speculations of the corporation's directors in Iowa. This, of course, was in addition to his salary as a company official. Dozens of towns were laid out by the Burlington associates and widely advertised as communities with an unbounded future. Actual conditions varied somewhat from the glowing verbal pictures used to attract settlers. As Perkins reported in 1864, Coalport consisted of ". . . two houses, one of which is a 'hotel,' and a store. The store is also the squire's office and post office, one man attending to all; with the help of his sister."[9]

As for the "towns" of Batavia, Whitfield, and Agency City, Perkins commented: "*Towns* they are on paper, meadows or timber land, with here and there a house, in reality."[10] And two years later when the land company began operations a few miles west of Ottumwa, Iowa, Perkins observed "I shall have two or three more towns to name very soon. . . . They should be short and easily pronounced. Frederic, I think is a very good name. It is now literally a cornfield, so I cannot have it surveyed, but yesterday a man came to arrange to put a hotel there. This is a great country for hotels."[11]

The surveyor arrived after the crop had been gathered in October, laid out the town, and received for his work the magnificent sum of seven dollars. Cut-rate professional fees helped profits.

The Burlington associates adapted a well-known dodge of frontier land-grabbers to its own town speculation purposes. Under the homestead laws of the time a settler was entitled to buy a quarter-section of land (160 acres) at the minimum price after presenting evidence to the government land office that he had erected certain "improvements" and had cultivated the land. At Lowell, Nebraska, the associates obtained land for the town site through the activities of four of their land agents. They built a house where quarter-section boundaries intersected, with one of the four corners of the house in each quarter-section. Each agent plowed a few acres in his quadrant, and their claim, as the saying went, was "proved."

All of the trans-Mississippi railroads engaged in the same kind of town development activities. The details varied, but almost

[9] Letter from Perkins to his wife, March 5, 1864, as quoted in Richard C. Overton, *Burlington West*, Cambridge, 1941, p. 184. Overton's account of the land policies of the Burlington line and its officers is brief but excellent.
[10] Letter from Perkins to his wife, April 18, 1864, *ibid*.
[11] Letter from Perkins to his wife, July 22, 1866, *ibid*.

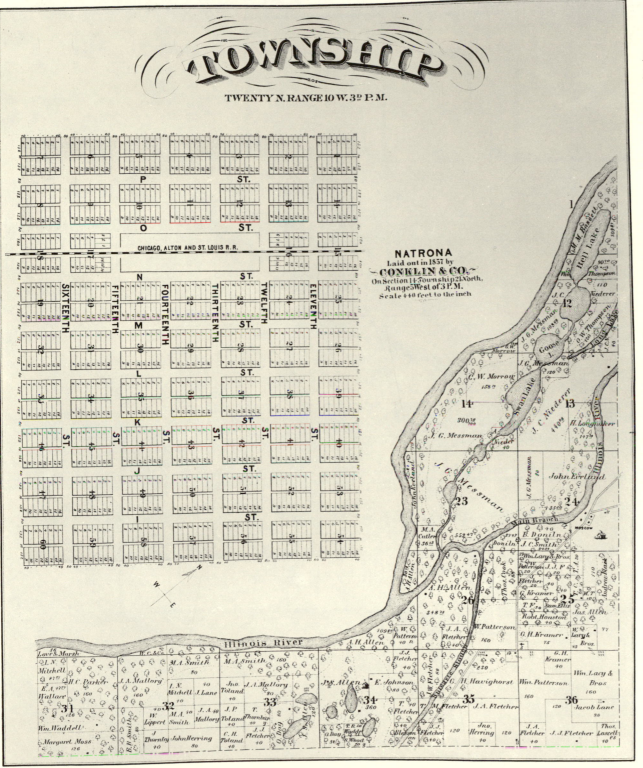

TOWNSHIP

TWENTY N. RANGE 10 W. 3ᴰ P. M.

NATRONA

Laid out in 1857 by

CONKLIN & CO.

On Section 14 Township 21 North,
Range 5 West of 3 P.M.
Scale 440 feet to the inch

Figure 235. Plan of Natrona, Illinois: 1874

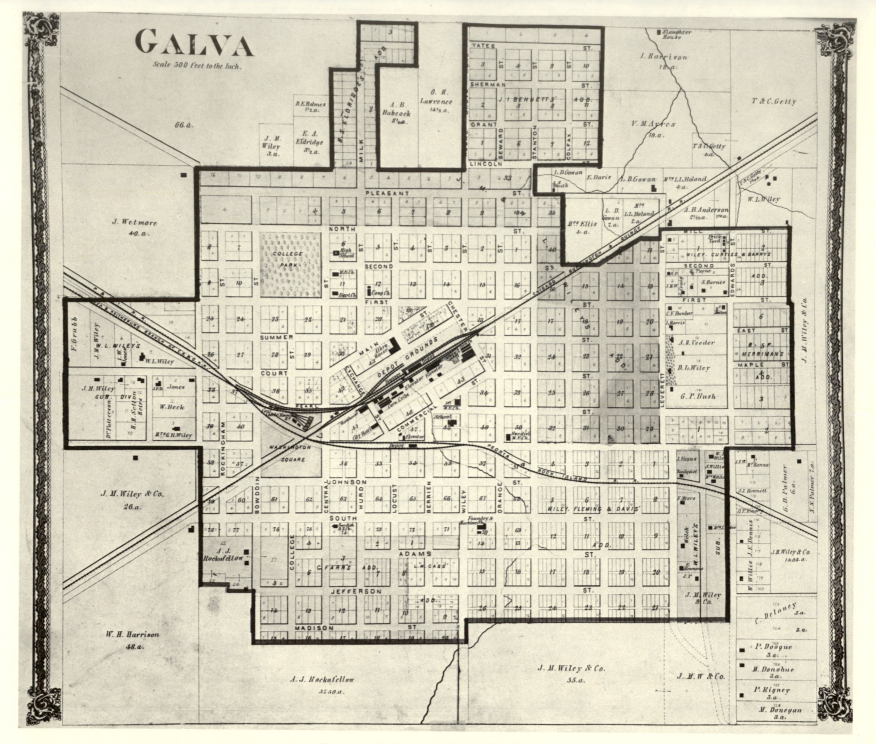

Figure 236. Plan of Galva, Illinois: 1875

without exception the physical results exhibited the impatience, the speculative greed, and the lack of taste which characterized the founders of these towns. Town builders they were, but they were town destroyers as well. As a member of the 1879 California Constitutional Convention said, describing the practice common throughout the railroad world:

"They started out their railway track and survey their line near a thriving village. They go to the most prominent citizens of that village and say, 'If you will give us so many thousand dollars we will run through here; if you do not we will run by,' and in every instance where the subsidy was not granted, that course was taken, and the effect was just as they said, to kill off the little town."[12]

Towns like Springfield, Missouri, which refused to meet the subsidy demands of what is now the St. Louis and San Francisco Railway, faced an uncertain future. There, in 1870, the railroad diverted its line a mile or so north of the original city and promoted a new town of North Springfield. For a time the new settlement prospered and the old town seemed doomed to stagnation or worse; but a few years later a new line was pushed through to the older development and the two towns were subsequently united. Other communities were not so fortunate and ceased to grow or vanished altogether.

New Tracks and New Towns Across the Continent

Probably the most colorful events of the association of town planning and railroad construction occurred during the race to complete the early transcontinental railroad systems. This period of railroad building excited the entire nation and focused the attention of the western world on activities taking place in hitherto little known sections of the great west. Fortunately, both the routine and the bizarre aspects of town development at this time were superbly recorded by participants and observers.

William A. Bell, Cambridge graduate, member of the survey party for the Kansas Pacific, and later Fellow of the Royal Geographical Society, tells how towns were built and abandoned as the railway progressed:

"Wholesale town-making may not be a romantic theme, or one capable of being made very attractive to the general reader; but it is the great characteristic of this part of our route, and is only to be seen to perfection along the line of these great railways. On the Platte, where the central line across the continent often advances at the rate of two miles a day, town-making is reduced to a system. The depot at the end of the line is only moved every two or three months; and . . . the town usually moves also, while nothing remains to mark the spot where thousands lived, but a station, a name, and a few acres of bare earth. Last winter, Cheyenne was the terminal depot on this route, and increased in size to 5,000 inhabitants. A man . . . told me that while he was standing on the railway platform, a long freight train arrived, laden with frame houses, boards, furniture, palings, old tents, and all the rubbish which makes up one of these mushroom 'cities.' The guard jumped off his van, and seeing some friends on the platform, called out with a flourish, 'Gentlemen, here's Julesburg.' "[13]

Apparently this occurred almost weekly on one line or another. John Morgan observed the destruction of one such town on the Denver and Rio Grande Railroad in 1878:

"Garland is emphatically a railroad town. It has no surrounding agricultural country, but is dependent entirely for support upon the business done at the terminus; consequently as Alamosa, forty-five miles further west, has been selected for the next terminus, Garland begins to move forward, and on every hand we see men tearing down the frail wooden structures with which it is built, and starting westward with them. Soon Garland will be a thing of the past and only battered oyster cans, castoff clothing, old shoes, and debris generally will mark the site of where once stood a flourishing city, with its hotels, its stores, its theatre comique, etc.

"The citizens appear to take it as a matter of course, and are getting ready to vacate the premises. Even the postoffice is getting ready to move out."[14]

[12] As quoted in Glenn Chesney Quiett, *They Built the West*, New York, 1934, p. 83. Quiett's work is a superb study of some of the more dramatic aspects of the western railroads during their construction. Chapter v, "Town-Building and Development of Resources," is especially valuable. I have followed Quiett in my treatment of Colorado Springs and Tacoma in this chapter.

[13] William A. Bell, *New Tracks in North America*, London, 1869, I, 17-18.
[14] Letter, March 13, 1878, State Historical Society of Colorado, *The Colorado Magazine*, XXV (1948), 261.

Figure 237. View of a Deserted Railroad Town in Kansas: 1874

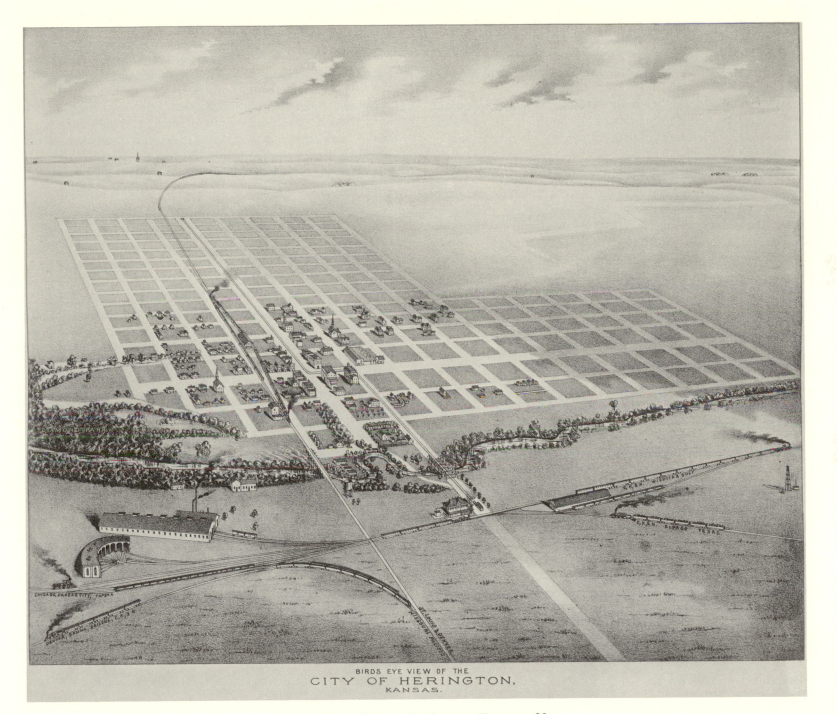

BIRDS EYE VIEW OF THE
CITY OF HERINGTON,
KANSAS.

Figure 238. View of Herington, Kansas: 1887

The typical result shows in Figure 237, although the coyotes rummaging through the debris and garbage probably represent the artist's license for dramatic overstatement more than anything else.

What were these towns like before the railroad terminals moved on? Bell describes one of the communities that managed to endure, Salina, Kansas, at the height of its glory:

"On the open grass land . . . several broad streets could be seen, marked out with stakes, and crossing each other like a chess-board. The central one was deeply cut up with cart-rucks, and strewn with rubbish. . . . On each side of this main street were wooden houses, of all sizes and in all shapes of embryonic existence. Not a garden fence or tree was anywhere to be seen. Still paddling about in the mud, we came to the most advanced part of the 'city,' and here we found three billiard saloons, each with two tables, and the everlasting bar. Then came an ice-cream saloon; then a refreshment saloon. Next . . . appeared the office of the *Salina Tribune*. . . . Opposite was a row of substantial 'stores' having their fronts painted. The builder here was evidently a rash speculator. . . . On each side was an 'hotel' . . . up a side street, we discovered the Methodist Chapel, the land Agency Office, labelled 'Desirable town lot for sale,' the Masonic Hall (temporary building), and the more pretentious foundations of the Free School, Baptist Chapel, and Episcopal Church. The suburbs consisted of tents of all shapes and forms, with wooden doors, shanties, half canvas, half wood. These were owned by squatters upon unsold lots. All around were scattered the empty tins of the period, labelled in large letters, 'desicated vegetables,' 'green corn,' 'pears,' 'peaches,' 'oysters,' and other untold luxuries."[15]

Bell also describes the speculative orgy in town lots that began after such a town was laid out and as the railroad line approached the city. Land prices soared in a kind of perpetual auction. The winners were those who managed to buy on credit when prices were low and who sold for cash when the peak was reached. As Bell observes, the game was played as much for "speculative amusement" as for financial advancement.

With the announcement of a new terminal and the date of its establishment, the game would come to an end. Bell concludes:

[15] Bell, *New Tracks*, 19-20.

· 400 ·

"The terminal depot must soon be moved forward, and the little colony will be left to its own resources. If the district has good natural advantages, it will remain, if not, it will disappear, and the town lots will fall to nothing."[16]

Where, as in Herrington, Kansas, shown in Figure 238, the town survived on a much reduced scale, the only consolation lay in the knowledge that no further costs for street and lot surveys would be needed for some time, if ever.

One curious settlement form of this general period and location was noted by an anonymous artist in *Harper's Weekly*. Reproduced in Figure 239, the subcaption reads as follows:

"Our readers will remember the curious and interesting sketch of a deserted railroad village, or rather settlement, published a short time since in the *Weekly*; in this number of our paper we give them, by way of contrast, a sketch of a village built on the under-ground plan, as if the hardy pioneers of civilization had taken a prairie-dog town as a model. Secure against the violent wind storms that sweep with irresistible fury over the plains, these 'dug-outs' form an excellent shelter. The style of architecture is certainly not imposing, but as temporary shelters these under-ground habitations, constructed at little expense, serve their purpose well until substantial buildings can be erected."[17]

How common this form of town was is not known. It resembles in some ways the sod houses of the 1870's in Nebraska and elsewhere on the frontier. For a transistory settlement at the temporary terminus of a railroad it must have been an admirable solution to the problem of securing a shack town against the winds that swept the treeless plains of western Kansas.

The Lunatic Fringe

Railroad town promotion attracted its share of eccentrics and fanatics. Aside from those thousands of lot purchasers with delusions of future wealth without work, certainly the most authentic lunatic, since a court finally declared him insane, was George Francis Train. It should be recorded, however, that he also exhibited genius for erecting complex financial structures as well as

[16] *ibid.*, 18.
[17] *Harper's Weekly*, Supplement, April 4, 1874, p. 306.

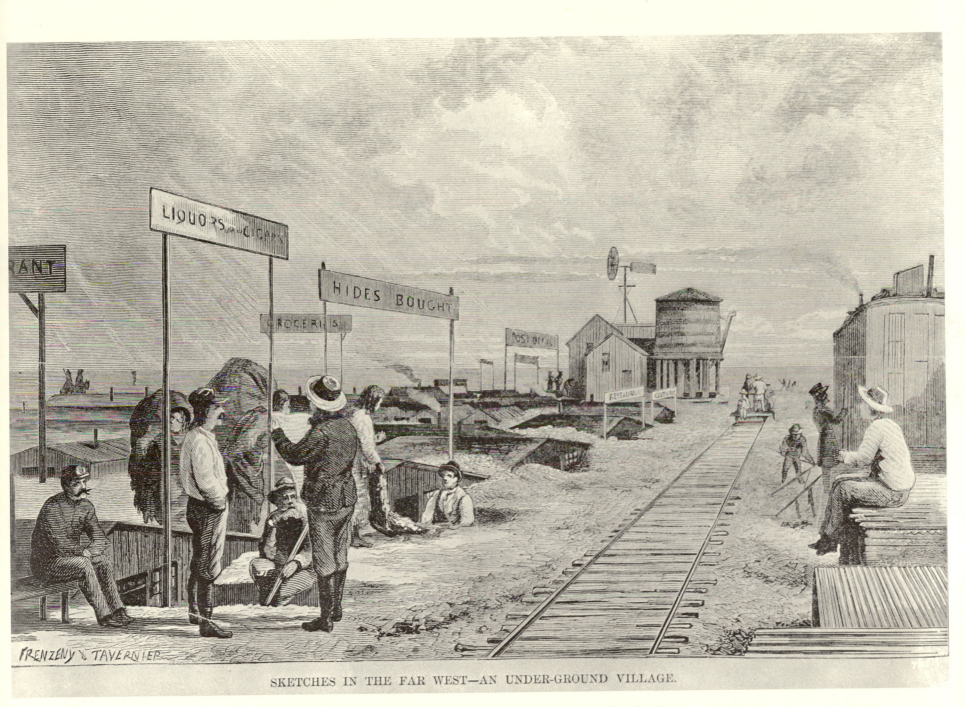

SKETCHES IN THE FAR WEST—AN UNDER-GROUND VILLAGE.

Figure 239. An Underground Town on a Western Railroad: 1874

a talent for enlisting the gullible and the greedy in his various enterprises.

In his autobiography Train modestly claimed credit for building the Union Pacific Railroad and then explained:

"But this enterprise was merely a beginning. I looked upon it only as the launching of a hundred other projects, which, if I had been able to carry them to completion, would have transformed the West in a few years. . . . One of my plans was the creation of a chain of great towns across the continent, connecting Boston with San Francisco by a magnificent highway of cities."[18]

Albert D. Richardson, whose *Beyond the Mississippi* is one of the most reliable as well as interesting accounts of the West at midcentury, observed Train's activities in Omaha in 1866. He records that Train owned some 500 acres in the growing city and was then head of the Credit Foncier, ". . . a great company . . . organized for dealing in lands and stocks—for building cities along the railway from Missouri to Salt Lake. This corporation had been clothed by the Nebraska legislature with nearly every power imaginable, save that of reconstructing the late rebel states."[19]

The Credit Foncier and the better known Credit Moblier were largely the creations of Train. The Credit Foncier operated principally as a townsite promotion organization along the lines of the Union Pacific road. Like all such companies it advertised in extravagant language. The following is a sample from a prospectus distributed to "boom" the new town of Columbus, Nebraska:

"Would you make money easy? Find, then the site of a city and buy the farm it is to be built on! How many regret the non-purchase of that lot in New York; that block in Buffalo; that acre in Chicago, that quarter section in Omaha. Once these city properties could be bought for a song. Astor and Girard made their fortunes that way. The Credit Foncier by owning the principal towns along the Pacific line to California, enriches its shareholders while distributing its profits by selling alternate lots at a nominal price to the public."[20]

[18] George Francis Train, *My Life in Many States and in Foreign Lands*, London, 1902, p. 293.
[19] Albert D. Richardson, *Beyond the Mississippi*, Hartford, 1867, p. 565.
[20] As quoted by A. M. Sakolski, *The Great American Land Bubble*, New York, 1932, p. 291.

Train later shifted his operations from Omaha to Denver and still later to Tacoma, which he adopted as the future great metropolis of the West. To prove the advantages of that railroad-founded city, he set out from Tacoma in 1891 to beat the round-the-world record of 72 days established the previous year by the celebrated Nellie Bly. Sixty-seven days later he returned, having trumpeted the advantages of the port of Tacoma to interested but amused audiences that he invariable attracted. However, for all his energy, Train died in poverty, his vision of a chain of cities stretching across the continent only partially realized.

A far more detached individual was P. Gerard, civil engineer and self-appointed advisor on city planning for the western railroads. Gerard published a sober treatise called, *How to Build a City, Designed for the Consideration of Founders of Towns, Architects, Civil Engineers, Sanitary Organizations, Municipal Authorities, Builders, and Especially the Managers of the Various Railroads of the Pacific*.[21] Many of Gerard's suggestions had merit, although they could hardly have been favorably received at the time. For example, he proposed that each state should enact regulations requiring ". . . every locality . . . to have some plan or map which all extensions should follow."

His city plan, shown in Figure 240, is a curious proposal. Specifically rejecting the use of diagonal streets because of traffic difficulties and the resulting building lots of odd shape, Gerard advocated an uncompromising grid pattern. All normal streets were to be 75 feet wide, but the large boulevards, marked "B" in the plan, would be 210 feet in width. The subtitle of the book shows Gerard's special concern with town planning by railroads, and his proposal includes depressed rail rights-of-way near the edges of the city. A similar depressed road was to be set aside as a "passage for livestock."

The large square with circular and radial drives was designed as a park, ". . . the best place of most amusements, even for horse races, for which can be used the great circle. . . ." Five tiers of small blocks, marked "A" on the drawing, were to be set aside for public building sites and for small parks. Gerard, as was typical of other mechanistic utopians of the era, included minute directions and specifications for houses, stables, horse-ponds, sidewalks and stairways, public baths and wash houses, chimneys, lamp-posts

[21] Philadelphia, 1872.

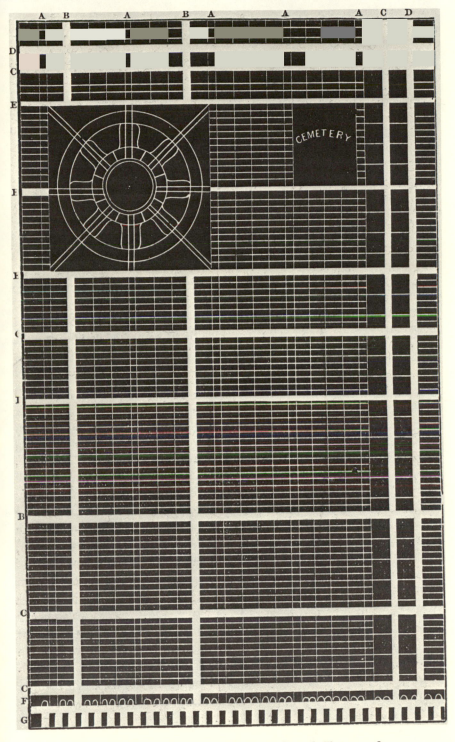

Figure 240. P. Gerard's Model Railroad Town: 1872

and a host of other details. No doubt this proposal went unnoticed. Certainly no concrete results materialized as far as can be discovered.

General Palmer's Resort in the Rockies

One of the towering figures in western railroad construction was General William J. Palmer. Following an early career as a surveyor for railroads in Pennsylvania and distinguished service during the Civil War, he was put in charge of surveying the route for the Western Pacific line from Kansas City to Denver. In 1870, when the line was completed, he resigned and organized his own line, the Denver and Rio Grande. Without the state or federal assistance enjoyed by other major railroads, Palmer succeeded in developing his line over probably the most difficult terrain yet encountered.

His initial construction connected Denver with Pueblo, 100 miles to the south. The need for funds plus the magnificent topography in the vicinity of Pike's Peak, including the Garden of the Gods and the mineral springs at Manitou, suggested that a city development project might be started. Palmer organized the National Land and Improvement Company to buy land for speculation along the railroad, including the site for his proposed city of Colorado Springs. A second company, the Colorado Springs Company, was called into existence to develop the new city.

When Palmer had first seen the Manitou springs and inspected the weird rock formations of the Garden of the Gods in 1869, he had written in his diary, "I am sure that there will be a famous summer resort here soon after the railroad reaches Denver." Now he set about making his own prophecy come true. In June 1871 the Colorado Springs Company first met in Denver to authorize the beginning of the project. Colonel Greenwood, the chief engineer of the Denver and Rio Grande, was directed to lay out the city. While Palmer and his associates did not enter into city development merely for amusement but for profit, Colorado Springs marked a distinct advance over previous towns built by railroads for speculative purposes. The founders determined that their city would form an oasis of culture and refinement in the wild and undisciplined west. Other speculative city plats frequently showed sites for such institutions as an opera house, a college, a luxurious hotel, and the like. At Colorado Springs these improvements were actually provided, along with the usual complement of schools, parks, and churches.

A further note of elegance appeared in the plan. Pike's Peak Avenue formed the central axis leading west to the splendid Antlers Hotel located between the business section and the railroad and standing in open ground. Two diagonal streets led from the northeastern and southeastern sections of the city terminating in two square-block parks at the edges of the business district. The bird's-eye view of the city in 1882, shown in Figure 241, reveals the basic plan with considerable clarity.

Greenwood, the planner, made the best of his splendid opportunity by using Pike's Peak as the backdrop for the Antlers Hotel. This majestic mountain, towering over the building, dominated the western vista along Pike's Peak Avenue. By contrast with other cities planned under similar sponsorship, Colorado Springs stands almost alone in its attempt to achieve some of the dignity and grandeur of its natural setting.

As the view demonstrates, settlement of the city was rapid. Palmer appointed a fellow army veteran, General Robert Cameron, manager of the enterprise. Cameron tirelessly stimulated the city's growth by all the usual means of advertising and promotion. The difference was that in this case the boasting and town "puffing," as it was usually termed, was true. Cameron retained a landscape architect to advise on city beautification, resort hotels were constructed, and a sanatorium was planned. Colorado Springs became the goal of ever-increasing streams of persons who visited the West for pleasure and to observe the settlement of what had shortly before been an Indian wilderness. No accurate record exists of the profits that flowed to Palmer and his business friends. Doubtless they were substantial, and certainly they were deserved. Colorado Springs demonstrated that not all railroad towns were unpleasant and that sound planning and good business were not incompatible.

The Railroad Land Boom in Southern California

Nowhere did the coming of the railroad generate more urban speculation and new town planning than in southern California. Hundreds of towns sprang up, almost literally overnight, beginning a tradition of high pressure land development that has been carried on to the present. Experienced townsite promoters flocked to

southern California during the 1870's and 1880's, and all their wiles and ingenious sales techniques were employed.

The first railroad-stimulated land boom in the area began in the mid-1870's. Until this time southern California lacked rail transportation. Transcontinental rail traffic passed far to the north, terminating at San Francisco Bay. In 1872 the Southern Pacific line reached south to the San Joaquin Valley at Tipton, but Los Angeles lay 250 weary stagecoach miles beyond. During the next four years the line was extended to Los Angeles, and by September 1876 the route was completed.

Land speculation and townsite promotion had in fact started well before the arrival of the railroad, anticipating that event by almost a decade. Drought conditions in the 1860's led to the break-up of the baronial ranchos, and small farm plots and town lots were created in their place. The six Stearns ranchos, totalling 70,000 acres, were subdivided in 1869. On one of them the city of Savana was platted, and its promotional literature described its splendid city hall, churches, and schools. A contemporary observer, however, who visited the site found conditions rather different: "A solitary coyote on a round-top knoll, possibly the site of the prospective city hall, gazed despondently down the street upon the debris of a deserted sheep camp. The other inhabitants of the city of Savana had not arrived, nor have they to this day put in an appearance."[22]

By the time the railroad project materialized the boom was in full bloom. Los Angeles, Santa Barbara, and San Diego were the centers of activity, as they would be in the more frenzied period of the 1880's. This later period of land speculation was touched off by the arrival of the Santa Fe Railroad in 1887. For the first time the Southern Pacific faced rail competition. In the ensuing rate war the passenger fare from Kansas to Los Angeles fell at one time to a low of one dollar. While fares soon rose, they remained at artificially low levels for many years. Such bargain fares and vigorous railroad advertising about the glories of southern California attracted hordes of migrants to the area.[23]

[22] James M. Guinn, "Los Angeles in the Later Sixties and Early Seventies," Historical Society of Southern California, *Annual Publications*, III (1893), 64.
[23] The best study of the period and place is the scholarly and entertaining Glenn S. Dumke, *The Boom of the Eighties in Southern California*, San Marino, 1944.

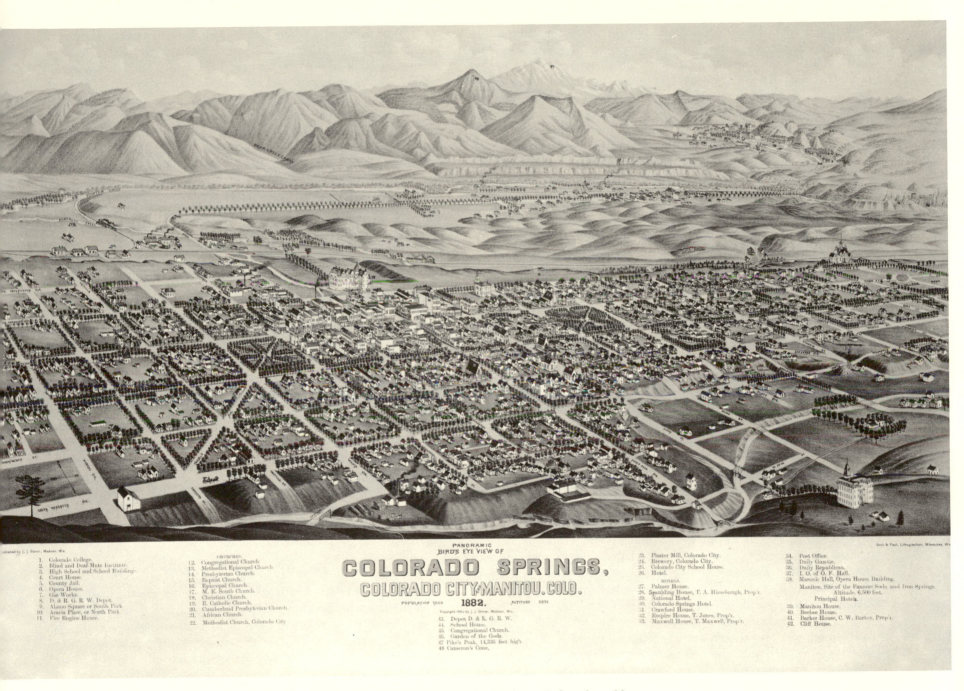

PANORAMIC
BIRD'S EYE VIEW OF
COLORADO SPRINGS,
COLORADO CITY·MANITOU·COLO.

POPULATION 7000   **1882.**   ALTITUDE 5975

Copyright 1882 by J. J. Stoner, Madison, Wis.

1. Colorado College.
2. Blind and Deaf-Mute Institute.
3. High School and School Building.
4. Court House.
5. County Jail.
6. Opera House.
7. Gas Works.
8. D. & R. G. R. W. Depot.
9. Alamo Square or South Park.
10. Acacia Place, or North Park.
11. Fire Engine House.

CHURCHES.
12. Congregational Church.
13. Methodist Episcopal Church.
14. Presbyterian Church.
15. Baptist Church.
16. Episcopal Church.
17. M. E. South Church.
18. Christian Church.
19. R. Catholic Church.
20. Cumberland Presbyterian Church.
21. African Church.
22. Methodist Church, Colorado City

23. Plaster Mill, Colorado City.
24. Brewery, Colorado City.
25. Colorado City School House.
26. Hotel.

HOTELS.
27. Palmer House.
28. Spaulding House, T. A. Hinebaugh, Prop'r.
29. National Hotel.
30. Colorado Springs Hotel.
31. Crawford House.
32. Empire House, T. Jones, Prop'r.
33. Maxwell House, T. Maxwell, Prop'r.

34. Post Office.
35. Daily Gazette.
36. Daily Republican.
37. I. O. of O. F. Hall.
38. Masonic Hall, Opera House Building.
Manitou, Site of the Famous Soda and Iron Springs.
Altitude, 6,500 feet.
Principal Hotels.
39. Manitou House.
40. Beebee House.
41. Barker House, C. W. Barker, Prop'r.
42. Cliff House.

43. Depot D. & R. G. R. W.
44. School House.
45. Congregational Church.
46. Garden of the Gods.
47 Pike's Peak, 14,336 feet high.
48 Cameron's Cone.

Figure 241. View of Colorado Springs, Colorado: 1882

Railroad advertising was but one type of promotional literature that soon threatened to flood the country. Existing southern California towns and cities loudly proclaimed their superiority in this new garden of Eden. Even more vehement were the hucksters of lots in new townsites platted along the railroads and at the outskirts of existing communities. Their advertisements in local and eastern newspapers proudly boasted of the unique merits and unusual opportunities that could be found in their particular developments. Local newspapers adopted the same techniques. All combined to establish an air of unbounded prosperity and a pervading feeling of confidence in the region and in the rising value of its town and farm lands.

Many of the new towns planned by speculators proved successful—at least they have survived. Glendale, Burbank, Azusa, Monrovia—to name but four in the Los Angeles area—were among these. Dozens of others, however, never existed in a form more permanent than wooden staked streets and lots and the printed posters advertising land sales. The difference between success and failure often seemed entirely fortuitous. The site of Azusa, according to one account, was nothing but sand, gravel, and boulder wash when Jonathan Slauson began its promotion in 1886. Extensive advertising produced crowds of buyers who stood in line all night before land sales began in the spring of 1887. Half of the platted town lots sold during the first three days, and at the end of two months the promoters were estimated to have cleared more than one million dollars. Similar events were recorded in scores of other developments, but Azusa became an established town where many others reverted to desert land when the boom collapsed.

The designs of these towns exhibited virtually the full range of plan forms that had been developed in the east and midwest. Many featured great central squares or were lavishly spotted with sites designated as parks. Prominent locations were set aside, on the printed plats at least, as spots for city halls, opera houses, luxury hotels, and like uses so favored by townsite promoters. Two of these cities, however, differed rather markedly from the grid layout normally employed by speculative town planners.

In 1885 Elisha Babcock of San Diego began the development of the town of Coronado on a sandy site at the end of the peninsula forming the northern edge of San Diego Bay. Land purchasers were lured with promises of free water for one year if they spent

$1,000 on improving their lot, as well as 130 tickets per month on the San Diego Electric Railway, the Coronado Ferry, and the Coronado Railway. An extensive local and national advertising campaign was launched, and the land sales were rapid. The Santa Fe Railway, which had been largely responsible for the land boom in San Diego, contributed its bit by printing a Coronado advertisement in its timetable and distributing 75,000 copies. Babcock opened what he boasted to be a one million dollar hotel early in 1888, and Coronado began to take form. The plan, which is reproduced in Figure 242, shows an interesting and rather skillful combination of formal, diagonal streets converging on a central square, the more normal grid street system, and the romantic, curvilinear roads around the rim of the development.

Equally unusual was the plan of Corona in San Bernadino County east of Los Angeles. Originally named South Riverside, the town was laid out in 1886 by the South Riverside Land and Water Company. Each purchaser of land received water rights, and the farm plots surrounding the town proper were said to be on "Choice, cultivable land." As can be seen from the plan reproduced in Figure 243, the town featured a great circular boulevard which described an area exactly one mile in diameter. Outside the circle, rural roads led off to the farm area like spokes from a wheel hub. Inside the circle a rigid grid layout of streets prevailed.

Corona's development was stimulated by plans for the Pomona and Elsinore Railroad, but the line was discontinued after only a short stretch was constructed. The town grew in spite of this disappointment. Its unique plan led to at least temporary fame in 1913, when Barney Oldfield, Ralph de Palma, and Earl Cooper used the great circular boulevard as a race track. The boulevard today provides facilities for more sedate movement than Cooper's winning time of 75 miles an hour.

Pears and Bananas in the Pacific Northwest

One final episode of railroad town planning remains to be told. It is the story of Tacoma and its three plans: one premature, one of epic quality but rejected, and one of surpassing mediocrity that was finally adopted. Because the story involves one who might fairly be called the first modern American city planner it is doubly interesting.

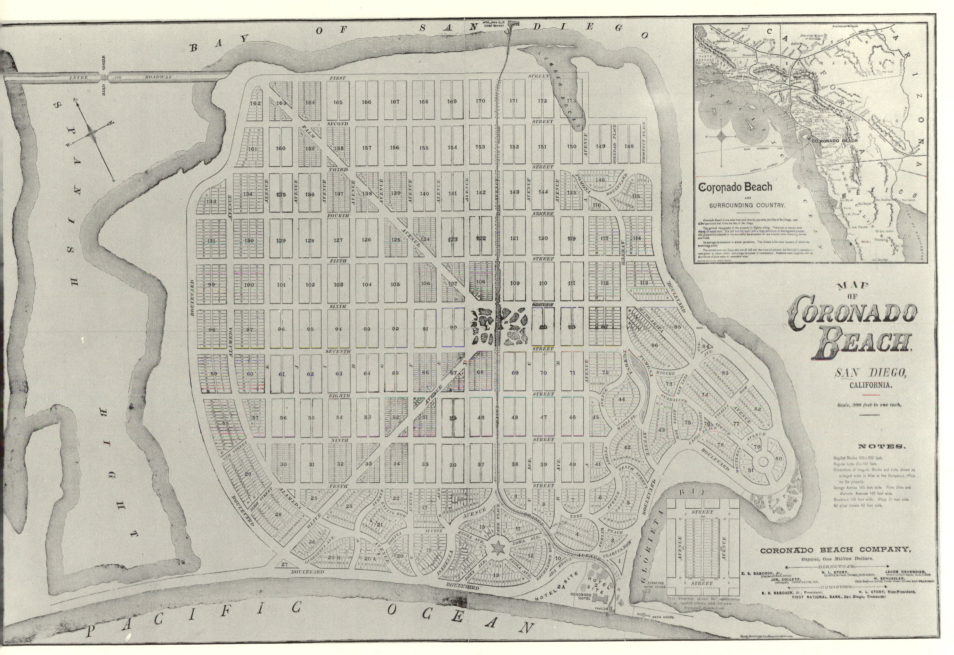

Figure 242. Plan of Coronado Beach, California: 1887

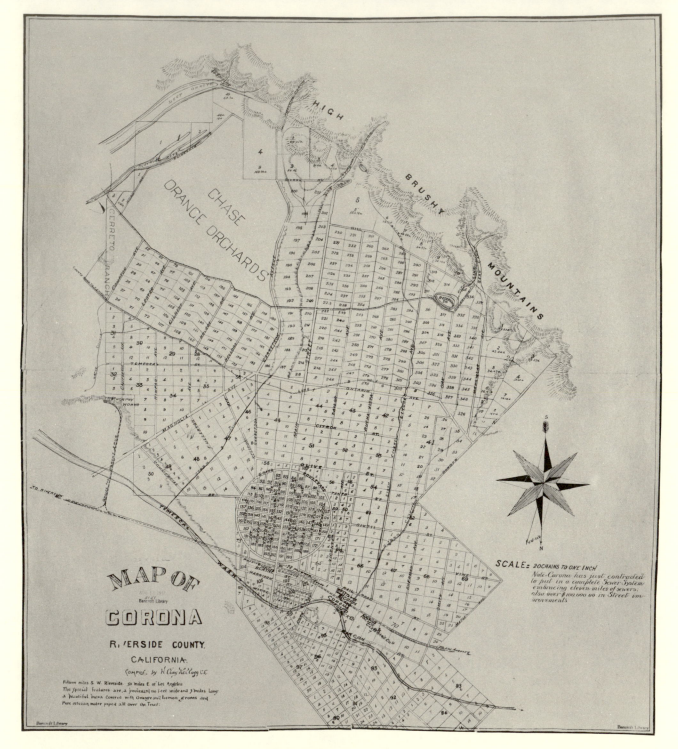

Figure 243. Plan of Corona, California: ca. 1900

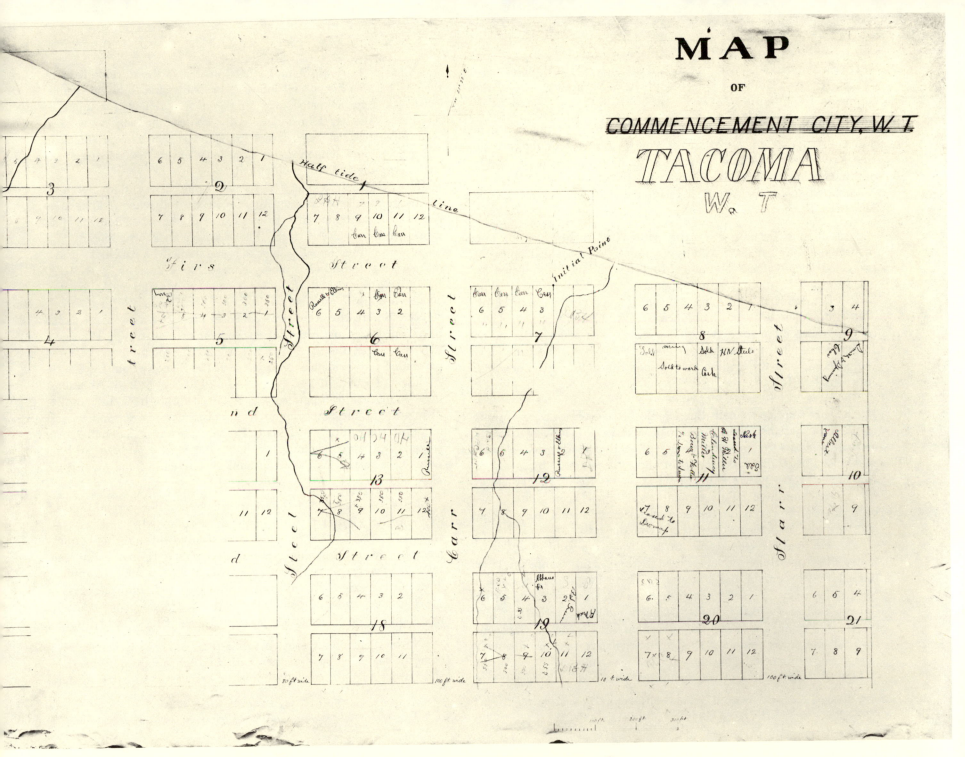

Figure 244. Plan of Tacoma, Washington: ca. 1873

On September 10, 1873, the Board of Directors of the Northern Pacific Railroad Company, meeting in New York City, passed the following resolution:

"*Resolved*, that the Northern Pacific Railroad Company locate and construct its main road to a point on Puget Sound on the southerly side of Commencement Bay . . . and within the limits of the City of Tacoma, which point in the same City of Tacoma is declared to be the Western terminus of the main line of the Northern Pacific."[24]

At that time Tacoma was a tiny settlement at the edge of Commencement Bay, an arm of Puget Sound that provided splendid protected deep-water anchorage. Much of the land was owned by one Morton M. McCarver, an experienced townsite promoter who had recognized the potentialities of the site on a visit there in 1868. The little town had originally been called Commencement City, but the more interesting name of Tacoma was adopted from the Indian name for Mount Rainier. Figure 244 shows the little saw-mill village, with the original name lined through and the new one substituted below.

McCarver's efforts to convince the officials of the Northern Pacific that Commencement Bay should be selected as the terminus of the line met first with amusement from the established towns of Seattle and Olympia and then with active resistance. A committee of the road's directors spent some time in the area, and of course each town put forward glowing claims for its favored location. The committee finally recommended the Tacoma site, however; it was approved by the executive committee in July 1873, and formally ratified by the directors in the fall.

The railroad developed the town through a subsidiary company, the Lake Superior and Puget Sound Land Company, later named the Tacoma Land Company. The actual location chosen for the new city lay some distance from McCarver's land, so he did not realize the full benefits of his promotional activities. The Northern Pacific, following the precedent set by earlier transcontinental lines, was reluctant to share speculative land profits with persons not connected directly with the company.

One of the members of the committee that had selected the site was Charles B. Wright of Philadelphia, and the development of the city became his special interest. Probably due to his influence, Frederick Law Olmsted was engaged to prepare the plan of Tacoma. Whether Olmsted actually visited the site or worked from topographical maps is not known. His plan is reproduced in Figure 245 and demonstrates Olmsted's efforts to adapt a street pattern to the difficult sloping site.

Here was truly a plan from another mold. One does not need to imagine the consternation this layout caused when it arrived in Tacoma. A contemporary declared it ". . . the most fantastic plat of a town that was ever seen. There wasn't a straight line, a right angle or a corner lot. The blocks were shaped like melons, pears, and sweet potatoes. One block, shaped like a banana, was 3,000 feet in length and had 250 lots. It was a pretty fair park plan but condemned itself for a town."[25]

Isaac Smith, therefore, was asked to prepare a new plan, which he claimed was patterned after Melbourne, Australia. Whatever may have been the merits of the Melbourne plan, they were not particularly in evidence as applied to the Tacoma site by Smith. A view of Tacoma in 1884 is reproduced in Figure 246. An almost undeviating gridiron pattern was followed throughout, in complete disregard for the topography. Railroad tracks, yards, and wharfs occupied the entire waterfront. Perhaps this was inevitable in a railroad sponsored community, but Olmsted's plan had at least reserved a portion of the steep bank at one end of the town for a park and lookout.

"Jealous rivals and indifferent strangers alike agree that no city on the continent is so splendidly planned," asserted one observer.[26] Perhaps his opinions were colored through his employment by the town-booming subsidiary of the railroad. But railroad cities were rarely reticent about their virtues and accomplishments. A stream of careful exaggerations poured from the press of the Tacoma Land Company and from local independent boosters. One loud singer of Tacoma's praises saw the brightest of futures:

"No one can doubt that the sum total of Tacoma's resources, domestic and foreign, together with the entire aspect of her own and the world's present environments, are vastly superior to those

[24] Tacoma Land Company, *Tacoma the Western Terminus of the Northern Pacific Railroad*, Tacoma, 1889, p. 1.

[25] As quoted by Quiett, *They Built the West*, 414.
[26] Tacoma Land Company, *Tacoma*, 13.

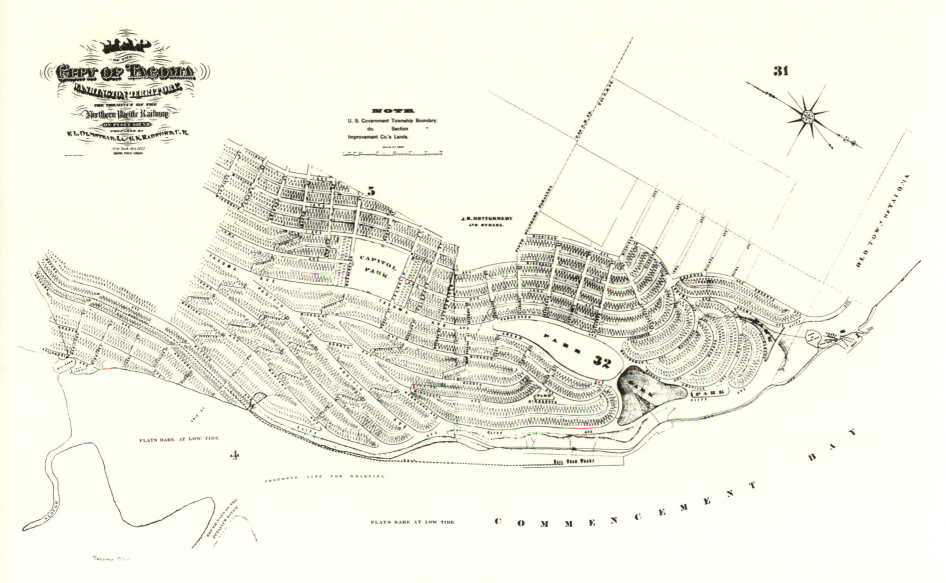

Figure 245. *Frederick Law Olmsted's Plan for Tacoma, Washington: 1873*

of Chicago in 1852, and that it is only a question of TIME when a greater city than Chicago or New York will flourish on the more salubrious shores of Puget Sound.

"With all these facts before us are we not warranted in postulating

GREAT EXPECTATIONS

for the growth of Tacoma and its environs on Puget Sound, within the period of the present generation?"[27]

Rudyard Kipling represented the other viewpoint. In the latter part of the 1880's he recorded these impressions in a highly critical description of Tacoma:

"Tacoma was literally staggering under a boom of the boomiest. I do not quite remember what her natural resources were supposed to be, though every second man shrieked a selection in my ear. . . . The rude boarded pavements of the main streets rumbled under the wheels of hundreds of furious men all actively engaged in hunting drinks and eligible corner-lots. They sought the drinks first. The street itself alternated five-story business blocks of the later and more abominable forms of architecture with board shanties. Overhead the drunken telegraph, telephone, and electric-light wires tangled on the tottering posts whose butts were half-whittled through by the knife of the loafer. . . . We passed down ungraded streets that ended abruptly in a fifteen-foot drop and a nest of brambles; along pavements that beginning in pine-plank ended in the living tree; by hotels with Turkish mosque trinketry on their shameless tops, and the pine stumps at their very doors."[28]

[27] C. Andrews, *Tacoma and "Destiny,"* Tacoma, 1891, p. 46.
[28] Rudyard Kipling, *From Sea to Sea*, New York. 1913, II, 43-44.

Of the boasting and booming and real estate promotions, Kipling commented:

"The hotel walls bore a flaming panorama of Tacoma in which by the eye of faith I saw a faint resemblance to the real town. The hotel stationery advertised that Tacoma bore on its face all the advantages of the highest civilization, and the newspapers sang the same tune in a louder key. The real-estate agents were selling house-lots on unmade streets miles away for thousands of dollars. On the streets—the rude, crude streets, where the unshaded electric light was fighting with the gentle northern twilight—men were babbling of money, town lots, and again money—how Alf or Ed had done such and such a thing that had brought him so much money; and round the corner in a creaking boarded hall the red-jerseyed Salvationists were calling upon mankind to renounce all and follow their noisy God. The men dropped in by twos and threes, listened silently for a while, and as silently went their way, the cymbals clashing after them in vain."[29]

Except for the speed with which cities were laid out and developed, the era of railroad expansion was not a notable period in American city planning. The philosophy of speculation, of treating land like a commodity to be put in handy packages for quick sale, or regarding townsite promotion as a means of raising ready cash to meet a railroad construction payroll, of making the physical layout of towns subservient to the railroad line and its requirements—these were the dominant attitudes of the railroad town builders. The country was settled—yes, and quickly—but at a price which generations since and those yet to come will be paying for in discomfort, danger, monotony and sterility.

[29] *ibid.*, 45-46.

VIEW OF THE CITY OF

TACOMA, W.T.

PUGET-SOUND

COUNTY SEAT OF PIERCE CO.

PACIFIC TERMINUS OF THE N.P.R.R.

1884.

Figure 246. View of Tacoma, Washington: 1884

CHAPTER 15

The Towns the Companies Built

THE industrialization of America contributed more than any other single factor to the development and growth of the nation's cities. New factories provided new jobs for new immigrants. Each additional person employed in manufacturing generated further employment in retail and service activities and eventually in secondary manufacturing. As employment increased, towns expanded to provide housing and the other physical requirements of city life, but the accelerated pace of industrialization in the latter half of the nineteenth century far outstripped the more leisurely tempo of urban improvements. The simple forms of government appropriate for an agrarian and village economy were inadequate for the expanded requirements of a rapidly industrializing society. The haphazard, largely unplanned urban expansion of this period created many of the undesirable features of our cities which modern planners have only recently begun to overcome.

From the middle of the nineteenth century on, most large-scale manufacturing establishments developed in already existing cities. Here were markets, labor, capital, and the hubs of transportation systems. Yet here and there isolated industrial enterprises developed. Some of these involved nothing more than the construction of a factory building and ancillary structures; these need not concern us. Our interest lies with the others, where the industrial enterprise not only built production facilities but also planned and constructed—and in many cases, managed as well—the town in which the factory stood.

Company town! The very phrase summons images of grimy tenements clustered about a pithead or forbidding factory, where over-worked laborers remained in perpetual debt to the company store. In truth, this picture hardly exaggerates reality, but its canvas is unduly restricted. By no means all company towns arose from the desires of employers to exploit their workers at artificially low wages or to keep them subservient to capitalist economic domination. Benevolent paternalism and practical necessity also led to the creation of new industrial towns, and the physical results were

not always unpleasant. In a few cases the most skilled designers available prepared the town plans.

The conclusion is inescapable, however, that town planning by American industry generally failed to produce communities significantly different or better than those which owed their layout to other sources. Nor were company towns leaders in the development of new standards or patterns of design; indeed, the reverse appears to be true. American industry, which prided itself on its inventiveness in the operations of machinery or in business administration, remained fundamentally conservative in its sporadic town planning activities. Like the myriad towns puffed into life by the American railroads, company towns in this country added little to our knowledge of how communities should be planned.

The stories of some of these towns, however, are not without interest. In a few of them developers combined sound planning with imaginative development to produce communities of substantial merit. Others proved dismal failures, but it would be well to remember that modern planners, too, have scarcely solved the complex problems of developing a model environment for industrial communities.

Textiles and Town Planning in Nineteenth-Century New England

At the beginning of the nineteenth century New England was the center of the textile industry in the United States. Hundreds of little spinning mills dotted the stream valleys where mill dams and races had been constructed at the falls of rivers. Around these mills clustered groups of houses in tiny industrial communities. These settlements had come into existence following the introduction into America by Samuel Slater of the Arkwright spinning machinery from England. Slater's machines converted cotton and wool into yarn, which was then woven into cloth on hand looms in the homes of weavers. The number of nearby looms established the capacity of the spinning mills, and the small scale of manufacturing operations thus limited the size of mill communities to mere hamlets and villages.

The development of power looms soon changed these conditions and led to the creation of new and much larger textile towns. Just as Slater had memorized the closely guarded details of the Arkwright machines in England, so Francis Cabot Lowell "re-invented" the new power looms he had inspected while visiting the flourishing mill towns of Lancashire. The quick popularity of the power looms, after Lowell introduced them in his Waltham mills, abruptly ended the era of handicraft in the textile industry. Much larger scale production now became an economic necessity if the complex and relatively expensive new machinery was to be used at maximum efficiency.

Adequate and suitable labor created certain problems. The old spinning mills had employed many children, but the more complicated new machines required adults for their operation. Lowell's Boston Manufacturing Company and other textile concerns found it difficult to recruit male employees because of the general labor shortage in the northeast caused by the War of 1812 and by westward migration. Lowell and his fellows of necessity turned increasingly to the young, unmarried women from the farms of New England.

Social pressures and mores affected the form and character of the emerging textile towns. Factory employment by women had long been regarded as degrading if not positively immoral. Respectable Yankee farmers seemed unlikely to permit their daughters to work in the new mills unless this stigma could be removed. The mill owners responded with typical ingenuity. Boardinghouses were built for young ladies watched over by matrons of impeccable reputation. Bible reading sessions and compulsory church attendance were established. Hours of work thought reasonable for young women were adhered to. The female loom operators found themselves in an atmosphere more akin to a convent than a conventional industrial enterprise.[1]

Such necessary paternalistic steps to win over the parents of

prospective laborers did not stop with the creation of model boardinghouses. The companies had to provide the entire range of town facilities if the industrial enterprise was to be a success. Lowell realized that the industrial plant could no longer exist apart from the community and that it was now a responsibility of industries to create the towns in which they would be located. He had apparently revealed to his associates his vision of the textile towns of the future before his death in 1817.

Lowell's concept of the physical plan was both simple and functional. The factory district was to be located along the river between it and a parallel canal that was to bring water to the mills. A major road was also to parallel the river at a distance of perhaps a quarter of a mile. Between the canal and the road lay the area for employee housing. The road served as the spine of the town, and here would be the stores, churches, and public buildings. Beyond the road the land could be developed for private residences. Such was Lowell's ideal plan. With variations for topography and other local conditions, it was to be repeated throughout New England.

In 1822 Lowell's plan received its first test. The Boston Manufacturing Company's mills at Waltham could no longer be expanded. Company officials purchased a new site on the Merrimac River and appointed Kirk Boott treasurer and agent for the new corporation. Soon construction was under way. Boott was evidently responsible for the plan of Lowell, as the new town was named, although he may have received help from others.

The city of Lowell departed somewhat from the ideas of the man for whom it was named. The plan of the town in 1832 appears in Figure 247 and clearly reveals the major existing elements and those proposed for the immediate future. Boott utilized the old Pawtucket Canal curving away from the Merrimac as part of the main canal system. From a point midway in its length he first cut a new canal to enter the river at right angles. Later, a second canal was added parallel with the first. Near these two canals he constructed the first plants and workers' housing. South of the mill and housing area Boott developed an elongated grid of streets which included some of the existing roads modified and straightened to conform to the new plan. Later development to the south and east was less clearly organized except for the plants and row housing of the Appleton and Hamilton Manufacturing Companies.

[1] For the background of the development of the New England textile mill towns see John Coolidge's splendid *Mill and Mansion*, New York, 1942, and the sources cited in his Chapter 2.

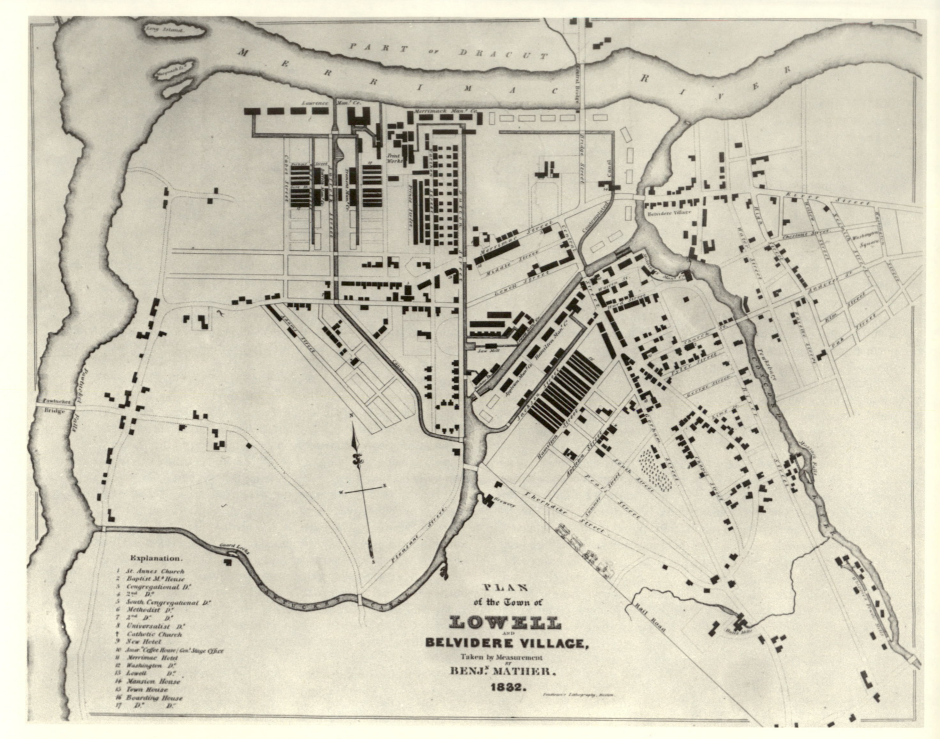

PLAN
of the Town of
LOWELL
AND
BELVIDERE VILLAGE,
Taken by Measurement
BY
BENJ.ⁿ MATHER.
1832.

Figure 247. Plan of Lowell, Massachusetts: 1832

Thus, the neat linear scheme that Francis Cabot Lowell envisaged emerged in a modified pattern.

Boardinghouses for the female employees took two forms in Lowell. Facing the new Merrimac Canal across Dutton Street and on both sides of a parallel street to the west Boott constructed rows of double houses. In the middle of each row stood quadruple houses of brick, contrasting in mass and material with the timber dwellings on either side. Most of the later boardinghouses in Lowell were row rather than semi-detached structures, and this was the pattern generally followed in the other New England textile towns of the period.

The first mill buildings, grouped along the river in a tidy, tree-shaded compound, as John Coolidge has pointed out, very much resembled an academic quadrangle. The whole effect, while somewhat mechanical in treatment, had a certain charm and order. Certainly the new community had every sign of permanence and respectability, both qualities being essential to attract the necessary female operatives. There is every evidence that Boott and his superiors sought quality in construction and strove for, if they did not entirely succeed, beauty as well.

Foreign visitors, such as Michael Chevalier in the mid 1830's, came away impressed both by Lowell's rapid growth and by its character. As Chevalier wrote,

"The town of Lowell dates its origin eleven years ago, and it now contains 15,000 inhabitants. . . . At present it is a pile of huge factories, each five, six, or seven stories high, and capped with a little white belfry. . . . By the side of these larger structures rise numerous little wooden houses, painted white, with green blinds, very neat, very snug, very nicely carpeted, and with a few small trees around them, or brick houses in the English style. . . . All around are churches and meeting-houses of every sect. . . Here are all edifices of a flourishing town in the Old World, except the prisons, hospitals, and theatres."[2]

Not all of Lowell was quite so idyllic. Irish laborers who had been brought to the site for canal and factory construction lived in unplanned squalor. By 1831 five hundred of them inhabited crude plank shacks along the canal southwest of the neat mill

village. One hundred and fifty children from these unfortunate families daily crowded into a small, single room schoolhouse. While in Lowell these slum conditions affected only a small part of the population, they foreshadowed the time when company towns would exhibit less desirable qualities.

Elsewhere in New England the founders of dozens of new communities followed the Lowell pattern of settlement. The new mill companies that had been formed to take advantage of power loom equipment and the growing demand for cotton textiles were often closely connected. The same men served as directors for many companies, and the chief investors of one company often held extensive interests in others. Then, too, the Lowell mills became an immediate financial success. It is, therefore, not difficult to understand why a standardized plan form quickly became accepted.

Only a year after the beginning of Lowell a new milling company purchased land and water rights on the Chicopee River, a tributary of the Connecticut. Near the falls of the river and on a site inside a bend, like that of Lowell, the town of Chicopee Falls was planned. An L-shaped area contained the mill next to the river, then a canal following the river's curve, a main street parallel to the canal, and the boardinghouses and other company-built residences beyond. As at Lowell, the remainder of the town lacked the clear form of the mill and boardinghouse district.

The same concern created another town a short distance down stream at the mouth of the Chicopee a few years later. Here the somewhat crude axial planning of Lowell was refined and, rather tentatively, symmetrical diagonal planning elements were introduced. Three streets radiated outward from a common point toward the three main mill buildings. Along the streets ranged the standard boardinghouse accommodations. The mills occupied the now familiar site between canal and river. This little essay in milltown baroque at Chicopee, Massachusetts, was apparently unique.

By far the best example of the Lowell ideal town was Manchester, New Hampshire. Land purchases begun in 1831 and extensive dam and canal construction culminated in a great linear community along the banks of the Merrimac. Ezekiel Straw, an engineer employed by the developing company, the Amoskeag Manufacturing Company, prepared the plan and applied here all the devices which had proved so successful elsewhere. The view

[2] Michael Chevalier, *Society, Manners and Politics in the United States*, Boston, 1839, pp. 128-29.

Figure 248. View of Manchester, New Hampshire: 1876

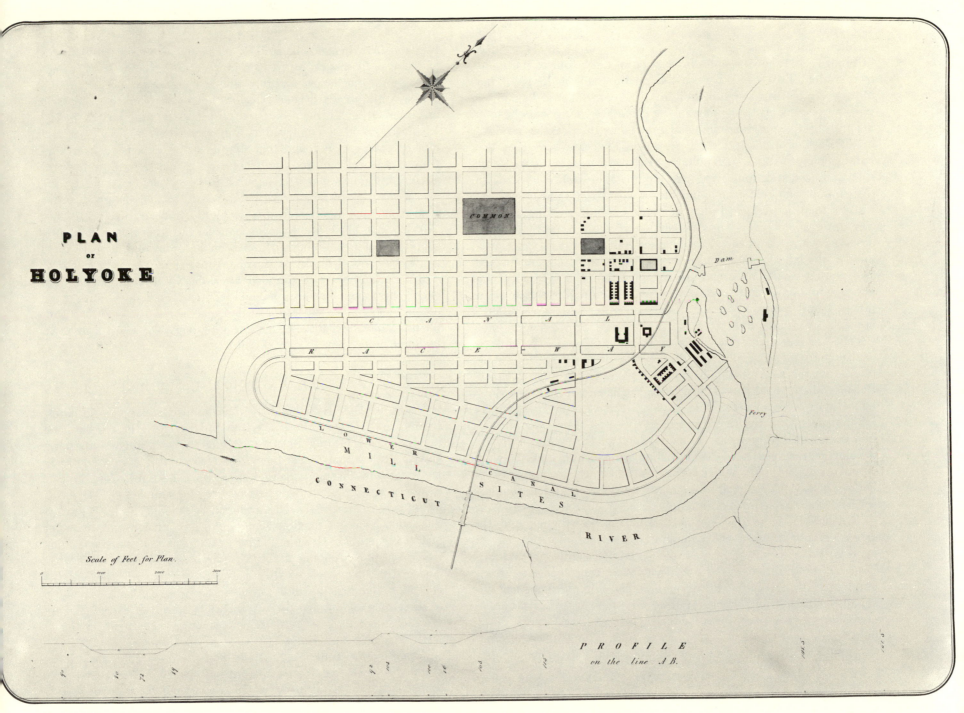

PLAN
OF
HOLYOKE

COMMON

Dam

C A N A L

R A C E W A Y

Ferry

L O W E R   M I L L   C A N A L   S I T E S

C O N N E C T I C U T   R I V E R

Scale of Feet for Plan.

PROFILE
on the line A B.

Figure 249. Plan of Holyoke, Massachusetts: ca. 1848

of Manchester at the height of its prosperity in 1876, reproduced in Figure 248, shows also an innovation in the layout of the industrial section. Two canals were led along the bank of the river, permitting double rows of mill buildings. The usual mill housing in rows perpendicular to the axis of the canal system appears beyond. Separating the mill and industrial housing district the straight, broad slash of Elm Street can be seen. The view also reveals a number of parks and open squares reserved for public use. While such public dedications were not unknown in earlier mill towns, their number and extent in Manchester seems to be uncommon.

As a final and relatively late example of the New England mill community, Holyoke, Massachusetts, on the Connecticut River deserves some comment. The Hadley Falls Company purchased most of the land in 1847 and proceeded with the ambitious project of damming the Connecticut River above the falls. The city plan appears in Figure 249 and shows the same duality as the other planned mill towns. The section set aside for industry and mill housing was quite distinct from the balance of the community. Because of the great fall of water at the site it was possible to utilize the water twice before discharging it downstream. In the middle of the town a canal and parallel raceway were planned. Between them stood the factory sites. Beyond the canal, boardinghouse sites were located. The raceway then looped to form the lower canal along the river, and here a second series of mill sites was established. Again, across the lower canal from the mills the developers reserved sites for boardinghouses. The land between the two rows of mills shows an awkward layout; the upper town had the usual grid pattern broken only by the rectangular common set aside by the company for public use.

Holyoke failed to develop as speedily as anticipated, and the extensive properties of the company were eventually put up for auction. Some of the mill sites were used for textile manufacturing, and the traditional boardinghouses were constructed for these employees. But Holyoke did develop on the original plan, and the canal system and mill sites proved admirably adapted for a variety of manufacturing processes of which paper making became dominant.[3]

The 1850's marked a change in the social conditions of New

[3] Constance McLaughlin Green, *Holyoke, Massachusetts*, New Haven, 1939.

· 420 ·

England that doomed the orderly and genteel planned mill towns of the Lowell model. Waves of immigrants, chiefly Irish, swept through the northeast. Largely illiterate, ignorant of urban life, and scornfully regarded as inferiors by native Yankees, the Irish in America found themselves a propertyless proletariat. Young Irish girls could be employed as mill operatives at low wages, and mill operators soon found that dignified and expensive boardinghouses were not required to attract them as workers. Daughters of old Yankee families reacted against this new element, and by the end of the 1850's factory work for young females of good native stock was once again regarded as highly undesirable.

With the need for boardinghouses and the other company-supplied facilities eliminated, much of the order and attractiveness of the mill towns began to vanish. Apparently relatively few new mill communities were founded after the Civil War, and in the older ones many of the original company housing units were divided and re-divided into crowded tenements. In New England, for the time being at least, the era of responsible, large-scale town building by industry was at an end.

From Civil War to Chicago Fair

The Civil War stimulated the development of large-scale industry in the North. In the years that followed, northern cities and the industries located in them expanded with almost alarming speed. Exploitation of the boundless resources of a rich continent had begun in earnest. Changes in social conditions arose in part from the new relationships between capital and labor. The scale of industrial enterprise brought an end to the older, almost family-like atmosphere of smaller factories where owner and manager often knew employees as individuals rather than as statistical units. Labor became a commodity to be purchased like raw materials. The first labor unions and their national organization, the Knights of Labor, founded in 1878, arose as the laboring man's response to these new conditions. Strikes and riots were the extreme manifestations of labor's desire to achieve some degree of power parity with industrial capital.

There seems little doubt that many of the company towns founded in the three decades before the turn of the century represented industry's reply to these threats against absolute power. If workers in a single plant could be isolated from their fellows, if no alternative sources of employment were readily available, and if employees were dependent on industry for housing, shopping facilities, and credit, then trouble might be avoided. At the same time some industrialists felt a genuine concern for workers' welfare and desired to establish better conditions for their labor. Both fear and philanthropy thus played parts in the development of new industrial communities.

Ample precedents existed. The New England textile towns furnished one model, but the special conditions of female labor there at the beginning of the century no longer prevailed. The coal mining communities of Pennsylvania and West Virginia were also available for study. Scores of little company towns, almost all of them drab, wretched places, had been founded at isolated pitheads to supply housing for miners and their families. No one could tell when coal seams would become exhausted, and the mining companies provided only the barest essentials in crude housing and the inevitable single company store. Clearly this type of town was unsuitable for modern enterprise. More satisfactory models existed in Europe. In Germany the Krupp enterprise had for some time provided decent housing for their workers in fairly well planned communities. Perhaps more familiar were the planned company towns in England of Saltair, founded in 1853, and Bourneville, dating from 1879. These and other European examples were well known, and the newly arrived American industrialist often included them as side excursions on his Grand Tour of the Old World.

Some of the earliest of the postwar efforts in America failed to produce much of interest. Homestead, Pennsylvania, which would achieve notoriety in the famous strike twenty years later, was laid out in 1872 south of Pittsburgh. The plan was an unrelieved grid, as was that of Duquesne, another steel town nearby, founded in 1885. These, perhaps, were typical of the period: routine plans, housing built to minimum standards, little concern for community facilities. An examination of the dozens of such company towns built in this period would be pointless.

A few of the company towns did, however, show evidence of more careful and systematic planning. Among these Pullman, Illinois, stands out as a company town project more in the European tradition of enlightened paternalism. Moreover, the developers of Pullman produced a three-dimensional plan in which the design of individual buildings received as much attention as the layout of streets, parks, and building sites. Professional designers, rather than a company engineer, had the responsibility for the plan, and they appear to have been given a fairly free hand. Pullman thus constitutes a valuable reference point in American planning—an example of a complete town, conceived and built as a unit, and under the direction of a team of designers who presumably embodied in the plan the most up-to-date theories and practices of town design.[4]

George Pullman's railway sleeping car products had become enormously successful and profitable during the vigorous expansion of the railways following the Civil War. In 1880 Pullman resolved to centralize all production in a modern complex of plants. Twelve miles south of Chicago on the western shore of Lake Calumet Pullman's agents had already purchased nearly four thousand acres of land. The lake front, so it was expected, would become a great port development providing sheltered anchorage and dock facilities. Pullman doubtless had in mind the increased value of the land after his own plants had been established and the possibility of selling choice sites at equally choice prices to other manufacturers. He fixed on the immediate goal of building a complete town where his workers could live in close proximity to the Pullman car plants.

Solon S. Beman, architect, and Nathan F. Barrett, landscape architect, received Pullman's commission to design the town and all of its buildings. Beman, who was only 27 at the time, later became one of the leading architects in Chicago. Little is known about Barrett, who had been the landscape architect for a number of estates in New York and whom Pullman had met when he was considering building a residence in New Jersey. Three hundred acres of the site between Lake Calumet and the Illinois Central tracks were selected as the town site. The factory area was located to the north, its southern boundary being the present 111th Street.

[4] Studies of Pullman are extensive. The following have proved most useful: William T. W. Morgan, "The Pullman Experiment in Review," *Journal of the American Institute of Planners*, XX (1954), 27-29; Robert M. Lillibridge, "Pullman: Town Development in the Era of Eclecticism," *Journal of the Society of Architectural Historians*, XII (1953), 17-22; and Richard T. Ely, "Pullman: A Social Study," *Harper's New Monthly Magazine*, LXX (1885), 452-66.

By 1881 production began in the first factory buildings, and within four years the population of the town reached 8,000. In these few years a stretch of flat Illinois prairie became a town of unique character and George Pullman's showplace.

The plan of Pullman and the accompanying view in Figure 250 reveal something of its quality. The basic grid plan is no surprise, but for the midwest the treatment of streets as enclosed ways lined with row houses or apartments was something of an innovation. Most of the houses were two- and three-story row structures of red or yellow brick. There were also a number of single-family detached houses for higher paid workers. On the Lake Calumet side of the town, blocks of two- and three-room tenements appear. Beman and Barrett appear to have anticipated modern recommendations for housing developments of mixed types. The young Richard T. Ely, only later to become famous for his contributions to land economics, was impressed by this combination of regularity and variety when he wrote these impressions in 1885:

"Unity of design and an unexpected variety charm us as we saunter through the town. Lawns always of the same width separate the houses from the street, but they are so green and neatly trimmed that one can overlook this regularity of form. Although the houses are built in groups of two or more, and even in blocks, with the exception of a few large buildings of cheap flats, they bear no resemblance to barracks. . . . Simple but ingenious designs secure variety, of which the most skillful is probably the treatment of the sky line. Naturally, without an appearance of effort, it assumes an immense diversity."[5]

Ely also found that the planners had found ways to add variety and interest to the grid plan:

"The streets cross each other at right angles, yet here again skill has avoided the frightful monotony of New York. . . . A public square, arcade, hotel, market, or some large building is often set across the street so ingeniously as to break the regular line, yet without inconvenience to traffic. Then at the termination of long streets a pleasing view greets and relieves the eye—a bit of water, a stretch of meadow, a clump of trees, or even one of the large but neat workshops. All this grows upon the visitor day by day.

No other feature of Pullman can receive praise needing so little qualification as its architecture."[6]

The major buildings and open spaces mentioned by Ely appear in the northwest section of the town. Here lay the entrance to the town by way of the Illinois Central station, which faced the southern end of an irregular park placed between the factories and the railroad. From this end of the park, one entered the public square. On two sides were residential buildings. At the northeast corner stood the Hotel Florence, a massive four-story building of eclectic design and an almost medieval roof line. Bordering the square on the west was the arcade building. This was vaguely Romanesque in appearance and contained a theatre, library, a bank, offices, and, lining its two-level arcade, the shops and stores of the town. Completing the grouping of major buildings was a church, that stood just off the square to the southeast, and a stable at the southwest corner.

The street forming the southern boundary of the square led eastward past the church to a second major urban space, the market square. Three other streets entered the square from the north, east, and south, all four intersecting the boundaries of the square at the midpoints of its sides. The market building in the middle originally resembled the other buildings of Pullman in its eclectic design. After a fire it was replaced in 1893 by a more impressive and simpler structure of classic derivation. At the same time new buildings were erected around the square for residential use with their first floors recessed behind round arched arcades that echoed the similar arches of the new market building.

Pullman was a remarkable achievement. Not since Williamsburg had an entire town been designed with equal attention to the ground plan and to the buildings that would form the third dimension. Beman and Barrett succeeded in creating in their two town squares real civic design. Despite the relatively small size of the town, the whole effect remained distinctly urban in character. The designers must be given full credit, but George Pullman deserves equal praise for his vision of what a model industrial town might be.

And yet Pullman proved to be no paradise. The company retained complete ownership of the land and all the buildings. Ely sensed the dissatisfaction and the feeling of impermanence of the

[5] Ely, "Pullman," 457.

[6] ibid.

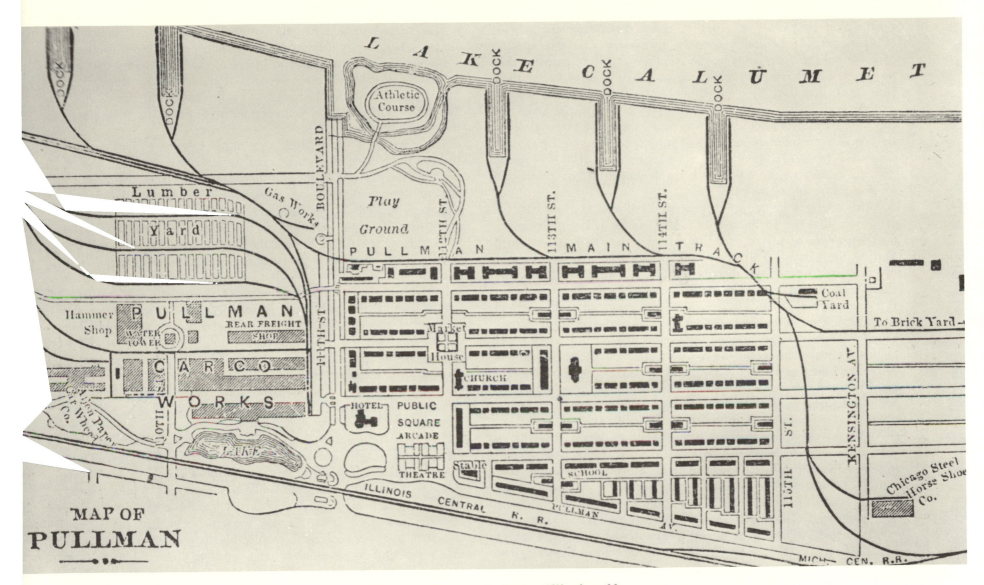

Figure 250. Plan of Pullman, Illinois: 1885

residents of Pullman and strongly criticized management policies in this respect. He pointed out too the uneasiness of the townspeople over their dependence on a single employer, their resentment that no voice of criticism was tolerated, and their fear of losing their right to occupy their homes at the whim of some company official. Ample, even lavish, residential accommodations and the luxury of the public buildings could not overcome what Ely referred to as the feudal system of land tenure and subjection to a single powerful combined landlord and employer. The absence of the ordinary political apparatus through which residents could have a voice in local affairs was keenly felt.

With different management practices Pullman might well have set a new direction for industry to follow in its inevitable influence on the growth of towns and cities during the twentieth century. During the Chicago Fair of 1893 Pullman received thousands of visitors, and a pamphlet distributed at the Palace Car Company exhibit made its name and general features familiar to many more. But the great Pullman strike of 1894 arose because wages and working schedules had been cut while rents in the company houses remained fixed. After an investigation of the conditions that led to this often violent protest on the part of the workers, the Illinois Supreme Court ordered the company to divest itself of all real property not required for strictly manufacturing operations. By 1908 all property had been sold, and Pullman, as a company town, ceased to exist. The unfavorable publicity resulting from these events convinced many industrialists that company towns on the Pullman model were undesirable. Most of the industrial communities founded after the turn of the century were on more conventional lines, far less lavish in their provision for community facilities, and often included provisions for workers to own their own property. Pullman itself has gone through a cycle of decay and rehabilitation. All land-use controls were removed and only in recent years have local activities restored some of the community's original character.

Three other company towns founded before the end of the last century deserve at least passing comment. In point of time Barberton, Ohio, was the first. Ohio Barber founded the town in 1891 near Akron as the site of his Diamond Match Company plant. W. A. Johnston, a civil engineer for the Pennsylvania Railroad devised the plan reproduced in Figure 251. The only remarkable feature in the otherwise standard grid pattern is Lake Anna, named for Barber's daughter, which stood in the center of the town. Between the little lake and the business street to the south, Johnston left one block open as a central green. Barber originally provided all municipal services and utilities, but as the town grew it was incorporated as Barberton and the new municipal government took over these activities.

Granite City, Illinois, began as a rather more ambitious project. In 1893 the Niedringhaus brothers bought 4,000 acres of land near the Mississippi River as the site for an enlarged plant manufacturing graniteware together with a town for its employees. The clumsy plan incorporated into its basic grid a single diagonal avenue running from the plant through the business district and on to the other side of the town. Where the diagonal slashed through the intersection of the central streets of the grid, a circle appeared. The purpose of this circle is difficult to determine, and in any event it has since vanished. The Niedringhaus name hardly lent itself for use in naming the town, and it was decided to call it after the product of the company. Although the company built the first houses for rent, it soon changed this policy and put all its non-manufacturing property up for sale. Other industries moved to Granite City, and its original character as a company town rapidly changed. Today the town is a grim symbol of industrial blight, and there is little evidence that any foresight whatsoever was exercised in its layout.

Far more interesting in its original concept, though scarcely exhibiting greater civic qualities today than Granite City, was Vandergrift, Pennsylvania. Here, northeast of Pittsburgh at a loop in the Kiskiminetas River, the Apollo Iron and Steel Company commissioned the firm of Frederick Law Olmsted and John Charles Olmsted to design a town for the workers at its new plant. The elder Olmsted was nearing the end of his distinguished career, and in all probability his nephew and stepson, John Charles, was responsible for the layout. The plan, reproduced in Figure 252, shows little of the genius that marked the best residential plans of Frederick L. Olmsted.

Only half of the town was built as originally planned—that portion to the left containing the factory, business district, and ten or so residential blocks. Although the streets are well adapted to the hilly site, the plan as a drawing is much more impressive than

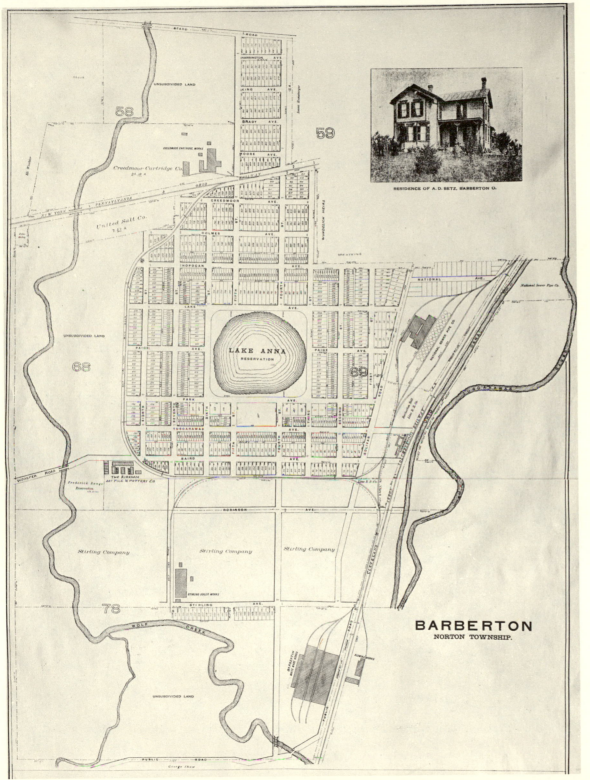

RESIDENCE OF A. D. BETZ, BARBERTON O.

BARBERTON
NORTON TOWNSHIP.

Figure 251. Plan of Barberton, Ohio: 1891

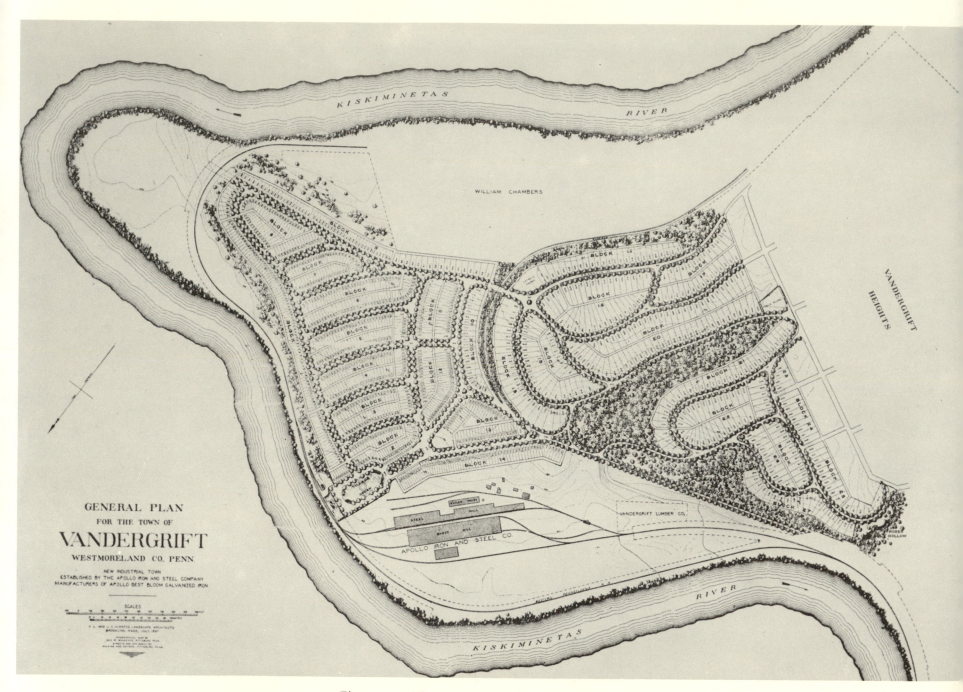

Figure 252. Plan of Vandergrift, Pennsylvania: 1895

when applied to the ground. The town has no central focus, no group of buildings that marks the center. Nor are the curving streets particularly well suited for business use, however admirable they may be for residential purposes. It is not known to what extent the Olmsteds were inhibited in their design by the wishes of the company, but the results must be catalogued among the small number of inferior designs associated with the name of Olmsted.

New Towns in a New Century

The years between the Chicago Fair and the First World War witnessed the founding of dozens of new company towns. The Fair itself brought new concepts of planning to the country and, as a later chapter will discuss, was responsible for the beginning of modern city planning in America. As far as company towns were concerned, the effects of the Fair were twofold. First, industrial leaders came away impressed by the idea of large-scale planning as a technique for better ordering the communities in which their plants might be located. Second, the formal, axial disposition of the Fair buildings came to be regarded by many industrialists as the desirable plan on which company towns might be shaped. The formal plan, as anticipated at Pullman, and the informal, curvilinear type of layout, as exhibited at Vandergrift, steadily replaced the old and standardized grid plans of previous years.

The grid, however, remained popular during the early years of the century, and the largest of the company towns founded at that time—Gary, Indiana—employed this type of street and lot planning exclusively. Gary was an enormous undertaking, one that only a giant corporation like its sponsor, U.S. Steel, could have attempted. Perhaps not even the corporation officers could have foreseen the magnitude of the task. Certainly this restrained announcement in the company's 1905 annual report failed to convey the scope of operations that soon would begin: "It has been decided to construct and put in operation a new plant to be located on the south shore of Lake Michigan in Calumet Township, Lake County, Indiana, and a large acreage of land has been purchased for that purpose."

The "large acreage" amounted eventually to nothing less than 11 square miles, a tract of baronial proportions. The single attraction of the site was its location midway between the iron ore of Minnesota and the coal of Pennsylvania and West Virginia and squarely in the center of a rapidly expanding market for steel products. In all other aspects the land seemed ill-suited for its purpose. Swamps and sloughs alternated with great stretches of deep sand heaped along the lake shore into enormous dunes. There was little ground cover and practically no trees except along the streams. Three railroad lines cut across the site, which was further broken by the Calumet River.

By 1907 the site bustled with activity. The river and the railroad lines were moved. Material dredged from the bottom of Lake Michigan to create harbors was used to fill the swamps. The dunes were leveled and the site of the first steel mill elevated 15 feet above its natural grade. At this time construction workers lived in a sprawling temporary camp stretched along a single sandy street. The Gary Land Company, created to develop the town itself, then took command.

A. P. Melton laid out the town which took its name from Judge Elbert Gary, head of U.S. Steel. Utility lines—water, gas, and sewer—were among the first projects. These were installed in alleys at the rear of residential and commercial lots. The company built some houses for rent, but the bulk of the town consisted of homes built by lot purchasers who did not acquire clear title until their houses were completed. Apparently the company exercised control over the design of commercial buildings, but here too it avoided following the policies of Pullman and placed maximum emphasis on private initiative. One reporter on the scene stated that by the fall of 1907 dozens of shops, a restaurant, theatre, two hotels, and two banks stood completed in the middle of the new town. According to Ida Tarbell, biographer of Judge Gary, the corporation had poured $50,000,000 into the project by this time, with an additional $30,000,000 marked for immediate expenditure. These sums, of course, included the costs of the complex modern steel manufacturing facilities, port development, and railroad relocation, as well as for the town proper. Certainly no one could charge the company with a failure to think in grandiose scale; the water system, for example, was designed for an ultimate population of 200,000.[7]

[7] Two contemporary accounts are of interest: John Kimberly Mumford, "This Land of Opportunity: Gary, The City that Rose from a Sandy Waste," *Harper's Weekly*, LII (1908), 22-23, 29; and Henry B. Fuller, "An Industrial Utopia," *Harper's Weekly*, LI (1907), 1482-83, 1495.

Melton's plan scarcely warranted such expenditures in money, time, and energy. The first area to be laid out by the Gary Land Company appears in Figure 253. The inset map in the upper right-hand corner indicates the relationship of this first subdivision to the industrial area along the lake and other lands available for residential growth. Trolley tracks along Fifth Avenue, running east and west, and along Broadway, north and south, indicate that the intersection of these two streets was intended as the center of the business district. The undeviating grid street pattern was broken in two places for park sites, one being the size of four standard blocks, the other being formed by combining two normal blocks. Three vacant blocks were set aside for public schools, and a half-block left open in the southwest corner was designated for a Catholic church and school. Other smaller sites were intended for churches, hotels, police and fire stations, and similar public and semi-public buildings. Melton at least provided locations for virtually the entire range of civic, educational, religious, and commercial uses that would be required in a town of substantial size. The Gary plat closely resembles the typical speculative plat of the nineteenth-century town boomers, most of which showed sites reserved for similar uses. The difference of course was that U.S. Steel had the financial resources and the determination to carry out the scheme.

Perhaps the most interesting feature of the Gary plan can be found not in the town plat but in the much broader plan for the development of the entire stretch of land owned by the company, of which Gary itself was but a part. The corporation intended to develop a whole series of plants, each having port facilities on the north and access to the railroads on the south. South of the railroads residential and commercial units, like Gary, would be laid out to provide housing for the workers of each plant together with civic and commercial facilities necessary for community life. The ultimate scheme, of which Gary was but the first increment, would be a vast linear metropolis running east and west. Whether consciously or not this great regional plan adopted the similar but much smaller system used in the planned New England mill towns of almost a century earlier. In the Gary region whole towns would replace the mill community boardinghouses. Lateral transportation along the Fifth Avenue axis of Gary would provide the link between adjacent communities.

It is just possible that Melton knew of the linear city proposals advanced in the 1880's by the Spanish engineer, Soria y Mata, and actually put into partial application outside of Madrid. More likely, Melton and other corporation officials simply applied what must have seemed to them intuitively a sound engineering and industrial solution to the site extending along the lake shore. It may be of interest to note that planners in the Soviet Union used the linear principle in the planning of new industrial communities during the late 1930's and also used this system in the reconstruction of war-damaged Stalingrad. More recently Le Corbusier and a French study group called ASCORAL advocated the use of lineal town planning patterns for the development of company towns in Europe. But it is highly doubtful that the Gary regional plan served either as inspiration or example for these later studies and projects.

The linear development projected for Gary did occur, but in rather unsystematic fashion. Additional steel plants and industrial concerns producing other products came to the area and sought sites along the lakefront. Gary is now but one, although the largest, of the cities of the Calumet. There appears to be a general tendency for workers to live near the plants in which they are employed, although the near-universal ownership of private automobiles has so increased mobility that a nearby residence is no longer as essential as it was in the days of trolley transportation. Gary itself remains indistinguishable in general character from hundreds of other industrial towns that grew largely without benefit of prior planning. U.S. Steel created a new industrial metropolis on the Indiana dunes but failed sadly in its attempt to produce a community pattern noticeably different or better than elsewhere. In this largest of all the company towns of America the greatest opportunity was thus irrevocably lost.

The other prewar company towns seem superior to Gary in plan and execution, although much smaller in scale. The list is long, and our treatment must be brief. First is Hershey, Pennsylvania, which preceded Gary and which, in its rectilinear plan, it resembles. Milton Hershey, a candy manufacturer, visited the Chicago Fair and came away the purchaser of some German chocolate manufacturing equipment exhibited there. It is likely that he also visited Pullman, and the idea of combining his proposed chocolate plant with a new town for its employees must have seemed logical. In 1903 he purchased a site between Harrisburg and Reading, suc-

Steel Works and Blast Furnaces, Indiana Steel Co.

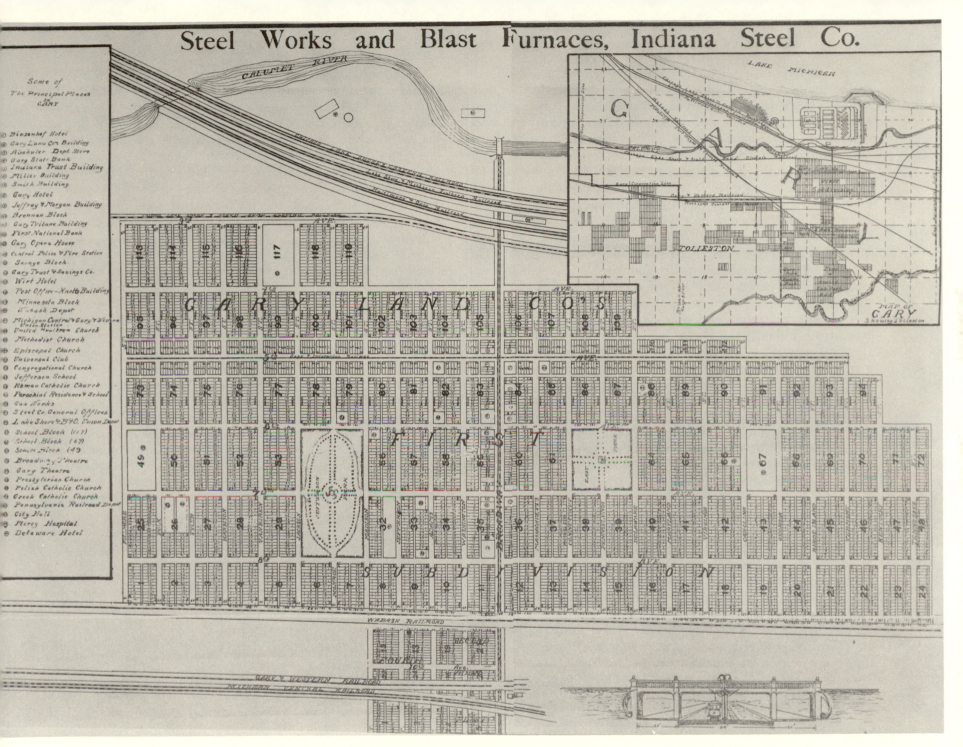

Figure 253. Plan of Gary, Indiana: 1907

ceeded in getting the railroad to erect a new station, and convinced the government that it should establish a post office. Hershey built his new plant north of the railroad and located a park and recreation fields nearby. Later he added a stadium, colosseum, zoo, and other cultural and recreational facilities. The business and residential portions of the community lay south of the tracks. Here Hershey adopted a completely regular plan without much interest except for the town square facing the plant on which fronted the important commercial and civic building. The paternalistic attitude of the founder largely continues to the present time, but the troubles that beset Pullman did not erupt in Hershey. The town remains small and, while not unpleasant, is not particularly distinguished. The country village atmosphere is marred only by the chocolate flavored smoke which, when the wind is from the north, pervades the town as a reminder of its reason for existence.[8]

Far more interesting and urban in character is Fairfield, Alabama, which illustrates the new forces of American site planning that had emerged by the first decade of the century. Robert Jemison, a real estate developer, hoped to create a model town on the best European and American patterns. He visited a number of company town projects and then in 1910 retained George H. Miller to design the community. Almost immediately the Tennessee Coal and Iron Company, a subsidiary of U.S. Steel, took over the development, contracting with the Jemison concern for the construction of houses. Miller's plan is reproduced in Figure 254 and shows the combination of a standard grid and a much freer curvilinear layout, with the introduction of a more formal element in the center. The greatest advance on the Gary plan is the development of a genuine community focal point. This appears as a plaza reached from the railroad by a broad street, with a group of civic buildings in a park-like setting beyond. The smaller lots fronting on the major streets were intended for commercial purposes and are far greater in number than were needed or have been utilized. Nor is the access to central Birmingham, whose boundaries adjoin Fairfield's, adequately handled. Yet the plan with all its shortcomings seems to have been approached with greater thought than the majority of previous company towns.[9]

[8] J. R. Snavely, "The Industrial Community Development of Hershey, Pa.," *American Landscape Architect*, III (1930), 24-36.
[9] George H. Miller, "Fairfield, a Town with a Purpose," *American City*, IX (1913), 213-19.

Another Alabama town, Kaulton, was founded in 1912 by the Kaul Lumber Company. Miller also designed this community. The little town takes the shape of a semicircle with the lumber mills located tangent to the curve at its midpoint. A street leads from the mills to the center, where a school and athletic field stand across the major circular street from the store, hotel, and offices. Walkways leading down the interior of the blocks furnish safe pedestrian access to the town center and the industrial district. The plan was considerably superior to the buildings that were erected in the town. These were of poor design and cheaply constructed.

Kohler, Wisconsin, a town founded in 1913 by a manufacturer of plumbing fixtures, was planned first by Werner Hegemann and Elbert Peets and later by the Olmsted firm. The plan as finally adopted appears in Figure 255. There is no central focal point, although most of the public buildings can be found in the northeast quadrant near the factory. Here the street system is rectangular, but west of Ravine Park, which divides the town, the streets follow freer lines. The Kohler Company constructed all the houses but, unlike Pullman, made them available for purchase at favorable terms. Kohler also was incorporated as a village, and the residents have full control over their governmental affairs.

Considerably more impressive in plan is Morgan Park, Minnesota. The town is another of the projects of the numerous subsidiaries of U.S. Steel. While Morgan Park is a suburb of Duluth, it enjoys a considerable degree of self-sufficiency. The plan by the firm of Morell and Nichols of Minneapolis is shown in Figure 256. The planners used a consistent and well-integrated combination of loop streets and diagonals radiating outward from the center. The park, school, and clubhouse form a central element which adjoins the business district extending from the east-west axis at right angles along one side of a principal street. At Morgan Park the steel company reversed its Gary policy and retained ownership of all the houses and apartments. This reversion to the old paternalism pattern seemed curiously out of keeping with its modern physical form.

Perhaps the most curious of the company town plans was that for Kincaid, Illinois, reproduced in Figure 257. The engineering firm of Albord and Burdick, assisted by O. C. Simmonds, landscape architect, produced a pattern of sinuous loops and curves superficially similar to those of the elder Olmsted but lacking his skill

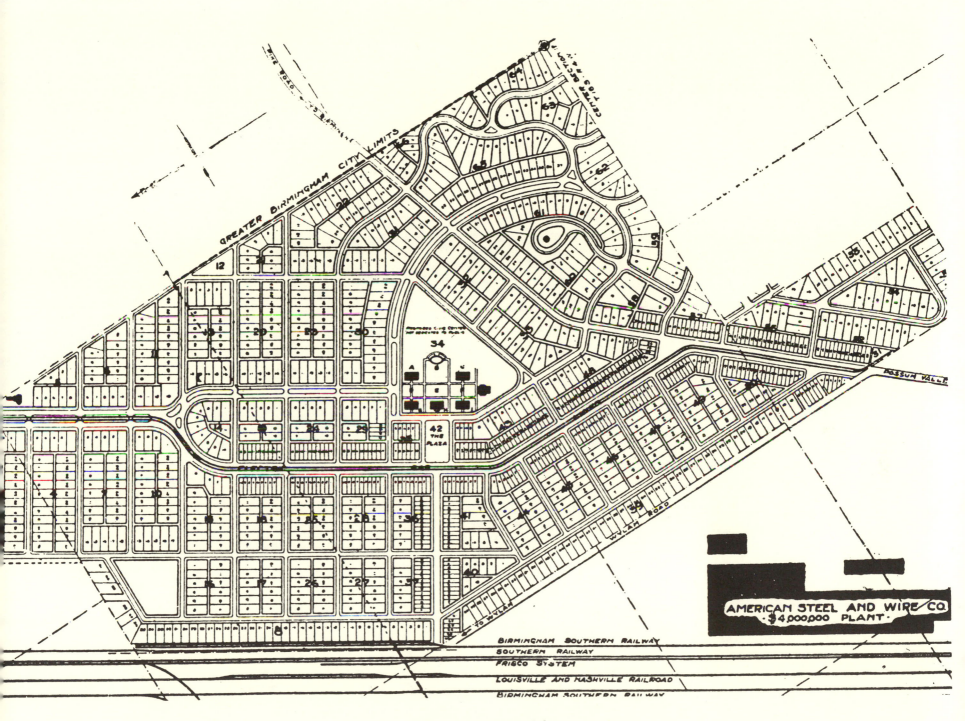

Figure 254. Plan of Fairfield, Alabama: 1910

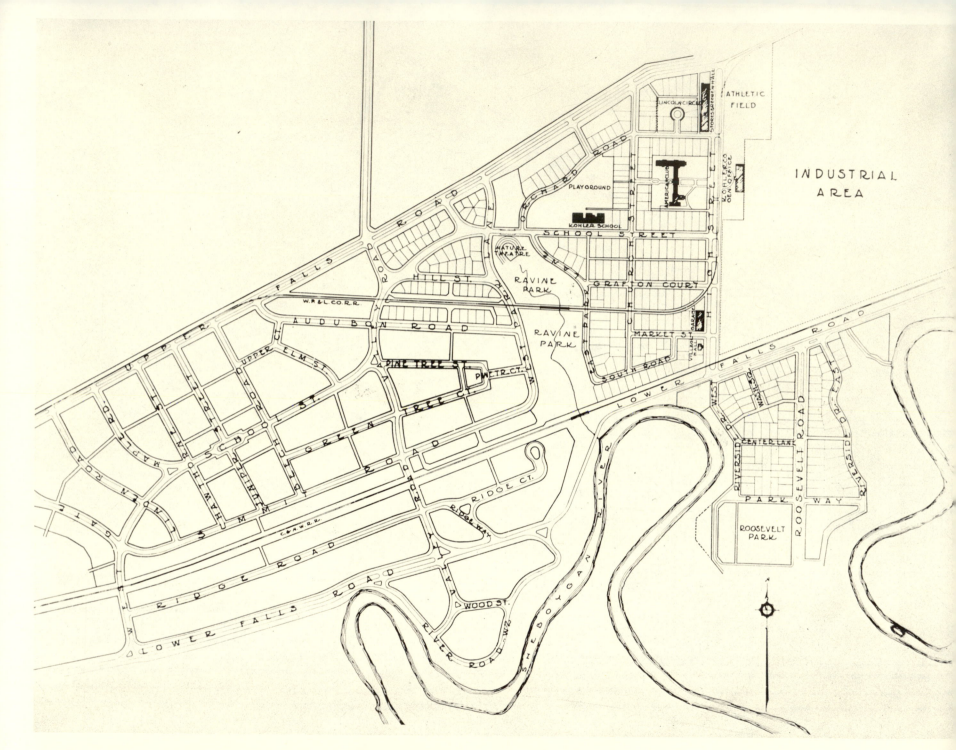

Figure 255. Plan of Kohler, Wisconsin: 1913

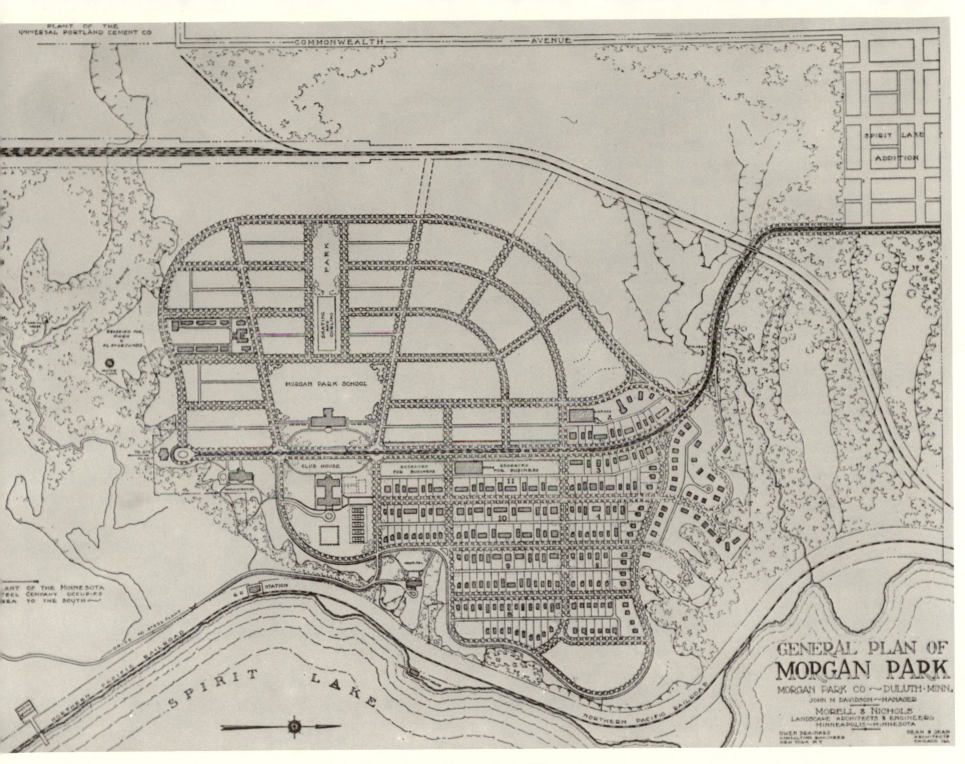

Figure 256. Plan of Morgan Park, Minnesota: 1917

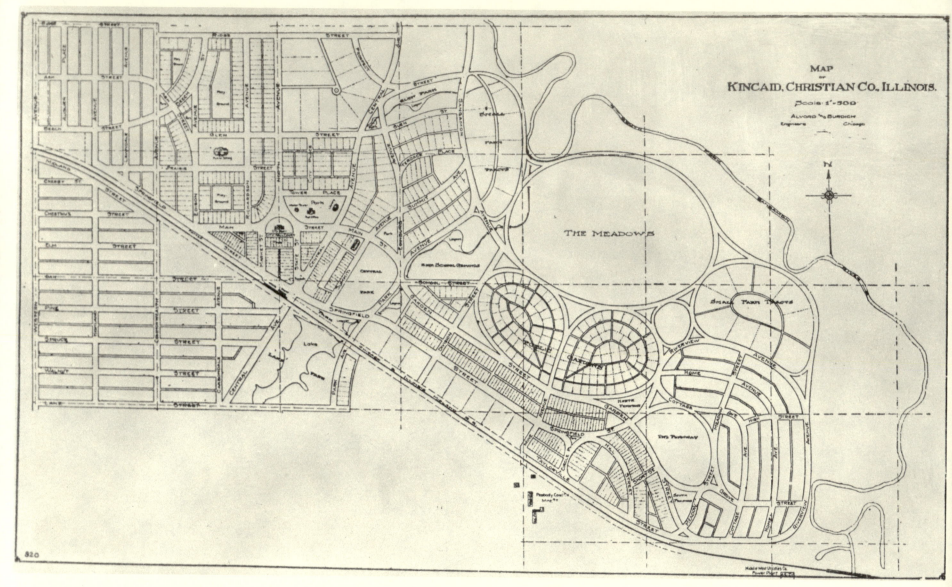

Figure 257. Plan of Kincaid, Illinois: 1915

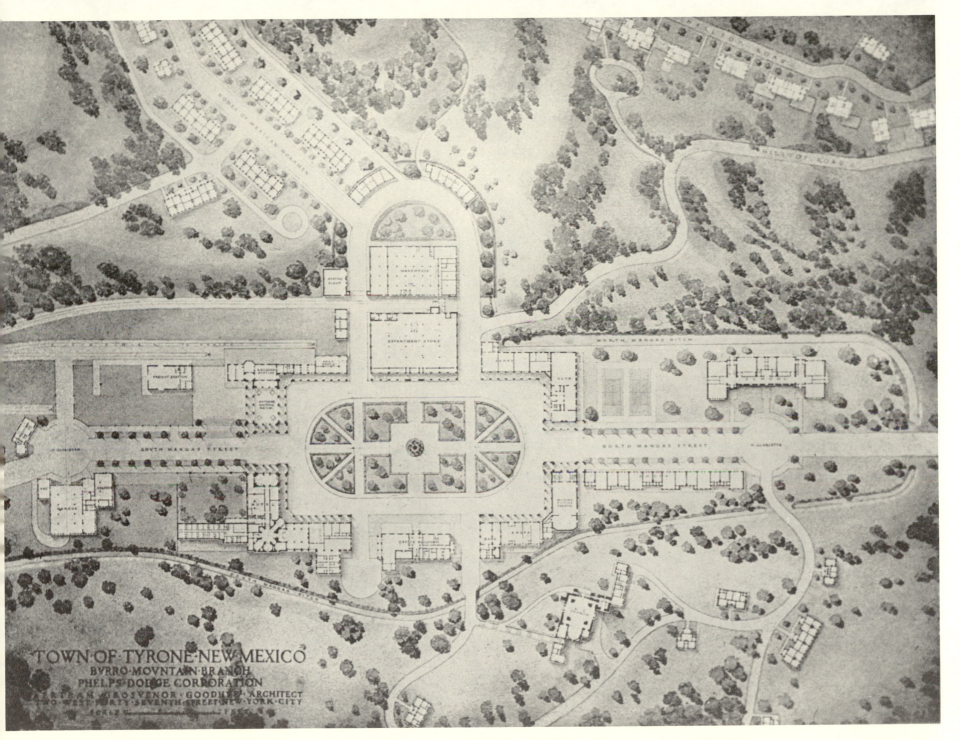

TOWN OF TYRONE NEW MEXICO
BVRRO·MOVNTAIN·BRANCH
PHELPS·DODGE·CORPORATION
BERTRAM·GROSVENOR·GOODHVE·ARCHITECT
TWO·WEST·FORTY·SEVENTH·STREET·NEW·YORK·CITY

Figure 258. Plan of Tryone, New Mexico: 1917

and feeling for the land. The plan serves as an excellent example of the deficiencies of curvilinear planning when attempted by unskilled hands. The awkward and dangerous intersections, unusable building lots near the ends of acute angled blocks, and the numerous remnants of strange shapes and sizes, all testify to the designers' lack of understanding of even the basic principles of free form design. Kincaid's chief claim to fame is that it probably represents the most intensive effort on the part of a coal mining company to provide a decent living environment for its workers.[10]

Another mining town, this one in the west, was begun at about the same time. In 1917 Bertram Goodhue prepared a plan for the town of Tyrone, New Mexico, for the Phelps Dodge Corporation's copper mining operations. Goodhue's scheme incorporated many of the traditional features of Spanish-American communities, an appropriate concept in view of the location and the expected use of Mexican laborers in the mines. The plan, reproduced in Figure 258, shows mainly the town center. Goodhue grouped a department store, shops, club, theatre, hotel, offices, and post office around a great plaza. Standing in open ground off one corner appears the Roman Catholic Church. The public school was nearby, facing the principal street, which entered the plaza at the midpoint of one of the shorter sides. Tyrone, however, was a center almost without a town. A single residential street led off at an angle flanked on both sides by groups of single-story row houses. While these may have represented improvements on traditional mining town residential accommodations, most of them consisted only of two rooms. Goodhue's superlative civic center and plaza thus stands almost alone and unsupported by residential planning of equal quality.

Finally, in this cursory survey of early twentieth-century company towns, we come to the plan of John Nolen at Kistler, Pennsylvania. Nolen by 1918 already had achieved leadership in the design of new towns, neighborhoods, and in the replanning of existing cities. Some of his work is summarized in his modest volume, *New Towns for Old*. Kistler, far from the best of his de-

signs, was undertaken for the Mount Union Refractories Company. The site was similar to Vandergrift, triangular in shape and bounded by a river on one side and the railroad on the other. The shape alone would have provided difficulty, but in addition a steep bank divided the land into two levels. Nolen's plan, shown in Figure 259, utilized the steep slope as a natural park. Adjacent to this he laid out an oval green on which he located the community hall. Facing the green and a major street on the top of the bank above the railroad were the shops. A smaller park separated the shopping district from the railroad station. The residential blocks are rectangular, but to add variety Nolen carefully located both detached and row houses with grouped setbacks. The modest houses provided by the company were attractively landscaped, and the whole effect was one of considerable charm.

Company Towns in American Planning

In 1938 the National Resources Committee reported the findings of its survey of planned communities in America, including a number of company towns.[12] The authors estimated the total population in all company towns at about two million persons. Even allowing some margin for underestimation the figure is not large as a percentage of the total population of the country, which was then 130,000,000. Company towns then must be regarded as a minor element in the American tradition of city planning. Although no accurate survey of recent activities has been carried out it would appear that the company town concept has declined in popularity. To be sure, new industrial communities continue to be created, but at a rate substantially less than during the period from the beginning of the century to the First World War.

Direct town founding and development by American industry has not therefore been of great importance in terms of population. Perhaps it is significant that no company town has become noted as a cultural or educational center. Even if measured by size, the achievement of company towns seems unimpressive; Gary's 1960

[10] A. T. Luce, "Kincaid, Ill.: A Model Mining Town," *American City*, XIII (1915), 10-13.

[11] John Nolen, *New Towns for Old*, Boston, 1927. See Chapter 5, "A Village for Factory Workers," 66-74.

[12] Arthur C. Comey and Max S. Wehrly, *Planned Communities*, Part I of the Supplementary Report of the Urbanism Committee to the U.S. National Resources Committee, Volume II, Washington, 1939. This study is a valuable source of material on company towns as well as other planned communities. For other surveys see Graham Romeyn Taylor, *Satellite Cities*, New York, 1915; and Budgett Meakin, *Model Factories and Villages*, London, 1905.

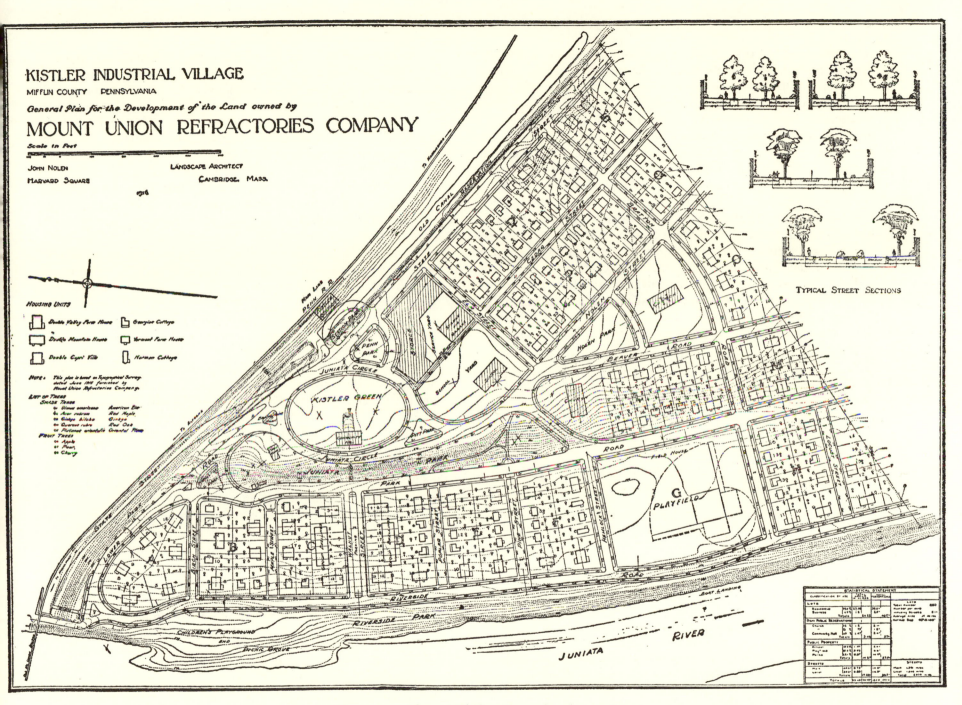

Figure 259. Plan of Kistler, Pennsylvania: 1918

population of 178,000 represents a considerable achievement, but it is not typical. Most of the towns founded by industry remain in the under-25,000 category.

In quality of design the record is mixed. Lowell, Pullman, and Kistler, to select three widely separated in time and character, produced environmental patterns superior to the average towns of their eras. Each in its way provided admirable solutions to the peculiar problems of fitting industry, housing, and civic activities to specific sites. Gary, however, stands as the more typical solution offered by company engineers throughout the country. For every Morgan Park, Kohler, or Fairfield, where attempts were made to create pleasant living patterns, there must have been ten Garys with their standardized grids very little different from the efforts of land speculators and town jobbers.

Even the best of the company towns appear to have exerted very little influence on subsequent town planning activities. Graham Taylor, in his reassessment of Pullman in 1915 had this to say about the town's impact on conditions elsewhere in the area:

"The substantial original construction of brick and the architectural scheme still give the houses of Pullman a distinct stamp in contrast with the stretches of dingy, frame houses characteristic of Chicago's poorer sections. They appear like a transplanted fragment of one of our eastern cities. Chicago housing seems not to have been influenced in the slightest degree by the "model" on its outskirts. While Chicago has only recently come up to the tenement light and air standards set up by Pullman thirty years ago, that progress seems part of the country-wide advance."[13]

Similar comments would be appropriate for many of the other company communities. Nevertheless, it was in the company towns during the decade preceding the First World War that some of America's first professional planning consultants found opportunities to experiment with site planning techniques that found later application in public projects and in city replanning studies.

One characteristic of company towns appears to have been widespread. This was the feeling, sometimes vague, sometimes strong, that the concept of a town in which an industry acted at the same time as employer, landlord, and governing agent somehow was contrary to American traditions. The failure of the company towns to enlist sympathetic and vigorous support from their residents

[13] Taylor, *Satellite Cities*, 38.

· 438 ·

stems from this attitude. Even where the companies sold houses to workers and permitted or encouraged incorporation of the town as a governmental unit the feeling persisted that the company continued to "run the town."

The paradox is plain. Where the towns were built and managed in a spirit of paternalism, as at Pullman, the physical results might be pleasing but the towns lacked the sense of true communities in the social-political sense. On the other hand, where the companies did not attempt to dominate the social and political aspects of community life, as at Gary, the physical results were often deplorable.

Some arrangement for joint corporation and governmental development might have avoided this unfortunate result. Under the conditions that prevailed at the time the towns came into existence, such a joint venture would have been impossible. Local governments were ill-equipped for activities of this sort even in the large cities. Their functions traditionally were limited, and these did not include large-scale building development. Moreover, business viewed governmental activities generally with considerable distaste and would hardly have welcomed the voice of government in determining company town policy. Finally, in many areas where company towns developed, only the most primitive types of rural governing units existed. Officials were for the most part non-professional and part-time. In these circumstances, association of government with industry in the development of industrial communities would have been ludicrous.

If the history of company town development offers lessons for the future it is this aspect that deserves further study. Joint public-private enterprise now exists in urban redevelopment activities. Company towns in the coming era might be formed by similar methods. With more than one industry participating, the old fears of economic domination could largely be eliminated. An equal share in the enterprise by metropolitan or state governments would assure representation of the public interest. Such a program must await extensive reorganization and reorientation of state and metropolitan governments, and in any event wholesale activity of this type seems unlikely. The old company town, with a single industry in full charge of both environment and administration, remains largely a thing of the past. The history of these communities provides few precedents that we would care to duplicate in the future. American industry, for all its success in production, signally failed in its attempt to manufacture noteworthy communities.

CHAPTER 16

Cities of Zion: The Planning of Utopian and Religious Communities

MARCHING across the continent with the planners of cities dedicated to Mammon—the grid surveyors, the town speculators, the creators of railroad towns, and the other men of affairs—were the reformers, the utopians, and the pariah religious sects in their restless quest for kingdoms of paradise on mortal earth. Their names are legion and their doctrines strange. But since many of these groups could boast of only a few dozen members and most of them were more concerned with enrichment of the spirit than with worldly wealth, it is not strange that the designs of the communities they founded often failed to match in interest and variety their doctrines for social, political, economic, or religious reforms. Nevertheless this is an aspect of American planning not without interest, and we shall find at least a few examples of sound achievements in the development of communities.

Almost from the beginning of settlement America seemed to be teeming with such groups, all busily engaged in their own special rituals, whether religious or secular. Indeed, since many of the religious sects practiced some brand of economic communism and the promoters of economic and social doctrines advanced their various causes with such fanatic zeal and dogmatism, it becomes difficult, if not impossible, to distinguish among them on such grounds. Therefore, no rigid classification of these groups and the communities they founded will be made, but they will be dealt with in rough chronological order.

Homes for Heretics: The Huguenots

Among the English colonies, Puritan New England, Quaker Pennsylvania, and Catholic Maryland owed their origins in large part to the strong desires of the settlers to escape religious persecutions and to follow their own beliefs in freedom and tranquility. In the French and Spanish colonies, religion furnished an added incentive to exploration, conquest, and settlement: the capture of the souls of the heathen for Rome.

But the Puritans, the Quakers, and the Catholics, at least in their own colonies, represented the majority and had the political power that usually accompanies superior numbers. Whatever may have been their position in England, the colonists in Maryland, Pennsylvania, and New England had secured official grants of both land and religious freedom.

This chapter, however, is concerned with other religious groups among those bands of settlers and colonizers loosely categorized as "utopians": those who remained in the minority, who commonly created new communities rather than taking up residence in established settlements, and who tended to work together as a community rather than as individuals who happened to share the same place of residence. Two such religious groups of colonial times stand out as planners of towns—the Huguenots and the Moravians.

The Huguenots, French Protestants, had long been persecuted by the Catholics. Tortures and executions, loss of property, heavy fines, and exclusion from public office or academic honors were widely practiced in an attempt to stamp out the heretical beliefs. It is little wonder that from the middle of the sixteenth-century Huguenots sought refuge abroad, including the New World. Under the sponsorship of Admiral Gaspard de Coligny, an expedition set out for Brazil in 1555 and succeeded in establishing a small settlement on the site of Rio de Janeiro. But this was broken up in 1560 by the Portuguese, and Huguenot eyes turned northward to the virtually unknown coast of Florida and the Carolinas.

In 1562, following renewed violence against them in France, a second Huguenot expedition under Jean Ribaut first landed at the mouth of the St. John's River in Florida, then proceeded northward along the coast of Port Royal harbor in what is now South Carolina. Here they built a small fortress, which they named Charlesfort. Ribaut, leaving a small group behind, returned to France to obtain reinforcements and additional supplies. At home the country was virtually in a civil war over the massacre of a group of Protestants in Champagne, and it was impossible at that time to organize a new expedition for Carolina. The tiny Charlesfort garrison meanwhile had quarreled among themselves, murdered their leader, constructed a small vessel, and finally managed to reach France after a voyage of unbelievable hardships.

Coligny managed to organize still a third settlement group which, with three ships and commanded by René de Laudonnière, managed to find the mouth of the St. John's River a second time. This little band established Fort Caroline on a site six miles inland. The plan of Fort Caroline is shown in Figure 260 as depicted in 1671 from the drawings made on the site more than a century earlier by Jacques LeMoyne. It was this settlement that the Spanish so quickly eliminated after they established St. Augustine as a military base nearby.

It should be remembered, too, that the first successful colonization of New France involved Huguenots. The Sieur de Monts, a wealthy Huguenot, had secured his grant from the former Huguenot leader, Henry IV. First at Ste. Croix Island, then Port Royal, and finally at Quebec this largely Huguenot group established the first settlements for France in the New World. The revocation of de Monts' exclusive trading rights, the assassination of Henry IV, and the early interest of the Jesuits and other Catholic orders in colonization brought an end to Huguenot influence in French America.

Much the same history was written in the founding of New Amsterdam. In the years following the bloody St. Bartholomew's Day massacres in 1572, thousands of Huguenots fled from France. Among them were the Walloons from northeastern France. Most of them went to Holland seeking freedom from religious tyranny, many of them settling in Leiden. Here in the early years of the seventeenth century they met another group searching for religious freedom, the Brownists or, as we know them, the Puritans. Doubtless the Walloons watched the Puritans depart for America in 1620 with some envy, and a year later the Walloon leaders petitioned the English ambassador at The Hague for similar settlement rights. This request subsequently was denied, but in 1622 the Dutch government agreed that the Walloons should take part in the colonization attempt of the newly formed Dutch West India Company. So it was that these refugees from French religious persecutions were largely responsible for the founding and early growth of New Amsterdam. Other Walloon and French Huguenot émigrés found

their way to the Dutch colony during the ensuing years and added to the development not only of New Amsterdam but the other settlements along the Hudson and on Long Island.[1]

Huguenot migration continued throughout the seventeenth century, but its volume sharply increased following the revocation of the Edict of Nantes in 1685. This formally eliminated the protection, more honored in the breach than in the observance, which had been extended to the French Protestants by Henry IV in 1598. Estimates of the number of migrants from France following this action vary, but certainly 200,000 and possibly 400,000 persons fled the homeland during the years of renewed and now official persecutions. It was only natural that many should come to America.

Oxford, Massachusetts, was perhaps the first of the Huguenot communities to be established in this period, dating from 1687. Here in south-central Massachusetts under the leadership of Daniel Bondet, a group of Huguenot refugees recently arrived from England established a settlement. The little town that resulted apparently closely resembled the other settlements of frontier New England, with a cluster of houses forming the village and with the farm and pasture lots lying beyond.

Virginia also received Huguenot refugees, and one of the settlements in that colony—Manakin—is of considerable interest because of its unusual plan. In the summer of 1700 a party of 200 Huguenots arrived in Virginia. Governor Francis Nicholson arranged for a tract of 10,000 acres on the James River, and William Byrd I escorted them to the site where cleared lands of the departed Manakin Indians provided favorable settlement conditions.

The only known plan of the town appears in Figure 261. Its details, scale, and author remain a mystery. The great square in the middle is named for Governor Nicholson. If the tiny rectangles represent individual houses the inside of the square would measure something like 800 feet across. This would also mean that Byrd Street would have a width of some 150 feet. All this is on the assumption that each house might be on the order of only 10 feet square. On the other hand the larger, only partially enclosed rectangles may be intended to represent houses, with the very small rectangles the chimneys. Unfortunately Byrd's report on the state

[1] Much of the material on the Huguenots prior to 1624 is based on Charles W. Baird, *History of the Huguenot Emigration to America*, New York, 1885, I.

Figure 260. View of Fort Caroline, Florida: 1671

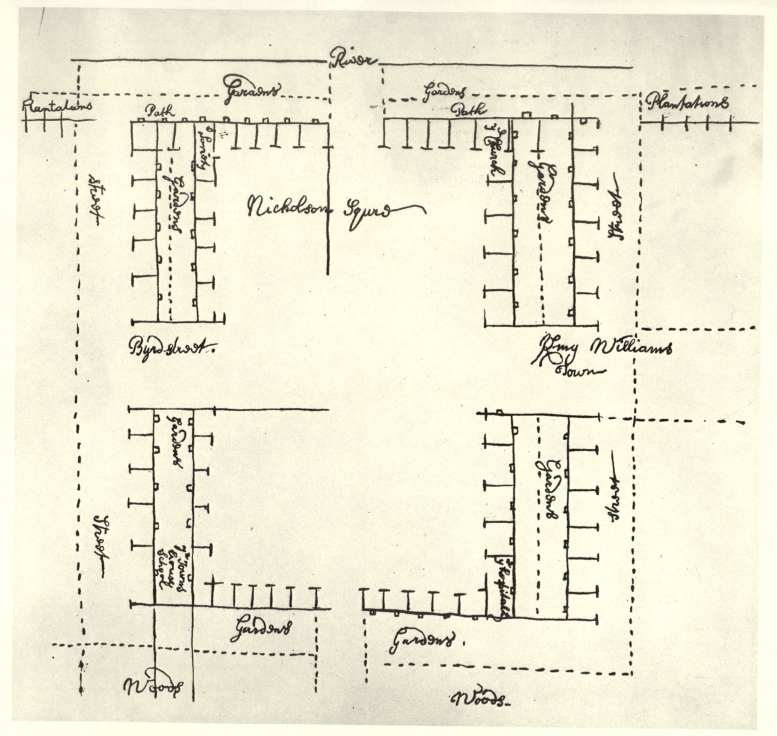

Figure 261. Plan of Manakin, Virginia: ca. 1700

of the settlement in May 1701 sheds little light. He mentions "about seventy . . . hutts, being, most of them, very mean . . ." but little else about the town's layout.[2]

The four corners of the square were reserved for public uses: hospital, church, laundry, and townhouse and school. Gardens were provided between the double rows of houses on two sides of the square and fronting the woods and the river on the other two sides. Farm fields evidently stretched along the James River on both sides of the settlement. Some 500 Huguenots eventually lived in and around Manakin and for many years spoke only their own language. But as the danger from Indians passed and the Huguenots became familiar with their new surroundings the original compact settlement gradually disappeared.

Other Huguenot settlements developed in South Carolina. North of Charleston on the Santee River a group of French refugees laid out the town of Jamestown in January 1705. The plan by Bartholomew Gaillard was on a grid system. The smallest lots fronted directly on the town common bordering the river. Larger lots extended back from the Santee. The common contained sites for church and cemetery. The town was not much of a success, and by 1720 apparently was almost abandoned. Today the site is largely unoccupied.[3]

A hundred miles up the Savannah River another group of Huguenots settled in 1764. In the summer of that year Patrick Calhoun, grandfather of John C. Calhoun, helped the Frenchmen lay out a township, in the center of which a tract of 800 acres was reserved for the village of New Bordeaux, vineyards, commons, and church glebelands. Village lots of 2½ acres and vineyard lots of 4 acres were surveyed, and sites were allotted for a fort, church, parsonage, market place, and parade ground.

Homes for Heretics: The Moravians

With few exceptions the Huguenot settlements in America did not last long as closed communities. Either their inhabitants drifted off to other towns not formed on religious lines or the original settlements opened their doors to outsiders. While Huguenot religious beliefs were strongly held, religious communalism was not contemplated. The Huguenots sought freedom of religious expression, but they did not attempt to create communities from which persons of dissimilar faith would be excluded.

Quite different in this respect were the towns planned by that remarkable sect, the Unitas Fratrum, the Church of the United Brethren, or, as it is usually referred to in America, the Moravian Church. Less numerous than the Huguenots and later in beginning their settlement activities, the Moravian communities nevertheless are of greater interest. A consistent policy governed their planning; moreover, the records of the church and its settlement activities have been carefully preserved. Further, church doctrines and settlement forms were considered to be closely related subjects.

The Moravians originated in Bohemia in the fifteenth century. Early in the seventeenth century they almost disappeared as a result of religious wars. A century later, following further persecutions in Moravia, the majority of the Brethren emigrated to Saxony and founded the town of Herrnhut in 1722 on the lands of Count Zinzendorf. But here again persecutions began, and in 1734 a few Moravians embarked on the long journey to America, landing in Philadelphia. Others went first to Georgia and then made their way northward to Pennsylvania. In 1741, on a site about 50 miles northwest of Philadelphia on the Lehigh River, work was begun on the town of Bethlehem. The first building, the *Gemeinhaus*, still stands, although in somewhat altered form. This structure was designed as a community center, serving as church, town hall, hospice, and church office, among its many functions. Two years later a large dormitory for single men was constructed, several small houses were built, and gradually other buildings were erected. During this same period work also proceeded on a second community nearby, called Nazareth.[4]

All of the buildings constructed at Bethlehem apparently were located only after careful deliberation, but it is not clear if any over-all village plan guided the gradual growth of the settlement. By 1757 the settlement was a busy, thriving community, virtually self-sufficient in industrial output. A bakery, tailor shop, shoemaker,

[2] Byrd's account, a reproduction of the plan, and genealogical information can be found in R. A. Brock, ed., *Documents Relating to the Huguenot Emigration to Virginia*, Richmond, 1886. The settlement is also described in Richard L. Morton, *Colonial Virginia*, Chapel Hill, 1960, I, 367-68.

[3] Arthur Henry Hirsch, *The Huguenots of Colonial South Carolina*, Durham, 1928, contains a brief account of the Jamestown settlement and a redrawn copy of its original plan.

[4] The early history of the Moravians as well as their settlement activities in and around Bethlehem are treated in Joseph Mortimer Levering, *A History of Bethlehem, Pennsylvania*, Bethlehem, 1903.

spinning and weaving establishment, grist mill, carpentry shop, blacksmith, potter, and other crafts were all represented. All worked under general church direction in a communal form of organization. Schools, dormitories for single members of the congregation, a tavern, and other buildings completed the town.

A view of Bethlehem in 1798 is reproduced in Figure 262. This is how the town appeared to Isaac Weld, whose description is of considerable interest:

"The town is regularly laid out, and contains about eighty strong built stone dwelling houses and a large church. Three of the dwelling houses are very spacious buildings, and are appropriated respectively to the accommodation of the unmarried females, and of the widows. In these houses different manufactures are carried on. . . .

"Attached to the young men's and to the young women's houses there are boarding schools for boys and girls. . . . These schools are in great repute. . . .

"Situated upon the creek, which skirts the town, there is a flour mill, a saw mill, an oil mill, a fulling mill, a mill for grinding bark and dye stuff, a tan yard, a currier's year; and on the Leleigh [Lehigh] River an extensive brewery, at which very good malt liquor is manufactured. These mills, &c. belong to the society at large, and the profits arising from them . . . are paid into the public fund. The lands for some miles round the town, which are highly improved, likewise belong to the society, as does also the tavern, and the profits arising from them are disposed of in the same manner as those arising from the mills. . . . The fund thus raised is employed in relieving the distressed brethren of the society in other parts of the world, in forming new settlements, and in defraying the expense of the missions for the purpose of propagating the gospel among the heathens."[5]

In 1753 the Moravian Brethren took possession of a tract of nearly 100,000 acres in the Piedmont region of North Carolina. Bishop Augustus Spangenberg had inspected the region a year earlier and purchased the land from Lord Granville. Spangenberg named the region Wachovia, probably for Wachau, Count Zinzendorf's Saxon estate. Late in 1753 the first settlers were dispatched from Pennsylvania to the region, and by the middle of November they had begun to clear land for their first town and its surrounding farms.

The town on which the colony centered was named Bethabara. Its plan as it appeared in 1766 is reproduced in Figure 263. Within five years after settlement the community included the traditional *Gemeinhaus*, a dormitory for single brothers, bakery, pottery, brewery, tavern, cobbler shop, family house, carpenter shop, dining hall, and other buildings. By 1766 a number of agricultural buildings and stables had been constructed, as well as a store, laboratory, gunsmith, smithy, apothecary, tailor's shop, and weaving and spinning establishments. As had Bethlehem, Bethabara became the most self-sufficient and industrialized settlement for many miles around.[6]

Other Moravian towns followed these initial settlements. In Pennsylvania, Nazareth was settled in 1742 and Lititz, shown in Figure 264, in 1757. Their patterns were essentially similar to Bethlehem's and, like all Moravian settlements, were designed as congregation towns with permanent residents limited to members of the church. In Carolina a second town, Bethania, was begun in 1759. Christian Gottlieb Reuter, a surveyor who had laid out Lititz, was also the planner of Bethania. A plan of this village and its surrounding lands appears in Figure 265. The village plan here is more regular than those of Bethlehem and Bethabara, with a rectangular town square being located at the intersection of two main streets. The farm fields surrounding the village are also perfectly regular in outline and location.

All of these Moravian villages in America closely resembled the three communities in Saxony from which the church was governed. The most important, Herrnhut, has already been mentioned. Nearby, two others had been planned—Nisky in 1742 and Klein Welke in 1756. The plans of these three towns are reproduced in Figure 266. While the details vary, they all have certain common features: a central square, a grid plan, a concentration of buildings in close proximity to the village square, and a surrounding

[5] Isaac Weld, *Travels Through the States of North America*, London, 4th ed., 1807, ii, 355-59.

[6] In the archives of the Moravian Church at Bethlehem there are two projected plans for Bethabara. One is square, the other a rectangle. Both plans show a large open square in the center, and both use a grid system of streets.

VIEW of BETHLEHEM _ a Moravian settlement.

Published Dec. 22. 1794. by I. Stockdale, Piccadilly.

J. Dadley sculp.t

Figure 262. View of Bethlehem, Pennsylvania: 1798

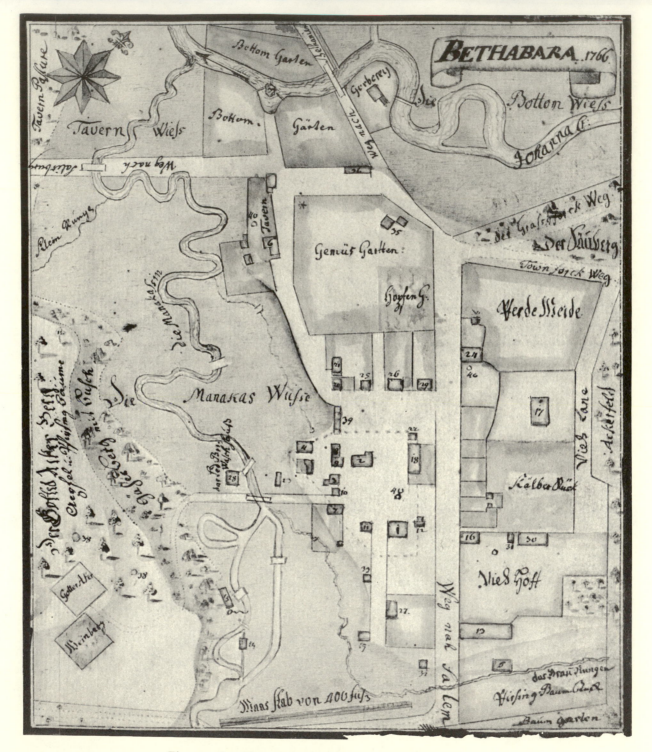

Figure 263. Plan of Bethabara, North Carolina: 1766

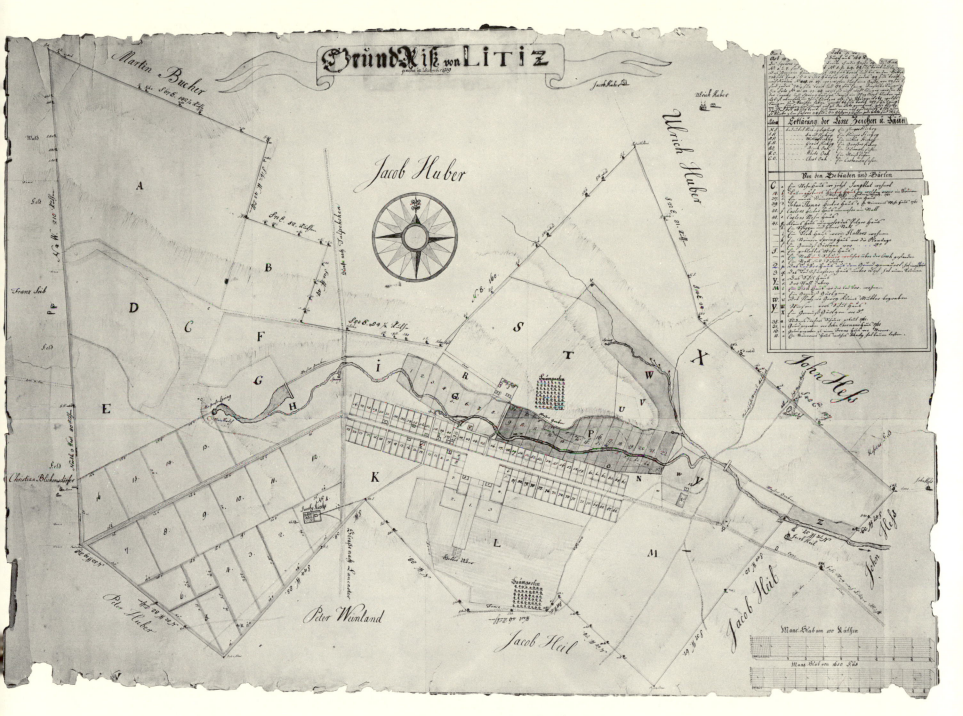

Figure 264. Plan of Lititz, Pennsylvania: 1759

belt of fields, orchards, and grazing lands that were farmed in common as a church enterprise. It seems obvious that the Moravians in the New World followed many of their colonial predecessors in reproducing on the frontier the community forms most familiar to them in their country of origin.

The most important town of the Wachovia region was not planned until 1766. Here, at Salem, all the accumulated Moravian experience in city planning was brought into use. Here, too, we have the clearest and most detailed statement by church authorities of the principles that the Moravians held most important in the development of towns.[7]

Mention of the site for a new town appears as early as 1759, but the search for a suitable location began in earnest in 1763 when Friedrich Marshall became head of the Wachovia Moravians and was directed by the church board in Herrnhut to choose a site for a central town. Many sites were examined, and in the selection process the Board of Elders called upon the Lord for assistance, using a method often employed by Moravian church leaders to decide important issues. The Board first narrowed the choice of sites as well as they could. Then they prepared "lots" with the name of the site on one and the other being a blank. Then, reverently asking for God's guidance, they drew one of the "lots." Thus, on February 14, 1765, the site for Salem was determined with Divine assistance.[8]

Christian Reuter laid out the town, but he was guided by a remarkable set of instructions and a model plan sent from Bethlehem in 1765 by Friedrich Marshall.[9] Marshall's "Remarks concerning the Laying Out of the new Congregation Town in the

[7] Adelaide L. Fries, ed., *Records of the Moravians in North Carolina*, Raleigh, 1922, I, has proved invaluable. See also John Henry Clewell, *History of Wachovia in North Carolina*, New York, 1902.

[8] See the account in the Bethabara Diary for 1765 and the Minutes of the Helfer Conferenz in Fries, *Records*, 298, 310.

[9] There was also a model plan sent to America from the Herrnhut Moravians. This unusual scheme had an octagonal open space at the center in which the communal buildings were to be grouped. Radiating outwards were no less than 32 streets, 8 of which were to be used as residential streets. A circular street linked the radial streets at point approximately halfway between the central open space and the outer limits of the town. Little seems to be known about the origins of this plan or why it was rejected. Clewell, in his *History of Wachovia*, reproduces it on p. 94 and dates it from about 1750 "or a little later."

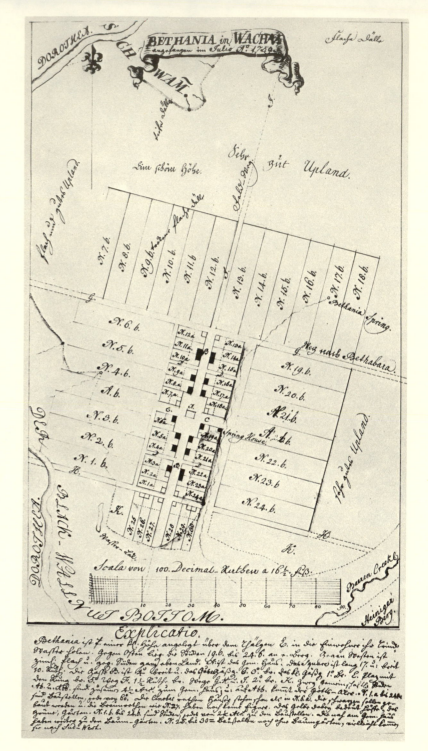

Figure 265. Plan of Bethania, North Carolina: 1759

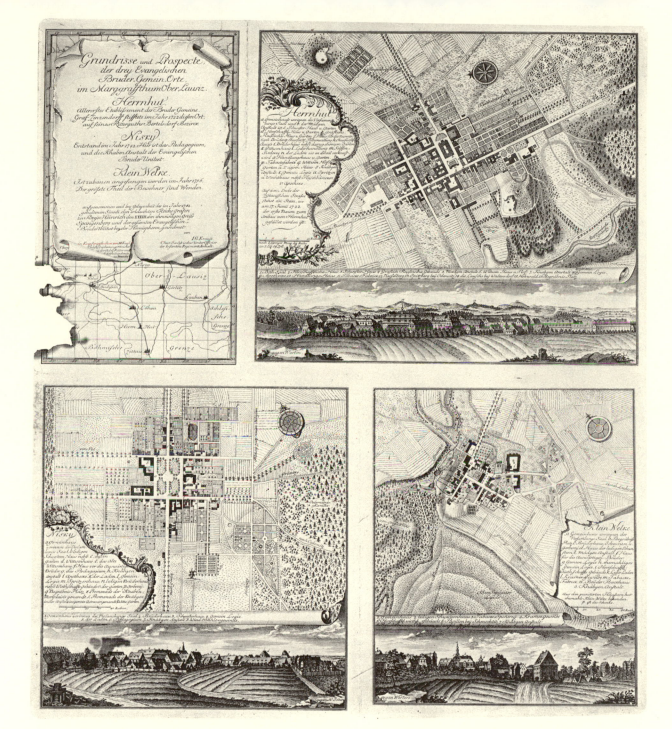

Figure 266. Plans of Herrnhut, Nisky and Klein Welke in East Germany: 1782

center of Wachovia" began by pointing out that Moravian towns of this type were closely knit socially. This, said Marshall, "must be considered in deciding the form of the Town Plan."

Close buildings or tall apartments seemed to him unsuitable. "Not more than two houses should be built side by side," and each family should have its separate house. This latter instruction reflected the dissatisfaction with communal living which had developed among the Moravians.

Marshall advocated lots large enough so that each family could have its own yard and garden in the rear of the house, adding that this was "particularly good for the children, who can thereby have room for their recreations under oversight." But lots should not be so large that the settlement would sprawl.

"The inconvenience of a wide-spread town is that the Brethren and Sisters can not so often attend the evening services or those of a day when there are many meetings, and the daily life of the Congregation, as one large family, cannot be so well supervised by the Ministers and other Congregation officers."[10]

Having stated these and other general principles to be observed, Marshall described many details of town layout to be followed, stating that he had prepared several plans but "of them all the enclosed has received the most approbation." This plan probably closely resembled that reproduced in Figure 267, which, with a few minor changes was followed in the planning of Salem.[11] Here is Marshall's analysis of the street system:

"Br. Reuter considers it important that the main street runs in a straight line from the Wach, through the town, and beyond it. . . . I have made it 60 ft. wide, as in Lititz where the main street was originally only 40 ft. but that was found to be too narrow. . . .; the other streets are 40 ft."[12]

[10] Friedrich Marshall, "Remarks concerning the Laying Out of the new Congregation Town in the center of Wachovia," Bethlehem, July 1765, in Fries, *Records*, 313-315.

[11] This plan is entitled "Copy of part of Br. Reuter's map of the new town site with a suggestion how it might be laid out. Bethl[ehem]: drawn to scale July, 1765." A close examination reveals that this is actually two plans: one has been cut out and superimposed over the other. I believe the cut-out portion showing the details of village layout is that sent by Marshall, while the remainder consists of Reuter's survey of the site.

[12] Marshall, "Remarks," 314.

Marshall then described the sites and buildings facing on the open square:

"The Gemein Haus, Saal [place of worship], Boys' and Girls' School, their kitchens and gardens are all together; then the Widows' House, and the House for the Single Sisters. . . . On the other side will be the Widower's House, or whatever of that kind of building may be needed. A Single Brothers' House is a manufacturing center, and an important business feature of the Congregation, and may well stand beside the Widowers' House, and keep all the business together; it would not be well to put these things among the family houses. . . . In order to keep the plan symmetrical the Store might be placed on the lower corner, since it also is larger than a family house."[13]

The instructions explain that Salem was not intended as an agricultural village "but for those with trades." However, until village industry and handicrafts could develop, each family should be provided with farm lots so that they could provide their own food. Marshall also suggested that the town lots not immediately used for building might be cultivated for a few years to make food production easier for the residents.

Salem, like Bethlehem, became the center of Moravian activity in its region. But the Moravians were not a passive Christian sect; they were dedicated missionaries who carried the Gospel to the Indians, even those tribes living beyond the frontier of white settlement. The profits from church-directed industrial and craft activities in such towns as Bethlehem and Salem supported missionary endeavors. In these efforts to convert the Indians the Moravian missionaries employed some of the town planning skills developed in Pennsylvania and Carolina.

The most interesting and best documented example is Schoenbrunn in eastern Ohio. Here, far beyond the scattered settlements in western Pennsylvania, the Reverend David Zeisberger gained the confidence of the Delaware Indians. In 1772 he laid out the little settlement of Schoenbrunn ("beautiful spring"), and a year later, 10 miles to the south, a second community named Gnadenhutten. Figure 268 shows the original design of the earlier town, which in its reconstructed form on the original foundations exists today as a state historical park.

[13] *ibid.*

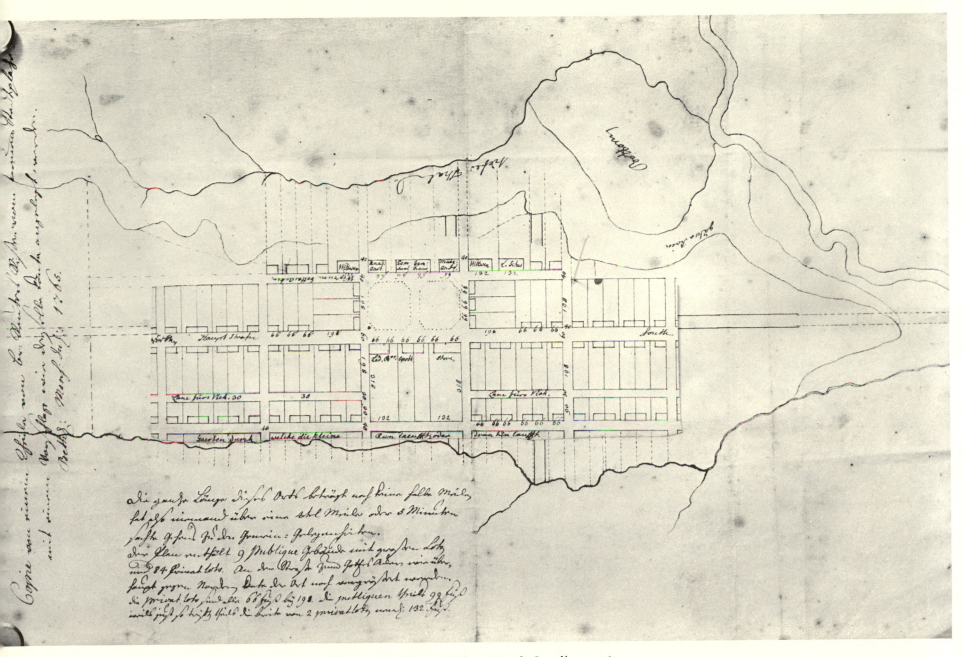

Figure 267. Plan of Salem, North Carolina: 1765

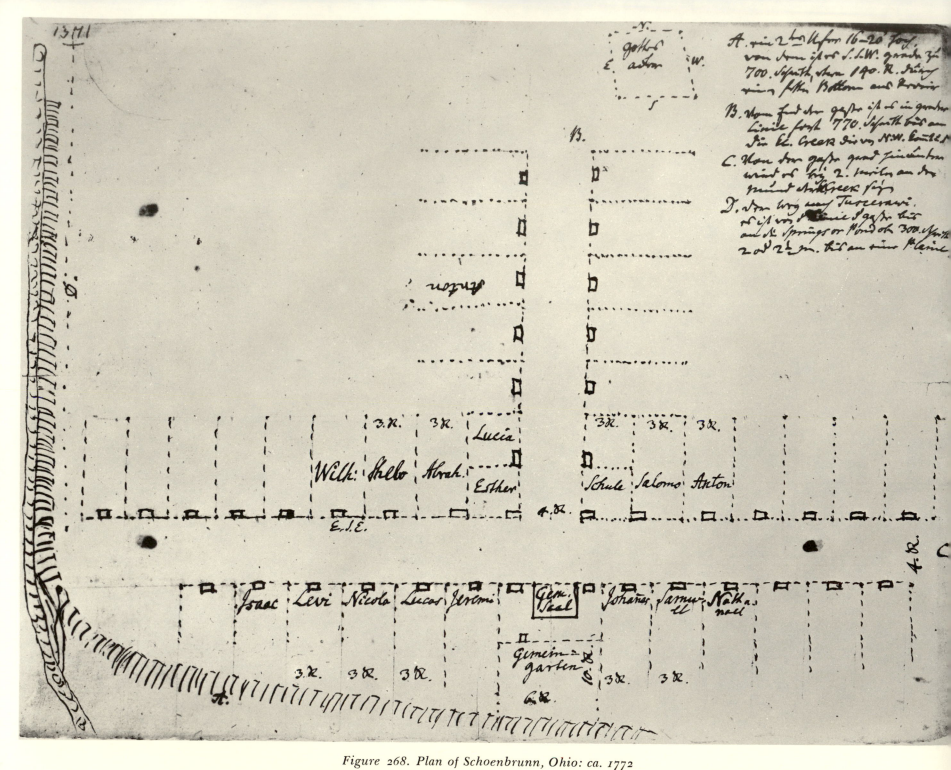

Figure 268. Plan of Schoenbrunn, Ohio: ca. 1772

Zeisberger placed his church as the central feature of the tiny village, thus completing the symbolical plan in the form of the Christian cross. The school building stood across the street at one corner. Along the two streets stood the houses of the Indians. The cemetery, or "God's Acre," was at one end of the village near the foot of the cross.

For several years the two communities maintained their precarious existence in the face of growing hostility from Indian tribes to the west. With the outbreak of the Revolution, the British enlisted the aid of these Indians to harass the western frontier settlements. Schoenbrunn was abandoned in 1778, and many of the Christian Indians were taken into Canada. Gnadenhutten was the scene of a brutal mass murder of 90 of Zeisberger's converts. After the war Zeisberger returned to the area and succeeded in reestablishing the missions on new sites. But the rapid influx of whites soon made missionary conditions difficult, and by the early years of the nineteenth century the effort had been abandoned.[14]

The Moravians built well. In Bethlehem and other Pennsylvania towns and in Salem their simple, sturdy buildings may still be seen. Modern restoration efforts have begun to recreate some of the original character and atmosphere these towns once possessed. Designed for a limited population and for a closed society, these Moravian communities were admirably suited for their purpose. They are also of interest because in their planning some thought was given to the buildings that would occupy assigned sites. While these towns cannot honestly be described as great works of civic design, the relationship of buildings to plan in both Bethlehem and Salem is at least fitting and comfortable.

George Rapp and his Towns of Harmony and Economy

The Lutheran province of Württemberg in Germany gave birth to at least two religious groups that ultimately planned towns in North America. The earliest of these and the one responsible for no less than three towns was the Harmony Society led by George Rapp. Rapp was born in 1757. While in his thirties he began to preach against the doctrines of the established church in Württemberg and attracted a small band of followers. In the face of persecutions by the Lutheran clergy he determined to lead his group to America where freedom of worship might be found in a community with common ownership of property. In 1803 he and a few disciples sailed for the United States where, on a tract of 5,000 acres in western Pennsylvania, they made their first settlement, which they called Harmony.[15]

Their little town became the center of a successful farming community, but in 1814 the group decided to locate farther west where they hoped to find more suitable soil for raising grapes and where additional land could be obtained to accommodate their growing numbers. They sold their village and its surrounding land, and with the proceeds purchased 30,000 acres of land along the Wabash River in Indiana. Once again they established a village, giving it the name of New Harmony. Within 10 years they succeeded in building a thriving community which attracted considerable attention. A visitor in 1824 has left this interesting description of the village and its principal buildings:

"The Village consisted of four streets running towards the river, & six crossing these. In the middle was an open space in which stood a wooded church. . . . In various streets stood large and small brick habitations, but the majority of the houses were either log houses or small wooden ones. At the back of the houses were gardens, all divided by wooden palings. . . .

"Adjoining to Mr. Rapp's house is a garden in which the old gentlemen takes pleasure to work. . . . Behind this is a lofty brick granary built in the german fashion, to keep the grain cool. There is another of wood at one corner of the village, near which are three wooden buildings, one a large barn, & thrashing machine moved by 8 horses, another a cotton and woolen manufactory & dying house, with a steam engine, and the third a cotton mill, worked by an inclined circular plane. . . . Under the new church are two cellars for wine, cider & beer. Over the church & under the roof

[14] James H. and Mary Jane Rodabaugh, *Schoenbrunn and the Moravian Missions in Ohio*, Columbus, 3rd ed., 1956.

[15] Two sources have proved of great value for the history of nineteenth-century American religious and utopian communities, including the Rappite settlements, Zoar, Bethel, and Aurora, Amana, the Fourier communities, and others: William Alfred Hinds, *American Communities and Co-Operative Colonies*, Chicago, 2nd rev., 1908; and Charles Nordhoff, *The Communistic Societies of the United States*, New York, 1875.

is a large room, where the population may meet when they give great entertainment. . . ."[16]

But in the mid-1820's the Harmonists decided to return to Pennsylvania, and they sold their Indiana holdings to Robert Owen and his followers, whose theories of society and town planning will be examined later. On the banks of the Ohio 20 miles north of Pittsburgh they laid out the town of Economy, the plan of which, as it existed in 1876, is reproduced in Figure 269. In plan Economy resembled the two earlier towns of Harmony and New Harmony. While there was nothing whatever remarkable about the regular grid layout, the buildings that lined these streets were sturdy and had a simple elegance about them that set the Rappite community apart from most other American towns of the period, as Figure 270 shows. Charles Nordhoff, who visited Economy in the early seventies, furnishes these impressions of the attractive little community:

"The town begins on the edge of the bluff; and under the shade-trees planted there benches are arranged, where doubtless the Harmonists take their comfort on summer evenings, in view of the river below and of the village on the opposite shore. Streets proceed at right angles with the river's course; and each street is lined with neat frame or brick houses, surrounding a square in such a manner that within each household has a sufficient garden. The broad streets have neat foot-pavements of brick; the houses, substantially built but unpretentious, are beautified by a singular arrangement of grape-vines, which are trained to espaliers fixed to cover the space between the top of the lower and the bottom of the upper windows. This manner of training vines gives the town quite a peculiar look, as though the houses had been crowned with green."[17]

The modern visitor may inspect Economy, substantial portions of which have been preserved and reconstructed by the state, and form his own opinion of the quality in town building achieved by the Harmonists. It is unlikely that he will fail to be impressed by the dignity, the excellent sense of proportion and scale, and the true urban character of the remaining buildings.

[16] *The Diaries of Donald MacDonald 1824-26*, Indiana Historical Society, *Publications*, Indianapolis, 1942, xiv, No. 2, 245-50.
[17] Nordhoff, *Communistic Societies*, 64.

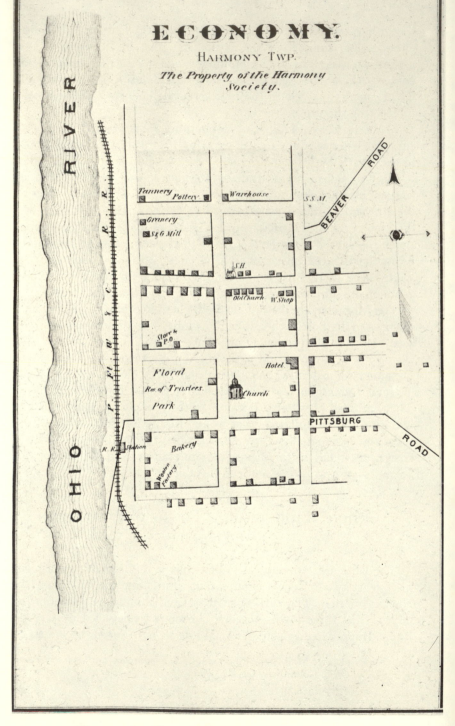

Figure 269. Plan of Economy, Pennsylvania: 1876

ASSEMBLY HALL—ECONOMY.

CHURCH AT ECONOMY.

Figure 270. Views of the Assembly Hall and Church in Economy, Pennsylvania: 1875

The Harmony Society came to an end early in the present century. Alfred Hinds, in his valuable survey of utopian communities, published in 1902, mentions that as late as 1900 the Society considered planning still a fourth community on farm lands owned near Economy. This apparently never worked out, and with the Society's dissolution its town planning activities came to an end.

Robert Owen's New View of Society in Theory and Practice

The Indiana Harmony, as has been mentioned, was taken over by Robert Owen in 1825. Here Owen expected to begin his transformation of modern industrial society in America.[18] Owen was a self-made man who had become a textile manufacturer of some renown in his native Britain. At his mills in New Lanark near Glasgow, he had introduced a number of labor reforms. Soon his interests centered on national social and economic problems. In 1813 he wrote *A New View of Society*, which was followed in 1817 by his proposal calling for the creation of a great many new towns in England as a measure to reduce unemployment and to provide a more humane setting for manufacturing activities. Because this type of community is what Owen evidently had in mind when he came to America, his ideas on the design of these new towns are worth investigating.

Owen believed that each town should contain about 1,200 persons in a quadrangle-like enclosure some 1,000 feet on each side. He was quite specific about the arrangement of buildings and uses within the town:

"Within the squares are public buildings, which divide them into parallelograms.

"The central building contains a public kitchen, mess-rooms, and all the accommodations necessary to economical and comfortable cooking and eating.

[18] Owenite literature is extensive. Among others, the following may be consulted with profit: Marguerite Young, *Angel in the Forest*, New York, 1945; Robert Owen, *The Life of Robert Owen*, London, 1858; Arthur E. Bestor, Jr., *Backwoods Utopias: The Sectarian and Owenite Phases of Communitarian Socialism in America 1663-1829*, Philadelphia, 1950; Everett Webber, *Escape to Utopia*, New York, 1959; and George B. Lockwood, *The New Harmony Movement*, New York, 1905.

"To the right of this is a building, of which the ground-floor will form the infant school, and the other a lecture-room and a place of worship.

"The building to the left contains a school for the elder children, and a committee-room on the ground floor; above, a library and a room for adults.

"In the vacant space within the squares, are enclosed grounds for exercise and recreation: these enclosures are supposed to have trees planted in them."[19]

On three sides of each square were to be the family lodgings. On the other side would be a dormitory for all children "exceeding two in a family" or more than three years old. Manufacturing buildings were to be located outside the quadrangle to one side, where also would be placed stables and farm buildings. Beyond would be the agricultural lands. In this rural-urban unit the residents would be almost self-sufficient and would produce goods necessary for the good life under a cooperative economic system.

Owen undoubtedly expected to carry out this plan at New Harmony. The drawing in Figure 271, prepared by Stedman Whitwell, symbolizes the high hopes with which the experiment began. But Owen's visionary plans were never to be realized. At the start, with the purchase of Rapp's village, Owen lost his chance to introduce his quadrangle town to America, and no further opportunity presented itself. The usual dissensions developed and the Owenites gradually realized that the perfect society was more easily talked about in the lecture hall than actually created on the Indiana frontier. Within two or three years the experiment was over, several splinter societies had been formed, and many of the original members of the group had departed for more conventional communities. Owen himself, however, remained convinced of the validity of his ideas, and he continued to lecture and write until his death in 1858.

Zoar, Bethel and Aurora, and Amana

There were a number of minor religious groups that, like the Harmonists, built towns in the early part of the nineteenth century.

[19] Robert Owen, "Report to the Committee of the Association for the Relief of the Manufacturing Poor" (March 1817), in Robert Owen, *The Life of Robert Owen*, Appendix I.

The examination of three of these from the dozens that were active must satisfy our curiosity. One such group was also from Württemberg. Calling themselves the Separatists and led by Joseph Bimeler, this sect arrived in America in 1817. With the help of some English Quakers they purchased 5,600 acres in eastern Ohio and laid out the community of Zoar. Like Economy, the plan of Zoar was a small gridiron. Its chief feature, however, as is shown in Figure 272, was a pleasant and unusual garden of 2½ acres. From the central spruce tree symbolizing salvation, which was surrounded by twelve trees representing the apostles, radiated twelve paths to righteousness. Other paths on a grid pattern stood for the routes to temptation. Many of the old buildings and the gardens have now been taken over by the state. Fortunately modern civilization has largely bypassed the village, and the residents have shown considerable interest and initiative in restoring individual houses outside of the area maintained by the state. Zoar remains as a reminder of what utopian America was like a century or so ago.

Considerably less attractive were the straightforward, rather grim communities of Bethel, Missouri, and Aurora, Oregon. These two towns were established by Dr. William Keil and his followers. Like Rapp and Bimeler, Keil was a German who came to America in 1838 and became an independent preacher after brief careers as a tailor and as an agent of the German Tract Society. In 1844 he and his group settled in Missouri 50 miles or so from Hannibal in a town they called Bethel. The character of the nondescript village is shown in Figure 273. Later, in 1856 another community was founded in Oregon and named Aurora. In both places ownership of the land was in common, but after the death of Keil this system was abandoned and the two communities as formal social structures ceased to exist.

Far more interesting were the settlements of the Inspirationists, first near Buffalo and later in Iowa. The Community of True Inspiration had its origins in the teachings of the German Mystics and Pietists. Led by Christian Metz, this group came to America from Germany in 1842. After some months spent in examining land in western New York the group purchased a 5,000-acre tract in Erie County and laid out its first town, Ebenezer. In 1843 the group organized itself under the name of the Ebenezer Society, with all but clothing and household articles to be held in common ownership. Later, other villages were planned at convenient loca-

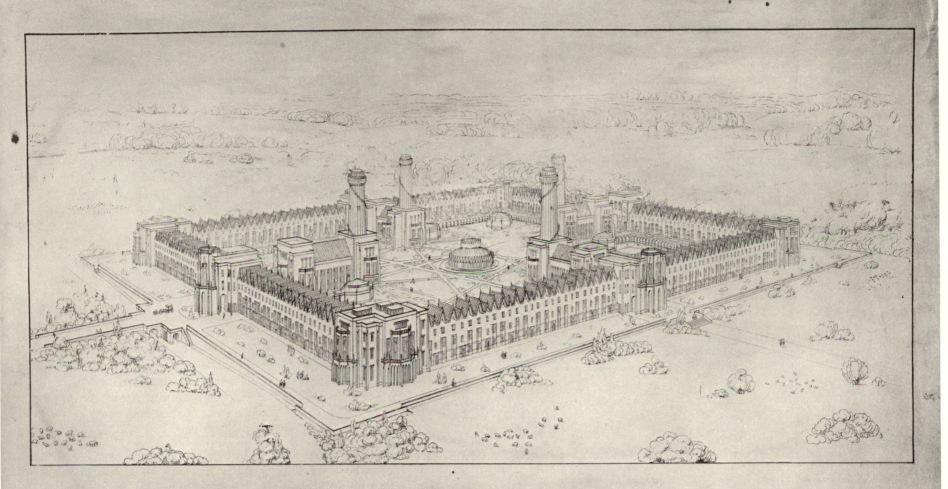

A BIRD'S EYE VIEW OF ONE OF THE NEW COMMUNITIES AT HARMONY.
IN THE STATE OF INDIANA NORTH AMERICA.
AN ASSOCIATION OF TWO THOUSAND PERSONS FORMED UPON THE PRINCIPLES ADVOCATED BY

ROBERT OWEN

STEDMAN WHITWELL, ARCHITECT.

THE SCITE IS NEARLY IN THE CENTRE OF AN AREA OF 2000 ACRES POSSESSED BY THE COMMUNITY, SITUATED UPON HIGH LAND, ABOUT THREE MILES FROM THE EASTERN SHORE OF THE GREAT WABASH RIVER AND TWELVE MILES FROM THE TOWN OF MOUNT VERNON, ON THE RIVER OHIO. BOTH THESE RIVERS ARE NAVIGATED BY STEAM BOATS OF CONSIDERABLE BURTHEN, WHICH MAINTAIN A COMMUNICATION BETWEEN NEW-ORLEANS IN THE GULPH OF MEXICO ON THE SOUTH AND PITTSBURCH IN THE EASTERN STATES ON THE ATLANTIC.
THE GENERAL ARRANGEMENT OF THE BUILDINGS IS A SQUARE, EACH SIDE OF WHICH IS 1000 FEET. THE CENTRES & THE EXTREMITIES ARE OCCUPIED BY THE PUBLIC BUILDINGS. THE PARTS BETWEEN THEM ARE THE DWELLINGS OF THE MEMBERS. IN THE INTERIOR OF THE SQUARE ARE THE BOTANICAL & OTHER GARDENS, THE EXERCISE GROUNDS &c. THE WHOLE IS RAISED ABOVE THE LEVEL OF THE NATURAL SURFACE, AND SURROUNDED BY AN ESPLANADE. THE DESCENT TO THE OFFICES IS UPON THE OUTSIDE OF THE WHOLE. — ONE OF THE DIAGONALS OF THE SQUARE COINCIDES WITH A MERIDIAN, AND THE DISPOSITION OF EVERY OTHER PART IS SO REGULATED BY A CAREFUL ATTENTION TO THE MOST IMPORTANT DISCOVERIES & FACTS IN SCIENCE, AS TO FORM A NEW COMBINATION OF CIRCUMSTANCES, CAPABLE OF PRODUCING PERMANENTLY, GREATER PHYSICAL, MORAL, AND INTELLECTUAL ADVANTAGES TO EVERY INDIVIDUAL, THAN HAVE EVER YET BEEN REALIZED IN ANY AGE OR COUNTRY.

INGREY & MADELLY, LITHO. 310. STRAND.

Figure 271. View of Proposed Community at New Harmony, Indiana: ca. 1825

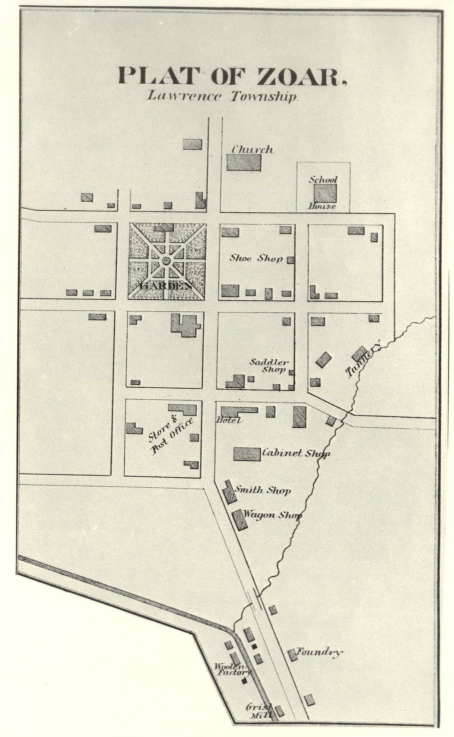

PLAT OF ZOAR,
Lawrence Township.

Church

School House

Shoe Shop

GARDEN

Saddler Shop

Tannery

Store & Post Office

Hotel

Cabinet Shop

Smith Shop

Wagon Shop

Foundry

Woolen Factory

Grist Mill

Figure 272. Plan of Zoar, Ohio: 1875

tions in the tract. In the European tradition members of the community lived in the villages, going out to the farm fields each day. The village boundaries and the rectangular agricultural lands can be seen on the map in Figure 274.

The community prospered, but as new members arrived from Germany and as the city of Buffalo expanded in the direction of the Society's lands it soon became evident that a new site would be desirable. Metz and three others journeyed west in 1854 to inspect possible locations in Kansas but returned dissatisfied. A new group went to Iowa and there, along the Iowa River it found a fertile tract which was purchased. In the summer of 1855 the first village of the new settlement was surveyed and named Amana. Five other villages were located and planned by 1862. The pattern of land division closely resembled that of the previous community. The plan of Amana Township as it existed in 1886 is reproduced in Figure 275. On this one can see the lands of the Society and the tight clusters of houses and shops comprising the villages.

Figure 276 shows a street view of Amana in 1875 when Charles Nordhoff visited the town and recorded these observations:

"The villages consist usually of one straggling street, outside of which lie the barns, and the mills, factories, and workshops. The houses are well built, of brick, stone, or wood, very plain; each with a sufficient garden, but mostly standing immediately on the street. They use no paint, believing that the wood lasts as well without. There is usually a narrow sidewalk of boards or brick; and the school-house and church are notable buildings only because of their greater size."[20]

At Amana the Inspirationists prospered to an even greater extent than at their former colony of Ebenezer. The sale of the Ebenezer lands at a considerable profit furnished capital for improvements, and the frugality of the Society and its individual members permitted additional investments. Here at least was one communistic society that became an economic success, and community ownership at Amana was not completely abandoned until 1932. In that year a system of corporate ownership was instituted, with Society members becoming shareholders. The modern corporation that produces home appliances, although no longer a part of the Society, has made the Amana name a familiar household word to those who

[20] Nordhoff, *Communistic Societies*, 32.

Figure 273. View of Bethel, Missouri: 1875

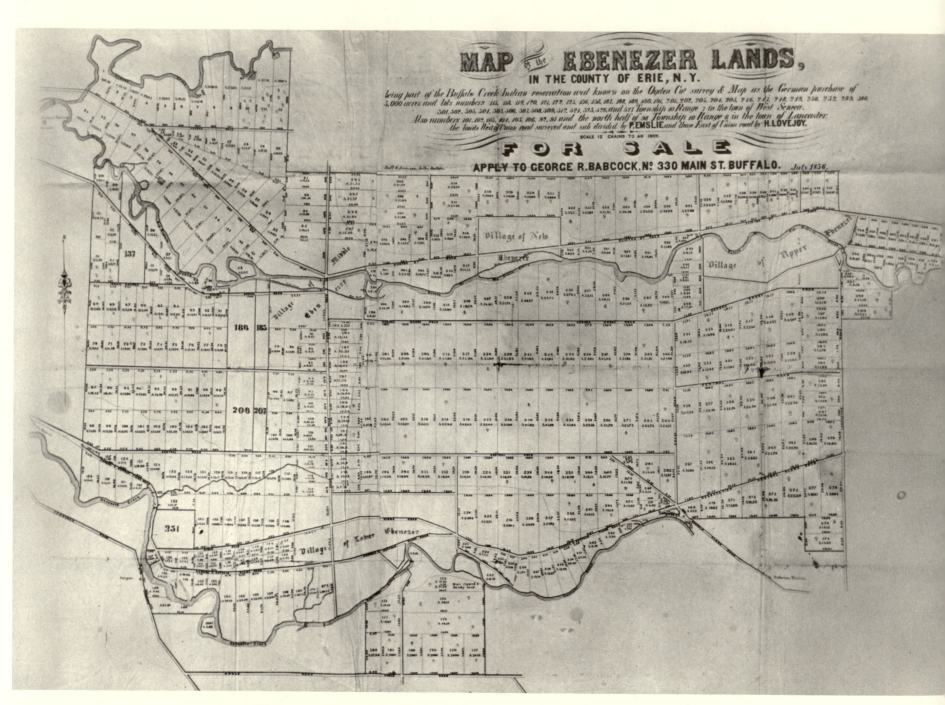

Figure 274. Map of the Inspirationists' Lands near Buffalo, New York: 1856

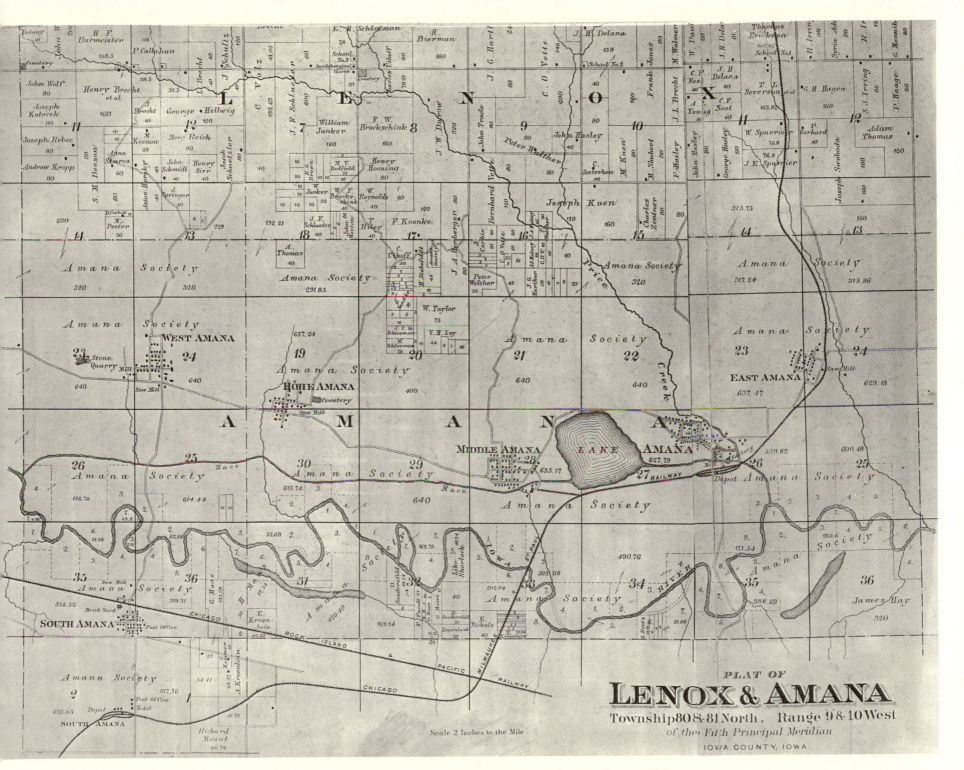

Figure 275. Map of Farm and Village Lands at Amana, Iowa: 1886

Figure 276. View of Amana, Iowa: 1875

have no idea of its origins or of the unusual settlement pattern established by its founders over a century ago.

Phalanstery, Phalanx, and Fourier

Most of the religious communities succeeded in producing towns or villages; but their plans were of no particular interest. The followers of Fourier, and later of Etienne Cabet, on the other hand, dreamed of elaborate and complex towns on unusual plans, but they were largely failures when it came to the practical matter of building them.

Charles Fourier was the son of a middle-class French merchant. The Revolution wiped out his inheritance, and he was forced to make his living as a shop clerk and traveling salesman. These mundane occupations did not keep him from philosophical speculation, and Fourier became absorbed with nothing less than the problem of reorganizing society on more rational lines. He viewed society as being composed of a multitude of individuals all with different aptitudes and interests. These "passions" as he called them could be combined into a harmonious unit only under certain conditions. The basic unit of society was the Group, composed of seven persons. Five Groups would form a Series, and a number of Series would unite to form a Phalanx of between 1,620 and 1,800 persons.

The Phalanx would be a communal society dwelling in a vast building called a phalanstery. Here would be all the physical elements needed for the creation of a new and better life. Fourier provided at tedious length all the details of his new society in his *L'Association Domestique Agricole*, published in 1822. With diagrams and plans, the vision of this new type of community was made public and immediately attracted a group of dedicated followers.

Nineteenth-century America was fertile ground for this kind of exotic plant, and Albert Brisbane, who had studied in France, was the man who transplanted it from Europe to America. Brisbane's writings apparently converted Horace Greeley, and the *New York Tribune* began to publish regular columns written by Brisbane explaining the new doctrines of Association which were to reform the world.

Figure 277 shows the plan of a phalanstery (Americanized to "The Edifice") which was to be established in the center of a tract of land 3 miles square. This great structure and its associated outbuildings were to contain all the dwellings, common eating rooms, shops, places of worship, meeting halls, and other facilities normally found in separate buildings in an ordinary community. Brisbane visualized groups of such buildings forming the city of tomorrow, "disposed with order and unity of design, surrounded by noble and extensive gardens and grounds, for the recreation and healthy occupation of the inhabitants, in which all the beauties of nature and the perfections of art will be combined and united to charm and delight."[21]

The phalanstery resembled somewhat the *maison á redents* that Fourier's countryman, Le Corbusier, would propose almost a century later as one element in his ideal city. As Corbusier was later to do so persuasively, Brisbane contrasted the proposed new order of cities with the disorganization that could be observed in the mid-1800's:

"A City at present is a heterogeneous mass of small and separate houses of all sizes, shapes, colors, styles and materials, which are crowded together without regard to architectural unity or design, convenience or elegance; it is cut up with irregular and narrow streets, dark lanes, confined courts, and cramped yards and alleys; it has its dirty and muddy streets, that annoy the inhabitants; its filthy gutters that fill the atmosphere with noxious exhalations which are injurious to health, and presents a scene of confusion, incoherence, waste and disorder."[22]

But, as most utopians have discovered, to criticize the existing world is far easier than to effect vast changes. Converts to Associationism made a number of attempts to found phalanxes. Hinds listed 30 of them in his review of communal societies published in 1902, and there undoubtedly had been others. Only a few of these lasted more than a year. The most successful, at least in terms of duration, was the North American Phalanx near Red Bank, New Jersey, begun in 1843 and not dissolved until twelve years later.

[21] Albert Brisbane, *A Concise Exposition of the Doctrine of Association*, New York (?), 2nd ed., 1844, p. 75.
[22] *ibid.*, 74.

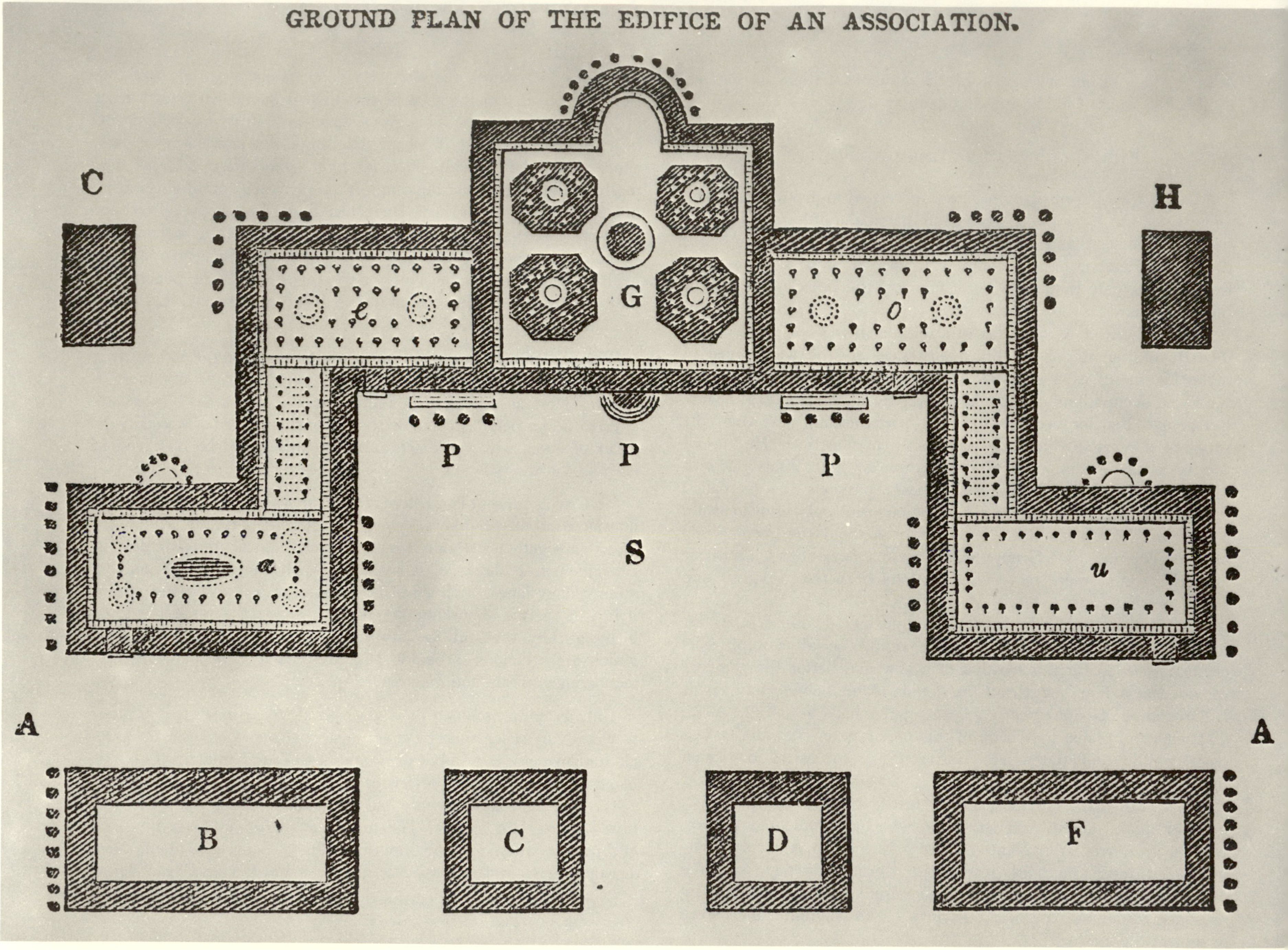

Figure 277. Plan of Albert Brisbane's Proposed Phalanstery: 1843

Here Brisbane, Greeley, and other supporters threw their energies into the experiment and did succeed in constructing a small phalanstery, mills, workshops, and farm buildings. Although this colony was mildly successful as a farm community, the initial wave of enthusiasm subsided and, after a fire destroyed many of the farm and shop buildings in 1854, the experiment came to an end.

Cabet and the Search for Icara

Fourier was not the only Frenchman whose social views resulted in an attempt to found new communities in America. His contemporary, Etienne Cabet, not only provided the intellectual stimulus for such an undertaking but himself led a group of followers to America for this purpose. Cabet was a lawyer who, because of his part in the Revolution of 1830 and later antigovernmental activities, was forced to leave France. In England he became acquainted with the theories of Robert Owen and was also influenced by a reading of More's *Utopia*. Returning to France, he wrote and published his own socialist utopia, *Voyage en Icarie*, in 1840.

Icara, the capital city of Cabet's imaginative kingdom, would have delighted the eye of an Alberti or a Palladio. Its streets were broad, and it was richly embellished with fountains, statues, and monuments. Icara was more than a simple village enlarged to the scale of a great city. Cabet anticipated the later development of the neighborhood unit by his proposal that the city be divided into a great many separate districts or quarters bounded by major streets and each provided with necessary public buildings and local facilities. Here is Cabet describing his city as he speaks through the voice of a citizen showing two visitors a map of Icara:

". . . Notice these areas distinguished by the light multicolored tints with which the entire city is marked. . . . They are the sixty quarters or communities, all very nearly equal and each one representing the extent of population in an ordinary town.

"Each quarter bears the name of one of the sixty principal cities of the ancient and modern world, and exhibits in its monuments and dwellings the architecture of one of the sixty principal nations. . . .

"Here is the plan of one of these quarters. All colored spots represent public buildings. Here is the school, the hospital, the temple. Red indicates the great factories, yellow the large retail shops, blue the places for public gatherings, violet the monuments.

"Notice that all these public buildings are so located that they are in all the streets and that every street contains the same number of houses. . . .

"Now here is a plan of a street. See! Sixteen houses on each side, with a public building in the middle and two other houses at the ends. These sixteen houses are treated alike on the exterior or combined to form a single building, but no street exactly matches any of the others."[23]

Cabet provided a complete description of the city, including such details as the design of sidewalks, the provisions for water supply and sewage disposal, methods of cleaning streets, and the use of raised paving blocks at street intersections for the convenience of pedestrian crossing. Although his greatest emphasis was on the system of political and social organization, his treatment at such length of the physical plan for his city indicates that his interest in such matters was greater than most other utopians who were primarily concerned with the reorganization of society.

The author soon had an opportunity to put his plans into effect. Icarian societies were organized, and Cabet rather reluctantly was prevailed upon to furnish the leadership for a practical experiment. On the advice of Robert Owen, Cabet contracted for 1,000,000 acres in the new state of Texas, and in the spring of 1848 the advance party of Frenchmen arrived in America. In Texas they learned to their dismay that only one-tenth of the land was actually available and that this had been allotted in alternate half-sections separated by land retained by the company with which Cabet had unfortunately contracted. Moreover, they were obliged to erect a house on each section before July in order to obtain title. By the time they arrived at the site, illness and desertions had reduced their number, and in the end they were able to claim but 10,000 acres.

Expected reinforcements from France were supposed to number 1,500. Only 19 finally left for America, and, of these, only 10 arrived at the site of the colony. Cabet himself came over in January 1849, accompanied by 450 followers; but this number dwindled quickly. Wisely deciding to abandon Texas, Cabet and 250 of his

23 Etienne Cabet, *Voyage en Icarie*, Paris, Rev. ed., 1848, p. 22.

disciples finally traveled up the Mississippi and established themselves at Nauvoo, which the Mormons had abandoned two years earlier. Here they attempted to organize their society, and for a number of years succeeded in maintaining an existence. But by 1856 Cabet's dictatorial tactics led to a split in the group, and although little Icarian societies were begun in St. Louis and Cheltenham, Missouri, Corning, Iowa, and Speranza, California, the brief, bright flame of the Icarians was all but extinguished.

Instead of the glorious Icara pictured in such detail by Cabet, the Corning Icarians had to be content with the little village described by Hinds on his visit there in 1876:

"A dozen small white cottages arranged on the sides of a parallelogram; a larger central building, containing a unitary kitchen and a common dining-hall, which is also used as an assembly-room and for community amusements, including an occasional dance or theatrical presentation; a unitary bake-room and laundry near at hand; numerous log-cabins, also within easy reach of the central building . . . behold the present external aspects of Icaria."[24]

The shattering of the Icarian vision was duplicated dozens of times during the nineteenth century. With few exceptions, the more bizarre the doctrine of the groups attempting to found such societies the greater was the incidence of failure. Those which succeeded, or at least were able to maintain some kind of existence, were those which diverged least from the established pattern of the world. Thus, a Fairhope, Alabama, could prosper because, except for its Georgian doctrine of the single tax, it resembled an ordinary industrial and real estate promotion. But for every Fairhope there were a hundred Icaras. Frontier America may have been the great proving ground for liberty and initiative, but in this respect at least it also proved too stern a test for most nonconformists. There were exceptions, of course, and to the greatest of these we now turn our attention.

The Mormon Cities of Zion

The year 1830 saw the birth of a new religion, one among the dozens spawned in the backwaters left by the advancing waves of the frontier. This Church of Jesus Christ of Latter-Day Saints—or the Mormons, as they soon were called—became the most successful city builder of all the religious and utopian societies.

From Fayette, in upstate New York, Joseph Smith and his followers began their much-interrupted march to the west; this march was not to end for many years and until a thousand miles and more had been covered. In Kirtland, Ohio, a town in the old Western Reserve northeast of Cleveland, they built the first Mormon temple and established a community.

The Mormon religion was based in part on the belief in divine revelation to God's chosen people. In July 1831 the prophet Joseph announced that it had been revealed to him that the future center of the Mormon kingdom was to be Jackson County, Missouri. From this spot near the center of the continent the Mormon doctrine would spread until it embraced the globe. Smith accordingly dispatched a group to Independence, Missouri, to prepare the way for a new settlement.

Two years later Smith sent detailed instructions to the Missouri church for the planning of the city that would be the center of activities for the Mormons. "We send by this mail a draft of the City of Zion," wrote Smith in June 1833. "Should you not understand the explanations . . . you will inform us so that you may have a proper understanding, for it is meant that all things should be done according to the pattern."

The plat that Smith sent is reproduced in Figure 278, and on it can be seen his instructions on the borders of the drawing. These directions are of considerable interest. Smith stated that the city was intended for a population of fifteen to twenty thousand persons. With only about 1,000 house lots, the average family size would work out to be between 15 and 20. Although the controversial doctrine of polygamy was not officially adopted until 1852, perhaps Smith had this in mind when he devised the plan of his city.

The three central blocks were designated as the sites for public buildings. Around them, in a grid pattern, were the blocks for commercial and residential use. Smith's specifications for the arrangement of lots were unusual.

"The plot contains one mile square; all the squares in the plot contain ten acres each, being forty rods square. You will observe that the lots are laid off alternately in the square; in one square

[24] William Alfred Hinds, Letter to the *American Socialist* (1876), as quoted in Hinds, *American Communities*, 378-79.

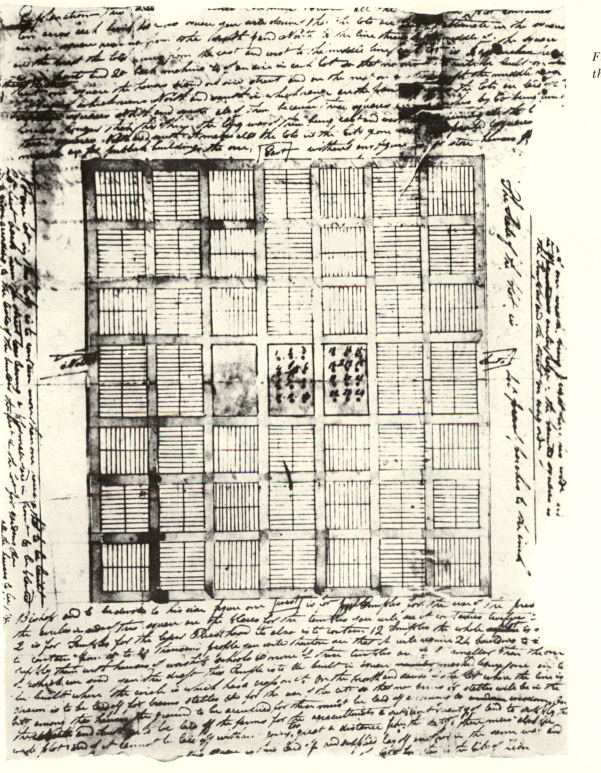

Figure 278. Joseph Smith's Plan of the City of Zion: 1833

running from the south and north to the line through the center of the square; and in the next, the lots run from the east and west to the center line. Each lot is four perches in front, and twenty back, making one-half of an acre in each lot, so that no one street will be built on entirely through the street; but on one square the houses will stand on one street, and on the next one, another, except the middle range of squares, which run north and south. . . ."[25]

All streets were to be 132 feet wide, and the houses were to be set back 25 feet from the street lines. Smith further specified that all houses were to be built of brick and stone; he obviously wished to create a spacious and impressive headquarters for his new religion. He also evidently had in mind some kind of permanent agricultural belt around the city which would limit its ultimate growth. After mentioning that the farm lands should be laid out beyond the town boundaries, he added: "When this square is thus laid off and supplied, lay off another in the same way, and so fill up the world in these last days; and let every man live in the city for this is the City of Zion."[26]

Acting under these instructions the church leaders in Missouri planned the city of Far West on a tract originally one mile square. Figure 279 shows the plan of the city and indicates that Smith's exact specifications had not been followed completely. While the 8 main streets leading to the central square were 132 feet wide, the others had been reduced to 82½ feet. The heavier lines enclosing the blocks in the center of the drawing evidently indicate the first blocks laid out, for this is exactly one mile square. But as more and more of the Saints made the long journey from Kirtland and as new church members were recruited from elsewhere, it apparently became necessary to expand the town.

The Mormons had been driven to Far West in Caldwell County, Missouri, by the older residents of Independence and other towns in Jackson County who resented the Mormon influx. Nor was Far West to remain for long a permanent resting place for these persecuted people. Once again they were driven away, this time eastward to the banks of the Mississippi in Illinois. Here, at a place they called Nauvoo ("the beautiful"), a great new city was

planned. Nauvoo in 1842 is shown in Figure 280, with the great temple that overlooked the river from its site on the bluff. Its plan differs from that of the City of Zion in that its streets were only 50 feet wide and the blocks were divided into four parcels about 100 feet square.

Nauvoo prospered and soon became the largest town in the state. It received a charter from the legislature, a university was organized, and here the Mormons apparently had found peace. However, once again their neighbors began a systematic series of persecutions which soon developed into full-scale warfare. After the brutal shooting of Joseph Smith by a mob which stormed the jail where he and a few companions had been thrown on some flimsy charge the Mormons resolved to abandon Nauvoo and begin again their quest for a new kingdom.

By the winter of 1847 many of them were encamped on the west bank of the Missouri River in Nebraska. Even here, at the temporary settlement they called Winter Quarters, the Mormons laid out a regular city. Their new leader, Brigham Young, described the town in a letter written that February: "Winter Quarters is platted in 41 blocks, numbering 20 lots to a block, 4 rods by 10 covered by about 700 houses divided into 22 wards, with 22 bishops and counsellers over whom preside a municipal High Council of 12 High Priests."[27]

Then, in the spring, the long trek westward began anew. Up the valley of the Platte and into the mountain passes the Mormons wound their way until Young, looking out over the valley of the Great Salt Lake uttered his famous words, "this is the place." Here in what they called the territory of Deseret the Mormons began to plan and build their great city of the Salt Lake.

Within 20 years the city had reached the sizeable proportions shown in the view reproduced in Figure 281. But the initial years were hard ones, and the town was anything but elegant. On his way to the gold fields of California one forty-niner recorded these impressions of the city in a letter to his wife:

"The buildings are mostly small; they are built some of logs, but mostly of what they call dobies. . . . When the Mormons first settled here, they put their buildings in the shape of a fort; they built two rows of buildings three-fourths of a mile in length

---

[25] As transcribed in Kate B. Carter, *The Mormon Village*, Daughters of Utah Pioneers, Lesson For November, 1954, pp. 133-34.
[26] *ibid.*, 135.

[27] As quoted in Ray West, *Kingdom of the Saints*, New York, 1957, p. 172.

· 468 ·

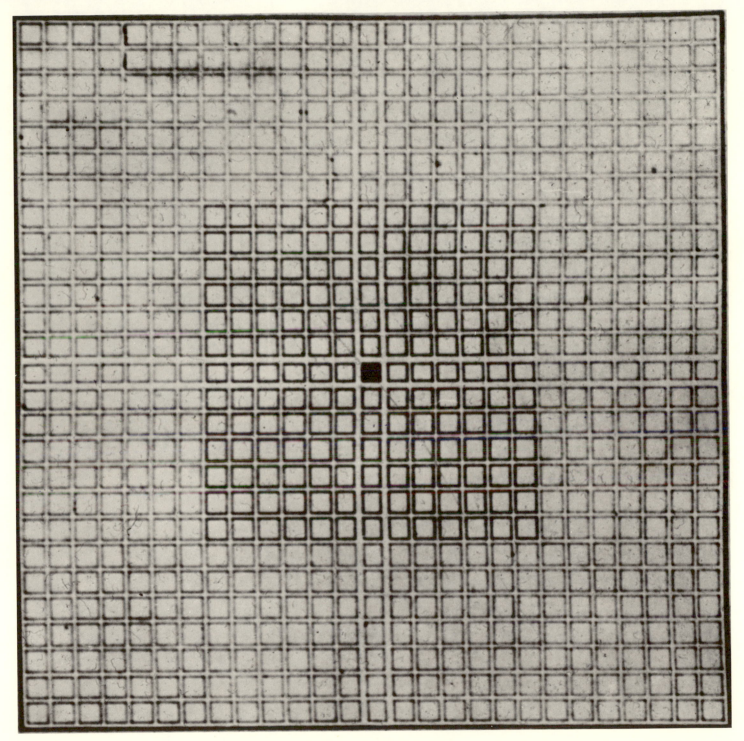

Figure 279. Plan of Far West, Missouri: ca. 1836

Figure 280. Plan of Nauvoo,
Illinois: ca. 1842

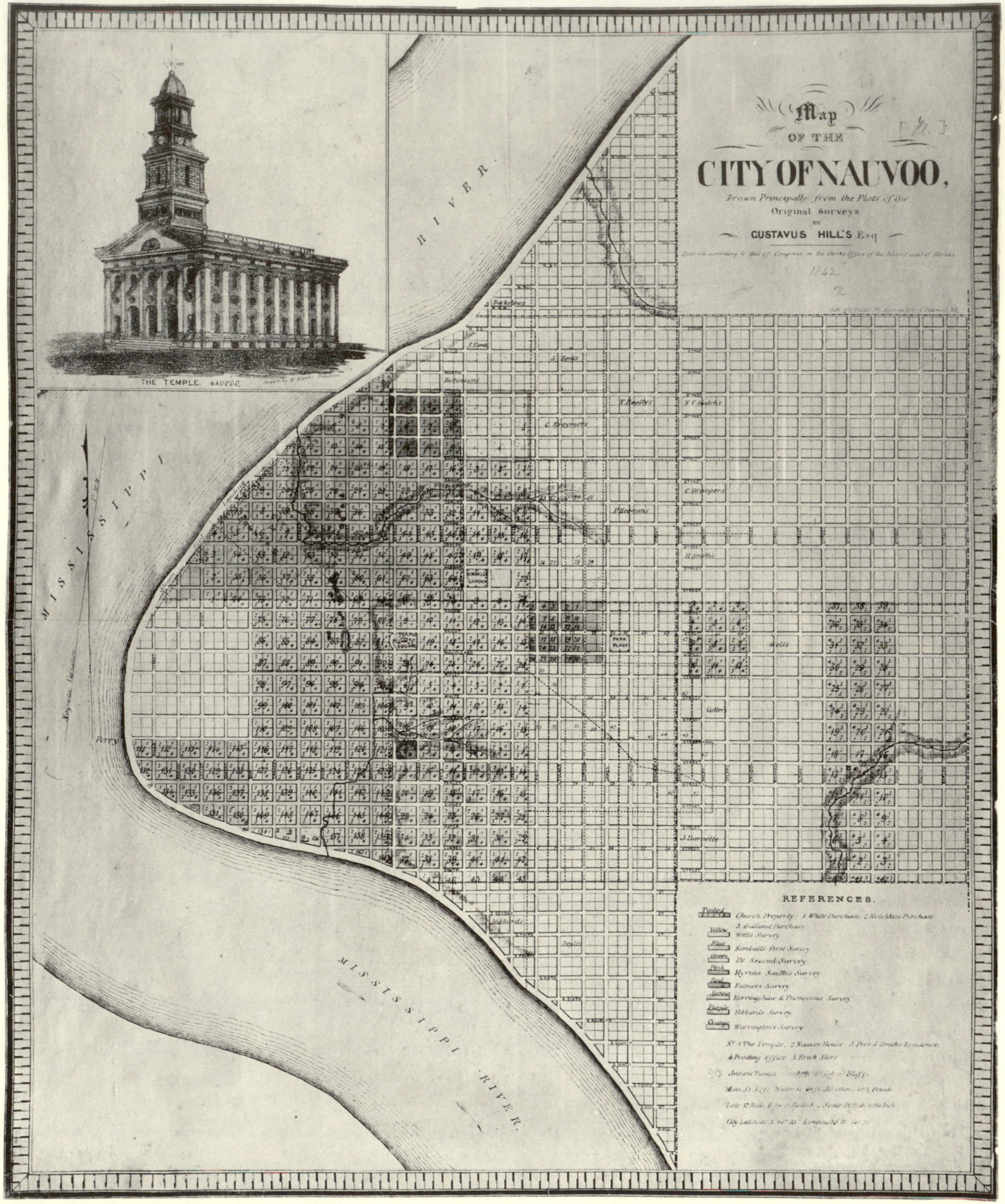

Figure 281. View of Salt Lake City, Utah: 1870

and [a] fourth of a mile apart, and shut up the ends by buildings across; inside of this they had three rows of buildings at equal distances across, forming four hollow squares, into which they could take all their cattle, wagons, etc., if they should be attacked by Indians. . . ."[28]

Howard Stansbury, who spent the winter of 1849-1850 in Salt Lake City during his official government survey of the Salt Lake valley, estimated that by that spring there were 8,000 inhabitants. The temple which appears in the view had not yet been started. Instead, on one of the central squares, an enormous shed with a roof supported by posts had been erected that was capable of sheltering 3,000 persons. Stansbury describes the plan as following in its essential the original City of Zion plat except for its larger size:

"A city had been laid out upon a magnificent scale, being nearly four miles in length and three in breadth; the streets at angles with each other, eight rods or one hundred and thirty-two feet wide, with sidewalks of twenty feet; the blocks forty rods square, divided into eight lots, each of which contains an acre and a quarter of ground. By an ordinance of the city, each house is to be placed twenty feet back from the front line of the lot, the intervening space being designed for shrubbery and trees. The site for the city is most beautiful; it lies at the western base of the Wahsatch mountains, in a curve formed by the projection westward from the main range, of a lofty spur which forms its southern boundary."[29]

Salt Lake City was by no means the only city planned following the City of Zion plat. Dozens of communities throughout Utah were soon laid out by the Mormons. While not all of them adhered to the strict prescriptions of Joseph Smith, they were all planned in the spirit of his original conception. One curious feature may still be observed. Square blocks were divided into four building sites of generous size. The houses, instead of being located near the middle of the plots, were grouped in fours at the street inter-

sections. That is, each house was built near the corner of its site formed by the two intersecting street lines.

While the origin of this method of siting houses remains obscure, the general derivation of the City of Zion type plan is fairly clear. Smith was a student of the Bible and no doubt was familiar with the description both of the cities of the Levites mentioned in Numbers 35: 1-5 and Leviticus 25 and the proposals by Ezekiel for the building of Jerusalem. Both called for square cities set in the middle of their agricultural lands and thus comprising the kind of rural-urban unit or city-state that Smith envisaged and Brigham Young later provided.[30]

Zion by the Lake

The Mormons were not the only group to use the name of Zion. Forty miles north of Chicago on the shore of Lake Michigan a strange new town began to take shape in the early years of the twentieth century. This was Zion City, Illinois, the creation of the Rev. John Alexander Dowie. Dowie had come to America from Australia and organized The Christian Catholic Church of Zion. A faith healer, fiery preacher in the Jonathan Edwards tradition, and fanatical believer in his own mission, Dowie soon attracted a large following in Chicago.

On the first day of 1900 Dowie announced to his flock that he had purchased 6,500 acres in Lake County, Illinois, and that there a town would be laid out. Here was to be the new headquarters of Dowie's church, from which the whole world would be converted.

Presumably Dowie himself originated at least the general outline of Zion City, the plan of which is shown in Figure 282, although Burton J. Ashley is listed as the designer. Certainly the generous scale of the town approached the inflated vision of his destiny that Dowie maintained in his own mind.

From the sides of the central square of 200 acres ran four main boulevards no less than 300 feet broad. Four diagonal streets diverged from the corners of the square and cut across the basic gridiron street pattern. Here and there, no doubt following natural

[28] Letter by A. P. Josselyn, July 15, 1849. Reprinted in William Mulder and A. Russell Mortensen, *Among the Mormons: Historic Accounts by Contemporary Observers*, New York, 1958, p. 236.
[29] Howard Stansbury, *Exploration and Survey of the Valley of the Great Salt Lake of Utah*, 32nd. Cong. Special Session, March 1851, Sen. Ex. doc. No. 3, Washington, 1853, p. 128.

[30] Discussions of Mormon town planning can be found in Lowry Nelson, *The Mormon Village*, Salt Lake City, 1952; Feramorz Young Fox, *The Mormon Land System*, unpublished Master's thesis, Northwestern University, 1932; and Charles L. Sellers, "Early Mormon Community Planning," *Journal of the American Institute of Planners*, XXVIII (1962), 24-30.

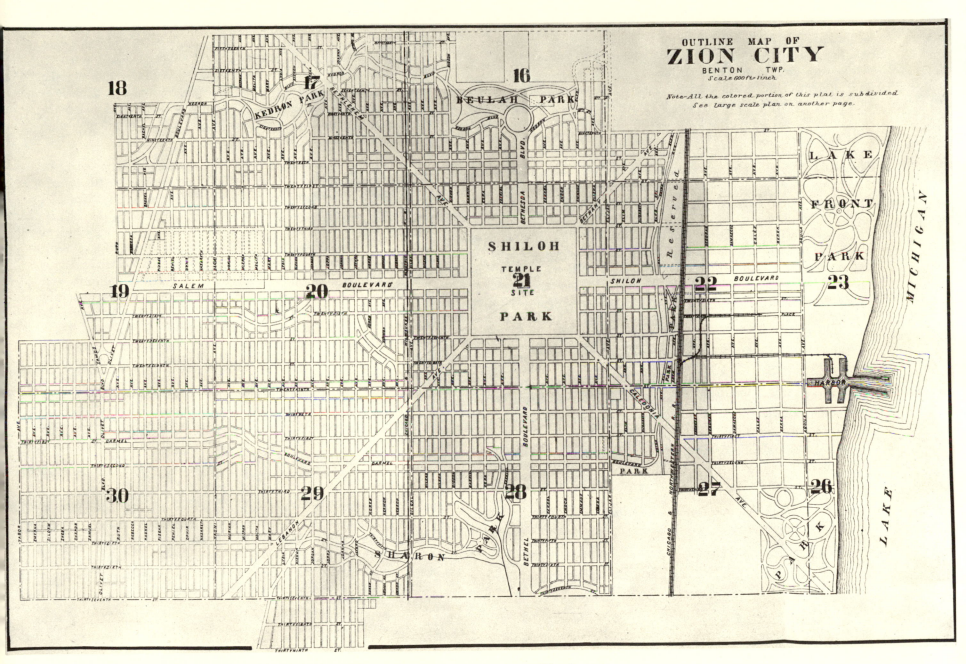

Figure 282. Plan of Zion City, Illinois: 1907

watercourses, the grid system was modified and incorporated winding park drives. Along the lake shore north and south of the harbor two large parks were provided.

The Zion Land and Investment Association was another creation of Dowie to manage the affairs of town development. The land policies followed were interesting and unusual. Land was to be granted on leases running to the year 3,000, but leasehold rights were to be declared forfeit if specific conditions of use of property were violated. All leaseholders were required to own stock in the Zion Land and Investment Association, and there is considerable evidence that Dowie was not above using the funds raised from stock sales for his own purposes.

In addition to restrictions on front yards and a limitation of one house to each lot, the leasehold restrictions, as summarized by one investigator, contained the following prohibitions as to use of land and buildings: "No saloons, no harlots' dens, no tobacco shops, no theatres, no gambling halls, no opium joints, no drug stores, no secret lodges, no pig markets, no surgeons' offices, no labor unions, no oyster traffic. . . ."[31]

Apparently there were enough devout Dowieites willing to forego oysters and the other manifestations of the sinful life in Chicago to warrant proceeding with construction. The city began to emerge from the plains, and within a few years had a substantial population. Dowie ruled the city like a little dictator. When the city was incorporated by the state legislature, he stated characteristically, "The City is governed municipally according to the law of the State of Illinois and of the United States of America, but I may as well tell you, the people would not vote a ticket if I did not approve it."[32]

Unlike some of the other communities founded in America under similar conditions, Zion City survived the death of its founder in

[31] Budgett Meakin, *Model Factories and Villages: Ideal Conditions of Labour and Housing*, London, 1905, p. 412n.
[32] As quoted in V. F. Calverton, *Where Angels Dared to Tread*, Indianapolis, 1941, p. 324.

1907. Wilbur Glenn Voliva became the new leader of the group and handled the affairs of the town until finally deposed in 1935. The land company went into bankruptcy in 1933, and under the subsequent reorganization the old leasehold system was abolished. Today, Zion City, except for its grandiose plan, is a relatively normal suburban community whose residents have little knowledge of its unique history.

The number of utopian groups in America was impressive. In the foregoing pages only a few of those responsible for the founding of communities have been described. There were, of course, many more: the Shakers, the Perfectionists of Oneida, the Labadists, the Society of the Woman in the Wilderness, the Ephrata Community, the Altruists, the Straight-Edgers, the Spirit Fruit Society, and others with exotic names and peculiar doctrines.

Although these groups were numerous, their influence on American society was modest. The bulk of the nation stubbornly pursued its old sinful and capitalistic ways, oblivious to the teachings of the new, self-appointed prophets who had arisen. Their neighbors viewed these sects and their leaders either with outright hostility or with the pity usually reserved for the dim-witted or the helpless.

The physical impact of the utopians was equally slight. With the exception of the Mormons no one of these groups made any significant impression on the pattern of towns in its region. Perhaps this is why we value all the more such artifacts as may have survived in a Bethlehem, a New Harmony, or an Amana.

If the heritage of bricks and mortar is meager, the utopians at least left a rich legacy of hopes and dreams. One should not be too harsh in judging what, with the advantage of a lengthened perspective, now appear as ludicrous or wildly impractical schemes to reconstruct society. The modern city planner, who himself must be something of a utopian if he is to maintain his idealism and sanity in an increasingly ugly and chaotic world, may appear equally absurd a century hence.

CHAPTER 17

Minor Towns and Mutant Plans

NOT all of America's ventures in city planning fall within the mainstream of tradition. Some were so short-lived or so little known that they were never used as models for later towns. Others show plan forms that can be regarded as mutants: patterns owing nothing to what had gone before and, like their biological counterparts, often failing to reproduce their kind. Despite this, or perhaps because of it, these episodes in American planning have more than passing interest. This chapter will sample a few of these mutant towns. Some of them may still be seen, while others no longer exist.

An Asylum for Marie

With the outbreak of the French Revolution and the slave insurrections of the French colonies in the West Indies, America became a refuge of thousands of émigrés. Philadelphia, then the capital and largest city of the nation, received many of them, including one Louis de Noailles, cousin and brother-in-law of Lafayette. It is not necessary to go into the details of his activities in Philadelphia, and in fact they remain partially obscure. In 1793 Noailles approached Robert Morris seeking help in the establishment of a colony of Frenchmen somewhere away from Philadelphia, where they might begin life again in a new environment.

Among Noailles' associates in this proposed venture were a number of Frenchmen who had pressed for liberal reforms in France while remaining loyal to the crown. There is a legend, largely undocumented, that this group in America hoped to establish a place of refuge for Louis and Marie Antoinette and were in touch with French loyalists who hoped to save the king and queen from the guillotine in exchange for permanent exile in America.

Morris was a friend of France and, as one of the principal American speculators in large-scale real estate ventures, was in a position to help Noailles and his group of Philadelphia Frenchmen.

He suggested a site on the Susquehanna River in northern Pennsylvania. Charles Boulogne, a member of the French group, was dispatched to investigate suitable sites in company with Major Adam Hoops, a surveyor who had become associated with Morris and who was later to plan his own town of Olean, New York.

Both Connecticut and Pennsylvania claimed the territory in question, and it was necessary to secure titles from two sets of land-owners who were rival claimants to the area. With this accomplished, the first group of settlers arrived late in 1793 and began to clear land and build houses. The plan of the little town appears in Figure 283. Whether this was prepared by Hoops, which seems probable, or by one of the French group is not known. With its central market square, rectangular street pattern, and system of town lots and farm lots, it resembles some of the little Pennsylvania towns near Philadelphia. Yet in the broad avenue leading up from the landing at the river to the market square and beyond, it has some of the qualities of the Grand Plan concept that would have been familiar to the former members of the French nobility and professional classes who came there to live. The name Asylum— or Azilum, as the members of the community spelled it—stood as a poignant reminder of what had been lost in France and what was hoped for in America.

The community enjoyed but a brief existence. There were conflicts over land titles arising from the claims of the two states. Many of the settlers found themselves ill-adapted for the rugged life of the frontier, and with the establishment of some measure of peace and order in France under Napoleon many of the refugees returned to their homeland. Others drifted south to Charleston, Savannah, and New Orleans. Only a few of the original colonists remained in the vicinity, and by 1812 much of the townsite was being farmed. Asylum is thus a candidate for the dubious distinction of being one of America's first ghost towns.[1]

[1] Louise Welles Murray, *The Story of Some French Refugees and Their "Azilum" 1793-1800*, Athens, Pa., 1903, rev. ed., 1917.

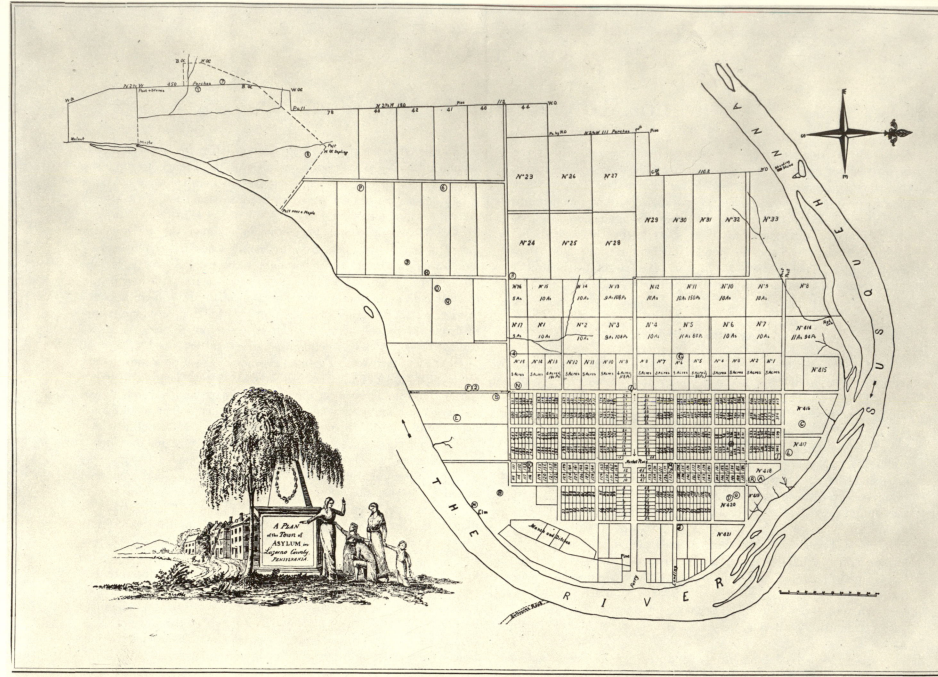

Houses built or inhabited by the French, location indicated on the map by letters: *a* Talon; *b* probably Boulogne; *c* Sibert, described in deed; *d* Schufeldt, afterward French; *e* Wheeler; *f* French, afterward A. P. Biles; *g* French, afterward J. Biles; *h* Homet; *i* French, afterward VanGorder; *j* French, afterward Miller; *k* French, afterward R. B. Kerrick; *l* Cottineau; *m* French, afterward Morey; *n* French, afterward Gordon; *o* F. X. Homet, now standing; *p* French, near C. Stevens' barn; *q* French, near Bacon's house; *r* House now standing built by Judge Laporte 1839, now Hagerman, visible from river, close to site of house of Talon; *s* House now occupied by George Laporte; *t* French still house; *u* Aubrey's smith shop; *w* location of Kerrick's famous camp, 1900; all original streets now used as roads are marked on map with arrows.

Cemeteries: Beginning with date of settlement up to present day, nine cemeteries have been established within original plot of Asylum, most of them afterwards abandoned. It is said more people are buried in this valley in comparison with population than is known in any such radius in this part of the country. These cemeteries are indicated on map in order of their establishment, by enclosed figures; the headstones are all gone from earliest ones. *1* old French; *2* abandoned about 1812; *3* abandoned about 1830; *4* Gordon family plot; *5* Laporte, first used 1836; *6* Homet, first used 1838; *7* Braun; *8* Gilbert; *9* In use 1903 at Methodist Church.

Figure 283. Plan of Asylum, Pennsylvania: 1793

New Madrid on the Spanish Frontier

In October 1788 a handbill appeared in New Jersey and other northeastern states describing a proposed city and colony on the western bank of the Mississippi in Spanish territory. Over the name of George Morgan, late Colonel in the Revolutionary Army, the notice set out the following terms of settlement:

"All Farmers, Tradesmen, &c. of good Characters, who wish to unite in this Scheme, and to visit the Country under my Direction, shall be provided with Boats and Provisions for the Purpose, free of Expence, on signing an Agreement, which may be seen by applying to me at Prospect, near Princeton, on or before the 8th Day of October; or at Fort Pitt, by the 20th Day of November next. . . . Every Person who accompanies me in this Undertaking, shall be entitled to 320 Acres of Land, at one eighth of a Dollar per Acre . . . ; 640 Acres, or more, being first reserved for a Town, which I propose to divide into Lots of One Acre each, and give 600 of them, in Fee, to such Merchants, Tradesmen, &c. as may apply on the Spot, and 40 of them to such Public Uses as the Inhabitants shall, from Time to Time, recommend; together with one Out Lot of 10 Acres to each of the first 600 families who shall build and settle in the Town.

"All Persons who settle with me at New-Madrid, and their Posterity, will have the free Navigation of the Mississippi, and a Market at New Orleans, free from Duties, for all the Produce of their Lands, where they may receive Payment in Mexican Dollars for their Flour, Tobacco, &c."[2]

Morgan's colonization activities were to include one of the most interesting, and perhaps the most futile, episodes in American town planning. Certainly they represented one of the earliest attempts by citizens of the new nation to lay out a town for more than speculative or utilitarian purposes. That Americans sought to carry out this project in Spanish territory requires some explanation.

Since the end of the Revolution the feeble Continental Congress had been confronted with problems affecting the territory beyond the Allegheny Mountains to the Mississippi River. These problems centered on the conflict between the American and Spanish governments over rights of navigation on the Mississippi, trading privileges at New Orleans, and customs collected by the Spanish on goods shipped through that port by western farmers.

Spanish policy was aimed at blocking westward expansion of the new nation. Closing the Mississippi to trade was a furtherance of that policy. Spain evidently hoped that settlement would be discouraged if the easiest and cheapest route to markets was denied to farmers in the old Northwest Territory. Spain may also have hoped to profit from the discontent of Kentucky settlers over the ineffectiveness of American representations to the Spanish authorities on trade and navigation rights. If Kentucky could be induced to establish itself as an independent republic, or if the settlers could be lured to Louisiana by generous land grants, Spain's position would be immeasurably strengthened. Both possibilities were explored by Don Esteban Miró, governor of Louisiana.

In the east the Spanish minister, Don Diego de Gardoqui, received instructions from his government to promote development of the Louisiana Territory through the extension of land grants to prospective colonists. It was at this time that George Morgan was attempting to negotiate a western land purchase with the Board of Treasury on behalf of the New Jersey Land Society, of which he was one of the leading figures. Morgan had previously been associated with other similar land companies, none of which had been successful in acquiring title to western lands.

When Morgan learned of the Spanish policy he quickly shifted his attention from the Treasury to Gardoqui. Morgan submitted to Gardoqui a number of proposals for colonization. The proposed colony was to consist of a large area of land extending westward from the Mississippi and north and south from a point opposite the mouth of the Ohio. Morgan was to be given command of the colony, freedom of religion was to be established, the colonists were to be permitted self-government although subject to the king, and the town to be established was to be a port of entry for the control of trade. Morgan was to be paid for his services and was to receive a land grant of at least 1,000 acres for each of his 5 children, himself, and his wife. Gardoqui was so impressed by Morgan's reputation and his evident understanding of how to organize such a venture that he quickly agreed to the proposal.

---

[2] From a reproduction of Morgan's handbill in Max Savelle, *George Morgan, Colony Builder*, New York, 1932, following p. 206. I have relied on Savelle for much of the background information in this section.

Morgan was eager to begin. Instead of waiting for Gardoqui to receive approval of the scheme from Spain, he requested and was granted permission to visit the area immediately, lay out the city, and make provisional land grants and sales subject to later affirmation by the king. Gardoqui wrote to Miró informing the Louisiana governor of his action:

"I enclose in this a duplicate of that which I had the satisfaction of writing to Your Lordship introducing to your protection Colonel Don Jorge Morgan. The latter laid before me after a few conferences a certain project for the formation of a new settlement on our western bank of the Mississippi river, south of Cape Cinque Hommes. It seems to me to be for the most part in accordance with the orders of the King. I regarded it as admissible, provided it were approved by his Majesty. . . .

"Contemplating this acquisition as one of the most important in the service of the King, I conducted myself in terms which I believe will have effect; and having proposed to me that he desired to take advantage of the rainy season to explore the land and fix on the place for settlement. I thought it best to grant it and contribute to his expenses, for I was certain that the end merits it and that his Majesty will approve it."[3]

It was on this authority that Morgan issued the handbill quoted at the beginning of this article. It attracted a number of persons willing to emigrate, and in January 1789 Morgan and some 70 companions started down the Ohio River from Fort Pitt.[4]

The party reached the Mississippi on February 14. After investigating possible sites for the colony, they finally settled on a location about 40 miles south of the mouth of the Ohio. Morgan had previously decided to call the town New Madrid out of respect for his sponsors. The town site was described in a letter from several settlers sent to friends in Pittsburgh early in April. It was situated, they said,

"... at a place formerly called Lance La Graise, or the Greasy Bend, below the mouth of a river, marked in Captain Hutchin's map Cheyousea or Sound river.

"Here the banks of the Mississippi, for a considerable length, are high, dry, and pleasant, and the soil westward to the river St. Francois, is of the most desirable quality for Indian corn, tobacco, flax, cotton, hemp, and indigo, though thought by some too rich for wheat; insomuch, that we verily believe that there is not an acre of it uncultivable, or even indifferent land, within a thousand square miles.

"The country rises gradually from the Mississippi into fine, dry, pleasant and healthful grounds, superior, we believe, in beauty and in quality, to every other part of America."[5]

The location of the town and the surrounding country are shown in Figure 284, "Plan of the Fort of New Madrid or Anse A La Graisse," drawn by Victor Collot following his visit in 1796. The swamps and marshes indicated on this map were conveniently overlooked by the first settlers in their description of the site. Also, as will be seen, other features of the area made it something less than an ideal location for a town.

Morgan had prepared detailed directions for the planning of the town. Probably he incorporated some of the features he had previously considered for town development during the many years he had endeavored to secure land grants elsewhere before and after the war. Some of these ideas he had summarized in the handbill already mentioned, and others were described in the settlers' letter of April 14. Morgan's town planning ideas were set forth in detail in a document of his handwriting endorsed "General Directions for Settlement at New Madrid" dated April 6, 1789. It is evident that Morgan was thinking of something more elaborate than merely another river hamlet. He envisaged New Madrid as the future metropolis of the central Mississippi Valley, and his town planning concepts matched this optimistic expectation.

[3] Letter from Gardoqui to Miró, October 4, 1788, in Louis Houck, *The Spanish Regime in Missouri*, Chicago, 1909, I, 284.

[4] Morgan's expedition caused some concern in the new government of the United States. On March 26, 1789, James Madison wrote to George Washington, enclosing a copy of the Morgan handbill and noting, "It is the most authentic & precise evidence of the Spanish project that has come to my knowledge." Gaillard Hunt, ed., *The Writings of James Madison*, New York, 1900-1910, v, 331.

[5] Letter to Messrs. Bedford and Turnbull from settlers at New-Madrid, April 14, 1789. There were apparently several versions of this letter printed in eastern newspapers in an attempt to attract additional settlers. The version quoted appeared in the *Virginia Gazette and Weekly Advertiser* for August 27, 1789, and was reprinted in the *Mississippi Valley Historical Review*, v (1918), 343-346, with a brief explanatory note by E. G. Swem. A slightly different version is in Houck, *Spanish Regime*, I, 279-283.

Morgan first repeated the terms of land grants and sales to the original and subsequent settlers, much as they appeared in the handbill. However, the size of city lots to be granted to each of the first 600 settlers was reduced from 1 to ½ acre, and the out lots from 10 to 5 acres.

Morgan specified a rectangular street pattern and rectangular lot layout:

"In laying out the city, all streets shall be at right angles and four rods wide, including the foot-paths on each side, which shall be fifteen feet wide, and shall be raised twelve or fifteen inches above the wagon road. No person shall be allowed to encroach on the foot-paths, with either porch, cellar door, or other obstruction to passengers.

"All the oblongs, or squares of the city, shall be of the same dimensions, if possible; viz.: extending from east to west eighty rods or perches, and from north to south twelve perches, so that each oblong or square will contain six acres, which shall be sub-divided by meridian lines, into twelve lots of half an acre each. . . . The lots shall be numbered from No. 1 upward, on each side of every street; extending from east to west; commencing at the east end."[6]

Street names were to be simplified by reference to compass directions from King Street, the main east-west street, and River Street, the street running north-south along the Mississippi:

"The streets shall be distinguished by names in the following manner: the middle street shall be a continuation of the middle range or road, extending from the first meridional line to the Mississippi river, and shall be called King street; and the streets north of this, extending from east to west, shall be called first North street, second North street, and so on, reckoning from King's street or middle street. In like manner all the streets south of Kings street or middle street . . . ; so also, all the streets extending North and South shall be distinguished by the names of first River street, second River street, and so on; reckoning the space between the eastmost squares and the river, as first or front River street."[7]

[6] George Morgan, "General Directions for Settlement at New Madrid," Houck, *Spanish Regime*, I, 303.
[7] *ibid.*, 303-304.

Figure 284. Map of New Madrid, Missouri and Vicinity: 1796

Although Morgan's directions mention no deviation from the gridiron plan, the settlers' letter written 8 days later indicates that this was contemplated. The letter describes a lake within the boundary of the town,

". . . of the purest spring water, 100 yards wide, and several leagues in length north and south, and emptying itself by a constant narrow stream through the center of the city. . . .

"On each side of this delightful lake, streets are to be laid out 100 feet wide, and a road to be continued round it of the same breadth, and the trees are directed to be preserved for ever, for the health and pleasure of its citizens."[8]

Morgan was generous in setting aside open spaces and sites for public uses and religious and educational purposes.

"Forty lots of half an acre each shall be reserved for public uses, and shall be applied to such purposes as the citizens shall from time to time recommend, or the chief magistrate appoint; taking care that the same be so distributed in the different parts of the city that their uses may be general, and as equal as possible."[9]

The two lots on either side of King Street nearest the river were to be dedicated for market places. Lot 13 on the south side of King Street was reserved for a Catholic school and Lot 13 on the north side for a Catholic church. Similarly the two lots number 13 on the north and south side of every fifth street above and below King Street were to be reserved for a church and school.

In addition to these 40 sites, Morgan directed that two large parks also be provided:

"There shall be two lots of twelve acres each laid out and reserved forever; viz.: one for the King, and one for public walks, to be ornamented, improved and regulated by or under the direction of the chief magistrate of the city, for the time being, for the use and amusement of the citizens and strangers."[10]

Morgan also reserved the bank of the Mississippi for public use.

"The space between the eastmost squares and the river, shall not be less than one hundred feet at any place, from the present margin or bank of the river, to be kept open forever for the security, pleas-

ure and health of the city, and its inhabitants; wherefore religious care shall be taken to preserve all the timber growing thereon."[11]

This reference to the preservation of trees obviously reflected a special concern of Morgan's, for he also specified that on the 40 reserved lots and the two large parks,

". . . the timber, trees and shrubs, now growing thereon, shall be religiously preserved as sacred; and no part thereof shall be violated or cut down, but by the personal direction and inspection of the chief magistrate for the time being, whose reputation must be answerable for an honorable and generous discharge of this trust, meant to promote the health and pleasure of the citizens."[12]

There was a similar injunction against removal of trees in any city street or county road without approval of the "magistrates of the police, or an officer of their appointment."

Finally, Morgan specified that, in the farm area surrounding the town, certain sites were to be dedicated for public uses:

"There shall be a reserve of one acre at each angle of every intersection of public roads or highways, throughout the whole territory, according to the plan laid down for settlement of the country; by which means, no farm house can be more than two miles and a half from one of these reserves, which are made forever for the following uses, viz.: one acre on the north east angle for the use of a school; one acre on the northwest angle for a church; one acre on the southwest angle for the use of the poor of the district, and the remaining acre in the south east angle for the use of the King."[13]

The original town plan has apparently not survived, and the earliest known map dates from 1794, by which time many changes had been made in Morgan's scheme. This map is shown in Figure 285, "Nouvelle Madrid en Avril 1794." Changes in street names, lot layout and numbers, reserved open spaces, and public building sites, and the addition of Fort Celeste in the center of the town are obvious. Morgan's ideal city and proposed western metropolis had actually developed as a conventional and rather dreary frontier village.

What had occurred may be briefly summarized. After Morgan

[8] Letter to Messrs. Bedford and Turnbull.
[9] Morgan, "General Directions."
[10] ibid., 302-303.

[11] ibid., 304.   [12] ibid., 303.   [13] ibid., 303.

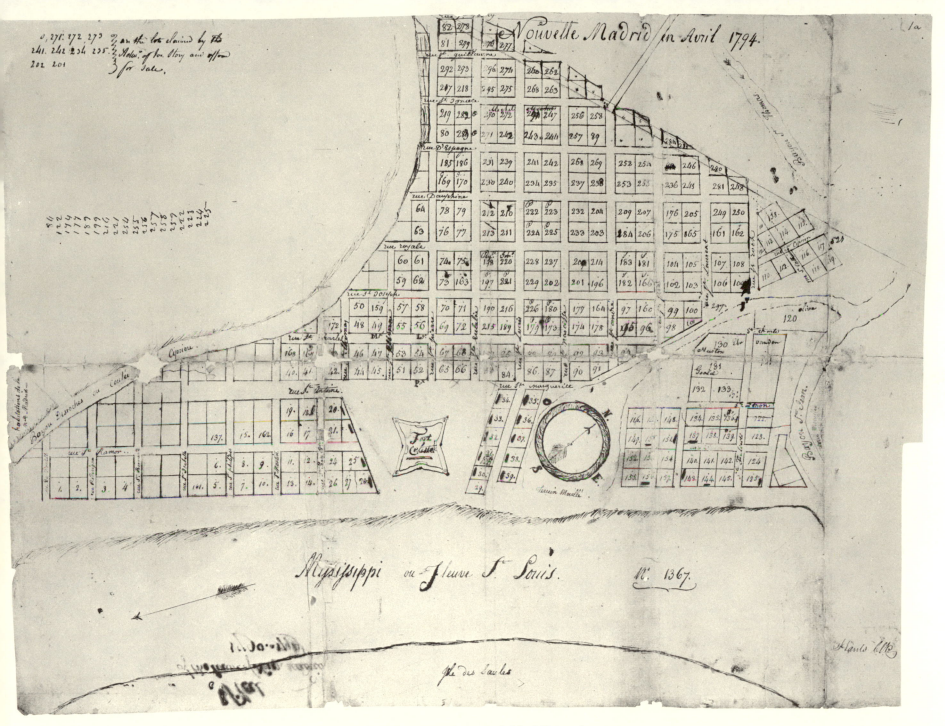

Figure 285. Plan of New Madrid, Missouri: 1794

Figure 286. Plan of New Madrid, Missouri: 1810

had laid out the town and made provisional land grants and sales to the first settlers, he set off to New Orleans to inform Miró of his progress. To his consternation and anger, Morgan discovered that Miró, far from being pleased, disapproved the terms of settlement and maintained that Gardoqui had exceeded his authority in making the conditional grant of land for the new colony. Miró's chief stated objection was that settlers should be given free land and that no individual like Morgan should be the recipient of large tracts to be laid out and sold for personal enrichment. Moreover, Miró felt that Morgan had been presumptuous in naming his settlement after Madrid. He also disagreed with the principle of religious toleration agreed to by Gardoqui. Miró refused to do more than confirm the titles already provisionally granted by Morgan and to recommend that he be given 1,000 acres for himself and his sons. Morgan returned to the east and reported his activities to Gardoqui, but after the death of his brother late in 1789 he appears to have lost all interest in the New Madrid colony.[14]

New Madrid, however, continued to attract settlers. The Spanish commander of the town could report that in the first four months of 1791 nearly 200 new persons had taken up residence. By the end of 1797 the total population was 569 plus 46 slaves, an increase of 116 over the previous year. When Francis Baily visited the town in April 1797 he found

". . . two or three hundred houses, scattered about at unequal distances within a mile of the fort, which stands in the centre of a square in the middle of the town, and which contains from thirty to forty men. Great encouragement is held out by the Spanish government to persons settling here; there being given to them from two hundred and forty to four hundred acres of land gratis. . . ."[15]

But as Baily and practically all other visitors observed, the future of the town was threatened by the eroding effects of the Mis-

sissippi. Collot described this danger which he witnessed on his visit in 1796:

"The river . . . carries away, at different periods of the year, a considerable quantity of the ground on which the town and fort are built; this ground being composed of earth, washed down by the waters, is easily dissolved, and extends .welve. miles inland, without changing either its nature or its level. Nothing can hinder this destructive effect. . . . Every annual revolution carries off from one to two hundred yards of this bank; so that the fort, built five years since at six hundred yards from the side of the river, has already lost all its covered way; and at the time we passed, the commander had given orders to empty the magazines and dislodge the artillery, having no doubt but that in the course of the winter the rest of the fort would be destroyed."[16]

By 1810 a considerable portion of the original town had vanished into the river. Figure 286, "Plat of the town of new madrid" shows the conditions in that year. The fort, two tiers of blocks and a portion of a third, and two streets paralleling the Mississippi had all disappeared. This gradual destruction would probably have eliminated all remaining traces of Morgan's plan in time, but in 1811 a still greater disaster occurred. In December of that year a violent earthquake shook the entire region, and the center of its force was at or near New Madrid. Here is the description of its results by the Reverend Timothy Flint who lived in the town for several months a few years after the tragedy:

". . . [w]hole tracts were plunged into the bed of the river. The graveyard at New Madrid, with all its sleeping tenants, was precipitated into the bend of the stream. Most of the houses were thrown down. Large lakes of twenty miles in extent were made in an hour. Other lakes were drained. . . . The trees split in the midst, lashed one with another, and are still visible over great tracts of country, inclining in every direction and in every angle to the earth and the horizon. They described the undulation of the earth as resembling waves, increasing in elevation as they advanced, and when they had attained a certain fearful height, the earth would burst, and vast volumes of water, and sand, and pit-coal were discharged, as high as the tops of the trees. . . .

[14] Morgan wrote to Gardoqui from his home at Prospect, N.J., on August 20, 1789. This long letter contains a full account of his negotiations with Miró, his comments on colonization policy, and a claim of compensation for his efforts. The entire letter is in Houck, *Spanish Regime*, I, 286-99. According to Savelle, Morgan also prepared an 8-page pamphlet on the New Madrid colony published shortly after his arrival in Philadelphia. This was evidently Morgan's last effort to promote further emigration. Savelle, *George Morgan*, 224.

[15] Francis Baily, *Journal of a Tour in Unsettled Parts of North America in 1796 & 1797*, London, 1856, p. 262.

[16] Victor Collot, *A Journey in North America* (Paris, 1826), reprinted, Florence, 1924, II, 17-18.

"After the earthquake had moderated in violence, the country exhibited a melancholy aspect of chasms of sand covering the earth, of trees thrown down, or lying at an angle of forty-five degrees, or split in the middle. The earthquakes still recurred at short intervals, so that the people had no confidence to build good houses, or chimnies of brick. . . . New Madrid again dwindled to insignificance and decay; the people trembling in their miserable hovels at the distant and melancholy rumbling of the approaching shocks."[17]

The ravages of erosion and the destruction caused by the earthquakes put an end to any remaining hope that Morgan's original concept of a beautiful and thriving town might survive. A brief period of activity occurred when Congress, in an effort to relieve the earthquake's victims, enacted a provision granting owners of New Madrid land the right to select tracts elsewhere in Missouri. Speculators promptly took advantage of this by purchasing worthless land in New Madrid, often from owners ignorant of this Congressional generosity, solely to acquire cheap title to land of their own selection. The confusion resulting from this law and its conflicting interpretations was to plague title-searchers for generations. The benefits, such as they were, were realized by only a few of those whom the law was designed to aid.

Despite the condition of the town, its reputation had been firmly established by the promotional literature of Morgan and his associates. Almost all travelers in this part of the country stopped at New Madrid, no doubt curious to see what portion of Morgan's elaborate scheme had been carried out. Without exception they were outspoken in their disappointment or ridicule. The following description appeared in *The Western Gazetteer, or Emigrants Directory*, published in 1817: "*New Madrid* is situated on a rich plain near the river bank, about seventy miles below the Ohio. This place has been finely described, and appears to better advantage on paper, than when under a *coup d'oeil*."[18]

[17] Timothy Flint, *Recollections of the Last Ten Years*, Boston, 1826, pp. 222-27. Flint also records a more ludicrous visitation on the town. This was a band of religious fanatics who rarely washed or changed their clothes, and who descended on New Madrid by boat. "They walked ashore in Indian file, the old men in front, then the women, and the children in the rear. They chanted a kind of tune, as they walked, the burden of which was 'Praise God! Praise God!' . . . . Sensible people assured me that the coming of a band of these Pilgrims into their houses affected them with a thrill of alarm which they could hardly express," p. 277.

[18] S. R. Brown, *The Western Gazetteer, or Emigrants Directory*, Auburn, 1817, p. 206.

And in a similar work, *The Emigrants' Guide*, which was published the following year, the town was also mentioned: "*New Madrid* has received a celebrity that must astonish those who ever visited the place in open day. The ground . . . is exposed to the ravages of . . . [the Mississippi] . . . to whose force it has, to a great measure, yielded. The town is environed, both above and below, with stagnant creeks."[19]

By the middle of the century practically all traces of Morgan's proposed metropolis had vanished. No features of the original plan have survived to the present time. Figure 287 is a view of the town as it existed one hundred years ago. A sleepy Mississippi River village then, and scarcely more than that today, New Madrid bears little resemblance to the generous vision of its now all but forgotten founder, George Morgan.

Nineteenth-Century Redevelopment: The Squaring of Circleville

In the annals of American city planning there is no more curious episode than the planning and subsequent redevelopment of Circleville, Ohio. It was probably the first and one of the very few towns in North America developed in a radio-concentric plan; it was probably the only city whose form was determined by earthworks constructed by aboriginal peoples; it was certainly one of the earliest examples of comprehensive urban redevelopment in the United States involving a complete change in the street pattern. If these assertions seem remarkable they are amply sustained by the singular facts of Circleville's history.

Pickaway County was established by the Ohio legislature in January 1810, and in the following month three commissioners were appointed to select a site for the county seat. During the spring the commissioners investigated a number of sites within the boundaries of the new county. Their attention soon centered on a location by the Scioto River occupied by geometrical earthworks of a long-vanished culture. This was but one of similar relics scattered throughout the Ohio Valley—the remains of prehistoric Indians commonly referred to as the Mound Builders.

Certainly the commissioners observed one of the most interesting of the Mound Builders' accomplishments. The first complete

[19] William Darby, *The Emigrants' Guide*, New York, 1818, p. 141.

Figure 287. View of New Madrid, Missouri: 1857

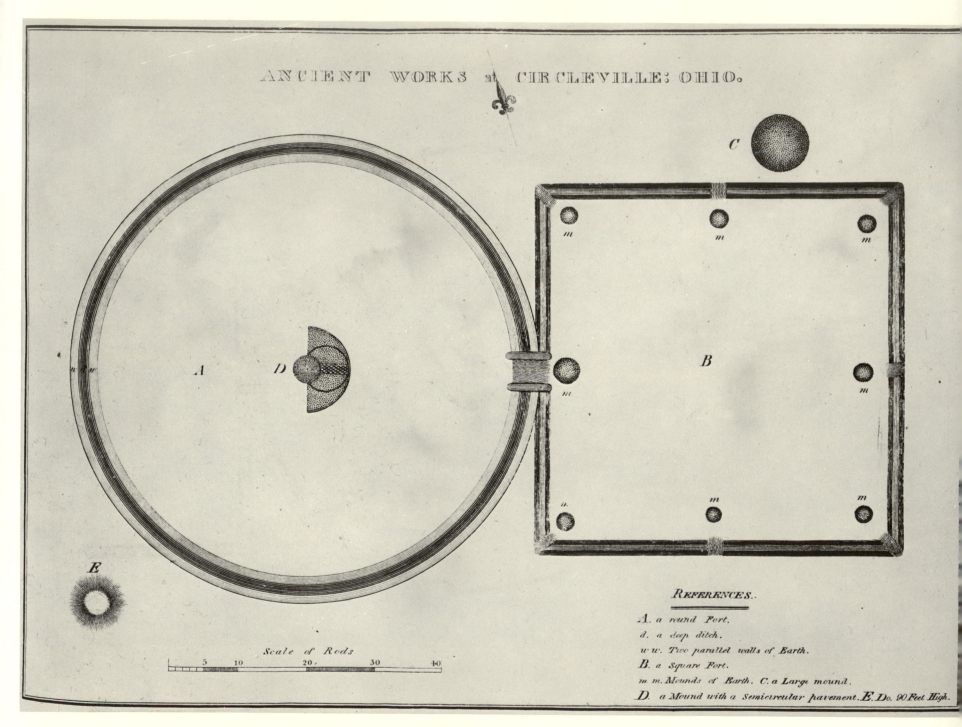

ANCIENT WORKS at CIRCLEVILLE: OHIO.

C

A *D* *B*

m *m* *m*

m *m*

n. *m* *m*

E

Scale of Rods

5   10   20.   30   40

Figure 288. Indian Mounds on the Site of Circleville, Ohio

scientific description was prepared by Caleb Atwater in 1820 and appeared in the first volume of the American Antiquarian Society's *Transactions*, from which Figure 288 and the following account are taken:

"There are two forts, one being an exact circle, the other an exact square. The former is surrounded by two walls, with a deep ditch between them. The latter is encompassed by one wall, without any ditch. The former was 69 rods in diameter, measuring from outside to outside of the circular outer wall; the latter is exactly 55 rods square measuring the same way. The walls of the circular fort were at least 20 feet in height, measuring from the bottom of the ditch. . . .

"What surprised me, on measuring these forts, was the exact manner in which they had laid down their circle and square; so that after every effort, by the most careful survey, to detect some error in their measurement, we found that it was impossible, and that the measurement was much more correct, than it would have been, in all probability, had the present inhabitants undertaken to construct such a work."[20]

The commissioners decided that this would be the site of the new town, and they reported their decision to the authorities. While there is some evidence that the commissioners felt that this might serve to protect and perpetuate these curious survivals of a previous age, it seems as likely they were attracted to a site already cleared and leveled, and with ready-made protection against hostile attack. Whatever their motives, their decision was approved, and on July 25 Daniel Driesbach was appointed to buy the land and lay out a town.

The purchase of land was quickly arranged: 200 acres were obtained from the owners for less than one thousand dollars. Driesbach was responsible for the survey of streets and lots which was soon completed. The first sales of land took place early in September, the new settlers immediately set to work building houses, and before the end of the year some 40 families were living in the new community.

[20] Caleb Atwater, "Description of the Antiquities Discovered in the State of Ohio," American Antiquarian Society, *Transactions and Collections*, I (1820), 141-45. In Atwater's account the dimension of the circular fort is given as 69 feet. This error was changed in the above quotation.

Presumably it was Driesbach's decision to adapt the street pattern to the shape of the circular enclosure. His plan of Circleville —the name, of course, followed inevitably—was at that time unique in this country. While one is inclined to give some credit to an unknown tribal chief or priest, the honors must surely go to Driesbach for realizing the potentialities of the peculiar site.

The original plan of streets and lots is shown in Figure 289. The circular portion is actually a double octagon, a pattern probably selected so that all property boundaries would be straight lines. In the center of the town Driesbach set aside a circular open space approximately 400 feet in diameter. This was soon occupied by the courthouse, an octagonal structure each side of which faced a radial street extending to Circle Street, which followed the outer limits of the original earthworks. Between the central open space and the outer circle was another circular street named Circle Alley. The four cardinal streets leading from the courthouse connected the circular portion of the city with four streets enclosing a square approximately 1,500 feet on each side.

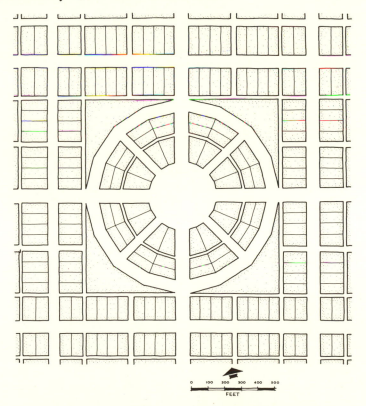

Figure 289. Plan of Circleville, Ohio: 1810

A view of the town as it existed in 1836 appears in Figure 290. Although we are told it was the work of an artist who "never had any instruction, and but very little practice, in drawing and painting," it is probably a generally accurate representation of the old portion of Circleville.

Certainly nothing quite like this town had ever been built in America. As events turned out, its unique plan was soon to be obliterated. James Silk Buckingham, the tireless English traveler and lecturer, visited Circleville in 1840 and recorded the changes then taking place:

"So little veneration . . . have the Americans for ancient remains, and so entirely destitute do they appear to be, as a nation, of any antiquarian taste, that this interesting spot of Circleville, is soon likely to lose all traces of its original peculiarities. The centre of the town contained, as its first building, an octagonal edifice . . . and the streets beyond this were laid out in a circular shape. . . . But though the octagonal building still remains, the circular streets are fast giving way, to make room for straight ones; and the central edifice itself is already destined to be removed, to give place to stores and dwellings; so that in half a century, or less, there will be no vestige left of that peculiarity which gave the place its name, and which constituted the most perfect and therefore the most interesting work in antiquity of its class in the country."[21]

What caused the abandonment of Circleville's distinctive plan? Why were these changes made? Local historians have pointed out that objections were raised to the original design as "a piece of childish sentimentalism," that the shape of the lots was awkward, and that the central circle had become a place where the local pigs ran at large. There were other arguments as well. The craze for land speculation and real estate development, which was to become the dominant force of nineteenth-century town building also affected Circleville. As one account has it,

[21] James Silk Buckingham, *The Eastern and Western States of America*, London, 1842, I, 351. In 1849 in his *National Evils and Practical Remedies* (London, 1849) Buckingham proposed the creation of model industrial towns in Britain. The book contains a plan and view of one of these ideal cities called "Victoria." The city was to be square, but with 8 main streets converging toward a central open space from the corners and the midpoints of the outer boundaries. In the middle of the central open space Buckingham showed an octagonal tower. It is possible the Circleville plan contributed to the details of this utopian proposal.

"It is not at all probable that any change in the town plat would ever have been made, if it had not occurred to somebody that by laying out the circular portion in a square form, several acres of waste ground—in the center of the circle, in the four angles where the square portion joined upon the circle, and in some of the avenues and alleys—would become available for building lots, and yield a fair profit over and above what the county would charge for it."[22]

In 1837 the first steps were taken by persons seeking to change the town plan. The state assembly was prevailed upon to pass enabling legislation to permit the replatting of Circleville. The act was brief and to the point. The county court was authorized to declare the circular portion of the original plat vacated and to establish a new street and lot layout on the application of real estate owners. One important condition was specified: all of the affected property owners had to give their consents before the redevelopment petition could be approved.

Difficulties developed in obtaining unanimous consent, and in the following year the assembly liberalized the replatting statute so that "the owners of real estate in any part of the circular part of the town" could initiate the change.[23] The next day the assembly also passed an act of incorporation, creating what was no doubt the first private urban redevelopment company in the country. The name selected suggests that the company's founders were not without an appreciation of the humorous aspects of their proposed project. The first section of the act of incorporation contained these provisions:

"Be it enacted . . . that Thomas Huston, Edson B. Olds, and Andrew Huston, and their associates, be, and they are hereby constituted a body corporate and politic, with succession for a period of twenty years, by the name and style of the 'Circleville Squaring Company. . . .' "[24]

As the revised legislation authorized, the Circleville Squaring Company proceeded with redevelopment of one segment of the

[22] *History of Franklin and Pickaway Counties, Ohio*, Cleveland, 1880, 179-80.
[23] An Act Supplementary to An Act to Authorize an Alteration in the Town Plat of the Town of Circleville, passed March 29, 1837. Local Acts, Thirty-Sixth General Assembly of Ohio, March 1, 1838.
[24] Local Acts, Thirty-Sixth General Assembly of Ohio, March 2, 1838.

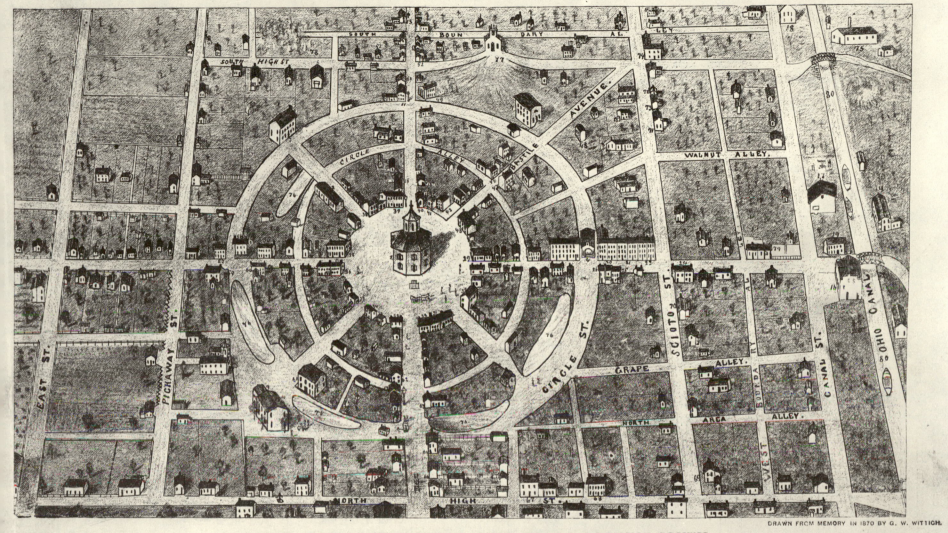

DRAWN FROM MEMORY IN 1870 BY G. W. WITTICH.

BIRD'S EYE VIEW OF CIRCLEVILLE, OHIO, IN 1836, LOOKING SOUTH.

Court House.
County Officers.
County Jail and Sheriff's Dwelling.
Market House.
Presbyterian Church.
Episcopal Church.
Lutheran Church.
Methodist Church.
District School.
Academy.
Henry House.
Margan's Tavern.
Red Lion Tavern, by Jacob Try.
Canal Hotel, by Cradlebaugh.

15, National House.
16, Rogers & Martin's Warehouse.
17, Wilkes & Wareh's Lumber Yard.
18, Finley's Warehouse.
19, J. & H. Smart's Provision Store.
20, Block built by James Bell.
21, Block built by M. M'Crea.
22, Block built by N. S. Gregg.
23, Block built by Sam. Rogers.
24, Block built by Francis Kinnear.
25, Bank of C——, H. Lawrence, Chr.
26, Wolfley & Duncan's Grocery.
27, M. Bright's Tin Shop.
28, Howard's Hat Store.

29, Westenhover's Grocery and Bakery.
30, Samuel Rogers' Store.
31, C. B. Crouse's Store.
32, Jacob Lutz's Store.
33, Francis Kinnear's Store.
34, Mrs. Jackson's Residence.
35, M. M. Gren's Residence.
36, Gossler's Tavern.
37, Dr. E. B. Olds' Drug Store.
38, Huston's Residence.
39, Diffenderfer's Grocery.
40, Hurst's Store.
41, H. Sage's Jewelry Store.
42, Jenkin's Grocery.

43, Israel Darst's Residence.
44, H. Sage's Residence.
45, Dr. Luckey's Office.
46, Dr. Luckey's Residence.
47, Geo. C. Gephart's Residence.
48, Wm. McLane Cabinet Shop.
49, Geo. W. Doane's Res. and Office.
50, W. B. Thrall's Residence.
51, Michael May's Residence.
52, W. M'Culloch's Residence.
53, S. Diffenderfer's Residence.
54, S. Marfield's Residence.
55, Dr. E. B. Olds' Residence.
56, Gen. Green's Residence.

57, Wm. P. Darst's Residence.
58, Thos. Pedrick's Residence.
59, Joseph Olds' Residence.
60, James Bell's Residence.
61, James Bell's Tannery.
62, Jos. Johnson's Residence.
63, Hy. Foresman's Residence.
64, Religious Telescope Office.
65, Circleville Herald Office.
66, F. G. Whittick's Book Bindery.
67, M. Myer's Chairshop and Res.
68, Wilkes' Brewery.
69, F. Williamson's Residence.
70, Hays' Residence.

71, H. Lawrence's Residence.
72, Tanus Crouse's Residence.
73, H. Robbins' Residence.
74, Thos. Wilkes' Residence.
75, T. Darst's Foundry.
76, Parts of Circular Ditch.
77, Mount Gilboa.
78, Lutheran Graveyard.
79, M. Arthur's Block, in progress.
80, Ohio Canal.

Figure 290. View of Circleville, Ohio: 1836

circle at a time. The four stages of replatting are shown in Figure 291. The southeast quarter of the town was vacated by court order and replatted by the end of March. Next came the northwest quarter, replatted early in October. For each project the company paid $750 to the county for public land deeded to it. The methods by which the company redeveloped these portions of the town are of interest.

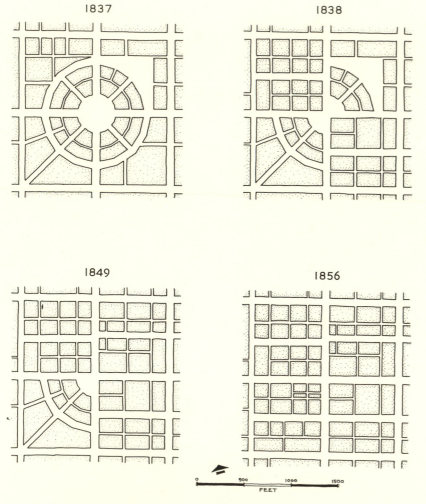

1837

1838

1849

1856

Figure 291. The Squaring of Circleville, Ohio: 1837-1856

"Many of the lots were purchased out and out by the parties making the change, and then resold after it was made. Of the lots unsold, some were increased in size, and others diminished by the change; and the owners of the former made, and those of the latter received suitable compensation.

"The buildings fronting the streets or avenues which were to be vacated (and which, of course, made acute angles with the main streets), were either removed, torn down or changed in position, so as to face the new streets."[25]

Subsequent action did not match the dispatch with which the first two quadrants were redeveloped. For eleven years company activities were suspended while the town remained half square and half circular. One can imagine that the original plan was not without its supporters, who refused to sell their land to the redevelopment company, perhaps feeling that half a circle, even in two parts, was better than none at all.

It was not until 1849 that the northeast quarter was replatted in conformity with the new plan. Then once again several years passed during which negotiations took place with the remaining adherents of the old order. Finally, in September 1854, the proposed plat for the southwest quadrant was submitted, and in March 1856 the remaining county land in the last portion of the old town was transferred. The squaring of Circleville had been accomplished.

Pinwheels and Cobwebs

Circleville may have been the first of the towns in America planned like a spiderweb, but it was not the last. Possibly Circleville influenced one or two of these cities laid out at later dates, but it seems more likely that the pinwheel plan used in each case arose simply from a desire of the founders to create something different from the ordinary grid pattern. In this respect they resembled the numerically more important diagonal towns, which were laid out in response to the same kind of impulse.

The most interesting of these towns, because the plan has remained unchanged to the present time, is Perryopolis, Pennsylvania, near the southwestern corner of that state. The original plat of this little city appears in Figure 292. Although the plat was apparently not recorded until 1834, the name gives a clue to its

[25] *History of Franklin and Pickaway Counties*, 180.

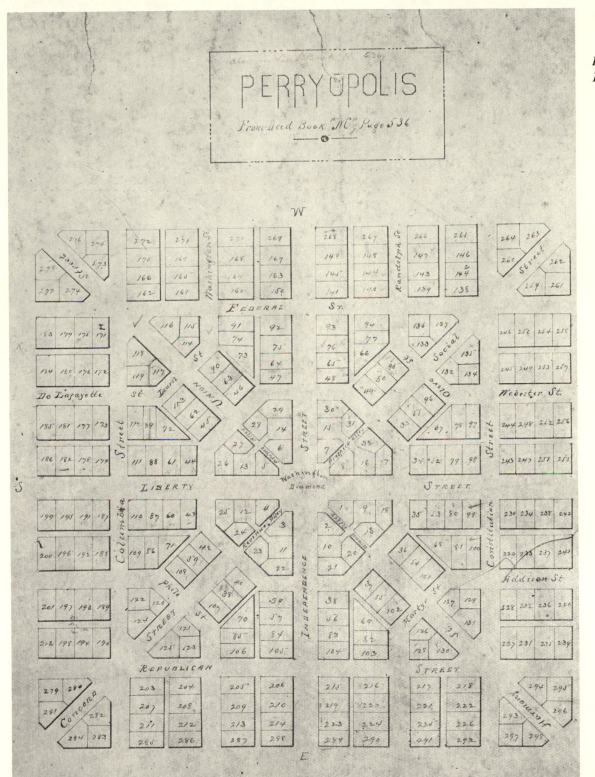

Figure 292. Plan of Perryopolis, Pennsylvania: 1834

actual founding date. The city was named in honor of Commodore Perry and was laid out in 1814 by one William Griffith, surveyor. Whether the peculiar plan was his idea or the inspiration of one of the three proprietors is not known. A cherished local legend is that the plan was suggested by George Washington, who once owned the land on which the city is located. Since he disposed of his interest in 1794, it seems highly unlikely that Washington had anything to do with the town's layout. Certainly the street names carry out the patriotic theme, with Constitution, Independence, Columbia, Liberty, Union, Federal, and Republican figuring prominently. Washington was remembered twice, with Washington Street and the name of the central square as Washington Diamond.

The town today is going through a minor renaissance, the result of an unusual bequest of $1,500,000 by Mrs. Mary Fuller Frazier. Mrs. Frazier left the town in 1887, returned only once in the 61 years before her death in 1948, and earned the reputation of being something of an eccentric. But in her will she remembered the town of her birth, and the interest from the money left in trust is now being used for municipal improvements ranging from a sewage treatment plant to new street lights. Perryopolitans are proud of their unique little city, and their recently prepared general development plan carefully preserves the original street system. In Perryopolis there will be no squaring of the circle.

Perryopolis may have been influenced by Circleville, but a more likely candidate is Lancaster, Ohio, about 25 miles east of Circleville. The original plan was a neat little gridiron with an elongated central square. With the development of one of Ohio's canals paralleling the river, the town experienced a mild boom. South of the original grid and along the banks of the canal a new addition was planned. There was not sufficient room for a full circular development, but a partial system of radial and octagonal streets was platted.

There were two other nineteenth-century cobweb plans in Pennsylvania and Ohio. About 1841 the town of Marienville in north central Pennsylvania was laid out by Cyrus Blood. Eight streets entered the central open space, and connecting them some distance from their intersection was an alley laid out on an octagonal pattern similar to Circle Alley in Circleville.

Somewhat different in plan and for another purpose was the layout platted on a 160-acre tract at the outskirts of Toledo in 1872. Shown in Figure 293, this plan was nothing less than a university city. Here was to be located the Toledo University of Arts and Trades. Academic buildings were to occupy the central circle, named University Place, which had a diameter of 500 feet. Houses for faculty members were to be located in the surrounding blocks. The streets were named for eminent inventors, landscape architects, and painters. Although some construction was begun, Toledo University was built on another site, and today the tract is a city park. One of the diagonal streets and a portion of the inner circle are the only remnants of the original plan.

Double octagons, circles, and octagons—only the hexagon, except as it appeared in Woodward's plan for Detroit, remained unused. Yet in the 1890's this geometric shape, too, became the basis for a city plan. North of San Francisco in the Santa Rosa Valley is Cotati, shown in Figure 294. It was planned by Dr. Thomas S. Page, who was the owner of the Cotati Rancho. In the early 1890's he platted the town in its hexagonal pattern, deeding the central plaza to the county. The six streets forming the boundary of the town lots and connecting the six diagonal streets he named for his six sons. One is tempted to speculate on what the town would have looked like if he had produced a different number of children. The plan appears to better advantage on paper than on the ground, since Cotati today is an unimpressive little hamlet with a weed-grown "plaza," surrounded by unsightly commercial buildings.

Vegetarians, Phrenologists, and Octagons

Mid-nineteenth-century America was the fertile ground from which blossomed the fruits of hundreds of social movements. One of the more exotic of these growths, the Vegetarian Movement, resulted in an attempt to plant a series of octagon cities in Kansas Territory. Vegetarianism flourished in the 1830's and 1840's when thousands of converts, renouncing the consumption of meat, munched dutifully on Sylvester Graham's new bread and devoured vegetables and fruits in increasing quantities. Championed by such intellectuals as Horace Greeley, Graham toured the country advocating his meatless diet as well as such other health measures as the use of hard mattresses and cheerfulness at meal times. But with Graham's death in 1851 the ranks of the vegetarians thinned and the movement began to die.

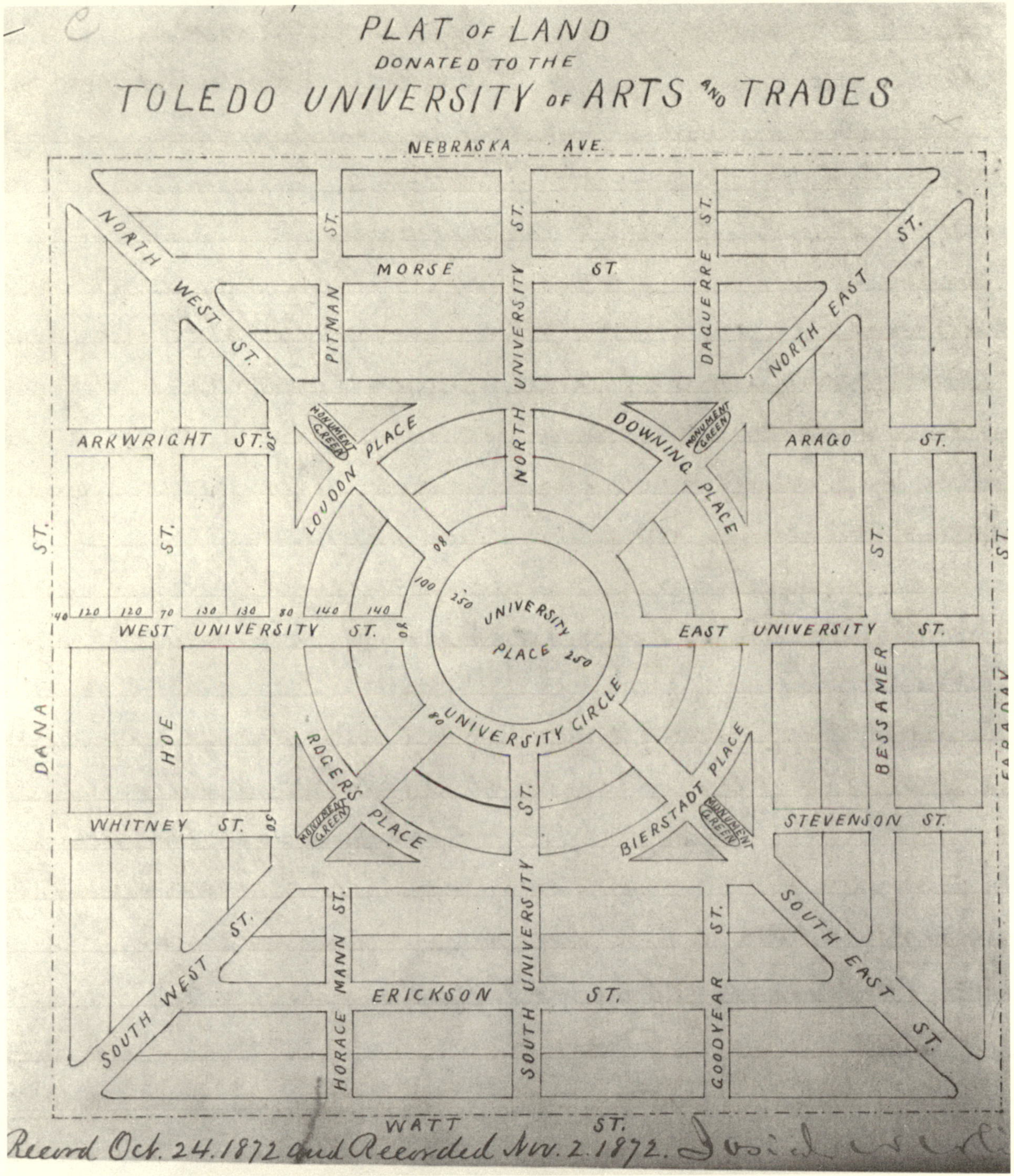

Figure 293. Plan of Proposed Toledo University Community: 1872

Figure 294. Plan of Cotati, California: 1898

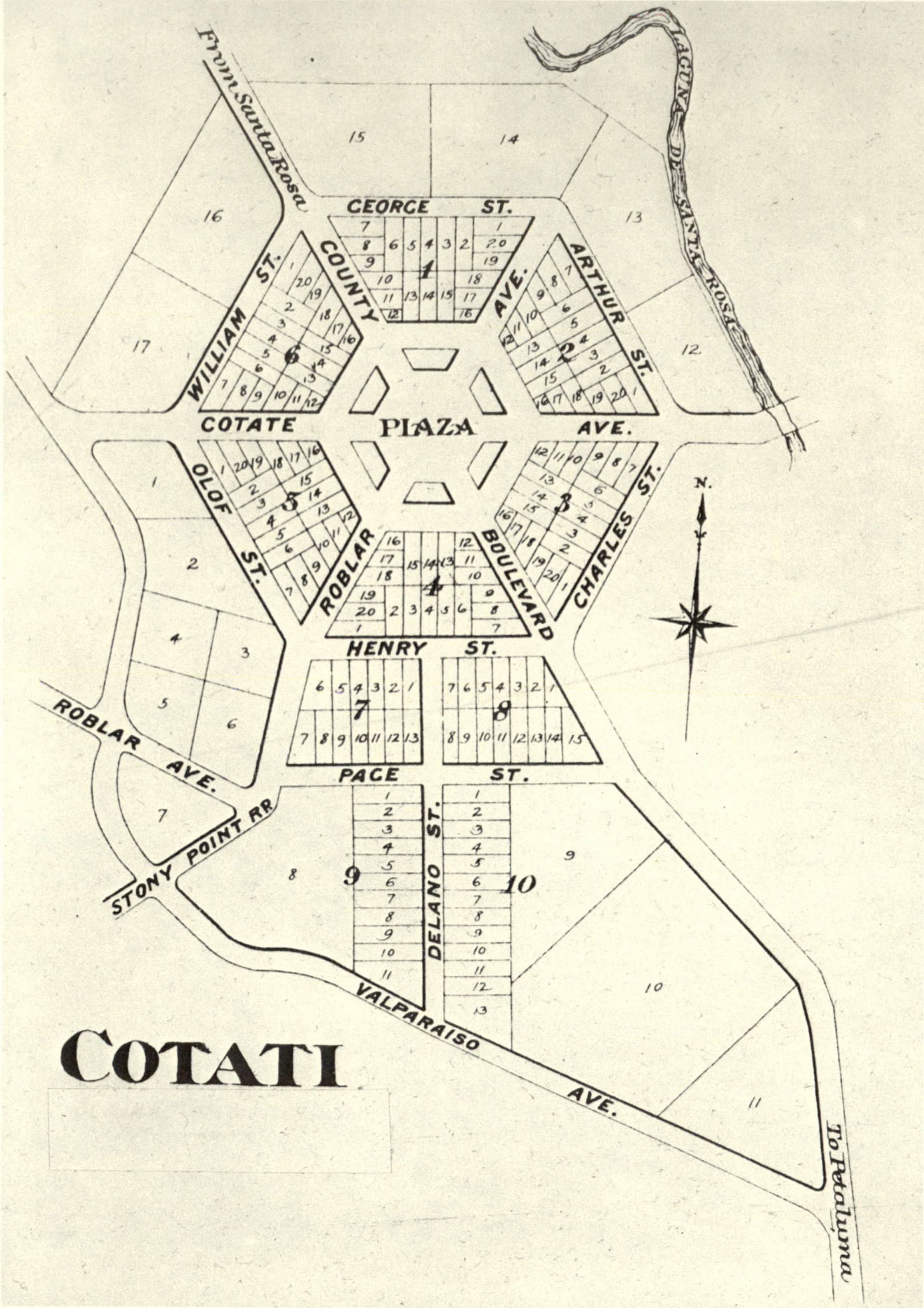

COTATI

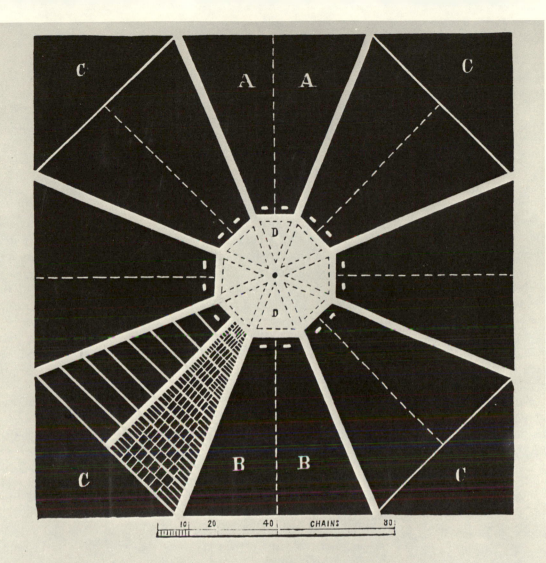

Figure 295. Plan of Octagon City, Kansas: 1856

THE OCTAGON PLAN OF SETTLEMENT.

[See page 5.]

ORIGINATED BY HENRY S. CLUBB

Henry Stephen Clubb, an ardent foe of any food that had once walked or swam, resolved to save his fellow man by establishing a model vegetarian colony from which the true word would be sent until all America was won over to the path of dietary righteousness. Clubb's reform tracts had been distributed by the publishing house of Fowler and Wells of New York. Orson Fowler, one of the publishers, by this time had already won fame as the leading authority on phrenology. By 1850 this science had as much popular acceptance as psychiatry has today, and Fowler was a figure of considerable stature. He had also written a little book advocating the use of the octagonal plan in the construction of houses. The popularity of this work is attested to by the dozens of octagonal houses still to be seen throughout the northeast.

Probably it was from his association with Fowler that Clubb hit upon the plan of using an octagonal layout for the villages that were to be planned. Clubb and his associates issued a prospectus of the settlement plan, including the diagram of a proposed village shown in Figure 295. The village and its surrounding farm lands were to occupy 4 square miles of land. Houses for 16 families would be grouped at the center of the tract on the outside of the octagonal street. Within the octagon the 8 triangular parcels formed by the 8 streets radiating from the center were to be held in common as a village green, as were the 4 triangles at the corners of the tract. Sixteen farms of 102 acres each lay between the diagonal streets.

Clubb envisioned a grouping of identical villages to form a small city. As his prospectus described this scheme: "The plan contemplated by the company embraces an area of four of these octagon villages, forming a city of sixteen square miles, with a square in the centre of 584 acres, to be appropriated to an agricultural college and model-farm, to be cultivated by the students, who will pay for their education by their labor."[26] The pamphlet also stated that two companies had already been formed: The Vegetarian Settlement Company and the Octagon Settlement Company, the latter evidently for those who might surrender to the urge for good red meat now and then.

The place selected for these settlements lay in eastern Kansas where a good deal of colonization by both free-staters and slave-staters had already been undertaken. Clubb announced that subscriptions would be received at the offices of Messrs. Fowler & Wells, and that in 1856 the first group would set out for Kansas. In his efforts to secure subscribers, Clubb was rather incautious in his statements of the facilities that would be provided and waiting for the weary travelers, improvements which were never constructed.

Clubb did not conclude his appeal with the advantages of vegetarianism or the superiority of the octagonal plan. He also held out the probability of vast financial rewards, pointing to the increase in land values that would arise from concentrated settlement in a reasonably compact village. In fact, the settlement prospectus was quite specific on this matter, since it described how the farms could be divided into city blocks and lots. On the diagram two of the farms are shown divided in this manner as an illustration and inducement for potential settlers.

In the spring of 1856 several small groups made the long journey from the east to the Kansas plains. One of these early arrivals, Mrs. Colt, has furnished an account of their first sight of Octagon City:

"We see that the city grounds, which have been surveyed, (and a log cabin built in the centre, where is to stand the large 'central octagon building,') are one mile from here. . . . Two or three families of us, and a few single men, take to our wagons again, drive over the roadless prairie, and around the head of a creek, to become the first residents in the 'Neosho, or Octagon City.' Find the city, as we had seen, to contain only one log cabin, 16 by 16, muddled between the logs on the inside, instead of on the outside; neither door nor window; the roof covered with 'shakes,' (western shingles,) split out of oak I should think, 3½ feet in length, and about as wide as a sheet of foolscap paper."[27]

Thus died the great dream of the octagon cities on the Kansas plains. The promoters were more adept at drawing diagrams and wording their glowing prospectus than in managing the practical affairs of a settlement enterprise. With her lost hopes Mrs. Colt buried her son and her husband who succumbed to the fever, and she returned to New England to publish the diary of her trip.

[26] The text of the prospectus appears in an appendix to Miriam Davis Colt, *Went to Kansas*, Watertown, 1862.

[27] Colt, *Went to Kansas*, 46-47.

CHAPTER 18

Chicago Fair and Capital City: the Rebirth of American Urban Planning

IN 1910 at the first great international meeting of city planners held in London under the sponsorship of the Royal Institute of British Architects, Daniel Burnham summarized the leading events in America during the previous two decades:

"The inception of great planning of public buildings and grounds in the United States was in the World's Fair in Chicago. The beauty of its arrangement and of its building made a profound impression not merely upon the highly educated part of the community, but still more perhaps upon the masses, and this impression has been a lasting one. As a first result of the object lesson the Government took up the torch and proceeded to make a comprehensive plan for the future development of the capital. Since then every considerable town in the country has gone into this study, and there are many hundreds of plan commissions at work at the present time throughout the United States. Then came the plan of Manila. . . . Next came Cleveland, Ohio. . . . Then came San Francisco, where an association of private men undertook to back the work; then Chicago, where the work was undertaken by the Commercial Club, which appointed a committee of fifteen of its members to conduct the enterprise."[1]

If Burnham, somewhat immodestly, cited only those city planning projects for which he had been responsible, he at least presented a true statement of the genesis of modern American planning. For Burnham unquestionably was the towering figure of the period—a gifted designer within the style he chose to adopt, the chosen leader of his associates, and a vigorous champion of civic order and beauty. From the Chicago Fair of 1893 through the Plan of Chicago in 1909 and until his death in 1912 Burnham was the acknowledged authority on city planning during this formative period. If today his plans may seem superficial in many

of their details and appear unrealistic in the magnitude of their proposals, they still stand as monumental essays illustrating magnificently the principles of one type of civic design. Impractical in the immediate sense they certainly were, yet they served their purpose well in supplying a vision of how cities might be replanned, in spurring the leaders of the community to direct their attention to such matters, and in providing an inspiration to all citizens at a time when it was most needed. We should judge Burnham and such lesser planners as Robinson, Brunner, Nolen, and the younger Olmsted, among others, not by how many of their specific proposals were carried out but in the manner by which they planted the seed and cultivated the growth of city planning in the relatively infertile ground of urban America at the beginning of the present century. In this respect the city planners of half a century ago succeeded far better than they may have realized.

This concluding chapter will trace the influences stemming from the Chicago Fair, the earliest attempts at modern city planning in America, and the initial development of the city planning movement. Necessarily this will be brief and provide little more than an outline of the principal events. It will not venture beyond the First World War, for this would exceed the intended scope of the present work and is too closely linked with modern planning activities to permit adequate evaluation.

The White City in Chicago

In the introduction to one of the numerous books published to celebrate the great World's Columbian Exposition held in Chicago in 1893, the president of the Fair Commission, Thomas W. Palmer, wrote these prophetic words:

"As an educational force and inspiration I believe the buildings, their grouping, and laying out of the grounds will in themselves do more good in a general way than the exhibits themselves, by the

---

[1] Daniel H. Burnham, "The City of the Future Under a Democratic Government," Royal Institute of British Architects, *Town Planning Conference Transactions*, London, 1911, pp. 368-78.

exaltation that it will inspire in every man, woman, and child who may have any emotions, and who has none, that may come to view it."[2]

Palmer was right. The Chicago Fair of 1893 changed the architectural taste of the nation and led to a new direction in American city planning. The sight of the gleaming white buildings disposed symmetrically around the formal court of honor, with their domes and columns echoing the classic buildings of antiquity, impressed almost every visitor. In comparison, the earlier Philadelphia exposition of 1876 seemed almost crude and unfinished. And in contrast with the dingy industrial cities of late nineteenth-century America, the Fair seemed a vision of some earthly paradise that might yet be created in the coming era.

The idea of a world exposition to commemorate the four hundredth anniversary of the discovery of America originated as early as 1882 when Dr. T. W. Zaremba suggested it to a group of New York leaders. While there was some interest in the proposal by these persons and later by a few individuals in Chicago, no immediate action was taken. In 1886 Dr. Zaremba renewed his suggestion at the meeting of the American Historical Society in Washington. The society established a committee to meet with the president and obtain his support. A number of cities, including Philadelphia, Chicago, and Washington expressed interest. Senator Cullom of Illinois in 1889 introduced a bill in the Senate providing for such an exposition, and, while this met with general approval, the location of the fair became a matter of bitter controversy. Finally, on February 24, 1890, Congress designated Chicago as the site. A national commission was formed with financial assistance from the city of Chicago and the state of Illinois.

The exact location of the exposition site in Chicago was not fixed. Frederick Law Olmsted was retained to advise on sites, and, after reviewing seven possibilities, he recommended the Jackson Park location. Before arriving at his recommendation Olmsted consulted Daniel H. Burnham, then in his early forties and already perhaps the leading Chicago architect. With his partner, John Root, he had designed such important structures as the Monadnock Building and the Masonic Temple in Chicago, a great many houses for members of Chicago society, and numerous railway

[2] Ben C. Truman, *History of The World's Fair*, Chicago (?), 1893, p. 19.

stations, banks, and office buildings elsewhere in the midwest. While their work was somewhat more conventional in design than such pioneers of the modern movement as Adler and Sullivan or Jenney and Mundie, their early buildings must be listed among those of the so-called Chicago School that paved the way to contemporary design. Indeed, from the time of the Chicago fire in 1871 to the Fair of 1893 hardly a major downtown building in Chicago showed more than superficial attempts to incorporate classical motifs. Most of them exhibited great originality in coping with the unfamiliar architectural problem of the design of tall office blocks on rather restricted sites. The result of this twenty years of building and expansion was a collection of buildings that expressed not only the new structural methods of the steel frame but the vigor and energy of a thriving commercial city.

Olmsted was retained as consulting landscape architect, A. Gottlieb was appointed consulting engineer, and Burnham and Root were designated consulting architects. Later the firm of Burnham and Root resigned; Burnham became Chief of Construction and later Director of Works, and Root served as consulting architect until his untimely death early in 1891. With Harry Codman, Olmsted's partner, this group was responsible for the general plan of the site and the location and size of the principal buildings.

Olmsted was familiar with Jackson Park because he had prepared a plan for its ultimate development several years before. Little had been done then, and this land along the lake shore remained much as he had found it previously. Three ridges of sandbars ran parallel with the shore. These and the marshy land between them were subject to floods, and the soil was almost saturated when the lake was at normal level. Olmsted and Codman quickly saw that a series of canals bordered by retaining walls along their banks and with the intervening spaces filled and piled for building sites would be the most feasible solution. At the outset, therefore, the formal nature of the ultimate plan was virtually dictated by the nature of the site.

No doubt the plans of the Philadelphia exposition fifteen years earlier were reviewed. It was obvious that the almost haphazard placement of buildings there should be avoided. Although there is no record of it being studied, the great Paris Exposition of 1889 could hardly have been overlooked. A view of that fair is

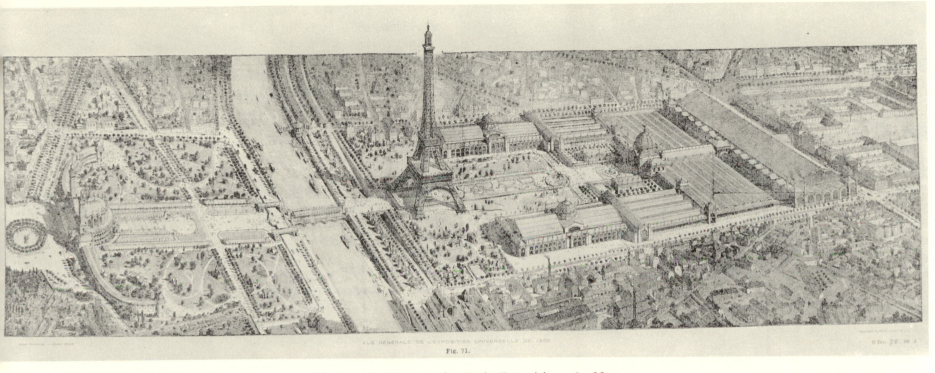

VUE GÉNÉRALE DE L'EXPOSITION UNIVERSELLE DE 1889
Fig. 71.

Figure 296. View of the Paris Exposition of 1889

reproduced in Figure 296. As at the earlier Paris Exposition in 1878 and that at Vienna in 1873, a symmetrical, formal layout was adopted, and, although the Eiffel Tower constituted a modern departure, the buildings themselves were of classical style and fronted a formal central mall.

A number of preliminary and very general schemes were prepared for the Chicago Fair, but time was pressing, and the National Commission urgently requested a final plan. Late in 1890, following a meeting of the design group, John Root hurriedly sketched a rough plan in pencil on brown paper. This was submitted along with some preliminary specifications and was adopted by the commission on December 1, 1890. Apparently the essential elements of the final plan appeared on this early sketch: the formal canal and great basin with an adjoining court, all surrounded by the

principal buildings, and beyond, the irregular lagoon with its informal island park separating the major structures from numerous minor buildings and state exhibits. The final plan appears in Figure 297, although it should be remembered that its details were not worked out until many months after Root's sketch of 1890.

At the time of the preliminary sketch no decision had been reached on the architectural style to be employed. According to Charles Moore, Root, the architectural consultant, favored the use of a variety of styles and the introduction of a variety of colors. Following the adoption of the general plan, Burnham, Root, Olmsted, and Gottlieb proposed to the Grounds and Buildings Committee that architects be selected to design the principal buildings. Burnham was subsequently authorized to do so and asked the following architects to participate: Richard Hunt; McKim, Mead

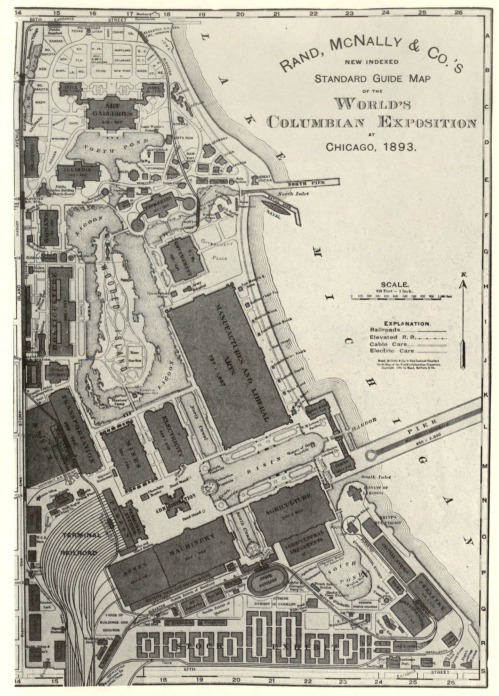

Figure 297. Plan of the World's Columbian Exposition in Chicago, Illinois: 1893

& White; and George B. Post, all of New York; Peabody & Stearns, of Boston; and Van Brunt & Howe, of Kansas City. In his letter inviting acceptance of this commission, Burnham wrote: "The Committee are disposed to leave the methods of designing to the five architects, and you may determine among yourselves whether to make a joint design of the whole as one, or each to take up separate parts to be modified to meet such views as shall be expressed in your conferences from time to time."[3]

The New York and Boston group held a preliminary meeting to discuss the proposal. According to William Mead it was generally agreed that the classic style should be adopted, although he does not record who introduced the idea. Probably the Paris Exposition exerted as powerful an influence on the style of architecture as has already been suggested that it had on the site plan. When Burnham came east to discuss the project with the architects, the general character of the five main buildings had thus already been established.

Five Chicago architects were then chosen to design other major structures. On January 10, 1891, the first meeting of the entire group took place in the office of Burnham and Root. After some preliminary discussion, individual buildings were assigned to the ten firms. The original site plan was reviewed and the sizes of the buildings, court, and canals agreed to. The height of a uniform cornice line was also established. Another meeting was scheduled for February at which time preliminary sketches were to be presented. Joining them at this time was the sculptor, Augustus Saint-Gaudens, who had come at the invitation of Burnham to advise on sculptural decoration and to help select the artists who were to execute the statues and fountains.

Burnham's account of this meeting reveals some of the events that took place:

"We had a breakfast for the visiting men. They were filled with enthusiasm. Charles McKim, with a good deal of repressed excitement, broke out, saying: 'Bob Peabody wants to carry a canal down between our buildings.' I said I would agree to that, even though it would cost something. . . . Next, Saint-Gaudens took a hand. He said the east end of the composition should be

[3] Letter from Burnham, December 12, 1890, in Charles Moore, *Daniel Burnham Architect Planner of Cities*, Boston, 1921, I, 40-41. Moore's two-volume study of Burnham and his work is thorough and well documented.

bound together architecturally. All agreed. He suggested a statue backed by thirteen columns, typifying the thirteen original States. All hailed this as a bully thing."[4]

A day or two later another meeting was held. Each architect exhibited sketches of his proposed building. First Hunt showed his Administration Building with its enormous dome. Then Post revealed his sketch for the Manufacturers and Liberal Arts Building. As Burnham tells it:

"George Post had a dome four hundred and fifty feet high. When they saw that dome a murmur ran around the group. George turned about, saying, 'I don't think I shall advocate that dome; probably I shall modify the building.' Charles McKim had a portico extending out over the terrace. It was extremely prominent. He did not wait as George had done, but explained that the portico had merely been under consideration and that he should withdraw it to the face of the building."[5]

So, one by one, the proposals were exhibited, discussed, and revisions agreed to where the composition as a whole would be improved and greater unity of design achieved. At the end of the long day, after all the plans had been exhibited, Burnham records that Saint-Gaudens, who had not said a word, ". . . came over to me, and taking both my hands said, 'Look here, old fellow, do you realize that this is the greatest meeting of artists since the fifteenth century!' "[6]

So it went through dozens of meetings and conferences, sometimes with the entire group, at other times in individual discussions by Burnham with the designers of single buildings. Charles Atwood was brought in to replace Root and contributed the design of the Art Building, the Peristyle between the basin and the lake, and a number of less important structures. The painters and sculptors who soon began to arrive added a Bohemian atmosphere to the project. Burnham himself spent most of his time in a rough shelter on the site. Here almost every night architects and artists met for dinner, talked far into the night, and then retired on cots. If it was not the greatest meeting of artists since the fifteenth century, it most certainly was the nearest thing to it that nineteenth-century America could furnish.

Despite the financial panic, the Fair opened in 1893 as scheduled and was an immediate success, at least as judged by popular acclaim, local enthusiasm, and national and international publicity. The high regard for Burnham by his professional peers was demonstrated by his election to the presidency of the American Institute of Architects, who convened their annual meeting in Chicago during July 1893. Yet there were dissenting views. Most critical of all was Louis Sullivan, the champion of architectural form that reflected the function of a building and its basic structural system. Sullivan had rebelled from the first at the decision to adopt the classical style. Of the major buildings only his Transportation Building escaped the coating of white stucco and paint that was finally adopted for the other buildings when no agreement could be reached on a plan for harmonized colors. In the bitterness of his old age Sullivan penned this evaluation of the effect of the Fair on American architecture:

"The virus of the World's Fair, after a period of incubation in the architectural profession and in the population at large, especially the influential, began to show unmistakable signs of the nature of the contagion. There came a violent outbreak of the Classic and the Renaissance in the East, which slowly spread westward, contaminating all that it touched. . . . Thus Architecture died in the land of the free and the home of the brave,—in a land declaring its fervid democracy, its inventiveness, its resourcefulness, its unique daring, enterprise and progress. Thus did the virus of a culture, snobbish and alien to the land, perform its work of disintegration; and thus ever works the pallid academic mind. . . .

"The damage wrought by the World's Fair will last for half a century from its date, if not longer. It has penetrated deep into the constitution of the American mind, effecting there lesions significant of dementia."[7]

But Sullivan's was a minority voice, joined by only a few other dissenters. More typical was the ecstatic view of a *Harper's Magazine* writer after her first view of the grounds:

"The fair! The fair! Never had the name such significance before. Fairest of all the World's present sights it is. A city of palaces set in spaces of emerald, reflected in shining lengths of water

[4] As quoted in Moore, *Daniel Burnham*, I, 46.
[5] *ibid.*, 47.   [6] *ibid.*

[7] Louis Sullivan, *The Autobiography of an Idea* (New York, 1924), new ed., New York, 1956, pp. 324-25.

which stretch in undulating lines under flat arches of marble bridges and along banks planted with consummate skill."[8]

The architectural style, the harmonious groupings of large building masses, the creation of unified and enclosed civic spaces—all these features excited and impressed the thousands who came to Chicago and stepped into this environment, so novel to America. What matter that the buildings were but temporary, that they constituted but an elaborate stage setting; for a time at least the illusion of reality had been created.

The perspective view of the Fair looking from Lake Michigan, reproduced in Figure 298 conveys something of the overwhelming scale and grandeur which the visitor encountered. This great formal composition with its strong axial relationships echoed in white plaster the noble cities of the ancient world. Thousands came and were impressed by the contrast between this gleaming, magical vision and the dingy, formless cities of industrial America.

The White City, as it came to be called, was not a real urban community. A few years were to pass before its design philosophy and its use of Renaissance planning devices found expression in true city planning. The Fair exerted its initial influence on architectural design, with the deadening results that Sullivan so caustically but accurately described. In less than a decade, however, the same design elements employed at the Fair and used by the same hands were applied in the replanning of an important American city.

Washington: A Century and a Decade after L'Enfant

By a coincidence which was to have profound influence on the subsequent course of American city planning, it was in the Washington of L'Enfant that the new doctrines of monumental planning were first carried out. Because the principles of Renaissance planning were so easily revived in this city, since its basic framework had been conceived in that spirit, the impression was soon created that these planning concepts could be successfully adopted elsewhere. Moreover, as Washington was the capital of the nation and the second city for all Americans wherever their place of residence,

the revised plan for the city attracted the immediate attention of the entire nation.

December 1900 was the centenary of the city of Washington as the seat of national government. Many persons both in and out of government advanced suggestions for the construction of some large building or memorial to commemorate the occasion. On this matter no agreement could be reached, and the year arrived with no specific project authorized.[9]

One interested party was Glenn Brown, secretary of the American Institute of Architects, whose office was in Washington and who was deeply interested in the history of the city. Brown arranged for the annual meeting of the Institute to be held in Washington in the centennial year and established as its theme the beautification of the Capitol. Such leading designers as Cass Gilbert, C. Howard Walker, Joseph C. Hornblower, Frederick Law Olmsted, Jr., and H. K. Bush Brown delivered papers on the grouping of government buildings, principles of monumental landscape design, the place of sculpture in the national capital, and related matters.

Attention naturally centered on the area occupied by the principal public buildings. Several plans for the redevelopment of this portion of the city were put forward for discussion. One of these, the plan by Cass Gilbert, appears in Figure 299. Gilbert's scheme, like others presented at the convention, anticipated several features of later official proposals. He suggested a formal treatment for the mall west of the Smithsonian Institution. A major avenue was to lead from the Capitol to the Washington Monument. While the monument was slightly off the Capitol axis, Gilbert felt that by tilting the axis of his composition slightly this minor deviation would not be noticed. The White House axis presented a more serious problem, since the monument had been built well to the east. Gilbert solved this by providing a second monument equidistant from the White House axis and located to the west. To terminate the vista from the White House he suggested a museum of history flanked by two smaller buildings and standing at one end of a circular formal garden. A large reviewing ground was to be located beyond the monument as part of the formal treatment

[8] Candace Wheeler, "A Dream City," *Harper's New Monthly Magazine*, LXXXVI (1893), 833.

[9] See the volume compiled by William V. Cox, *Celebration of the One Hundredth Anniversary of the Establishment of the Seat of Government in the District of Columbia*, Washington, 1901.

Figure 298. View of the World's Columbian Exposition in Chicago, Illinois: 1893

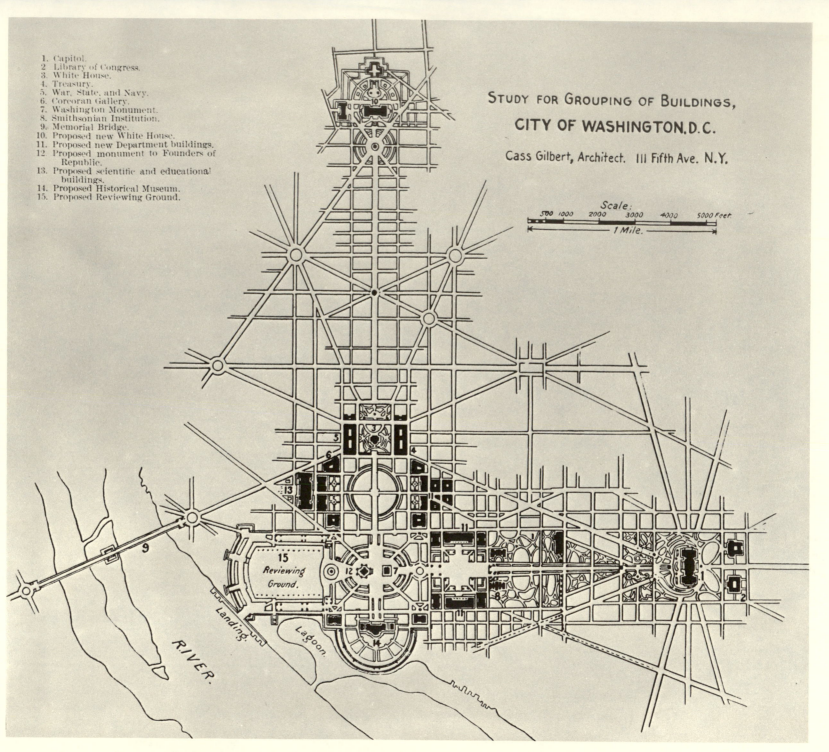

1. Capitol.
2. Library of Congress.
3. White House.
4. Treasury.
5. War, State, and Navy.
6. Corcoran Gallery.
7. Washington Monument.
8. Smithsonian Institution.
9. Memorial Bridge.
10. Proposed new White House.
11. Proposed new Department buildings.
12. Proposed monument to Founders of Republic.
13. Proposed scientific and educational buildings.
14. Proposed Historical Museum.
15. Proposed Reviewing Ground.

STUDY FOR GROUPING OF BUILDINGS,

CITY OF WASHINGTON. D.C.

Cass Gilbert, Architect. III Fifth Ave. N.Y.

Scale:
500 1000 2000 3000 4000 5000 Feet
1 Mile.

Figure 299. Cass Gilbert's Plan for the Mall and Central Washington, D.C.: 1900

of the mall. Around the mall and White House grounds Gilbert grouped the major buildings of the government.[10]

The papers presented at this meeting attracted wide attention, and not only from members of the architectural profession. Through his secretary, Dr. Charles Moore, Senator James Mc-Millan of Michigan learned of the interest of the Institute and its members. McMillan, senator from Michigan, was the Chairman of the Senate Committee on the District of Columbia and would become the political figure behind whom rallied those concerned with the improvement of the city of Washington. Moore acted as go-between, strategist, confidential adviser, and skilled publicist.

Early in March 1901 the Senate authorized the District Committee to study and prepare plans for the improvement of the park system of the District of Columbia and to employ such experts as might be needed. On March 19 a subcommittee met with representatives of the American Institute of Architects to discuss how these plans might best be prepared. As a result of these discussions, Daniel Burnham and Frederick Law Olmsted, Jr., were selected for what became known as the Senate Park Commission. They were given authority to add to their number and within a short time asked Charles F. McKim and, later, Augustus St. Gaudens to serve with them. Thus once again three of the leading members of the Chicago Fair group, together with the younger Olmsted, became associated in a project of enormous scale and of great importance.

The approach of the park commission to their great work was interesting. In April 1901 Burnham announced to his colleagues: "I have talked the matter over with Senator McMillan. The four of us are going to Europe in June to see and to discuss *together* parks in their relations to public buildings—that is our problem here in Washington and we must have weeks when we are thinking of nothing else."[11]

After a preliminary trip to visit estates in Virginia and to inspect Williamsburg, Burnham, McKim, Olmsted, and Moore sailed for Europe in June; St. Gaudens, who had just been added to the commission, did not accompany the group because of ill health. With

them they took maps, drawings, and photographs of Washington and such preliminary plans as they had been able to prepare. Between visits to the principal parks and buildings in Paris, Rome, Venice, Budapest, Frankfurt, Berlin, and London, they reviewed the problems confronting them in Washington and discussed and sketched tentative design solutions. In the seven weeks the little group spent together the revised plan for Washington thus took shape in the shadows of some of the same examples of monumental civic design that had inspired L'Enfant himself.

Replanning the center of Washington depended in large part on the treatment of the grounds stretching from the Capitol westward to the Potomac. L'Enfant had clearly intended this as a vast formal mall having a width in scale with its great length and lined with important buildings. In the more than one hundred years that had passed since his plan was adopted for the city this great central axis had remained little more than an open pasture bordered by the canal. One serious attempt at replanning the area took place in 1851, when President Millard Fillmore commissioned Andrew Jackson Downing to prepare a design for the mall. Downing's plan, reproduced in Figure 300, brought about a number of changes, but the result was a series of unrelated informal parks and groves that failed to provide the unity of design that L'Enfant had envisaged.

The location of the Washington Monument in this area presented special difficulties because, as has already been mentioned, it had been built on the axis of neither the White House nor the Capitol. A more serious and certainly incongruous element, and obviously the most difficult to rectify, was the rail line of the Baltimore and Potomac which, by act of Congress in 1872, had been allowed to cross the mall on grade at 6th Street. To compound this blunder Congress also granted a site for the railroad station on the mall itself lying west of 6th Street. This discordant feature can be seen in Figure 301, which shows a portion of a model of central Washington which the Senate Park Commission had prepared.

While still in Europe the commission members met with President Cassatt of the Pennsylvania Railroad, which operated the Baltimore and Potomac line and which had just acquired controlling interest in the Baltimore and Ohio. The latter line had already received permission to construct its new station north of the Capitol. Burnham, as architect for the proposed new Baltimore and

[10] For Gilbert's proposal and others presented at the 1900 meeting of the American Institute of Architects, see Glenn Brown (comp.), *Papers Relating to the Improvement of the City of Washington*, Washington, 1901.

[11] As quoted in Moore, *Daniel Burnham*, I, 142.

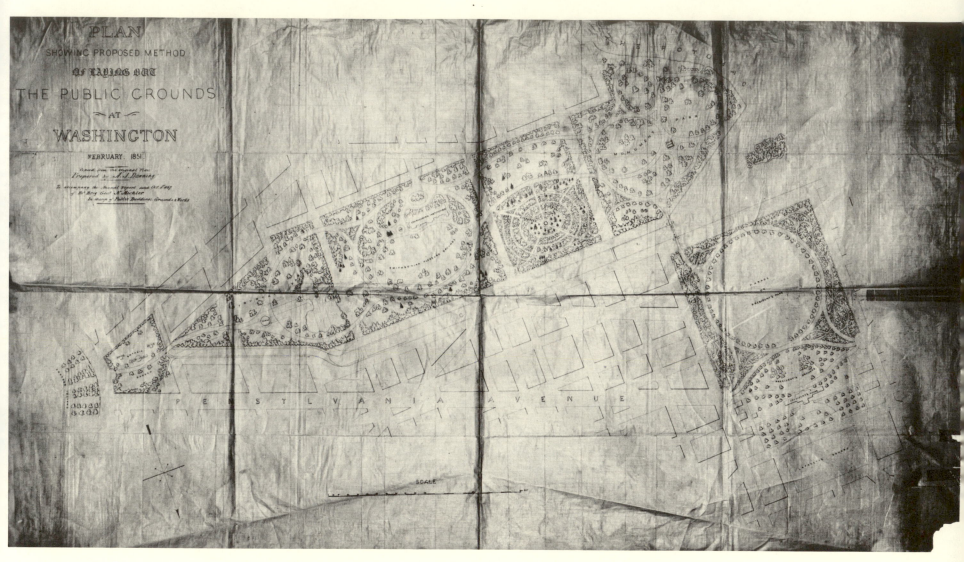

Figure 300. Downing's Plan for the Mall in Washington, D.C.: 1851

Figure 301. Model of the Capitol in Washington, D.C. and Surrounding Area in 1901

Potomac station, had already urged the withdrawal of the line from the mall and the construction of its new station to the south. Cassatt, however, proposed a bolder move. He indicated his willingness to combine with the Baltimore and Ohio in a union station north of the Capitol if the government would pay a portion of the cost of the tunnel necessary to reach the station site from the south. Here was the key to the replanning of the mall.[12]

When the commission returned from Europe on August 1, after seven weeks of travel, discussion, and sketching, the main elements of their plan had been generally decided. Much hard work remained in translating these broad decisions into design specifications. In New York, above the architectural offices of McKim, Mead, and White, the commission established a drafting room and design studio. McKim, who initially with characteristic modesty had suggested that his role would be minor, found himself inevitably the key figure in the commission's work. Burnham, Olmsted, and St. Gaudens were, of course, consulted, and on occasion all the members of the commission met for discussions. The evidence is clear, however, that the park commission plans for central Washington owe their inspiration largely to Charles McKim.

By December the text of the report, prepared by Moore and Olmsted, had been unanimously approved, and on January 15, 1902, the proposals were made public. Under McKim's direction some two hundred drawings, photographs, and models were arranged for display at the Corcoran Gallery of Art. As Moore records the momentous occasion:

"Senator McMillan, Senator Gallinger, and other members of the Senate Committee on the District of Columbia received the guests. There came President Roosevelt, interested, curious, at first critical and then, as the great consistent scheme dawned on him, highly appreciative. Secretary Root had been consulted from the inception of the work. Secretary John Hay was especially interested in the location and design of the memorial to Lincoln. . . . Secretary Hitchcock was particularly interested in the fountains, the play of waters recalling Versailles and Peterhof. There were senators and members of the House, and a few other invited guests."[13]

[12] Charles Moore, *The Life and Times of Charles Follen McKim*, Boston, 1929, p. 198. Chapter xv of this work is particularly valuable for its account of the commission's European tour.

[13] Moore, *Daniel Burnham*, I, 167-68.

The "great consistent scheme" as shown in plan and perspective drawings from the commission's report appears in Figures 302 and 303. The mall, extended, strengthened, and replanned, provided the feature around which the commission fashioned its plan for central Washington. By tilting the Capitol axis of the mall very slightly, much as Cass Gilbert and others had suggested, the commission recaptured the original L'Enfant concept. The Washington Monument became the center of this realigned axis, which was extended beyond the monument to the banks of the Potomac.

The formal character of the mall was to be emphasized by two lines of elms to be planted in rows of four on either side. This would confine the views down its center and strengthen the axial effect. Figure 304 shows how the commission proposed to treat the mall and its termination near the Capitol. Here was to be located a great plaza containing equestrian statues of Generals Grant, Sherman, and Sheridan—a proposal which has now largely been realized.

The commission proposed special treatment for the Washington monument. A formal, terraced base to be reached from the west by a wide flight of steps would stress the monumental character of the mighty shaft. Surrounding this area was to be a formal walled garden to function as a suitable enclosure from which the monument could be viewed at close hand. Figure 305 shows the commission's proposals and also indicates their suggestions for locating major buildings along the mall.

Owing to the location of the Washington Monument well to the east of the White House axis, the commission plan provided a substitute termination of the view south from the White House. The perspective drawing reproduced in Figure 303 shows a group of buildings directly south of the presidential mansion at the end of a short, wide mall. The view from the White House past the Washington Monument to this proposed memorial building complex is shown in Figure 306. This site is now occupied by the Jefferson Memorial.

Beyond the Washington Monument to the west the commission proposed to extend the mall axis on land reclaimed from the Potomac River. Here they planned the Lincoln Memorial. It would be approached from Virginia by a new bridge with the Lincoln Memorial at one end of its axis and the Lee Mansion in Arlington Cemetery at the other. Between the Washington Monument and

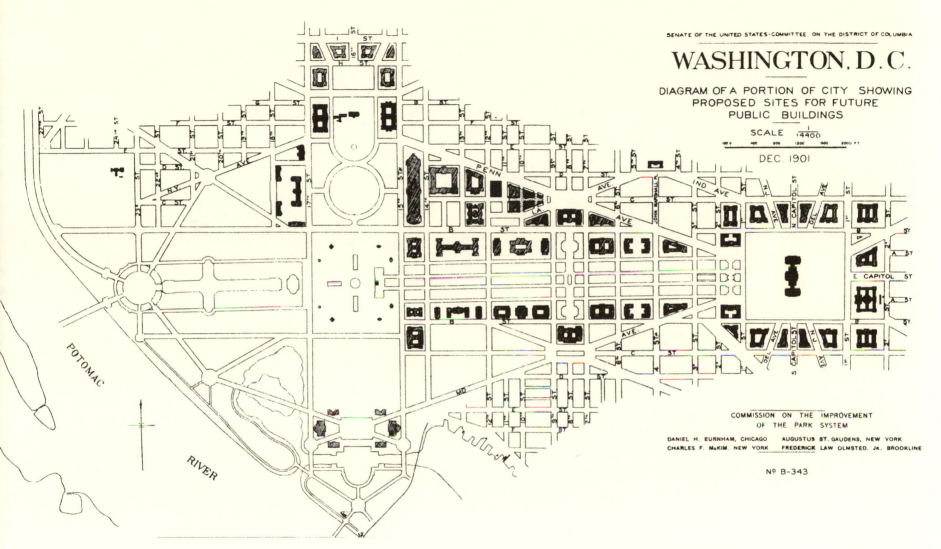

Figure 302. The Senate Park Commission Plan for Central Washington, D.C.: 1901

Figure 303. The Senate Park Commission Proposals for Central Washington, D.C.: 1901

*Figure 304. The Senate Park Commission Proposals for the Approaches to the
Capitol in Washington, D.C.: 1901*

*Figure 305. The Senate Park Commission Proposals for the Washington Monument
Terrace and the Mall in Washington, D.C.: 1901*

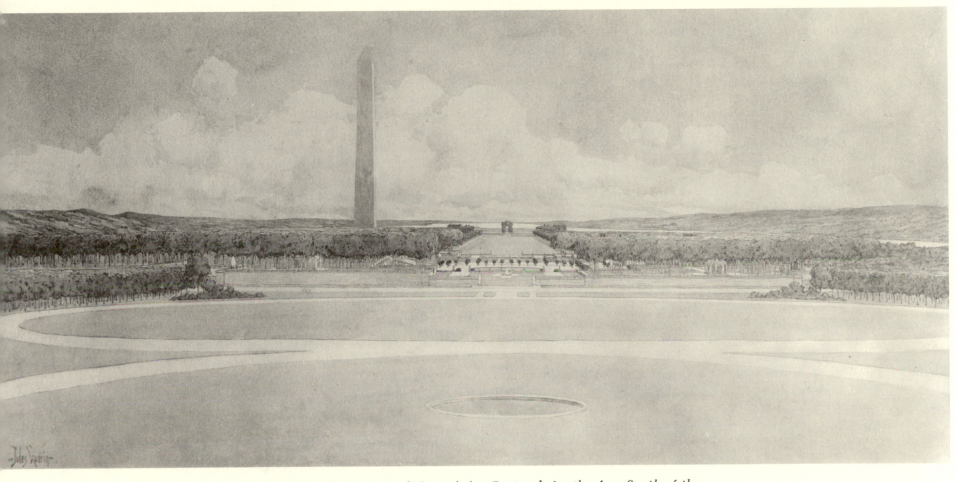

Figure 306. The Senate Park Commission Proposals for the Area South of the White House in Washington, D.C.: 1901

the Lincoln Memorial the commission proposed a long, shallow reflecting pool with a formal park on either side, much like the similar composition at Versailles. Here, again with but minor changes in detail, the commission's plan has been carried out.

In addition to the sites along the mall, public buildings were to be grouped in three areas: surrounding the Capitol, in the triangle between the mall and Pennsylvania Avenue, and flanking the White House and around the adjoining Lafayette Square. These locations can be seen in Figure 302. The modern visitor to Washington will find that these recommendations, too, have been followed.

There were, of course, many other features of the plan, which embraced all of the park lands of the district, including nearly two thousand acres of land recently acquired in the Rock Creek area. The commission's report contained recommendations for the treatment of this land as well as suggestions for further acquisitions to connect existing parks and to provide additional recreation facilities. It also suggested principles to be followed in siting buildings, statues, and monuments, and the general embellishment of the city. For its time the commission's report was a major achievement and may still be read with profit as a remarkable essay in civic beautification and the handling of monumental settings for public buildings.[14]

The McMillan Commission plan attracted widespread interest and attention. Not only the journals of architecture in this country and abroad but popular magazines and newspapers reviewed the proposals and reprinted the maps and drawings from the report. This publicity was overwhelmingly favorable and came at a time when improvement and reform activities in other fields had already caught the public fancy. It was entirely natural that to the enthusiasm for trust-busting, overcoming graft and corruption in city government, and alleviating a variety of social ills should be added excitement about remaking the dingy industrial cities of America to a new pattern. The plan for Washington devised by McKim and his colleagues provided the model for other cities to imitate. A wave of enthusiasm for civic planning and beautification swept the country, and soon groups of business men and civic leaders in major cities began to discuss the possibilities of preparing such a plan for their own communities.

[14] *Report of the Park Commission to the Senate Committee on the District of Columbia*, Senate Report No. 166, Fifty-Seventh Congress, First Session, Washington, 1902.

That the cost of such planning and much of the responsibility for carrying out any resulting proposals was logically a task for city government was usually overlooked. The prevailing attitude was that the city government was too dishonest or inefficient or apathetic for such a project, and, in any event, the local officials could be persuaded by one means or another that plans prepared under private auspices should be followed. Local administration was thus viewed with both distrust and disgust by men of means and influence. Clearly the way to accomplish planning was to retain one of the half-dozen persons with some competence in the field, pay them to prepare a city plan, and worry later about how it would be received by local officials.

It must be admitted that, in this line of reasoning, there was more than a grain of truth. The history of municipal government is full of similar examples where a new service was first provided by wholly private groups and only later accepted as a proper function of government itself. Thus, when private business or civic betterment groups underwrote the costs of the early city plans they were following a long tradition in American municipal affairs, and one which was perhaps quite inevitable. While in an important sense the plans produced under such sponsorship were almost always unrealistic, at least they laid the foundation for modern planning which combines governmental support and somewhat broader citizen participation.

The Haussmanns of Urban America

Early in 1902 Burnham visited San Francisco as the architect for the Merchants Exchange Building. At that time he agreed to prepare a plan for the city. In the following year the Association for the Improvement and Adornment of San Francisco was formed by a number of leading citizens. Other groups, including the Outdoor Art League and the California chapter of the American Institute of Architects, indicated their interest and intention to cooperate. The work was begun in the fall of 1904. Burnham volunteered his services, stipulating only that a cottage and work rooms be built for him on the side of Twin Peaks, from which he commanded a view of the entire city. While the published report is dated 1905, the actual presentation of the plan was made by Burnham on May 21, 1906. Printed copies of the report are now com-

Figure 307. Daniel Burnham's Plan for San Francisco, California: 1905

Figure 308. View of the Burnham Proposals for San Francisco, California: 1905

paratively rare, since most of them were destroyed in the great earthquake and fire a month before the presentation.

This vast destruction of the city presented an almost unparalleled opportunity to rebuild along the lines suggested by Burnham. Perhaps if the plan had appeared many months before and had been generally understood this would indeed have occurred. As it turned out, so little was known about the proposals and so imperative did the need for rebuilding appear that the Burnham plan was almost entirely ignored. As in the case of London two and a half centuries earlier, a unique opportunity for civic improvement was thus forever lost.

Burnham's plan is revealing and foreshadows the greater contribution he was soon to make in Chicago. Here and in Manila,

the plan for which was completed and submitted to the Secretary of War in June 1905, Burnham was testing the principles of planning applied first at the Chicago Fair and then in the city of Washington. The plan for Washington had been limited to proposed improvements of parks and public buildings. There the L'Enfant street pattern provided a suitable framework for the monumental grouping of buildings and the formal gardens, monuments, and mall. San Francisco, however, was a gridiron city, and the effects to which Burnham was committed could not be achieved with such a street system. He proposed nothing less than a reshaping of the basic street layout in order to provide new vistas, grand boulevards, and magnificent plazas.

Figure 307 shows the general plan for the city. Burnham's perspective drawing showing the effect of these proposed changes is reproduced in Figure 308. The general character of Burnham's work is clearly evident. In each major sector of the city he introduced a system of diagonals. Where they met or at the intersections of the diagonals and existing major streets or boulevards, squares, ovals, or circles were to be created.

The plan of the proposed civic center appears in Figure 309. Here, instead of a closely grouped complex of buildings, Burnham suggested a much looser arrangement. The existing city hall was to be retained, but with views opened to it and its commanding dome. New buildings on large, open plazas were to be provided at intervals of several blocks, with all these sites connected by imposing boulevards.

The plan also called for a vast increase in land set aside for parks, playgrounds, and reservations. Land to be acquired in order to carry out the Burnham proposals is shown on Figure 310, which reveals the scope of the entire program. That practically none of the proposals was carried out was due in part to the date the plan was released, as has already been explained, but the plan itself disregarded the limitations of finances and energy that could be marshalled for such an undertaking. Burnham's San Francisco plan has more merit as an abstract design than as a serious proposal for public improvement. The obsession with diagonal boulevards which was to affect most of the planners of the day led Burnham to make proposals for new streets whose only apparent function was to complete a symmetrical pattern. Burnham himself admitted, perhaps unconsciously, his limited views of the scope of city planning when he wrote in the introduction to the report, "A city plan must ever deal mainly with the direction and width of its streets."[15]

In the Chicago plan of 1909, however, Burnham demonstrated a greater understanding of city planning. This was his unquestioned masterwork, and he entered into it as much with his heart as with his brain. No other achievement, with the possible exception of the Fair, gave him as much satisfaction as this comprehensive plan for his native city. With all the weaknesses which the modern critic, having the advantage of time, may be able to discover, the Chicago plan remains one of the great accomplishments of American planning. Coming as it did at the very threshold of

[15] Daniel H. Burnham, assisted by Edward H. Bennett, *Report on a Plan for San Francisco*, San Francisco, 1905, p. 36.

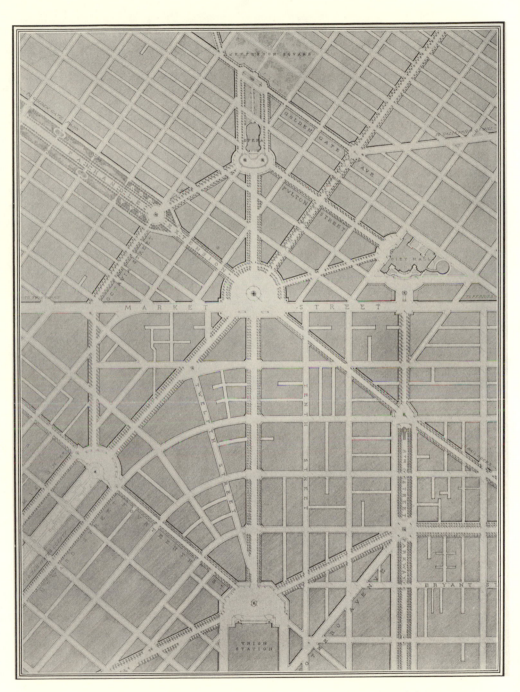

Figure 309. Burnham's Plan for the San Francisco, California Civic Center: 1905

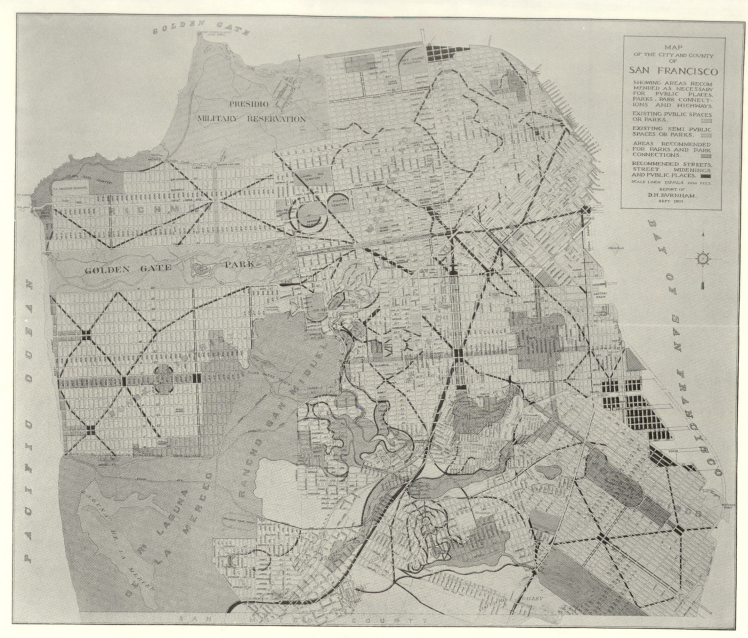

Figure 310. The Burnham Plan for San Francisco, California: Streets, Public Spaces, and Parks: 1905

the modern era, it at once established a high technical standard toward which other and later planners might strive and at the same time it aroused and stimulated laymen not only in Chicago but through the country.

As in San Francisco, Burnham donated his services as a public contribution. The salaries of his associates and the expenses for the operation of the office were borne by the Commercial Club, an organization of leading merchants and members of the professions. Work began in 1907, and in July 1909 the results were published in an elaborate and beautifully printed volume. Only a few elements of the Chicago plan can be discussed, and these inadequately, in this work. In general the plan resembled the earlier proposal for San Francisco only in the design philosophy from which both were conceived. The Chicago plan is much more thorough, dealt with many additional facets of the city, and exhibits an intimate familiarity with the details of the city that was lacking in Burnham's earlier plans for San Francisco and Manila.

The introductory chapter of the report discusses the growth of Chicago, the planning of the Fair, and the studies Burnham had done for the development of the lake front in 1896 and 1904. A second chapter reviews planning in Europe and the recent American projects in Washington, Cleveland, San Francisco, and Manila. It is significant that Haussmann's improvements in Paris receive considerable attention. A colored map shows the street openings and widenings carried out in Paris from 1854 to 1889, and the report contains this passage:

"The task which Haussmann accomplished for Paris corresponds with the work which must be done for Chicago in order to overcome the intolerable conditions which invariably arise from a rapid growth of population. At the time he began, the population of Paris was half a million less than the population of Chicago to-day."[16]

Burnham's own Haussmann-like plan can be seen in Figures 311 and 312. One major feature was the proposal to create a great half-crescent boulevard enclosing in its arc the central portion of the city. A monumental lake entrance to the city was also to be created and tied in with Jackson Park stretching southward along the shore of Lake Michigan.

[16] Daniel H. Burnham and Edward H. Bennett, *Plan of Chicago*, Chicago, 1909, p. 18.

Leading from the waterfront and a group of civic and cultural buildings Burnham proposed a broad boulevard to run westward to the civic center. The details of these proposals for the core of the city may be seen in Figure 313. The great plaza of the civic center from which 10 principal avenues were to radiate appears in the detailed drawing reproduced in Figure 314.

The length of presentation and the attention given to the drawings illustrating the treatment of the civic center and new parks and plazas in the central core indicate that these were the aspects of the plan that most excited Burnham. However, the Chicago plan sounded new notes. The regional implications of metropolitan growth were discussed. The plan dealt as well with the need for improved rapid transit, the possibilities for control of outlying subdivisions, requirements for railroad line and terminal relocation and consolidation, and other features not normally covered in the planning reports of the day. Note, too, these prophetic words:

"The slum exists today only because of the failure of the city to protect itself against gross evils and known perils, all of which should be corrected by the enforcement of simple principles of sanitation. . . . Chicago has not yet reached the point where it will be necessary for the municipality to provide at its own expense . . . for the rehousing of persons forced out of congested quarters; but unless the matter shall be taken in hand at once, such a course will be required in common justice to men and women so degraded by long life in the slums that they have lost all power of caring for themselves."[17]

In an appendix to the plan, prepared by Walter L. Fisher, there was a long and carefully prepared examination of the legal powers necessary to carry out the proposals. The Chicago plan was also noteworthy in its attention to the techniques of visual presentation. The exquisite perspectives in color by Jules Guerin were particularly outstanding, and the use of clear and attractive maps and diagrams to illustrate the various recommendations also established a standard of graphic analysis that has seldom been equalled.

The Chicago plan was Burnham's major contribution to American planning, and it not only led to many improvements in Chicago but stimulated similar planning and improvement programs in other cities. When the American Institute of Architects in 1917

[17] *ibid.*, 108-109.

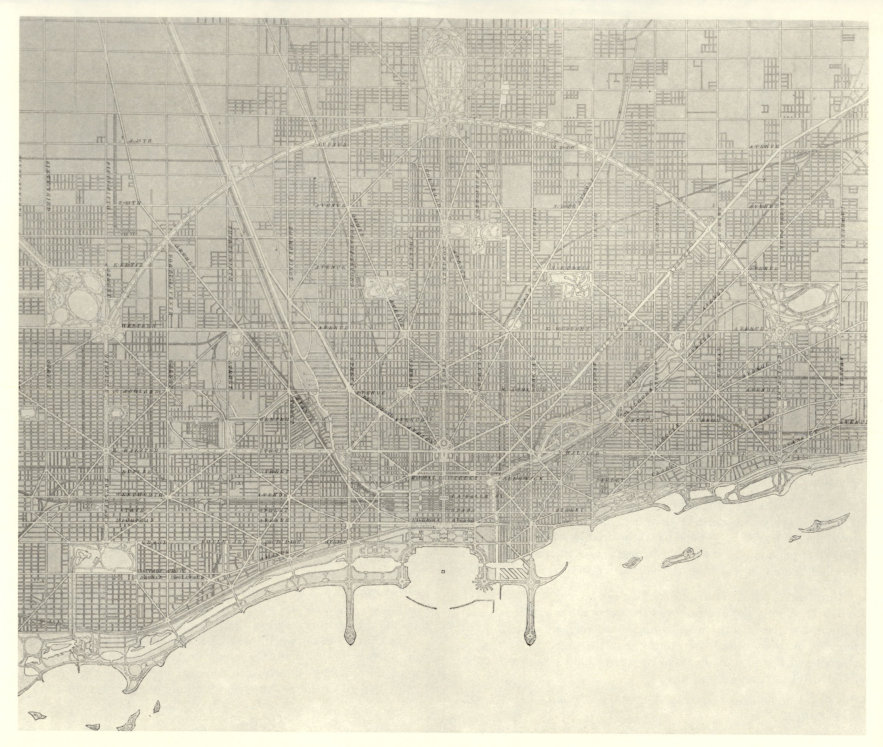

Figure 311. Daniel Burnham's Plan for Chicago, Illinois: 1909

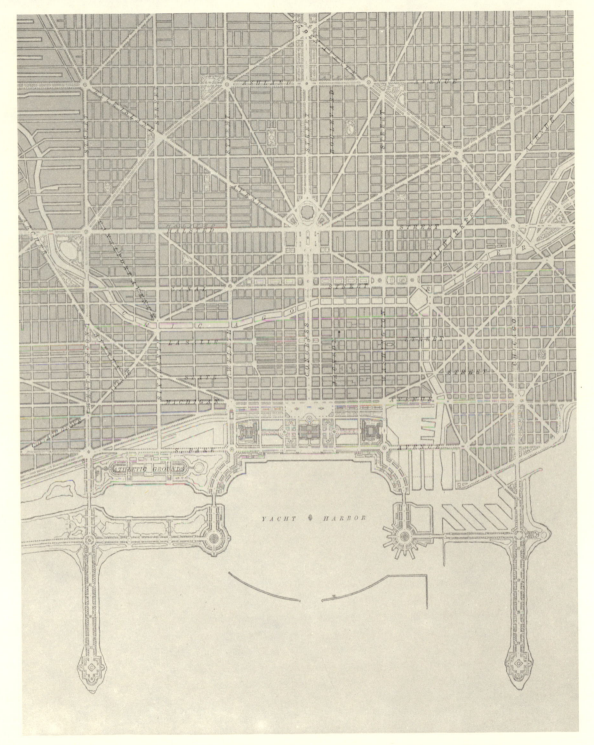

Figure 312. The Burnham Plan for the Central Area of Chicago, Illinois: 1909

Figure 313. Burnham's Proposals for the Business Center of Chicago, Illinois: 1909

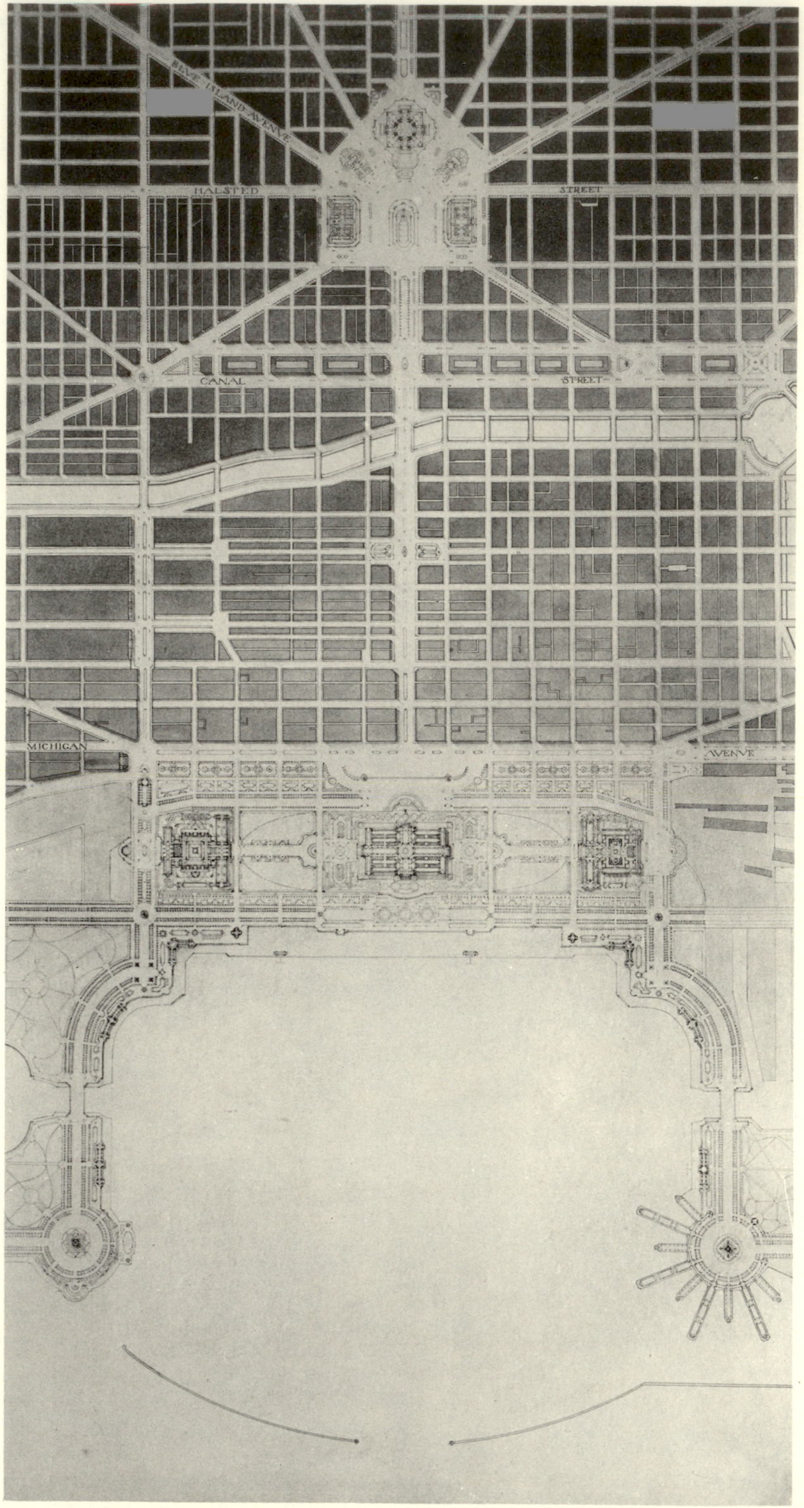

Figure 314. The Burnham Plan for the Civic Center in Chicago, Illinois: 1909

issued its *City Planning Progress in the United States,* a review of activity in this new field, improvement programs of one sort or another could be described in 233 cities. True, many of those mentioned were for isolated construction projects, but in a number of these cities comprehensive studies of municipal needs had been carried out and long-range development plans had been prepared.

In examining this publication, which is an important historical document that perhaps has not been adequately recognized, one finds major emphasis on the proposals for new radial boulevards and on the grouping of public buildings in a civic center composition. No one knows who originated the phrase or under what circumstances it was first applied, but the description of this approach to planning as "The City Beautiful Movement" is certainly appropriate. In more recent times this preoccupation with the appearance of the city and the concentration of improvement efforts on the erection of a few monumental structures of classical design has been much derided. This attitude is not without justification when one considers that these early planners overlooked more pressing social and economic ills, as well as other physical inadequacies of the city, in their striving to ape the effects created by Haussmann in Paris or to remake grid cities to the image of L'Enfant's Washington.

Inevitably there was a reaction from this approach that emphasized the appearance of the city almost to the exclusion of other matters. During the 1920's and 1930's a shift in emphasis occurred. The City Efficient replaced the City Beautiful as the main goal of city planners. Today planners are beginning to rediscover the merits of the earlier position of Burnham and his contemporaries and are attempting to combine the two approaches without sacrificing the interests of either.

In the first decade and a half of this century, however, the dominant motifs in American city planning were the civic centers, the landscaped parks, the boulevards, and the parkways. In report after report issued in such cities as Pittsburgh, St. Louis, Dallas, Detroit, Los Angeles, and Minneapolis, these elements were emphasized by the consultants who prepared the comprehensive development plans.[18] If many of their recommendations were wildly

impractical, they at least served as an inspiration for those who sought after and fought for civic improvements on a more modest scale.

American Planning: New Dimensions and New Directions

How did the city planning of the early twentieth century differ from that which had gone before? To begin, there was a new— or more correctly, a renewed—attention to the vertical dimension. Where most American planning from colonial times to the end of the last century had been concerned with the width and alignment of streets and the pattern of open spaces, the planning of Burnham's era brought attention to the design, location, and mass of buildings that should be erected on the two-dimensional plan. That the architectural taste and the theories of enclosing urban spaces exhibited by Burnham and his contemporaries differed from ours is not as important as the fact that they saw planning as something more than mere street layout.

The physical elements which were seen as comprising the modern city, and hence those subject to planning, became more numerous. In addition to streets and squares, some early planners turned their attention to public buildings, parks and playgrounds, docks and harbors, railroads, and in a few cases, mass transit. Burnham's plan of Chicago was particularly noteworthy in this respect.

Although initially supported by private sponsors, city planning rather quickly became a function of local government. The Mayor's City Plan Commission in Chicago, appointed in 1909, represented an early stage. On firmer ground was the planning commission in Hartford, Connecticut, established by charter amendment in 1907. While many of the early plan commissions had little funds and still less power or authority and were created without any clear definition of their place in the hierarchy of local government, at least there was recognition that planning was an official duty of city officials.

With this development came efforts to control urban growth,

---

[18] A list of typical American city planning reports of this period appears in Theodora Kimball, *Manual of Information on City Planning and Zoning,* Cambridge, 1923, pp. 43-46. See also John Nolen's presidential address before the National Conference on City Planning in 1927, "Twenty Years of City Planning Progress in the United States," National Conference on City Planning, *Planning Problems of Town, City and Region,* Philadelphia, 1927, pp. 1-44.

including privately owned land. Regulations of land use, building height, and building bulk through comprehensive zoning were introduced in New York in 1916. Control of private land subdivision, which had been exercised in some cities many decades earlier, became widespread and was a power often conferred on the new planning commissions.

In response to the rise in interest in city planning and the growing demand for technical assistance in plan preparation, a new profession came into being. In 1909 the first National Planning Conference was held in Washington at the suggestion of the New York Committee on Congestion of Population. This brought together a number of persons who were professionally interested in one aspect or another of city planning. In 1917 the American City Planning Institute was organized within the National Planning Conference. For the most part architects, landscape architects, and engineers, but with a few representatives of the fields of housing, administration, and law, these pioneers constituted the beginning of the present American Institute of Planners with a membership approaching four thousand. Specialized training in planning began at Harvard University, and there was growing recognition that city planning was an art or science which, although related to other disciplines, constituted a separate and increasingly complex field of endeavor.

Because the basic framework of most cities had already been established by the beginning of the century, modern planning necessarily concentrated on needed changes in the existing urban pattern. While new towns were yet to be established in America, the city planning of the period more and more became synonymous with urban redevelopment. Vastly more difficult than planning on a virgin site, city replanning called for skills other than land surveying or civil engineering. Although plans for city extensions and suburban growth were and remain important, it is the attention to devising remedies for existing city problems that characterizes much of modern planning and makes it so different in scope and approach to earlier efforts when the founding of new towns was the prevalent task.

Finally, there was a gradual realization during these formative years that the arrangement of the physical elements of the city vitally affected the people who dwelt in it. At first this was limited to considerations of the impact of monumental groupings of public buildings on the visual sensibilities of the beholders. Then came a growing awareness of the effect of housing accommodations and the provision of neighborhood open spaces on city dwellers. As early as 1911, with the creation of the experimental planned neighborhood unit of Forest Hills Gardens on Long Island, the consequences of convenient grouping of schools, parks, shopping center, and churches in a planned neighborhood environment began to receive attention. It is worth noting that Clarence Perry, who later was to formulate his influential theories of the neighborhood unit as a social force, lived in Forest Hills Gardens and there obtained much of his practical knowledge of group interaction within a unified composition of spaces and buildings.

So it was that in the period of a few years at the beginning of the century the course of American city planning was altered. Despite distracting trends and the vagueness of its goals, for half a century American planning has moved ever more steadily in the directions first charted when Burnham and those who followed in his wake ventured beyond the bounds marked out by such earlier explorers as Champlain, Penn, Nicholson, Oglethorpe, L'Enfant, Olmsted and the countless others who created the cities of America.

Notes on the Illustrations

This list contains bibliographic information about the illustrations reproduced in this work. An explanation of the capital letter symbols following each entry, which indicate the collection from which it has been reproduced, will be found at the end of the list.

All illustrations are reproduced by permission of copyright holders or through the courtesy of the libraries, offices, or collections indicated. The several plans from the Archives of the Moravian Church in Bethlehem, Pennsylvania, are used by special permission of the Provincial Archives Committee and may not be reproduced without its written permission.

Illustrations

Figure 1. *Plan Partiel de la Ville de Monpazier en Périgord (Dordogne)*. Plan of a portion of Monpazier, France, drawn by F. de Verneilh, from Didron (ed.), *Annales Archeologiques*, vol. 6. Paris, 1847. BN

Figure 2. *Vitry-le-François*. View of Vitry-le-François, France, from Nicolas Tassin, *Les Plans et Profils de Toutes les Principales Villes et Lieux Considerables de France*. Paris, 1634. LC-M

Figure 3. *Charleville, sur le Bord de la Meuse dans la Principaute Souveraine Darches*. Plan of Charleville, France, from Martin Zeiller, *Topographia Galliae*. Frankfort, 1656. A

Figure 4. *Philippeville*. Unsigned, undated plan of Philippeville, Belgium. Details of publication unknown. A

Figure 5. *Wilhelmostadum*. Plan of Willemstad, Holland, from Joannes Blaeu, *Stedenatlas van de Vereenigde Nederlanden*. Amsterdam, 1647. A

Figure 6. Untitled vertical aerial photograph of Santa Fé, Spain, taken in 1958. Supplied by Arquitecto Valentin Picatoste, Madrid, Spain. A

Figure 7. *The Plat of the Cittie of Londonderrie, as it Stand Built and Fortyfyed*. Copy of a plan of Londonderry drawn in 1622, from Sir Thomas Phillips, *Londonderry and the London Companies, 1609-1629*. Belfast, 1928. LC-GC

Figure 8. *A Plan for Rebuilding the City of London after the Great Fire in 1666*. Plan for the rebuilding of London in 1666 by Christopher Wren, from John Knox, *A New Collection of Voyages, Discoveries*, and *Travels*. London, 1767. LC-GC

Figure 9. *London Restored or Sir John Evelyn's Plan for Rebuilding that Antient Metropolis after the Fire in 1666*. Plan for the rebuilding of London in 1666 by John Evelyn, from William Maitland, *The History and Survey of London from its Foundation to the Present Time . . .* , London, 1756, Vol. 1. A

Figure 10. *Grundtriss der Statt London wie solche vor, und nach dem Brand anzusehen sampt dem Newen Model, wie selbige widrum Aussgebauwet werden solle*. Unsigned, undated plan of the London Fire in 1666, the details of publication of which are unknown. The insert plan for rebuilding the city has been attributed to Robert Hooke. A

Figure 11. *La Place Royale*. View of the Place Royale in Paris, France, from Israel Silvestre, *Recueil de Cent Vues Différentes . . . de la Ville de Paris . . . .* Paris, 1652. BN

Figure 12. *Delphum urbs Hollandiae cultissima, ab eiusdem nominis fossa, vulgo, Delfft appellata*. Plan of Delft, Holland, from Braun and Hoggenberg, *Civitates Orbis Terrarum*. Cologne, 1582. A

Figure 13. *Plan de Versailles*. Plan of the town, chateau, and gardens of Versailles, France, drawn by Abbé Delagrive. Paris, 1746. A

Figure 14. *Urbs Domingo in Hispaniola*. Plan of Santo Domingo, Dominican Republic, from Arnoldus Montanus (Arnald van den Berg), *De Nieuwe en Onbekende Weerld: of Beschryving van America*. Amsterdam, 1671. A

Figure 15. *Saint Augustine*. View of the Harbor, Fort, and Town of St. Augustine, Florida in 1586, from *Expeditio Francisci Draki Equitis Angli in Indias Occidentalis*, Leyden, 1588. NY-S

Figure 16. *A New & Accurate Plan of the Town of St. Augustine*. Unsigned, undated plan of St. Augustine, Florida based on a survey by Don John de Solis drawn ca. 1770. Details of publication unknown. LC-M

Figure 17. *Plano dela Poblacion*. Plan of the Pueblo of San Fernando de Béxar (San Antonio), Texas, ca. 1730, drawn by D. Joseph de Villaseñor. Reproduction of the original in the Archivo General y Público, Mexico, Provincias Internas, from Herbert E. Bolton, *Texas in the middle eighteenth century*. Berkeley, 1915. CU-O

Figure 18. Untitled and undated manuscript plan of the Pueblo of San Fernando de Béxar (San Antonio), Texas, drawn ca. 1777, from the manuscript of Fray Juan Augustín Morfi, *Historia de Texas*. LC-MS

Figure 19. *Mapa dl Presidio d San Antonio d Bexar.* . . . Unsigned manuscript map of San Antonio, Texas, and vicinity drawn in 1764. JCB

Figure 20. *Carolo Ignante, Urbem adificat amox, Galvez ad honoxem, nomen dedit que suum.* Unsigned manuscript plan of Galvez, Louisiana, drawn in 1778. LC-M

Figure 21. *Gezigt van't Spaansch Hek Pensacola, aan de Baay van dien naam, in de Golf van Mexiko, beoosten den uitloop van de Rivier Mississippi.* Unsigned, undated view of Pensacola, Florida, as it existed in 1743. Details of publication unknown. NY-S

Figure 22. *A Plan of Pensacola and its Environs.* Manuscript plan of Pensacola, Florida, drawn by Joseph Purcell in 1778. LC-M

Figure 23. *Plano Dela Villa de Santa Fee Capital del Reino del nuebo Mexico.* . . . Photocopy of a manuscript plan of Santa Fé, New Mexico, in the British Museum, drawn by Joseph de Urrutia ca. 1766. LC-M

Figure 24. *Santa Fe.* View of Santa Fé, New Mexico, in 1848, from U.S. Engineer Department, *Notes of a Military Reconnoissance from Fort Leavenworth, in Missouri, to San Diego in California.* . . . By W. H. Emory. New York, 1848. LC-P

Figure 25. *Vue de la Mission de Saint Louis Roi de France dans la Nouvelle California.* View of the Mission of San Luis Rey, California, from Eugene Duflot de Mofras, *Exploration du Territoire de l'Oregon, des Californies et de la Mer Vermeille.* Paris, 1844. LC-P

Figure 26. *The Presidio of San Francisco in 1820.* Manuscript copy of a plan of the Presidio of San Francisco, California, made in 1905 from the original copy drawn in 1880. UC-BL

Figure 27. *The City of Monterey, California 1842.* View of Monterey, California, drawn by Larkin, printed by D'Avignon. New York, 1842. HEHL

Figure 28. Untitled, undated manuscript copy of a plan showing Los Angeles, California, ca. 1781 prepared for Hubert Howe Bancroft in the nineteenth century from an early plan of unknown date. UC-BL

Figure 29. *Los Angeles.* View of Los Angeles, California by Charles Koppel, from U.S. War Department, *Reports of Explorations and Surveys, to Ascertain the Most Practicable and Economical Route for a Railroad from the Mississippi River to the Pacific Ocean.* LC-P

Figure 30. *Los Angeles, Los Angeles County, Cal. 1857.* View of Los Angeles, California, drawn by Kuchel & Dresel, published by Hellman & Bro. San Francisco, 1857. CPS

Figure 31. *Plan of Sonoma.* Manuscript plan of Sonoma, California, drawn by Otto v. Geldern in 1875. UC-BL

Figure 32. *Isle de sainte Croix.* Map of Sainte Croix (Douchet) Island, Maine, drawn by Samuel de Champlain in 1604. From a facsimile reproduction in H. P. Biggar (ed.), *The Works of Samuel de Champlain.* Toronto, 1922. UC

Figure 33. *Habitasion de l'iles Ste. croix.* View of Champlain's settlement on Sainte Croix (Douchet) Island, Maine, drawn by Samuel de Champlain in 1604. From a facsimile in Biggar (ed.), *The Works of Samuel de Champlain.* UC

Figure 34. *Abitasion du port royal.* View of Champlain's settlement at Port Royal, Nova Scotia, drawn by Samuel de Champlain in 1605. From a facsimile in Biggar (ed.), *The Works of Samuel de Champlain.* UC

Figure 35. *Abitation de Quebecq.* View of the first buildings at Quebec, drawn by Samuel de Champlain in 1608. From a facsimile in Biggar (ed.), *The Works of Samuel de Champlain.* UC

Figure 36. *Quebec, The Capital of New-France, a Bishoprick, and Seat of the Soverain Court.* View of Quebec, Canada, drawn and published by Thomas Johnston. Boston, 1759. JCB

Figure 37. *Vray Plan du haut & bas de quebec comme il est en lan 1660.* Manuscript plan of Quebec, Canada drawn in 1660. PAC

Figure 38. *A Plan of the City of Quebec.* Plan of Quebec, Canada in 1759, from Thomas Jefferys, *The Natural and Civil History of the French Dominions in North and South America.* London, 1760. CU-O

Figure 39. *Plan de la Ville de Louisbourg.* Plan of Louisbourg, Canada, in 1764, from J. N. Belin, *Le Petit Atlas Maritime.* Paris, 1764. CU-O

Figure 40. *Plan of the Town and Fortifications of Montreal or Ville Marie in Canada.* Plan of Montreal, Canada, in 1758, from Jefferys, *The Natural and Civil History of the French Dominions in North and South America.* CU-O

Figure 41. Untitled, unsigned, and undated manuscript plan of Montreal, Canada, drawn ca. 1644 by Jehan Bourdon. McGL

Figure 42. *Plan du Fort du Détroit.* Plan of Detroit, Michigan, in 1764, from Belin, *Le Petit Atlas Maritime.* CU-O

Figure 43. *A Plan of Cascaskies.* Plan of Kaskaskia, Illinois, drawn by Thomas Kitchin in 1770, from Philip Pittman, *The Present State of the European Settlements on the Missisippi.* London, 1770; reprinted, Cleveland, 1906. CU-O

Figure 44. *Saint Louis des Illinois.* Manuscript copy made in 1846 of the plan of St. Louis, Missouri, in 1764, drawn by Auguste Chouteau. MHS

Figure 45. *Plan de la Ville de St. Louis des Illinois.* . . . Photocopy of a manuscript plan of St. Louis, Missouri, drawn by George de Bois St. Lys in 1796. Location of original unknown. MHS

Figure 46. *Plan de la Ville et Fort Louis de la Louisiane.* . . . Copy of the original manuscript plan of Mobile, Alabama, by the Sieur Cheuillot, from Peter J. Hamilton, *Colonial Mobile.* Boston, 1897. CU-O

Figure 47. *A Plan of Mobile.* Plan of Mobile, Alabama, drawn by Thomas Kitchin in 1770, from Pittman, *The Present State of the European Settlements on the Missisippi.* CU-O

Figure 48. *Plan de la Nouvelle Orleans.* Photocopy of an unsigned and undated manuscript plan of New Orleans, Louisiana, in the French National Archives, drawn ca. 1720. LC-M

Figure 49. *Plan de la Nouvelle Orleans.* Plan of New Orleans, Louisiana, in 1764, from Belin, *Le Petit Atlas Maritime.* CU-O

Figure 50. *Plan of the City and Suburbs of New Orleans.* Plan of New Orleans, Louisiana, drawn by I. Tanesse, published by Charles Del Vecchio and P. Maspero. New York, 1817. LC-M

Figure 51. *City of New Orleans and Suburbs.* View of New Orleans, Louisiana, published by Gustave Koeckert, 1883. NYHS

Figure 52. *James Forte at Jamestowne.* Plan of Jamestown, Virginia, in antique style, drawn by John Hull, published by the A. H. Robins Co., Inc., Richmond, 1957. A

Figure 53. *Virginiae Pars.* Map of the Coast of Virginia and the James River from Francus (Jacobus, pseud. for Conrad Memmius), *Relations Historicae Continvatio, oder Warhafftige Beschreibunge aller. . . . Historien . . . dieses 1613.* Frankfort, 1613. NY-R

Figure 54. *A Platt of the towne belonging to York County.* Manuscript plan of Yorktown, Virginia, drawn by Lawrence Smith in 1791. VSL

Figure 55. *Tappahanock Town: A Platt of fifty Acres of Land lying at Hob's hole in Essex County.* Manuscript plan of Tappahanock, Virginia, drawn by Harry Beverley in 1706. VSL

Figure 56. *The Town of Marlborough.* Manuscript plan of Marlborough, Virginia, drawn by John Savage in 1731 from the original survey of 1691 by William Buckner and Theodorick Bland. John Mercer Letter Book. VSL

Figure 57. *Plan of the Town of Fredericksburg.* Manuscript plan of Fredericksburg, Virginia, drawn by Royston Buckner in 1721. VSL

Figure 58. *A Plan of Alexandria now Belhaven.* Unsigned, undated manuscript plan of Alexandria, Virginia, drawn by George Washington ca. 1749. LC-M

Figure 59. *Eden in Virginia.* Map of Eden in Virginia with a plan of one of the proposed towns from William Byrd, *New-gefundenes*

Eden. Oder: Auss fuehrlicher Bericht von Sun- und Nord-Carolina, Pensilphania, Mary Land, & Virginia . . . Helvetischen Societät, 1737. JCB

Figure 60. *The Mappe of Vienna Town.* Unsigned and undated manuscript plan of Vienna Town, Maryland, drawn in 1706. MHR

Figure 61. Untitled, unsigned manuscript plan of Charlestown, Maryland, drawn in 1742. LC-M

Figure 62. *A Grand Plat of the City and Port of Annapolis.* Manuscript copy made in 1748 of a manuscript plan of Annapolis, Maryland, drawn by James Stoddert in 1718. MHR

Figure 63. *Bird's Eye View of the City of Annapolis, Md.* View of Annapolis, Maryland, in 1864, published by Charles Magnus. New York, 1864. NY-S

Figure 64. *Plan de la ville et environs de Williamsburg en virginie america.* Unsigned manuscript plan of Williamsburg, Virginia, drawn in 1782. CWML

Figure 65. Untitled, unsigned, and undated manuscript plan of Williamsburg, Virginia. CWML

Figure 66. *The draught of St. Georges fort Erected by Captayne George Popham Esquier.* . . . Unsigned, undated plan of St. George's Fort, Maine, from a reproduction of the original manuscript drawn in 1608 in Henry O. Thayer, *The Sagadahoc Colony.* Portland, 1892. CU-O

Figure 67. Conjectural view of a portion of Plymouth, Massachusetts in 1630, prepared for Plimoth Plantation, Inc. by Strickland, Brigham and Eldredge. Boston, 1956. PP

Figure 68. *Wethersfield, Connecticut: 1640.* Manuscript redrawing by John Gibson in 1962 of a map of Wethersfield, Connecticut, in 1640, from Charles M. Andrews, *The River Towns of Connecticut.* Baltimore, 1889. CU-DP

Figure 69. *Springfield, Massachusetts: 1640.* Manuscript redrawing by John Gibson in 1962 of a plan of Springfield, Massachusetts, in 1640, from Henry M. Burt, *The First Century of the History of Springfield.* Springfield, 1898. Vol. 1. CU-DP

Figure 70. Untitled, unsigned manuscript map of Little Compton, Rhode Island, in 1681 drawn in the late eighteenth or early nineteenth century from the original map of 1681. JCB

Figure 71. *Meredith, New Hampshire: 1770.* Manuscript redrawing by John Gibson in 1962 of a map of Meredith, New Hampshire, in 1770, from C. P. Paullin, *Atlas of the Historical Geography of the United States.* Washington, 1932. CU-DP

Figure 72. *Salem, Massachusetts: 1670.* Manuscript redrawing by John Gibson in 1962 of a plan of Salem, Massachusetts, in 1670, from Sidney Perley, *The History of Salem, Massachusetts*. Salem, 1924, Vol. 1. CU-DP

Figure 73. *Cambridge, Massachusetts: 1637*. Manuscript redrawing by John Gibson in 1962 of a plan of Cambridge, Massachusetts, in 1637 prepared by Erwin Raisz from data compiled by Albert P. Norris, from Samuel Eliot Morison, *The Founding of Harvard College*. Cambridge, 1935. CU-DP

Figure 74. *A Plan of the Town of New Haven With all the Buildings in 1748*. Plan of New Haven, Connecticut, in 1748, drawn by William Lyon, published by T. Kensett, 1806. NYHS

Figure 75. *Hartford, Connecticut: 1640*. Manuscript redrawing by John Gibson in 1962 of a plan of Hartford, Connecticut, in 1640, from DeLoss Love, *The Colonial History of Hartford*. Hartford, 1914. CU-DP

Figure 76. *Fairfield, Connecticut: 1640*. Manuscript redrawing by John Gibson in 1962 of a plan of Fairfield, Connecticut in 1640, from Elizabeth Hubbell Schenck, *The History of Fairfield, Fairfield County, Connecticut*. New York, 1889. Vol. 1. CU-DP

Figure 77. *A Plan of the Compact Part of the Town of Exeter, at the Head of the Southern Branch of Piscataqua River*. Plan of Exeter, New Hampshire, in 1802 drawn by P. Merrill. DCL

Figure 78. *Woodstock*. Plan of Woodstock, Vermont, from Beers, Ellis, and Soule, *Atlas of Windsor County, Vermont*. New York, 1869. DCL

Figure 79. *Lebanon, Grafton County, N.H.* View of Lebanon, New Hampshire, published by Geo. E. Norris. Brockton, Mass., 1884. DCL

Figure 80. *Fair Haven*. Plan of Fair Haven, Vermont, from F. W. Beers and Company, *Atlas of Rutland County, Vermont*. New York, 1869. DCL

Figure 81. *Ipswich*. Plan of Ipswich, Massachusetts, from D. G. Beers and Company, *Atlas of Essex County, Massachusetts*. Philadelphia, 1872. CU-O

Figure 82. *Providence, Rhode Island: 1638*. Manuscript redrawing by John Gibson in 1962 of a plan of Providence, Rhode Island, in 1638, from Cady, *The Civic and Architectural Development of Providence*, Providence, 1957. CU-DP

Figure 83. *Greenfield, Massachusetts: 1774*. Manuscript redrawing by John Gibson in 1962 of a plan of Greenfield, Massachusetts, in 1774, from the Centennial Edition of the *Greenfield Gazette*. Greenfield, February 1, 1892. CU-DP

Figure 84. *Boston, Massachusetts: 1640*. Manuscript redrawing by John Gibson in 1962 of a reconstruction of street and property lines in Boston, Massachusetts, in 1640, prepared by Samuel C.

Clough in 1927 and reproduced in Walter M. Whitehill, *Boston: a Topographical History*. Cambridge, 1959. CU-DP

Figure 85. *The Town of Boston in New England*. Plan of Boston, Massachusetts, drawn by John Bonner, printed by Fra. Dewing. Boston, 1722. NY-S

Figure 86. *A View of Part of the Town of Boston in New England and Brittish Ships of War Landing their Troops*. View of Boston, Massachusetts, drawn and published by Paul Revere. Boston, 1768. NY-S

Figure 87. *A New Plan of Boston from Actual Surveys*. Plan of Boston, Massachusetts, drawn by Osgood Carleton. Boston, 1800. Manuscript additions by George Lamb, 1879. NY-S

Figure 88. *Bird's Eye View of Boston*. View of Boston, Massachusetts, drawn by J. Bachman, published by Williams and Stevens. New York, 1850. NYHS

Figure 89. *Concept C. Het Fort; Concept A. Het plein van het Fort; Concept B. De Landen*. Conjectural Dutch Plans for the fort and town of New Amsterdam (New York City) in 1625, from F. C. Wieder, *De Stichting van New York en Juli 1625*. Amsterdam, 1925. CU-O

Figure 90. *Redraft of the Castello Plan. New Amsterdam in 1660*. Manuscript redrawing in 1916 by John Wolcott Adams and I. N. Phelps Stokes of the manuscript plan of New Amsterdam in the Medici Library, Florence, Italy, drawn in 1660. NY-S

Figure 91. *Kingstone*. Plan of Kingston, New York, in 1695, from John Miller, *A Description of the Province and City of New-York*. London, 1843. CU-O

Figure 92. *Albany*. Plan of Albany, New York, in 1695, from Miller, *A Description of the Province and City of New-York*. CU-O

Figure 93. *A Plan of the City of New York from an actual Survey*. Plan of New York City, drawn by James Lyne. New York, 1731. NY-S

Figure 94. *Plan of the City of New York, in North America: Surveyed in the Years 1766 and 1767*. Plan of New York City, drawn by B. Ratzer, published by Jefferys and Faden. London, 1776. LC-M

Figure 95. *Christina shantz*. Manuscript plan of Fort Christina and Christinahamm, Delaware, drawn by Per Martensson Lindeström in 1654. SAS

Figure 96. *A Plan of the Island of Burlington and a View of the City from the River Delaware*. Plan of Burlington, New Jersey, drawn and published by William Birch. Philadelphia, 1797. LC-M

Figure 97. *A Portraiture of the City of Philadelphia in The Province of Pennsylvania in America*. Plan of Philadelphia, Pennsylvania in 1682 drawn by Thomas Holme, sold by Andrew Sowle. London, 1683. From a restrike in John C. Lowber, *Ordinances of the City of Philadelphia, 1812*. Philadelphia, 1812. CU-O

Figure 98. *The ffirst of the Mapp of the designe for Cytie of London*. Manuscript plan for rebuilding London in 1666, drawn by Richard Newcourt. Retouched from a reproduction in T. F. Reddaway, "The Rebuilding of London After the Great Fire: A Rediscovered Plan," *Town Planning Review*, Vol. 18, No. 3 (1939). A

Figure 99. *A Mapp of Ye Improved Part of Pensilvania in America*. Plan of Philadelphia, Pennsylvania, and vicinity with an inset plan of Philadelphia, drawn by Thomas Holme, published by Ino Harris. ca. 1720. LC-M

Figure 100. *Philadelphia*. Plan of Philadelphia, Pennsylvania, drawn by Nicholas Scull. Philadelphia, 1762. LC-M

Figure 101. . . . *Plan of the City and Suburbs of Philadelphia*. Plan of Philadelphia, Pennsylvania, drawn by A. P. Folie in 1794. LC-M

Figure 102. *A Ground Plan of the City of Philadelphia*. Inset plan of Philadelphia, Pennsylvania, from a facsimile drawn by Charles Warner in 1870 of a map prepared by John Reed in 1774. Philadelphia, 1870. LC-M

Figure 103. *Philadelphie*. View of Philadelphia, Pennsylvania, drawn by Asselineau from a water color by John Bachman, published by Wild. Paris, ca. 1855. NYHS

Figure 104. *A Plan of Charles Town from a survey of Edward Crisp*. Plan of Charleston, South Carolina, drawn by Edward Crisp, from David Ramsay, *The History of South Carolina*, Vol. 2. Charleston, 1809. CU-O

Figure 105. *The Ichnography of Charles-Town at High Water*. Plan of Charleston, South Carolina, drawn by G. H., published by B. Roberts and W. H. Toms. London, 1739. Photocopy of plan in British Museum, King George III Collection, No. 122-67. LC-M

Figure 106. Unsigned, untitled portion of a view of Charleston, South Carolina, drawn by Smith and Smith, published by Smith Brothers & Co., London, 1851. NY-S

Figure 107. *A Plan of the Town of Newbern in Craven County North Carolina*. Manuscript plan of New Bern, North Carolina, drawn by C. J. Sauthier, 1769. WLC

Figure 108. *A Plan of the Town & Port of Edenton in Chowan County, North Carolina*. Manuscript plan of Edenton, North Carolina, drawn by C. J. Sauthier, 1769. WLC

Figure 109. *A Plan representing the Form of Setling the Districts,*

or County Divisions in the Margravate of Azilia. Plan of the proposed Margravate of Azilia in Georgia, drawn by Sir Robert Mountgomery, from a facsimile of the original published in London, 1717, in George P. Humphrey (ed.), *American Colonial Tracts*, No. 1. Rochester, 1897. CU-O

Figure 110. *A Map of the County of Savannah*. Map of the County of Savannah, Georgia, from Samuel Urlsperger. *Ausfuhrliche Nachricht von den Saltzburgischen Emigranten*, Vol. 1, Part 4. Halle, 1735. JCB

Figure 111. Untitled, map of the Savannah, Georgia common, garden, and farm lands ca. 1800, drawn by John McKinnon, published privately by J. F. Minis. London, 1904. LC-M

Figure 112. *A View of Savannah as it stood the 29th of March, 1734*. View of Savannah, Georgia, drawn by Peter Gordon. London (?), 1734. LC-P

Figure 113. *A Plan of the Town of Savannah as began and intended to be carried on in Georgia*. Unsigned, undated manuscript plan of Savannah, Georgia, ca. 1740. AMCB

Figure 114. *Plan Von Neu Ebenezer*. Plan of New Ebenezer, Georgia, drawn by Matthew Seutter. Augsburg, ca. 1740. A

Figure 115. Photocopy of an untitled, unsigned, and undated manuscript map in the British Museum of St. Simons Island, Georgia, drawn by John Thomas ca. 1740. LC-M

Figure 116. *Plan of the Town of Frederica on the Island of St. Simon*. Manuscript resurvey of Frederica, Georgia, by Joshua Miller in 1796. GSGD

Figure 117. *An Exact Plan of George Town*. Manuscript plan of George Town (Hardwick), Georgia, drawn by Henry Yonge in 1754. LC-M

Figure 118. *Map of the City of Savannah*. Unsigned plan of Savannah, Georgia, published by John M. Cooper & Co. New York, 1856. LC-M

Figure 119. *Savannah, Georgia: 1733-1856*. Manuscript plans of Savannah, Georgia, drawn by John W. Reps in 1959. A

Figure 120. *Savannah Ga. 1855*. View of Savannah, Georgia, drawn by J. W. Hill, published by Endicott & Co. New York, 1856. NYHS

Figure 121. *Plan of the Lots Laid out at Pittsburgh and the Coal Hill*. Manuscript plan of Pittsburgh, Pennsylvania, drawn by Tobin Mills. Philadelphia, 1787. LC-M

Figure 122. *Plan of Pittsburg and Adjacent Country*. Plan of Pittsburgh, Pennsylvania, drawn by William Darby, published by R. Patterson and William Darby. Pittsburgh, ca. 1815. LC-M

Figure 123. *Fort Boonesborough*. View of Fort Boonesborough, Kentucky, drawn by George Ranck after a plan by Judge Richard Henderson, from George W. Ranck, Boonesborough, Louisville, 1901. CU-O

Figure 124. *Kentucke*. Map of Kentucky, drawn and published by John Filson. Philadelphia, 1784. LC-M

Figure 125. *Plan of Louisville 1779*. Photocopy of manuscript plan of Louisville, Kentucky, in 1779, attributed to George Rogers Clark. FCL

Figure 126. *City of Louisville and its Enlargements*. Plan of Louisville, Kentucky, drawn by E. D. Hobbs, published by Gabriel Collins in 1836. LC-M

Figure 127. *Plat of the Seven Ranges of Townships*. Map of the first townships surveyed in eastern Ohio, drawn by Mathew Carey after surveys by Thomas Hutchins, published by Mathew Carey. Philadelphia, 1796. WLC

Figure 128. *A Map of the Federal Territory from the Western Boundary of Pennsylvania to the Scioto River*. Unsigned, undated map of the eastern portion of Ohio, probably prepared by Manassah Cutler ca. 1787. LC-M

Figure 129. *Plan of the Ancient Works at Marietta*. Plan of Marietta, Ohio, and the Indian Earthworks, drawn by Charles Whittlesey in 1837. WRHS

Figure 130. *Marietta*. Plan of Marietta, Ohio, drawn by C. Sullivan ca. 1837. LC-M

Figure 131. *Campus Martius, in 1791*. View of the Campus Martius at Marietta, Ohio, from *The American Pioneer*, Vol. 1. Cincinnati, 1842. LC-P

Figure 132. *Gallipolis in 1791*. View of Gallipolis, Ohio, from Henry Howe, *Historical Collections of Ohio*. Cincinnati, 1847. A

Figure 133. *Plan of Cincinnati, Including All the late Additions & Subdivisions*. Plan of Cincinnati, Ohio, drawn by Thomas Darby, from Daniel Drake, *Natural and Statistical View*, or *Picture of Cincinnati and the Miami Country*. Cincinnati, 1815. DCL

Figure 134. Unsigned, undated, and untitled manuscript plan of Zanesville, Ohio, drawn ca. 1815. WLC

Figure 135. *Map of the Town of Columbus*. Unsigned manuscript plan of Columbus, Ohio, drawn in 1817. WRHS

Figure 136. *A Plan of the City of Cleaveland*. Redrawing in 1855 by L. M. Pillsbury of the original plan of Cleveland, Ohio, by Seth Pease in 1796, from *Journal of the Association of Engineering Societies, Transactions*. Vol. 3, No. 10 (1884) LC-M

Figure 137. *Cleveland, Ohio*. View of Cleveland, Ohio, drawn by Thomas Whelpley in 1833. New York, 1834. LC-P

Figure 138. *Jefferson*. Plan of Jefferson, Ohio, from Titus, Simmons

& Titus, *Atlas of Ashtabula County, Ohio*. Philadelphia, 1874. CU-O

Figure 139. *Town Plat of Canfield*. Unsigned, undated manuscript plan of Canfield, Ohio, ca. 1800. WRHS

Figure 140. *Map of Elyria, Lorain County, Ohio*. Unsigned, undated plan of Elyria, Ohio, printed by Miller & Co. New York, ca. 1850. WRHS

Figure 141. *Bird's Eye View of the Town of Elyria*. View of Elyria, Ohio, drawn by A. Ruger in 1868. LC-M

Figure 142. *Tallmadge Center*. Plan of Tallmadge Center, Ohio, from Tackabury, Mead and Moffett, *Combination Atlas Map of Summit County Ohio*. Philadelphia, 1874. CU-O

Figure 143. *Tallmadge Center Park*. View of the Central Green in Tallmadge, Ohio, from Tackabury, Mead and Moffett, *Combination Atlas Map of Summit County Ohio*. Philadelphia, 1874. CU-O

Figure 144. *Sketch of Washington in Embryo*. Map showing the division of land on the site of the national capital, drawn by E. F. M. Faehtz and F. W. Pratt, based on research by Dr. Joseph M. Toner. Washington, 1874. LC-M

Figure 145. Untitled manuscript marginal sketch by Thomas Jefferson showing suggested land division in a city block, from a manuscript note dated November 29, 1790, entitled "Proceedings to be had under the Residence Act." Papers of Thomas Jefferson. LC-MS

Figure 146. Untitled manuscript marginal sketch by Thomas Jefferson of a plan for a capital city on the site of Carrollsburg, District of Columbia, from a manuscript note dated November 29, 1790, entitled "Proceedings to be had under the Residence Act." Papers of Thomas Jefferson. LC-MS

Figure 147. Untitled, undated manuscript plan for a town on the site of Washington, D.C., with notes in Thomas Jefferson's hand. Probably drawn by Jefferson in March 1791. Papers of Thomas Jefferson. LC-MS

Figure 148. *Plan of the City intended for the Permanent Seat of the Government of the United States*. Copy by the United States Coast and Geodetic Survey in 1887 of the manuscript plan for Washington, D.C., drawn by Pierre Charles L'Enfant, 1791. A

Figure 149. *Plan of the City of Washington in the Territory of Columbia. . . .* Plan of Washington, D.C., drawn by Andrew Ellicott, published by Thackara & Vallance. Philadelphia, 1792. Restrike in 1962 from the original plate. A

Figure 150. *City of Washington from beyond the Navy Yard*. View of Washington, D.C., drawn by W. J. Bennett from a painting by George Cooke, published by Lewis P. Clover. New York, 1834. LC-P

Figure 151. *View of Washington.* View from the Capitol to the White House in Washington, D.C., drawn and published by Robert P. Smith, 1850. LC-P

Figure 152. *Washington City, D.C.* View of Washington, D.C., drawn by Theo. R. Davis, from *Harper's Weekly*, March 13, 1869. LC-P

Figure 153. *The City of Washington. Birds-Eye View from the Potomac Looking North.* View of Washington, D.C., published by Currier & Ives, 1892. LC-P

Figure 154. *To the Citizens of Philadelphia This New Plan of the City and its Environs is respectfully dedicated by the Editor.* Plan of Philadelphia, Pennsylvania, drawn by P. C. Varlé. Philadelphia (?), 1802. LC-M

Figure 155. *A Plan of the City of Detroit.* Manuscript plan of Detroit, Michigan, drawn by Abijah Hull in January 1807. DP-BC

Figure 156. *A Plan of one Section of Detroit.* Unsigned manuscript plan for a portion of Detroit, Michigan, dated January 1, 1807, probably drawn by Abijah Hull. DP-BC

Figure 157. *Plan of Detroit.* Unsigned, undated plan of the central portion of Detroit, Michigan, as planned by Judge Woodward in 1807, from *American State Papers*, Public Lands Series, Vol. 6. Washington, 1860. CU-O

Figure 158. *Plan of Detroit.* Plan of Detroit, Michigan, in 1830, drawn by John Mullett, from *American State Papers*, Public Lands Series, Vol. 6. CU-O

Figure 159. *Plat of the Town of Indianapolis.* Plan of Indianapolis, Indiana, published by H. Platt. Columbus, 1821. ISL

Figure 160. *Plat of Madison the Capital of Wisconsin. Map of the Four Lake Country.* Plan of Madison, Wisconsin, and map of the Four Lake Country, drawn by John V. Suydam, published by P. Desobry. New York, 1836. LC-M

Figure 161. *View of Madison the Capital of Wisconsin.* View of Madison, Wisconsin, drawn by S. H. Donnel, published by C. Curriers. New York, 1856. NY-S

Figure 162. *Topographical Plan of the City and Battle-Field of Baton Rouge, La. Fought on the 5th of August 1862.* Plan of Baton Rouge, Louisiana, drawn by Joseph Gorlinski, from U.S. War Department, *Atlas to Accompany the Official Records of the Union and Confederate Armies.* Washington, 1891-1895. LC-M

Figure 163. *Map of Cleveland and its Environs.* Plan of Cleveland, Ohio, drawn and published by Ahaz Merchant. New York, 1835. LC-M

Figure 164. *The Town of Sparta. . . .* Manuscript plan of Sparta, Ohio, submitted as a record plat in 1815 by Amos Jenney, Proprietor. STCO

Figure 165. *Map of Perrysburg Township.* Plan of Perrysburg, Ohio, from Andreas & Baskin, *An Illustrated Historical Atlas of Lucas and Part of Wood Counties.* Chicago, 1875. CU-O

Figure 166. *City of Sandusky.* Plan of Sandusky, Ohio, drawn by A. Doolittle. New Haven, 1818. WRHS

Figure 167. *City of Sandusky, O.* Unsigned view of Sandusky, Ohio, published by A. J. Hare. Sandusky, 1883. LC-M

Figure 168. *Hatfield.* Unsigned Plan of Hatfield, Kansas, from L. H. Everts, *Official State Atlas of Kansas.* Philadelphia, 1887. LC-M

Figure 169. *Hugoton.* Unsigned plan of Hugoton, Kansas, from L. H. Everts, *Official State Atlas of Kansas.* Philadelphia, 1887. LC-M

Figure 170. *Montezuma.* Unsigned plan of Montezuma, Kansas, from L. H. Everts, *Official State Atlas of Kansas.* Philadelphia, 1887. LC-M

Figure 171. *Palmyra.* Plan of Palmyra, Nebraska, from Everts & Kirk, *The Official State Atlas of Nebraska.* Philadelphia, 1885. NY-M

Figure 172. Untitled, unsigned and undated plan illustrating principles of urban design, described in "Architecture in the United States," *American Journal of Science and Arts*, Vol. 17. New Haven, 1830. CU-O

Figure 173. *General Plan for Enlarging & Improving the City of Boston.* Plan for Boston, Massachusetts, drawn by Robert Fleming Gourlay, from Robert Gourlay, *Plans for Beautifying New York, and for Enlarging and Improving the City of Boston.* Boston, 1844. HU-GD

Figure 174. *A New & Accurate Plan of the City of New York in the State of New York in North America.* Plan of New York City, drawn by B. Taylor. New York, 1797. NY-S

Figure 175. *A Plan of the Commons Belonging to New York. . . . Common Land . . . Belonging to the Corporation of the City of New York.* Photocopies of two manuscript surveys of Manhattan Island by Casimir Goerck in 1785 and 1796, from originals in the office of Francis W. Ford's Sons, Surveyors, and the Office of the Comptroller of New York. CU-DP

Figure 176. *Map of the City of New York and Island of Manhattan.* Commissioners' Plan of New York City, from William Bridges, *Map of the City of New-York and Island of Manhattan; with Explanatory Remarks and References.* New York, 1811. NYHS

Figure 177. *Chicago with the School Section, Wabansia, and Kinzie's*

Illinois, drawn by H. Wellge, published by Henry Wellge & Co. Milwaukee, 1888. LC-M

Figure 233. *Plan of.* Unsigned, undated town plat used by the Illinois Associates, in the Rantoul-Neal Collection. HU-BA

Figure 234. *Outline Map of Illinois.* Map of the Illinois Central Railroad lines, stations, and lands, from Illinois Central Railroad, *A Guide to the Illinois Central Railroad Lands.* Chicago, 1860. CU-O

Figure 235. *Natrona, Laid out in 1857 by Conklin & Co.* Plan of Natrona, Illinois, from W. R. Brink & Co., *Illustrated Atlas Map of Mason County, Illinois.* Edwardsville, Illinois (?), 1874. CU-O

Figure 236. *Galva.* Plan of Galva, Illinois, from Warner & Beers, *Atlas of Henry County and the State of Illinois.* Chicago, 1875. CU-O

Figure 237. *"Busted!"—A Deserted Railroad Town in Kansas.* View from *Harper's Weekly*, February 28, 1874. LC-P

Figure 238. *Birds Eye View of the City of Herington, Kansas.* View of Herington, Kansas, from L. H. Everts, *Official State Atlas of Kansas.* Philadelphia, 1887. LC-M

Figure 239. *Sketches in the Far West—An Under-Ground Village.* View from *Harper's Weekly*, Supplement, April 4, 1874. LC-P

Figure 240. *Section of City.* Plan of a model town, from P. Gerard, *How to Build a City.* . . . Philadelphia, 1872. LC-GC

Figure 241. *Panoramic Bird's Eye View of Colorado Springs, Colorado City and Manitou, Colo.* View of Colorado Springs, Colorado, published by J. J. Stoner. Madison, 1882. LC-M

Figure 242. *Map of Coronado Beach, San Diego, California.* Plan of Coronado Beach, California, published by Rand, McNally & Co. Chicago, 1887. LC-M

Figure 243. *Map of Carona, Riverside County, California.* Undated plan of Carona, California, drawn by H. Clay Kellogg, ca. 1900. UC-BL

Figure 244. *Map of Commencement City, W. T. Tacoma, W. T.* Unsigned, undated plan of Tacoma, Washington, ca. 1873. WSHS

Figure 245. *Map of the City of Tacoma.* Plan of Tacoma, Washington, drawn by F. L. Olmsted and R. K. Radford. New York, 1873. WSHS

Figure 246. *Tacoma, W. T.* View of Tacoma, Washington, published by J. J. Stoner. Madison, 1884. LC-M

Figure 247. *Plan of the Town of Lowell and Belvidere Village, Taken by Measurement.* Plan of Lowell, Massachusetts, drawn by Benjamin Mather. Boston, 1832. MAHS

Figure 248. *Manchester, N.H., 1876.* View of Manchester, New Hampshire, drawn and published by H. H. Bailey & [illegible] Hazen. Milwaukee, 1876. DCL

Figure 249. *Plan of Holyoke.* Unsigned, undated plan of Holyoke, Massachusetts, ca. 1848. MAHS

Figure 250. *Map of Pullman.* Plan of Pullman, Illinois, from Richard T. Ely, "Pullman: A Social Study," *Harper's New Monthly Magazine*, Vol. 70, No. 417, 1885. A

Figure 251. *Barberton.* Plan of Barberton, Ohio, from Akron Map & Atlas Co., *Illustrated Summit County Ohio.* Akron, 1891. NY-M

Figure 252. *General Plan for the Town of Vandergrift.* Plan of Vandergrift, Pennsylvania, drawn by F. L. and J. C. Olmsted, from U.S. National Resources Committee. Supplementary Report of the Urbanism Committee, *Urban Planning and Land Policies.* Washington, 1939. Vol. 2. A

Figure 253. *Steel Works and Blast Furnaces, Indiana Steel Co.* Plan of Gary, Indiana, drawn by Albert Jewett. Gary, 1907. GI

Figure 254. Untitled, unsigned plan of Fairfield, Alabama in 1910, from Graham Taylor, *Satellite Cities.* New York, 1915. CU-FA

Figure 255. Untitled, unsigned plan of Kohler, Wisconsin, in 1913, from L. L. Smith, "The Industrial City of Kohler, Wisconsin," *American Landscape Architecture*, September, 1930. CU-FA

Figure 256. *General Plan of Morgan Park.* Plan of Morgan Park, Minnesota, from National Resources Committee. Supplementary Report of the Urbanism Committee, *Urban Planning and Land Policies.* Washington, 1939. Vol. 2. A

Figure 257. *Map of Kincaid, Christian Co. Illinois.* Plan of Kincaid, Illinois, from A. T. Luce, "Kincaid, Illinois, a Model Mining Town," *American City* (Town and Country Edition), July 1905. CU-FA

Figure 258. *Town of Tyrone, New Mexico.* Plan of Tyrone, New Mexico, from "New Mining Town of Tyrone, New Mexico," *Architectural Review*, April 1918. CU-FA

Figure 259. *Kistler Industrial Village.* . . . John Nolen, *New Towns for Old.* Boston, 1927. A

Figure 260. *Arx Carolina.* View of Fort Caroline, Florida, from Arnoldus Montanus (Arnald van den Berg), *De Nieuwe en Onbekende Weerld: of Beschryving van America.* Amsterdam, 1671. A

Figure 261. Untitled, unsigned, and undated manuscript plan of Manakin, Virginia, ca. 1700. VSL

Figure 262. *View of Bethlehem, a Moravian settlement.* View of Bethlehem, Pennsylvania, in 1798, from Isaac Weld, *Travels Through the States of North America*, Vol. 2. London, 4th ed., 1807. CU-O

Figure 263. *Bethabara. 1766.* Unsigned manuscript plan of Bethabara, North Carolina, drawn in 1766. MAWS

Figure 264. *Grund Ritz von Litiz.* Unsigned manuscript plan of Lititz, Pennsylvania, drawn in 1759. AMCB

Figure 265. *Bethania in Wacha.* Unsigned manuscript plan of Bethania, North Carolina, drawn in 1759. AMCB

Figure 266. *Grundrisse und Prospecte der drey Evangelischen Bruder Gemein Orte im Marggrassthum Ober Lausiz: Herrnhut . . . Nisky . . . Klein Welke . . .* Plans and views of Herrnhut, Nisky, and Klein Welke in East Germany, drawn by I. G. Krause in 1782. AMCB

Figure 267. *Copy of part of Br. Reuter's map of the new town site with a suggestion how it might be laid out.* [title in German]. Manuscript plan of Salem, North Carolina drawn in Bethlehem, Pennsylvania, July 1765, from a drawing by Christian Reuter. LC-M

Figure 268. Untitled, unsigned, undated manuscript plan of Schoenbrunn, Ohio, ca. 1772. AMCB

Figure 269. *Economy.* Plan of Economy, Pennsylvania from Joseph A. Caldwell, *Caldwell's Illustrated, Historical Centennial Atlas of Beaver County, Pennsylvania.* Condit, Ohio, 1876. LC-M

Figure 270. *Assembly Hall—Economy. Church at Economy.* Views of Economy, Pennsylvania, from Charles Nordhoff, *The Communistic Societies of the United States.* New York, 1875. UC

Figure 271. *A Bird's Eye View of one of the New Communities at Harmony in the State of Indiana North America.* Undated view of New Harmony, Indiana, drawn by Stedman Whitwell, published by Ingrey & Madelly. London, ca. 1825. NYHS

Figure 272. *Plat of Zoar, Lawrence Township.* Plan of Zoar, Ohio, from L. H. Everts & Co., *Combination Atlas Map of Tuscarawas County.* Philadelphia, 1875. CU-O

Figure 273. *The Bethel Commune, Missouri.* View of Bethel, Missouri, from Nordhoff, *The Communistic Societies of the United States.* New York, 1875. UC

Figure 274. *Map of the Ebenezer Lands in the County of Erie, N.Y.* Map of the lands of the Community of True Inspiration near Buffalo, New York, printed by Scott and Jamison. Buffalo, 1856. BHS.

Figure 275. *Plat of Lennox & Amana.* Map of Amana Township, Iowa, from George Warner and C. M. Foote, *Plat Book of Iowa County, Iowa.* Minneapolis, 1886. LC-M

Figure 276. *Amana, A General View.* View of Amana, Iowa, from Charles Nordhoff, *The Communistic Societies of the United States.* New York, 1875. UC

Figure 277. *Ground Plan of the Edifice of an Association.* Plan of a proposed Phalanstery, from Albert Brisbane, *Association; or, a Concise Exposition of the Practical Part of Fourier's Social Science.* New York, 1843. UC

Figure 278. *Plat of Zion City.* Manuscript plan of the ideal Mormon city, with descriptive text, drawn by Joseph Smith, 1833. HLDS

Figure 279. *Plat of Far West, 1836.* Plan of Far West, Missouri, from Lowry Nelson, *The Mormon Village.* Salt Lake City, 1952. CU-O

Figure 280. *Map of the City of Nauvoo.* Plan of Nauvoo, Illinois, drawn by Gustavus Hill's, printed by J. Childs. New York, ca. 1842. LC-M

Figure 281. *Bird's Eye View of Salt Lake City.* View of Salt Lake City, Utah, drawn and published by Augustus Koch. Chicago, 1870. LC-M

Figure 282. *Outline Map of Zion City.* Plan of Zion City, Illinois, from George A. Ogle, *Standard Atlas of Lake County, Illinois.* Chicago, 1907. LC-M

Figure 283. *A Plan of the Town of Asylum in Luzerne County, Pennsylvania.* Plan of Asylum, Pennsylvania, from Louise Welles Murray, *The Story of Some French Refugees and Their "Azilum."* Athens, Pennsylvania, 1903. A

Figure 284. *Plan of the Fort of New Madrid or Anse a la Graisse.* Map of New Madrid, Missouri, and vicinity. From Victor Collot, *A Journey in North America.* Atlas. From a facsimile of the Paris edition of 1826. Florence, 1924. NYSL

Figure 285. *Nouvelle Madrid in Avril 1794.* Unsigned manuscript plan of New Madrid, Missouri, 1794. MHS

Figure 286. *Plat of the town of new-madrid, in Louisiana—1810-.* Unsigned manuscript plan of New Madrid, Missouri, 1810. MHS

Figure 287. *New Madrid Missouri.* View of New Madrid, Missouri, from Henry Lewis, *Das Illustrirte Mississippthal.* Dusseldorf, 1857. NY-S

Figure 288. *Ancient Works at Circleville: Ohio.* Plan of Indian Mounds on the site of Circleville, Ohio, from Caleb Atwater, "Description of the Antiquities Discovered in the State of Ohio," American Antiquarian Society, *Transactions and Collections.* Worcester, Mass., 1820. Vol. 1. CU-O

Figure 289. *Circleville, Ohio: 1810.* Manuscript redrawing by John W. Reps in 1955 of a copy of the original town plat of Circleville, Ohio, as reconstructed by the Pickaway County, Ohio Engineer. A

Figure 290. *Bird's Eye View of Circleville, Ohio, in 1836, Looking South.* View of Circleville, Ohio in 1836, from a painting by G. W. Wittich in 1870, in Williams Brothers, *The History of Franklin and Pickaway Counties, Ohio.* Cleveland, 1880. CU-O

Figure 291. *Circleville, Ohio: 1837-1856*. Manuscript plans of Circleville, Ohio, drawn by John W. Reps in 1955. A

Figure 292. *Perryopolis*. Unsigned, undated manuscript redrawing of the original plat of Perryopolis, Pennsylvania, 1834. FCP

Figure 293. *Plat of Land Donated to the Toledo University of Arts and Trades*. Unsigned plan of a proposed Toledo University Community recorded October 24, 1872. LCO

Figure 294. *Cotati*. Plan of Cotati, California, from Reynolds & Proctor, *Illustrated Atlas of Sonoma County, California*. Santa Rosa, 1898. LC-M

Figure 295. *The Octagon Plan of Settlement*. Plan for Octagon City, Kansas, from Octagon Settlement Company, *The Octagon Settlement Company, Kansas*. New York, 1856. KHS

Figure 296. *Vue Generale de L'Exposition Universelle de 1889*. View of the Paris Exposition of 1889, from Glenn Brown (comp.), *Papers Relating to the Improvement of the City of Washington*. Washington, 1901. CU-FA

Figure 297. *Standard Guide Map of the World's Columbian Exposition at Chicago, 1893*. Plan of the World's Fair at Chicago, Illinois, published by Rand, McNally & Co. Chicago, 1893. NY-M

Figure 298. *Bird's Eye View, World's Columbian Exposition*. View of the Chicago Fair of 1893, from Hubert Howe Bancroft, *The Book of the Fair*. Chicago, 1893. CU-O

Figure 299. *Study for Grouping of Buildings, City of Washington, D.C.* Plan for Washington, D.C., drawn by Cass Gilbert in 1900, from Brown, *Papers Relating to The Improvement of the City of Washington, District of Columbia*. CU-FA

Figure 300. *Plan Showing Proposed Method of Laying Out the Public Grounds at Washington*. Unsigned manuscript copy in 1867 of Andrew Jackson Downing's plan for the mall in Washington, D.C., of 1851. Prepared to accompany the annual report of Br^t Brig. Genl N. Michler, in charge of Public Buildings, Grounds, and Works. October 1, 1867. FAC

Figure 301. Untitled photograph of model of the Capitol and surrounding area in Washington, D.C., as existing in 1901. FAC

Figure 302. *Washington, D.C. Diagram of a Portion of City Showing Proposed Sites for Future Public Buildings*. Plan for Central Washington, D.C., from Senate Park Commission, *The Improvement of the Park System of the District of Columbia*. Washington, 1902. A

Figure 303. *Bird's-Eye View of General Plan, from Point Taken 4,000 Feet above Arlington*. View drawn by F. L. V. Hoppin for the Senate Park Commission in 1901 showing the proposals for Washington, D.C. FAC

Figure 304. *View Showing the Proposed Treatment of Union Square at the Head of the Mall*. View drawn by C. Graham for the Senate Park Commission in 1901 showing the proposals for Washington, D.C. FAC

Figure 305. *General View of the Monument Garden and Mall, Looking toward the Capitol*. View drawn by C. Graham for the Senate Park Commission in 1901 showing the proposals for Washington, D.C. FAC

Figure 306. *View of the Monument and Terraces from the White House*. View drawn by Jules Guerin for the Senate Park Commission in 1901 showing the proposals for Washington, D.C. FAC

Figure 307. *San Francisco. Plan Showing System of Highways, Public Places, Parks, Park Connections, etc. . . . Daniel H. Burnham, Report on a Plan for San Francisco*. San Francisco, 1905. A

Figure 308. *Bird's-Eye Perspective of the City from the East, Showing the Proposed Changes*. View of San Francisco, California, from Burnham, *Report on a Plan for San Francisco*. A

Figure 309. *Plan of Civic Center*. Plan of the Civic Center for San Francisco, California, from Burnham, *Report on a Plan for San Francisco*. A

Figure 310. *Map of the City and County of San Francisco Showing Areas Recommended as Necessary for Public Places, Parks, Park Connections and Highways*. Plan of San Francisco, California, from Burnham, *Report on a Plan for San Francisco*. A

Figure 311. *Chicago. Plan of a Complete System of Street Circulation and System of Parks and Playgrounds. . . .* Plan for Chicago, Illinois, from Daniel H. Burnham and Edward H. Bennett, *Plan of Chicago*. Chicago, 1909. TWM

Figure 312. *Chicago. Plan of the Complete System of Street Circulation; Railway Stations; Parks, Boulevard Circuits and Radial Arteries; Public Recreation Piers, Yacht Harbor, and Pleasure-Boat Piers; Treatment of Grant Park; the Main Axis and the Civic Center. . . .* Plan for Chicago, Illinois, from Burnham and Bennett, *Plan of Chicago*. TWM

Figure 313. *Chicago. The Business Center of the City, within the first Circuit Boulevard, showing the Proposed Grand East-and-West Axis and its Relation to Grant Park and the Yacht Harbor; the Railway Terminals Schemes on the South and West Sides, and the Civic Center*. Plan for Chicago, Illinois, from Burnham and Bennett, *Plan of Chicago*. TWM

Figure 314. *Chicago. Plan of the Proposed Group of Municipal Buildings or Civic Center, at the Intersection of Congress and Halsted Streets*. Plan for Chicago, Illinois, from Burnham and Bennett, *Plan of Chicago*. TWM

Explanation of Symbols

A	Author's Collection
AMCB	Archives of the Moravian Church, Bethlehem, Pennsylvania
BHS	Buffalo Historical Society, Buffalo, New York
BN	Bibliothèque Nationale, Paris, France
CCI	Clark County, Indiana Official Records, Jeffersonville, Indiana
CHS	Chicago Historical Society, Chicago, Illinois
CPL	Cairo Public Library, Cairo, Illinois
CPS	California Pioneer Society, San Francisco, California
CU-DP	Cornell University, Department of City and Regional Planning, Ithaca, New York
CU-FA	Fine Arts Library, Cornell University, Ithaca, New York
CU-M	Mann Library, Cornell University, Ithaca, New York
CU-O	Olin Library, Cornell University, Ithaca, New York
CU-UA	University Archives, Cornell University, Ithaca, New York
CWML	College of William and Mary Library, Williamsburg, Virginia
DCL	Dartmouth College Library, Hanover, New Hampshire
DP-BC	Burton Historical Collection, Detroit Public Library, Detroit, Michigan
FAC	Fine Arts Commission, Washington, D.C.
FCL	Filson Club Library, Louisville, Kentucky
FCP	Fayette County, Pennsylvania Official Records, Uniontown, Pennsylvania
GI	Gary, Indiana Official Records
GSGD	Georgia Surveyor-General Department, Atlanta, Georgia
HA-U	Widener Library, Harvard University, Cambridge, Massachusetts
HEHL	Henry E. Huntington Library, San Marino, California
HLDS	Church Historian, Church of Jesus Christ of Latter-Day Saints, Salt Lake City, Utah
HU-BA	Harvard University, Library of the Graduate School of Business Administration, Cambridge, Massachusetts
HU-GD	Harvard University, Library of Graduate School of Design, Cambridge, Massachusetts
ISL	Indiana State Library, Indianapolis, Indiana
JCB	John Carter Brown Library, Brown University, Providence, Rhode Island
KCL	Kenyon College Library, Gambier, Ohio
KHS	Kansas Historical Society, Topeka, Kansas
KNCL	Knox College Library, Galesburg, Illinois
LC-GC	Library of Congress, General Collection, Washington, D.C.
LC-M	Library of Congress, Map Division, Washington, D.C.
LC-MS	Library of Congress, Manuscripts Division, Washington, D.C.
LC-P	Library of Congress, Prints and Photographs Division, Washington, D.C.
LCO	Lucas County, Ohio Official Records, Toledo, Ohio
MAHS	Massachusetts Historical Society, Boston, Massachusetts
MAWS	Moravian Archives, Winston-Salem, North Carolina
McGL	McGill University Library, Montreal, Canada
MDAH	Mississippi Department of Archives and History, Jackson, Mississippi
MHR	Maryland Hall of Records, Annapolis, Maryland
MHS	Missouri Historical Society, St. Louis, Missouri
NCPC	National Capital Planning Commission, Washington, D.C.
NYHS	New York Historical Society, New York, New York
NY-M	Map Division, New York Public Library, New York, New York
NY-R	Rare Books Division, New York Public Library, New York, New York
NY-S	Stokes' Collection, New York Public Library, New York, New York
NYSL	New York State Library, Albany, New York
PAC	Public Archives of Canada, Ottawa, Ontario, Canada
PP	Plimoth Plantation, Inc., Plymouth, Massachusetts
SAS	State Archives of Sweden, Stockholm, Sweden
STCO	Stark County, Ohio Official Records, Massillon, Ohio
TWM	Collection of Thomas W. Mackesey, Ithaca, New York
UC	General Collection, University of California Library, Berkeley, California
UC-AE	University of California, Office of Architects and Engineers, Berkeley, California
UC-BL	Bancroft Collection, University of California Library, Berkeley, California
VSL	Virginia State Library, Richmond, Virginia
WHS	Wisconsin Historical Society, Madison, Wisconsin
WLC	William L. Clements Library, University of Michigan, Ann Arbor, Michigan
WRHS	Western Reserve Historical Society, Cleveland, Ohio
WSHS	Washington State Historical Society, Tacoma, Washington

Note on Cartographic Research Methods

MUCH of the material appearing in this book was obtained through the use of conventional research techniques and methods. Special attention to cartographic sources was required because of the nature of the subject. A brief note on this aspect of the research may be of assistance to others concerned with the history of urban planning of a particular era, region, or type of plan.

The study began with a list of cities known to be significant because of their size and importance, some peculiarity of their plan which set them apart, their position as a dominant community whose plan was reproduced in later communities of the same or other areas, their place in time as an early example of a major plan form, or some other distinguishing characteristic. This initial list included such cities as Washington, Philadelphia, New York, New Haven, Williamsburg, Annapolis, Savannah, St. Augustine, to mention only a few on the Atlantic coast.

Collection of conventional historical materials on the founding and development of these cities was accompanied by a search for significant cartographic items. Local historical societies and libraries were consulted as well as most of the major map libraries of the country whose collections are not limited to a particular region. Photostat copies of maps and views dating from the founding of the city and its earlier years were obtained for study purposes.

One library collection deserves special mention because of its usefulness. This is the Stokes Collection of American historical prints in the New York Public Library. This magnificent collection contains several hundred plans and views of American cities. The printed catalog of the collection has full bibliographical descriptions of all items included as well as historical and interpretative comments. Copies of every view and plan in this collection were studied with profit.

As efforts were made to trace the origins of the plan forms used in these cities and to determine their influence in the planning of cities subsequently laid out, it became obvious that the inquiry should be widened. A more ambitious research plan was conceived, aimed at a broader view of towns and cities without regard for any known importance of their plans. An attempt was made to look at maps showing the plan of every city, town, and village in the United States. This could not be done completely because some of the maps do not exist, but a major portion of the country was covered using a variety of sources. While this required much time, the results amply repaid the effort. Several sources of cartographic materials were employed.

All United States Geologic Survey topographic quadrangle maps in print by the summer of 1957 were examined in the Cornell University Library collection. The number of these sheets probably exceeds 10,000. Their scales vary from the recent series at 1:24,000 (1 inch to 2,000 feet) to the older maps of the series dating from the 1880's and 1890's at 1:125,000. The entire country is not yet mapped, but the parts for which there is still no coverage are sparsely settled or uninhabited. Notes were made of any cities showing unusual street patterns, large amounts of open space, parks and recreation areas with symmetrical distribution patterns, large or unusually designed central squares, or other features setting them apart from the more typical undeviating gridiron pattern unrelieved by parks, squares, or open space. It may be useful to note that many of the older quadrangles were more revealing as far as the pattern of parks and squares is concerned than the modern series of maps. More recent quadrangles use a red tint for built up areas. While this does not prevent a study of the street pattern, it does obscure individual city blocks that may have been set aside as parks or open spaces.

An effort was made to examine all state and county atlases that were published in such large numbers during the three decades after the Civil War, particularly in eastern and midwestern states. The Cornell University Library has a large and representative collection of these atlases, which contain detailed street and property line plans of all cities and villages and many unincorporated hamlets. Major collections of these atlases in the New York Public Library and the Library of Congress were also consulted as well as those in many smaller regional libraries and historical societies. In all, probably 800 to 1000 of these atlases were examined and photostats of significant plans were obtained for further study.

Visits were made to most of the libraries in the United States with major map collections. Many smaller collections were also visited. The best results were obtained from looking at every item in these collections. This required more time than selecting maps to be seen from a card catalog, but it brought to light plans of many cities with unusual characteristics that would otherwise have remained unknown. With few exceptions map librarians were willing to permit this kind of search once the nature of the study was explained to them. Additional photostat study copies were obtained at this stage of the research. Where suitable plans were not found in map collections and where previous information indicated that the plans of certain cities were probably significant, copies of the original town plats were obtained from the county clerks or registers of deeds of the counties in which the communities were located.

Four types of books provided additional hints of unusual town plans or of events in the planning or development of communities that warranted further search for cartographic materials. Early travel accounts proved of some value, and dozens of these were skimmed for any mention of peculiar or outstanding features of town layout. The state and city guidebooks produced in the depression years by the Federal Writers' Program were particularly useful, although of uneven quality. All of the state guides and many of those for cities in this series were reviewed for any mention of noteworthy planning characteristics. Also of great help were the catalogs of the Library of Congress exhibitions of state centennial or sesquicentennial celebrations. These catalogs reproduce many of the early plans and views of chief cities of the states and give full bibliographic listings of other cartographic items.

A final series of books that proved of material assistance were the delightfully illustrated historical works by John Warner Barber, Sherman Day, and Henry Howe. Typically, these volumes contain brief accounts of the principal features of all of the cities of the states or territories covered, together with wood engravings of views or plans of many of them. The accuracy and detail varies from book to book, but generally they present a good impression of the appearance of American cities in the middle of the last century.

County histories, publications and collections of local and state historical societies, and works on state, regional, and local history also suggested cities and towns for which plans should be obtained. In addition, articles and books by others concerned directly with the history of city planning in a particular city, state, or region were useful. Valuable suggestions were also made by many persons whose ideas on cities and towns to be included in the investigation were solicited or volunteered.

Finally, most of the towns and cities selected for description and analysis in the text of the book were visited, inspected, and photographed. There is no completely adequate substitute for such field inspection.

These trips included examination of all of the European cities or projects discussed in the opening chapter dealing with the background of North American colonial settlement and town planning.

This research effort has been both arduous and rewarding. Much still remains for city planning historians of a particular period, area, or plan form. There is a wealth of manuscript and archival material that remains virtually untouched by those concerned with the history of town development. The use of aerial photographs in the present study was limited, but this tool has great possibilities for research in a state or region. In special cases the techniques of the field archaeologist can be profitably employed as in such localities as Williamsburg, Schoenbrunn, and Fort Raleigh. The author is under no illusions that he has exhausted even the obvious and more readily obtainable cartographic evidence and hopes only that this note will be of help to future historians who may correct, amplify, or confirm the findings, conclusions, and judgments contained in this study.

Acknowledgments

This book could not have been written without the encouragement, advice, and assistance of many persons and organizations and without access to research and library facilities of many institutions. I am deeply indebted to all these sources of help. It is inevitable that in the acknowledgments to follow I have omitted some names of persons and organizations who have been of assistance to me. Let me here extend my apologies for any such oversights and record my gratitude for their aid.

Thomas W. Mackesey, Professor of Regional Planning and Vice-Provost of Cornell University, was Dean of the College of Architecture during most of the time this study was conceived and carried out. Dean Mackesey is an authority in city planning history and made helpful suggestions on many occasions. Both he and his successor, Burnham Kelly, extended constant encouragement and understanding throughout the eleven years of research on this work.

The cost of travel and assembling the large number of map and plan reproductions would have been beyond my means except for generous financial assistance. I am particularly grateful to the John Simon Guggenheim Foundation for a fellowship grant in 1958 which permitted seven months of uninterrupted travel, research, and writing. The Foundation also provided a supplementary grant in 1963 to meet the substantial cost of photographs reproduced in the text. I am indebted also to the Cornell University Faculty Research Committee for several grants to pay costs of travel and map reproduction. Inspection of several foreign map collections was made possible through the generosity of the Eisenhower Exchange Fellowship, under whose sponsorship I traveled in Europe in 1959.

For three months in 1958 the University of California at Berkeley generously extended its hospitality to me as a Visiting Scholar. The Department of City and Regional Planning provided office space, and the following members of that department were generous with their help in many ways: Francis Violich, Jack Kent, Donald Foley, Catherine Bauer Wurster, Barclay Jones, Melvin Webber, and Holloway Jones.

The staff of the Reference and Rare Books Departments of the University Library and the Fine Arts Library of Cornell University were of major assistance in gathering material for this study. I am especially grateful to the following: Etta Arntzen, David Shearer, Josephine Tharpe, Frances Lauman, Barbara Berthelsen, Caroline Spicer, Michael Jasenas, Billy Wilkinson, Virginia Reid, and Evelyn Greenberg. Sandra Rowe, Assistant Librarian of the Fine Arts Library, spent many hours checking, correcting, and verifying the bibliographic entries.

Two chapters draw heavily on Master's theses prepared under my supervision by Fred Roy Frank and David G. Sheffield. Neither should be held responsible for certain conclusions I have reached with which they may not entirely agree. One other Master's thesis at Cornell, by Ralph Gakenheimer, proved extremely useful as a check on my research and conclusions.

Briefer studies of various aspects of American city planning history have been prepared over the years by former students as course or seminar papers. Among the most helpful were those written by the following persons: Edward Street, John Stainton, Walter Muir, Frederick Mayer, Charles Rogers, Jonathan Meigs, Eduardo Molinari, Luigi Horne, David Brandon, Richard West, and James Vandervoort. After the completion of the first draft five students listened to seminar presentations of a major portion of the work: David Sheffield, Bruce Hyland, Andre Wallays, Robert Smart, and Phillip Chamberlain. Their constructive questions and critical comments proved valuable in the work of rewriting and revision. The same students reviewed the status of town planning in European countries responsible for American colonial settlement. These seminar papers helped materially in the preparation of the introductory chapter.

A number of my colleagues at Cornell have made useful suggestions for which I am grateful. They include Morris Bishop, Stephen Jacobs, Barclay Jones, Kermit Parsons, Martin Dominguez, Paul Gates, David Davis, Stuart Barnette, Frederick Marcham, Henry Detweiler, and Frederick Edmondson. I am also indebted to Grady Clay, R. V. Tooley, Robert Morris, Edward Heiselberg, Myer R. Wolfe, Robert Lillibridge, Walter Creese and L. M. Wilson for similar aid.

My debt to Carl Feiss is substantial. Mr. Feiss generously allowed me to use an unpublished manuscript prepared by him and Frederick R. Stevenson some years ago covering much the same ground as this book. This proved of major assistance in confirming or correcting many of my ideas and in suggesting areas for further investigation. Beyond this, Mr. Feiss has given me many valuable suggestions and has encouraged and helped me in matters of detail and interpretation.

I appreciate also the aid of Professor Gerald Breese who read and commented in great detail on the penultimate draft of the book. Although it has not been possible to incorporate all of his suggestions, many have resulted in substantial improvements. Useful editorial and substantive help was also received from Mrs. Helen Duprey Bullock, who read and commented on an earlier draft of several of the chapters. Edward S. Riley also reviewed a portion of the material appearing herein. To all of these I wish to express my thanks, while absolving them of any errors of fact or interpretation which may remain.

The research necessary for this study has taken me to many libraries, historical collections, museums, archives, and public records. I have received assistance also by mail from others that could not be visited. Space does not permit detailed acknowledgment of the many special services and collection searches that were required by staff members of these institutions and offices. My indebtedness to all those who rendered assistance is very great, for it would have been impossible to complete this book without the help that was so willingly and promptly extended.

To this aspect of the work staff members of the following historical societies contributed: Massachusetts Historical Society, Kansas Historical Society, State Historical Society of Wisconsin, American Antiquarian Society, American Philosophical Society, Missouri Historical Society, Burlington County, New Jersey Historical Society, Western Reserve Historical Society, Washington State Historical Society, California Historical Society, Arizona Pioneers' Historical Society, Society of California Pioneers, Colorado State Historical Society, Columbia Historical Society, Florida Historical Society, St. Augustine Historical Society, Georgia Historical Society, Chicago Historical Society, Illinois State Historical Society, Indiana Historical Society, Kansas State Historical Society, Louisiana Historical Society, Detroit Historical Society, Minnesota Historical Society, Buffalo Historical Society, Long Island Historical Society, Holland Purchase Historical Society, Firelands Historical Society, Ohio Historical Society, York County Historical Society, Bennington Battle Monument and Historical Association, Antiquarian and Numismatic Society of Montreal and the New York Historical Society.

I also wish to thank librarians of the following: Dartmouth College Library, Harvard University Library, Harvard University Graduate School of Business Administration Library, Harvard University Graduate School of Design Library, Toledo, Ohio Public Library, College of William and Mary Library, Detroit Public Library, Virginia State Library, Colorado State Library, Huntington Library, University of California Library, University of California College of Environmental Design Library, Cairo, Illinois Public Library, Circleville, Ohio Public Library, Northampton, Massachusetts Public Library, Tacoma, Washington Public Library, William L. Clements Library, John Carter Brown Library, Marietta College Library, Knox College Library, San Francisco, California Public Library, Ohio State Library, Indiana State Library, Illinois State Library, New York State Library, Athens, New York Public Library, Library of the American Institute of Architects, Pittsfield, Massachusetts Public Library, Louisiana State Library, Koninklijke Bibliotheek in The Hague, and the Bibliotheek der Rijksuniversiteit in Leiden.

Because of special assistance rendered in three libraries on many occasions I wish to express my thanks especially to the following: Richard Stephenson of the Map Division and Milton Kaplan of the Division of Prints and Photographs in the Library of Congress, Gerard L. Alexander, Chief of the Map Division of the New York Public Library, and John Barr Tompkins of the Bancroft Collection in the University of California Library.

Officials of the following organizations also provided assistance: The Filson Club of Louisville, Kentucky; Colonial Williamsburg; Plimoth Plantation, Inc.; Detroit Museum of History; Louisiana State University Department of Archives and Manuscripts; Maryland Hall of Records; Mississippi Department of Archives and History; New York State Division of Archives and History; North Carolina State Department of Archives and History; Campus Martius Museum of Marietta, Ohio; Archives of the Moravian Church in Bethlehem, Pennsylvania; Moravian Archives in Winston-Salem, North Carolina; Bishopsgate Institute in London; the British Museum; the Public Archives of Canada; and the Riksarkivet in Stockholm.

I appreciate also the help rendered by Suzanne Bergeon of Paris and Valentine Picatoste of Madrid in obtaining graphic materials from libraries in France and Spain for study and reproduction purposes. For original drawings used for some of the illustrations I am obligated to John Gibson and Ray Weisenburger. I am grateful to the following who typed various portions of several drafts of the manuscript: Lois Teeter, Kathleen Chandler, Lynn Walsh, Christine Dauber, and Jacqueline Haskins. For skillful and painstaking assistance in photocopy work for many of the illustrations I am deeply indebted to Frederick Keib of the Cornell Photo Science Studios.

Portions of several chapters originally appeared in somewhat different form in two journals which have authorized their use in this book. To the editors of the *Town Planning Review* and the *Journal of the Society of Architectural Historians* I owe not only the usual formal acknowledgment but also deep appreciation for their editorial help in the past and for the encouragement their publication of my articles has given me.

I also wish to acknowledge with gratitude permission to use copyrighted materials in the possession of the following: Appleton-Century-Crofts, Inc., Martinus Nijhoff, A. H. Robins Co. Inc., Marshall Jones Co., and the Commercial Club of Chicago. The difficult task of editing the manuscript was skillfully performed by Mrs. Gail Filion.

Finally, with deepest appreciation I wish to thank my wife, Constance Peck Reps for her understanding, patience, and encouragement over the many years in which this work has been in preparation.

Selected Bibliography of Sources Consulted

This bibliography is divided into twenty sections: one for general sources, one for sources dealing in whole or part with urban topography, and one for each of the eighteen chapters. It is far from exhaustive, but it should prove helpful to those who wish to pursue further the subjects treated in this book.

General Works

Andrews, Charles McLean, *The Colonial Period of American History.* 4 vols. New Haven: Yale University Press, 1934-38.

Bannister, Turpin C., "Early Town Planning in New York State," *Journal of the Society of Architectural Historians*, Vol. 3, Nos. 1-2 (January-April, 1943), pp. 36-42.

Billington, Ray Allen, *Westward Expansion, a History of the American Frontier.* New York: The Macmillan Co., 2nd ed., 1960.

Bolton, Herbert Eugene and Thomas M. Marshall, *The Colonization of North America.* New York: The Macmillan Co., 1920.

Bridenbaugh, Carl, *Cities in the Wilderness: The First Century of Urban Life in America, 1625-1742.* New York: The Ronald Press Co., 1938.

————, *Cities in Revolt: Urban Life in America, 1743-1776.* New York: Knopf, 1955.

Brown, Ralph H., *Historical Geography of the United States.* New York: Harcourt, Brace and Co., 1948.

Chitwood, Oliver Perry, *A History of Colonial America.* New York: Harper, 3rd ed., 1961.

Churchill, Henry S., *The City is the People.* New York: Reynal & Hitchcock, 1945.

Dick, Everett, *The Story of the Frontier.* New York: Tudor Publishing Co., 1941.

Feiss, Carl, "The Heritage of Our Planned Communities," *Journal of the Society of Architectural Historians*, Vol. 1, Nos. 3-4 (July-October, 1941), pp. 27-30, 32.

Gabriel, Ralph Henry (ed.), *The Pageant of America.* 15 vols. New Haven: Yale University Press, 1926-29.

Green, Constance McLaughlin, *American Cities in the Growth of the Nation.* New York: John DeGraff, 1957.

Griffith, Ernest S., *History of American City Government.* New York: Oxford University Press, 1938.

Hamlin, Talbot F., *Greek Revival Architecture in America.* New York: Oxford University Press, 1944.

Handlin, Oscar, and Others, *Harvard Guide to American History.* Cambridge: Belknap Press, 1954.

Havighurst, Walter (ed.), *Land of the Long Horizons.* New York: Coward-McCann Inc.

————, *Land of Promise: The Story of the Northwest Territory.* New York: The Macmillan Co., 1946.

Morrison, Hugh, *Early American Architecture from the First Colonial Settlements to the National Period.* New York: Oxford University Press, 1952.

Mumford, Lewis, *Sticks and Stones: A Study of American Architecture and Civilization.* New York: Dover, 2nd ed., 1955.

Nelson, Howard J., "Walled Cities of the United States," *Annals of the Association of American Geographers*, Vol. 51 (1961), pp. 1-22.

Newcomb, Rexford, *Architecture of the Old Northwest Territory.* Chicago: University of Chicago Press, 1950.

Riegel, Robert E., *America Moves West.* New York: Holt, 3rd ed., 1956.

Tallmadge, Thomas E., *The Story of Architecture in America.* New York: Norton, rev. ed., 1936.

Trewartha, Glenn T., "Types of Rural Settlement in Colonial America," *Geographical Review*, Vol. 36, No. 4 (October 1946), pp. 568-96.

Tunnard, Christopher, *The City of Man.* New York: Charles Scribner's Sons, 1953.

————, and Henry Hope Reed, *American Skyline: The Growth and Form of Our Cities and Towns.* Boston: Houghton Mifflin, 1955.

U.S. Library of Congress, *A Guide to the Study of the United States of America.* Prepared under the Direction of Roy P. Basler by Donald H. Mugridge and Blanche P. McCrum. Washington: U.S. Government Printing Office, 1960.

U.S. Works Progress Administration and Works Projects Administration, Federal Writers' Project and Writers' Program, *American Guide Series.* 153 vols. Various publishers, 1936-1943.

Wade, Richard C., *The Urban Frontier: The Rise of Western Cities, 1790-1830.* Cambridge: Harvard University Press, 1959.

Winsor, Justin (ed.), *Narrative and Critical History of America.* 8 vols. Boston: Houghton Mifflin and Co., 1884-89.

————, *The Westward Movement.* Boston: Houghton Mifflin and Co., 1897.

Urban Cartography and Topography

Barber, John Warner, *Connecticut Historical Collections.* New Haven: Dure & Peck and J. W. Barber, 1838.

————, *Historical Collections . . . of Every Town in Massachusetts.* Worcester: Dorr, Howland & Co., 1839.

————, *Pictorial History of the State of New York.* Cooperstown: J. & E. Phinney, 1846.

————, and Henry Howe, *All the Western States and Territories.* Cincinnati: Howe's Subscription Book Concern, 1868.

Barber, and Howe, *Historical Collections of the State of New Jersey*. New York: S. Tuttle, 1844.

——, ——, *Our Whole Country: A Panorama and Encyclopedia of the United States*. 2 vols. Cincinnati: Charles Tuttle, 1863.

Day, Sherman, *Historical Collections of the State of Pennsylvania*. Philadelphia: George W. Gorton, 1843.

Freeman, Graydon LaVerne (ed.), *Historical Prints of American Cities*. Watkins Glen: Century House, 1952.

Haskell, Daniel C., *American Historical Prints. Early Views of American Cities, Etc.* New York: New York Public Library, 1927.

Howe, Henry, *Historical Collections of Ohio*. Cincinnati: Henry Howe, 1847.

Lewis, Henry, *Das Illustrirte Mississippithal*. Dusseldorf: Arnz & Comp., 1857.

Lowery, Woodbury, *A Descriptive List of Maps of the Spanish Possessions within the Present Limits of the United States, 1502-1820*. Edited with notes by Philip Lee Phillips. Government Printing Office, 1912.

Paullin, Charles O., *Atlas of the Historical Geography of the United States*. Washington: Carnegie Institution of Washington and American Geographical Society of New York, 1932.

Phillips, Philip Lee, *A List of Geographical Atlases in the Library of Congress*. 5 vols. (vol. 6 in preparation as of July 1963). Beginning with vol. 5, the List is compiled by Clara Egli LeGear. Government Printing Office, 1909.

——, *A List of Maps of America in the Library of Congress, Preceded by a List of Works Relating to Cartography*. Government Printing Office, 1901.

——, *List of Maps and Views of Washington and District of Columbia in the Library of Congress*. Government Printing Office, 1900.

Stokes, I. N. Phelps and D. C. Haskell (comps.), *American Historical Prints:*

Early Views of American Cities. New York: New York Public Library, 1932.

U.S. Library of Congress, *An Exhibition Commemorating the Settlement of Georgia, 1733-1948*. Government Printing Office, 1948.

——, *California: The Centennial of the Gold Rush and the First State Constitution*. Government Printing Office, 1949.

——, *Centennial of the Oregon Territory*. Government Printing Office, 1948.

——, *Centennial of the Settlement of Utah*. Government Printing Office, 1947.

——, *Centennial of the Territory of Minnesota*. Government Printing Office, 1949.

——, *Colorado: The Diamond Jubilee of Statehood*. Government Printing Office, 1951.

——, *District of Columbia Sesquicentennial of the Establishment of the Permanent Seat of the Government*. Government Printing Office, 1950.

——, *Florida's Centennial*. Government Printing Office, 1946.

——, *Indiana: The Sesquicentennial of the Establishment of the Territorial Government*. Government Printing Office, 1950.

——, *Iowa Centennial*. Government Printing Office, 1947.

——, *Kansas and Nebraska: Centennial of the Territories, 1854-1954*. Government Printing Office, 1954.

——, *Michigan: Sesquicentennial of the Territory, 1805-1955*. Government Printing Office, 1955.

——, *Ohio: The Sesquicentennial of Statehood, 1803-1953*. Government Printing Office, 1953.

——, *Oklahoma: The Semicentennial of Statehood*. Government Printing Office, 1957.

——, *Old New Castle and Modern Delaware*. Government Printing Office, 1951.

——, *Tennessee's Sesquicentennial Exhibition*. Government Printing Office, 1946.

——, *Texas Centennial Exhibition*. Government Printing Office, 1946.

——, *United States Atlases: A Catalog*

of National, State, County, City, and Regional Atlases in the Library of Congress and Cooperating Libraries. Compiled by Clara Egli LeGear. Government Printing Office, 1953.

——, *United States Atlases: A List of National, State, County, City, and Regional Atlases in the Library of Congress*. Compiled by Clara Egli LeGear. Government Printing Office, 1950.

——, *Washington: Centennial of the Territory, 1853-1953*. Government Printing Office, 1953.

——, *Wisconsin Centennial*. Government Printing Office, 1948.

Winsor, Justin, *The Kohl Collection (now in the Library of Congress) of Maps Relating to America*. Government Printing Office, 1904.

1. *European Planning on the Eve of American Colonization*

Alberti, Leone Battista, *Ten Books on Architecture*. Translated into Italian by Cosimo Bartoli and into English by James Leoni. Edited by Joseph Rykwert. London: Tiranti, 1955.

Blunt, Anthony, *Art and Architecture in France, 1500 to 1700*. London: Penguin Books, 1953.

Burke, Gerald L., *The Making of Dutch Towns: A Study in Urban Development from the Tenth to the Seventeenth Centuries*. London: Cleaver-Hume Press, 1956.

Camblin, Gilbert, *The Town in Ulster: An Account of the Origin and Building of the Towns of the Province and the Development of Their Rural Setting*. Belfast: W. Mullan, 1951.

Chancellor, Edwin Beresford, *The History of the Squares of London*. London: Kegan Paul, Trench, Trubner and Co., 1907.

Eden, W. A., "Studies in Urban Theory: The De Re Aedificatoria of Leon Battista Alberti," *The Town Planning Review*, Vol. 19, No. 1 (1943), pp. 10-28.

Gakenheimer, Ralph Albert, *The Spanish*

King and His Continent: A Study of the Importance of the "Laws of the Indies" for Urban Development in Spanish America. Unpublished Master's Thesis, Cornell University. Ithaca, New York, 1959.

Gothein, Marie Louise, A History of Garden Art. 2 vols. Translated from the German by Mrs. Archer-Hind. Edited by Walter P. Wright. London: J. M. Dent and Sons, Ltd., 1928.

Hautecoeur, Louis, Histoire de l'Architecture Classique en France.... Vol. 1, La Formation de l'Ideal Classique. Paris: A. Picard, 1943-55.

Hegemann, Werner and Elbert Peets, The American Vitruvius: An Architect's Handbook of Civic Art. New York: Architectural Book Publishing Co., 1922.

Hiorns, Frederick R., Town-Building in History. London: G. G. Harrap, 1956.

Hughes, Thomas Harold and E. A. G. Lamborn, Towns and Town Planning, Ancient and Modern. Oxford: Clarendon Press, 1923.

Korn, Arthur, History Builds the Town. London: Lund, Humphries, 1953.

Lavedan, Pierre, Histoire de l'Urbanisme. 3 vols. Paris: H. Laurens, 1926-1952.

Mackesey, Thomas W., History of City Planning: A Bibliography. Edited by Rolland W. Mills. Oakland: Council of Planning Librarians, 1961.

Morley, Henry (ed.), Ideal Commonwealths. London: G. Routledge and Sons, Ltd., 1885.

Mumford, Lewis, The City in History: Its Origins, Its Transformations, and Its Prospects. New York: Harcourt, Brace & World, 1961.

———, The Culture of Cities. New York: Harcourt, Brace and Co., 1938.

Palladio, Andrea, The Architecture of A. Palladio: In Four Books. Revised, designed, and published by Giacomo Leoni. Translated from the Italian original with notes and remarks of Inigo Jones. 3rd edition. London: A. Ward, 1742.

Rasmussen, Steen Eiler, Towns and Buildings Described in Drawings and Words. Cambridge: Harvard University Press, 1951.

———, London: The Unique City. New York: Macmillan Company, 1937.

Reddaway, T. F., "The Rebuilding of London After the Great Fire: A Rediscovered Plan," The Town Planning Review, Vol. 18, No. 3 (July 1939), pp. 155-61.

Reps, John W., Ideal Cities. Unpublished Master's Thesis, Cornell University. Ithaca, New York, 1947.

Stewart, Cecil, A Prospect of Cities. London: Longmans, Green, 1953.

Summerson, John Newenham, Georgian London. New York: Charles Scribner's Sons, 1946.

Torres Balbas, Leopoldo, Resumen Histórico del Urbanismo en España. Madrid: Instituto de Estudios de Administración Local, 1954.

Tout, Thomas Frederick, Medieval Town Planning. Manchester: Manchester University Press, 1934.

Triggs, Harry Inigo, Garden Craft in Europe. London: B. T. Batsford, 1913.

Tunnard, Christopher, The City of Man. New York: Scribner, 1953.

Zucker, Paul, Town and Square from the Agora to the Village Green. New York: Columbia University Press, 1959.

2. Spanish Towns of Colonial America

Bancroft, Hubert Howe, History of California. 7 vols. San Francisco: The History Company, 1884-90.

Beck, Warren A., New Mexico: A History of Four Centuries. Norman: University of Oklahoma Press, 1962.

Blackmar, Frank Wilson, Spanish Institutions of the Southwest. Baltimore: Johns Hopkins Press, 1891.

Bolton, Herbert Eugene, Outpost of Empire: The Story of the Founding of San Francisco. New York: A. A. Knopf, 1931.

———, Texas in the Middle Eighteenth Century: Studies in Spanish Colonial History and Administration. Berkeley: University of California Press, 1915.

———, "The Spanish Occupation of Texas, 1519-1690," The Southwestern Historical Quarterly, Vol. 16, No. 1 (July 1912), pp. 1-26.

Chatelain, Verne Elmo, The Defenses of Spanish Florida, 1565-1763. Washington, D.C.: Carnegie Institution of Washington, 1941.

Corner, William (ed.), San Antonio de Bexar. San Antonio: Bainbridge & Corner, 1890.

Cox, Isaac Joslin, "The Founding of the First Texas Municipality," Texas Historical Association Quarterly, Vol. 2, No. 3 (January 1899), pp. 217-26.

Cutter, Donald C., Malaspina in California. San Francisco: John Howell, 1960.

Dominguez, Francisco Atanasio, The Missions of New Mexico, 1776: A Description with Other Contemporary Documents. Translated and annotated by Eleanor B. Adams and Angelico Chavez. Drawings by Horace T. Pierre. Albuquerque: University of New Mexico Press, 1956.

Duflot de Mofras, Eugène, Duflot de Mofras' Travels on the Pacific Coast. 2 vols. Translated, edited and annotated by Marguerite Eyer Wilber. Santa Ana: Fine Arts Press, 1937.

Forbes, Alexander, California: A History of Upper and Lower California from Their First Discovery to the Present Time. London: Smith, Elder and Co., 1839.

Gakenheimer, Ralph Albert, The Spanish King and His Continent, a Study of the Importance of the "Laws of the Indies" for Urban Development in Spanish America. Unpublished Master's Thesis, Cornell University. Ithaca, New York, 1959.

Gregory, Thomas Jefferson, History of Sonoma County, California. Los Angeles: Historic Record Company, 1911.

Hall, Frederic, The History of San José and Surroundings. San Francisco: A. L. Bancroft and Co., 1871.

Hammond, George P. and Agapito Rey (eds. and trans.), Don Juan de Oñate: Colonizer of New Mexico, 1595-1628. 2 vols. Albuquerque: University of New Mexico Press, 1953.

Instituto de Estudios de Administración Local, *Planos de Ciudades Ibero-americanas y Filipinas Existentes en el Archivo de Indias*. 2 vols. Madrid: 1951.

Instruccion para la Fundacion de Los Angeles. Archives of California, State Papers, Missions and Colonization, Vol. 1. As translated and used in evidence in *Annis Meril v. J. S. Joerenhout*, et al., filed in California Superior Court, Los Angeles County, May 10, 1869.

Johnson, John Everett (trans.), *Regulations for Governing the Province of the Californias*. 2 vols. San Francisco: Grabhorn Press, 1929.

Lowery, Woodbury, *The Spanish Settlements within the Present Limits of the United States, 1513-1561*. New York: G. P. Putnam's Sons, 1901.

————, *The Spanish Settlements within the Present Limits of the United States: Florida, 1562-1574*. New York: G. P. Putnam's Sons, 1905.

Morfi, Juan Augustin, *History of Texas, 1673-1779*. 2 vols. Translated by Carlos Eduardo Castañeda. Albuquerque: Quivira Society, 1935.

Moses, Bernard, *The Establishment of Municipal Government in San Francisco*. Baltimore: Publication Agency of Johns Hopkins University, 1889.

Nuttall, Zelia, "Royal Ordinances Concerning the Laying Out of New Towns," *The Hispanic American Historical Review*, Vol. 5 (1922), pp. 249-54.

Pittman, Philip, *The Present State of the European Settlements on the Missisippi*. London, 1770. Reprinted, Cleveland: A. H. Clark Co., 1906.

Pourade, Richard F., *The History of San Diego: The Explorers*. San Diego: Union-Tribune Publishing Company, 1960.

Ramsdell, Charles, *San Antonio: A Historical and Pictorial Guide*. Austin: University of Texas Press, 1959.

Richman, Irving Berdine, *California Under Spain and Mexico, 1535-1847*. Boston: Houghton Mifflin Company, 1911.

Scott, Mellier Goodin, *The San Francisco Bay Area: A Metropolis in Perspective*. Berkeley: University of California Press, 1959.

Smith, Robert C., "Colonial Towns of Spanish and Portuguese America," *Journal of the Society of Architectural Historians*, Vol. 9, No. 4 (December 1955), pp. 3-12.

Stanislawski, Dan, "Early Spanish Town Planning in the New World," *The Geographical Review*, Vol. 37, No. 1 (January 1947), pp. 94-105.

Violich, Francis, "Evolution of the Spanish City: Issues Basic to Planning Today," *Journal of the American Institute of Planners*, Vol. 28, No. 3 (August 1962), pp. 170-79.

Vitruvius, Pollio, *The Ten Books of Architecture*. Translated and edited by Morris Hicky Morgan. Cambridge: Harvard University Press, 1926.

3. *The Towns of New France*

Alvord, Clarence Walworth, *The Illinois Country, 1673-1818*. Springfield: Illinois Centennial Commission, 1920.

American State Papers. Public Lands Series, Vol. 2. Washington: Gales and Seaton, 1834.

Atherton, William Henry, *Montreal, 1535-1914*. 3 vols. Montreal: The S. J. Clarke Publishing Company, 1914.

Baily, Francis, *Journal of a Tour in Unsettled Parts of North America, in 1796 and 1797*. London: Baily Brothers, 1856.

Belting, Natalia Maree, *Kaskaskia Under the French Regime*. Urbana: University of Illinois Press, 1948.

Brackenridge, Henry Marie, *Views of Louisiana: Together with a Journal of a Voyage up the Missouri River in 1811*. Pittsburgh: Cramer, Spear and Eichbaum, 1814.

Calnek, W. A., *History of the County of Annapolis*. Edited and completed by A. W. Savary. Toronto: William Briggs, 1897.

Cauthorn, Henry S., *A History of the City of Vincennes, Indiana from 1702 to 1901*. Vincennes: Margaret C. Cauthorn, 1902.

Champlain, Samuel de, *The Works of Samuel de Champlain*. 6 vols. Reprinted, translated and annotated by six Canadian scholars under the general editorship of H. P. Biggar. Toronto: Champlain Society, 1922-36.

Charlevoix, Pierre François Xavier, *History and General Description of New France*. 6 vols. Translated by John Gilmary Shea. New York: John Gilmary Shea, 1866.

————, *Journal of a Voyage to North America*. 2 vols. Translated and edited by Louise Phelps Kellogg. Chicago: Caxton Club, 1923.

Collins, Earl A. and Felix Eugene Snider, *Missouri: Midland State*. Cape Girardeau: Ramfire Press, 1961.

Crouse, Nellis M., *Lemoyne d'Iberville: Soldier of New France*. Ithaca: Cornell University Press, 1954.

Davis, Edwin Adams, *Louisiana: The Pelican State*. Baton Rouge: Louisiana State University Press, 1959.

Dollier de Casson, François, *A History of Montreal, 1640-1672*. Translated and edited by Ralph Flenley. London: J. M. Dent & Sons, 1928.

Douglas, James, *Old France in the New World: Quebec in the Seventeenth Century*. Cleveland: Burrows Brothers Company, 2nd ed., 1906.

Federal Writers Project, Works Progress Administration, *New Orleans City Guide*. Boston: Houghton Mifflin Co., 1938.

Flint, Timothy, *Recollections of the Last Ten Years*. Boston: Cummings, Hilliard, and Co., 1826.

Hamilton, Peter Joseph, *Colonial Mobile*. Boston and New York: Houghton Mifflin Co., Rev. and enl. ed., 1910.

Hugo-Brunt, Michael, "The Origin of Colonial Settlements in the Maritimes," Town Planning Institute of Canada, *Plan*, Vol. 1, No. 2 (June 1960), pp. 78-114.

Jefferys, Thomas, *The Natural and Civil History of the French Dominions in North and South America*. London: Thomas Jefferys, 1760.

Leacock, Stephen Butler, *Montreal, Seaport and City*. Garden City, New York: Doubleday, Doran & Company, Inc., 1942.

McDermott, John Francis, *Old Cahokia*. St. Louis: The St. Louis Historical Documents Foundation, 1949.

Pénicant, André, *Fleur de Lys and Calumet: Being the Pénicant Narrative of French Adventure in Louisiana*. Translated and edited by Richebourg Gaillard McWilliams. Baton Rouge: Louisiana State University Press, 1953.

Pittman, Philip, *The Present State of the European Settlements on the Missisippi*. London, 1770. Reprinted, Cleveland: A. H. Clark Co., 1906.

Quaife, M. M., *This is Detroit: 250 Years in Pictures*. Edited by William White. Detroit: Wayne University Press, 1951.

Reid, J. H. Stewart, Kenneth McNaught, and Harry S. Crowe, *A Source Book of Canadian History*. Toronto: Longmans, Green and Co., 1959.

Roberts, W. Adolphe, *Lake Pontchartrain*. Indianapolis: Bobbs-Merrill Co., 1946.

Schaaf, Ida M., "The Founding of Ste. Genevieve, Missouri," *Missouri Historical Review*, Vol. 27, No. 2 (January 1933), pp. 145-50.

Traquair, Ramsay, *The Old Architecture of Quebec*. Toronto: The Macmillan Company of Canada, Ltd., 1947.

Winsor, Justin, *Cartier to Frontenac: Geographical Discovery in the Interior of North America in Its Historical Relations, 1534-1700*. Boston: Houghton Mifflin and Co., 1894.

————, *The Mississippi Basin: The Struggle in America Between England and France, 1697-1763*. Boston: Houghton Mifflin and Co., 1895.

Woestemeyer, Ina Faye, *The Westward Movement*. New York: D. Appleton-Century Co., 1939.

4. *Town Planning in the Tidewater Colonies*

Andrews, Matthew Page, *Virginia: The Old Dominion*. Garden City: Doubleday, Doran & Co., Inc., 1937.

Beverley, Robert, *The History and Present State of Virginia* (London, 1705). Edited by Louis B. Wright. Reprinted, Chapel Hill: University of North Carolina Press, 1947.

Brewington, M. V., *Chesapeake Bay: A Pictorial Maritime History*. Cambridge, Maryland: Cornell Maritime Press, 1953.

Brown, Alexander (ed.), *The Genesis of The United States*. 2 vols. Boston: Houghton Mifflin and Co., 1890.

Brown, William H. (ed.), *Archives of Maryland*. 65 vols. Baltimore: Maryland Historical Society, 1883-1952.

Bruce, Philip Alexander, *Economic History of Virginia in the Seventeenth Century*. 2 vols. New York: Macmillan Co., 1896.

Dalton, Charles, *George The First's Army, 1714-1727*. 2 vols. London: Eyre and Spottiswoode, Ltd., 1910-1912.

Eddis, William, *Letters from America*. London: The Author, 1792.

Forman, Henry Chandlee, *Jamestown and St. Mary's, Buried Cities of Romance*. Baltimore: Johns Hopkins Press, 1938.

————, *Tidewater Maryland Architecture and Gardens*. New York: Architectural Book Publishing Co., 1956.

————, *Virginia Architecture in the Seventeenth Century*. Williamsburg: Virginia 350th Anniversary Celebration Corp., 1957.

Hall, Clayton Colman (ed.), *Narratives of Early Maryland, 1633-1684*. New York: Charles Scribner's Sons, 1910.

Hamor, Ralph, *A True Discourse of the Present Estate of Virginia, and the Successe of the Affaires There Till the 18 of June, 1614. Together with a Relation of the Severall English Townes and Fortes. . . .* London: William Welby, 1615.

Harrington, J. C., "Archeological Explorations at Fort Raleigh National Historic Site," *North Carolina Historical Review*, Vol. 26, No. 2 (April 1949), pp. 127-49.

Harris, Malcolm H., " 'Delaware Town' and 'West Point' in King William County, Virginia," *William and Mary Quarterly*, Second Series, Vol. 14, No. 4 (October 1934), pp. 342-51.

Hatch, Charles E., *Jamestown, Virginia: The Townsite and Its Story*, U.S. National Park Service Historical Handbook Series, No. 2. Government Printing Office, rev. ed., 1957.

Hening, William Waller, *The Statutes at Large . . . of Virginia*. Richmond: Samuel Pleasants, 1812.

Johnston, George, *History of Cecil County, Maryland*. Elkton, Maryland: The Author, 1881.

Jones, Hugh, *The Present State of Virginia*. London: J. Clarke, 1724.

Labaree, Leonard Woods (ed.), *Royal Instructions to British Colonial Governors, 1670-1776*. 2 vols. New York, London: D. Appleton-Century Co., 1935.

Land, Robert Hunt, "Henrico and Its College," *William and Mary Quarterly*, Second Series, Vol. 18, No. 4 (October 1938), pp. 453-98.

Lorant, Stefan (ed.), *The New World*. New York: Duell, Sloan & Pearce, 1946.

Mayer-Rotermund, Gerda, *Alte Gerichtsbegaude in Virginia*. Unpublished Dr. Ing. Dissertation, Technischen Hochschule. Braunschweig, 1958.

Mereness, Newton Dennison, *Maryland as a Proprietary Province*. New York: Macmillan Co., 1901.

Morton, Richard L., *Colonial Virginia*. 2 vols. Chapel Hill: University of North Carolina Press, 1960.

Oldmixon, John, *The British Empire in America*. 2 vols. London: J. Nicholson, B. Tooke, 1708.

Radoff, Morris Leon (ed.), *The Old Line State: A History of Maryland*. 3 vols. Hopkinsville, Ky.: Historical Record Association, 1956.

Riley, Edward M., "The Town Acts of

Colonial Virginia," *The Journal of Southern History*, Vol. 16, No. 3 (August 1950), pp. 306-23.

Riley, Elihu S., "The Ancient City": *A History of Annapolis, in Maryland. 1649-1887.* Annapolis: Annapolis Record Printing Office, 1887.

Shurcliff, Arthur A., "The Ancient Plan of Williamsburg," *Landscape Architecture*, Vol. 28, No. 1 (January 1938), pp. 87-101.

"Speeches of Students of the College of William and Mary Delivered May 1, 1699," *William and Mary Quarterly*, Second Series, Vol. 10, No. 4 (October 1930), pp. 323-37.

Tyler, Lyon Gardiner (ed.), *Narratives of Early Virginia, 1606-1625.* New York: Charles Scribner's Sons, 1907.

Whiffen, Marcus, *The Public Buildings of Williamsburg.* Williamsburg: Colonial Williamsburg, 1958.

Yonge, Samuel H., *The Site of Old "James Towne," 1607-1698.* Richmond: Association for the Preservation of Virginia Antiquities, 1904.

5. *New Towns in a New England*

Akagi, Roy Hidemichi, *The Town Proprietors of the New England Colonies: A Study of Their Development, Organization, Activities, and Controversies, 1620-1770.* Philadelphia: University of Pennsylvania Press, 1924.

Allen, Francis Olcott, *The History of Enfield, Connecticut.* 3 vols. Lancaster, Pennsylvania: The Wickersham Printing Co., 1900.

Andrews, Charles McLean, *The River Towns of Connecticut: A Study of Wethersfield, Hartford, and Windsor.* Baltimore: Publication Agency of Johns Hopkins University, 1889.

Atwater, Edward Elias, *History of the Colony of New Haven to Its Absorption into Connecticut.* New Haven: The Author, 1881.

Bidwell, Percy Wells and John I. Falconer, *History of Agriculture in the Northern United States, 1620-1860.* Washington: The Carnegie Institution of Washington, 1925.

Bigelow, Edwin Victor, *A Narrative History of the Town of Cohasset, Massachusetts.* Boston: S. Usher, 1898.

Bradford, William, *Bradford's History of Plymouth Plantation, 1606-1646.* Edited by William T. Davis. New York: Charles Scribner's Sons, 1908.

Bronson, Henry, *The History of Waterbury, Connecticut.* Waterbury: Bronson Brothers, 1858.

Bunting, Bainbridge, "The Plan of the Back Bay Area in Boston," *Journal of the Society of Architectural Historians*, Vol. 13, No. 2 (May 1954), pp. 19-24.

Burrage, Henry Sweetser, *The Beginnings of Colonial Maine, 1602-1658.* Portland: Marks Printing House, 1914.

Burt, Henry M., *The First Century of the History of Springfield: The Official Records from 1636-1736.* 2 vols. Springfield, Mass.: H. M. Burt, 1898-99.

Cady, John Hutchins, *The Civic and Architectural Development of Providence, 1636-1950.* Providence: Providence Book Shop. 1957.

Daniels, George Fisher, *History of the Town of Oxford, Massachusetts.* Oxford: The Author, 1892.

Egleston, Melville, *The Land System of the New England Colonies.* Baltimore: N. Murray, Publication Agent, Johns Hopkins University, 1886.

Felt, Joseph Barlow, *History of Ipswich, Essex, and Hamilton.* Cambridge: C. Folsom, 1834.

Garvan, Anthony W. B., *Architecture and Town Planning in Colonial Connecticut.* New Haven: Yale University Press, 1951.

Gray, Howard Levi, *English Field Systems.* Cambridge: Harvard University Press, 1915.

Green, Samuel Abbott, *Ten Fac-simile Reproductions Relating to Old Boston and Neighborhood.* Boston: J. Wilson and Son, 1901.

Hunnewell, James Frothingham, *A Century of Town Life: A History of Charlestown, Massachusetts, 1775-1887.* Boston: Little, Brown and Co., 1888.

Hurd, Duane Hamilton, *History of Middlesex County, Massachusetts.* 3 vols. Philadelphia: J. W. Lewis and Co., 1890.

Jameson, John Franklin (ed.), *Narratives of New Netherland, 1609-1664.* New York: Charles Scribner's Sons, 1909.

Labaree, Leonard Woods, *Milford, Connecticut: The Early Development of a Town as Shown in Its Land Records.* New Haven: Yale University Press, 1933.

Lambert, Edward Rodolphus, *History of the Colony of New Haven, Before and After the Union with Connecticut.* New Haven: Hitchcock & Stafford, 1838.

Love, William DeLoss, *The Colonial History of Hartford.* Hartford: The Author, 1914.

Maclear, Ann Bush, *Early New England Towns: A Comparative Study of Their Development.* New York: Longmans, Green & Co., 1908.

Meeks, Carroll L. V., "Lynx and Phoenix: Litchfield and Williamsburg," *Journal of the Society of Architectural Historians*, Vol. 10, No. 4 (December 1951), pp. 18-23.

Morison, Samuel Eliot, *The Founding of Harvard College.* Cambridge: Harvard University Press, 1935.

Mussey, Barrows, *Old New England.* New York: A. A. Wyn, Inc., 1946.

Perley, Sidney, *The History of Salem, Massachusetts.* 3 vols. Salem: S. Perley, 1924-28.

Schenck, Elizabeth Hubbell Godfry, *The History of Fairfield, Fairfield County, Connecticut, from the Settlement of the Town in 1639 to 1818.* 2 vols. New York: The Author, 1889-1905.

Scofield, Edna, "The Origin of Settlement Patterns in Rural New England," *Geographical Review*, Vol. 28, No. 4 (October 1938), pp. 652-63.

Sheldon, George, *A History of Deerfield, Massachusetts.* 2 vols. Deerfield: E. A. Hall & Co., 1895-96.

Shurtleff, Nathaniel Bradstreet, *A Topographical and Historical Description of Boston.* Boston: Printed by request of the City Council, 1871.

Smith, Joseph Edward Adams, *The History of Pittsfield (Berkshire County), Massachusetts.* 2 vols. Boston: Lee and Shepard, 1869-76.

Stiles, Henry Reed, *The History of Ancient Windsor, Connecticut.* New York: C. B. Norton, 1859.

Strachey, William, *The Historie of Travaile into Virginia Britannia.* Edited from the original manuscript by R. H. Major. London: Hakluyt Society, 1849.

Thayer, Henry Otis, *The Sagadahoc Colony.* . . . Portland: Gorges Society, 1892.

Trewartha, Glenn T., "Types of Rural Settlement in Colonial America," *Geographical Review,* Vol. 36, No. 4 (October 1946), pp. 568-96.

Trumbull, James Russell, *History of Northampton, Massachusetts.* 2 vols. Northampton: Gazette Printing Co., 1898-1902.

Weeden, William B., *Economic and Social History of New England, 1620-1789.* 2 vols. Boston: Houghton, Mifflin and Co., 1890.

Whitehill, Walter Muir, *Boston, a Topographical History.* Cambridge: Belknap Press of Harvard University Press, 1959.

Wilcoxson, William Howard, *History of Stratford, Connecticut, 1639-1939.* Stratford: Stratford Tercentenary Commission, 1939.

Winsor, Justin (ed.), *The Memorial History of Boston, Including Suffolk County, Massachusetts, 1630-1880.* 4 vols. Boston: J. R. Osgood and Co., 1880-81.

Woodard, Florence May, *The Town Proprietors in Vermont: The New England Town Proprietorship in Decline.* New York: Columbia University Press, 1936.

Woodruff, George Catlin, *History of the Town of Litchfield, Connecticut.* Litchfield: C. Adams, 1845.

Young, Alexander, *Chronicles of the First Planters of the Colony of Massachusetts Bay, from 1623-1636.* Boston: C. C. Little and J. Brown, 1846.

————, *Chronicles of the Pilgrim Fathers of the Colony of Plymouth, from 1602 to 1625.* Boston: C. C. Little and J. Brown, 1841.

6. *New Amsterdam, Philadelphia and Towns of the Middle Colonies*

Bailey, Paul, *Long Island.* New York: Lewis History Publishing Co., 1949.

Board of Proprietors of the Eastern Division of New Jersey, *The Minutes of the Board. . . . from 1685 to 1705.* Introductory Essay by George J. Miller. Perth Amboy: Board of Proprietors of the Eastern Division of New Jersey, 1949.

Campanius Holm, Thomas, *A Short Description of the Province of New Sweden.* Translated by Peter S. Du Panceau. Pennsylvania Historical Society, *Memoirs,* Vol. 3, Part 1, pp. i-vi, 13-166. Philadelphia: Pennsylvania Historical Society, 1834.

Danckaerts, Jasper, *Journal of Jasper Danckaerts, 1679-1680.* Edited by Bartlett Burleigh James and J. Franklin Jameson. New York: Charles Scribner's Sons, 1913.

De Cou, George, *Burlington: A Provincial Capital.* Philadelphia: Harris and Partridge, Inc., 1945.

Diffenderffer, Frank Ried, ". . . . Early Local History as Revealed by an Old Document," *Lancaster County Historical Society, Journal,* Vol. 2, No. 1 (1897), pp. 1-27.

Eckman, Jeannette, *Crane Hook on the Delaware, 1667-1699.* Newark: Institute of Delaware History and Culture, University of Delaware, 1958.

Elting, Irving, *Dutch Village Communities on the Hudson River.* Baltimore: W. Murray, 1886.

Flick, Alexander C. (ed.), *History of the State of New York.* 10 vols. New York: Columbia University Press, 1933-37.

Ford, James, *Slums and Housing.* 2 vols. Cambridge: Harvard University Press, 1936.

Frank, Fred Roy, *The Development of New York City: 1600-1900.* Unpublished Master's Thesis, Cornell University. Ithaca, New York, 1955.

"Governor Thomas Pownall's Description of the Streets and the Main Roads about Philadelphia, 1754," *Pennsylvania Magazine of History and Biography,* Vol. 18, No. 2 (1894), pp. 211-18.

Hazard, Samuel, *Annals of Pennsylvania, from the Discovery of the Delaware, 1609-1682.* Philadelphia: Hazard and Mitchell, 1850.

Hough, Oliver, "Captain Thomas Holme, Surveyor-General of Pennsylvania and Provincial Councillor," *Pennsylvania Magazine of History and Biography,* Vol. 19 (1895), pp. 413-27 and Vol. 20 (1896), pp. 128-31, 248-56.

Innes, J. H., *New Amsterdam and Its People.* New York: Charles Scribner's Sons, 1902.

Jameson, John Franklin (ed.), *Narratives of New Netherland, 1609-1664.* New York: Charles Scribner's Sons, 1909.

Johnson, Amandus, *The Swedish Settlements on the Delaware, 1638-1664.* 2 vols. Philadelphia: University of Pennsylvania, 1911.

Kouwenhoven, John A., *The Columbia Historical Portrait of New York: An Essay in Graphic History in Honor of the Tercentennial of New York City and the Bicentennial of Columbia University.* New York: Doubleday & Co., 1953.

Laws of the Commonwealth of Pennsylvania. Philadelphia: John Bloren, 1810.

Lingelbach, William E., "William Penn and City Planning," *The Pennsylvania Magazine of History and Biography,* Vol. 68, No. 4 (October 1944), pp. 398-418.

MacCoun, Townsend, *Early New York. A Portfolio of Five Maps.* New York: Townsend MacCoun, 1909.

Miller, The Rev. John, *A Description of the Province and City of New York with Plans of the City and Several Ports as They Existed in the Year, 1695.* London: Thomas Rodd, 1843.

Myers, Albert Cook (ed.), *Narratives of*

Early Pennsylvania, West New Jersey, and Delaware, 1630-1707. New York: Charles Scribner's Sons, 1912.

Nederlandsche West-Indische Compagnie, *Documents Relating to New Netherland, 1624-1626, in the Henry E. Huntington Library.* Translated and edited by A. J. F. van Laer. San Marino, California: The Henry E. Huntington Library and Art Gallery, 1924.

O'Callaghan, E. B., *The Documentary History of the State of New York.* 4 vols. Albany: Weed, Parsons & Co., Public Printers and Charles van Benthuysen, Public Printer, 1849-51.

Penn, William, *A Further Account of the Province of Pennsylvania and Its Improvements.* London: n. p., 1685.

Philadelphia Select and Common Councils, *A Digest of the Acts of Assembly Relating to the City, the (late) Incorporated Districts of the County, and the Said City and Districts, in Force 1st January, 1856.* Compiled and edited by W. Duane, W. B. Hood, and L. Meyers. Philadelphia: n. p., 1856.

Reddaway, T. F., "The Rebuilding of London After the Great Fire: A Rediscovered Plan," *Town Planning Review,* Vol. 18, No. 3 (July 1939), pp. 155-61.

Reed, John, "An Explanation of the Map of the City and Liberties of Philadelphia," *Pennsylvania Archives,* Third Series, Vol. 3 (1894), pp. 295-401.

Reps,. John W., "William Penn and the Planning of Philadelphia," *Town Planning Review,* Vol. 27, No. 1 (April 1956), pp. 27-39.

Sachse, Julius F., "Penn's City on the Susquehanna," Lancaster County Historical Society, *Journal,* Vol. 2, No. 8 (1898), pp. 223-37.

Smith, Samuel, *The History of the Colony of Nova-Caesaria, New Jersey.* Trenton: W. S. Sharp, 1877.

Stokes, I. N. Phelps, *The Iconography of Manhattan Island, 1498-1909.* 6 vols. New York: R. H. Dodd, 1915-28.

Tatum, George B., *Penn's Great Town.* Philadelphia: University of Pennsylvania Press, 1961.

Thompson, Benjamin F., *History of Long Island.* 3 vols. New York: Robert H. Dodd, 3rd ed., 1918.

Valentine, David T., *History of the City of New York.* New York: G. P. Putnam & Co., 1853.

Van Rensselaer, Mariana Griswold, *History of the City of New York in the Seventeenth Century.* 2 vols. New York: Macmillan Co., 1909.

Ward, Christopher, *New Sweden on the Delaware.* Philadelphia: University of Pennsylvania Press, 1938.

————, *The Dutch and Swedes on the Delaware, 1609-1664.* Philadelphia: University of Pennsylvania Press, 1930.

Wieder, Frederik Caspar, *De Stichting van New York in July, 1625.* The Hague: M. Nijhof, 1925.

Wootten, Bayard and Anthony Higgins, *New Castle, Delaware, 1651-1939.* Boston: Houghton Mifflin Co., 1939.

7. Colonial Towns of Carolina and Georgia

"A Contemporary View of Carolina in 1680," *The South Carolina Historical Magazine,* Vol. 55 (1954), pp. 153-59.

Bannister, Turpin B., "Oglethorpe's Sources for the Savannah Plan," *Journal of the Society of Architectural Historians,* Vol. 20, No. 20 (May 1961), pp. 47-62.

Buckingham, James Silk, *The Slave States of America.* 2 vols. London: Paris, Fisher, Son & Co., 1842.

Chandler, Harry A., "Map of a Portion of Historical Savannah," *Georgia Historical Quarterly,* Vol. 1, No. 4 (December 1917), frontispiece.

Coulter, E. Merton, *Georgia: A Short History.* Chapel Hill: University of North Carolina Press, 3rd ed., 1960.

DeBrahm, John Gerar William, *History of the Province of Georgia; with Maps of Original Surveys.* Wormsloe, Georgia: Privately printed by George Wymberley-Jones, 1849.

Dill, Alonzo Thomas, *Governor Tryon and His Palace.* Chapel Hill: University of North Carolina Press, 1955.

Ettinger, Amos Aschbach, *James Edward Oglethorpe: Imperial Idealist.* Oxford: Clarendon Press, 1936.

Fleming, Berry (comp.), *Autobiography of a Colony: The First Half-Century of Augusta, Georgia.* Athens: University of Georgia Press, 1957.

Graffenried, Christopher von, *Baron Christopher von Graffenried's Account of the Founding of New Bern.* Edited with an historical introduction and an English translation by Vincent H. Todd . . . in cooperation with Julius Goebel. Raleigh: Edwards and Broughton Printing Co., 1920.

Johnston, Frances Benjamin, *The Early Architecture of North Carolina.* Chapel Hill: University of North Carolina Press, 1941.

Jones, Charles Colcock, *The Dead Towns of Georgia.* Georgia Historical Society, *Collections,* Vol. 4, Part 1. Savannah: Georgia Historical Society, 1878.

————, *The History of Georgia.* 2 vols. Boston: Houghton, Mifflin & Co., 1883.

Lee, E. Lawrence, Jr., "Old Brunswick, The Story of a Colonial Town," *North Carolina Historical Review,* Vol. 29, No. 2 (April 1952), pp. 230-45.

Lefler, Hugh Talmage and Albert Ray Newsome, *North Carolina: The History of a Southern State.* Chapel Hill: University of North Carolina Press, 1954.

Martyn, Benjamin, *An Account, Showing the Progress of the Colony of Georgia, in America, from its First Establishment.* London, 1741. Reprinted, Georgia Historical Society, *Collections,* Vol. 2, pp. 265-325. Savannah: Georgia Historical Society, 1842.

————, *Reasons for Establishing the Colony of Georgia.* London, 1733. Reprinted, Georgia Historical Society, *Collections,* Vol. 1, pp. 203-38. Savannah: Georgia Historical Society, 1840.

Moore, Francis, *A Voyage to Georgia, Begun*

in the Year, 1735. London, 1744. Reprinted, Georgia Historical Society, *Collections,* Vol. 1, pp. 79-152. Savannah: Georgia Historical Society, 1840.

Mountgomery, Sir Robert, *A Discourse Concerning the Design'd Establishment of a New Colony to the South of Carolina in the Most Delightful Country of the Universe.* London, 1717. Reprinted. Washington: Peter Force, 1835.

Nichols, Frederick Doveton, *The Early Architecture of Georgia.* With a Pictorial Survey, by Frances Benjamin Johnston. Chapel Hill: University of North Carolina Press, 1957.

"Observations in Several Voyages and Travels in America," *The London Magazine,* Vol. 14 (December 1745), pp. 602-04.

Oglethorpe, James Edward (Attributed), *A New and Accurate Account of the Provinces of South Carolina and Georgia.* London: Printed for J. Worrall . . . and sold by J. Roberts, 1732.

Reps, John W., "Town Planning in Colonial Georgia," *The Town Planning Review,* Vol. 30, No. 4 (January 1960), pp. 273-85.

————, "The Green Belt Concept," *Town and Country Planning,* Vol. 28, No. 7 (July 1960), pp. 246-50.

Salley, Alexander S. (ed.), *Narratives of Early Carolina, 1650-1708.* New York: Charles Scribner's Sons, 1911.

South Carolina Gazette, 1733. Charleston, S.C.

Spalding, Thomas, "A Sketch of the Life of General James Oglethorpe," Georgia Historical Society, *Collections,* Vol. 1, pp. 239-95. Savannah: Georgia Historical Society, 1840.

Stevenson, Frederick R. and Carl Feiss, "Charleston and Savannah," *Journal of the Society of Architectural Historians,* Vol. 10, No. 4 (December 1951), pp. 3-9.

Tailfer, Patrick, Hugh Anderson, David Douglass and Others, *A True and Historical Narrative of the Colony of Georgia in America.* Charles Town, 1741. Reprinted with Comments by the Earl of Egmont, Athens: University of Georgia Press, 1960.

Temple, Sarah B. and Kenneth Coleman, *Georgia Journeys.* Athens: University of Georgia Press, 1961.

Wallace, David Duncan, *South Carolina: A Short History.* Chapel Hill: University of North Carolina Press, 1957.

8. *Pioneer Cities of the Ohio Valley*

Baily, Francis, *Journal of a Tour in Unsettled Parts of North America, in 1796 and 1797.* London: Baily Brothers, 1856.

Birkbeck, Morris, *Notes on a Journey in America from the Coast of Virginia to the Territory of Illinois.* London: James Ridgway, 3rd ed., 1818.

Bond, Beverley W., *The Foundations of Ohio.* Vol. 1 of The History of the State of Ohio, edited by Carl Wittke, 6 vols. Columbus: Ohio State Archaeological and Historical Society, 1941.

Buckingham, James Silk, *The Eastern and Western States of America.* 3 vols. London: Fisher, Son & Co., 1842.

Caruso, John Anthony, *The Great Lakes Frontier: An Epic of the Old Northwest.* Indianapolis: The Bobbs-Merrill Co., 1961.

Craig, Neville B., *The History of Pittsburgh, with a Brief Notice of Its Facilities of Communication, and Other Advantages for Commercial and Manufacturing Purposes.* Pittsburgh: J. H. Mellor, 1851.

Durrett, Reuben Thomas, *The Centenary of Louisville.* Louisville: J. P. Morton and Co., 1893.

Feiss, Carl, "Tallmadge, Township No. 2, Range 10, Connecticut Fire Lands: An Early Ohio Planned Community," *Journal of the Society of Architectural Historians,* Vol. 12, No. 2 (May 1953), pp. 25-26.

Flower, George, *History of the English Settlement in Edwards County, Illinois.* Chicago: Fergus Printing Company, 1882.

Ford, Amelia C., *Colonial Precedents of Our National Land System as It Existed in 1800.* Madison: University of Wisconsin, 1910.

Harris, Isaac, *Pittsburgh Business Directory for the Year, 1837.* Pittsburgh: n.p., 1837.

Hatcher, Harlan, *The Western Reserve: The Story of New Connecticut in Ohio.* Indianapolis: Bobbs-Merrill Co., 1942.

Havighurst, Walter, *Land of Promise: The Story of the Northwest Territory.* New York: The Macmillan Co., 1946.

————, *Wilderness for Sale: The Story of the First Western Land Rush.* New York: Hastings House, 1956.

Hening, William Waller, *The Statutes at Large . . . of Virginia.* Richmond: Samuel Pleasants, 1812.

Hibbard, Benjamin H., *A History of the Public Land Policies.* New York: The Macmillan Co., 1924.

Howe, Henry, *Historical Collections of Ohio.* 2 vols. Cincinnati: State of Ohio, 1900.

Hulbert, Archer B. (ed.), *The Records of the Original Proceedings of the Ohio Company.* 2 vols. Marietta: Marietta Historical Commission, 1917.

Kennedy, James Harrison, *A History of the City of Cleveland.* Cleveland: Imperial Press, 1896.

Lester, William Stewart, *The Transylvania Colony.* Spencer, Indiana: Samuel R. Guard & Co., 1935.

Mahoning Valley Historical Society, *Historical Collections of the Mahoning Valley.* Vol. 1. Youngstown: Mahoning Valley Historical Society, 1876.

Mason, Kathryn Harrod, *James Harrod of Kentucky.* Baton Rouge: Louisiana State University Press, 1951.

Melish, John, *Travels in the United States of America, in the Years, 1806 and 1807, and 1809, 1810 and 1811.* 2 vols. Philadelphia: The Author, 1812.

Mendenhall, Thomas Corwin, "The Town of Tallmadge—The Bacons and Shakespeare," Ohio Archaeological and Historical Society, *Publications,* Vol. 32 (1923), pp. 590-612. Columbus: Ohio Archaeological and Historical Society, 1923.

Newcomb, Rexford, *Architecture in Old Ken-*

tucky. Urbana: University of Illinois Press, 1953.

Pattison, William D., "The Survey of the Seven Ranges," *The Ohio Historical Quarterly*, Vol. 68, No. 2 (April 1959), pp. 115-40.

Pittsburgh Regional Planning Association and Pittsburgh City Planning Commission, *North Side Study*. Pittsburgh: Pittsburgh Regional Planning Association, 1954.

Putnam, Rufus, *The Memoirs of Rufus Putnam*. Boston: Houghton Mifflin Co., 1903.

Ranck, George Washington, *Boonesborough; Its Founding, Pioneer Struggles, Indian Experiences, Transylvania Days and Revolutionary Annals*. Louisville: J. P. Morton & Co., 1901.

Randall, Emilius O., "Tallmadge Township," Ohio Archaeological and Historical Society, *Publications*, Vol. 17 (1908), pp. 275-306. Columbus: Ohio Archaeological and Historical Society, 1908.

Riebel, R. C., *Louisville Panorama*. Louisville: Liberty National Bank and Trust Co., 1954.

Robbins, Roy M., *Our Landed Heritage: The Public Domain, 1776-1936*. Princeton: Princeton University Press, 1942.

Roseboom, Eugene H. and Francis P. Weisenburger, *A History of Ohio*. Edited and illustrated by James H. Rodabaugh. Columbus: The Ohio State Archaeological and Historical Society, 1953.

Sato, Shosuke, *History of the Land Question in the United States*. Baltimore: Publication Agency of the Johns Hopkins University, 1886.

Saugrain de Vigni, Antoine François, *L'Odyssée Américaine d'une Famille Française*. Baltimore: Johns Hopkins Press, 1936.

Smith, William (ed.), *Historical Account of Bouquet's Expedition Against the Ohio Indians, in 1764*. Cincinnati: R. Clarke & Co., 1868.

Treat, Payson Jackson, *The National Land System, 1785-1820*. New York: E. B. Treat & Co., 1910.

Upton, Harriet Taylor, *History of the Western Reserve*. 3 vols. Chicago: Lewis Publishing Co., 1910.

Vance, John L., "The French Settlement and Settlers of Gallipolis," Ohio Archaeological and Historical Society, *Publications*, Vol. 3 (1895), pp. 45-81. Columbus: Ohio Archaeological and Historical Society, 2nd ed., 1895.

Volney, Constantin Francois Chasseboeuf, Comte de, *A View of the Soil and Climate of the United States of America*. Translated by C. B. Brown. Philadelphia: J. Conrad & Co., 1804.

Williams Brothers, *History of Ashtabula County, Ohio*. Philadelphia: Williams Brothers, 1878.

Wright, Alfred J., "Joel Wright, City Planner," *Ohio Archaeological and Historical Quarterly*, Vol. 56, No. 3 (July 1947), pp. 287-94.

9. *Planning the National Capital*

Baily, Francis, *Journal of a Tour in Unsettled Parts of North America in 1796 and 1797*. London: Baily Brothers, 1856.

Birkbeck, Morris, *Notes on a Journey in America from the Coast of Virginia to the Territory of Illinois*. London: J. Ridgway, 3rd ed., 1818.

Bryan, Wilhelmus Bogart, *A History of the National Capital from its Foundation Through the Period of the Adoption of the Organic Act*. 2 vols. New York: The Macmillan Co., 1914-16.

Caemmerer, H. Paul, "The Life of Pierre Charles L'Enfant," Columbia Historical Society, *Records*, Vol. 50 (1952), pp. 323-340. Washington: Columbia Historical Society, 1952.

———, *The Life of Pierre Charles L'Enfant, Planner of the City Beautiful, The City of Washington*. Washington: National Republic Publishing Co., 1950.

———, *Washington, the National Capital*. Senate Document No. 332, 71st Congress, 3rd Session. Government Printing Office, 1932.

Clark, Allen C., "Origin of the Federal City,"

Columbia Historical Society, *Records*, Vols. 35-36 (1935), pp. 1-97. Washington: Columbia Historical Society, 1935.

Committee on the Centennial Celebration of the Establishment of the Seat of Government in the District of Columbia, *Celebration of the One-Hundredth Anniversary of the Establishment of the Seat of Government in the District of Columbia*. Compiled by William V. Cox. Government Printing Office, 1901.

Ellis, John B., *The Sights and Secrets of the National Capital*. New York: United States Publishing Company, 1869.

Goff, Frederick, "Early Printing in Georgetown (Potomak), 1789-1800 and the Engraving of L'Enfant's Plan of Washington, 1792," Columbia Historical Society, *Records*, Vols. 51-52 (1955), pp. 103-19. Washington: Columbia Historical Society, 1955.

Green, Constance McLaughlin, *Washington: Village and Capital, 1800-1878*. Princeton: Princeton University Press, 1962.

Hamilton, A. B., *Maps of the District of Columbia and City of Washington, and Plats of the Squares and Lots*. Washington: A. B. Hamilton, 1852.

Jefferson, Thomas, *Thomas Jefferson and the National Capital*. Edited by Saul K. Padover. Government Printing Office, 1946.

"Journal of William Loughton Smith, 1790-1791," Massachusetts Historical Society, *Proceedings*, Vol. 51 (1917-1918), pp. 20-88. Boston: Massachusetts Historical Society.

King, Nicholas, *The King Plats of the City of Washington in the District of Columbia, 1803*. Washington: N. Peters, 1888.

Kite, Elizabeth Sarah, *L'Enfant and Washington, 1791-1792*. Baltimore: The Johns Hopkins Press, 1929.

Lear, Tobias, *Observations on the River Potomack, the Country Adjacent, and the City of Washington*. New York, 1793. Reprinted, Baltimore: S. T. Chambers, 1940.

Mathews, Catherine Van Cortlandt, *Andrew*

Ellicott: His Life and Letters. New York: The Grafton Press, 1908.

Morgan, James Dudley, "Major Pierre Charles L'Enfant, the Unhonored and Unrewarded Engineer," Columbia Historical Society, *Records*, Vol. 2 (1899), pp. 116-57. Washington: Columbia Historical Society, 1899.

Morrison, Alfred J. (comp.), *The District in the XVIII Century . . . as Described by the Earliest Travellers*. Washington: Judd & Detweiler, 1909.

Nicolay, Helen, *Our Capital on the Potomac*. New York: The Century Co., 1924.

Peets, Elbert, "Famous Town Planners: L'Enfant," *Town Planning Review*, Vol. 13, No. 1 (July 1925), pp. 30-49.

———, "L'Enfant's Washington," *Town Planning Review*, Vol. 15, No. 3 (May 1933), pp. 155-64.

———, "The Genealogy of L'Enfant's Washington," *American Institute of Architects Journal*: Part I, Vol. 15, No. 4 (April 1927) pp. 115-19; Part II, Vol. 15, No. 5 (May 1927), pp. 151-54; Part III, Vol. 15, No. 6 (June 1927), pp. 187-91.

Phillips, Philip Lee, *List of Maps and Views of Washington and District of Columbia in the Library of Congress*. Senate Document 154, 56th Congress, 1st Session. Government Printing Office, 1900.

———, *The Beginnings of Washington, as Described in Books, Maps, and Views*. Washington: The Author, 1917.

Sunderland, Byron, "Washington as I First Knew It, 1852-1855," Columbia Historical Society, *Records*, Vol. 5 (1902), pp. 195-211. Washington: Columbia Historical Society, 1902.

Thatcher, Erastus, *Founding of Washington City*. Washington: The Law Reporter Co., 1891.

"The L'Enfant Memorials," Columbia Historical Society, *Records*, Vol. 2 (1899), pp. 72-110. Washington: Columbia Historical Society, 1899.

"The Writings of George Washington Relating to the National Capital," Columbia Historical Society, *Records*, Vol. 17 (1914), pp. 3-232. Washington: Columbia Historical Society, 1914.

Tindall, William, *Origin and Government of the District of Columbia*. Government Printing Office, 1908.

———, *Standard History of the City of Washington*. Knoxville: H. W. Crew & Co., 1914.

Twining, Thomas, *Travels in America 100 Years Ago*. New York: Harper & Brothers, 1894.

U.S. National Capital Park and Planning Commission, *Reports and Plans, Washington Region*. Supplementary Technical Data to Accompany Annual Report. Government Printing Office, 1930.

Varnum, Joseph Bradley, *The Seat of Government of the United States: A Review of the Discussions, in Congress and Elsewhere, on the Site and Plans of the Federal City*. Washington: R. Farnham, 1854.

Washington, George, *President Washington's Diaries, 1791 to 1799*. Transcribed and compiled by Joseph A. Hoskins. Summerfield, N. C.: n.p., 1921.

10. *Boulevard Baroque and Diagonal Designs*

American State Papers, Public Lands Series, VI. Washington: Gales & Seaton, 1860.

"Architecture in the United States," *American Journal of Science and Arts*. Vol. 17 (January 1830), pp. 99-110, 249-73.

Bolton, Nathaniel, *Early History of Indianapolis and Central Indiana*. Indianapolis: The Bowen-Merrill Co., 1897.

Carmony, Donald F., "Genesis and Early History of the Indianapolis Fund, 1816-1826," *Indiana Magazine of History*, Vol. 38, No. 1 (March 1942), pp. 17-30.

Chapman, Edmund H., "City Planning Under Industrialization: The Case of Cleveland," *Journal of the Society of Architectural Historians*, Vol. 12, No. 2 (May 1953), pp. 19-24.

———, "City Planning Under Mercantile Expansion: The Case of Cleveland, Ohio," *Journal of the Society of Architectural Historians*, Vol. 10, No. 4 (December 1951), pp. 10-17.

Copeland, Robert Morris, *The Most Beautiful City in America: Essay and Plan for the Improvement of the City of Boston*. Boston: Lee & Shepard, 1872.

"Documents Relating to Detroit and Vicinity, 1805-1813," *Michigan Historical Collections*. Lansing: Michigan Historical Commission, 1929.

Farmer, Silas, *History of Detroit and Michigan*. 2 vols. Detroit: Silas Farmer, 2nd ed., 1889.

Heald, Edward Thornton, *The Stark County Story*, Vol. I. Canton, Ohio: Stark County Historical Society, 1949.

"Judge Woodward's Resolution on Sundry Subjects, and the Report of the Committee on the Same, December 31, 1806," Michigan Pioneer and Historical Society, *Historical Collections*, Vol. 12 (1888), pp. 462-73. Lansing: Thorp & Godfrey, 1888.

Laws of the Territory of Michigan. Lansing: W. S. George & Co., 1811. Vol. I.

Merz, Charles, "Masonic Plat of Sandusky," *Sandusky Masonic Bulletin*, Vol. 25, No. 1 (September 1944). Sandusky, Ohio: Sandusky Masonic Lodge, 1944.

Michigan Commission on Land Titles, *Proceedings of the Land Board of Detroit*. Governor and Judges Journal. Edited by M. Agnes Burton and compiled by Clarence M. Burton. Detroit: n.p., 1915.

Moore, Charles, "Augustus Brevoort Woodward—A Citizen of Two Cities," Columbia Historical Society, *Records*, Vol. 4 (1901), pp. 114-27. Washington: Columbia Historical Society, 1901.

"Naming of Madison and Dane County," State Historical Society of Wisconsin, *Report and Collections*, Vol. 6 (1872), pp. 388-96. Madison: Atwood & Culver, 1872.

Nolan, Jeannette Covert, *Hoosier City: The Story of Indianapolis*. New York: Julian Messner, 1943.

Pickins, Buford L., "Early City Plans for Detroit, A Projected American Metropolis,"

The Art Quarterly, Vol. 6, No. 1 (Winter 1943), pp. 34-51.

"Protest by Judge Woodward Against the Sale of Certain Lands in Detroit, June 1, 1818," Michigan Pioneer and Historical Society, *Historical Collections*, Vol. 12 (1888), pp. 473-83. Lansing: Thorp & Godfrey, 1888.

Report of the Governor and Judges of Michigan Territory to Congress, October 10, 1805. Michigan Pioneer and Historical Society, *Historical Collections*, Vol. 36 (1908), pp. 103-11. Lansing: Michigan Pioneer and Historical Society, 1908.

Reps, John William, *Ideal Cities*. Unpublished Master's Thesis, Cornell University. Ithaca, New York, 1947.

———, "Planning in the Wilderness: Detroit, 1805-1830," *The Town Planning Review*, Vol. 25, No. 4 (January 1955), pp. 240-50.

Root, W. D., *Sandusky in 1855: City Guide and Business Directory*. Sandusky, Ohio: Bill, Cooke & Co., 1855.

Smith, Alice Elizabeth, *James Duane Doty*. Madison: State Historical Society of Wisconsin, 1954.

Steele, Fletcher, "Robert Fleming Gourlay, City Planner," *Landscape Architecture*, Vol. 6, No. 1 (October 1915), pp. 1-14.

Strong, Moses M., *History of the Territory of Wisconsin from 1836 to 1848*. Madison: Democrat Printing Co., 1885.

Thornbrough, Gayle and Dorothy Riker (comps.), *Readings in Indiana History*. Indianapolis: Indiana Historical Bureau, 1956.

Tipton, John, *The John Tipton Papers*, Vol. 1. Compiled by Glen A. Blackburn, edited by Nellie Armstrong Robertson and Dorothy Riker. Indianapolis: Indiana Historical Bureau, 1942.

Woodford, Frank B., *Mr. Jefferson's Disciple: A Life of Justice Woodward*. East Lansing: Michigan State University Press, 1953.

11. *Checkerboard Plans and Gridiron Cities*

Andreas, A. T., *History of Chicago*. 3 vols. Chicago: A. T. Andreas, 1884.

Baily, Francis, *Journal of a Tour in Unsettled Parts of North America in 1796 and 1797*. London: Baily Brothers, 1856.

Baird, Lewis C., *Baird's History of Clark County, Indiana*. Indianapolis: B. F. Bowen & Co., 1909.

Balestier, Joseph N., *The Annals of Chicago*. Chicago, 1840. Reprinted, Chicago: Fergus Printing Co., 1876.

Bridges, William, *Map of the City of New York and Island of Manhattan with Explanatory Remarks and References*. New York: William Bridges, 1811.

Buckingham, James Silk, *The Eastern and Western States of America*. 3 vols. London: Fisher, Son & Co., 1842.

Frank, Fred Roy, *The Development of New York City, 1600-1900*. Unpublished Master's Thesis, Cornell University. Ithaca, New York, 1955.

Herrington, James, "A Letter of James Herrington Written from Chicago in 1831," *Bulletin of the Chicago Historical Society*, Vol. 1, No. 2 (February 1935), pp. 45-46.

Hillman, Arthur and Robert J. Casey, *Tomorrow's Chicago*. Chicago: University of Chicago Press, 1953.

History of the Ohio Falls Cities and Their Counties with Illustrations and Bibliographical Sketches. 2 vols. Cleveland: L. A. Williams & Co., 1882.

Hoyt, Homer, *One Hundred Years of Land Values in Chicago*. Chicago: The University of Chicago Press, 1933.

Jefferson, Thomas, *The Writings of Thomas Jefferson*. 20 vols. Andrew R. Lipscomb, editor-in-chief. Washington: Thomas Jefferson Memorial Association of the U. S., 1903-04.

Laws of the State of Indiana Passed at the First Session of the General Assembly. Corydon: Cox and Nelson, 1817.

Lewis, Oscar (ed.), *This Was San Francisco*. New York: David McKay Co., Inc., 1962.

Martineau, Harriet, *Retrospect of Western Travel*. London: Saunders and Otley, 1838.

Pierce, Bessie Louise, *A History of Chicago*. 3 vols. New York: A. A. Knopf, 1937-57.

Reps, John W., "Thomas Jefferson's Checkerboard Towns," *Journal of the Society of Architectural Historians*, Vol. 20, No. 3 (October 1961), pp. 108-14.

Rowland, Dunbar, *History of Mississippi: The Heart of the South*. 2 vols. Chicago-Jackson: S. J. Clarke Publishing Co., 1925.

Scott, Mellier Goodin, *The San Francisco Bay Area: A Metropolis in Perspective*. Berkeley: University of California Press, 1959.

Soule, Frank, John H. Gihon and James Nisbet, *The Annals of San Francisco*. New York: D. Appleton & Co., 1855.

Stokes, Isaac Newton Phelps, *Iconography of Manhattan Island, 1498-1909*. 6 vols. New York: R. H. Dodd, 1915-28.

Tryon, Warren Stanson, *A Mirror for Americans: Life and Manners in the United States, 1790-1870, as Recorded by American Travelers*. 3 vols. Chicago: University of Chicago Press, 1952.

U. S. Department of State, *The Territorial Papers of the United States*. Vol. 7, *The Territory of Indiana, 1800-1810*. Compiled and edited by Clarence Edwin Carter. Government Printing Office, 1939.

———, *The Territorial Papers of the United States*. Vol. 9, *The Territory of Orleans, 1803-1812*. Compiled and edited by Clarence Edwin Carter. Government Printing Office, 1940.

12. *Cemeteries, Parks, and Suburbs: Picturesque Planning in the Romantic Style*

American Communities Company, *Lake Forest*. Chicago: American Communities Company, 1916.

"A Residence Section Planned on Nature's Lines: The Laying Out of Roland Park, near Baltimore," *The American City*, Vol. 9, No. 2 (August 1913), pp. 115-20.

Charles Eliot: Landscape Architect. Boston: Houghton Mifflin Co., 1902.

Cleveland, H. W. S., *A Few Words on the Arrangement of Rural Cemeteries*. Chicago: George K. Hazlitt & Co., 1881.

———, *Landscape Architecture as Applied to the Wants of the West*. Chicago: Janson, McClurg & Co., 1873.

Cook, Clarence Chatham, *A Description of the New York Central Park*. New York: F. J. Huntington and Co., 1869.

Copeland and Cleveland, *A Few Words on the Central Park*. Boston: Copeland & Cleveland, 1856.

Dearborn, Nathaniel, *Dearborn's Guide Through Mount Auburn*. Boston: n.p., 1851.

Downing, Andrew Jackson, *A Treatise on the Theory and Practice of Landscape Gardening*. New York: O. Judd & Co., 8th ed., 1859.

———, *Rural Essays*. Edited by George William Curtis. New York: G. P. Putnam and Co., 1853.

Hubbard, Theodora Kimball, "H. W. S. Cleveland: An American Pioneer in Landscape Architecture and City Planning," *Landscape Architecture*, Vol. 20, No. 2 (January 1930), pp. 92-111.

Menhinick, Howard, "Riverside Sixty Years Later," *Landscape Architecture*, Vol. 22, No. 2 (January 1932), pp. 109-17.

Mumford, Lewis, "Frederick Law Olmsted's Contribution," *Roots of Contemporary American Architecture*. New York: Reinhold, 1952, pp. 101-16.

New York City Board of Commissioners of the Central Park, *First Annual Report on the Improvement of the Central Park, January 1, 1857*. New York: Charles W. Baker, 1857.

New York City Board of Commissioners of the Central Park, *Minutes of Proceedings for the Year Ending April 30, 1859*. New York: William C. Bryant & Co., 1859.

Olmsted, Frederick Law, *Frederick Law Olmsted, Landscape Architect, 1822-1903*. 2 vols. Edited by Frederick Law Olmsted, Jr. and Theodora Kimball. New York: G. P. Putnam's Sons, 1922.

———, "Riverside Illinois." Selections from the Papers of Frederick Law Olmsted. Edited by Theodora Kimball Hubbard. *Landscape Architecture*, Vol. 21, No. 4 (July 1931), pp. 257-91.

Olmsted, Vaux & Company, *Preliminary Report in Regard to a Plan of Public Pleasure Grounds for the City of San Francisco*. New York: William C. Bryant & Co., 1866.

———, *Preliminary Report upon the Proposed Suburban Village at Riverside, Near Chicago*. New York: n.p., 1868.

———, *Report upon a Projected Improvement of the Estate of the College of California, at Berkeley, Near Oakland*. New York: William C. Bryant & Co., 1866.

Parsons, Samuel, *Memories of Samuel Parsons*. Edited by Mabel Parsons. New York: G. P. Putnam's Sons, 1926.

Proctor, John Clagett, "The Tragic Death of Andrew Jackson Downing and the Monument to His Memory," Columbia Historical Society, *Records*, Vol. 27 (1925), pp. 248-61. Washington: Columbia Historical Society, 1925.

Strauch, Adolphus, *Spring Grove Cemetery: Its History and Improvements*. Cincinnati: R. Clarke & Co., 1869.

Swift, Samuel, "Llewellyn Park, Orange, New Jersey," *House and Garden*, Vol. 3, No. 6 (1903), pp. 327-35.

"The Central Park," *Harper's Weekly*, Vol. 1, No. 48 (November 28, 1857), pp. 756-57.

The Central Park Association, *The Central Park*. New York: Thomas Seltzer, 1926.

Tunnard, Christopher, "The Romantic Suburb in America," *Magazine of Art*, Vol. 40, No. 5 (1947), pp. 184-87.

Walter, Cornelia W., *Mount Auburn Illustrated*. New York: R. Martin, 1847.

13. *Cities for Sale: Land Speculation in American Planning*

Alley, John, *City Beginnings in Oklahoma Territory*. Norman: University of Oklahoma Press, 1939.

Baily, Francis, *Journal of a Tour in Unsettled Parts of North America in 1796 and 1797*. London: Baily Brothers, 1856.

Bingham, Robert Warwick, *Cradle of the Queen City, a History of Buffalo to the Incorporation of the City*. Buffalo: Buffalo Historical Society, 1931.

Birkbeck, Morris, *Notes on a Journey in America from the Coast of Virginia to the Territory of Illinois*. London: J. Ridgway, 3rd ed., 1818.

Bullock, William, *Bullock's Journey from New Orleans to New York in 1827*. Reuben G. Thwaites (ed.), *Early Western Travels, 1748-1846*, Vol. 19, Cleveland: A. H. Clark Co., 1905.

Dalington, W. M. (ed.), *Christopher Gist's Journals*. Pittsburgh: J. R. Weldin & Co., 1893.

Day, Sherman, *Historical Collections of the State of Pennsylvania*. Philadelphia: G. W. Gorton, 1843.

Dick, Everett, *The Sod-House Frontier, 1854-1890*. New York: D. Appleton-Century Co., 1937.

Downes, Randolph Chandler, *Canal Days*. Toledo: Historical Society of Northwestern Ohio, 1949.

Dumke, Glenn S., *The Boom of the Eighties in Southern California*. San Marino, California: Huntington Library, 1944.

Ellicott, Joseph, *Reports of Joseph Ellicott as Chief of Survey (1797-1800) and as Agent (1800-1821) of the Holland Land Company's Purchase in Western New York*. 2 vols. Edited by Robert W. Bingham. Buffalo: The Buffalo Historical Society, 1937-41.

Evans, Paul D., *The Holland Land Company*. Buffalo: Buffalo Historical Society, 1924.

Ferguson, Donald W., "The Proposed Town of Cornish, Ohio," *Ohio State Archaeological and Historical Quarterly*, Vol. 44, No. 2 (April 1935), pp. 245-49.

Flint, Timothy, *Recollections of the Last Ten Years*. Boston: Cummings, Hilliard, and Co., 1826.

Gittinger, Roy, *The Formation of the State of

Oklahoma, 1803-1906. Norman: University of Oklahoma Press, 1939.

Guinn, James Miller, *History of California and an Extended History of Los Angeles and Environs*. 3 vols. Los Angeles: Historic Record Company, 1915.

Havighurst, Walter, *Wilderness for Sale: The Story of the First Western Land Rush*. New York: Hastings House, 1956.

Hedrick, Ulysses Prentiss, *A History of Agriculture in the State of New York*. Albany: New York State Agricultural Society, 1933.

History of Greene County, New York. New York: J. B. Beers & Co., 1884.

La Rochefoucauld Liancourt, François Alexandre Frederic, *Travels Through the United States of North America, the Country of the Iroquois, and Upper Canada, in the Years 1795, 1796, and 1797*. 4 vols. London: R. Phillips, 2nd ed., 1800.

Livermore, Shaw, *Early American Land Companies*. New York: The Commonwealth Fund, 1939.

McMaster, Guy H., *History of the Settlement of Steuben County, New York*. Bath: R. S. Underhill & Co., 1853.

Prettyman, William S., *Indian Territory, a Frontier Photographic Record*. Selected and edited by Robert E. Cunningham. Norman: University of Oklahoma Press, 1957.

Prospectus of the New York Lumber, Manufacturing and Improvement Company. Albany: New York Lumber, Manufacturing and Improvement Co., 1867.

Quiett, Glenn Chesney, *They Built the West; an Epic of Rails and Cities*. New York, London: D. Appleton-Century Co., 1934.

Richardson, Albert Deane, *Beyond the Mississippi: From the Great River to the Great Ocean, Life and Adventure on the Prairies, Mountains, and Pacific Coast . . . 1857-1867*. Hartford: American Publishing Co., 1867.

Sakolski, Aaron Morton, *The Great American Land Bubble*. New York: Harper & Brothers, 1932.

Scott, Angelo Cyrus, *The Story of Oklahoma City*. Oklahoma City: Times-Journal Publishing Co., 1939.

Smith, Alice Elizabeth, *James Duane Doty, Frontier Promoter*. Madison: State Historical Society of Wisconsin, 1954.

"Some Ingalls Letters," Kansas State Historical Society, *Collections*, Vol. 14 (1915-18), pp. 94-122.

Trollope, Frances, *Domestic Manners of the Americans*. London: Whittaker, Treacher, 4th ed., 1832.

Van Dyke, Theodore S., *Millionaires of a Day: An Inside History of the Great Southern California "Boom."* New York: Howard & Hulbert, 1890.

Weld, Isaac, *Travels through the States of North America and the Provinces of Upper and Lower Canada, during the Years 1795, 1796, and 1797*. 2 vols. London: J. Stockdale, 4th ed., 1800.

Wicks, Hamilton S., "The Opening of Oklahoma," *Cosmopolitan*, Vol. 7, No. 5 (September 1889), pp. 460-70.

Winterbotham, William, *An Historical, Geographical, Commercial, and Philosophical View of the United States of America, and of the European Settlements in America and the West Indies*. 4 vols. New York: J. Reid, 1796.

Woestemeyer, Ina Faye, *The Westward Movement; a Book of Readings on Our Changing Frontiers*. New York: D. Appleton-Century Co., 1939.

14. *Towns by the Tracks*

Andrews, Charles, *Tacoma and "Destiny"* . . . Tacoma: Puget Sound Printing Co., 1891.

Bell, William Abraham, *New Tracks in North America. A Journal of Travel and Adventure whilst Engaged in the Survey for a Southern Railroad to the Pacific Ocean during 1867-8*. 2 vols. London: Chapman and Hall, 1869.

Buckingham, James Silk, *America; Historical, Statistic, and Descriptive*. 3 vols. London: Fisher, 1841.

Clark, Ira G., *Then Came the Railroads: The Century from Steam to Diesel in the Southwest*. Norman: University of Oklahoma Press, 1958.

Dickens, Charles, *American Notes for General Circulation*. London: Chapman and Hall, 1842.

Dumke, Glenn S., *The Boom of the Eighties in Southern California*. San Marino: Huntington Library, 1944.

Gates, Paul, *The Illinois Central Railroad and Its Colonization Work*. Cambridge: Harvard University Press, 1934.

Gerard, P., *How to Build a City. Designed for the Consideration of Founders of Towns, Architects, Civil Engineers, Sanitary Organizations, Municipal Authorities, Builders, and Especially the Managers of the Various Railroads, to the Pacific. . . .* Philadelphia: Review Printing House, 1872.

Guinn, James M., "Los Angeles in the Later Sixties and Early Seventies," Historical Society of Southern California, *Annual Publications*, Vol. 3 (1893), pp. 63-68. Los Angeles: Historical Society of Southern California, 1893.

Harper's Weekly. Supplement, Vol. 18, No. 901 (April 4, 1874), pp. 305-08.

Haswell, A. M., "The Building of a City—Springfield," *Missouri Historical Review*, Vol. 19, No. 3 (April 1925), pp. 397-403.

Kipling, Rudyard, *From Sea to Sea*. 2 vols. New York: Doubleday, Page & Co., 1913.

Lansden, John McMurray, *A History of the City of Cairo, Illinois*. Chicago: R. R. Donnelley & Sons Co., 1910.

Long, Henry C., *Report of Captain Henry C. Long, on the Condition and Prospects of the City of Cairo, September 2, 1850*. New York: Narine & Co., 1850.

Morgan, John, "Garland City, Railroad Terminus, 1878," *The Colorado Magazine*, Vol. 25, No. 6 (November 1948), pp. 259-62.

Overton, Richard G., *Burlington West: A Colonization History of the Burlington Railroad*. Cambridge: Harvard University Press, 1941.

Quiett, Glenn Chesney, *They Built the West:*

An Epic of Rails and Cities. New York: D. Appleton-Century Co., 1934.

Reps, John W., "Great Expectations and Hard Times: The Planning of Cairo, Illinois," *Journal of the Society of Architectural Historians*, Vol. 16, No. 4 (December 1957), pp. 14-21.

Richardson, Albert Deane, *Beyond the Mississippi: From the Great River to the Great Ocean, Life and Adventure on the Prairies, Mountains, and Pacific Coast . . . 1857-1867.* Hartford: American Publishing Co., 1867.

Riegel, Robert E., *The Story of the Western Railroads.* New York: The Macmillan Co., 1926.

Sakolski, Aaron Morton, *The Great American Land Bubble.* New York: Harper & Brothers, 1932.

Tacoma Land Company, *Tacoma, the Western Terminus of the Northern Pacific Railroad.* Tacoma: n.p., 1889.

Train, George Francis, *My Life in Many States and in Foreign Lands.* London: D. Appleton and Co., 1902.

Wild, J. C., *The Valley of the Mississippi, Illustrated in a Series of Views.* St. Louis: Published by the Artist, 1841.

15. *The Towns the Companies Built*

Atterbury, Grosvenor, "Model Towns in America," *Scribner's Magazine*, Vol. 52, No. 1 (July 1912), pp. 20-35.

Chevalier, Michel, *Society, Manners and Politics in the United States: Being a Series of Letters on North America.* Translated from the 3rd Paris edition. Boston: Weeks, Jordan and Co., 1839.

Comey, Arthur C. and Max S. Wehrly, *Planned Communities.* Part I of Supplementary Report of the Urbanism Committee to the U. S. National Resources Committee. Volume II, *Urban Planning and Land Policies*, pp. 3-161. Government Printing Office, 1939.

Commissioners of State Bureaus of Labor Statistics, *Report of the State Bureaus of Labor Statistics on the Industrial, Social and Economic Conditions of Pullman, Illinois, 1884.*

Coolidge, John, *Mill and Mansion: A Study of Architecture and Society in Lowell, Massachusetts, 1820-1865.* New York: Columbia University Press, 1942.

Davis, Horace B., "Company Towns," *Encyclopaedia of the Social Sciences*, Vol. 4, pp. 119-23. New York: The Macmillan Co., 1930.

Doty, Mrs. Duane, *The Town of Pullman, Illustrated: Its Growth with Brief Accounts of Its Industries.* Pullman: T. P. Struhsacker, 1893.

Ely, Richard T., "Pullman: A Social Study," *Harper's Magazine*, Vol. 70, No. 417 (February 1885), pp. 452-66.

Fuller, Henry Blake, "An Industrial Utopia," *Harper's Weekly*, Vol. 51 (October 12, 1907), pp. 1482-83, 1495.

Gould, E. R. L., *The Housing of the Working People.* Eighth Special Report of the Commissioner of Labor. Prepared under the Direction of Carroll D. Wright, Commissioner of Labor. Government Printing Office, 1895.

Green, Constance McLaughlin, *Holyoke, Massachusetts: A Case History of the Industrial Revolution in America.* New Haven: Yale University Press, 1939.

Hunt, Edward S., F. G. Tryon, and Joseph H. Willits, *What the Coal Commission Found.* Baltimore: The Williams and Wilkins Co., 1925.

Institute of Local Government, Queen's University, *Single-Enterprise Communities in Canada.* A Report to Central Mortgage and Housing Corporation. Kingston: Institute of Local Government, 1953.

Lillibridge, Robert M., "Pullman: Town Development in the Era of Eclecticism," *Journal of the Society of Architectural Historians*, Vol. 7, No. 3 (October 1953), pp. 17-22.

Luce, A. T., "Kincaid, Illinois—Model Mining Town," *American City*, Vol. 13 (July 1905), pp. 10-13.

Meakin, Budgett, *Model Factories and Villages: Ideal Conditions of Labour and Housing.* London: T. F. Unwin, 1905.

Miller, George H., "Fairfield, a Town with a Purpose," *American City*, Vol. 9 (September 1913), pp. 213-19.

Morgan, William T. W., "The Pullman Experiment in Review," *Journal of the American Institute of Planners*, Vol. 20 (Winter 1954), pp. 27-29.

Mumford, John Kimberly, "This Land of Opportunity: Gary, the City that Rose from a Sandy Waste," *Harper's Weekly*, Vol. 52 (July 4, 1908), pp. 22-23.

Nimmons, George C., "Modern Industrial Plants," *Architectural Record*, Vol. 44, No. 5 (November 1918), pp. 414-21.

Nolen, John, *New Towns for Old: Achievements in Civic Improvement in Some American Small Towns and Neighborhoods.* Boston: Marshall Jones Co., 1927.

Sheffield, David G., *Town Planning by Industry in the United States.* Unpublished Master's Thesis, Cornell University. Ithaca, New York, 1961.

Shlakman, Vera, *Economic History of a Factory Town: A Study of Chicopee, Massachusetts.* Northampton: Department of History of Smith College, 1936.

Snavely, J. R., "The Industrial Community Development of Hershey, Pennsylvania," *American Landscape Architect*, Vol. 3, No. 5 (November 1930), pp. 24-36.

Taylor, Graham Romeyn, *Satellite Cities; a Study of Industrial Suburbs.* New York: D. Appleton and Co., 1915.

"The New Mining Community of Tyrone, New Mexico, Now Building for the Burro Mountain Branch of the Phelps Dodge Corporation: Bertram Grosvenor Goodhue, Architect," *Architectural Review*, Vol. 6 (April 1918), pp. 53-56, 59-62.

16. *Cities of Zion: The Planning of Utopian and Religious Communities*

Baird, Charles Washington, *History of the Huguenot Emigration to America.* 2 vols. New York: Dodd, Mead & Co., 1885.

Bestor, Arthur Eugene, *Backwoods Utopias:*

The Sectarian and Owenite Phases of Communitarian Socialism in America, 1663-1829. Philadelphia: University of Pennsylvania Press, 1950.

Brisbane, Albert, *A Concise Exposition of the Doctrine of Association.* New York: J. S. Redfield, 2nd ed., 1844.

Brock, Robert Alonzo (comp. and ed.), *Documents Relating to the Huguenot Emigration to Virginia and to the Settlement at Manakin-Town.* Richmond: Virginia Historical Society, 1886.

Cabet, Etienne, *Voyage en Icarie.* Paris: Au Bureau du Populaire, 1848.

Calkins, Earnest Elmo, *They Broke the Prairie.* New York: Charles Scribner's Sons, 1937.

Calverton, Victor Francis, *Where Angels Dared to Tread.* Indianapolis: The Bobbs-Merrill Co., 1941.

Carpenter, Garrett R., *Silkville: A Kansas Attempt in the History of Fourierist Utopias, 1869-1892,* The Emporia State Research Studies, Vol. 3, No. 2. Emporia: Graduate Division, Kansas State Teachers College, 1954.

Carter, Kate B., *The Mormon Village.* Salt Lake City: Daughters of Utah Pioneers, 1954.

Clewell, John Henry, *History of Wachovia in North Carolina: The Unitas Fratrum or Moravian Church in North Carolina during a Century and a Half, 1752-1902.* New York: Doubleday, Page & Co., 1902.

Comey, Arthur C. and Max S. Wehrly, "Zion, Lake County, Illinois," *A Study of Planned Communities.* Manuscript in Library of Graduate School of Design, Harvard University. November 1939.

Dobbs, Catherine R., *Freedom's Will: The Society of the Separatists of Zoar, an Historical Adventure of Religious Communism in Early Ohio.* New York: William-Frederick Press, 1947.

Ely, Richard T., "Amana: A Study of Religious Communism," *Harper's Monthly Magazine,* Vol. 105 (October 1902), pp. 659-68.

Fox, Feramorz Young, *The Mormon Land System.* Unpublished Master's Thesis, Northwestern University. Evanston, Illinois, 1932.

Fries, Adelaide (ed.), *Records of the Moravians in North Carolina.* Vol. I. Raleigh: Edwards & Broughton Printing Co., 1922.

Graffenried, Christoph von, *Christoph von Graffenried's Account of the Founding of New Bern.* Edited and translated by Vincent H. Todd. Raleigh: Edwards & Broughton Printing Co., 1920.

Hinds, William Alfred, *American Communities and Cooperative Colonies.* Chicago: C. H. Kerr & Co., 2nd revision, 1908.

Hine, Robert V., *California's Utopian Colonies.* San Marino: Huntington Library, 1953.

Hirsch, Arthur Henry, *The Huguenots of Colonial South Carolina.* Durham: Duke University Press, 1928.

Holloway, Mark, *Heavens on Earth: Utopian Communities in America, 1680-1880.* London, Turnstile Press, 1951.

Knoedler, Christiana, *The Harmony Society: A 19th Century American Utopia.* New York: Vantage Press, 1954.

Lefler, Hugh Talmage and Albert Ray Newsome, *North Carolina: The History of a Southern State.* Chapel Hill: University of North Carolina Press, 1954.

Levering, Joseph Mortimer, *A History of Bethlehem, Pennsylvania, 1741-1892, with Some Account of Its Founders and Their Early Activity in America.* Bethlehem: Times Publishing Co., 1903.

Lockwood, George B., *The New Harmony Movement.* New York: D. Appleton and Co., 1905.

MacDonald, Donald, "The Diaries of Donald MacDonald, 1824-1826," Indiana Historical Society, *Publications,* Vol. 14, No. 2 (1942), pp. 245-50 Indianapolis: Indiana Historical Society, 1942.

Meakin, Budgett, *Model Factories and Villages: Ideal Conditions of Labour and Housing.* London: T. F. Unwin, 1905.

Morton, Richard Lee, *Colonial Virginia.* 2 vols. Chapel Hill: University of North Carolina Press, 1960.

Mulder, William and A. Russell Mortensen (eds.), *Among the Mormons: Historic Accounts by Contemporary Observers.* New York: Knopf, 1958.

Nelson, Lowry, *The Mormon Village: A Pattern and Technique of Land Settlement.* Salt Lake City: University of Utah Press, 1952.

Nordhoff, Charles, *The Communistic Societies of the United States.* New York: Harper & Brothers, 1875.

Ohio Historical Society, Department of Research and Publications, *Zoar, an Ohio Experiment in Communalism.* Columbus: Ohio State Archaeological and Historical Society, 1952.

Owen, Robert, *The Life of Robert Owen.* 2 vols. London: E. Wilson, 1857-58.

Parrington, Vernon Louis, Jr., *American Dreams: A Study of American Utopias.* Providence: Brown University Press, 1947.

Perkins, William Rufus, and Barthinius L. Wick, *History of the Amana Society, or Community of True Inspiration.* Iowa City: Iowa State University, 1891.

Rodabaugh, James H. and Mary Jane Rodabaugh, *Schoenbrunn and the Moravian Missions in Ohio.* Columbus: The Ohio Historical Society, 3rd ed., 1956.

Sellers, Charles L., "Early Mormon Community Planning," *Journal of the American Institute of Planners,* Vol. 28, No. 1 (February 1962), pp. 24-30.

Shambaugh, Bertha Maud, *Amana That Was and Amana That Is.* Iowa City: The State Historical Society of Iowa, 1932.

Stansbury, Howard, *Exploration and Survey of the Valley of the Great Salt Lake of Utah, Including a Reconnaissance of a New Route through the Rocky Mountains.* Senate Executive Document No. 3, 32nd Cong., Special Session, March, 1851. Washington: R. Armstrong, 1853.

The History of Iowa County, Iowa. Des Moines: Union Historical Co., Birdsall, Williams & Co., 1881.

Vaughan, Isabel Ann, "The Community of True Inspiration," Buffalo Historical Society, *Publications*, Vol. 34 (1947), pp. 79-96. Buffalo: Buffalo Historical Society, 1947.

Webber, Everett, *Escape to Utopia: The Communal Movement in America*. New York: Hastings House, 1959.

Weld, Isaac, *Travels Through the States of North America, and the Provinces of Upper and Lower Canada During the Years 1795, 1796, and 1797*. 2 vols. London: J. Stockdale, 4th ed., 1807.

West, Ray, *Kingdom of the Saints: The Story of Brigham Young and the Mormons*. New York: Viking Press, 1957.

Young, Marguerite, *Angel in the Forest: A Fairy Tale of Two Utopias*. New York: Reynal & Hitchcock, 1945.

17. *Minor Towns and Mutant Plans*

"A Letter from New Madrid, 1789," *Mississippi Valley Historical Review*, Vol. 5, No. 3 (December 1918), pp. 343-46.

Atwater, Caleb, "Description of the Antiquities Discovered in the State of Ohio and other Western States," American Antiquarian Society, *Transactions and Collections*, Vol. 1 (1820), pp. 105-267. Worcester: American Antiquarian Society, 1820.

Baily, Francis, *Journal of a Tour in Unsettled Parts of North America in 1796 and 1797*. London: Baily Brothers, 1856.

Brown, Samuel R., *The Western Gazetteer; or Emigrant's Directory, Containing a Geographical Description of the Western States and Territories*. Auburn: H. C. Southwick, 1817.

Buckingham, James Silk, *The Eastern and Western States of America*. 3 vols. London: Fisher, Son & Co., 1842.

Callot Georges Henri Victor, *A Journey in North America*. 2 vols. Paris, 1826. Reprinted, Florence: O. Lange, 1924.

Colt, Miriam Davis, *Went to Kansas: Being a Thrilling Account of an Ill-Fated Expedition to that Fairy Land and its Sad Results*. Watertown: L. Ingalls & Co., 1862.

Darby, William, *The Emigrant's Guide to the Western and Southwestern States and Territories*. New York: Kirk & Mercein, 1818.

Flint, Timothy, *Recollections of the Last Ten Years*. Boston: Cummings, Hilliard, and Co., 1826.

[Author unknown,] *History of Franklin and Pickaway Counties, Ohio*. Cleveland: Williams Brothers, 1880.

Houck, Louis, *The Spanish Regime in Missouri*. 2 vols. Chicago: R. R. Donnelley & Sons Co., 1909.

Madison, James, *The Writings of James Madison*. 9 vols. Edited by Gaillard Hunt. New York: G. P. Putnam's Sons, 1900-1910.

Murray, Louise Welles, *The Story of Some French Refugees and Their "Azilum," 1793-1800*. Athens: n.p., 1903.

Reps, John W., "New Madrid on the Mississippi: American 18th Century Planning on the Spanish Frontier," *Journal of the Society of Architectural Historians*, Vol. 18, No. 1 (March 1959), pp. 21-26.

————, "Urban Redevelopment in the Nineteenth Century: The Squaring of Circleville," *Journal of the Society of Architectural Historians*, Vol. 14, No. 4 (December 1955), pp. 23-26.

Savelle, Max, *George Morgan, Colony Builder*. New York: Columbia University Press, 1932.

18. *Chicago Fair and Capital City: The Rebirth of American Urban Planning*

Babcock, J. R., "The Campaign for a City Plan for Dallas," *American City*, Vol. 3, No. 4 (October 1910), pp. 157-62.

Bancroft, Hubert Howe, *The Book of the Fair*. Chicago: The Bancroft Co., 1893.

Bennett, Edward H., *Plan of Minneapolis*. Edited and written by Andrew Wright Crawford. Minneapolis: The Civic Commission, 1917.

Boston Society of Architects, Committee on Municipal Improvement, *Report*. Boston: Boston Society of Architects, 1907.

Brown, Glenn, *1860-1930 Memories*. Washington: W. F. Robert Co., 1931.

Buel, J. W., *The Magic City: A Massive Portfolio of Original Photographic Views of the Great World's Fair*. Philadelphia: Historical Publishing Co., 1894.

Burnham, Daniel H., "A City of the Future under a Democratic Government," Royal Institute of British Architects, Town Planning Conference, *Transactions*, pp. 368-78. London: Royal Institute of British Architects, 1911.

————, *Report on a Plan for San Francisco*. Edited by Edward F. O'Day. San Francisco: Sunset Press, 1905.

————, and Edward H. Bennett, *Plan of Chicago Prepared under the Direction of the Commercial Club during the Years MCMVI, MCMVII, and MCMVIII*. Edited by Charles Moore. Chicago: The Commercial Club, 1909.

Caemmerer, H. Paul, "Charles Moore and the Plan of Washington," Columbia Historical Society, *Records*, Vols. 46-47 (1944-1945), pp. 237-58. Washington: Columbia Historical Society, 1947.

————, "Problems in Restoring the Plan of Washington," *Journal of the Society of Architectural Historians*, Vol. 4, No. 1 (January 1944), pp. 34-40.

Carrere and Hastings, Advisory Architects, *A Plan of the City of Hartford*. Hartford: The Commission on the City Plan, 1912.

Columbus Plan Commission, *The Plan of the City of Columbus*. Columbus: Columbus Plan Commission, 1908.

Committee on the Centennial Celebration of the Establishment of the Seat of Government in the District of Columbia, *Celebration of the One Hundredth Anniversary of the Establishment of the Seat of Government in the District of Columbia*. Compiled by William V. Cox under the Joint Committee on Printing. Government Printing Office, 1901.

Fairmount Park Art Association, *The Fairmount Parkway*. Philadelphia: Fairmount Park Art Association, 1919.

Gilbert, Cass and Frederick Law Olmsted, *Report of the New Haven Civic Improvement Commission to the New Haven Civic Improvement Committee*. New Haven: New Haven Civic Improvement Committee, 1910.

Harrisburg Executive Committee, *Proposed Municipal Improvements for Harrisburg, Pennsylvania*. Harrisburg: The Executive Committee, 1901.

Hegemann, Werner, *Report on a City Plan for the Municipalities of Oakland and Berkeley*. Oakland: The Municipal Governments of Oakland and Berkeley, etc., 1915.

Hubbard, Theodora Kimball, *Manual of Information on City Planning and Zoning, Including References on Regional, Rural, and National Planning*. Cambridge: Harvard University Press, 1923.

Kelsey, Albert (comp. and ed.), *The Proposed Parkway for Philadelphia*. Philadelphia: The Parkway Association, 1902.

Moody, Walter D., *Wacker's Manual of the Plan of Chicago*. Chicago: H. C. Sherman & Co., 1911.

Moore, Charles, *Charles Moore Papers*, Park Commission Correspondence. Manuscript Division, Library of Congress.

———, *Daniel H. Burnham, Architect, Planner of Cities*. 2 vols. Boston: Houghton Mifflin Co., 1921.

———, (comp.), *Park Improvement Papers*. Government Printing Office, 1903.

———, *The Life and Times of Charles Follen McKim*. Boston: Houghton Mifflin Co., 1929.

"Mr. Burnham's Address Before the World's Congress of Architects," *The American Architect and Building News*, Vol. 41, No. 920 (August 12, 1893), pp. 103-106.

Newark City Plan Commission, *Comprehensive Plan of Newark*. Newark: H. Murphy, 1915.

Nolen, John, *Madison: A Model City*. Boston: John Nolen, 1911.

———, "Twenty Years of City Planning Progress in the United States," National Conference on City Planning, *Planning Problems of Town, City, and Region: Papers and Discussions, 1927*. pp. 1-44. Philadelphia: National Conference on City Planning, 1927.

Parsons, William E., "Burnham as a Pioneer in City Planning," *Architectural Record*, Vol. 38, No. 1 (July 1915), pp. 13-31.

Papers Relating to the Improvement of the City of Washington, District of Columbia. Compiled by Glenn Brown. Government Printing Office, 1901.

Report of the Park Commission to the Senate Committee on the District of Columbia. Senate Report No. 166, Fifty-Seventh Congress, First Session. Government Printing Office, 1902.

Schuyler, Montgomery, "Last Words About the World's Fair," *Architectural Record*, Vol. 3 (January-March, 1894), pp. 271-301.

———, "The Art of City Making," *Architectural Record*, Vol. 12, No. 1 (May 1902), pp. 1-26.

Seattle Municipal Plans Commission, *Plan of Seattle*. Seattle: Lowman & Hanford Co., 1911.

Sullivan, Louis Henry, *The Autobiography of an Idea*. New York: Dover Publications, 1956.

Taft, William Howard and James Bryce, *Washington the Nation's Capital*. Washington: The National Geographic Society, 1915.

The Civic League of St. Louis, *A City Plan for St. Louis*. St. Louis: The Civic League, 1907.

Tindall, William, "A Sketch of Alexander Robey Shepherd," Columbia Historical Society, *Records*, Vol. 14 (1911), pp. 49-66. Washington: Columbia Historical Society, 1911.

———, "The Origin of the Parking System of this City," Columbia Historical Society, *Records*, Vol. 4 (1901), pp. 75-99. Washington: Columbia Historical Society, 1901.

Topham, Washington, "First Railroad into Washington and Its Three Depots," Columbia Historical Society, *Records*, Vol. 27 (1925), pp. 175-247. Washington: Columbia Historical Society, 1925.

Truman, Benjamin Cummings, *History of the World's Fair*. Chicago: Mammoth Publishing Co., 1893.

U. S. Commission of Fine Arts, *The Plan of the National Capital*. From the Ninth Report of the Commission of Fine Arts. Government Printing Office, 1923.

U. S. National Capital Park and Planning Commission, *Plans and Studies: Washington and Vicinity*. Supplementary Technical Data to Accompany Annual Report, 1928. Government Printing Office, 1929.

U. S. Senate, Committee on the District of Columbia, *City Planning*. Senate Document No. 422, Sixty-First Congress, Second Session. Government Printing Office, 1910.

Wacker, Charles and Edward H. Bennett, "Technical Features of the Plan of Chicago," *American City*, Vol. 1, No. 2 (October 1909), pp. 55-58.

———, "The Plan of Chicago," *American City*, Vol. 1, No. 2 (October 1909), pp. 49-53.

Walton, William, *World's Columbian Exposition MDCCCXCIII: Art and Architecture*. 2 vols. Philadelphia: George Barrie & Son, 1893.

"Washington: The Development and Improvement of the Park-System," *American Architect and Building News*, Vol. 75, No. 1362 (February 1, 1902), p. 33; Vol. 75, No. 1367 (March 8, 1902), pp. 75-77.

Wheeler, Candace, "A Dream City," *Harper's Magazine*, Vol. 86 (May 1893), pp. 830-46.

Wrigley, Robert L., Jr., "The Plan of Chicago: Its Fiftieth Anniversary," *Journal of the American Institute of Planners*, Vol. 26, No. 1 (February 1960), pp. 31-38.

Index

Abercorn, Ga., 195, 198

Alabama, French settlement at Mobile, 78; company towns in, 430, 438

Albany, N.Y., fort near, 147; planned by Stuyvesant, 150; park in, 339

Alberti, Leon Battista, influence, 1; theories of city planning, 4; civic grandeur described by, 6; doctrines familiar to Spanish, 9

Albord and Burdick, 430

Alexandria, Va., 97

Allegheny, Pa., 206

Allentown, Pa., 174

Altruists, 474

Amana, Iowa, 458

American City Planning Institute, 525

American Institute of Architects, 501, 502, 505, 514, 519

American Institute of Planners, 525

Amoskeag Manufacturing Co., 417

Amsterdam, Holland, 22

Andreae, Johann Valentin, ideal city of, 5

Annapolis, Md., made capital of Maryland, 106; plan, 106-08; deficiencies in plan, 108; description, 108; part of American planning tradition, 174; temporary site of national capital, 240

Anne Arundel, Md., 106

Antoinette, Marie, 475

Apollo Iron and Steel Co., 424

Appalachian Mountains, barrier to settlement, 204

architecture, classical revival, 325; picturesque style, 325; in Pullman, 422; new attention to in city planning, 524

Ashley, Burton, 472

Association for Improvement and Adornment of San Francisco, 514

Associationism, 463

Asylum, Pa., 475

Atwater, Caleb, 487

Atwood, Charles, 501

Augusta, Ga., 195

Aurora, Ore., 456

Azusa, Calif., 406

Babcock, Elisha, 406

Bacon, David, 234

Bacon, Francis, 5

Baily, Francis, description of New Orleans, 81-84; description of Louisville, 214; description of national capital, 257; advocated combination of grid and radial streets, 294; impressions of gridiron street plans, 294; description of land speculation techniques, 358; description of New Madrid, 483

Baker, R. S., 380

Ballona, Calif., 380

Baltimore, Md., growth, 108; temporary site of national capital, 240; park, 336

Barber, Ohio, 424

Barberton, Ohio, 424

Barlow, Joel, 222

baroque planning. See radial street plan

baroque planning principles, used at Annapolis, 106-08; used at Williamsburg, 111

Barrett, Nathan, 421, 422

bastide towns, in Europe, 2; influence on Laws of the Indies, 31

Batavia, Iowa, 394

Batavia, N.Y., 352

Bates, Frederick, 264

Bath, N.Y., land office opened, 350; planned by Williamson, 351; described by Rochefoucauld, 351

Baton Rouge, La., 277

Beacon Hill district, Boston, 145

Beaver, Pa., 361

Bell, William, description of railroad towns, 397; description of Salina, Kans., 400

Belmont, Wisc., 364

Beman, Solon S., 421, 422

Benicia, Calif., 308

Berkeley, Calif., 342-44

Bermuda City, Va., 91

Bethabara, N.C., 444

Bethania, N.C., 444

Bethel, Mo., 456

Bethlehem, Pa., settlement by Moravians, 443; early growth, 443-44; description by Weld, 444; model plan sent from, 448; buildings restored, 453

Beverly, Robert, description of Williamsburg, 110

Bienville, de Sieur, 78

Bigelow, Jacob, 326

Bimeler, Joseph, 456

Birkbeck, Morris, description of capital, 257; description of land speculation techniques, 358

Birmingham, Ala., 430

Bloomsbury Square, Annapolis, 106

Bloomsbury Square, London, 106, 163, 199

Boonesborough, Ky., 208, 210, 212

Boott, Kirk, 415, 417

Border City, Calif., 378

Boston Manufacturing Co., 415

Boston, Mass., settled, 140; described by Josselyn, 141; development in 18th century, 141; irregular streets, 141; in 1800, 141-45; Beacon Hill district, 145; projects designed by Bullfinch, 145-46; in 1850; 146; plan for by Copeland, 290-93; plan for by Gourlay, 290-93

Boudinot, Elias, 225

Boulogne, Charles, 475

Bouquet, Henry, 210

Bourneville, England, 421

Brackenridge, Henry, description of St. Louis, 75-76

Brahm, de, William, description of Savannah, 187-92

Branciforte, Calif., 51

Brawley, Calif., 293, 380

Briggs, Joseph, description of land speculation techniques, 358-60

Brisbane, Albert, 463, 465

Brooks, Peter Chardon, 234

Brown, Glenn, 502

Brunner, Arnold, 497

Bryant, William Cullen, 331

Buckingham, James, description of Savannah, 201-02; description of Pittsburgh, 206; description of Cairo, 383-86; description of Circleville, 488; proposed town of Victoria, 488n

Buffalo, N.Y., 263-64, planned by Ellicott, 351; plan, 351-52; speculation in, 352; utopian community near, 456-58

Columbus, Ohio, 227
common land, at Plymouth, 117; in New England communities, 120; in Savannah, 187; in Louisville, 214; in Marietta, 222; in New York City, 296; in Jackson, 322
Community of True Inspiration, 456-58
company towns, in America, 414; in New England, 414-20; Lowell's plan for, 415; after Civil War, 420-27; in 20th century, 427-36; population, 436; influence, 438; possibilities in future, 438
congestion, in 19th century American cities, 330
Connecticut Land Company, 230
Connecticut, settlement in, 122, 128-31
Continental Congress, adoption of land policy, 216-17
Coolidge, John, 417
Copeland, Robert Morris, plan for Boston, 290-93; planned Oak Bluffs, 348
Cornell, Ezra, 374
Cornell University, 374
Cornell, Wisc., 374
Corning, Iowa, 466
Cornish, Ohio, 371
Corona, Calif., 380, 406
Coronado, Calif., 293, 380, 406
Cotati, Calif., 293, 492
court house squares, in Virginia, 99
Covent Garden, London, 21, 163, 199
curvilinear street plan, first applied to cemetery design, 325; at Greenwood, 326; at Laurel Hill, 326; at Mount Auburn, 326; used in Central Park, 333-36; in Llewellyn Park, 339; in Lake Forest, 339-42; in Berkeley, 342-44; justification of by Olmsted, 344; in Riverside, 344-48; in Oak Bluffs, 348; in Ridley Park, 348; in Roland Park, 348; in Tarrytown Heights, 348; widely used in subdivisions, 348; in Coronado, 406; in Kincaid, 430-36; in Tacoma, 410; in Vandergrift, 424-27
Cutler, Manasseh, 217

Dale, Thomas, 91
Darien, Ga., 192, 198
David, Alexander, 339, 348
Davila, Pedrarias, 28
Dayton, Jonathan, 225, 227
Dayton, Ohio, 227
Deerfield, Mass., 138-40
Delaware Town, Va., 97n

Delft, Holland, 22
Denman, Matthias, 225
Denver, Colo., 402, 403
Derry, see Londonderry
Detroit, Michigan, French plan of, 71-73; destroyed, 264; lots sold in, 266; planned by Woodward, 266-70; plan compared to Washington, 266-70; demand for land in, 270; land board, 270, 271; Woodward plan abandoned, 271-72
De Witt, Simeon, 297
diagonal street plans. See radial street plans
Dickens, Charles, description of Cairo, 386, 386n
Dominguez, Francisco, description of Santa Fe, New Mexico, 43
Doty, James Duane, planned Madison, 275-77; land speculator, 364
Douglas, Stephen, 389
Dowie, John, 472
Downing, Andrew Jackson, plan for mall in Washington, 262; comments on rural cemeteries, 325; reported on visitors to cemeteries, 326; advocated public parks, 330; commented on London parks, 331; death, 333; effect of Washington mall plan, 505
Drake, Francis, 33
Driesbach, Daniel, 487
Duer, William, 217, 222
Duquesne, Pa., 421
Dutch colonial planning, in New Amsterdam, 147-50; on the Hudson river, 150
Dutch West India Company, 147, 440

Eastburn, Benjamin, 169
Eaton, Theophilus, 129
Ebenezer, Ga., 192, 198
Ebenezer, N.Y., 456-58
Economy, Pa., 454
Eden, Va., 99
Edenton, N.C., 180
Edict of Nantes, 440
Elburg, Holland, 9
Ellicott, Andrew, 230; appointed surveyor of national capital site, 242; met with Washington, 249; completed plan of national capital, 254
Ellicott, Joseph, brother of Andrew, 351; planned Buffalo, 351; land speculator, 352
Ely, Herman, 234

Ely, Richard T., description of pullman, 422
Elyria, Ohio, 234
English colonial planning, in Northern Ireland, 12-15; in Virginia and Maryland, 88-114; in New England, 115-41; in New York, 150-54; in New Jersey, 158; in Pennsylvania, 160-69; in South Carolina, 175-77; in North Carolina, 177-83; in Georgia, 183-99
Ephrata Community, 474
Erie Canal, 300
Española, Spanish colonial towns on, 26-28
Esperanza, N.Y., 263-64, 352, 355
Evelyn, John, plan for rebuilding London, 15, 163
Exeter, N.H., 131-32
Eximenic, ideal city of, 5-6

Fairfield, Ala., 430, 438
Fairfield, Conn., 131
Fair Haven, Vt., 132
Far West, Mo., 468
Fayette, N.Y., 466
Federal Housing Administration, 348
Fillmore, Millard, 505
Filson, John, 210, 225
Fisher, Walter, 519
Flint, Timothy, description of New Orleans, 84; description of New Madrid, 483
Flint, Wales, 2
Florida, French settlement at Fort Caroline, 32-33; Spanish settlements, 32-33, 40-43; Huguenot settlement, 440
Fond du Lac, Wisc., 364
Forest Hills Gardens, N.Y., 349, 525
Fort Boone, Ky., 208
Fort Caroline, Fla., 32-33, 440
Fort Christina, Del., 154-57
Fort Duquesne, Pa., 204
fortification methods, influence on Renaissance city plans, 4-5
Fourier, Charles, 463
Fowler, Orson, 496
Franklin, Benjamin, 350
Franklin Place, Boston, 145-46
Franklinville, Ky., 355
Frazier, Mary, 492
Frederic, Iowa, 394
Frederica, Ga., settled, 192; decline, 195; description of, 195; similarity to Ulster plantation towns, 198

· 566 ·

influence on plans of Georgia towns, 198; open spaces, 201; national capital located in, 240; radial plan for extension of, 264; as model for gridiron plans, 294; squares, 314; Laurel Hill cemetery, 326; open spaces of, 330; park planned for, 339; exposition of 1876, 498

Philip II of Spain, proclaims Laws of the Indies, 29

Philippeville, Belgium, 9, 148

piazza, *see* public squares

Piazza di San Marco, Venice, 19

Pike's Peak, Colo., 403, 404

Pilgrims, at Plymouth, 117

Pittman, Philip, description of Pensacola, 43; description of Kaskaskia, 73

Pittsburgh, Pa., Fort Duquesne at, 73; early plan, 204; early description by Washington, 204; description by Buckingham, 206; description by Melish, 206; park at, 339

Pittsfield, Mass., 131

Place Dauphine, Paris, 19

Place de la Concorde, Paris, 19, 252

Place de l'Etoile, Paris, 24, 252

Place de l'Opera, Paris, 19

Place des Vosges, Paris, 19

Place Royale, Paris, 19, 21

planning commissions, development of, 524

plantation system in Virginia, effect on towns, 93

Plymouth Company, 88, 115

Plymouth, Mass., settled, 115; description by de Rasieres, 117; land allocation in, 117; land system of, 117-19

Popham, John, 115

Port Royal, Nova Scotia, Champlain's description of, 59; Champlain's plan of settlement for, 59; similarity to later American frontier forts, 59; Huguenots in, 440

Port Royal, S.C., 439

Post, George, 500, 501

Pownall, Thomas, description of Philadelphia, 167-69

presidios, Spanish, 33-36; in Texas, 36; in California, 48-51

Princeton, N.J., 240

Providence, R.I., 138, 339

public squares, in Renaissance cities, 6, 19-21; in Spanish colonial towns, 29; in New Orleans, 81, 84; in Annapolis, 108; in Williamsburg, 111; in New Haven,

128; in Boston, 145-46; in New York City, 154; in Philadelphia, 172-74; at New Bern and Edenton, 180; in Western Reserve communities, 230-34; plan for in national capital, 252; in Indianapolis, 272; in Madison, 275; in San Francisco, 314; in California towns, 406. *See also* open spaces

pueblos, Spanish, in Texas, 36; in California, 51; land system in, 54; resemblance to New England towns, 54

Pullman, George, 421, 422

Pullman, Ill., designers, 421; site, 421; buildings in, 422; description by Ely, 422; plan, 422; difficulties in, 424; sale, 424; paternalism, 438

Pulteney Purchase, 350

Pulteney, William, 350

Puritans, 440

Putnam, Rufus, 217, 218, 317

Quakers, in New Jersey, 158; at Gravesend, 165; in Philadelphia, 172

Quebec, Canada, French character of, 56; Champlain's description of founding, 61; at end of French rule, 61-65; described by Charlevoix, 65; linear plan of lower town, 65; plan of upper town, 65; compared to Montreal, 68; Huguenots in, 440

radial street plan, in Renaissance cities, 5; in Tallmadge, 234; L'Enfant's justification for, 249-50; in Paterson, 263; in Detroit, 266-70; in Indianapolis, 272-75; in Madison, 275; in Baton Rouge, 277; in Cleveland, 277; in Greentown, 277; in Perrysburg, 277; in Sparta, 277; in Sandusky, 277-84; in Colorado Springs, 284; in Hatfield, 284; in Hugoton, 284; in Montezuma, 284; in Palmyra, 284; theories of by anonymous critic, 284-90; misunderstanding of purposes by American planners, 293; proposed for Boston, 290-93; in Esperanza, 352; in Hygeia, 358; in Coronado, 406; proposed for Salem, 448n; in Circleville, 487; in Perryopolis, 490-92; in Cotati, 492; in Lancaster, 492; in Marienville, 492; for Toledo University of Arts and Trades, 492; impracticability of proposals for in San Francisco, 517

railroad lines, Santa Fé, 378; Southern Pa-

cific, 378; Illinois Central, 389-92; Chicago, Alton and St. Louis, 392; Chicago, Burlington and Quincy, 392; Peoria and Rock Island, 392; St. Louis and San Francisco, 394; Kansas Pacific, 397; Denver and Rio Grande, 397, 403; Union Pacific, 402; Western Pacific, 403; Southern Pacific, 404; Pomona and Elsinore, 406; Northern Pacific, 410

railroads, effect on existing cities, 382, 392; town planning activities in Illinois, 389-92; town planning by in mid-west, 392-97; as town destroyers, 394; abandoned towns along, 397; town planning along transcontinental lines, 397-400; responsible for California land boom, 404; effects of town planning activities, 412; replanning of Washington made difficult by, 505-08

railroad towns, Cairo, 382-89; in Illinois, 389-92; in Iowa, 392-94; in Nebraska, 394; in west, 397-400; in Kansas, 400; model for, 402-03; in Colorado, 403-04; in California, 404-06; in Washington, 406-12

Raisieres, de, Isack, description of Plymouth, 117

Raleigh, N.C., 174

Raleigh, Walter, 88

Ralston, Alexander, 272

Rapp, George, 453

Reading, Pa., 174, 240

Red Bank, N.J., 463

redevelopment, in Jeffersonville, 319-21; in Circleville, 484, 488-90

Red Lion Square, London, 106, 199

Reed, John, 169

Regent Street, London, 19

religious groups, towns founded by, *see* utopian communities.

Residence Act, provisions, 241; amended, 242

residential squares, in Renaissance cities, 19-21; in London, 21; in Boston, 145; in Savannah, 199; in New York, 296. *See also* public squares

Reuter, Christian, planned Bethania, 444; planned Salem, 448

Ribaut, Jean, 32, 439

Richardson, Albert, description of land speculation in Kansas, 364-71; description of Sumner, 371; description of Train, 402

L'Enfant, 247; further negotiations with proprietors, 249; diary entry concerning plan, 249; report to by L'Enfant, 249-50; received revised plan from L'Enfant, 250-52; policies toward land sales, 253; warned L'Enfant to obey commissioners, 254; dismissed L'Enfant, 256

land company activities, 350, owned site of Perryopolis, 492

Washington Monument, D.C., 262, located off axis, 505; plan for area of, 508

Waterbury, Conn., 128

Wautauga, Tenn., 208

Weld, Isaac, description of Bethlehem, 444

western lands, claims by states after Revolution, 214; cession of state claims, 214-16; disposal of, 216-17

Western Reserve, establishment, 227; survey, 230; characteristics of towns, 230; public squares in towns, 234

West Point, Va., 97n

West Virginia, mining towns, 421

Wethersfield, Conn., 121

White House, Washington, 262; Senate park commission plan for, 508

Whitfield, Iowa, 394

Wicks, Hamilton, 374

Wilkinson, James, 227

Willemstad, Holland, 9

William and Mary, College of, 105, 110, 111

Williamsburg, N.Y., 351

Williamsburg, Va., description by Beverly, 110; description by Jones, 110; made capital, 110; planned by Nicholson, 110; early plan lost, 110-11; plan, 111; 19th-century plan, 111-14; merits of plan, 114; modern restoration, 114; as part of American planning tradition, 174; compared to Pullman, 422

Williamsport, Pa., 351

Williamstadt, Md., 103n, 106

Wilmington, Del., 240

Wilson, James, 350

Winchelsea, England, 2

Windsor, Conn., 122, 127, 130

Winston Salem, N.C., see Salem

Winter Quarters, Neb., 468

Winterbotham, William, 355

Wisconsin, capital site selected, 275; capital planned on radial system, 275; land speculation in, 364, 374

Wisconsin City, Wisc., 364

Woodstock, Vt., 132

Woodward, Augustus, appointed to replan Detroit, 264; early life, 264; plan for Detroit, 266-70; resolution of condemned by Hull, 271; statement of legal basis of plan, 271-72

World's Columbian Exposition, see Chicago World's Fair of 1893

Wren, Christopher, plan for rebuilding London, 15, 163; possible influence on Nicholson, 105

Wright, Joel, 227

Wye, Md.,103n

York, Pa., 174, 240

Yorktown, Va., 97

Young, Brigham, 468

Zane, Ebenezer, 227

Zanesville, Ohio, 227

Zaremba, T. W., 498

Zeisberger, David, 450, 453

Zinzendorf, Nikolaus, 443, 444

Zion City, Ill., founded, 472; plan, 472-74; restrictions on land use, 474

Zion Land and Investment Association, 474

Zoar, Ohio, 456